Lone Star
Navy

Other Naval and Maritime Titles from Potomac Books

Success Is All That Was Expected:
The South Atlantic Blockading Squadron during the Civil War
Robert M. Browning, Jr.

The Last of the Cape Horners:
Firsthand Accounts from the Final Days of the Commercial Tall Ships
Spencer Apollonio

All the Factors of Victory:
Adm. Joseph Mason Reeves and the Origins of Carrier Airpower
Thomas Wildenberg

Hunters in the Shallows: A History of the PT Boat
Curtis L. Nelson

War in the Boats: My WWII Submarine Battles
William J. Ruhe

The U.S. Navy in Vietnam: An Illustrated History
Edward J. Marolda

The Liberty *Incident: The 1967 Israeli Attack on the U.S. Navy Spy Ship*
A. Jay Cristol

Lone Star
Navy

TEXAS, THE FIGHT FOR THE GULF OF MEXICO, AND THE SHAPING OF THE AMERICAN WEST

JONATHAN W. JORDAN

Potomac Books
An imprint of the University of Nebraska Press

First Paperback Edition 2007
Copyright © 2006 by Jonathan W. Jordan.

Published in the United States by Potomac Books, Inc. All rights reserved. No part of this book may be reproduced in any manner whatsoever without written permission from the publisher, except in the case of brief quotations embodied in critical articles and reviews.

Library of Congress Cataloging-in-Publication Data

Jordan, Jonathan W., 1967–
    Lone Star navy : Texas, the fight for the Gulf of Mexico, and the shaping of the American West / Jonathan W. Jordan.— 1st ed.
      p. cm.
    Includes bibliographical references (p.) and index.
    ISBN 978-1-59797-053-2 (paperback : alk. paper)
    1. Texas. Navy—History. 2. Texas—History, Naval—19th century. 3. Mexico, Gulf of—History, Naval—19th century. 4. Texas—History—Revolution, 1835–1836—Naval operations. 5. Texas— History—Republic, 1836–1846.
I. Title.

F390.J67 2005
976.4'0345—dc22

2005006911

Jay Karamales, Cartographer

Printed in the United States of America on acid-free paper that meets the American National Standards Institute Z39-48 Standard.

First Edition

For my darling Kate

Contents

Acknowledgments	ix
OVERTURE: SHIFTING WINDS	xi

PROLOGUE: PRELUDE TO REVOLUTION (1832–1835)

One: The Troubled Texas Waters	1
Two: Drawing Blood	9
Three: The Influence of Naval Power on the Texas Revolution	19

ACT ONE: FLEET OF THE REVOLUTION (1835–1836)

Four: A War of Privateers	25
Five: The Fleet That Sank Its Government	36
Six: Iron Men for Wooden Ships	42
Seven: The Revolution at Sea	49

ACT TWO: A NATIONAL FLEET (1836–1837)

Eight: Defending the Lone Star	63
Nine: The General at the Helm	74
Ten: A Clash of Flagships	83
Eleven: Mister Fisher's Revenge	89
Twelve: Death of a Navy	98
Thirteen: Hell to Pay	101

INTERMISSION: THE PAPER NAVY (1837–1839)

Fourteen: Managing a Ghost Fleet	109
Fifteen: Vive la France!	115

ACT THREE: THE SECOND TEXAS NAVY (1839–1846)

Sixteen: Houston, Lamar, and Shifting Political Currents	121
Seventeen: Phoenix of the Sea	129
Eighteen: Wintertime in New York	139
Nineteen: The Seafaring Life	142

Twenty: Gunboat Diplomacy	151
Twenty-one: At Sea	156
Twenty-two: Second Thoughts	177
Twenty-three: The Great Game	188
Twenty-four: Red Skies in Morning	192
Twenty-five: The Wooden Aegis	195
Twenty-six: Mutiny on the *San Antonio*	201
Twenty-seven: The Horse Latitudes	208
Twenty-eight: The Plan	231
Twenty-nine: Amateurs in Command	236
Thirty: "To Save the Republic"	246
Thirty-one: The Last Hurrah	250
Thirty-two: Cat and Mouse	259
Thirty-three: The Showdown	263
Thirty-four: The Pirate Navy	272
Thirty-five: The War at Home	279
Thirty-six: A Slow Death	287
Thirty-seven: Flotsam and Jetsam	297
Thirty-eight: Ghosts and Graves	304
Epilogue: The Verdict	307
Appendix A: The Texas Navy and the San Jacinto Campaign	310
Appendix B: Glossary of Selected Naval Terms	316
Notes	321
Bibliography	358
Index	369
About the Author	381

Acknowledgments

THIS BRIEF CHRONICLE OF THE maritime drama that unfolded during the heady days of Texas independence would not be possible without the support of the following scholars: Dr. Clive Cussler, known to the world as a great adventure novelist, but one of the country's most successful nautical archeologists in his own right; Walter Nass of the Texas Navy Association, the man who brought the story of the Texas Navy to the internet; Texas historian and author Jim Haley; gifted archeologist and historian Gregg Dimmick; Professor James E. Crisp of North Carolina State University; Wayne Gronquist of the National Underwater & Maritime Agency; Billy Bob Crim of the Texas Navy Association; naval history expert Mark Lardas; Kurt Voss of Galveston's Texas Seaport Museum; Allegra Young, Kate Jordan, David Bissinger and John O'Neill, for editorial, literary and common-sense help; Shannon Jordan Dollinger, a gifted scientific and technical illustrator; Will Fisher IV, descendant of Texas' most colorful Navy Secretary; Jerry Drake of Texas's General Land Office; Dr. Robert V. Remini; John S.D. Eisenhower; Professor Linda Arnold of Virginia Tech; Amy Borgens; Dr. Michael Crawford of Washington's Naval Historical Center; B. Rice Aston of the Sons of the Republic of Texas; and the helpful staffs of the Texas State Library and Archives, University of Texas's Center for American History and Benson Latin American Library, Sam Houston Library and Research Center, Texas Tech University Library, Galveston's Rosenberg Library, the National Archives and Records Administration, Star of the Republic Museum, Texas Seaport Museum, Naval Historical Center, Daughters of the Republic of Texas Library, Historical New Orleans Collection, Chicago's Newberry Library, Rockport's Texas Maritime Museum, Houston's San Jacinto Museum, and the Brazoria County Historical Museum. Thanks also to Patricia Barriga Robles of Mexico City and Kristin Konschnik of Austin, Texas, for providing research assistance; Jaime Fernandez, Benjamin Mendoza III and Rose Buckley of Austin for essential translation help; and to Herb McCreary for early inspiration.

OVERTURE

Shifting Winds

Yet Zeus the all-seeing grants to Athene's prayer, that the wooden walls only shall not fail...
—Herodotus, THE HISTORIES, Book VII

IN THE EARLY DECADES OF THE American experiment, a small, impoverished nation, conceived in revolution and tutored in the American school of democracy, struggled to build a government from the ashes of war. In time, a small band of frontier patriots assembled the basic necessities of government: bodies to create and execute laws, infrastructure to supply rudimentary public services, and institutions to assure the national defense.

That nation was Texas, a curious mix of fighters and farmers, lawyers and merchants, doctors and ranchers, all drawn together by a thirst for land, wealth, adventure, and freedom. The republic they founded would last a mere ten years, but in that short span, it would experience the full range of growing pains felt by larger democracies struggling to balance freedom and security, individualism and collective action. And—oddly enough for a country dominated by plains, deserts, and mesas—this internal struggle was most openly observed, debated and fretted over in the naval affairs of the Republic of Texas.

The early 1830s was a time of awakening and uncertainty for the two great democracies that occupied the land between the Great Lakes and the Yucatán peninsula. In the United States of America, the old order, represented by the revolutionary generation of eastern gentlemen, gave way to a new breed of rough frontiersmen from the West, exemplified by Andrew Jackson, Henry Clay, and Davy Crockett. As the heavy hand of the British Empire drew back from America's shores, confidence became the nation's watchword. America's spirit stretched its wings and turned towards the wild lands of the West.

The United States of Mexico, for its part, was struggling with a fundamental question that had haunted republicans since the constitutional debates of the 1780s: the proper balance between local autonomy and central government control. This question came to the forefront when Mexico shook off the imperial yoke of Spain and set off a chain of violence that caused rivers of blood to be spilled in the deserts, cities, and jungles of Zacetecas, Yucatán, Tabasco, Coahuila, and Campeche. Although veterans of Mexico's revolutionary years long dominated Mexican politics, the great cultural diversity of that budding empire frustrated efforts to forge a national consensus. As the 1830s dawned, the rise of Generalissimo Santa Anna set the stage for a tragic cycle of instability, uprisings, and repression punctuated by infrequent spasms of national unity and peace.

Texas broke away from Mexico in the fall of 1835 for a number of reasons, chief among them an innate thirst for individualism that resisted central control—particularly by a government that immigrants from the American South regarded as foreign. But the spirit of independence that compelled Texan colonists to shake off the loose bridle of Mexican control also defied the efforts of Stephen F. Austin, Sam Houston, David Burnet, and other leaders to harness this spirited people. And nowhere was this freedom flaunted more brazenly than on the worn pine decks of the Texas warships.

The pages that follow tell the story of a little fleet of wooden warships, bought on credit by an impoverished band of revolutionaries and sent to sea on a single mission: to win independence for Texas. After Texas won its freedom, the Texas Navy's mission changed as the fledgling Texas government, bereft of funds, was forced to weigh the heavy costs of defense against a reduced need for security along its southern border. Coastal defense was pushed to the margin as new priorities vied for the young government's attention.

But the spirit of Texas's mariners, like that of their kinsmen on the frontier, could not be easily restrained. When they saw an enemy flag on the waters, their instincts were to fight without regard to diplomatic niceties or considerations of cost. Once dispatched, a fully-armed man-of-war could not be recalled without the consent of its captain. Texas leaders like Houston and Burnet fought an uphill battle, often unsuccessfully, to rein in their captains and commodores and maintain control over foreign policy back at the capital, where it belonged.

Complicating this struggle between the government and its sea captains was a deep-seated clash of visions over what Texas should become. The martial spirit of the frontiersman, at first dampened by President Sam Houston in the interest of economy, was stoked to the boiling point by President Mirabeau Lamar, the cultured paladin who dreamed of an empire of the west. For nearly seven years, the Texas Navy was pulled between these conflicting political tides. The rushing rivers of imperialism, economy, and diplomacy thus collided with a deafening roar, dashing old ideals and throwing new ones to the surface.

The men who sailed for Texas, fought on the seas, then faded into history's dim kaleidoscope are a permanent part of Texas's legendary past. Like a wave that breaks against the coastline, dispersing on the shore but shaping the land in the process, the Texas Navy shaped the Republic of Texas, and in doing so, helped shape the American West.

A Note on Quotations

THE LEGENDARY CHARACTERS WHO CREATED the Republic of Texas and its navy were a rough bunch, usually educated in the backwoods of the American South or aboard merchant or naval sailing ships. In an age where letters were written in longhand, often without the assistance of clerks or secretaries, the correspondence of Sam Houston, Commodore Moore, Stephen F. Austin, and other Texas pioneers is replete with misspellings, grammatical errors, and awkward or archaic phrasings that ring poorly in the modern ear. All of these idiosyncrasies are left as they are found in their originals, to remain true to the direct, coarse prose of the Texas frontier.

PROLOGUE

*Prelude to Revolution
(1832–1835)*

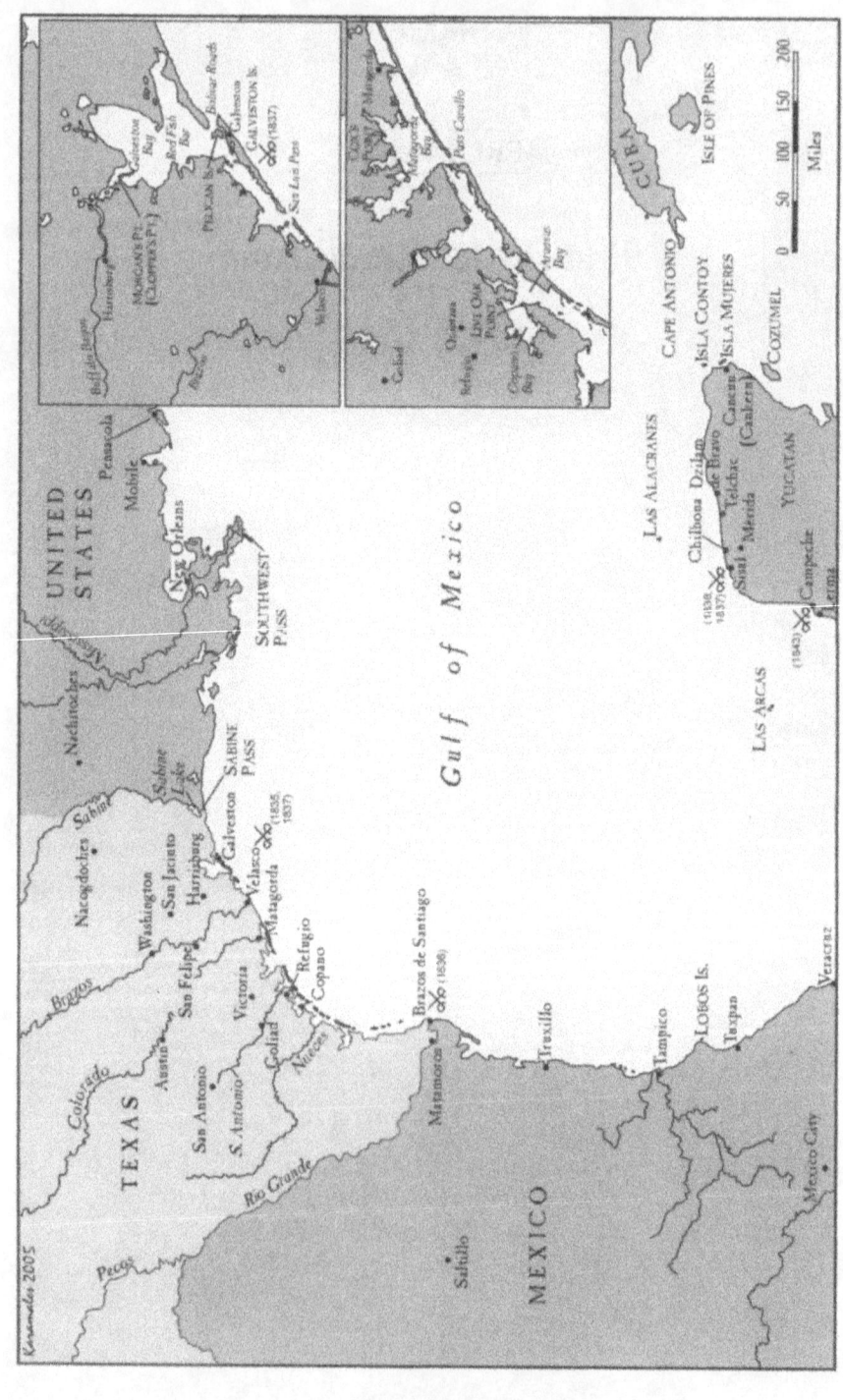

CHAPTER ONE

The Troubled Texas Waters

Our sea coast for years has produced nothing but a scene of fraud, corruption and piracies, to the unfortunate, who either by misfortune or design have been drawn upon our shores....
—Henry G. Smith, provisional governor of Texas, November 1835

THE STORM SWELLS OF REVOLUTION were awakened by a tide of Anglo-American immigration that swept the Mexican state of Coahuila y Tejas in the late 1820s. By the early 1830s, Texas had become culturally and economically unique within the Mexican federation, being largely populated by Anglo-Americans from the United States who began referring to themselves as "Texians" rather than Mexicans. As one French traveler observed, "Texians are radically different from most North Americans in their social temperament. They are in large part emigrants from the Western regions and possess that vivacity of character and especially that combative spirit which is characteristic of the American frontiersman." Texian émigrés, a fiercely independent people, chafed at Mexican policies towards immigration, states' rights, slavery, trade, and a host of other political and economic issues.

Mexican leaders feared that the flood of *norteamericanos* would spawn dreams of secession from Mexico or even—God forbid—annexation to the ever-expanding United States. By 1831, Mexico's darkest fears became reality; fueled by a cycle of Anglo agitation and ineffective Mexican response, Texas began drifting away from its legal guardian and into the arms of its biological parent.

To remedy the problem of demographics, the Mexican government resorted to military occupation. Gen. Manuel de Mier y Terán, commander of Mexico's northern forces, stationed troops at four strongpoints around Texas to impose the government's will on the increasingly dissatisfied Anglo community. Besides the main garrison at Béxar, modern-day San Antonio, soldiers were sent to Fort Velasco, at the mouth of the Brazos River (the most important river in early Texas), Anáhuac at the north end of Galveston Bay—Texas's deepest port—and Nacogdoches in northeastern Texas. With this show of national authority, law and order would be maintained, and Texas would remain fixed within Mexico City's orbit. Or so Mexican leaders hoped.

It was a daunting task. Texas, the northern half of Coahuila y Tejas, covered over 200 million acres and boasted a 300-mile coastline. Its most fertile land was segmented by a dozen major rivers that impeded overland travel. From east to west, these waterways included the Neches River, the western fork of the Sabine River; the Trinity, which empties into Galveston Bay; the Brazos, which connected Texas's largest colony to the Gulf of Mexico; the Colorado, on which present-day Austin stands; the Navidad, Guadalupe, and San Antonio Rivers of south Texas; and the Nueces River, running to modern-day Corpus Christi, the traditional border of Texas and the Mexican state of Tamaulipas. (The Rio Bravo del Norte, now called the Rio Grande, would not become the formal southern boundary of Texas until 1848.) Along the shallow, sandy coast, Galveston Bay and a succession of inlets provided hundreds of hiding places for pirates and smugglers sailing in from New Orleans or Florida. These treacherous, snag-strewn bays—Galveston, Matagorda, Aransas, and Copano—and the rivers that fed them would leave a deep mark on the character and people of early Texas.

As Texian discontent with government policies grew in the early 1830s, Mexico's forces took on the unhappy character of an army of occupation rather than a national defense force. The proud but chronically impoverished soldiers stationed at Béxar and Nacogdoches had little to fear for the moment, being in the heart of *Tejano* country, those portions of Texas inhabited by ethnic Mexicans. But during the hot, steamy summer of 1832, Texian anger vented itself at Anáhuac, on Galveston Bay, and Brazoria, the principal port on the Brazos River. The Anáhuac and Brazoria garrisons were deep inside Anglo territory, and like the settlements they controlled, they depended heavily on water traffic for communications, supplies, and reinforcements. Though they did not know it yet, the unfortunate troops at these towns would soon witness the colonists' first experiments in naval combat.

For the Mexican government, the trouble all began at Anáhuac.

In 1832, the garrison at Anáhuac was commanded by a fighting Kentuckian named John Davis Bradburn. To most colonists, he was not a pleasant man. A former Louisiana militia officer, Coloniel Bradburn was high-handed, arbitrary, and to many Texians, a traitor to his race for selling out to the Mexicans. As military commander of Anáhuac and the surrounding environs, "Juan" Bradburn earned the bitter hatred of local inhabitants by marching into the nearby municipality of Liberty—a state-chartered settlement thought to be too close to federal property—and forcibly dissolving the town. He redistributed settlers' lands to men he considered loyal to the central government, arrested land grant commissioners, confiscated slaves without compensating their owners, and declared martial law along the coast. Bradburn tended to think in purely military terms, and his power, zealousness, and lack of finesse made him the wrong man at the wrong time to protect Mexico's political interests.

In June of 1832, Colonel Bradburn earned the wrath of a small group of hotheaded political activists, including John Austin, the mayor of Brazoria, and a fiery twenty-three-year-old William Barret Travis, who would meet his legendary end at the Alamo. After a series of civil disturbances, Bradburn had several ringleaders, including Travis, arrested for sedition. He held the agitators in a converted brick kiln until they could be sent to Matamoros, Mexico's stronghold on the Rio Grande, for trial. The arrests sent the prisoners' enraged friends and relatives into surrounding towns, where they recruited some one hundred armed volunteers to march on Anáhuac and free their "American" comrades.

The motley band of frontiersmen had enough horse sense to see that they needed support from the sea if they were to force Bradburn to come to terms. As Bradburn himself once observed, armed schooners would be required for any assault on Anáhuac, since the fort could easily be resupplied through Galveston Bay. So Francis Johnson, a thirty-three-year-old frontiersman elected as the militia's leader, appealed to local ship captains for support of a blockade effort. Soon three small merchant vessels—the *Water Witch*, the *Stephen F. Austin*, and the *Red River*—were loaned to the insurgents, and the Texians were ready to take over the bay.

Water Witch was a tiny sloop with a four-and-a-half-ton hold commanded by Capt. James Spillman. She took on four riflemen, and weighed anchor to patrol Cedar Point, west of Anáhuac. *Stephen F. Austin*, a five-ton boat with five armed men, went out under Capt. William Scott to patrol the waters between Anáhuac and Double Bayou to the southeast. The third vessel, *Red River*, was commanded by David Kokernot; she was dispatched to cover Anáhuac. With this "sea militia," Texas fielded its first unofficial fleet.

The tiny flotilla spent several days in late June merrily playing havoc on supply vessels bound for Anáhuac, cutting off the garrison's supply of food, gunpowder, and men. *Stephen F. Austin* captured a Mexican boat at the mouth of Double Bayou, while *Water Witch* seized a vessel ferrying supplies to the garrison. As *Red River*'s captain recalled, the makeshift squadron cut off all support to Anáhuac's Fort Davis, "so that none of the [pro-government] Tories could carry provisions to the enemy." The vessels drew fire from the fort's six-pounders as they dashed across its field of fire, but they managed to evade the splashing six-pound cannon balls and flying bullets long enough to capture three government-chartered boats loaded with butter, eggs, chickens, beef, and pork.

After several days of sporadic shooting, Colonel Bradburn knew his position was untenable. Provisions were running low, and there was no chance of resupply or reinforcement. So on the first of July, an embittered Bradburn agreed to a very one-sided settlement brokered by his worried commander in Nacogdoches: Bradburn relinquished all command of the fort, and the prisoners were immediately released. Stripped of his powers and fearing for his life, Bradburn attempted to flee Anáhuac in a small boat, but the rebel blockade was too tight. Abandoning this effort, he fled by night across east Texas to Louisiana, never to darken this damp, wooded corner of Texas again.

The Texians' victory over Colonel Bradburn whetted the small navy's appetite for destruction, and soon the squadron sailed throughout Galveston Bay, where it captured the customs house, arrested the deputy collector, and looted the building's offices. The motley fleet then sailed back to Anáhuac.

The insurrectionists had shattered their government's hold on Galveston's vital harbor.

As the makeshift militia was gathering at Anáhuac, a call went out for volunteers and cannon to assist the rebels, sparking another, more serious clash at Fort Velasco, a stockade was built in early 1832 at the mouth of the Brazos River on orders of Colonel Bradburn. Its commander, Lt. Col. Domingo de Ugartechea, built a wooden wall to protect the fort's hundred-man garrison, and placed an eight-pounder (a cannon firing an eight-pound ball) on a tall mound overlooking the entry to the Brazos and the nearby town of Velasco. This menacing gun was sited to control the entrance to the Brazos, which in turn regulated all river traffic to Stephen Austin's thriving Anglo colony of San Felipe. By the summer of 1832, free entry to San Felipe was impossible.

Somewhat unintentionally, the schooner *Brazoria* came to the rescue. A local shipmaster, John G. Rowland, offered to fit out his small vessel and have her ready to run the blockade by June 22. A thirty-year-old North Carolinian named William J. Russell took command of the boat, which was armed with two cannon—a brass nine-pounder and a swivel-mounted four-pounder—and brought aboard thirty rough-hewn volunteers to add small arms fire to his boat's arsenal. *Brazoria* sailed peacefully down the muddy Brazos, but Ugartechea's soldiers blocked her way at Fort Velasco. As Captain Russell retreated back up the river, Ugartechea's troops called out to *Brazoria*, ordering the rogue ship to return.

Brazoria obeyed the following day, but not in the way the soldiers had expected. Captain Russell sailed back, accompanied by around 150 Anglo sharpshooters, who escorted him from the river's thickly wooded banks. When they arrived at Fort Velasco around June 26, the militia fanned out and directed a murderous fire on the redoubt while *Brazoria*'s small cannon bombarded it from the river.

The Mexicans attempted to work their eight-pounder, but the gun's mount rose high above the fort's walls, making it an easy target for the Texas sharpshooters firing from the thick woods and the decks of the schooner, which was lined with bullet-stopping cotton bales. To Russell's relief, the cannon—incapable of being depressed enough to hit the nearby *Brazoria*—proved useless to the garrison. Texas musket balls picked off an alarming number of artillerymen, and the survivors scrambled down the hill to the safety of the stockade's walls. With casualties mounting, his main cannon out of action, and no foreseeable help, Colonel Ugartechea offered to surrender the fort on honorable terms.

His troops marched out on June 27. In the fighting around Fort Velasco, some seven Texians and forty-two Mexican troops died in the most violent confrontation yet between Anglos and government troops. As with many of the confrontations Texas would force with Mexico, however, no one thought to ask the question, "What next?"

With the fall of Fort Velasco and the loss of Anáhuac, Mexican control over the upper Texas coast was broken. By mid-July the Nacogdoches garrison had quit the town, and the presidio at Tenoxtitlán on the upper Brazos was quickly disbanded. The outer reaches of Mexico's power were thus pushed back to San Antonio de Béxar, essentially turning the clock back to 1829, when Texians lived and traded with virtually no government regulation.

But the success of the "War Party" radicals also invited reprisals against the upstart colonists, who had shed Mexican blood and openly defied their government. Mexico may have been embroiled in another round of political crises for the moment, but the more politically astute Anglos knew better than to underestimate Mexican patriotism in the face of a national insult. They also understood that 20,000 farmers could not withstand a battle-hardened army supported by a nation of over six million.

To head off a full-scale invasion by a vengeful government, the more coolheaded leaders published a series of proclamations in which they announced that the actions at Velasco and Anáhuac were aimed at the centralist faction, and not the Mexican Republic, to which they remained loyal. The rebels, they claimed, were actually supporting Gen. Antonio López de Santa Anna and his federalist party. These proclamations were presented to Mexico's local commandant amidst lavish celebrations and banquets when he arrived in Texas at the head of 400 regulars, an act of shrewd diplomacy that averted bloody reprisals. The Texas proclamations were a thinly veiled cover to allow the government to save face, and most observers knew it. But they contained enough truth to defuse a confrontation for the time being, and Texas was spared further bloodshed for another three years.

From the outbreak of violence in 1832 until the beginning of the Texas Revolution, at least three countries—the United States, Great Britain, and Mexico—maintained significant naval presence in the Gulf of Mexico, while two other powers, Spain and France, sent warships into the Gulf from time to time to keep an eye on their present and former colonies. The United States's principal bases for Gulf of Mexico operations were Pensacola, in the Florida Territory, the headquarters of its West Indies Squadron, and, at New Orleans to the West. The U.S. Navy fielded one frigate, the *Constellation*, and a number of sloops and smaller warships, to protect its commerce from pirates and intercept illegal slave shipments from the Caribbean and Africa. While officials in Pensacola carefully maintained a neutral stance as the Texas-Mexico rift widened, commanders in New Orleans—like much of that city's population— tended to side with their kinsmen to the west. Until the Texas Navy reached its peak of professionalism in the early 1840s, the U.S. fleet was the most effective fighting force in the Gulf, although warships were never deployed in significant numbers along the coastline.

Great Britain's interests in the Gulf included protecting its merchant ships from predators, interrupting the slave trade, and preventing the United States from gobbling up too much former Spanish territory. As the principal arm of British foreign power, the Royal Navy operated from bases in the western Caribbean, and it maintained close ties to the Mexican fleet at Veracruz. The heavy ships-of-the-line that fought at Trafalgar were rarely sent to the Gulf, being unnecessary to protect British interests and generally too big to be of much use in the Gulf's shallow ports. Britain did send smaller sloops-of-war into Mexican waters on diplomatic missions, however, and as Mexico's grip on Texas began to slip, the Royal Navy kept an even closer eye on Mexico's eastern coast.

After its break with Spain in 1821, Mexico began building up a fleet to protect itself from another invasion by Spain and to enforce its laws along coastal regions from Texas to Yucatán. Two heavy Spanish ships—the seventy-four-gun frigate *Asia* and the brig *Constante*—defected from Spain's Pacific fleet, and by 1826, the Mexican Navy included the frigates *Libertad*, *Victoria*, and *Guerrero*, the brigs *Bravo* and *Hermon*, the schooners *Papaloapan*, *Tampico*, and *Orizaba*, and the warships *Félix*, *Luciana*, *Perdenal*, and *Chalco*.

This impressive roster was, however, a wooden tiger. The Mexican Navy— like much of Mexico's military—was hampered by chronic political instability, irregular pay, and a lack of coherent strategy. Worse yet, Mexico's fleet lacked enough officers and sailors to put all her ships into action. As one U.S. consul in Mexico informed Secretary of State Henry Clay, "The navy of Mexico consists of a small frigate, two brigs and two or three small schooners, all of which are in wretched condition. On board the frigate there is but one seaman. The brig Victoria is in nearly the same state . . . There are not, in all their vessels of war, seamen enough to man either of the brigs of war."

Lacking qualified sailors and officers, the Mexican government recruited them from foreign navies. Lured by promises of faster promotion, better pay, prize money from captured Spanish ships, and of course, adventure, officers from the United States and Great Britain flocked to the Mexican ensign and infused new life into the young republic's navy. The long European peace that began with Napoleon's exile in 1815 sorely limited a junior officer's ability to advance, so adventurers like Britain's Lord Cochrane began using their leave time to earn extra money in mercenary service.

In 1826 the Mexican government decided to appoint foreigners to several senior positions. Command of the Mexican Navy was given to Commodore David Porter, a distinguished American captain who had made a name for himself in the War of 1812, and afterwards as commander of the United States West Indies Squadron. Commodore Porter—suspended from U.S. naval command for insulting the mayor of Fojardo, Puerto Rico—brought with him a number of veteran officers, many of whom would offer their services to Texas in the coming years. Porter's tenure with the Mexican Navy got off to a rocky start due to his broken Spanish and his demands for the extravagant sum of $13,000 per month to cover expenses, but he was able to retain command of Mexico's naval forces until 1829, when shifting political tides and harsh fiscal realities brought foreign dominance of the Mexican Navy to a close.

In the early 1830s, Mexico's support for its navy was limited to unfunded appropriations and proclamations that were never implemented, and by 1834 the Veracruz fleet was reduced to a handful of small warships, including the schooners *Moctezuma, Veracruzana, Campecheana,* and *Papaloapan.* Of these, all but the *Moctezuma* were stuck in port for want of crews and maintenance. Despite efforts to improve the navy by Minister of War and Marine José de Herrera and his energetic successor, José Maria Tornel, by mid-1835, Mexico's eastern fleet boasted only the schooners *Veracruzana* and *Moctezuma.*

But for the moment, none of this really mattered much to Texas. Mexico's prescient northern commander, General Terán, was wary of United States designs on Texas. He tried to impose order along the coast in the late 1820s by summoning a frigate to convoy ships sailing between Matagorda, Brazoria, and Galveston. He also frequented Texas ports aboard the armed schooner *Constante* until it ran aground and broke up in 1830. But with Terán's death in 1832 and the withdrawal of Mexican detachments from east Texas, Mexican naval operations in Texas waters were limited to revenue enforcement, and these efforts were half-hearted.

Even Mexico's infrequent use of revenue cutters and pirate hunters occasionally caused trouble. In the spring of 1834, army Col. Juan Alamonte conducted an extensive survey of Texas which, to no one's surprise, found smuggling to be rampant. He quickly dispatched troops to Anáhuac, which had remained abandoned after the uprising of 1832, and sent for the armed schooner *Moctezuma*. The schooner did its job too well, detaining a number of Spanish, Texan, and neutral vessels, and became yet another symbol of Mexican "oppression." William Travis, the young hothead whose protests sparked the siege of Anáhuac, wrote that *Moctezuma*'s operations "aroused the indignation & resentment of the whole people" like no other issue had done before.

Moctezuma went too far in early 1835, however, when it seized the U.S. merchant vessel *Martha*. Suspecting *Martha* to be a Texas smuggler, *Moctezuma* forced her to drop her anchors, boarded her, and towed her towards Matamoros for legal proceedings. As *Moctezuma* escorted her prisoner to the mouth of the Rio Grande, the two vessels stumbled across the U.S. revenue cutter *Ingham*. Believing *Ingham* to be another Texas smuggler, *Moctezuma* bore down upon the American schooner in an attack posture. *Ingham* suddenly heeled about and fired a broadside at the Mexican warship, which broke off the attack and fled to the mouth of the Rio Grande, running aground so badly that she was put out of action for several months. *Ingham*'s captain, Ezekiel Jones, pulled alongside the helpless *Moctezuma*, chastised her skipper, and berated him into releasing all "American" citizens aboard *Martha*, underscoring the impotence even of Mexico's best warships.

Such were the animosities of "American" Texians to the renewed Mexican naval presence by early 1835. And Texian anger and frustration over Mexican control of their seaports would come to the forefront when the pot boiled over in the fall.

CHAPTER TWO

Drawing Blood

> *The issue of the suit is indeed a very remarkable one ... the pirates set at liberty and the Attorneys committed to jail.*
> —*New Orleans Courier*, January 18, 1836

THE WAR BEGAN WHEN AN obscure Mexican army captain tried to rebuild an old, abandoned customs house. In early 1835, the Mexican government ordered Capt. Antonio Tenorio to take forty soldiers to Anáhuac, a frontier town of roughly a thousand souls at the north end of Galveston Bay. The captain's mission was to reestablish the customs house for the collection of import duties on goods shipped to Texas.

Tenorio's superiors were worried. Rebuilding the customs house at Anáhuac would infuriate Anglo-American settlers, who had been living on Mexican land virtually tax-free for over a decade. These "Texian" colonists had built farms, homes, and businesses from the Gulf of Mexico to San Antonio. They were a prickly bunch, having lived for years with little interference from a generous and usually distracted Mexican government, and they were not about to submit to taxation, import duties, and those other aspects of Mexican life they feared and despised: Roman-style civil law, a strong central government, enforced Catholicism, and the abolition of slavery.

Word quickly spread among local commanders that armed vigilance committees were forming to oppose the government's bureaucrats and soldiers. Mexican fears of insurrection must have seemed justified: as Captain Tenorio set up his command post in the heart of Anglo country, colonists began venting hostility at their "oppressors" at a level not seen since 1832. The ranking military commander in Texas, Col. Domingo de Ugartechea, complained of them to Captain Tenorio, "Nothing is heard but God damn Santa Anna. God damn Ugartechea."

The Texians' rebellious attitude was a sign of the times. In the hot, tense summer of 1835, passions ran high within that most Americanized of the Mexican provinces. To the south, Mexico was in a state of civil war over the level of autonomy state governments would retain within the Mexican federation. The federalists, whom the Texians passively supported, believed in strong state and local government, as envisioned by Mexico's liberal Constitution of 1824. Centralists, now championed by the turncoat federalist hero, General Santa Anna, believed in weak, unarmed state governments held in check by Mexico City's standing army. The violence reached Coahuila in April 1835, when Santa Anna sent his brother-in-law, Gen. Martín Perfecto de Cós, with a centralist army into the state capital of Saltillo to enforce subservience to the Supreme Government.

As Cós battered down his federalist opponents in neighboring Coahuila, the usually boisterous Texians sat out the fray. That is, until June 30, 1835, when William Barrett Travis, the fire-eating frontier lawyer from Liberty, decided to close down Captain Tenorio's garrison. He sailed to Anáhuac aboard the sloop *Ohio* with twenty armed men and a crude six-pounder cannon mounted on a pair of sawmill truck wheels. Disembarking at the Trinity River mouth, Travis's insurgents surrounded Tenorio's men. The sensible army captain promptly surrendered without violence, trekking to San Felipe on the Brazos for a brief stay as a fêted guest of the worried colonists there.

Most Texians were furious at "Buck" Travis's impulsive, reckless move. Elders from Liberty condemned his actions as "unwise, ill-timed and criminal," but the town's retraction did no good; the Texians' affront to the central government was serious enough to justify sending General Cós north to deal with the insurrectionists. Before moving against the rebels, Cós brought up reinforcements, and sent for one of the most notorious sea dogs on the Gulf Coast—Thomas "Mexico" Thompson. Life on Galveston Bay was about to get worse.

"Mexico" Thompson, a second lieutenant in the Mexican Navy, was a man to whom Destiny seemed to take a natural dislike. Giving up a meager living as tavern owner and a merchant captain, Thompson was driven by grinding poverty into the Mexican naval service. He was described by one who knew him as a "a frank and good-natured man, but of the most desperate and reckless character," prone to violence, especially after indulging in one of his fierce bouts with liquor. The short, thick-set Englishman's light blue eyes, huge blonde mustache, and ruddy complexion set him apart from his colleagues physically, and his English heritage distinguished him culturally. Regardless of his outward differences, though, Thompson dutifully served Mexico while awaiting an opportunity to improve his fortunes.

Fortune, among others, would get a chuckle out of Thompson's orders to pacify Texas, because he was one of the worst possible candidates for such a dicey task. Caring little for the ungrateful Yankees who lived along the rivers and bays of Texas, Thompson viewed Mexico's rebellious province as a gold mine for an opportunistic official like himself. The Texians, for their part, saw him as simply the latest in a long line of petty tyrants, a pirate under a Mexican flag. His "administration" of this region would be nasty, brutish, and short.

Thompson sailed his warship, the *Correo Mejicano,* into Texas waters in the summer of 1835, escorting the supply vessels *Josepha* and *Ana Maria.* The *Correo* was a trim, low-lying schooner, meaning that she carried two masts with her sails rigged "fore and aft" (as opposed to a classic "square-rigger," whose sails are set perpendicular to the vessel's keel). Built in New Orleans under the name *Henrieta*, she was sold to the Mexican government on June 19, 1835, and the Mexican Navy hastily outfitted her with arms from the schooner *General Bravo.* Weighing a mere thirty-three tons loaded, *Correo* carried one, possibly two cannon (accounts differ), and some small arms for her ten soldiers who acted as marines. In addition to her soldiers, the *Correo Mejicano* carried fourteen sailors and three officers.

Around July 5, Thompson was sent from Matamoros to Anáhuac with orders to determine whether Captain Tenorio's men had been massacred or expelled from the region, and report his findings to General Cós, the ranking officer in Texas. While at Matamoros, army Lt. Jiminez Carlos Ocampo boarded *Correo* with a small detachment of soldiers and $1,000 in payroll and expense money for Tenorio's garrison. After escorting a landing force to Copano Bay near Matagorda, halfway down the Texas coast, Thompson's *Correo* made its way to the cradle of rebellion, to shed the first blood of the Texas Revolution.

Once *Correo* dropped anchor at Anáhuac in late July, Thompson lost no time in alienating the local population. He declared martial law and warned all citizens against organizing an armed militia, a violation of Santa Anna's new centralist laws. In early August, he confiscated a merchant sloop leaving Galveston Bay and sold it back to its owner for $100. He refused to allow ships to deliver basic staples such as flour or coffee to Anáhuac, declared a blockade of the Texas coast, and impressed another small sloop into his service. Decreeing that "there were no slaves legally indented in Texas," he also warned the colonists that he would confiscate any slaves he found, with a promise to free the captives after one year's servitude—to himself, of course. He also offered a $1,000 reward for the capture of William Travis, whom he vowed would swing from his yardarm within a half-hour of his capture. By the time he spotted the merchant brig *Tremont* at the mouth of the Brazos River on the morning of September 1, "Mexico" Thompson was one of the most hated men in Texas.

As *Correo Mejicano* bullied her way along the upper Texas coast, Stephen F. Austin—freed from a Mexican prison after eighteen months' captivity—was in New Orleans, packing his bags for a long-awaited voyage home. Having watched Mexico drift away from its republican ideals before and during his imprisonment, the embittered *empresario* who founded the largest colony in Texas now considered Santa Anna an "unprincipled bloody monster" for defying the Mexican Congress and Mexico's venerated Constitution of 1824. It was with the intention of forcing Mexico to accept the Americanization of Texas that Austin boarded the ship named for his capital city, the armed schooner *San Felipe*.

San Felipe was owned by the trading company of McKinney & Williams. Based at the twin cities on the mouth of the Brazos River, Quintana and Velasco (south of present-day Houston), the firm's owners—Thomas F. McKinney and Samuel May Williams—purchased *San Felipe* in New Orleans for the moderate price of $8,965, "including freight on board when taken." ("Freight on board" was a veiled reference to contraband items such as cannon, muskets, and gunpowder that McKinney & Williams was hastily importing into the volatile region.) Mounting two twelve-pounder carronades, *San Felipe* carried twelve sailors and thirty passengers, and was placed under the command of a McKinney & Williams employee, Capt. William Hurd.

A contemporary described Captain Hurd as a "plain man, evidently accustomed only to the management of trading vessels," but like most hard-boiled Texians, Captain Hurd was a quick study and always ready to jump into the thick of a fight when provoked. By the end of August, Hurd had armed and provisioned his ship, and *San Felipe* lay at anchor, ready to take her very important passenger home, where she would rendezvous with destiny and an American merchant vessel called the *Tremont*.

Tremont was a brig—a two-masted craft with square-rigged sails—carrying goods from Pensacola to Brazoria, the major port on the Brazos River and the lifeline to Austin's colony. Too heavily laden to cross the shallow Brazos bar, *Tremont* hovered off the town of Velasco, at the Brazos mouth, and was "lightening," or transferring her cargo of lumber to a shallower McKinney & Williams vessel, the steamboat *Laura*. As she did so, Thompson stopped her, later claiming that he suspected that she did not have proper import papers. He also may have suspected *Tremont* of importing slaves to Texas, a practice strictly forbidden by international and Mexican law.

Bellowing through a speaking trumpet, Thompson ordered *Tremont*'s captain and mates to come aboard *Correo* with the brig's papers. When *Tremont*'s master could not produce a satisfactory manifest, Thompson, with his usual inflexibility, sent over a rowboat and a small sloop loaded with soldiers to take possession of the brig.

Watching from the shore, Thomas McKinney flew into a rage. McKinney, a Kentuckian who had carved out a small shipping company from the coastal wilderness, was not a man to be trifled with; Stephen Austin's nephew, Moses Austin Bryan, described the rough-hewn magnate as "no ordinary man, bold and outspoken, generous, warm-hearted, enthusiastic and devoted to his friends, and a bitter enemy, of strong partialities and prejudices," who "could see no faults in his friends and no virtue in enemies." As *Correo*'s marines boarded *Tremont*, McKinney and his fellow citizens cursed, threatened, then finally took matters into their own hands. Some thirty of their number ran to their homes, grabbed their rifles, and came back to join McKinney aboard the steamer *Laura*, prepared to teach *Correo*'s captain a lesson he wouldn't forget.

Laura, rifles bristling from her decks, paddled alongside *Tremont*, and the vigilantes opened fire on *Correo*'s boarding party. Other volunteers stood on the beach, firing their rifles at the Mexican vessels, and Thompson reported that the vigilantes even fired a cannon at him from the shore. Thompson's men, chased off the *Tremont* by hot musket balls, jumped back in their boats. The rowboat paddled back to *Correo*, while four marines in the sloop attempted to haul up *Tremont*'s anchor, to bring her alongside Thompson's warship.

Correo hove about and loosed three cannon shots at *Laura*, each missing the mark. After fifteen minutes of gunfire, Thompson, shocked at the Texians' violent reaction, backed off to take stock of the situation. *Laura*, meanwhile, sent eight gunmen to safeguard *Tremont*, and then steamed east to intercept a mysterious sail on the horizon.

The two schooner captains, Hurd and Thompson, had been looking for each other for several weeks. Thompson had bragged to a sailor from *Tremont* that he would take *San Felipe* to Matamoros as a prize, while Captain Hurd reportedly told one New Orleans sailor that he had armed *San Felipe* to capture Thompson, whom the locals wanted to see hung from the nearest yardarm. The two captains were about to find out who was tougher.

San Felipe, sailing west from New Orleans, made sight of Velasco on September 1, just as the evening breeze was dying. Almost immediately, the schooner's lookouts spotted the notorious *Correo Mejicano* bobbing on the waves outside the Velasco landing. Seeing trouble ahead, Captain Hurd cleared his deck and readied his cannon for action, as *Laura* paddled out to meet *San Felipe*. When the two boats got close enough to see each other's passengers, McKinney spotted Austin on the deck. Overjoyed at the return of Texas's founding father, McKinney waved his hat in the air and threw it into the gulf as far as he could, while *Laura* tossed a line to *San Felipe* and towed her up the choppy green waters to Velasco.

Aboard *Correo*'s single deck, an anxious Lieutenant Thompson watched *San Felipe* approach through his spyglass. The wind and currents were running against him, so there was little he could do. He loaded his cannon with iron scraps, nails, and handfuls of musket balls, then settled back to watch *Laura* and *San Felipe* as they churned through the currents towards Velasco.

When the tandem vessels reached the Brazos mouth, both dropped anchor, and *Laura* began ferrying the schooner's cargo—including her very noted passenger—to the river mouth. Before Thompson's squinting eyes, about twenty heavily armed frontiersmen left *Laura* and boarded *San Felipe*. To those men, the night was still young, and their lethal brand of protest had not been heard clearly enough. Yet.

Around 8:00 that evening, as darkness fell, a hopeful evening breeze rippled over the schooners' canvas sails. Thompson, weighing his options carefully, quietly sent out his sloop with nine armed men for a closer look, giving them a signal lantern to warn him if the enemy began to sail. When *San Felipe* began to weigh anchor, the sloop's commander decided to inform Thompson personally, and heeled his boat around, back towards *Correo*. A Texian lookout spotted the sloop's movement in the faint moonlight, and *San Felipe* began firing. Barking out orders rapidly in his Cockney-accented Spanish, Thompson ordered his men to clear *Correo*'s deck for battle, and placed Lieutenant Ocampo in charge of *Correo*'s marines. He spotted *San Felipe* moving to get the weather gage, interposing herself between *Correo* and the wind—in a classic attack maneuver. The Englishman stood fast, grimly determined to fight off the insolent rebels.

San Felipe sailed within hailing distance, when "Mexico" Thompson ordered the schooner to halt, bellowing, "Let go your anchors, you damned Yankees!" Ignoring the order, *San Felipe* bore straight for *Correo*. After a nerve-wracking pause, Thompson ordered his men to open fire. One cannon shot ripped through *San Felipe*'s topgallant sail, and three more were loosed at the Texian schooner in rapid succession. Captain Hurd, his blood boiling, responded with two of his own. A fat burst of white smoke spewed from *San Felipe*'s sides as her stout carronades bucked violently on their slotted carriages. Neither shot scored a hit.

The men took to battle. Smoke built up faster than the light breeze could blow it away as the two schooners traded cannon shots and musket fire in the darkness. Commanders bellowed orders as they maneuvered to cross the unarmed bow or stern of the enemy. Gun captains harangued their men to load their cannon faster and aim carefully, while riflemen and musketeers knelt behind the boats' bulwarks and traded shots across each other's decks. Meanwhile, *Correo*'s sloop maneuvered around *San Felipe*'s stern, and Mexican marines fired their muskets at Hurd's crew from the cutter. At one point, Captain Hurd charged, intending to board *Correo*, but somehow he sprung his rudder, and Thompson easily tacked his ship out of harm's way.

All the while, spectators ashore strained to catch a glimpse of the ships through the swirling haze of smoke and darkness. They measured the battle's progress through disembodied orange flashes knifing through the black sky, followed by booms echoing over the rippling waters as the cannons' thunder vainly chased the flying projectiles.

The shooting lasted about forty-five minutes, and in the confusion of orders, screams and smoke, shots from *San Felipe* somehow managed to cut down several unlucky sailors aboard *Correo Mejicano* who lay bleeding on the ship's single deck. Among the casualties was Thompson himself, wounded twice in the thighs by rifle balls, and Thompson's small cannon, which a lucky shot had unshipped. Seeing *Correo*'s sloop cut off from her mother ship, Captain Hurd luffed his schooner around and chased the tiny boat, giving *Correo* a chance to escape. Corporal Lino Perez, the ranking soldier aboard the cutter, later reported to his superiors, "Since we couldn't join the *Correo* we started to sail towards land with the schooner following us. It was about eleven or midnight that they fired their last two cannonballs." In the darkness, *Correo*'s sloop eluded *San Felipe*, giving the schooner the slip by midnight, and its thoroughly unnerved men beached their craft at the Aransas Bar, marching south to the safety of the Mexican base at Matamoros, near the mouth of the Rio Grande.

After midnight, the enemy sloop lost for good, Captain Hurd ordered his tense, exhausted crew back to Velasco to take on ammunition and fresh volunteers in hopes of resuming the battle. *San Felipe* pulled into the harbor and brought aboard fresh stores of black powder and balls, but the dark night, brooking no further interruptions, shielded the enemy gunboat from prying eyes on the Velasco beaches. It was obvious to Hurd and McKinney that *Correo Mejicano* could not be found that night, much less captured, so the two men decided to wait for daybreak to see whether the she would come back.

Peering into the darkness, Thompson pondered his next move. His sloop and several valuable men were gone. He was low on ammunition, his cannon was dismounted, and he had wounded sailors in hostile waters. Thompson saw only one option left—to run south to Matamoros. At Thompson's bitter orders, the exhausted crew wore their ship around, and *Correo* swung out into the dark sea.

Throughout the night, "Mexico" Thompson cursed the Gulf's miserly winds and his own bad luck. The evening breeze calmed after he broke off the fight, and he had made damned little progress distancing himself from the Brazos mouth. As darkness broke before the sun's steady climb, his little warship was still within sight of Velasco. And if he could see the port, the Texas pirates could see him. His only hope was for a fresh land breeze to push him into the Gulf towards the safety of Matamoros.

To his dismay, Thompson saw a faint puff of smoke coming from the direction of Velasco. The steamer *Laura*, her boilers up, slowly chugged her way out to the drifting seas with *San Felipe* in tow. Lining the decks of both vessels were about twenty-five volunteers from Velasco, standing, crouching, ready to pour hot lead onto anyone foolish enough to resist them. As *Laura* towed *San Felipe* within a half-cannon shot of *Correo*, Lieutenant Thompson knew his luck had run out, and he sent Lieutenant Ocampo in a small boat to negotiate terms of surrender.

Under the muzzles of Texian rifles, the army lieutenant climbed aboard *San Felipe* and asked to parley with the schooner's commander. The dark-eyed lieutenant later complained that Hurd, "on being informed of my object, replied that it was no time for offering conditions after we had been beaten." Hurd took Ocampo prisoner aboard *San Felipe*, while several heavily armed frontiersmen clambered into an old whaleboat with a flag of truce and rowed out to the Mexican schooner.

Hurd's boarding party rounded up *Correo*'s marines and crew and sent them ashore in a boat. The boarding party then sent Lieutenant Thompson and four other men back to *San Felipe* to keep Lieutenant Ocampo company. The wounded were treated, although one sailor, a native of Baltimore named Blackburn, died two days later. *Correo Mejicano* came back to Velasco, not as a blockader, but as a spoil of Texas's first naval victory. "Mexico" Thompson's days of tyrannizing the Texas coast were over.

For four days, the prisoners were held aboard *San Felipe* as Hurd's men went through *Correo*'s papers and effects. They seized the ship's small arms and helped themselves to the passengers' baggage, including the army payroll carried by Lieutenant Ocampo. Lacking a court of admiralty jurisdiction in Texas, Velasco's citizens decided to send Thompson and his crew to New Orleans on piracy charges, on the grounds that *Correo* had fired on an American-registered vessel. On September 6, Hurd's men put the six prisoners in irons aboard *Correo Mejicano*, now flying an American flag, and set sail for New Orleans in the company of *San Felipe*.

When he arrived at New Orleans around September 15, Captain Hurd swore out an affidavit before Judge Galien Preval, a reliable Texas supporter, accusing *Correo*'s captain of attacking *San Felipe* with the intent to plunder the ship's cargo. Thompson and Ocampo were promptly arrested by the United States Marshal and held for trial in the county jail. The Mexican consulate protested to the local U.S. attorney, arguing that as a duly commissioned officer of the Mexican Navy, Thompson could not be jailed for enforcing Mexican laws. But Thompson and Ocampo did not have their paper commissions with them, and they were ultimately held in a local jail until the next district court could sit in session.

The case *United States v. Thompson* produced a sensation in New Orleans society, since the Mexican government strongly protested the charges against Thompson, and since the case was argued by two of the Crescent City's most prominent lawyers—future ambassador Pierre Soulé for the defendants, and district attorney Henry Carleton for the prosecution, a longtime associate of outspoken Texas advocate Felix Huston of Natchez, Mississippi.

Several Texas partisans, including Hurd and Peter Grayson, the *Laura's* captain, testified for the prosecution; the Mexican *chargé d'affaires* took the stand in Thompson's defense. According to New Orleans papers, at one point in the emotionally-charged trial tempers became uncontrollable: the opposing barristers began insulting each other in open court, then hurled law books and inkwells at each other across the courtroom. After the judge and bailiff restored order in the court, the judge suspended the proceedings and sentenced each lawyer to jail for six hours for contempt of court.

When the case resumed, closing arguments were long and flowery; Soulé's oratory was delivered in French. After eighteen hours of deliberation, Thompson's jury deadlocked, while a separate jury acquitted Lieutenant Ocampo of all charges. With a marked lack of enthusiasm for his case, Carleton decided not to retry Thompson, and on January 17, the two prisoners were set free. The New Orleans *Courier* remarked the next day: "The issue of the suit is indeed a very remarkable one—such, it may be said, as never happened before—the pirates set at liberty and the attorneys committed to jail." The news was somewhat premature, however, as less than twenty-four hours later, Thompson's creditors had him arrested on charges that are not entirely clear. Thompson spent the next few weeks ensnared in further legal proceedings, while Ocampo tarried in New Orleans, bringing charges against Captain Hurd for the theft of the Mexican garrison's payroll.

The case against "Mexico" Thompson died with a whimper, but the *San Felipe* incident pushed Mexico and Texas closer to war. Word of *Correo's* seizure reached Colonel Ugartechea, who forwarded the news to General Cós. An irate Cós ordered Ugartechea to investigate the matter so that Mexican officials could punish the American pirates, and called up the armed schooner *Veracruzana* to bring up artillery, military supplies, and several dozen pairs of leg irons for the insurrectionists. Reflecting these sentiments, the Mexican Navy schooner *Bravo* fired into Velasco in late October 1835.

In central Mexico, officials demanded severe reprisals for the Texians' acts of piracy and defiance. Mexico City newspapers claimed the seizure of a government vessel was further evidence of a Jacksonian conspiracy against America's southern neighbor, and clamored for a strong military response to this slap in the face of Mexican honor. The official government daily, *Diario del Gobierno*, editorialized, "Mexican blood boils while seeing such degradation and treason by the rebels. And whatever their excuses are, [*Correo's* seizure] has contributed to the hatred [borne] by any patriotic Mexican." Secretary of War José Maria Tornel would later write, "Would not the United States have protested with unexcelled indignation if the schooner *Grampus*, or any other of their war vessels, had been captured by the *Correo* and brought at once with its entire crew into a Mexican port?"

For their part, the Texas "war party" regarded the incident as just another example of the central government's abuse of power. Citizens of Brazoria held a drunken celebration over Thompson's capture, according to Jeremiah Brown, a local Brazos pilot. One week after the *San Felipe* incident, at a dinner held in Brazoria to welcome him back to Texas, Stephen Austin warned the town's citizens, "This country is now in anarchy, threatened with hostilities; armed vessels are capturing every thing they can catch on the coast, and acts of piracy are said to be committed under cover of the Mexican flag."

The *San Felipe* incident also set off a diplomatic firestorm between Mexico and the United States. Thompson's arrest prompted a series of heated exchanges between the Mexican *chargé d'affairs* in New Orleans, the Mexican legate at Philadelphia, and Andrew Jackson's secretary of state, John Forsyth. While defending the prosecution of Thompson and Ocampo, Forsyth pressured federal officials in New Orleans to enforce U.S. neutrality laws in a more evenhanded manner. Captain Hurd was thus arrested and tried on piracy charges. A sympathetic New Orleans jury promptly acquitted him, and his acquittal predictably set off another round of charges by Mexican diplomats, accusing the United States of siding with the Texas insurgents.

But what of the little ships that started the uproar? *Correo Mejicano* ultimately made its way back to the Mexican government, but several months of neglect while she was in the hands of Texas sympathizers took a severe toll on the craft. She was released on January 27, 1836, to head off another complaint visit from a Mexican official, but due to her decrepit condition she was sold for $450 on May 10. *San Felipe*, property of the McKinney & Williams firm, was pressed into Texas service, and began ferrying artillery, guns, and ammunition from New Orleans to the Texas rebels, as we shall soon see. *Laura* paddled on, a faithful servant of the Texas cause, until she too was lost on the Brazos in early 1836.

All told, the shooting between *San Felipe* and *Correo Mejicano* died down in less than two hours. But echoes of the two ships' small guns would thunder for the next ten years.

CHAPTER THREE

The Influence of Naval Power on the Texas Revolution

Where is your navy? Stop those ports, and they are ruined.
—James Walker Fannin, February 16, 1836

IF THE UNITED STATES WAS Texas's biological parent, then shipping lanes from New Orleans were the umbilical cord that kept the rebellion alive during its embryonic months. Because overland trade was impeded by Louisiana's swamps and the "Big Thicket" of East Texas, virtually all small arms, ammunition, artillery, and volunteers came to Texas by boat, along with the hard currency and imported goods that sustained life.

From Mexico's perspective, the countryside of northern Coahuila and southern Texas—"extensive and frightful deserted lands," as Santa Anna's top general called them—could not hope to sustain an army of six thousand hungry soldiers on an extended campaign. Napoleon's early victories, the model for Santa Anna's campaigns against Zacatecas and Texas, took the French army through the prosperous Italian and Austrian countryside. But Texas was different, and the self-proclaimed "Napoleon of the West" disregarded history when planning his campaign through Texas; had they dared, his staff officers might have reminded him that the *Grande Armeé* suffered its greatest losses while slogging through the impoverished frontiers of Poland, Lithuania, and Russia—country more fertile than the South Texas scrublands. In the days before railroads, marching an army hundreds of miles from central Mexico into the heart of Texas resistance would be a tremendous challenge for any commander; overland supply once the army arrived would prove impossible. Timetables and troop morale would be burdened, perhaps fatally, by poor logistics during the biting Texas winter. Later Gen. Vicente Filisola, Santa Anna's Italian-born second-in-command, would lament bitterly how poor roads, swollen rivers, mud, deserts, and marauding Indians doomed supply efforts from the start. He pointedly concluded, "the posts of Texas are not sustainable, whilst a maritime force does not co-operate with the operations of the land service."

The solution, of course, was the sea. A straight line on a map from Mexico City to Galveston runs across the Gulf of Mexico. With the port cities of Matamoros, Tampico, and Veracruz safely under government control, Mexican transport boats could quickly move thousands of conscripts—or at least a large holding force—from Mexico's interior to Velasco, cutting off the main rebel armies at San Antonio and Goliad from their government and supply bases. This would be an amphibious version of a tactic Napoleon had used against Austria thirty-six years earlier, and it would work well for future generals in southern France and Korea. Threatened from the rear, the Texas volunteers would be forced to withdraw from their western positions to protect their homes, farms, and government to the east. Then, with a foothold established between the Colorado River and Galveston Bay, Mexico's battalions could be supplied and reinforced quickly and efficiently. All that was required was control of the Texas coast.

The Texians were well aware of this threat. As future navy lieutenant Francis Wright warned Stephen Austin and Sam Houston at the beginning of the war: "[Your] foe may sail up and down your Coast plundering your inhabitants and those you would wish to assist them, preventing an intercourse upon the high seas between yourselves and your friends more Northerly, restricting that assistance which is necessarily essential for you to receive, blockading your harbours, terrifying the inhabitants along your sea coast, and rendering every assistance to their countrymen with whom you are at war on shore—should not some measure be adopted to remedy this evil?"

Wright was right. Control of the Gulf, once established, presented tremendous opportunities for the Texians. James Fannin, commander of the Texas volunteers at Goliad, wrote as early as August 1835 of the need to muster a flotilla of fighting ships. Once letters of marque and reprisal were issued to volunteer captains, he predicted, "we will have afloat a sufficient naval force to guard our coast and cripple their trade from the Campeachy banks to N. Orleans—the land party will, thus closed in, be an easy prey." When the revolution was in full swing, Fannin pleaded with the revolutionary government. "Provisions are very scarce in Matamoras and the adjoining country, and they must depend upon New Orleans. Where is your *navy*? Stop those ports, and they are ruined."

Fannin's words contained much force, because Santa Anna was running out of time. As late as February 1836, the Mexican government was receiving credible reports that the army's provisions were running low, and Santa Anna would be unable to operate in the wastelands of South Texas without additional supplies.

As it turned out, however, Santa Anna paid scant attention to naval affairs. The real contest, he felt, would be decided exclusively by his veteran army on land. Indeed, the impetus for closing down the Texas ports of Galveston and Matagorda in January 1836 came from the government, not from its absent commander in chief. The warships *Moctezuma* (recently rechristened *Bravo*) and *Veracruzana* patrolled the Texas coastline during the waning months of 1835, and other ships began fitting out in New Orleans, Veracruz, and Tampico in early 1836. But Mexico's fleet never made any serious effort to dominate the coastal waters during the rebellion. Her national vessels were employed against Texas only as escort ships, when they sailed at all.

Santa Anna's dismissal of the coast as a significant theater is reflected in the disposition of his troops. General Filisola suggested hugging the Texas coastline as the army drove north, at least until the troops reached Gonzales. This strategy, similar to one Persia's King Xerxes used in his invasion of Greece in 480 BC, would permit the Mexican Army to be resupplied by sea and eliminate some of the problems of living off barren land in wintertime. The *generalissimo* rejected this advice, and when he invaded Texas, he spared only about 550 of his 6,200 troops to drive up the coast, through Matamoros, San Patricio, and Goliad, under Gen. José de Urrea.

The land campaign began in earnest in the fall of 1835. Believing that a majority of the colonists remained loyal to the government, Santa Anna sent his brother-in-law, Gen. Martín Perfecto de Cós, north to San Antonio with 500 regulars to reinforce Colonel Ugartechea. Cós's troops landed at Copano Bay south of the San Antonio River, and marched north to San Antonio by early October. Shocked into action, the Texians began organizing volunteer companies. Stephen Austin led 618 volunteers west from Gonzalez, while Capt. George Collingsworth moved south with fifty-two men, capturing Matagorda and La Bahia.

When word of the Texian advance reached Mexico City, Santa Anna called up recruits, and ordered Gen. Joaquín Ramírez y Sesma to march his 1,400-man brigade north from Saltillo, the capital of Coahuila y Tejas, to relieve General Cós in San Antonio. Before Ramírez y Sesma arrived, however, the Texians drove Cós out of his stronghold. Cós's men were permitted to leave the presidio under arms, with the promise that they would not return to Texas. Immediately breaking his oath, Cós linked up with Ramírez y Sesma's division in late December and prepared to drive north.

By January 1836, Santa Anna's main force was assembled at Saltillo, and soon he was on the march. The Vanguard, First, and Second Brigades, under Santa Anna's command, were to form the main body, thrusting north through Laredo towards San Antonio. From there they would turn east, sweeping through San Felipe in Austin's colony to the heart of Texas resistance. General José de Urrea, taking a third brigade, would move along the coast towards Goliad, guarding the right flank of Santa Anna's corps.

After capturing San Patricio on February 27, 1836, Mexico's Army of Operations was in a position to attack Colonel Travis—the troublemaker from Anáhuac—and a small band of sharpshooters who had walled themselves up inside the Alamo at San Antonio. But while Santa Anna marched overland virtually unimpeded, the Texas government prepared to inflict losses on Mexico at sea.

ACT ONE

Fleet of the Revolution
(1835–1836)

CHAPTER FOUR

A War of Privateers

I recommend granting Letters of Marque and Reprisal; by doing which we can not only prevent invasion by sea, but we can blockade all ports of Mexico and destroy her commerce, and annoy and harrass the enemy more in a few months, than by many years' war, carried on within our own limits.
—Provisional Governor Henry Smith, November 1835

IN OCTOBER 1835, TEXAS WAS a swirling kaleidoscope of confused political and military activity. Planters, merchants, and politicians generally agreed that they faced grave danger, perhaps even extinction, but they lacked a consensus on how to deal with it. As General Cós threatened San Antonio, a significant faction of planters and landowners advocated reconciliation with the central government. Among the "war party," opinions clashed on the aims of the rebellion: Was Texas fighting for independence? Separate statehood? Or perhaps a return to the federalist structure of 1824 as part of Coahuila?

To provide some direction to these disparate factions, representatives from each Texas municipality gathered at San Felipe's clapboard Council Hall in November 1835 to form a provisional government. This "Consultation," as it was known, elected Henry Smith as Texas's provisional governor, James Robinson as its lieutenant governor, and a General Council to act as its legislative body. Sam Houston was appointed commander in chief of the nonexistent regular army, and Stephen Austin—a better politician than general—was appointed Texas's commissioner to the United States. This frontier government began its work in mid-November, and proceeded to bring order out of chaos as best it could.

Recognizing the vulnerability of its coastline, one of the first items the General Council took up was the creation of a navy. Two immediate options presented themselves. The government could purchase an official fleet, or it could commission privateers—privately owned armed vessels—to prey upon Mexican warships and merchantmen.

Thomas McKinney had suggested the latter course in late October to a future member of the Consultation, and Governor Smith advocated the privateer option in his inaugural address to the General Council: "I recommend granting Letters of Marque and Reprisal; by doing which we can not only prevent invasion by sea, but we can blockade all ports of Mexico and destroy her commerce, and annoy and harrass the enemy more in a few months, than by many years' war carried on within our own limits. My own mind is satisfied that the whole of our maritime operations can be carried on by foreign capital and foreign enterprise. Already applications for commissions have been made; they are willing to take the hazard, as such afford them every encouragement."

To Smith and the General Council, a privateer option made good sense. The government had little money and even less time, and a "national" fleet would require a great deal of both. There was precedent for this approach, as privateers had been used successfully in the Latino revolutions against Spain, and against Great Britain during the American Revolution. By the time the Council met, Augustus Allen, an entrepreneur who later co-founded the city of Houston, had proposed to "arm, man and fit out a vessel mounting nine guns, and fifty stand of small arms, with fifty volunteers on board and four months' provisions, to cruise off our coast as a privateer." So it was only logical that the revolutionary government would turn to the private sector to give the rebels a naval force during the opening weeks of hostilities.

On November 13, after a lengthy but hardly practical discussion of organic law and inalienable rights of man, the General Council concluded that it was vested with the power to issue letters of marque and reprisal, the official documents that gave legal sanction to privateering activities. Without these documents, privateers' use of force to capture vessels would be considered acts of piracy by any foreign navy.

Unconfirmed reports of *Moctezuma* and *Veracruzana* patrolling the Texas coast prompted the government to act. The Texas General Council's first move to authorize a privateer fleet came on November 18, when its three-member Committee on Naval Affairs drafted the country's first privateering law, which it adopted on November 19. Unaware that a preliminary resolution had been passed the previous day, on November 20 Smith sent the General Council a strong message urging them to enact whatever measures were necessary to grant letters of marque. "Commissions granting letters of Marque and Reprisal," he complained, "have been earnestly solicited, both by our own citizens and foreigners, and as yet have not been acted on." Smith deemed this subject "of the most urgent and vital importance," and admonished the Council that the subject "should receive prompt attention."

Governor Smith's message set the tone for his future dealings with the General Council. Smith, an ardent supporter of Texas independence, was an imperious executive who believed one of his principle tasks was to herd the sheep that made up the General Council towards wise and expedient legislation. Smith's message of November 20 shows that even at this early date, tactful persuasion of the General Council was not his strong suit. And relations between the two branches of government would only worsen over time to the point of stalemate.

On November 22, two days after Smith's message urging prompt action, the General Council met in special session. Governor Smith forwarded a letter from Captain Edward Hall, also suggesting the propriety of issuing letters of marque to qualified sea captains, and a final vote on the measure was taken. The bill passed on its third reading and was sent to Governor Smith for his signature.

The bill set out a number of requirements for would-be privateers. First, applicants must be men of "character and skill" as naval tacticians. Second, no license would be granted to any ship weighing less than eighty tons burthen, or mounting fewer than four twelve-pounder carronades "or their equivalent in metal." Cruising would be restricted to the Gulf of Mexico, and prizes could only be taken if they were sailing under the flag and commission of the Mexican government. Captured prizes must be brought into a Texas port and adjudicated by a competent tribunal, with five percent of the proceeds of sale going to the governmental treasury. Privateers also had to post a bond to insure that no misdeeds were committed on the high seas. Finally, letters of marque would expire within three to six months, unless the war between Texas and Mexico ended sooner.

Two days later, Smith returned the bill without his approval. He felt that the government's share of the proceeds was too small, given the expense of selling captured prizes and the government's potential liability for illegal seizures. "Besides," Smith warned, "privateers would have an unbridled license to roam at large, without being particularly under the control of the Government, and kept within limits calculated to protect our own commerce, and might, in the end, be productive of more injury than good."

Smith's comments were not designed to placate the strong wills of the council members, and the councilmen, who had spent several days drafting and rewriting the law, were highly displeased with Smith's objection. A vote was quickly taken to override the governor's veto, but it failed by a margin of eight to three, and the matter was referred back to the standing committee on naval affairs for revisions. The following day, November 25, the Naval Affairs Committee presented legislation increasing the government's share to 10 percent, and on the third reading, the measure was approved by the General Council. On November 27, Governor Smith signed a version of the resolution that gave the government a 20 percent commission, evidently due to a scrivener's error.

On November 30, the Council amended the privateer law to authorize three blank commissions each for Thomas McKinney and Silas Dinsmore of Velasco, and two others for Samuel Whiting of the Trinity River area. While they were supplementing the privateer law, the councilmen also decided to clarify a few details about the privateer fleet. Councilman Wyatt Hanks moved to reduce the government's share from 20 percent to 10 percent, notwithstanding any prior law to the contrary.

The Council also designated an official privateer flag, which would become famous as the flag that legend claims flew from the ramparts of the Alamo. Section two of the supplemental law stated:

> *Be it further ordained and decreed, etc.*, That all vessels sailing under Licenses, as Letters of Marque and Reprisal, which have been, or may hereafter be granted by the Governor and Council, or by the Governor, as provided in this supplementary Ordinance, or under any register or license of this Government, shall carry the flag of the Republic of the United States of Mexico, and shall have the figures 1, 8, 2, 4 cyphered in large Arabics on the white ground thereof.

Governor Smith signed the amendment, and quickly began issuing letters of marque to sea captains and ship owners. Silas Dinsmore received his commissions on November 30. Another was issued to Ira Lewis and the owners of the schooner *William Robbins* on December 5, while on December 6, Benjamin Smith and the Committee of Safety of Matagorda received another. In all, a total of eleven letters of marque were issued by the provisional government, although it does not appear that many were actually used.

Texas's first privateer, acting under the authority of a local vigilance committee, was the familiar McKinney & Williams schooner *San Felipe*. In October 1835, before a revolutionary government was even created, local communities began raising militia companies, purchasing arms and ammunition, and mustering volunteers for the cause. The McKinney & Williams firm, for its part, sent Samuel May Williams to the United States, to use his connections with the New York and Baltimore banking establishments to secure funds and supplies for the rebels. Meanwhile, McKinney kept *San Felipe* busy ferrying arms and equipment from New Orleans to the makeshift Texas army. By late October, *San Felipe* was back in Brazoria, laden with muskets and artillery for the network of volunteer forces operating under independent commanders.

Throughout October, municipalities in the heart of Texas began forming committees of safety, copying a practice of the American Revolution. One such committee, based in Columbia, Texas (near the Brazos river mouth), formally pressed McKinney's vessel into service, and issued its own letter of marque on November 1, 1835:

> The Schooner San Felipe having been impressed into the public service of Texas for the defence of the country. We the undersigned members of the committee of safety of the Jurisdiction of Columbia grant the Said Schooner San Felipe this Sea Letter for her protection and to constitute her a legal cruiser of the Free and sovereign State of Texas. Under the Command of William A. Hurd Master Commandant.
>
> In witness whereof we have hereunto set our hands this 1st day of November 1835.
>
> Silas Dinsmore Jr.
Jn. G. McNeel

This brief note is the first evidence of any privateer being awarded official sanction.

San Felipe's tenure as a Texas privateer was short-lived. One week after her commission was signed, she ran aground in Matagorda's treacherous bay. In a letter to the General Council, McKinney provided dubious information that *San Felipe*, while aground, had exchanged shots with a Mexican schooner—apparently the *Moctezuma*. McKinney optimistically predicted that *San Felipe* would make its way off the Matagorda bar soon, and would accompany the privateer *William Robbins* to New Orleans.

The stubborn McKinney clung to his belief that his schooner would be saved, but his hopes were soon broken on the Matagorda shores; reports from local sources confirmed that *San Felipe* had indeed been lost. Her cannon and cargo were saved, and on November 13 the privateer *William Robbins* was sent to Bird Island with the intention of recovering her guns. On January 17, 1836, Councilman R. R. Royall was appointed by the General Council to take charge of the wrecked schooner, which was reportedly lying on a beach "in or near Passo Cabello." So ended the brief but storied career of Texas's first privateer.

In November 1835, the central Texas coast was rife with rumors of a Mexican blockade. *Moctezuma* and *Veracruzana* were said to be patrolling Texas waters, and the panic these two warships incited was multiplied by the reported presence of *General Bravo*, which was actually the rechristened *Moctezuma*.

Enter the schooner *William Robbins*. Built in Matthews County, Virginia, in 1833, she was in many ways typical of the armed vessels that prowled the Gulf during the war for Texas. Weighing about seventy tons fully loaded, the sixty-seven-foot schooner carried three guns on her single deck. With a shallow draft and stout construction, she was perfectly suited to prey on Mexican shipping and defend Texas's lifeline to New Orleans.

The Matagorda Committee of Safety began raising funds for a warship to drive away the Mexican cruisers. The committee appointed Ira Lewis and Samuel Rhoads Fisher to purchase *William Robbins* from her captain and owner, and the $3,500 purchase price was paid by a draft of the ubiquitous Thomas McKinney.

The first assignment for *William Robbins* was to escort the damaged *San Felipe* to New Orleans for repairs. When *San Felipe* turned out to be a lost cause, *William Robbins* was given the task of recovering her guns. With *San Felipe* permanently out of commission, McKinney moved his fighting captain, William Hurd, to *William Robbins* as her new commander.

In mid-November, *William Robbins* was caught up in an incident that almost proved her backers' undoing, and became a distraction to the provisional government at a time when it desperately needed to focus on the defense of Texas. The incident was the seizure of the Texas arms smuggler *Hannah Elizabeth*, and it would give the General Council a reason to second-guess its decision to rely on privateers.

The story began when *Hannah Elizabeth* left New Orleans on November 13 bound for Matagorda. On her deck, the schooner mounted two six-pounder cannon and a small four-pounder, while in her hold she carried a cache of 500 muskets with bayonets, and eighteen kegs of gunpowder destined for the Texas rebels. (One Texas agent sardonically wrote that *Hannah Elizabeth* bore "provisions and merchandise for *family use*, as they say.") The schooner also carried fifteen American and five Mexican passengers, and a few thousand dollars' worth of legitimate cargo on her journey west.

As *Hannah Elizabeth* approached Paso Cavallo, at the entrance to Matagorda Bay, she was spotted by *General Bravo*, which had been patrolling the South Texas coast. After a brief chase, she ran aground, and a prize crew of twenty-one soldiers under a Lieutenant Mateo rowed over to take control of the stranded vessel. As the prize crew was being lowered in *Bravo*'s boats, an American businessman named Peter Kerr and several other merchants interested in protecting *Hannah Elizabeth*'s legitimate cargo began throwing contraband items—cannon, ammunition, and muskets—into the sea to prevent the remaining goods from being seized as lawful prizes. As the prize crew's boat thumped against the hull of the merchantman, *Hannah Elizabeth* surrendered without resistance. The owners of the weapons, José Carbajal and

Fernando de León, together with several Americans, were taken aboard *Bravo* for transportation to Matamoros, the closest major port in Mexican hands.

News of *Hannah Elizabeth*'s capture reached Matagorda on November 19. The good citizens of Matagorda dispatched *William Robbins*, which sailed to the scene the next day under the command of Captain Hurd, with a small force of volunteer marines commanded by "Colonel" S. Rhoads Fisher. (At the time, respectable Southern gentlemen were commonly addressed as "Colonel," "Judge," "General" or some similarly authoritative-sounding title.)

On the evening of November 21, *William Robbins*, anchoring to the north of the pilot house at Paso Cavallo, discovered that a norther which struck the Gulf the day before had driven *Bravo* back out to sea. While accounts differ, it appears that the expedition from Matagorda easily recaptured the vessel and took Lieutenant Mateo and his prize crew prisoners. When Fisher, the commanding officer, arrived on the scene, Lieutenant Mateo offered his sword to "Colonel" Fisher, arguably sparing Mexico the disgrace of surrendering a military command to a volunteer rabble. The prisoners were marched off to the nearby home of Dr. Peter Kinsey, where they were held until December 19. They were then transferred to Fisher's home for two more weeks before being paroled.

Hannah Elizabeth soon foundered upon the breakers, and her cargo was hustled ashore. A question then arose over what to do with her merchandise. At Captain Hurd's suggestion, the privateers took *Hannah Elizabeth's* wares to Matagorda, and sold them as legitimate booty captured from Mexico. In a letter to Councilman Royall, Fisher requested that the General Council rule that *Hannah Elizabeth* was either a legal prize taken from the Mexican Navy, or was salvage; under either theory, Fisher's men would collect prize money as salvors or captors.

When word of the events circulated, irregularities surrounding the sale prompted a heated exchange between Fisher and militia commander James Fannin, a longtime business and political rival of Captain Hurd and his employer, Samuel May Williams. The controversy, which sparked a divisive, inconclusive investigation and a challenge to a duel between Fisher and Fannin, lasted until March 1836, and ended with Fannin's death at the hands of his Mexican captors at Goliad. The purchase of *William Robbins* by the Texas government in January 1836 brought to a close her short and controversial career as a privateer.

Two other private vessels, the schooner *Flash* and the steamboat *Yellow Stone*, also provided valuable assistance to the Texas rebels, although they never actually fired a shot. *Flash,* a flat-bottomed schooner owned by Col. James Morgan, had worked the Texas waters as a merchant vessel since 1832.

As the threat of a Mexican blockade became real in late 1835, Morgan bought his vessel "an eighteen Pounder, Muskets, Cutlasses and every thing necessary, and came out in company with the Schooner Pennsylvania and the brig Durango bound for the Brazos as far as Galveston." Under Capt. Luke Falvel, *Flash* sailed to New Orleans in early January 1836, presumably to bring volunteers and arms back to Texas.

The revolutionary Texas government must have found *Flash* useful, as its secretary of state, Samuel Carson, offered to buy *Flash* from Morgan for $8,500 for the Texas Navy on April 1, 1836, one month after Texas declared its independence. Carson needn't have offered: the patriotic Morgan kept *Flash* busy doing quasi-governmental work, assisting Anglo refugees and their slaves fleeing before the oncoming army of Santa Anna, in an exodus that became known as the "Runaway Scrape." *Flash* was dispatched to the lower Brazos to pick up all women and children, and carry them to Morgan's Point at the head of Galveston Bay. From there, *Flash* would defend the point in the event of attack. Captain Falvel later claimed *Flash* also had aboard two small but critical artillery pieces nicknamed the "Twin Sisters," gifts from the citizens of Cincinnati, Ohio. She transferred the Twin Sisters to the sloop *Opie* for delivery to Sam Houston's army in time to participate in the Battle of San Jacinto on April 21.

On the morning of April 19, *Flash* sailed down Galveston Bay to a landing between Clopper's Point and Red Fish Bar, where Interim President David G. Burnet came aboard in a small boat. *Flash* continued down the bay to Galveston Island, anchoring off the old Mexican customs house near what is now the corner of Avenue A and 11th Street.

For six harrowing days, the inhabitants of Galveston scrounged for food, water, and shelter, awaiting news of the Mexican army's approach. By April 26, some 150 refugees were aboard *Flash*, preparing to sail to New Orleans and safety. Captain Falvel was ordered to set sail, but adverse winds made crossing the bar dangerous, and he refused to weigh anchor. About that time, news of the decisive Texas victory at San Jacinto arrived, which, said one observer, "put a quietus on the terror stricken inhabitants of Texas who were fleeing the country."

After the war, the government evidently purchased *Flash* and placed her in a limited commission. Around April 1837, *Flash*, under a Captain Marstella, ran aground at the west end of Galveston Island. One account claims that Marstella mistook the San Luis Pass for the eastern entrance to Galveston Harbor, and the ship wrecked on one of the many treacherous bars there. The final resting place of *Flash* will, however, probably never be known.

Yellow Stone, under the command of Capt. John E. Ross, was a sidewheel steamer built in Louisville in 1831. Weighing 144 tons, she was 122 feet long, twenty and a half feet wide, and blew thick black smoke through two stacks rising proudly from her single engine. Built for John Jacob Astor's American Fur Company, she had worked the Missouri River beaver routes until the last day of 1835, when she paddled her way down to Texas.

In a few short months, *Yellow Stone* became the steamboat most closely associated with the Texas Revolution. She brought the famed Mobile Grays to Velasco, transported Sam Houston's army over the swollen Brazos during the retreat to San Jacinto, and evacuated refugees from Harrisburg as Mexican soldiers were burning it (pulling away from the dock under fire, while Mexican cavalry troopers attempted to throw their lassos over her chimneys). She ferried Houston, Santa Anna and a number of troops and prisoners to Galveston after San Jacinto, and the following year, she carried the body of Stephen F. Austin home to his final resting place.

The ultimate fate of this legendary Texas steamer is unclear; some historians say she snagged on Buffalo Bayou and was lost in 1837, but there is also evidence that she returned to the United States and worked the Ohio River, presumably under a different name. The only souvenir *Yellow Stone* left for Texas is her ship's bell, which is now on display at the Alamo in San Antonio.

A wide variety of other merchant vessels served Texas in various capacities, generally as transport ships for arms and volunteers. Most of these vessels carried only small arms for protection, although a few mounted cannon. Typical of these was the armed merchantman *Julius Caesar*, which began ferrying volunteers to Texas in November 1835, and was captured by the Mexican Navy in 1837 with a cargo of small arms and merchandise. The schooner *Mary Jane* also played a part in the early conflict, ferrying 150 volunteers to General Mexía for his raid on Tampico in early 1836.

The steamboat *Cayuga*, a small craft carrying two light guns, was pressed into the defense of Galveston Island briefly in late April 1836, and like *Flash*, she ferried refugees from Harrisburg to Galveston during the Runaway Scrape. On May 27, she arrived at Galveston laden with Mexican prisoners who were put to work constructing a fort on the island. After the war, *Cayuga* was commissioned as a national vessel. Before the summer of 1837, she was sold under the supervision of Texas Navy Secretary S. Rhoads Fisher.

The American brig *Durango* was in Texian service as early as January 3, 1836. By March, John A. Wharton, adjutant general of the Army of Texas, and William S. Brown, "of Texan schr. *Liberty*," certified that they had pressed *Durango* into service, and that the Texas government would be responsible for any loss or damage that should befall her.

A number of other private vessels came to Texas to assist the rebels in various capacities. Harrisburg's *Telegraph and Texas Register* reported that a fine six-gun Boston schooner named *Bounty* arrived off the Texas coast to fight for the rebels; this appears to have been an unfounded rumor, as nothing further is mentioned of a warship by that name. The same newspaper reported in October 1835 that the *Columbus* arrived with two artillery pieces and some ammunition for the Texas army. The schooner *San Jacinto* ferried some sixty volunteers to Texas a month after the battle that ended the war, as did the merchant schooners *Pennsylvania, Congress,* and *Santiago.* The private schooner *Flora* also conveyed a wounded General Houston to New Orleans after the war so doctors could treat injuries he received at the Battle of San Jacinto.

The privateer fleet of 1836 was born out of desperation, a wartime expedient dictated by an acute lack of time and money. It inflicted little damage on Mexico's navy and shipping, but the privately-owned vessels performed a great service to Texas by ferrying supplies and men where they were needed most. With no fear of capture by Mexican cruisers, the armed ships could move men and arms from New Orleans to points along the Texas coast with impunity. Later in the conflict, their willingness to attack Mexican merchantmen also created a climate of fear among New Orleans merchants, putting a damper on Mexican-American trade and thereby hindering Mexico's ability to wage war.

As offensive weapons, however, privateers came with a number of liabilities, not the least of which was the government's inability to control them. With no leash on the reckless sea dogs, the government could neither implement a coherent naval strategy nor ensure that its privateers only attacked legitimate targets. England's greatest admiral, Lord Nelson, summed up the low opinion of privateers held by the "Great Powers" of Europe a half-century before: "The conduct of all privateering is, as far as I have seen, so near piracy that I only wonder any civilized nation can allow them. The lawful as well as the unlawful commerce of the neutral flag is subject to every violation and spoliation."

Texas would surely incur the ill will of the Great Powers if armed vessels sailing under its flag captured innocent ships. By the first month of 1836, one Texas agent had already begun to report home that "opinion [was] setting so strongly through the United States against the system of Letters of Mark & Reprisal on the part of Texas." The New Orleans *Bee* complained bitterly that pirates could easily use the Texas flag as a cover to enter United States ports, since all that was needed to impersonate a privateer was "a piece of cloth with a star in the middle." The final tally of captured and damaged ships—none of which were ever condemned by a court of admiralty jurisdiction—did not justify the political and economic risks, at least in the minds of the Texas leaders.

So as early as January 1836, the General Council began having second thoughts about the wisdom of sponsoring privateers. A note from the council's journal for January 7 reads, "On motion of Mr. Barrett it was ordered that the committee on Naval affairs be requested to examine into the expediency of retracting all letters of marque and reprisal heretofore granted by this Council." The committee never completed its task. Four days later, a rift between Governor Smith and the General Council effectively shut down the government, and no official action was taken until a new government was formed on March 2.

Interim President David G. Burnet was elected to head up the Texas government on March 17, 1836—two weeks after Texas declared her independence, and eleven days after the Alamo fell to Santa Anna. Burnet, a heavy-set empresario from New Jersey with huge muttonchops and an entrepreneurial flair, quickly moved to reorganize the country's naval defenses and end its dependence upon privateers. On March 25, as Santa Anna's army marched relentlessly towards San Felipe, Burnet issued a proclamation suspending all letters of marque issued by the government and demanding their return. While several private vessels later would fight on behalf of the Texas Republic, the official practice of authorizing privateers would not be resumed until long after the dead of San Jacinto had been buried.

Texas needed a navy, not a privateer fleet. And one of the first orders of business for the provisional government was to find a navy, and find it fast.

CHAPTER FIVE

The Fleet That Sank Its Government

Mr. Allen is in treaty for a fine vessel [the Brutus], to be well armd & Equipd, to cruise off the coast, a small Mexican Scho called the Venus from Campeachy is fitting out for the Mexican service, which may be made a prise to Mr. Allens vessel if he can get her out in time.
—Edward Hall to Texas Governor Henry Smith

Captain Allen has no intention to cruise against Mexican vessels, nor has on board [the Brutus] any marine or soldier in his service other than his crew.
—Edward Hall to U.S. District Attorney Henry Carleton

MILES AWAY FROM THE BREWING cauldron of the Gulf, representatives of Texas's principal towns gathered in Austin's capital of San Felipe to form a provisional government. When the disorganized menagerie of merchants, lawyers, and planters met at San Felipe's Council House in November 1835, they knew that time was running out. General Cós was awaiting reinforcements in San Antonio, and Santa Anna's wrath was sure to vent its fury on the Texians for their many insults to Mexican honor.

The various factions of the General Council, bracing for the approaching storm, put aside their differences long enough to focus on the defense of Texas. A volunteer army was already in the field, and the regular army had a commander—albeit with no soldiers to lead—so the next issue was the protection of the long coastline.

Four days after assuming power, the General Council's Committee on Naval Affairs proposed legislation to establish an official Texas Navy, recommending to the council:

Your committee would further most earnestly represent that the establishment of a small Naval force for the security of our extended coast and the protection of our own commerce would seem to them highly necessary and indispensable, and under that conviction would recommend the purchase, arming and equipping of two schooners of twelve, and two schooners of six guns each, to cruise in and about the bays and harbors of our coast. This arm of the service should be confided and entrusted only to men whose nautical skill and experience are well known and established, and whose activity and efficiency would with greater certainty secure the objects of its creation and organization.

The council coupled the navy bill with the privateer law, and sent both measures to Governor Smith for his approval. On November 24, Smith vetoed the bill because it incorporated the privateer provisions to which he objected, so the next day, the council passed a bill detaching the privateer provisions from the navy bill. The bill was signed by Governor Smith on November 25, 1835, and with it, Texas authorized its first navy.

Efforts to turn the paper navy into a wooden one moved quickly. On December 2, the Committee on Naval Affairs reported that Samuel May Williams, business partner of *San Felipe* owner Thomas McKinney, had obtained funds from New York to purchase a twelve-gun brig, a six-gun schooner, and several thousand firearms for the Texas cause. Five days later, the provisional government sent Stephen F. Austin, Dr. Branch Archer, and William H. Wharton to New Orleans to procure additional vessels, funds, and supplies. These commissioners appointed Edward Hall as their purchasing agent and William Bryan as Texas's general agent. These five civilians would oversee the supply pipeline from the United States, and would prove as vital to Texas's maritime defense as any sea captain.

New Orleans was the perfect place to buy warships, men, and equipment for operations against Mexico. By 1830, New Orleans had become the third largest U.S. city, behind New York and Baltimore, and it boasted maritime resources Texas would only dream of until well into the twentieth century. Over 18 percent of U.S. exports—goods of every kind—flowed down the "Father of Waters," as the Indians called the Mississippi River, through the Southwest Pass and out to sea.

The New Orleans harbor, sitting between the Algiers district and the French Quarter, teemed with maritime activity of every description. Scores of large commercial and military vessels—frigates, barks, steamboats, clippers, sloops, schooners, and brigs—and untold smaller boats lined the wharves, taking on or unloading wares, moving up and down the river, or patiently waiting for repairs by the hundreds of contractors, shipwrights, sailmakers, carpenters, blacksmiths, armorers, barrelwrights, boilermakers, or other specialists who made their living off the sea trade from the safety of dry land.

Beside these specialists, thousands of landsmen, officers, seamen, and boys thronged the wharves, mingling with the carriages, wagons, slaves, and frock-coated pedestrians that packed the brick-paved streets connecting the docks and warehouses with the red-brick buildings of the city's mercantile offices.

By night these men, be they Irish, British, French, Creole, Caribbean, or American, could be recruited by the handful by any recruiter adventurous enough to step into the French Quarter's crowded theaters, restaurants, saloons, gambling houses, and places of ill-repute frequented by sailors making the most of their precious shore leave. If ships and sailors were to be found anywhere, New Orleans was the place to find them.

The schooner *Liberty*, Texas's first official warship, began its naval career as the privateer *William Robbins*. Bought by McKinney & Williams for $3,500, the firm offered the schooner to the government at cost. *William Robbins* arrived in New Orleans on January 3, 1836, and seven days later Austin, Archer, and Wharton informed Governor Smith that they had purchased *William Robbins* during the trip and rechristened her *Liberty*. The General Council, evidently unaware of the purchase, separately passed a resolution calling for the inspection and potential purchase of *William Robbins* on January 7. Governor Smith, now thoroughly alienated from the council, vetoed the measure on the grounds that his commissioners were already authorized to purchase the vessel. As a mark of his growing contempt for the meddling sheep of the council, Smith brusquely stated that he gave the measure "the attention which I considered the subject merited," and signed his veto message "Respectfully, Henry Smith," rather than with the customary "Respectfully, Your obedient servant, Henry Smith."

Once *Liberty* anchored off the Crescent City, Texas partisans lost no time in fitting her out for combat. She was equipped with a medium-range twelve-pounder pivot gun and two heavy six-pounders on her waist, and a pair of twelve-pounder gunades (a type of carronade). By late January she was ready to sail with a crew of forty, whom one crewman described as "long, wiry fellows, who were on their first visit to the city, and having been enticed to the gambling dens, had, by the turn of a card or roulette-wheel, lost the proceeds of months of toil and exposure." In fitting her out, the conscientious Stephen Austin noted with some alarm that *Liberty* had quickly become a drain on the revolution's precious finances, and warned that if strict accountability were not instituted within the naval procurement system, "carelessness, confusion, and waste, and perhaps fraud will creep into the treasury department, which will totally destroy all confidence and credit & ruin our cause." His comment, proved prophetic, but for the time being, Texas could boast a working fleet of one.

The second warship to enter Texas waters was the schooner *Invincible*. Built in October 1835 for the illicit African slave trade, *Invincible* was a fast Baltimore clipper with one deck and two masts. Weighing 126 tons fully loaded, the sharp-hulled schooner stretched over eighty-three feet in length, and drew water to a depth of eight feet. She carried a battery of eight or nine guns, including two twelve-pounder pivot guns, four six-pounders, and two nine-pounders. Samuel May Williams dispatched her from Baltimore in late 1835, and she arrived at Galveston on New Year's Day, 1836, where she sat idle for the next few weeks while her newly-adopted government debated her fate.

Once *Invincible* had cruised into Galveston Bay, the General Council's Committee on Naval Affairs reported: "Messrs. McKinney and Williams, through Mr. Williams, have made a purchase of, and equipped a schooner of about one hundred and twenty-six tons burthen, adapted to the object of protecting our commerce against the enemy. This vessel, called the 'invincible,' is now in the Bay of Galveston, and is generously offered to the Government of Texas, by the owners, at first cost and charges." "First cost and charges" included the $12,613.02 price of the ship, plus 12.5 percent to cover shipping and insurance, plus outfitting costs, bringing the total price tag to around $20,000. Not cheap, but not a bad price for a fast new warship, either.

In early January, the General Council dispatched Edmund Andrews and William Harris to inspect the schooner and purchase it, if it proved satisfactory. The stated objective was to protect Texas from the war schooner *Moctezuma*, which was again rumored to be prowling the coast. But the immediate use the council had in mind was an expedition against the Mexican base at Matamoros on the Rio Grande. *Invincible* was expected to ferry troops and protect transport ships en route to the target. This ambitious plan clashed with the strategy of General Houston and Governor Smith to fight a defensive war, trading Texas's ample space for time. Given Mexico's superior resources, Houston and Smith quite reasonably believed that any invasion of the mother country would be a dangerous and foolhardy expedition.

When the resolution to buy *Invincible* was brought to Governor Smith for his signature, he became suspicious. On January 6, he asked for particulars on the warship and its purpose. Rather than comply, on January 8 the council met in a special evening session to pass a resolution commissioning *Invincible* under "Captain" McKinney, ordering McKinney to prepare her for a cruise against the enemy.

Two councilmen carried the January 8 resolution to Governor Smith, who exploded with fury. Having once been pressured to commission privateers to fight the ghost ship *Moctezuma*, he was not about to give the General Council a weapon to invade Mexico under the same pretense. In a reply delivered on January 10, Smith castigated the council with as many fighting words as ever were fired by a Texas chief executive at the legislature. Smith said:

> You urge me by resolutions to make appointments, fit out vessels, as government vessels, registering them as such, appointing landsmen to command a naval expedition by making representations urgent in their nature.... You have acted in bad faith, and seem determined by your acts to destroy the very institutions which you are pledged and sworn to support.... Mexican like, you

are ready to sacrifice your country at the shrine of plunder.... Base corruption has crept into your councils, men who, if possible, would deceive their God.... The appointment and instructions founded on the resolutions predicated on false premises, shall now be tested. I will immediately countermand the order made out in such haste.... [Y]ou would do the Government serious injury by meddling with matters which you have put out of your power by special appointment.

With that, Smith shut down the government, adjourning the General Council until March 1, 1836, and stating his intention to act as commander in chief of the army and navy until Texas formed a permanent government. The next day, the council passed resolutions dismissing Governor Smith and appointing Lt. Gov. James Robinson in his place. The council then published a proclamation styled "To the People of Texas," defending *Invincible*'s purchase and claiming that *Moctezuma* was cruising off Galveston and preying upon Texas shipping. For the next few weeks, Smith and the General Council ignored each other; Smith vainly ordered one official to seize the council's papers relating to *Invincible*'s purchase, while the General Council transacted its business with Acting Gov. James Robinson.

But the business of war had to go on. While the government languished in gridlock, government agents bought *Invincible* and commissioned her on January 16, 1836. She sailed off to New Orleans to prepare for battle, the only thing she had sunk so far being her own squabbling government.

Next came *Independence*. This New York-built schooner hailed from New Orleans as the United States revenue cutter *Ingham*, the warship that ran down *Moctezuma* after her attack on the merchant vessel *Martha* in 1835. The 112-ton *Ingham*, a *Morris*-class revenue cutter built at the Webb & Allen shipyards in New York, was a slow sailer, somewhat smaller than *Invincible*, and initially carried six guns, evidently medium range six-pounders. She was already six years old, but with a few repairs, she would be good as new, and her battery and shallow draft would fit Texas's coastal needs perfectly. Details of the *Ingham*'s purchase are sketchy, but it appears that she was purchased and fitted out for about $10,000 in mid January 1836, and by January 18 she had been rechristened the *Independence*. With a proven battle record, she would soon become the flagship of the Texas Navy.

The last vessel to join the original Texas fleet was supposed to have been its first. Built in Franklin County, Maine, the Maine schooner *Brutus* was sitting calmly at anchor in New Orleans when she caught the eyes of agents Edward Hall and Augustus Allen.

The two men agreed she would make a fine man-of-war. Slightly larger than *Invincible*, *Brutus* was a slow but sturdy sailer. Her firepower was similar to that of *Invincible*; she carried a half-dozen six-pounders and one long-range eighteen-pounder pivot gun. Gus Allen bought *Brutus* in December 1835, and agreed to sell her to the Texas government for the very reasonable price of $15,000.

Brutus was being fitted out in New Orleans during late December, when a rumor published in the New Orleans *Union* claimed that she was being armed to prey on shipping between New Orleans and Mexican ports. The day after Christmas, a group of twenty-five insurance and shipping presidents sent a petition to District Attorney Henry Carleton, claiming: "The schooner Brutus has been purchased, and is now fitting out, armed with six cannon, and one large one on a pivot, for the purpose of capturing Mexican vessels, which, with their cargoes are principally insured by the underwriters of this city; and as our country is at peace with Mexico, we, the undersigned, request that immediate measures may be taken to prevent said vessel from leaving this port."

Carleton, a Texas partisan, coolly replied that he could not prosecute the Texians without witnesses. When the shipping group rounded up its witnesses, Carleton interviewed twenty men under oath, but found no credible evidence that *Brutus* was planning attacks against Mexico. His findings were based in large part on the testimony of Edward Hall, who swore that Captain Allen had no "intention to cruise against Mexican vessels, nor that he has on board any marine or soldier in his service other than his crew." Hall also testified that *Brutus*'s heavy armament was purely for self-defense in the dangerous Texas waters. Hall's story was affirmed by William Bryan, the Texas purchasing agent.

Hall and Bryan were lying, of course. Hall had previously informed the governor and General Council that *Brutus* was fitting out to seize the Mexican schooner *Venus*, which was itself fitting out for Mexican military service in New Orleans. But the story stuck long enough to allow Allen to get *Brutus* out of United States waters. The case was dropped, and *Brutus* cleared New Orleans as a merchant vessel, carrying seven cannon and one hundred riflemen of the Alabama Red Rovers, ostensibly to protect her forty barrels of sundry merchandise. She proceeded forthwith to Matagorda, and when her transfer to Texas was registered on February 12, *Brutus* became the final warship of the initial Lone Star fleet.

With four armed schooners—*Liberty, Invincible, Independence,* and *Brutus*—Texas finally had a fleet of its own. Never mind that it plunged the infant nation into tremendous debt, or that it brought down its civil government in the process. Texas had acquired bragging rights to the best warships in the Gulf, if only it could find the right men to lead them.

CHAPTER SIX

Iron Men for Wooden Ships

[Captain Hawkins] is a gentleman whose experience and ability in naval affairs would render his services acceptable in any govt—and more particularly in ours, which is just emerging from chaos.
—Gov. Henry Smith to Stephen F. Austin

SHIPS, WITHOUT MEN TO SAIL THEM, do not make a navy. Mexico, like many other countries, learned this lesson the hard way, spending the first half of the 1830s with an impressive number of fighting ships that were mere driftwood without competent officers and sailors. Unlike militia, which could be called up from farms and villages and handed muskets, told to fight, then disbanded on short notice, sailors were skilled professionals who could only be recruited in sufficient numbers from established seaports like New Orleans, Mobile, or Pensacola. Good commanders were even harder to find. The navy captain of the 1830s had to be a warrior, sailor, and ambassador; a gentleman and a strict disciplinarian; a strategist; and an obedient servant to his government, his commander, and Neptune. Subordinate officers had to serve their captains with competence, efficiency, and enthusiasm. So it was only logical that, after sending out agents to find ships, the next priority was to locate officers and men to sail them.

The navy of the 1830s—any sizeable navy, that is—was organized along fairly standard lines refined by Britain's Royal Navy over the previous three centuries. At the very top stood the civil government; naval administration was overseen by a secretary of the navy in the United States, or by the First Lord of the Admiralty in the British system. Unlike today, where the Navy secretary's functions may be delegated to hundreds of bureaucrats and uniformed professionals, the navy secretary of the 1830s was responsible for virtually all details of naval life, from routine administration (such as granting furloughs to junior officers) to issuing orders for specific missions.

The highest rank in the Age of Sail was *Admiral*, or commander of a fleet, a title used only in European and Latin navies. (The U.S. Navy would not adopt admiral grades until much later.) Since the entire Texas navy consisted of only four ships, this rank was never conferred, and the designation of *Commodore*, or commander of a squadron, was the title for the commander of the Texas Navy. A commodore was generally the senior *Post Captain*, the highest official rank ever held by a Lone Star naval commander.

Just under post captain fell the rank of *Commander*, who was, in theory, an officer in charge of a small warship. Below commanders came *Lieutenants*, who executed the commanding officer's orders. There were no official grades of lieutenants, and a lieutenant's status and promotion hopes were based solely on seniority, determined by the date of his commission. Designations of "First Lieutenant," "Second Lieutenant," and so on, were used on Texas warships, but they were indications of seniority, not rank, while the temporary designation of "Lieutenant Commanding," as the name implied, denoted a lieutenant in command of a vessel of any kind.

Lieutenants were the lowest rank of commissioned officers. They were usually drawn from a pool of *Midshipmen*, who were basically apprentice lieutenants. Midshipmen, generally young teenage boys, assisted the lieutenants and studied the arts of sailing and naval command, as well as hard sciences such as gunnery, mathematics, geography, and astronomy. Midshipmen were required to keep detailed logbooks that recorded weather, position readings and significant events on board ship each day. After a term of satisfactory performance they could take the midshipman's examination and apply for a lieutenant's commission. In the U.S. Navy of the 1830s, midshipmen who passed their examination (*Passed Midshipmen*) could also be temporarily appointed sailing masters until their promotion to lieutenant.

After commissioned officers came the *warrant officers*, senior specialists who were not in line for promotion to lieutenant or captain. This class included the *Purser* (the ship's storekeeper and accountant), the *Master* (chief navigation officer), the *Surgeon*, *Boatswain* (caretaker of the ship's sails and rigging), *Gunner*, *Carpenter*, and *Sailmaker*. Aboard steam warships, it would also include the *Chief Engineer*. Below these ranks were a lower class of warrant officers (called *petty officers*), which included the *Cook* (the senior petty officer), *Chaplain*, *Clerk*, and *Quartermaster*. Some of these officers—particularly surgeons, pursers, clerks, and chaplains—were typically recruited from civilian ranks, while gunners, carpenters, sailmakers, and boatswains could be promoted from talented sailors.

After officers came the sailors—*Able Seamen*, *Ordinary Seamen*, and *Landsmen*. These men were not permanently attached to a ship, and held no commission; they were paid an enlistment bonus and "shipped" to serve the navy for a certain period of time. Like officers, they theoretically received both regular wages and a share of prize money from captured enemy vessels. They were usually recruited from port cities such as New Orleans, Mobile,

Charleston, Baltimore, or New York. Able seamen and ordinary seamen performed specialized ship's duties (such as working with the more difficult or hazardous rigging), while landsmen performed less specialized duties such as hauling anchors and rowing boats. Occasionally, a seaman would beg off the more dangerous duties in the upper rigging by understating his experience and signing on as a landsman. But on at least one occasion, a Texas "landsman's" instincts gave him away; when the man cried out "Sail ho!" to a miniscule speck on the horizon (which turned out to be an approaching brig), he was recognized for the old salt he really was, and was sent topside to become an excellent main topyard captain.

A final class of seafarers was the *Marines*. The marines were the ship's soldiers; they would spearhead boarding and landing parties, act as snipers and riflemen during battle, and maintain order aboard ship. At other times, they performed the chores of landsmen, but they could never be ordered to go up into the rigging. On shore, they guarded naval stores and prisoners. Private marines were ultimately commanded by a major or captain, whose orders devolved upon lieutenants, sergeants, and corporals.

Eventually, Texas established a navy yard at Galveston, and created the posts of Naval Storekeeper and Naval Agent. But that was in the not-so-distant future; in early 1836, Texas's primary worry was finding qualified men to put aboard its ships.

The Texas Navy's first civilian commander was Secretary of the Navy Robert M. Potter. Potter was one of those colorful, often violent rogues who had what could charitably be called a "checkered past." A native of North Carolina, the dark-haired, dark-eyed Potter joined the U.S. Navy as a midshipman at the end of the War of 1812. Tiring of sea life, he returned to his home state, where he became a lawyer, a member of the North Carolina House of Commons, and a U.S. congressman. Convinced that his wife was having an affair with a Methodist minister and another man, Congressman Potter tracked them both down one dark night, beat them unconscious, then savagely worked them over with a knife, disfiguring both men for life. The vicious attack earned him a short prison sentence for simple assault (on the books, the only crime he had committed), and ejection from the House. The enraged North Carolina legislature quickly passed a law against "Potterizing," as the crime was designated. The penalty for Potterizing was death by hanging, "without the benefit of clergy."

After serving a portion of his sentence, the locally popular Potter won reelection to the North Carolina House of Commons, only to be removed on ethical charges. His wife divorced him in 1834, and the following year thirty-six-year-old Robert Potter pulled up his withered roots and moved to Texas, where his character as a fighter could be put to better use in the brewing rebellion.

Potter applied for a privateer's commission in December 1835, and when Texas declared its independence the following March, Interim President Burnet appointed Potter Secretary of the Navy. The two men worked together at the Texas capital of Washington-on-the-Brazos from a one-story, unfinished wooden building, its thick curtains covering the open windows to block out the blustery March wind. Like Burnet, the hotheaded Potter was dismayed by General Houston's strategy of trading space for time, and he quickly aligned himself with the anti-Houston faction. His scathing criticism would never be forgotten by Sam Houston, who years later would write, "[Potter's] infamy was wider than the world and deeper than perdition." (Evidently some of Potter's neighbors felt the same way; he would die in a hail of shotgun slugs six years later during a feud that became known as the Regulator-Moderator War.) While Secretary Potter would play a major role in the defense of Galveston, and would take credit for the design of the Texas Navy's flag, the real work of the revolutionary navy fell to its captains, not its civilian leadership.

After Old Hickory's victory over the British at New Orleans and Napoleon's defeat at Waterloo, the navies of the western world were at peace, and would remain so, more or less, for several years. As they became inactive, their restless officers looked abroad for more action, faster promotion, and better pay. Following the traditions of other young Latin American republics, Texas recruited its senior naval officers from experienced merchant captains and former U.S. and Mexican officers. The first commander the provisional government hired was a veteran of both the U.S. and Mexican navies, Commodore Charles E. Hawkins.

Charles Edward Hawkins was born in New York in 1802. He came from a family of means, and according to Lewis Washington, a fellow Texas seafarer, Hawkins "imbibed at an early period of his life, those ostentations, notions and habits, which characterize aristocratic arrogance." At age sixteen he left his life on land to join the U.S. Navy as a midshipman, serving aboard the frigates *Constitution, Constellation,* and *Guerriere* in the Atlantic before being transferred to the West Indies Squadron under Commodore David Porter. In early 1826, when Porter resigned to join the Mexican Navy, Hawkins followed him and spent the next few years playing havoc on Spanish shipping in the Gulf from an abandoned U.S. naval base at Key West, commanding a small squadron aboard the five-gun brig *Hermon.* Hawkins's notoriety became such that, as one Havana resident recalled, "Captain Hawkins was Havana's greatest scourge—his very name was a terror to every master of a vessel that was in the Spanish West Indies trade."

When U.S. authorities discovered that Hawkins was waging war on Spain from Key West, they arrested him. He was promptly released on bail, and returned to Veracruz. When money became tight in Mexico, and Admiral Porter and his colleagues fell out of favor with the government, Hawkins resigned his commission. He fled legal troubles in Florida (dueling and a murder charge in Key West), and became a successful Georgia steamboat captain on the Chattahoochee River. For the next few years, Hawkins was a flamboyant socialite among the southern aristocrats of the bustling city of Columbus, Georgia.

When war broke out in Texas, Hawkins joined Gen. José Antonio Mexía in an expedition to capture the Mexican port of Tampico. At Tampico, Hawkins served as Mexía's aide-de-camp and personally led the attack on the city's fortifications. The attack failed miserably, and Hawkins and Mexía escaped on a passing ship to Brazoria. Undaunted, Hawkins headed to San Antonio; having missed the battle against General Cós there, he offered his services as a naval commander to the fledgling government.

Sam Houston commended Hawkins to the government as a worthy officer who "is familiarly acquainted with the coast of the Gulph." Gov. Henry Smith, even more impressed, recommended Hawkins to the Texas commissioners in New Orleans as "a gentleman whose experience and ability in naval affairs would render his services acceptable in any govt—and more particularly in ours, which is just emerging from chaos." Hawkins traveled to New Orleans and presented himself to the Texas commissioners, who hired him on the spot.

Hawkins had a healthy ego. One woman described him as "a handsome man, and fully conscious of this fact." Always wearing his dashing captain's uniform, he carried himself with the swagger of a Napoleonic cavalry marshal. Following in the footsteps of his mentor, Commodore Porter, Hawkins gave the Texas agents fits by demanding extravagant sums to outfit *Independence* for her first sea cruise. As Texas agent William Bryan wrote to his government, "The disbursements of the Independence have been extremely large, much beyond what the government could afford & part of it in a great measure useless. . . . Your astonishment can hardly equal mine that Capt Hawkins should have gone to such an expense upon that small vessel . . . the expenditure of Capt Hawkins has troubled me more than all my other business."

Having fitted out *Independence* in a style becoming a national flagship, Hawkins began sailing in late January. But while Hawkins had a ship, he had no official commission; if captured, he and his fellow officers would be tried as pirates if they were not hanged immediately. Agents in Texas and Louisiana reminded Governor Smith that officers captured without commissions would very likely suffer "an ignominious death." On March 12, 1836, Interim President Burnet commissioned Hawkins as post captain and commodore of the fleet, and placed Hawkins in command of the warship *Independence*. As naval commander for the Republic, Commodore Hawkins would have primary responsibility for riding herd over an unruly, sometimes insubordinate, group of brother captains.

The hard-bitten William A. Hurd was already famous as the commander of the privateers *San Felipe* and *William Robbins*. He was given charge of *Brutus* in late January by William Bryan, who recommended him to the government as "a brave & meritorious man who has suffered much in your cause." A frustrated Hurd spent February in New Orleans, waiting for the government to supply him with men, provisions, and a commission. Unfortunately Hurd, like Hawkins, would have to wait until mid-March to receive his formal appointment.

Jeremiah Brown, like William Hurd, was another of the "old school" Gulf captains. Barely literate, the Rhode Islander operated a coastal packet after his arrival in Texas in 1830, and made a name for himself as captain of the *Sabine*, a merchant schooner that smuggled some of Texas's first cotton to market. A riverboat pilot along the Brazos, he also ran a tavern at Velasco and did some small-time land speculation before joining the cause in December 1835. He was appointed master of the warship *Liberty* in late January 1836, and soon Thomas McKinney—the official commander of the larger *Invincible*—asked the eager Brown to take *Invincible*'s helm.

In early March, Commodore Hawkins promoted Acting Lt. George Washington Wheelwright to captain, and assigned him command of *Liberty*, vacated by Captain Brown's move to the *Invincible*. The Texas government on March 14 recognized the gallant Wheelwright's promotion, but before Wheelwright was appointed, Adj. Gen. John Wharton placed William S. Brown—brother of Jeremiah Brown and a veteran of the siege of Béxar—in charge of *Liberty*. William Brown, a tall, dapper, fair-haired mariner, had *Liberty* out on a cruise at the time of Wheelwright's appointment, and Wheelwright could not find his vessel until she returned to Matagorda. When Wheelwright rowed over from *Independence* with a small detachment of marines to assume command, Brown had the marines' arms confiscated and refused to surrender his ship. For the time being, Wheelwright would be the only "charter captain" of the Texas Navy without a fighting ship.

In mid-January 1836, Lieutenant Governor Robinson recommended the creation of a Texas "corps of marines," and commissioned a United States Marine lieutenant, Francis Scott Nevill, as a marine. On March 12, 1836, Arthur Robertson was appointed captain of the Texas Marine Corps, making him the highest-ranking officer in a body to which over 350 enlisted men and 18 officers would eventually be attached.

The Texas government quickly concluded that it needed naval regulations if it were to keep its subordinate officers and men in line. On January 3, 1836, the General Council's Committee on Naval Affairs recommended adoption of those regulations used in the navy of the "United States of the North," and two days later, the General Council adopted U.S. naval regulations for use in the Texas Navy. Since the measure was part of the same ordinance that approved the purchase of *William Robbins* and *Invincible*, Governor Smith refused to sign it, so the council overrode Smith's veto by a constitutional majority. With this simple legislative action, Texas had a regulated navy.

One final item remained: the creation of a naval ensign. The "1824 Flag" was the official ensign of the privateer fleet, and it was carried aboard Lone Star warships prior to the Texas declaration of independence on March 2, 1836. But when Texas declared itself independent, the Mexican Constitution of 1824 no longer symbolized why Texians fought and died, and a new flag was in order. On April 9, Interim President Burnet decreed that the flag of the Texas Navy would be identical to the national flag of the United States, except that it would carry a single star in the blue field, in place of the twenty-four stars of the union to the north. Whether intended or not, the design would serve Texas well, since when the "star and stripes" hung limp, it could easily be mistaken for a United States flag. The public and the Navy must have liked the design, since Burnet's decree was later ratified by Sam Houston, and the flag would be left unchanged for the life of the Republic.

With a flag, regulations, officers, and men, Texas could finally boast a national fleet. But how well would a hastily organized group of amateurs fare against an established naval power? The world would find out by early March.

CHAPTER SEVEN

The Revolution at Sea

A dark cloud was resting on the affairs of Texas—they were being driven to their last strong hold—an expedition was fitting out at Matamoras for Galveston. On their Navy alone could they rely for protection and defence.

—Samuel Ellis, May 20, 1836

FOR THE FIRST MONTH OF ITS LIFE, the Texas Navy spent most of its time escorting transport and supply ships between New Orleans and Matagorda, and shipping volunteers and supplies to Texas. But the little fleet soon proved to be a potent weapon. To the delight of the beleaguered Texans—who had been beaten on land at every turn—the Texas Navy scored its first victory the day after Texas declared its independence. The spoils of war were brought to Galveston under the guns of Capt. William Brown's *Liberty.*

William Brown was getting restless. Clad in a second-hand officer's coat with gilt buttons, dapper epaulets, and a blue captain's hat, the handsome Captain Brown spent January 1836 skulking around New Orleans in search of men and supplies. He was unable to get *Liberty* out to sea until almost February—on convoy duty—and by March he still had nothing to show for his efforts. Defeat of a Mexican warship or merchantman would mean glory, fame, and riches, since naval prize regulations decreed that such vessels and their cargo would be sold, and the proceeds would be divided among the officers and crew, the captain garnering the lion's share.

But Brown found none of this along the Louisiana coast. Although the Texas Navy had not captured a single prize, exaggerated fears of *Brutus, Liberty* and the privateers made New Orleans shippers cautious, and the Mexican Eagle and Snake ensign was seldom seen in the northern Gulf.

Lacking any guidance from the provisional government, and refusing to recognize orders from Commodore Hawkins, Captain Brown decided to look for targets elsewhere.

Perhaps the hunting would be better off the Yucatán coast, the heart of Mexico's shipping industry. So Brown shaped his course for Sisal, a heavily armed port on the northwest side of the Yucatán peninsula. Running under fair winds, on the evening of March 5 Brown's schooner crept within sight of the city. There, his lookouts spotted a large merchant brig anchored among the barques and schooners of Sisal's busy harbor. Running up the Mexican flag, he shortened his sails and hung back, waiting outside the harbor until after dark. His plan was simple: that night he would send thirty men in *Liberty*'s boats to pluck the slumbering brig from her berth.

The dark seas were choppy, and *Liberty* lost two of her three boats as they were lowered into the churning waves. After some caucusing, Brown crammed fourteen men into the remaining boat, passed around a horn of grog to steady their spirits, and sent them off toward the flickering lights of the harbor.

Liberty's dangerously overcrowded launch paddled its way silently through the bouncing waters to the nearest vessel, the schooner *Sabine*, and Brown's men quietly cut her stern boat loose while her crew was sleeping. The party then divided itself and rowed in the two boats up to either side of the merchant brig.

The port's commandant, however, had spotted the suspicious ship hovering in the distance earlier that evening, and had wisely taken precautions. As the rowboats neared the brig from opposite sides, a platoon of double-armed Mexican soldiers hidden on the brig's deck suddenly stood up on the starboard side and loosed two volleys of musket fire in the oncoming boat's direction. No one was hit, and the Texians pulled with all their might, trying to close the gap as the soldiers frantically reloaded their flintlocks.

The Texians managed to clamber up the brig's side before another organized volley could be fired, and went to work with cutlasses and knives, hacking at their attackers and picking up muskets and pistols to return fire. Just then, *Liberty*'s second rowboat, thus far undetected, thudded against the brig's slick wooden hull, and several Mexican soldiers rushed to the port side to repel the attack from that direction. The Texas boarding party pushed the encircled enemy back, killing a half dozen of them and injuring three to five others. Mexican soldiers jumped overboard and dove down the hatches for safety. The ship was secure for the moment.

An alarm rang out over the wharves and houses, and the Texians could hear the sound of drums mustering soldiers out of their barracks. Under the direction of a lieutenant and sailing master, the party worked furiously to back the brig out of the harbor before reinforcements could arrive.

They almost didn't make it. The headsails and mainsail had been taken ashore by the prudent Mexican commander, and the main-boom had been immobilized with an iron spike. But the foresails, topsail, and topgallant were left, and several seamen quickly scrambled up the rigging to shake out the sails while others desperately pulled and hacked at the ship's mooring cables. Someone found a large awning on the quarterdeck, and the sailors frantically lashed it to the jib boom to make an improvised jibsail. An awful sail, but it would have to do.

Once the brig was cut loose and her makeshift rigging was set, the sailing master steered her out of the harbor. A cannonball launched by an angry port commandant flew high over the mastheads, but the fourteen men brought their vessel back under the protection of *Liberty*'s guns on the dark Yucatán sea, to the fading screams and curses of the port authorities.

The prize turned out to be the *Pelicano*, a 100-ton Baltimore-built schooner that had cleared New Orleans in late February. The haul was decent—550 barrels of flour, plus apples, potatoes, and other foodstuffs. At least, that was what was listed on the manifest prepared by J.W. Zacharie & Company, a pro-Mexican mercantile firm that had lobbied for the seizure of *Brutus* the previous December. Upon close inspection, however, Brown's crew found a number of secret compartments containing china, jewelry, dry goods, and other valuable items. Brown had stolen a smuggler! *Liberty*'s jubilant crew escorted *Pelicano* to Matagorda Bay, where she was to be condemned as a lawful prize and sold, making them rich men.

But Brown's luck ran out on the unforgiving Texas shore. *Pelicano* ran aground and broke up while crossing the treacherous Matagorda Bar on March 18, and the most valuable portions of her cargo were lost with the ship. Her barrels of foodstuffs were recovered, however, and were offloaded by *Liberty*'s crew with local help. When a smashed barrel was inspected, someone discovered a keg of gunpowder hidden inside. Other barrels were searched, and more kegs were discovered. Some 300 kegs of Santa Anna's gunpowder were eventually recovered from the wreckage, and were sent to Sam Houston's retreating army, where they would be put to good use at the Battle of San Jacinto.

A proclamation by General Houston heralded the dramatic victory, but public opinion in the Navy's unofficial home, New Orleans, was quite different. New Orleans was happy to support the Texas cause in the abstract, but when it interfered with the city's lucrative Mexican trade, the newspapers and shipping industries were quick to condemn Brown's Texians as pirates. At the end of March, Stephen Austin's cousin Henry Austin warned Texas agents, "If our armed vessels are to be employed to rob the very citizens of this city who furnished the money to purchase them . . . the disposition to aid our cause which has been so ardently evinced by the citizens of New Orleans will speedily be changed to an extreme disapprobation." William Bryan, writing to his government, was more circumspect. "The capture of the Mexican vessel, she being owned by Americans & Insured here, has caused great excitement, and some bad feelings. It is however to be expected."

The uproar did not seem to bother the swashbuckling Captain Brown, who penned a defiant letter to the editor of the New Orleans *True American*. He described the illicit cargo hidden aboard *Pelicano*, and warned the *American*'s readers, "My situation requires that I should keep a constant lookout, and when I see a Mexican flag flying, I shall either take it or be taken. I can not fly from a Mexican, and will not."

However livid New Orleans merchants might have been, William Brown had good reason to be pleased. Despite the loss of the smuggled valuables, the District Court of Brazoria County ultimately condemned *Pelicano* and her cargo as a legal prize, and awarded $3,792.02 to her captors. (In keeping with maritime custom, the award was later doubled to $7,584.05 on the grounds that *Pelicano*'s tonnage was more than one-third greater than *Liberty*'s.) Besides, the fact that Mexican suppliers were now hiding war materiel among civilian goods spoke volumes about the reputation of the Texas Navy and her sister privateers in the Gulf.

Soon after *Pelicano*'s capture, Capt. Jeremiah Brown's *Invincible* scored a critical victory off the Mexican coast. With provisions running low, Santa Anna's army desperately needed supplies and reinforcements. Shortages of food and basic equipment became more acute the further the *generalissimo* drove into the Texas heartland, and Mexico City obligingly prepared a convoy of supplies and men to give its army the momentum to finish off the rebels.

Reinforcements, ammunition, food, and supplies for Santa Anna's army were concentrated at Matamoros, a military base some twenty miles up the Rio Grande. The local commandant ordered the port sealed off to keep the buildup a secret. The war schooner *General Bravo* stood guard at the river's mouth with the two-gun schooner *Segundo Correo de Mexico*. When additional supplies and intelligence, expected any day, arrived from New Orleans, the two warships would convoy the transports *John M. Bandel*, *New Castle*, and *Pocket* to Copano Bay to resupply the army. This concentration of fat targets presented a perfect opportunity for an intrepid sea dog like *Invincible*'s Captain Brown.

Jeremiah Brown had spent the early part of 1836 fitting out *Invincible* for combat, and shuttling volunteers from New Orleans to Texas. When President Burnet took the reins of government, Brown anxiously requested orders to sail. By late March, he was cruising along the Texas coast, searching for the infamous *Bravo*. He found her on the morning of April 3.

Sailing south towards Matamoros under United States colors, Captain Brown peered through his spyglass at *General Bravo* sitting off Brazos de Santiago, at the mouth of the Rio Grande, in company with *Segundo Correo*. Something was amiss. The warship did not maneuver for position, and there was unusual activity around her stern. Brown ordered his schooner to move closer, decks quietly cleared for action, and soon he realized that *Bravo*'s rudder had been damaged on the Rio bar, leaving her helpless. Moving in around noon, his Stars and Stripes still flying, Captain Brown hailed *Bravo* and sent passenger William Leving aboard dressed in the uniform of a United States naval officer. Leving told the Mexicans that he was there at the behest of the U.S. government to complain about the treatment of American vessels and citizens.

Bravo's commander, Lt. Fernando R. Davis, was wary of this unfamiliar guest. He or "Mexico"Thompson, who was assisting in the *Bravo*'s repair, may have recognized Leving as a Texas officer. Either way, around noon Leving's cover was blown, and a shot from *Invincible* blew into *Bravo*'s rail, wounding two men.

Brown barked out orders to his lieutenants, and *Invincible* turned loose a furious broadside on *Bravo*. Lieutenant Davis returned the barrage, and a general gun battle opened between the two vessels. For an hour or so, guns bucked and cannons roared as blackened, sweaty gun crews worked their guns, while *Invincible* wore around for a better position. *Bravo*'s shots inflicted only minor damage to *Invincible*'s rigging, while *Invincible* sent some round shot through *Bravo*'s poop deck and rigging. Between *Bravo*'s missing rudder and the bombardment from *Invincible*'s guns, *Bravo* ran aground on the river's north shore, out of action for good.

The one-sided battle could have raged much longer. But around 2:00 p.m., on the faint line that divides the sky from the sea, a speck appeared. In the Age of Sail, specks were important, and the battling ships' lookouts watched the speck intently until it took on the shape of a sizeable brig. No one knew if it was armed, and neither captain wished to be outgunned, so *Invincible* broke off the engagement while the immobilized *General Bravo* had no choice but to watch and wait.

The ship hailed from New Orleans, and flew an American flag. She was the brig *Pocket*, and judging from her manifest, she carried a typical load of commercial goods. What was not on her manifest, however, was any reference to the cache of military supplies and ammunition bound for the Mexican Army. What was also unusual was her passenger list, which included at least three Mexican Navy officers—one of whom was Lieutenant Ocampo of the old *Correo Mejicano*, returning home from his extended stay at New Orleans.

Invincible ran straight for *Pocket*, and the brig's master, Elijah Howes, made no effort to run. When *Invincible* sailed within shouting distance, Howes told the Texians that *Pocket* was an American ship bound for Matamoros. Brown tacked his ship into the wind and got closer, then sent over a boarding party under *Invincible*'s menacing guns. The marines ordered Howes to come aboard *Invincible* with *Pocket*'s papers, while the crew and cargo of the brig were thoroughly searched.

The Texians were delighted at what they found. In addition to 600 barrels of flour and other foodstuffs, they found the ammunition and supplies intended for the reinforcement operation, dispatches to Santa Anna revealing plans to land 1,000 men at Galveston, a detailed chart of the Texas coast, and the Mexican officers. Given the obvious hostility of this brig to the Texas cause, the Texas officers felt justified in liberating a number of personal articles during their search. The 1824 flag was hoisted at the *Pocket*'s mast, and over vehement protests from Captain Howes, *Pocket* was placed under the command of a prize crew.

After waiting two more days off Matamoros, *Pocket* and *Invincible* sailed back to Galveston. *Invincible*'s departure, however, sealed the fate of U.S.-uniformed Lieutenant Leving, left aboard the *Bravo*, who was taken to Matamoros in irons and executed before a Mexican firing squad in conformity with Mexico's "no quarter" policy towards Texas rebels. Brown never explained his decision to leave the unfortunate officer in Mexican hands, although there was probably little he could do once Leving was taken below decks.

On the voyage home, the two ships were joined by *Brutus*, and the Mexican officers—Ocampo, three other Mexicans, and three Americans in Mexican service—were transferred to Captain Hurd's vessel. Under the gleeful eye of *Brutus*'s Lieutenant Damon, the prisoners were strip-searched, and four officers were placed in double irons below decks. According to U.S. *chargé d'affaires* Alcée LaBranch, the personal trunk of an American named Taylor was broken open, and Lieutenant Damon relieved him of $800 worth of cash and personal property; when Taylor demanded a receipt for his lost property, he too was placed in double irons, where he was kept for seven weeks.

Captain Hurd must have cracked a wicked smile when he reunited with Lieutenant Ocampo, the army lieutenant who had accused Hurd of stealing $1000 of Mexican payroll money from *Correo Mejicano*. Ocampo's presence aboard *Pocket* was, in fact, partly due to his lingering in New Orleans to prosecute his lawsuit against Hurd.

Hurd, who liberally ordered floggings of his own men for lesser infractions, must have found the irony delicious. He ordered Ocampo and Hogan tied down over the barrel of *Brutus*'s eighteen-pounder and treated to one hundred lashes each with a cat-o'-nine-tails. After the officers recovered from their bloody thrashing, Captain Hurd ordered that they be hanged. He braced up the foreyard and let the unfortunate men quiver under the yardarm with ropes about their necks for some time before putting them back in irons below.

On April 7, the ships arrived in Galveston. Captain Brown dropped off his prisoners, and President Burnet recruited a district judge to try the case and determine whether *Pocket* was a lawful prize. Brown took *Invincible* back to New Orleans for additional supplies, while *Pocket*'s military stores were forwarded to Houston's army. Captain Howes and his crew were detained at the tent city on Galveston Island until the end of the month, while *Pocket* was tethered off Galveston as a storage ship and sick bay for the next few months.

News of *Pocket*'s capture reached New Orleans around April 9, and a furor broke out within the city's shipping and insurance industries. The brig's owners filed piracy charges against Captain Brown and his crew, and when *Invincible* arrived in the Crescent City the following month, William Bryan immediately ordered her back to Galveston.

While *Liberty* was prowling the Yucatán coast, Commodore Hawkins was busy escorting convoys and capturing small merchantmen aboard the flagship *Independence*. While details of Hawkins's actions at this point are sketchy, notes later compiled by Lt. William A. Tennison indicate that between January and early March, *Independence* cruised throughout the Gulf, boarding and burning a number of small Mexican supply vessels. During the first few months of the year, *Independence* had her baptism of fire, allegedly engaging the Mexican brigs of war *Urrea* and *Bravo*, which evidently were escorting a supply schooner to Mexico. According to Tennison, the two brigs carried twenty-two guns to the Texian's eight, and Captain Hawkins, with a dramatic flair to match the bravado that came naturally to him, assembled his men and asked if he should attack. The crew responded with three hearty cheers, and *Independence* attacked, loosing broadside after broadside at the enemy ships, and driving them off without significant damage.

As the Texas Army withdrew from South Texas in late March 1836, Hawkins knew that his supply base at Matagorda was becoming untenable. He abandoned it, sending a landing party to burn the supply depot at Cox's Point. He butted heads with Captain William S. Brown, attempting to replace him with the properly appointed Captain Wheelwright.

The engagements of *Independence*, when coupled with the captures of the *Pelicano* at Sisal and *Pocket* at Matamoros, helped establish the Texas Navy's reputation as an effective, semi-piratical force that made Mexico's suppliers think twice before shipping goods across the Gulf. But as Santa Anna's army swept across central Texas, the naval center of gravity shifted to the last refuge of the revolutionary government, Galveston Island.

Virtually deserted before the war, in April 1836 Galveston Island's east end was crammed with hundreds of terrified refugees who had fled their homes and farms before Santa Anna's killing machine. News of the Alamo and the massacre of Colonel Fannin's men at Goliad drove most of the Anglo population eastwards, to seek shelter in the patchwork tents and driftwood lean-to's amidst the sand, rain, mud, and insects. The muddy, rain-soaked isle was crowded with the families of farmers, merchants, and slaves, huddled together in a semi-tropical tent city, as if Margaret Mitchell's Atlanta refugees had removed themselves to *Gilligan's Island*. The Texas government, having abandoned San Felipe for Washington-on-the-Brazos (west of modern-day Houston), again fled its capital to move officials and their families to Harrisburg, then fled again down the San Jacinto River to a tent city on the Galveston shore via the *Cayuga, Yellow Stone,* and *Flash.* By now, these settlers were not fighting for the Constitution of 1824, or for separate statehood, or independence. They were fighting to stay alive.

The tattered remnants of Texas aristocracy spent most of April fortifying Galveston for a last stand; if that failed, the survivors would evacuate to New Orleans, most likely never to return. Navy Secretary Robert Potter recalled the fleet to Galveston, and President Burnet nationalized the island as a fortified naval base, placing it under Potter's command. *Brutus* transferred civilians and supplies from Matagorda in early April, and the Navy's surgeons stayed busy making bandages for expected battle casualties. By the end of the month, Commodore Hawkins had gathered *Brutus, Invincible* and *Independence* close to the island to support the land forces and ward off any attack from the sea, while Col. James Morgan organized a local militia group to prepare defensive earthworks, sight artillery pieces, and prepare for the expected invasion.

Each passing day brought fresh rumors of disaster, magnified by the reality that General Houston's army was in headlong retreat. But as Burnet, Potter, Hawkins, and Morgan were circling the wagons around Galveston, the outnumbered Sam Houston launched a surprise attack on Santa Anna's advance guard, encamped between Buffalo Bayou and the San Jacinto River. On the afternoon of April 21, 1836, some 900 Texians attacked roughly 1,200 Mexicans commanded by Santa Anna and General Cós. Although Santa Anna knew the rebels were trapped on a small patch of land near his camp, he failed to take even the most rudimentary precautions, and the attack inexplicably came as a total shock to the Mexican leader. Within twenty minutes, the Mexican force was shattered; Santa Anna's capitulating soldiers were butchered by the hundreds by vengeful Texians, whose brothers, sons, and friends had been massacred at Goliad and the Alamo. When the Texians' blood-lust was quenched, roughly (very roughly) 600 Mexicans lay dead, and a near-equal number were taken prisoner—including *El Presidente* himself, disguised in a private's uniform. The cost to Texas was eight killed and twenty-three wounded.

The Battle of San Jacinto ended Mexican rule in Texas. But no one knew it yet. The largest part of the Mexican Army, now under the command of General Filisola, was still moving through the burned-out farmlands of central Texas. And word of Houston's victory would not reach the defenders at Galveston for another six days.

On April 27, *Invincible*'s lookouts spotted a small skiff moving towards the island. The four men in the boat, Col. Robert Calder, Pvt. Benjamin

Franklin, and two other soldiers, had rowed all the way from the mouth of the San Jacinto River. Slowly, the exhausted men paddled their way toward *Invincible*'s hull as Jeremiah Brown and his men curiously peered at the visitors from the deck. Old Captain Brown leaned over the ship's rail, put a speaking trumpet to his lips and shouted, "What's news?"

"When I told them," recalled Calder, "his men literally lifted us on board, and in the midst of the wildest excitement, Brown took off his hat and gave us three cheers, and threw it as far as he could into the bay." As the word of their deliverance spread, Brown called out, "Turn loose Long Tom!" whereupon *Invincible*'s eighteen-pounder boomed three times, startling the panic-ridden refugees.

Brown quickly thought better of the ruckus he was starting; he suddenly caught himself, saying, "Hold on, boys, or old Hawkins will put me in irons again." He ordered his men to lower the captain's gig and take Calder and Franklin across the harbor with the good news, but not before directing the purser to break out the ship's best liquor and pour some drinks for the two envoys of destiny.

As *Invincible*'s seamen rowed the two exhausted heroes to the landing, their path took them athwart *Independence*. Commodore Hawkins, spying them through his glass, frantically hailed them for news. The men shouted back and forth until they were close enough to be heard. The news hit the flagship like a carronade blast, and pandemonium broke out. Word spread from vessel to vessel, and a tidal wave of laughter, cheering and relief spread over the island. *Independence* fired thirteen guns, and Hawkins summoned the two messengers aboard for a feast and celebration.

During the festivities aboard *Independence*, it dawned on the revelers that no one had notified President Burnet, and Commodore Hawkins hinted that Calder and Franklin should go ashore immediately and report to the president. The two men excused themselves and rowed out from *Independence* to the shore, where they were coldly received by a red-faced Burnet, who was more than a little annoyed that everyone on the island should have heard the news before their president did. Eventually, however, the infectious feeling of relief took hold even in Burnet. Warming up, he treated the men, in Calder's words, "with that grace and genial courtesy for which, throughout life, he was ever distinguished."

With a cannon salute from the Texas flagship, the revolutionary government entered a new age. Its *raison d'être* no longer was survival; its job was now to protect and govern its people. At the same time, the Texas Navy entered a murky, ill-defined phase. Its new function was not to win a war, but to behave like a modern, civilized navy. And for the next sixteen months, the Texas Navy would fight a cold war at sea while competing for legitimacy in the eyes of the world.

Before moving on to the Texas-Mexican struggle of the next seven years, Capt. Jeremiah Brown's April 3 engagement off Matamoros bears a closer look, since his little adventure with *Bravo, Correo Segundo,* and *Pocket* quite possibly saved Texas, and thereby altered the course of American history. This unlikely-sounding conclusion begins with a look at the military picture from the Mexican side.

While Santa Anna was moving rapidly through central Texas in February and March 1836, his supply lines had dwindled to almost nothing. His men had been cold and hungry since they left Saltillo; in the "frightful and deserted lands" of south Texas, as General Filisola called them, the Mexicans had virtually no access to food or other essential supplies except by sea. The thirteen-day siege of the Alamo forced Mexico's *Ejército de Operaciónes* to consume valuable rations, and cost the corps over 600 casualties. As Santa Anna's advance guard pushed towards Galveston Bay in mid-April, generals Filisola, Ramírez y Sesma, and Urrea watched in dismay as swollen rivers delayed their advance and forced them to eat most of their food. As the troops marched, they became hungry, and soon one conclusion became obvious: they desperately needed provisions, if not reinforcements, to sustain operations in Texas.

After Santa Anna's defeat at San Jacinto on April 21, General Filisola, whose force substantially outnumbered Houston's, meekly accepted Santa Anna's orders to withdraw, despite the urgings of his fellow generals. Filisola defended his decision to evacuate, among other things, on the ground that the army was desperately short of food and essential supplies. But the relief expedition from Matamoros—equipment, food, maps, ammunition, and men packed aboard *Correo Segundo, Bravo, John M. Bandel, New Castle,* and *Pocket*—would undoubtedly have solved Filisola's dilemma. Land a few hundred reinforcements and three shiploads of supplies at Copano, the Brazos mouth, or Galveston, and Filisola would have no excuse for retreat. Encamped within striking distance of San Jacinto on April 25, Filisola could have easily linked up with the relief force, fed his hungry men, and Sam Houston's army—heavily outnumbered in artillery, cavalry, and infantry—would probably have been annihilated, or else driven into Louisiana as an exiled guerilla band. Unless the lightning of San Jacinto struck a second, even more improbable time, Texas would have ended up exactly as Santa Anna had intended: a military buffer state in which the Anglo population had been driven out at the point of a bayonet. (See Appendix A.)

But the relief flotilla never came, its timetable disrupted by the arrival of *Invincible* and the capture of the *Pocket*. Captain Brown's bold incursion into Mexico's northern base effectively scrubbed the planned effort until the end of the month, by which time Filisola's army was inexorably committed to a retreat to Mexican territory.

Texas secession in turn had a profound impact on the subsequent history of the American west. Santa Anna's secretary of war, José María Tornel y Mendivil, predicted, "The loss of Texas will inevitably result in the loss of New Mexico and the Californias. Little by little our territory will be absorbed. . . ." Tornel would prove clairvoyant in this regard; the annexation of Texas in 1845 became the spark that exploded into war the following year, resulting in the American acquisition of New Mexico, Arizona, California, and parts of Utah, Colorado, and Nevada.

Cataclysmic events such as the Mexican War rarely occur in a vacuum, and to be sure, the undulating pressures of Manifest Destiny might have made war with Mexico inevitable. Washington had long coveted Mexico's northwestern lands, and the California Gold Rush of 1849 would have Anglicized the Pacific coast to a far greater degree than the immigration rush to Texas in the early 1830s. But it was Texas, not California or New Mexico, that presented a *causus belli* to Mexico and the United States, and ultimately led to the acquisition of six western states through the Treaty of Guadalupe Hidalgo in 1848. (In Mexico, the 1846 war was popularly referred to as the "Texas War" until Gen. Winfield Scott took the conflict to Mexico.) By contrast, with Texas firmly in Mexico's grasp, there very likely would have been no Mexican War (at least, not in 1846), and the lands that became the spoils of that conflict would not have devolved to the *Estados Unidos del Norte* until much later, if ever. The Texas Navy, as much as the Battle of San Jacinto, saved Texas, and thereby altered the history of the American west.

ACT TWO

A National Fleet
(1836–1837)

CHAPTER EIGHT

Defending the Lone Star

> *So far in our struggle with Mexico, our navy has proved adequate to the protection of our seacoasts, and to the annoyance of the enemy. But the navy of the enemy has lately been increased by the addition of several vessels of the most splendid description. . . .*
> —Texas Naval Affairs Committee, October 26, 1836

THE "HOT" WAR HAD ENDED. Mexico's army—those elements that had not been slaughtered or enslaved at San Jacinto—retreated to the Rio Grande under Santa Anna's orders. As Filisola withdrew, Santa Anna, his back almost literally to the hangman's tree, signed two Treaties of Velasco, recognizing Texas's independence and promising to work for Mexican approval of his agreements.

But the end of the hot war was merely the beginning of a warm one. The enraged Mexican Congress resolved to prosecute the war with even greater vigor, and quickly disavowed the peace treaties signed by Santa Anna. Over the next few months, the Mexican government concentrated troops and supplies at Matamoros for a second invasion, and commissioned a new schooner-of-war, the nine-gun *Vencedor del Alamo*, to provide additional naval protection. As a result, rumors of war wafted through Texas during the hot summer of 1836.

Against this backdrop, the Texas Navy began scrounging for new recruits and supplies. But a deficit of competent civilian leadership hampered the Navy's ability to do its job. As would happen again and again, the Navy got itself into crippling financial and legal trouble, starting with its next excursion to New Orleans.

One of General Houston's basic needs after the Battle of San Jacinto was medical treatment. A musket ball had found its way to his left ankle during the battle and, according to Houston, the wound required better medical care than his army surgeons could provide. President Burnet, sensing a political rival rising from the haze of battle, refused to provide Houston with a warship to take him to New Orleans. Houston therefore booked a passage on the schooner *Flora*, and *Liberty* went along as *Flora*'s escort. The two vessels left Galveston on May 15, 1836, and arrived in New Orleans on May 22.

Secretary Potter, who left Galveston for New Orleans shortly after the Texas victory, lost no time in preparing *Liberty* for another cruise. He dismissed the insolent William Brown—whose lack of military discipline stood out even by the Texas Navy's loose standards—and replaced him with Captain George Wheelwright. He then ordered around $7,000 worth of repairs and supplies for *Liberty*, heedless of the fact that Texas had no money in her coffers to pay for them. Exasperated fiscal agents were forced to admit to *Liberty*'s creditors that they could not pay for the schooner's overhaul.

Liberty quickly sank into trouble. The swarm of carpenters, sailmakers, painters, and laborers threatened to walk off the job by the beginning of June, and despite a $5,000 loan by Col. Robert Triplett, repair costs quickly outstripped the agents' meager ability to pay for them. By the end of the summer, the vessel was sequestered in New Orleans, encumbered by more than $10,000 in debts. Resigned to the loss of his warship, President Burnet instructed his general agent, the firm of Thomas Toby & Brother, to allow *Liberty* to be sold to use any leftover repair funds for other needs. Ignominiously, *Liberty* became the Texas Navy's first casualty—lost not to fiery Mexican batteries or the Gulf's impromptu hazards, but to a mob of New Orleans merchants who had been stiffed by the well-meaning but bankrupt republic.

While William Brown's *Liberty* was shoving off for New Orleans, his brother's warship, *Invincible*, was just arriving there, and would be met with a much different reception. Although Jeremiah Brown did not know it, a group of shipping and insurance executives had singled out *Invincible* for piracy charges over the *Pocket* affair, and in April they pressed Commodore A.J. Dallas of the West Indies Squadron to arrest the vessel and her crew if she dared enter American waters. Dallas, under pressure from the Jackson administration to enforce U.S. neutrality laws evenhandedly, dispatched the sloop *Warren* to apprehend *Invincible* when she arrived at the Balize. *Invincible* was duly seized at the mouth of the Mississippi, and on May 2, her crew (without Captain Brown, who was not aboard at the time) was led through the streets of New Orleans in handcuffs by a U.S. marshal.

The unfortunate sailors were held for three days in a jail that one British observer characterized as "a dungeon, the exact model of the 'Black Hole.'" One problem for the defense was that Judge Benjamin C. Franklin of the

District of Brazoria had not gotten around to condemning *Pocket* as a lawful prize, so the status of the capture was unresolved, even in Texas. On May 4 the case, involving forty-seven officers and men, was called to trial at the Royal Street courthouse, but owing to a lack of prosecution witnesses, the case was reset. Taking their case to the New Orleans public, Texas agents used the delay to circulate a broadside, which read:

To the Friends of Civil Liberty!
The examination of the officers and crew of the Texian Man of War Schooner Invincible, will take place at Judge Rawle's office, on Royal Street, at 11 o'clock today.
The public will there have an opportunity of seeing who are the aiders and abetters of the Bloody Massacres of Santa Anna.

Two days later, the case was called before Judge Edward Rawle, a state judge sitting in for his absent federal counterpart. Three officers of the *Warren* testified about *Invincible*'s capture, but no evidence of *Pocket*'s circumstances could be produced—the prosecution's witnesses all being held in Texas—so Judge Rawle freed the prisoners. With the acquittal, Texas agents in New Orleans enjoyed a brief wave of public support. *Invincible*'s crew was released to the cheers of Texas sympathizers, who treated them en masse to a feast and an evening at the theater in the French Quarter. The New Orleans *Commercial Bulletin* glowingly opined, "Never have we seen a finer collection of robust, honest-faced tars than the prisoners, and in a good cause, we should ever hope, that they might prove invincible."

The feeling didn't last. Three days later, a haggard, angry Captain Howes arrived from Galveston aboard the schooner *Congress* and immediately filed new charges against his captors, prompting another round of outrage in the fickle city. Insurance underwriters pressed Commodore Dallas to provide armed escorts for vessels traveling to Mexico, complaining that the American flag was "no protection whatever" from Texan marauders, especially Captains Brown and Hurd. Local newspapers—even those friendly to Texas—began denouncing *Pocket*'s capture; the New Orleans *Bee* summed up the Crescent City's misgivings when it commented, "As much as we love Texas, we love America more, and can not connive at any violation of the American right and commerce by Texas."

To head off a second round of piracy charges, William Bryan and the Thomas Toby firm quickly paid Captain Howes $3,500 for his losses and bought *Pocket* to settle his claims. They compensated several passengers for their detention and for personal losses, and made Captains Brown and Hurd publicly swear that they would never again molest American merchant vessels. By early June, Texas's auditor in New Orleans reported to the Texas treasury secretary that "[t]o prevent a second arrest of the Crew of the Invincible on the Charge of Piracy it was deemed necessary to settle with such Citizens of the United States as had suffered damage, and by that means silence them. It was accordingly done."

Individuals could be bought off. But silencing the enraged insurers and the United States government turned out to be a bigger problem. The Louisiana State Marine and Fire Insurance Company, which insured *Pocket*'s cargo, filed suit against Jeremiah Brown on May 19. Captain Brown was taken into custody the next day, and was released on a $9,000 bond posted by Thomas Toby and William Bryan. (The case dragged on for over four years, dying from lack of interest sometime in 1840, some two years after Brown's death.) The United States government also presented formal claims against the Republic of Texas, and Texas eventually settled the governmental claims for $11,750 with a treaty ratified by the U.S. Senate on June 14, 1838.

While lawyers, diplomats, and insurers sparred in New Orleans, Jeremiah Brown was able to extricate his warship from American waters. For all the trouble he caused the Republic by capturing *Pocket*, Captain Brown could at least take satisfaction in the knowledge that he had struck a great blow for the Texas war effort. And that feeling would have been even sweeter had Captain Brown known that by the end of May, General Filisola was complaining bitterly to his government that *Pocket*'s seizure had caused the Mexican army's New Orleans supplier to cancel future deliveries.

While *Invincible* was detained in New Orleans, Commodore Hawkins assumed the role of watchdog against counter-revolutionaries. Hawkins and James Morgan, commander of the Galveston militia, rounded up a number of local "Tories" and held them in double irons aboard *Independence*, with express orders that no officer or crewman could speak with the prisoners. In Hawkins's mind, "Tories" included Capt. William Brown, and he used this political roundup to settle scores with *Liberty*'s captain. In Brown's words, Hawkins, "ordering my crew on shore from the Flora, and placing a pistol to my head, and saying that he would blow my brains out if I should say one word to him, [took] me at the same time on board his vessel a prisoner." He clapped *Liberty*'s commander in irons and held him aboard *Independence* overnight, until Secretary Potter ordered his release.

Independence, now augmented with a fine brass nine-pounder captured at San Jacinto, did little else that summer. Hawkins spent his time disbursing funds, purchasing naval supplies, and squabbling with Secretary Potter over command appointments.

After *Invincible*'s legal problems were addressed and provisions were obtained, Jeremiah Brown sailed her back to Velasco, where she got into a scrape with her sister ship. Brown came ashore to Velasco on May 28, leaving Lt. Francis Johnson in charge of the anchored *Invincible*. At dusk the next day, Johnson's lookouts spotted a strange sail about a mile-and-a-half off the port quarter. The stranger fired a signal (a single shot from a musket), which *Invincible*'s sailing master recognized as a standard Mexican port signal. Thinking the interloper to be a Mexican warship, Johnson ordered the crew to weigh anchor and clear the decks for action. Men scurried about, loading guns, shaking out sails, and throwing up protective netting under the rigging, while volunteer riflemen camped ashore at Quintana poured onto a nearby steamer to assist *Invincible* if need be.

By 11:00 a.m., *Invincible*'s crew was able to make out two musket flashes repeated every two minutes. After consulting the fleet's signal book, the officers decided the approaching vessel must be *Brutus*. *Invincible* replied with her signal, when *Brutus* fired three cannon—two blank and one with a ball—directly at *Invincible*.

Fortunately, the ball struck the water about forty yards from *Invincible*'s port quarter, and while it caused a great commotion among her crew, no one was hurt. *Invincible* continued signaling, and soon *Brutus*, carrying Commodore Hawkins as well as Captain Hurd, ceased firing. Both ships tacked for their anchorage. Captain Hurd and *Brutus*'s surgeon, Dr. Albert Moses Levy, came aboard *Invincible* and informed the commanding lieutenant that Commodore Hawkins himself had sighted the gun that had been shotted. Lieutenant Johnson was ordered aboard *Brutus*, and Hawkins curtly informed him that Captain Brown was to be dismissed and replaced by someone from New Orleans.

Although Commodore Hawkins wanted to remove the brother of the insubordinate William Brown, he was unsuccessful. Jeremiah Brown informed President Burnet of the bizarre incident, and requested an explanation of any charges leveled against him. No charges were ever raised, and Brown remained in command. The explanation for the Texan commodore's strange behavior has been lost to history.

During the spring of 1836, *Invincible* moved from controversy to controversy with the ease of a clipper ship gliding through a quiet harbor. After the unexpected attack by *Brutus*, President Burnet selected *Invincible* for holding Santa Anna, who had recently signed the Treaties of Velasco, which paved the way for Mexican recognition of Texas. On June 1, she was ready to repatriate the *generalissimo*, his secretary, and Col. Juan Almonte, all prisoners since April 21.

Santa Anna was not a popular man in Texas at the time (nor, for that matter, at any time over the next two centuries). If he had a Yankee dollar for every time his life had been threatened since his capture, he probably could have bribed his way home. President Burnet and General Houston nevertheless stood firm against his execution, on legal grounds (the idea of war crimes was not really formalized in the 1830s), political grounds (Texas had just ratified a treaty ending the war, and couldn't very well execute the man who signed it), and military grounds (it was convenient to have someone who could order General Filisola to withdraw to the Rio Grande). For his own protection, President Burnet decided to place Santa Anna aboard *Invincible* and send him home with Texas diplomats Lorenzo de Zavala and Bailey Hardeman.

Invincible was supposed to weigh anchor on June 1, but delays in getting instructions to the commissioners kept the warship in port until June 4, when the steamboat *Ocean* chugged into Velasco with Gen. Thomas Jefferson Green and some 200 roughneck volunteers from New Orleans. When they learned Santa Anna's whereabouts, they blockaded *Invincible* at the river mouth and formed a large, ugly lynch mob, threatening to shoot anyone—including the president—who got in their way.

Even hard-line critics of the diplomatic approach were worried. Secretary of War Mirabeau Buonaparte Lamar, Houston's antagonistic cavalry commander at San Jacinto, sided with the president and Houston in a rare show of unity, declaring, "Mobs must not intimidate the government. We want no French Revolution in Texas!" Burnet, standing firm against a flagrant violation of international law, ordered Santa Anna safely removed from *Invincible*, and dispatched enough troops to back up his orders.

In a scene that did little credit to either Texas or Mexico, Santa Anna, believing that he was about to be executed, struggled desperately to stay on board the schooner, pleading for his life. He was eventually dragged off the warship under heavy guard, and moved from safe house to safe house until he could be sent to Washington, D.C., for repatriation to Mexico.

Mexico refused to concede the loss of Texas, but for the moment she was helpless to recover her province. Learning from the disasters of the Texas campaign, Secretary of War and Marine José Maria Tornel y Mendivil began rebuilding a fleet to provide interdiction and convoy services for a second invasion. He sent agents to Baltimore and New Orleans to purchase new warships, and soon reports of armed brigs heading to Veracruz began drifting back to Texas. The tireless William Bryan informed President Burnet in June that Mexico was raising 15,000 men to reconquer Texas, and he urged the government to provide funds to buy new arms and supplies.

A strange event at Copano Bay seemed to confirm Bryan's worst fears. Responding to rumors of an invasion, on May 29 Gen. Thomas J. Rusk ordered Maj. Isaac Burton to take a company of twenty mounted rangers to patrol the coast near Refugio and the mouth of the San Antonio River. Five days later, while staking out Copano Bay, the rangers spotted a schooner approaching from the south. Hiding most of their number in nearby bushes, Burton had a few unarmed men frantically hail the schooner in Spanish, which obligingly dispatched a boat with five men to pick up the castaways. The rangers quietly captured the boat at gunpoint as it landed and moved sixteen heavily armed men into it. Rowing out to the schooner, the rangers easily captured *Watchman*, a supply ship from Matamoros carrying 520 barrels of food intended for General Filisola's army.

Burton's rangers ordered *Watchman*'s master to take the schooner to Velasco, but adverse winds delayed the voyage for nearly two weeks. On June 18, two other supply ships, *Fanny Butler* and *Comanche*, approached Aransas Pass, and Burton, six rangers, and a local captain named James D. Boylan lured the vessels by running up *Watchman*'s usual ensign. When the two ships crossed the bar, Burton sent over rangers disguised as sailors, who invited the two captains aboard *Watchman* for a glass of grog. When the unsuspecting captains came aboard, they were taken prisoner, and the fleet of captured ships sailed for Velasco the next day.

By June 23, the rangers anchored their flotilla at Velasco, where the local admiralty court condemned *Fanny Butler* and *Comanche* as prizes. The freight, valued at nearly $20,000, was distributed to the army, and the following month Burton distributed prize money to his rangers, who achieved local fame in song and legend as the "Horse Marines."

Among the many things the Texas Navy had to improvise during 1836 was civilian leadership. After the Battle of San Jacinto, Navy Secretary Robert Potter left his post to pursue other interests, which included an abandoned married woman he picked up during the refugee exodus of the Runaway Scrape. (He eventually persuaded the young woman to marry him by convincing her that her previous union was not legal under Mexican law, since it had never been certified by a Catholic priest.)

President Burnet did his best to fill the vacuum created by Potter's absence. Writing orders as if he were a navy secretary, Burnet decided to put Mexico's *Vencedor del Alamo* out of business before she could take on provisions and menace Texas. Admonishing Jeremiah Brown that "I find it important that our little navy be on the alert," Burnet ordered *Invincible* to rendezvous with *Brutus* at Matagorda; the two warships would then launch a coordinated attack on a naval squadron said to be fitting out at Veracruz. *Independence*, then at New Orleans, would meet the two vessels along the way. One New Orleans newspaper predicted a swift Texian victory. "Captain Hawkins and the other officers of the Texas Navy will not allow Mexican ships to cross the Gulf near Matagorda."

But *Vencedor* was closer to home than the Texians knew. As *Invincible* weighed anchor at Velasco in mid-June, *Vencedor* was sitting outside Matagorda Bay, bottling up *Brutus* in the harbor. When word of this one-ship blockade reached Velasco, *Invincible,* the schooner *Union,* and the steamboat *Ocean,* all laden with volunteer riflemen, ran down the Texas coast to relieve Captain Hurd. At the sight of this makeshift squadron, *Vencedor del Alamo* unbent her sails and "skinned out" to Veracruz; the Texas squadron, it appears, was content to let her go for the moment.

After running a few errands for the government, *Invincible* returned to the task of threatening Veracruz. Reacting to reports of prizes leaving New Orleans under the protection of the United States, on July 21 President Burnet issued a blockade proclamation against Matamoros, and ordered his warships to the Rio Grande. Four days later, *Invincible* was sitting outside the harbor at Veracruz, single-handedly blockading the Mexican Navy's main base. Captain Brown challenged the idle *Vencedor* to a duel in open water, but *Vencedor*'s captain declined on the grounds that his crew, having gone without their wages for some time, was in no condition to fight. By the end of the month, *Independence,* in New Orleans, reported that three Texas vessels, presumably *Invincible, Brutus,* and the schooner *Union,* had Matamoros completely bottled up. "Mexico" Thompson's *Correo Segundo* slipped out towards Veracruz, but wrecked along the way, and all aboard except the resilient Thompson and two lucky marines perished.

The naval threat was gone, for the moment. With no inviting targets and provisions running short, Captain Brown returned home, encountering on the way a French vessel whose captain mistook the warship for a pirate vessel; it seems the Frenchman had not heard of this strange new republic on Mexico's northern border.

One of President Burnet's improvisations that tense summer was to grant an informal commission to the privateer *Terrible.* There are few surviving records of the exploits of the one-gun schooner owned by the future mayor of Galveston, but it appears that *Terrible,* formerly the schooner *Union,* reported for duty on June 28, 1836. The following day, Burnet informed Capt. Jeremiah Brown, "We have given a letter of Marque to Capt [John] Allen for the little Schooner Terrible, one long pivot 6 pd, a clipper."

Captain Allen wasted no time getting his six-pounder into action. In early August *Terrible* ventured between Sisal and Campeche on the Yucatán peninsula's west coast, and captured the merchant sloop *Matilda,* bearing dry goods from New Orleans to Mexico. The captain of the merchant schooner *San Jacinto* reported that *Terrible* also ran down and destroyed another Mexican vessel on August 5. Sending *Matilda* to Galveston under a prize crew, Allen's vessel returned to New Orleans, searching in vain for *Invincible* for a rendezvous at the mouth of the Rio Grande. By August 16, the *Telegraph and Texas Register* reported that *Terrible* was on patrol again in Mexican waters.

The seizure of *Matilda*, a New Orleans merchant vessel, stoked fresh outrage among New Orleans' shipping tycoons, and soon powerful coastal interests demanded that the U.S. Navy take a more active interest in protecting U.S. shipping. Commodore Dallas obligingly dispatched the sloop of war *Boston* to apprehend *Terrible*. *Boston* tracked her down and arrested the crew, sending them to Pensacola for further proceedings. (The charges were eventually dropped.) Dallas dispatched additional warships to New Orleans to convoy merchant vessels clearing customs for Matamoros, Tampico, and Veracruz; his move quelled much of the political uproar, and kept the Texas sharks at bay for the moment.

With the momentary lull in the Gulf, *Invincible* headed back to New Orleans. In August, Capt. Jeremiah Brown convinced President Burnet that his schooner was "totally unfit to perform another cruise from the want of many essential repairs, and also, from the insubordinate state of the crew." Brown advised Burnet that *Invincible* needed repairs, men, and supplies that could best be obtained in New York, rather than New Orleans, given the tropical diseases that ran rampant there in late summer.

Burnet granted Brown's request and ordered him to proceed there via New Orleans, where he could pick up funds from Thomas Toby. *Invincible* arrived there on August 19, and Brown discharged his crew except for those needed to sail to New York. Evidently nervous about a rumored military buildup at Matamoros, Burnet countermanded his order four days later, and instructed Brown to return to Velasco. Brown, receiving his recall orders in New Orleans, replied that he could not comply due to the decrepit condition of his vessel.

While Captain Brown was pleading for orders to proceed to New York, Captain Hurd took *Brutus* there, arriving on August 31. He had absolutely no authority for his voyage. Hurd's arrival in New York, the first by a Texas national vessel, was big local news, and one New York paper reported, "Yesterday, for the first time, the flag of Texas was seen floating on our harbor, and from the main peak of a *real* Texian vessel of war, the Brutus." What the papers did not know was that the flag of Texas flew over an AWOL vessel.

After docking, Hurd began ordering repairs and supplies for his ship on credit. Hurd's first letters from New York stressed the need for substantial repairs to his ship, and bemoaned the mutinous state of his underpaid crew, which Hurd said compelled him to shoot two of his men. News of the purchases alarmed Texas agents, who foresaw huge bills and lost opportunities to capture Mexican vessels leaving New Orleans.

Their fears proved well founded. Invoices from local merchants began rolling in some six days after Hurd's vessel dropped anchor: cider, rum, champagne, brandy, sherry, and Madeira wine; potatoes, eggs, vegetables, ham, salt and raisins; wood, lanterns, coffee mills, paper, screws, fuses, sight glass, spoons, plates, duck trousers, blue jackets, shirts, and socks. In short, everything including the kitchen sink (actually, two of them). The officers, as was typical of the times, bought their own food with advances on their uncertain pay: London porter, claret, ham, wine, beef, mackerel, butter, cheese, molasses, currants, tripe, honey, pickles, and other fine foods. In mid-September, Captain Hurd borrowed $4,500 to pay off his men, pledging his country's warship as collateral for the loan. By October, Texas agents were vainly working to pay off $6,500 in debts for *Brutus*, and collection proceedings had commenced. The schooner was seized, and an officer was appointed by a New York court to take charge of the warship. By December the mounting bills included fees for lawyers working to keep *Brutus* from meeting the same fate that had befallen *Liberty* the previous summer.

Following Hurd's lead, Captain Brown sailed *Invincible* for New York around August 24, arriving there on September 11. Like Hurd, Captain Brown immediately plunged his little ship, and the republic responsible for her, into debt by ordering repairs, additional men, and supplies. With creditors clamoring to sell both warships, the two Texas captains settled in for a long stay in Manhattan.

By September 1836, Texas was losing the battle for naval supremacy in the Gulf of Mexico. The Mexican government embarked on a program to convert merchant vessels into fighting ships, and soon would field a fleet consisting of the warships *Vencedor del Alamo, General Bravo, General Urrea, Independencia,* and *Libertador* in the northern Gulf. Texas, meanwhile, had lost *Liberty* to creditors, and her two largest warships to their prodigal captains.

With his term of office coming to an end, Burnet tried to reconstitute the Navy any way he could. He commissioned privateer James Boylan as captain of the armed schooner *Passaic*, which Boylan renamed *Viper*, and ordered Boylan to cruise down the Gulf coast. (Burnet's acting navy secretary asked Boylan not to rename his schooner the *Sam Houston*, as Boylan had planned, since it was much too small a craft to dignify the Hero of San Jacinto.) Burnet commissioned the schooner *Thomas Toby* as a privateer, and recommissioned *Liberty*'s Capt. William Brown on the condition that he find and fit out a vessel to be christened *Benjamin R. Milam*. (Brown died before his ship could be fitted out.) Burnet sent *Thomas Toby* and *Viper* out to patrol the Mexican coastline, and signed commissions for the steamboat *Cayuga* and the sloop *Water Witch*. To buttress the loyalty of *Independence* and her crew, he wrote a personal letter of commendation to the flagship's officers. He also reiterated his orders to Jeremiah Brown to return to Velasco, and ordered agents in New Orleans and New York to do whatever it took to free the

Invincible and *Brutus* from their creditors, including using land scrip—promissory notes that could be redeemed for acreage in Texas if not paid by the maturity date. In all, Burnet did quite a bit for the Navy that eventful summer. But as a dissatisfied Burnet grumbled before leaving office, "the present condition of the navy is by no means commensurate with the importance of that arm of the public defence." With the departure of *Independence* for New Orleans in late September, Texas had no war vessels to guard its coasts as a new administration prepared to take the reins of government.

CHAPTER NINE

The General at the Helm

Where is our Navy? Where are the privateers which were on our coast some time since? Our navy is almost in a state of mutilation, torn to pieces—without men, without provisions, almost without officers, several having resigned in consequence of the dilatory movements of our government, in furnishing the means to man and provision their vessels for service. Great God! What is Texas coming to?

—Velasco *Herald*, 1836

DURING THE LONG, UNEASY SUMMER OF 1836, Texas settled into the business of creating a permanent government with permanent military institutions. In July 1836, *ad interim* President Burnet, tired of incessant criticism, public debts, and the demands of office, called for a general election to be held in September, opening the door to the man who would dominate Texas politics for the next two decades, Gen. Sam Houston.

Houston, commander in chief of the Texas Army, came to Texas a wreck of a man. The six-foot three-inch veteran of the Creek Indian Wars hailed from Tennessee, but he had run away from home as a teenager to live among the Cherokee Indians for three years, earning the nickname "The Raven." After military service under Andrew Jackson, Houston's star rose rapidly as a Jackson protégé; he was elected to Congress, then became governor of Tennessee. Like Jackson, Houston's thoughts were occupied with the expansion of the Union into the west, fulfilling the charter Destiny had assigned to the Americans. But disaster struck in 1829 when his politically-connected bride left him under unexplained circumstances, ruining Houston's career in Tennessee. He left the Volunteer State for a life of exile among the Cherokee in Oklahoma, who derided the once-great man as "Big Drunk."

When disturbances began shaking Texas in 1832, Houston went west. Revolution broke out in 1835, and Governor Smith appointed Houston commander of the regular army. The problem was that Texas had volunteers and militia, but no regular army. For several months, Houston unsuccessfully tried to impose some kind of strategy on the disparate, headstrong volunteer commanders scattered throughout South Texas—Fannin, Johnson, Grant, and Travis. Thoroughly frustrated, he furloughed himself and quit the army until March 1, when a convention assembled to decide once and for all the question of Texas independence.

On March 3, 1836, the convention appointed Houston commander of all Texas forces, both regular and volunteer, giving him as much authority as the embryonic government could bestow. Saddling up his white horse Saracen, he galloped off to a campaign of retreat-and-regroup from central Texas to the headwaters of Galveston Bay. Houston's victory at San Jacinto, and his wisdom in sparing Santa Anna's life, saved the Texas rebels from probable extinction.

Sam Houston was one of the greatest visionaries Texas produced—after, next to, or notwithstanding Stephen Austin, depending on how one views these two frontier giants. Houston's defensive campaign against Santa Anna, his two successful presidential bids and his diplomatic maneuverings with Britain, France, Mexico, and the United States evinced both strategic brilliance and the expansive Jacksonian vision he held for Texas and the United States. But for all Houston's strengths as a politico-military strategist, he was a questionable military tactician, and a miserable failure as commander in chief of his navy.

Houston's inability to wield his fleet effectively stemmed from two fundamental misconceptions he held about navies of the nineteenth century. First, he believed that navies, like militia forces, could be assembled as needed on short notice. This conviction did not take into account the specialized nature of naval warfare, which required unique equipment, skilled sailors, and experienced officers. Logistics was another difference. Armies could live off the land, if necessary, or send their baggage trains along behind the main force. In fact, this approach was often preferable. For a warship, however, there was no land to live off; a man-of-war's crew had to pack everything needed for its survival, including food, water, supplies, and ammunition, before it weighed anchor. A navy therefore needed to be maintained during peacetime, if it was to be of any timely use when war broke out.

Houston's second misconception was that a small navy is more effective when held close to shore rather than roaming the high seas. In Houston's view, the best defense was a close-in defense, and the best offense was none at all. His conduct of the San Jacinto campaign (essentially, a scaled-down version of Russia's defense against Napoleon in 1812) illustrates Houston's defensive orientation. On land, this approach held some appeal, considering the relative sizes of the Mexican and Texas armies and the vast uninhabited lands Texas could trade for time. But keeping a fleet bottled up did little except protect its own harbor, which could be done much more cheaply with shore batteries. And harbor defense was useless if the merchantmen sailing in and out of the harbor were captured as soon as they left the limited zone protected by the warships. Besides, tethering Texian warships to Galveston or the Brazos mouth would concede the Gulf to the enemy, permitting Mexico to purchase military supplies in the United States and transport troops wherever they were most useful. Houston's philosophy also failed to acknowledge that a vessel outside the Galveston Bar at low tide was almost as isolated as one off the coast of Veracruz, and had much less room to maneuver.

On the other hand, a small squadron could easily draw off more than its size in enemy ships sent to chase it. The Confederates demonstrated this many times during the American Civil War with the armed sloops *Alabama* and *Florida*, and Germany proved this twice during the next century, with the battle cruiser *Goeben* and pocket battleship *Graf Spee*. In short, Houston may have been popularly known as "The General," but no one, least of all Houston, would ever think of calling him "The Admiral."

The General's popularity had not waned during his convalescence in New Orleans, and the Hero of San Jacinto handily beat Stephen F. Austin and Henry Smith in the presidential race of 1836, capturing over 75 percent of the vote. The public elected Houston's former cavalry commander and frequent critic, Mirabeau Lamar, as vice-president. On October 22, 1836, Houston made an impromptu inaugural address in the patrician style of George Washington, then settled down to the business of running a country.

Setting up his government in the small two-story Executive Office building in Columbia, Texas (near Velasco), Houston's first order of business was to appoint his cabinet. Four days after his inauguration, Houston submitted his choices to the Texas Senate for its approval, and the person he nominated to head up his naval force was "S. Rhoades [sic] Fisher, Secretary of the Navy."

Samuel Rhoads Fisher, a forty-two-year-old native of Philadelphia, had settled at Matagorda in 1831. As the owner of the schooner *Champion*, he had tried unsuccessfully to establish a trade route between Galveston Bay and Tampico on the Mexican coast. When revolution broke out, Fisher became active in the defense of the South Texas coast, figuring prominently in the recapture of *Hannah Elizabeth* by the privateer *William Robbins*. His violent quarrel with James Fannin—whom Houston had denounced for ignoring orders and sacrificing his command (and life) at Goliad—did not hurt Fisher's standing with the General, and as a signatory to the Texas Declaration of Independence, Fisher's patriotism was unquestioned. Although Fisher briefly held a job in the Philadelphia Naval Yard, his credentials would have been considered thin anywhere except in the young republic. To Houston, however, "Judge" Fisher would make a fine candidate to help him implement his cornerstone policies.

But what were Houston's cornerstone policies? Simplistically, Houston wanted to restore Texas's battered economy, place the military firmly under civilian control, reconcile with neighboring Indian tribes, avoid provoking Mexico, and annex Texas to the United States. Unfortunately for the Navy's commanders, none of these objectives were consistent with a robust navy, and four of them ran directly counter to the Navy's interests. From the start, Fisher and Hawkins would have an uphill battle to keep the Navy strong enough to defend Texas's shores.

Undoubtedly guided by Commodore Hawkins and Secretary Fisher, the Texas Congress set to work rebuilding the Texas Navy. The day Fisher's name was submitted to the Senate, the Committee on Naval Affairs summed up the state of the service: "That arm of the national defense appears to be in a most deplorable and crippled condition. The 'Brutus' and the 'Invincible' are both in New York, in a situation which prevents their services from being immediately available, and the 'Liberty' is detained in New Orleans. Thus, while momentarily in expectation of a blockade from the enemy, our whole line of sea-coast is defended by but one national vessel, the 'Independence,' mounting seven guns, and four small privateers, each pursuing its own prey, and not immediately subject to the orders of the Government. While our navy remains in this condition, it is in the power of the enemy, at his pleasure, to cut off our supplies, and seize upon our seaports."

Chastised by the committee's report, Congress went to work on a naval appropriations bill. Never mind that the government was broke; this was Texas, the land of big dreams and tremendous, if rarely realized, potential. In November Congress approved "An Act Providing for an Increase in the Navy," which called for the purchase of a twenty-four-gun sloop of war, "of such draft of water as will enable her to enter the port of Galveston." The bill also directed the executive to purchase two steam vessels, each able to transport 750 men with provisions, and two eleven-gun topsail schooners. Houston signed the bill without complaint on November 18, 1836, and with a stroke of a pen, Texas took its first step on a long and rocky path to a truly professional navy.

As Congress was rebuilding the Navy, President Houston was feeling his first pangs of discomfort with his sea captains. In a letter to the Thomas Toby firm in New Orleans, he commented, "It is very desirable to have our little Naval force once more at home, and to confer with the officers in command prior to the adoption of new measures, or the formation of new plans." To Houston, these "new measures" almost certainly included the dismissal of Captains Hurd and Brown.

Houston must have turned the matter over in his mind that night, because the very next day he wrote another, more insistent letter to Mr. Toby. "The

Invencible [sic] and the Brutus are at present both absent and without orders from this Government. The former indeed was ordered there to refit by my predecessor in office, but he has since disobeyed an absolute injunction to return and report. The Brutus absented himself in the night without leave or license from the proper functionaries, and has brought upon us a species of discredit which cannot be slightly overlooked. . . . This is a dereliction from duty and a contempt of authority which merits the highest reprobation."

In these two letters, we find the first hints of Sam Houston's dissatisfaction with his navy. Unlike the army, which with effort could be brought under Houston's personal control, a ship at sea could not be recalled without the consent of its commander. The presence of *Brutus* and *Invincible* in New York underscored Houston's impotence to control his fleet from land-locked Columbia.

But for the time being, Houston made the best of the situation. As a sign of goodwill to Mexico, he lifted the blockade President Burnet had imposed upon Matamoros the previous July. After all, there was no point in imposing a blockade if he didn't have the ships to do the job. On the home front, he signed the naval appropriations bill, formalized naval regulations, and sent Fisher to find additional warships.

One privateer did come to the aid of Texas during its time of trouble, a one-gun vessel named for Texas's agent in New Orleans. *Thomas Toby* began life as the schooner *DeKalb*, built in Dorchester County, Maryland, in 1829. Weighing 112 tons, seventy-three feet long and seven feet wide, the *Toby* was one of the larger vessels in the privateer flotilla. When she began serving the Texas cause, she carried a single nine-pounder pivot gun and a variety of small arms, including cutlasses, muskets, and pistols. Her principal commander, a fiery Scotsman named Nathaniel Hoyt, was a veteran captain of the schooners *Pennsylvania* and *Mentor*.

Captain Hoyt's first adventure aboard *Thomas Toby* began in October 1836, when he ran the *Toby* down the Mexican coast. Around October 12, he captured a Mexican merchantman (apparently the *Mentor*, his former ship), and soon afterwards, the emboldened Scotsman arrived at Tampico, a major port half-way between Veracruz and Matamoros. On November 3, the New Orleans *Commercial Bulletin* provided its readers with an account of Captain Hoyt's exploits, probably taken from the merchant vessel *Louisiana*:

> [The *Toby*] run in towards the fort at the mouth of the river, and playing her "long tom" upon it for some time, without however, doing much damage, except frightening the good people of the town nearly out of their wits, who supposing her to be the van guard of the Texian Navy turned out *en masse*, repaired to the fort and along the river banks determined to repel any hostile

movement of the imaginary Texian fleet. The commander of the privateer soon after transmitted a challenge to the commandant of Tampico requesting a meeting with any armed Mexican vessel which might be in port; but receiving no answer within a reasonable time, she stood off and spoke the *Louisiana* determined to capture all Mexican property she fell in with."

Soon afterwards, Hoyt, holding court in a New Orleans tavern, issued a public challenge to fight any Mexican Navy vessel on the seas (a challenge undoubtedly issued after an epic battle with the local fire-water). His announcement drew sharp rebukes from some quarters of New Orleans. The editor of *Bee* admonished his readers, "This may be very fine sport to these gentlemen, but they must be careful that our commercial relations and trade with the Mexican Republic be not disturbed or invaded."

It appears that during the latter part of 1836, *Thomas Toby* did little else of note, most likely going back into the commercial trade until the summer of 1837, when she resurfaced as a privateer. At one point, it appears, the *Toby* sailed to Havana to pick up two brass cannon purchased by the society ladies of Havana for the Republic of Texas. During the winter months, *Thomas Toby* engaged in no reported military activity, and this inactivity may have contributed to a mutiny, which occurred in February 1837 as the vessel lay off New Orleans. *Toby*'s doctor and purser were murdered, but the mutiny was put down, and the insurgents were thrown into a New Orleans prison.

Thomas Toby's exploits, while locally sensational, did little to further Texas interests. While she was frolicking in the Gulf, Houston and Fisher could only sit tight and wait for *Brutus* and *Invincible* to come home.

They would not return until the following spring. As Houston was haranguing his agents to get *Brutus* and *Invincible* back to Texas (and prohibiting the use of land scrip to do so), Texas officials in New York were desperately trying to sell land scrip authorized by President Burnet to pay off the two vessels' debts. One land speculator, New York port collector Samuel Swartwout, purchased $10,000 in scrip in late October, and on December 26, Texas agent Charles Sayre closed a deal with *Brutus's* creditors that released the schooner from her debts. On January 5, 1837, Captain Hurd, some fifty crewmen, and twenty-five marines breathed a sigh of relief as they cleared the Port of New York and sailed home for Texas via New Orleans. A month later, the beleaguered Texas agents similarly rescued *Invincible*, which sailed home at the end of February.

With *Independence* docked in New Orleans, the Republic of Texas was in desperate need of aggressive, creative leadership to compensate for its lack of firepower. But it was not to come from the dashing Commodore Hawkins, who died of smallpox on February 11, 1837. He was buried with full military honors in New Orleans, the *Telegraph* eulogizing him with a touching if somewhat overstated tribute: "A more gentlemanly or chivalrous spirit never graced a quarterdeck and his loss will be deplored, and his memory respected by his gallant comrades of the navy so long as merit in the naval profession claims esteem." In New Orleans, the *Courier* emoted, "In him Texas has lost an able officer, society, a good citizen, and the cause of freedom, a great defender." With Hawkins's death, command of *Independence*, which was tantamount to command of the Texas Navy, devolved to *Liberty*'s Capt. George Wheelwright.

While Houston, Fisher, and the Navy sat mired in debts and muddled reorganization, Mexico's government, now under President Anastasio Bustamente, began resuscitating its national dream of reconquering Texas. On February 11, 1837, the central government declared a blockade of all Texas ports, set to take effect on March 11. To back up its announcement, Mexico assembled a formidable fleet, consisting of the brigs *Vencedor del Alamo, Libertad, General Urrea,* and *General Terán,* and the schooner *Hidalgo*, all commanded by Capt. Francisco de Paula López, a capable Spaniard from the Canary Islands who was a court favorite of Santa Anna. For Texas, it was a sign of bad tidings to come.

Mexican warships were soon reported cruising within twelve miles of Galveston, stinging the Texians into action. In New Orleans, Algernon Thruston, Texas's local agent, asked Captain Wheelwright to prepare *Independence* for a two-month cruise, and Secretary Fisher frantically urged Thruston to purchase the armed schooners *Urchin* and *Thomas Toby* for the government. On March 3, Fisher accepted an offer to sell the *Toby* to the Republic, but negotiations bogged down and Texas authorities never ratified the contract.

On March 11, the wayward *Brutus* suddenly appeared off the Balize at the mouth of the Mississippi, returning to New Orleans after an uneventful and unauthorized cruise to Matamoros. When Captain Hurd caught word that he was going to be dismissed, his officers informed Texas agents that *Brutus* would not return home to Velasco until Hurd received a guarantee of an honorable discharge from the Navy Department. Thruston dispatched *Independence* to rein in the insubordinate vessel, but to no avail.

By the end of March, however, both *Brutus* and *Invincible,* desperately short of supplies, dropped anchor at Galveston. Captains Hurd and Brown were immediately sacked, and their crews promptly deserted. *Brutus* was placed under the command of Lt. James Boylan, former prize master of the *Comanche* and captain of the schooner *Viper*, while *Invincible* was assigned to Commander Henry L. Thompson, a former Mexican Navy officer and captain of the schooner *Colonel Fannin*.

Notwithstanding the return of *Brutus* and *Invincible,* President Houston had good reason to be worried about the condition of the Texas fleet. In an address to Congress, he lamented: "The insufficiency of our navy must be a subject of serious consideration.... Our commerce has suffered to some extent, and a small portion of supplies for the army has been captured and taken into Mexican ports." On April 5, he ordered Secretary Fisher to meet the threat: "You will proceed to Velasco forthwith, and if true as reported there should be a Mexican Naval force, off the mouth of Brazos, you will, devise such measures for the defence of the coast, as may seem to you best, with all the means, which you can command. Do the best you can, as you will be upon the spot and can judge of the course most proper to be pursued."

Communications over the rural Texas countryside were slow and sporadic, and Houston's orders must have seemed a reasonable delegation of power. Consistent with his nonaggression policy towards Mexico, Houston limited Fisher's authority to "the defence of the coast." With all three warships under the control of reliable men—not buckskin swashbucklers like Hurd and Brown—Sam Houston had some assurance that his military would not exceed its authority.

Naval action certainly seemed warranted. As many as five Mexican warships began patrolling the coast from Galveston to Matagorda at the beginning of April. On April 3, the American schooner *Champion*, loaded with muskets, swords, flints, and other military supplies, was captured by the five-gun brig *General Urrea* and sent to Matamoros under a prize crew. The next day *Urrea* captured the merchantman *Louisiana* and escorted her to the mouth of the Rio Grande. Soon afterwards, the six-gun brig *General Terán* took two more prizes, the Texas-registered *Julius Caesar* and the American *Climax*, bringing the total captures to four. Later that month, it was reported that the Mexican fleet captured the gun-runner *Vigilant* east of Matagorda, and chased the schooner *Flash* onto shore at Galveston Island.

Thus, by May 1837, President Bustamente had clamped an unyielding tourniquet on the arteries that fed the fragile Texian economy. Galveston, and with it Texas, was in danger of being crippled by the strongest Mexican fleet ever to sail in Texas waters. This was not the beaten, demoralized Mexico of nearly twelve months previous; it was a very real threat to Texas's economic life. The New Orleans *True American* warned, "unless our vessels of war will protect them, all the vessels that have sailed for Texas will fall prey to the Mexicans."

The situation became so bad that in a complete reversal from the previous year, the U.S. West Indies Squadron began protecting vessels engaged in the Texas trade. While investigating matters off the Rio Grande, the U.S. sloop-of-war *Natchez* captured *General Urrea* on April 8, sending her to Pensacola under a prize crew on piracy charges. The next day *Natchez* sailed into Matamoros and, after a polite exchange with the Mexican authorities, her captain ejected the prize crew from the *Louisiana* and escorted the liberated vessel back into the Gulf. And at the end of the month, New Orleans newspapers published an announcement signed by a young U.S. Navy lieutenant,

Edwin Ward Moore, declaring that the U.S. sloop *Boston* would cruise off the Texas coast for the next few weeks to protect merchant shipping to the Lone Star Republic.

Back in Texas, Secretary Fisher's first order of business was to get his undermanned navy up to fighting strength. Lacking sailors, he requisitioned one hundred men from the army and sent for more provisions from New Orleans. He then ordered Captain Wheelwright to bring *Independence* home so that the Navy's firepower would be concentrated in Texas waters.

It was this order that would lead to the Texas Navy's next great disaster.

CHAPTER TEN

A Clash of Flagships

Sir, I am your prisoner, but my sword you shall never receive.
—Lt. John W. Taylor to Lt. Fernando R. Davis

On April 10, 1837, Captain Wheelwright ordered the crew of the *Independence* to weigh anchor for Texas. The flagship quietly slipped her berth cables and was towed to the Southwest Pass of the Mississippi's toothy mouth, which led out to the open sea. As his vessel slid past the barques, schooners, kedges, steamers, and sloops milling about the harbor, the commodore undoubtedly projected that air of quiet confidence expected of all naval commanders since the days of Jason's Argonauts.

In truth, there was much to be worried about. The warship was severely undermanned, carrying only twenty-five landlubbers and six seamen under the command of Wheelwright, and thirteen officers—roughly a third of her normal complement. She also carried several locally prominent passengers to protect. If the Mexican corvettes known to be prowling the coast set upon her, she would barely be able to maneuver and work half her guns at the same time. The absence of any marines meant that in close fighting, *Independence* would be all but helpless. Under those conditions, Wheelwright had no choice but to rely upon Fate, that mysterious lady who so often determines the difference between greatness and a bloated, briny death.

Despite the lack of experienced sailors, *Independence* made her way safely out to sea. After plowing the choppy waters against uncooperative headwinds, *Independence*, sailing with no flag at her gaff, made her way past Galveston and crept into the heart of the blockade.

Commodore López, commander of the *Escuadrilla del Mar del Norte*, still had a formidable fleet cruising off the Texas coast. López had sent the brigs *Urrea* and *Terán* back to Matamoros with captured prizes, but he kept two large brigs-of-war, the sixteen-gun *Libertador*, under Lt. Fernando Davis, and the nine-gun *Vencedor del Alamo*, under Capt. Blas Godines, to intercept any Texas warships that tried to break the blockade.

Of all the warships cruising the Gulf, *Libertador* was to be the most feared. A fast Baltimore brig, she could outsail and outgun anything in the Texas Navy, as well as most local ships of the U.S. and British navies. Her crew of 140 consisted of the best men in the northern squadron, mostly Mexican veterans, with a few American and English sailors. It was no wonder that López chose *Libertador* to be the flagship of the northern squadron.

In the early morning hours of April 17, lookouts atop *Independence* spotted two sails about six miles to windward, flying no colors. With luck, they would be a merchant convoy from the United States, but Wheelwright was taking no chances. He ordered his drummer to beat "to quarters," and cleared the flagship's deck for action. Men scurried about, readying the great guns, stacking shot, priming muskets, and throwing protective netting into the rigging, while Wheelwright paced the afterdeck, ensuring that his lieutenants had their stations under control.

The two brigs spotted the unidentified schooner coming out of the rising sun, signaled each other, then bore down upon her with all sails. Wheelwright did not need to know more; it was perfectly clear that a fight was coming, and it would begin the moment the oncoming vessels reached cannon range.

As the brigs closed on *Independence*, *Vencedor del Alamo* bore away, then wore around to bring her bow guns to bear on the Texians' stern. *Libertador* pulled back, hovering off Wheelwright's weather quarter so that López could rush the Texas flagship when the time was right.

Bellowing through a brass speaking trumpet, Captain Wheelwright ordered his officers to hoist the Lone Star ensign; a few minutes later, the brigs replied with the Eagle and Snake. With these simple gestures, the political and financial problems that dogged the Texas officers no longer mattered. What counted now was powder, shot, and wind. This was what the commodores, captains, and lieutenants had trained for all their careers. This was their moment. The Texians had always been outnumbered—at the Alamo, at San Jacinto, and now at sea. The world would soon see whether Texas courage and determination would defeat Mexico's advantages of numbers, guns, and skill.

From about a mile out, *Libertador* opened with a broadside, missing her target, and Wheelwright ordered his weather battery—three six-pounders and his long nine-pounder pivot—to return the favor. The guns boomed out, bucking against the thick ropes that fixed their carriages to the bulwarks, but they too missed their mark. The wind began blowing harder, and *Independence* leaned so far that her lee guns dipped below the waterline; as the schooner rocked back, even her weather guns' muzzles occasionally kissed the warm, salty sea.

For nearly two hours, the three ships traded a brisk fire, but given the inaccuracy of naval artillery at long range, the battle was going to be a race rather than a slugging match. Cutting into the wind, a schooner generally had an advantage over square-riggers like *Vencedor* and *Libertador*, but *Independence* did not have the crew to take full advantage of her fore-and-aft rigging. Moreover, one of the schooner's chief advantages—fewer sails to allow for a smaller crew—made the flagship extremely vulnerable to shots through her canvas. As the vessels raced to Velasco, *Vencedor* kept up an ineffective raking fire from behind *Independence*, doing but little damage to her rigging, while *Libertador* closed in from the windward side. Lacking enough men to work all guns and sail the ship at the same time, Wheelwright kept his weather battery hot on *Libertador* and ignored the harassing *Vencedor* at his stern.

At 9:30 a.m., *Libertador* pulled within two cable lengths of *Independence* (about 400 yards), luffed around so that her bow turned into the wind, and opened up a vicious broadside of round shot, grape, and canister. The two flagships exchanged fire for fifteen minutes—*Independence* outnumbered two-to-one on her weather beam—then *Libertador* suddenly drew off, to fire round shot from afar. As cannonballs threw up white plumes of spray around his ship, Captain Wheelwright bellowed more orders through his speaking trumpet, then went below deck.

After some ineffective long-range bombardment, Commodore López decided to make another run at *Independence*. He ran close to Wheelwright's weather quarter and gave him another broadside of grape shot and canister, then backed off to pelt *Independence* with round shot. By now his gunners had "found the range," and worked their guns with deadly competence. One ball smashed through the protective copper on *Independence*'s lower hull. Others pierced the rigging, punching jagged holes into *Independence*'s canvas. Another crashed through the quarter gallery, sending a hail of wooden splinters into Wheelwright's right side and hand, dropping him to the deck. As he was carried off by the ship's surgeon, Dr. Albert Moses Levy, the wounded Wheelwright ordered his first lieutenant, John W. Taylor, to take command.

Taylor rallied the men, exhorting them to keep up a steady stream of fire, but it was a losing game. With her rigging lacerated and several sails split, *Independence* began slowing as the old *Vencedor* crept up on her stern, blasting away.

Soon, the racing warships were within sight of the Velasco shore; if Taylor could hold the Mexicans off just a little longer, he might be able to take refuge among the small batteries at the Brazos mouth. If need be, he could also beach the flagship, salvaging the ordnance later and sparing the men the humiliation of capture. He pressed ahead, hoping for some miracle that would get him under those friendly shore guns. As the ships coasted within sight of the Brazos landing, an excited crowd turned out to watch the battle.

Seeing his prey struggling for the shore, López went in for the kill. He signaled for *Vencedor* to cut into the wind and pull alongside the Texian's weather quarter while he tacked back and pulled within pistol range of the Texian's stern. His eight starboard guns backed up an unspoken ultimatum: surrender or die.

To Lieutenant Taylor, it looked hopeless. *Vencedor* held its position, waiting for the signal to blast the schooner's battered weather quarter, while off the stern *Libertador* sat in perfect position to mow down every man on Taylor's deck. Seeing no way out, Taylor consulted with Captain Wheelwright, who gave him permission to surrender the flagship. Just before noon, the Lone Star fluttered down from the gaff, and the flagship was in Mexican hands.

The official surrender observed a standard formula dictated by European custom, save one incident. Lt. Fernando Davis, former commander of the *General Bravo*, came aboard *Independence* to accept the vessel's surrender. Lieutenant Taylor greeted him coolly, remarking, "Sir, I am your prisoner, but my sword you shall never receive." With a flourish, he flung his saber into the brine, and led his men into captivity.

For all the fireworks, there was surprisingly little structural damage to any vessel. Aboard *Libertador*, two Mexican sailors were killed, her main topgallant was cut, a gun was unshipped, her foremast was nicked, and some rigging was sliced. *Independence* suffered holes in her hull and quarter gallery, badly split sails and rigging damage, but the only casualty was the injured Captain Wheelwright. *Vencedor del Alamo* finished the battle unscathed.

Damaged or not, *Independence* was a tremendous prize for the Mexican Navy. She was the first Texas warship to strike her colors, and she netted a bounty of prominent prisoners, including the Texas Navy's commander and the minister plenipotentiary to the United States, William H. Wharton. But the crowning trophy was a brass eight-pounder, subsequently known as the "Golden Standard," which had been captured from Santa Anna by General Houston's army at the Battle of San Jacinto. The Mexican government's official newspaper, *Diario del Gobierno*, reported that it had been engraved with "the initials of the leading ladies of Texas, where the cannon is esteemed as one of the best trophies capricious fortune conceded to them."

The crew of the *Independence* was divided and put aboard the two brigs. A prize crew raised the Mexican colors over the former flagship, sailing with the gallant Commodore López to Brazos de Santiago, at the mouth of the Rio Grande. At anchor sat *Libertador, Vencedor*, the six-gun *Terán*, and the three-gun *Bravo*. Counting *Independence* and the absent *Urrea*, Mexico now had six manned warships that could cover the Texas coast; Texas had none.

It seemed to the prisoners that if the Mexican government did not execute them as pirates, it would probably exchange them for Mexican prisoners from San Jacinto still held in Texas. The crew—excepting the wounded Captain Wheelwright and his surgeon, Dr. Levy—were marched to Matamoros with prisoners from *Julius Caesar, Champion*, and other captured merchantmen. The sailors were treated "rather rudely," according to two passengers from *Julius Caesar*, but the officers were treated kindly by Commodore López, Captain Davis, and, oddly enough, *Bravo*'s current commander, Thomas "Mexico" Thompson.

Thompson, it seems, had grown tired of life in the Mexican Navy. Having done his part for Mexico, suffering deprivation and abuse during the Texas Revolution, he still commanded only a small, dilapidated three-gun boat, while other officers around him were being assigned to the larger, newer brigs-of-war. As William Wharton's younger brother John frantically organized an expedition to exchange William for thirty San Jacinto prisoners, Mexico Thompson secretly hatched a plot to free the elder Wharton and desert with him to Texas. When word leaked out to the Mexican authorities, Thompson found himself unable to free Wharton, but he offered freedom to Wheelwright and his surgeon, who were still held at Brazos de Santiago. Wheelwright escaped with Dr. Levy and Thompson—possibly under the blind eye of Commodore López—and made it back to Matagorda in mid-July. William Wharton, disguised as a Catholic priest (some accounts say he was dressed as a nun), also escaped, and he arrived back at his plantation on the Brazos River in late August. His brother John, who in his bid to rescue Wiliam had been shipwrecked off Brazos de Santiago and taken prisoner, was eventually released and made his way home by early September. Before long, Thompson, still reviled in the Galveston Bay region for his oppression of the inhabitants in 1835, would appear in the Texas port ("as bold and confident as Hector himself," one Galvestonian put it), brandishing a brace of pistols and vainly trying to charm the locals who, while careful not to provoke him, quietly wished him dead.

The capture of the Texas flagship was a heavy blow to the country's morale, and created a counterproductive sense of urgency in Congress, whose reaction seemed to be, "Do something. Anything." In May the dispirited legislators passed a joint resolution to send *Brutus* and *Invincible* to Brazos de Santiago to negotiate a prisoner exchange. Houston vetoed the resolution, pointing out that armed ships off the mouth of the Rio Grande would probably unnerve the Mexican commander into moving his prisoners to Mexico's interior, or perhaps even massacring them as the Mexicans had done at Goliad and the Alamo. If Mexico were willing to negotiate, he argued that an unarmed ship would suffice; if not, Texas would be risking her last two warships by sending them into hostile waters where they could be outgunned and captured. Having dealt with unreliable commanders and the loss of his flagship, Houston now had little faith in his fleet. He put it plainly, "I have every reason to believe that Mexico has a navy that would greatly overpower our ships of war, should they be sent as proposed. The consequence would be to give them the entire command of the Gulf, and permit the most insignificant armed vessel, which they might send, not only to annoy our coast, but to entirely cut off our trade on the ocean—the consequences of which must be manifestly ruinous."

President Houston's message to Congress in May 1837 closed the book on the sorry episode as far as official Texas policy was concerned. The president wanted his ships at home, guarding the coastline, not miles away off the Mexican coast, and he made sure everyone knew it.

But the man most humiliated by the fiasco was not satisfied to wait for the enemy to come back to Texas. He wanted to take the war to Mexico. And whether Houston approved of it or not, he would have his revenge.

CHAPTER ELEVEN

Mister Fisher's Revenge

I do not wish a fool hardy expedition, or an attack when there is but little hope, and should the contest be decidedly unequal avoid it if possible but if it is not to be avoided sustain the glory of our flag to the last.
   —S. Rhoads Fisher to Commander H.L. Thompson, May 23, 1837

IN THE CROWD THAT THRONGED THE BEACHES to watch *Independence* fight for her life, the loneliest face belonged to S. Rhoads Fisher, the secretary of the navy. The main battle had taken place out of sight of Velasco, so local townsfolk only witnessed the final act in which their mighty flagship, apparently undamaged, struck its colors with shameful promptitude. The *Telegraph and Texas Register* reported the crowd's reaction to the apparent cowardice of Captain Wheelwright and his crew. "We confess that when the first news of this combat arrived, containing the intelligence that the Independence had surrendered to two Mexican brigs without having received any injury, and her crew unhurt, a flash of shame and indignation mantled our cheeks and the exclamation '30 or 40 cowards and an old hulk are no loss,' almost involuntarily fell from our lips."

The irate crowd soon turned its curses, shouts, and jeers on the representative of the "imbecile government" who was supposed to bring the fleet success and glory. Secretary Fisher listened to the angry citizens vent their anger with "the deepest mortification and chagrin," one lieutenant later wrote. He assured the good people that he would do something, somehow, to retrieve the lost honor of the Navy, and he resolved to take revenge for the personal humiliation he endured that fine April morning.

Fisher did not need any further incentive to put his ships to sea, but he soon got it. Two weeks after the *Independence* fiasco, he received word from a Texas spy in Anne Arundel County, Maryland, that Baltimore shipwrights were constructing a new 300-ton sloop-of-war for Mexico, its largest warship yet—bigger even than *Libertador.* Fisher dispatched an agent to see about acquiring a small armed schooner to intercept the sloop just as it left U.S. territorial waters, as United States law prohibited American-built ships sold to foreign nations from arming themselves until they were outside American waters. Fisher then prepared orders to his new commanders for an offensive that would take the war to Mexico.

The man Fisher chose to lead the expedition was *Invincible*'s Henry Livingston Thompson. Thompson, a hard-drinking, foul-mouthed sea dog, was prone to bravado and carelessness, but he was politically reliable and had a burning desire to make Mexico pay for its capture of the *Independence*. Supporting Thompson would be Commander James Boylan, aboard *Brutus*.

On May 23, Fisher ordered Thompson to rendezvous with *Brutus* at Paso Cavallo, on Matagorda Bay, and obtain a crew of landsmen from the idlers at the local army base. He cautioned Thompson to take "none but sound and healthy men, and for this purpose I will suggest the propriety of a surgeon of the fleet being sent to examine them." Once he selected the men he wanted, Thompson was to give their commander a receipt for them, then take them into the Gulf for exercises and drill. "Once you are satisfied that the discipline and trim of your fleet may justify your run south," instructed Fisher, "seek the enemy whenever you may think you can find him." Cautioning Thompson to avoid unnecessary risks, especially those associated with the capture of neutral vessels, Fisher warned, "I will here observe that the present cruise will in all probability fix the character and reputation of the Navy, for his Excellency rather considers that we are running an improper risk and requires some persuasion to induce him to extend his consent to the present cruise."

"Requires some persuasion," indeed. In fact, the commander in chief had expressly forbidden the mission, believing that the two warships were needed to break the Mexican blockade of the Texas coast. When Fisher first brought the idea of an offensive to the president, Houston peremptorily refused. Fisher then requested a furlough to go home to Matagorda for health reasons, and the unsuspecting Houston granted Fisher a six-week leave. Fisher quickly packed his bags and rode to Matagorda where, not coincidentally, *Invincible* was picking up men for the summer offensive.

While the Navy was preparing for operations south of the border, another privateer began an offensive of her own, although it would not join Fisher's expedition. In late May, the redoubtable *Thomas Toby* was busy again, sailing off Sisal on the Yucatán peninsula. On June 2, she captured the brig *Phoenix*, which was evidently intended for the Mexican Navy. The *Telegraph and Texas Register* reported on June 8, 1837:

The *Thomas Toby* has just sent into Galveston harbor a very valuable prize, being a large fine brig, strongly built, and capable of being fitted out as a man of war, bearing guns heavier than any now in the Mexican Navy. She was captured on the coast of Campeachy and has on board 200 tons of salt. The Tom Toby when last seen was in hot pursuit of two Mexican schooners; this pursuit will undoubtedly prove successful, as "Fortune ever favors the brave."

Phoenix proved to be a potentially valuable warship, and Texas sorely needed a morale boost in the summer of 1837. Mexico was clearly frustrated by the little privateer's exploits, and one Yucatán newspaper fumed, "The evils that a pirate so insignificant as the *Thomas Toby* causes daily to our extended commerce are very grave." But an incident or two involving a lone privateer would pale in comparison to what Fisher's squadron was about to do.

By June 10, 1837, *Invincible* was in Matagorda Bay, ready to move out. The next day *Brutus* went scurrying down the coast to join her sister ship, pick up additional crewmen, and return to Galveston with *Invincible*. When Houston got wind of the fleet's moves, he sent Fisher specific orders forbidding him to authorize a cruise against Mexico. Unaware of Fisher's exact whereabouts, Houston sent copies of his orders to both Galveston and Matagorda.

They arrived too late. By June 12, Fisher was safely aboard *Invincible* off the coast of Velasco, requesting additional supplies from agents in New Orleans. He lamented the sorry state of ships and men to the agents, imploring, "[when] we return to Galveston, our men will be entirely destitute unless you succeed in sending supplies. The men are naked, many only having part of a shirt. Canvass is also much needed, and some Bunting and paints."

Notwithstanding the squadron's poor state, in the early morning hours of June 12 the two-ship fleet left the Texas coast on a journey that would keep them in foreign waters until the end of August. A few days later, Fisher sought to justify his participation in the voyage in a lengthy letter to the editor of the New York *Albion*:

> I know, you gentlemen of systematized governments will smile at the idea of the "secretary of the navy" turning sailor, and may be inclined to consider it better adapted to the adventure seeking disposition of the knight of rueful countenance; but my opinion is that it will inspire great confidence in the men, and stimulate our Congress to do something for us; for it appears that this branch of national defense has never been popular in its infancy in any country; it has ever been compelled to fight itself into notice and government patronage; such

at least I am satisfied is our case, and I think that my present step is precisely such as will suit the meridian of the views of our Texas population.

Summing up the Texas spirit of self-reliance, he continued:

We must be governed and actuated by such course as may best suit us; we are acting and legislating for ourselves and not for the world, and however at variance our system of policy may be with the preconceived ideas of right or wrong amongst the world at large, I humbly conceive that as we have to lie in the bed, we have the right to make it. Therefore, it is that however quixotic my present step may appear, and indeed for the United States or Great Britain would be, *I* am satisfied that it is right.

Fisher was correct in believing that his mission would be applauded by the Texas populace, and he was also realistic about how his actions would be viewed by other nations with more stable civil governments. But most of all, his orders met with the utter disapproval of the one man who counted most, and Fisher knew he would have to face Sam Houston upon his return. As Lord Nelson demonstrated at Copenhagen in 1801, however, success in war can marginalize flagrant displays of insubordination. Fisher was confident that the resulting glory for the Navy and its Republic would shelter him from Houston's momentary anger.

The first stop was New Orleans, in search of easy Mexican prey. The two warships hovered off the mouth of the Mississippi River for two days, but finding no sign of the enemy, they turned south for the Yucatán coast. By July 1, with storms approaching and visibility dropping, the schooners separated, agreeing to meet back in one week at the Isla de Mujeres, on the Caribbean side of the peninsula near present-day Cancún. *Brutus* sailed east to Cape Antonio off Cuba, while *Invincible* sailed to Cankern Island, where she took on wood, salt, and sea turtles, the latter being kept aboard the vessel as a source of fresh meat. By July 8, the two schooners made their rendezvous at Mujeres, taking on additional water and resting for a few days while the commanders plotted their next move.

Leaving Mujeres, the two ships headed south to the Island of Cozumel. The men disembarked at the southwest tip of the island on July 13, and were instantly enchanted with what they found. Commander Boylan wrote, "The anchorage are indeed safe & commodious for any number of Vessels the soil is delightful the climate salubrious the forest abound in the finest kinds of Timber Logwood, Mahogony, & Spanish ceder and abundance of fruits of various kinds there is also an abundance of water." Commander Thompson recalled that the "salubrious trade wind, beautiful roadstead and anchorage" inspired the high-spirited Texians to claim the island for Texas. They "hoisted the Star Spangled Banner at the height of forty five feet with acclamation both from the inhabitants of the Island and our small patriotic band." The ships fired a twenty-three-gun salute in honor of Texas's latest conquest, while a tiny group of bewildered natives obligingly swore allegiance to the strange country that claimed ownership of their island. The Texians surveyed the island as best they could, lingered in the tropical paradise for a few more days, then sailed off, allowing the islanders to return to their otherwise pastoral lives.

Leaving Cozumel behind, the squadron headed north, stopping first at the Isle of Contoy, where they found houses, turtle pens, and small boats that had been abandoned by the villagers at the sight of the armed landing parties. Helping themselves to more turtles, water, and anything else they could carry back, they began moving west along the Yucatán coast, commencing a merry adventure of pillage and arson.

Reports later claimed that the squadron burned eight to ten towns on the coast and picked up some $30,000 in loot. These stories were greatly exaggerated, but one raid, on the northern Yucatán village of Dzilam de Bravo on July 21, was well documented by Mexican authorities and appears to be fairly typical of the Texians' rough approach. At Dzilam, local fishermen spotted two warships approaching the coast around 11:00 that morning, beating against the wind until they were close enough to lower three crowded launches and one canoe. About eighty men rowed up to the beaches, each armed with a sword, a dagger, a carbine, and a brace of pistols. The villagers fled, most of them hiding in a cave behind a hill, although two fishermen who wandered near the landing party were captured. The Texians marched up to the tree line and planted a flag "which was green at its beginning and at the end [had] some white and red stripes with a star in the green." (The sea spray had evidently bleached the blue field of the Texas naval ensign to a mottled sea green.) Posting a guard near the boats, the marines declared, "We are Texans, sworn enemies of the Mexicans, [and have] brought orders from [our] government to burn all the ports of the coast." They asked their captives the way to the nearest town, the name of the village, the whereabouts of the town's mayor, and so forth.

Guided by Mayan natives whose faces were disguised with heavy war paint (but whose dialects betrayed them as Campecheanos), the Texians roamed about the hamlet, rummaging through the small wooden shacks, taking with them everything they could carry—old pots, pans, and utensils, nets, broken pitchers, even the doors off houses. They found the town watchman's house and rifled through his papers until 4:00 p.m., when *Invincible*'s guns boomed out. The party scurried back to their boats with their loot, and ordered one of the captured fishermen to accompany them back to their boat as a guide (the other one had escaped by then). When the fisherman pleaded that his wife was blind and would not survive without him, the Texians let him go, then rowed back out to their warships. The tiny armada sailed off into the distance, never to bother the bucolic little community again.

Sailing west, the squadron "captured" the port city of Telchac in a night raid. Commander Boylan dispatched a landing party under Lieutenant Wright to rouse the local *alcalde*, or mayor, from his sleep and demand tribute from the town. The surprised *alcalde* collected some fifty dollars—a considerable sum in those parts—and affected the formal surrender of the port. The argonauts moved on.

Throughout the squadron's adventure, Commodore Thompson ruled his ship as a tyrant king. To the lowly crewmen, that was to be expected—the cats, irons, reduced rations, and burly marines were standard methods of maintaining discipline aboard ship. But when harsh treatment was doled out to his officer corps, Thompson crossed the line. Lt. James Simons later accused Thompson of "ungentlemanly and unofficerlike conduct," stating, "[d]uring the whole cruise he has been accustomed to damn his officers...he cursed me calling me and others lubbers and damnable sons of bitches." The master's mate and another lieutenant complained that to his officers, Thompson would "make use of the words God damn you sir! Why don't you do this and why don't you do that?" Thompson's vocabulary, saltier than the Gulf's waters, was such that the ship's purser later complained, "I felt awful at the blasphemy and feared the Almighty would inflict severe punishment on us for his wickedness." In another episode, Thompson locked one offending lieutenant below decks and put a pistol to his temple, threatening to shoot him dead.

But this was just the beginning. Thompson's use of liquor was almost as excessive as his profanity. One officer charged that Thompson "was in the habit of being intoxicated four or five times a week," while another stated more circumspectly, "[c]annot say that I ever saw him drunk but that I have seen him frequently when he has drank too much spirits." Thompson's appropriations of prize property for his own use—gin and personal effects, including "six pair pantaloons"—drew the ire of his officers, as did his refusal to provide any water to Lieutenant Wright's crew manning a prize ship, even though *Invincible* had over seven hundred gallons of water aboard. Thompson's use of the cats on the seamen was also considered excessive by his officers, who cited his liberal flogging policy as evidence of "Oppressive and Tyrannical Conduct."

The day after their visit to Telchac, the Texian squadron spotted the Mexican merchant schooner *Union*. They ran it down, boarded it, and sold the vessel and its cargo of logwood back to its master for $660. Commodore Thompson then distributed $527.37 of this sum to his men as advance prize money. They chased a number of other vessels, all of which turned out to be neutral, and captured several *pirogues*, or pontoon boats, helping themselves to whatever they could find. Thompson cursed *Invincible*'s slow sailing qualities ("which I can with an open heart assure you is not nor never was what they have been cracked up to be," he told the Navy Department), and pursued small merchant vessels until he reached Chilbona (evidently, present-day Chuburna), near Telchac.

At Chilbona, Fisher, Boylan, and a small landing party decided to go ashore and survey the area. Leaving their long arms in the boat, the group wandered a few hundred yards from shore when they were ambushed by a squadron of Mexican cavalry. About twenty riders charged them, carbines and pistols blazing, from one hundred yards away. Their shots went wild, and Fisher, the only man who thought to bring his pistols, calmly squeezed off two rounds, dropping one caballero from his saddle. The other Texians managed to rush back to the boats, holding off the Mexicans with sporadic gunfire until everyone could get to the launches and shove off for the safety of the *Brutus*.

The impertinence of the local militia in firing upon the Texians—a "rascally reception," in Thompson's words—sent the commodore into a rage. He later wrote to his superiors: "Previously to this we had acted with every degree of humanity towards the enemy, but from that time our feelings became excited and I gave an order to this effect—To burn, sink and destroy everything we came athwart and then commenced burning their towns, names which, at present, I cannot remember." Boylan's subsequent report corroborates Thompson's recollection, stating that on one day the expedition "maned & Armed too boats went on shore and burned Two Towns. . . ."

As they were burning their way along the Yucatán coast, the Texas squadron captured the merchantmen *Adventure* and *Telegrafo* off Sisal, a major port on the northwest corner of the peninsula. They kept these vessels alongside as they made their way closer to the city in late July.

Arriving at Sisal on July 26, the Texas officers found a creative means of financing their expedition. Thompson sent ashore a canoe with a letter directing the town's commandant to deliver $25,000 in return for his pledge that Sisal would not be attacked by any Texas vessel for six months. If he refused, the squadron's guns would level the town. The town's only reply was to send a cannonball in the direction of the two enemy vessels, a move designed to draw the Texians in close to the thickly wooded beaches, where several heavy field pieces were concealed. Commodore Thompson later recorded the exchange:

> [W]e engaged under many disadvantages on our part—small guns, bad powder, want of shells, port fires, Congreve rockets, small arms &cetera. We stood them a fight of two hours and forty minutes, close under their castle which was mounted with six pieces of cannon, calibres from eighteen to thirty two pounders independently of some guns they had planted behind the bushes which opened a severe fire upon us from a quarter we least expected. I finding nothing was to be gained from the enemy and my vessel lying in fifteen feet water, thought it best to weigh anchor and get to sea our vessels and men. We rec'd no damage from their shot, but directing ours in as well as we knew how

and be assured that few of ours was wasted. . . . the hot shot which we fired was merely cold shot warmed and did not have the desired effect or we could have burned the whole town which consisted of about one hundred houses.

Commander Boylan, concerned about the quality of the squadron's powder, agreed that the prudent course was to retire. The only apparent effect of the three-hour bombardment was to prompt Yucatán authorities to send word of the squadron's presence to Commodore López at Veracruz. López immediately ordered his heavies, *Libertador* and *Iturbide*, and the brig *Independencia*, to prepare for a cruise east in search of the troublesome raiders.

Concerned that their reception was getting hot, the Texians burned the slow-sailing *Adventure,* and sent *Telegrafo* to Matagorda along with *Abispa,* a captured vessel laden with crockery. They released their prisoners near Sisal, then sailed west to Las Alacranes, a small three-island atoll that they also claimed for the Republic of Texas. There they allegedly picked clean the wreck of the English schooner *Little Penn,* which had run aground on its journey from Liverpool to Tabasco.

The two commanders' subsequent reports are filled with disappointed entries of merchant vessels that got away. But on August 3, lookouts perched atop *Brutus* spotted a nice, slow prize in the offing. Spotting *Brutus,* the stranger wore about with all sails set, and Boylan ordered his men to give chase. Beating into the wind, *Brutus* soon overhauled the merchant schooner *Eliza Russell*, sailing from Liverpool to Sisal under a British flag. After two shots across her bow, *Eliza*'s captain hove to, and Boylan boarded the merchantman. Over the master's protest, Boylan put a prize crew aboard *Eliza Russell,* and escorted her back to Las Alacranes for Thompson's decision on her fate.

Rifling through her papers, Thompson found that nearly half her cargo was shipped by a Mexican trading house in London, so Thompson ordered her to Galveston for condemnation proceedings. A week later, the squadron dropped off additional prisoners in a canoe at Campeche Bay, then proceeded down Yucatán's west coast to Tabasco, at the southern end of the Gulf.

Off the Tabasco bar, the two men-of-war captured *Correo de Tabasco*, a small mail schooner. Correspondence aboard *Correo* revealed Commodore López's plans for the Texas Navy: the former Texas flagship *Independencia* and the heavy brigs *Libertador* and *Iturbide* were to sail under Commodore José de Aldana from Veracruz to Campeche in search of the Texas squadron.

Although both Boylan and Thompson claimed they quickly moved to intercept the Mexican ships, they must have known that time was running out for the expedition. Thompson put Lieutenant Wright in charge of *Correo,* and the trio sailed north to drop off additional prisoners and get home. The captives were relatively well-treated, as the local commandant was quite friendly to the Texas officers, ordering his men to supply them with fruit and water to speed them on their way. The squadron sailed off, capturing the one-gun schooner *Rafaelita*. (*Rafaelita* evidently was formerly known as the *Correo Segundo*, as Henry Thompson referred to her as "formerly the war Sch'r com'd by Capt. Thompson," and the men all called her *Correo*.)

The small fleet reached Tampico, halfway between Veracruz and Matamoros, on August 15. They boarded a few vessels, all American, British, or French, and let them go, heading back up the coast to Matamoros. There they learned of William Wharton's escape and, being short of water, they made their way back to Galveston. They passed Velasco around 5:00 on the afternoon of August 26, and reached the Galveston bar by 9:00 p.m., laying off for the night.

At 8:00 the next morning, with the tide up, Thompson signaled to Boylan to proceed into Galveston's harbor in company with *Correo*. *Invincible* stood guard outside the bar. According to two officers, the sleepy squadron commander, probably having "spliced the main brace" the night before, lay atop of a large wooden trunk for a long, deep siesta that lasted until early afternoon.

When he awoke, he would be facing two large enemy brigs.

CHAPTER TWELVE

Death of a Navy

Our long tom spoke the Texian Language and almost every shot told well, and with a small assistance rendered me the same two brigs of war could have been ours.
    —Commander Henry L. Thompson, August 29, 1837

COMMODORE ALDANA WAS DISAPPOINTED, but not surprised, when he dropped anchor at Campeche. His squadron arrived there too late to catch the pirates, who thoughtlessly did not leave any clues as to their next stop. The perceptive commander, however, guessed that the warships would be heading back to Galveston soon. From interrogations of local witnesses, it must have sounded like the Texians were in wretched condition—exactly the way a man-of-war would look after a long cruise, when the officers and men were itching to come home. Not much to go on, but it was an educated guess. At a minimum, if Aldana blockaded their home base for a while, he would eventually meet the Texas squadron on its return trip, and perhaps take some prizes in the bargain.

Leaving the painfully slow *Independencia* behind, Commodore Aldana took his flagship, *Iturbide,* and her sixteen-gun sister, *Libertador,* to Galveston. Spotting a strange vessel on the horizon heading there on the morning of August 27, he made all sail and chased the little schooner *Sam Houston* towards the bar. As he drove towards the island up the Bolivar Roads, his lookouts spotted their original target, *Invincible*, isolated and at anchor outside the bar.

Aboard *Invincible*, lookouts scrambled up the pitch-covered ratlines while officers began clearing the deck. Commodore Thompson, sound asleep, did not rouse until his first lieutenant had called to him six times for orders. When the lookouts confirmed that the intruders were Mexican vessels, Thompson, by then wide awake, ordered his officers to prepare for battle, and to distribute round, grape, and canister shot among the gun stations.

Inside the harbor, A. S. Thruston scrambled aboard *Brutus* and informed Commander Boylan that the enemy was bearing down on *Invincible*. Boylan sent boats dashing about the harbor to collect volunteer riflemen and got under way. But the tide was too low to allow *Brutus* to pass, and a soft, sliding sound all too familiar to Texas sea captains soon told an appalled Commander Boylan that his vessel was grounded on the bar. He set all sail in an attempt to ride over the sand, but *Brutus* was stuck fast.

Help was on the way, or so it seemed. The steamboat *Branch T. Archer* soon pulled alongside to help the stranded warship. While maneuvering around *Brutus*, however, *Archer's* hawser ran afoul of the warship's decaying rudder and tore it right off. *Brutus*, stuck in the sand and unmaneuverable even if it got free, was now out of action, so Boylan frantically waved his armed men aboard *Archer* to make a boarding run at one of the enemy brigs.

If the East Pass was too shallow for *Brutus*, it was also too shallow for the slightly larger *Invincible*. Instead of running in, which would almost certainly leave *Invincible* stuck and helpless, Commodore Thompson, in true swashbuckling style, ordered his ship's master to take *Invincible* straight for the nearest enemy brig and bring his vessel to close range, where grape and canister shot would clear the enemy decks. About 3:00 in the afternoon, he charged within short range, then luffed around and gave them a blast from his port battery. Aldana's brigs replied, and the cornered Texian exchanged short, ineffective broadsides with the Mexican vessels. Thompson wore around, then backtracked to the island's east end in hopes of luring the Mexicans into shallow water—a risky maneuver at low tide. Aldana was too savvy a sailor to take the bait; after all, *Brutus* appeared to be stuck, and no other warships were in the neighborhood. He decided to wait and see what would happen.

Thompson crept towards the harbor, hoping to draw the enemy in, but by early evening disaster had struck: *Invincible* grounded on a sandbar. Trying to push through under all sail, her rudder—the most vulnerable part of the schooner—sheared off. Stuck fast, she began to list, like a weary tiger mired in a tar pit. *Invincible* was now helpless.

Desperate for help, Commodore Thompson ordered his gig over the side and became the first man off the ship. Men followed in other boats, assisted by the steamboat *Archer*, while a few stalwarts fought through the evening to save the stricken vessel. Broad, sinister waves began lapping at the stranded schooner's hull. Higher and harder, the tide pounded the schooner with growing intensity as darkness cast its shadow over land and sea. In the inky waters, the ghost ship began leaning, her timbers groaning eerily, and the sea began pouring in. Before midnight, the few remaining crewmen gave up on the doomed schooner and abandoned her to the waves.

Invincible's fate was sealed. The Mexican brigs drew off, and the Gulf's pitiless current did the job for them. Timbers bowed, then snapped as *Invincible* went to pieces during the night. As dawn broke the next morning, all the officers could do was bring *Correo* to the site of the wreck and begin salvaging what little they could.

The water was swift, dangerous, and murky, but Lieutenant Wright managed to retrieve the topmost yards and some worn sails from the wreck, and Commander Boylan hired a private captain for a four-day salvage operation. The equally-helpless *Brutus* was eventually floated and moored safely at her anchorage, near Pelican Island, although her rudder remained firmly ensconced under six feet of mud and water.

Brutus was not long in following her sister to the grave, but her final resting place would be on land, not water. By mid-September, she was in no condition to put to sea; her sails were worn, her rigging was dangerously weak, her hull's copper plating was cracked, and her guns—cannon and small arms—needed powder. As Commander Boylan informed the Navy Department, "There is not a musket or pistol that is fit for use, her powder is good for nothing.... The vessel herself is good and remarkably strong, but a miserably dull sailer." Boylan's men were destitute and hungry ("living on charity, or by fishing," he noted), and the weather, Boylan complained, was too unfavorable for sailing anyway.

Boylan did not know it, but the weather was about to get much worse. Since late September, the British sloop *Racer* had been warning other ships of a huge storm brewing in the Caribbean. As the tropical depression built up momentum, it dipped into the warm Gulf waters and swelled into one of the most violent hurricanes ever to hit Texas. Dubbed "Racer's Storm," this maelstrom drove north up the Texas coast from Matamoros, and on October 7 it lashed into Galveston with the fury of an angry god. Its screaming gusts and six-foot storm surge threw the brig *Jane* against a three-story McKinney & Williams warehouse, smashing both to splinters. Galveston's new Tremont Hotel, the new customs house, and two churches—along with nearly everything else on the island—were flattened by the deadly rush of wind and water. Vessels were pushed as far as five miles onto the mainland—some fifteen being destroyed or damaged, including the prize *Correo*, the privateer *Thomas Toby*, and *Brutus*—before the monster thundered up the coastline to Louisiana. The destruction was so complete that fifty years later, a Texas Navy midshipman would recall vividly that on his first visit to Galveston, two years after the storm blew through, "The storm which had swept over the Island in '37 had left many reminders of the visit. One schooner was imbedded in the sand just where we landed. I saw another at the Sand Hills over on the Gulf side of the Island." Racer's Storm became the final death blow to the once-feared Lone Star fleet.

As the winds died away and the waters receded, the soaked inhabitants of Galveston trickled back to rebuild their homes and restore their town. It would be hard, frustrating work, often visited by misfortune and disappointment. And for the next two years, disappointment and misfortune would visit the Texas Navy time and again.

CHAPTER THIRTEEN

Hell to Pay

The trial of Mr. Fisher was continued to-day by Mr. John Wharton, in a most furious tirade against President Houston; it was the bitterest invective I ever heard uttered by man.
—Rev. Littleton Fowler, November 25, 1837

SAM HOUSTON WAS BEYOND MERE FURY. He had already sacked one pair of insubordinate commanders—Captains Hurd and Brown—only to be defied by a trio whose reliability he should have been able to take for granted. The actions of Fisher, Thompson, and Boylan were irresponsible, dangerous, and worst of all, an affront to the prestige and authority of His Excellency, the President. What could these men have been thinking?

To add insult to injury, the public was hailing the mutineers as heroes! Each prize sent into port, each exaggerated report of the Navy's exploits, was received with public acclaim—particularly along the Gulf coast, where Francis Moore's *Telegraph and Texas Register* sang the praises of the little fleet. The *Telegraph* waxed eloquently over the return of Fisher and his prodigal brethren.

> The gallant tars with whom he has shared the dangers and privations of this desperate cause have thrown a new luster around the national flag and accomplished an enduring valor, which shall long illumine the pages of the Texian story. The gratitude of an admiring nation, shall dictate his and their reward.

The public knew Fisher's cruise was strictly against Houston's orders, but the egalitarians among them delighted in the president's impotence to bring his valiant fleet to heel. One Galveston resident summed up the feelings of many Texians in a letter to his wife with the words, "S. Rhoads Fisher has done honor with his little fleet—six prizes, burnt 8 or 10 towns in the sea coast, and got $30,000—this has excited the feeling of the General, who does not like to be eclipsed in glory or fame."

Houston's orders had been explicit: there was to be no cruise away from the Texas coast, where his warships were needed most. Fisher violated this directive, using his furlough for "health reasons" as a ruse, then committed gross nonfeasance by leaving the seat of government, where he belonged, and sailing off as an amateur marine.

Commodore Thompson, for his part, committed a host of acts that violated both Texas and international law. He claimed two Mexican islands for Texas, having no authority to do so and no way to back up his claim. He robbed and burned a number of villages, and fired his cannon into coastal cities without provocation. He seized neutral ships, in violation of Fisher's own orders, burned one merchant schooner, and ransomed another, also in violation of orders. He divided his force in enemy waters, where it might be outgunned and captured, and sent his shallowest vessels into Galveston at high tide, leaving *Invincible* stranded outside the Galveston Bar when she was attacked. His conduct during the engagement with the two Mexican brigs was deplorable, and reports from his officers indicated that his conduct at sea was ungentlemanly, to say the least.

A dark cloud of suspicion also hung over *Brutus's* Commander Boylan, but as the junior commander, he was presumably following orders from Thompson and Fisher. Boylan would not become the focus of the president's wrath.

Houston had already taken steps to rid himself of Secretary Fisher. Shortly after Fisher's departure, Houston appointed a new secretary of the navy, a former army surgeon named William M. Shepherd; Houston could therefore simply ignore his former minister. Commodore Thompson, however, needed to be court-martialed, so Houston directed Acting Secretary Shepherd to collect whatever evidence was necessary to drum the rogue out of the service.

Shepherd delegated to Commander Boylan the unpleasant task of interviewing *Invincible*'s officers to support charges against their former commander. At least five officers jumped at the chance, testifying to military crimes ranging from drunkenness to tyranny and embezzlement.

Through his chief clerk, Peter W. Humphreys, Secretary Shepherd directed a series of pointed questions to Commodore Thompson, berating the commander for taking actions without proper authority, or in violation of direct orders and international law. Thompson defiantly wrote back: "With regard to the charges brought against me . . . I shall be able to repel them when I am brought before that tribunal which the laws of my country have guaranteed to all her citizens." Shortly afterwards, Houston dismissed Thompson, setting the stage for a terrific battle before a court-martial board. Unfortunately for both Thompson and his accusers, Thompson abruptly died on the first of November, sparing Texas an ugly public spectacle.

Thompson's death transformed him from a petty sea tyrant into a lion among the fallen Texas heroes. The *Telegraph* reported that after his funeral oration, delivered in Houston by Gen. T. J. Rusk, "his remains were followed to the grave by the largest and most respectable assemblage of citizens which has ever attended a similar occasion in this city." The *Telegraph* compared the inebriated, foul-mouthed sea dog to Themistocles of Athens, proclaiming, "He has displayed in the cause of Texas a devotedness, a zeal and a daring courage which have shed a glowing lustre on the flag which he delighted to honor." The Senate adjourned its proceedings early on November 1, "as a mark of respect to the memory of Captain H.L. Thompson, of the Texian Navy," and the plethora of legal questions about Thompson's acts during the 1837 expedition died with him.

The problem of Secretary Fisher would not, however, go away quite so conveniently. When Fisher returned to Texas, the public hailed him as a naval hero, a Nelson of the west, a man of action who had avenged the murders at Goliad and the Alamo. Mexico was still legally at war with Texas, and it was high time someone took the war to the enemy. One navy lieutenant wrote that a public meeting was held by the leading citizens of Galveston, "for the purpose of expressing their high admiration for the character of the honorable S. Rhoads Fisher, Secretary of the Navy of Texas, and of tendering him an invitation to partake of a public dinner." A letter of invitation to Fisher declared that the Navy's gallant exploits "have thrown a hallo around the 'single star' which will animate the future hero, and be the glorious beacon light of coming combat." In reply, Fisher praised the courage and determination of his officers, and predicted that if Congress would extend genuine support to the Navy, the names of Wheelwright, Thompson, and Boylan "would stand brightly conspicuous in the pages of our national history." He wrote the *Telegraph,* "It is highly gratifying to my personal feelings to have my official conduct approved by the PEOPLE."

Whatever the PEOPLE may have thought, it was the PRESIDENT who counted most, and he was thoroughly poisoned against his navy secretary. Having replaced him with Dr. Shepherd, Houston initially tried to ignore Citizen Fisher. His fury was rekindled by Fisher's mild comments to the *Telegraph* on September 10, which indicated that during the previous May Fisher had planned to resign as secretary of the navy if Houston denied him the furlough he used to take the voyage.

Sam Houston may have considered Fisher to be "without portfolio" after June 1837, but the Texas Congress felt differently. Houston had made many enemies in Congress, and an anti-Houston faction had emerged under the leadership of ex-president Burnet, General Rusk, and Vice-President Lamar. The president's opponents in Congress thought the Fisher controversy would be a perfect opportunity to take a political jab at Houston's eye. Indeed, the Senate had a legitimate interest in the matter, since the Texas

Constitution prohibited the president from dismissing a cabinet member without the advice and consent of that honorable body.

On October 11, the Senate passed a resolution disapproving of Fisher's dismissal as "disrespectful, dictatorial and evincive of a disposition on the part of the Executive to annihilate these co-ordinate powers conferred upon the senate." A week later, the Senate passed another resolution reinstating Fisher and directing him to resume "active exercises of his duties as Secretary of the Navy."

On November 7, President Houston weighed in again, charging Fisher with exceeding the limits of his authority, usurping the executive's power, behaving insubordinately, committing acts incompatible with his office, and bringing reproach upon the government. He accused Fisher of smuggling tobacco to Mexico in exchange for horses and mules, embezzling funds from the sale of the steamboat *Cayuga* and the brig *Pocket*, and publishing comments disrespectful to the president in the *Telegraph and Texas Register*. He followed up his charges with an angry message to Congress about the *Eliza Russell's* seizure.

> Orders were issued to the commander of the navy *that all neutral flags should be respected, unless the vessel was bound to an enemy's port, and had on board articles contraband of war.* In violation of these orders, the Eliza Russell, an English brig, was seized and sent into port, with a valuable cargo of fine goods, but containing nothing *contraband of war!* Other acts connected with the cruise of a character not calculated to elevate us in the scale of nations, were done either without orders, or in direct violation of those which had been issued by the department.

After reviewing Houston's evidence, the anti-Houston faction introduced a resolution contesting Houston's reasons for suspending Fisher, and on November 9, the Senate agreed to take up the case. On November 24, hearings on the Fisher resolution, which were tantamount to an impeachment trial of Fisher, commenced in the new capital city of Houston, in the small two-story wooden building that passed for the Senate chambers. The Senate's chaplain, Rev. Littleton Fowler, noted in his journal for that day, "[S. Rhoads Fisher] stands impeached by President Houston. Gray and Kaufman are counsel for the prosecution. Ex-President Burnet and General Rusk for the defense. [Gray] was followed by Burnet at some length and with much bitterness towards the Chief Executive; his speech disclosed a burning hatred for the President." The next day Fowler reported, "The trial of Mr. Fisher was continued to-day by Mr. John Wharton, in a most furious tirade against President Houston; it was the bitterest invective I ever heard uttered by man." The emotionally-charged trial continued until November 27, and the next day the Senate passed a resolution sustaining Houston's decision to remove Fisher in the interest of governmental harmony, but declaring, "at the same time we must do S. Rhoads Fisher the justice to say that there has been no evidence before us to prove that he has been guilty of any crime." Five days later, Houston submitted Shepherd's name to the Senate, which unanimously confirmed the new secretary of the navy.

With the Senate's consent, Fisher's eventful public career was over. He returned to his home in Matagorda, basking in popular support but holding no other national office until an assassin cut short his life on March 13, 1839. The leaders of the original Texas Navy had been purged, and Houston's new man, Doc Shepherd, was at last unquestionably the head of the Navy Department. As 1837 drew to a close, Shepherd, under Houston's watchful eye, settled into the unenviable task of managing a navy that had no warships, little money, and questionable purpose.

INTERMISSION

*The Paper Navy
(1837–1839)*

CHAPTER FOURTEEN

Managing a Ghost Fleet

While the country has been gradually rising from the effects of the revolution, our navy has become almost extinct. The embarrassed situation for our financial affairs, has heretofore rendered it impossible to make the necessary appropriations for keeping it up; and we have now but one small vessel afloat to guard a coast of more than six hundred miles in length.
—Navy Secretary William M. Shepherd, September 30, 1837

WHEN WILLIAM SHEPHERD TOOK OVER the Navy Department after his predecessor's bizarre absence, he had two unspoken directives: build up the seacoast's defenses, and never, never cross Sam Houston. The second task was easy enough: he had no warships to command, so he could not very well order them to do anything that displeased the president. The first was much more difficult, however, as a navy's primary means of defense usually includes ships, preferably ones that can inflict injury on enemy vessels. For Shepherd, the calendar may as well have been flipped back to November 1835, when the denuded Texas coast lay exposed to attacks from even the most insignificant armed Mexican vessel. Fortunately for Texas, federalist uprisings in Guadalajara, Oaxaca, California, and the Rio Grande kept the Mexican government's hands full for the moment.

William Shepherd was one of the more thorough and competent administrators the Texas Navy ever had. He was careful to never violate his directives, and lacked the boldness to force Houston to create a potent fleet, but he consistently prodded the president for incremental reforms that would provide sailors and officers with better lives and regular pay. He pressed for the establishment of a navy yard in Galveston, pursued efforts to rebuild the Navy after the disasters of 1837, and raised the need for a survey of the Texas coast. He advocated land bounties for sailors—something army soldiers had enjoyed since the revolution—and worked hard to convert the receiving brig *Potomac* into a fighting vessel. Had he had more to work with, he probably would have done more for the Texas Navy than more colorful secretaries such as Potter or Fisher (who deserted their posts) or later appointees of Presidents Mirabeau Lamar, Sam Houston, and Anson Jones.

Shepherd's obvious starting point for a "close-in" defense was Galveston. The Galveston of 1837 had come a long way from the "wild, desolate" wilderness Stephen Austin beheld in the early 1830s. Gail Borden, Jr., an eccentric inventor, surveyor, customs officer, missionary, and future founder of a condensed milk company, designed the City of Galveston in a large gridiron pattern centered on the eastern half of the island. By September 1837 it boasted a fine hotel, several commercial buildings and churches, and an increasingly busy anchorage with schooners, brigs, and steamers running between Galveston and Matagorda, and New Orleans and Mobile. Snakes, alligators, and feral pigs still plagued the islanders, and mosquitoes occasionally brought yellow fever to the inhabitants, but these natural hazards would not stand between Galvestonians and the great progress they expected from the finest harbor in Texas.

At first, Secretary Shepherd had little to work with. Texas had purchased the brig *Potomac* from Capt. L. M. Hitchcock for $8,000, for use as a harbor boat. *Potomac* was not, at the moment, a combat vessel, but it would at least give the officers a ship on which to bunk until others could be obtained. In December, Shepherd ordered his officers to convert her into a brig of war, but President Houston refused to approve the expenditures necessary to convert her. By April 1838 she had not even been modified to receive a battery, and a number of important alterations (such as the addition of a magazine, storerooms, and shot lockers) were only half-finished. Despite Shepherd's urgings and sunk costs of $8,000, the project was abandoned.

The one-gun *Correo*, captured off Tabasco, had been damaged by Racer's Storm, but she was in good enough shape that the government considered refitting her as a warship. Before his death, Commodore Thompson had recommended that the government commission her as a reconnaissance vessel. Shepherd agreed, and ordered Lt. Francis Wright to inspect *Correo* to see if she would function as a warship. Wright rated the sixty-five-ton schooner an "admirable vessel of her class," and recommended that Shepherd transport the long eighteen-pounder on Boylan's *Viper*, nicknamed the "Widow Porter," to *Correo*, and give her two six-pounders from *Thomas Toby*, so she would pack the punch of a light cruiser. With topsails from *Invincible*, Wright wrote, she would be ready to put to sea "in a short space of time and at a verry moderate expense." The government impressed *Correo* into service, and in December 1837, Shepherd ordered Captain Wheelwright, once again commander of the fleet, to have the beached *Correo* prepared for defensive action along the coast. Unfortunately, by the following April, *Correo* still was not seaworthy, due to the lack of tools and funding to complete the job.

Another possibility was the heavy brig *Phoenix*, the prize taken by *Thomas Toby* off Sisal. Thanks to her two large anchors and two tethered cannon thrown overboard, she had ridden out the October storm in relative safety. Before his dismissal, Commodore Thompson had recommended that the government fit her out with fifteen guns, a twenty-four-pounder pivot and fourteen medium eighteens. Shepherd agreed, and ordered Lieutenant Wright to inspect the vessel in greater detail. Wright found *Phoenix* to be a splendid vessel, in "better than new" condition, requiring few modifications to make her an outstanding twelve-gun warship. But for some unrecorded reason, probably financial, nothing ever came of Wright's recommendations.

In desperation, Houston appealed to the class of military men he had the most reason to mistrust. On September 15, 1837, he published a proclamation calling for privateers to defend Texas. Houston, it seemed, viewed privateers as a kind of seagoing militia, one that could be called up and disbanded at the whim of the executive. But Houston's fundamental misunderstanding of the naval profession did not alter the facts, or improve the results: although the Texas Congress sanctioned Houston's request, and reduced the government's fee to 2.5 percent—a quarter of its former share—the lack of urgency by the maritime community, and seafarers' general reluctance to risk hanging while outnumbered by Mexican warships, doomed Houston's call to arms from the start.

A related problem for Shepherd was finding a permanent berth for the Navy's future warships. During the darkest days of the revolution, President Burnet declared all of Galveston Island a naval depot, but that decree was rescinded soon after the war in favor of commercial development. The Navy urgently needed a place to store supplies, shelter its sea craft and concentrate men when not at sea. Prompted by, among others, a former U.S. Navy midshipman named John Grant Tod, Secretary Fisher had dispatched Alexander Thompson, a former officer in the U.S. and Mexican navies, to New Orleans to purchase surveying equipment with which to plot out a Navy Yard for Galveston.

In mid-September, Secretary Shepherd ordered Thompson to draft a plan for the Navy Yard, which would be submitted to Congress, and on October 5 Thompson obliged. He proposed enclosing eighty-two acres with a harbor frontage of 800 yards, onto which he planned to add watering tanks and several buildings, plus a drainage system to stave off flooding from continual rains and high tides.

In early February 1838, Captain Wheelwright and Secretary Shepherd turned to an unlikely sailor for help with the Navy Yard project. They asked the ubiquitous "Mexico" Thompson to take command of the Yard, establish the necessary facilities there, and assist with *Correo*'s overhaul. Thompson, full of energy whether oppressing the Texians or aiding them, went right to work, and by April the Navy Yard consisted of a blacksmith's shop with two forges, an armorer's shop, a carpenter's shed with a sail loft, mechanics' shops, and officers' quarters.

Evidently most of these improvements were made with private donations solicited by Captain Wheelwright, although some apparently compromised the government's already precarious credit. Near the end of April, Shepherd asked the eager Mr. Tod to conduct an audit of expenditures on stores and manpower needs for the Navy Yard. Unfortunately for the Navy, the additional expenses came to Sam Houston's attention, and in early May he lamented to Tod, "Oh God what splendid villainy and stupendous waste have been practiced on this government." Heads would undoubtedly roll.

One thorny problem left over from Fisher's cruise was what to do with the various prize vessels. Texas was not about to compensate Mexico for the burning of *Adventure*, but judicial proceedings had to be followed to condemn *Abispa, Correo,* and *Telegrafo* as proper prizes.

Even more problematic were the British merchantmen *Eliza Russell* and *Little Penn*. President Houston had been courting Great Britain to extend formal recognition to Texas, and the last thing he needed was a charge of piracy influencing British opinion. Asa Brigham, acting secretary of the treasury, quickly ordered Port Collector Gail Borden to release Eliza Russell, whose "capture was made contrary to instructions from the Navy Dep't. to the commanding officer of the fleet," and reimburse her captain for any losses he had suffered. Borden immediately complied, but the Court of St. James continued to press its case for several years, and claims of over $4,000 were ultimately paid by Texas on account of *Eliza Russell's* seizure. Evidently nothing was ever done about *Little Penn*, as the evidence against the Texas Navy was much more equivocal.

The solution to the Navy's host of problems was, of course, money. But Texas had little or nothing to spend on programs Houston favored, much less those he intuitively disliked. Texas had no national currency until late 1837, and its credit in the United States was withering fast.

Recognizing that Houston needed some convincing if the Navy were to receive anything from its government, Shepherd prepared a well-reasoned report on September 30, 1837, stressing the need for a few thousand dollars to avoid a military disaster that would cost Texas millions, perhaps even her survival, once Mexico finished rebuilding her fleet. Recounting the importance of a navy to Texas's independence, Shepherd noted

While the country has been gradually rising from the effects of the revolution, our navy has become almost extinct.... We have now but one small vessel afloat to guard a coast of more than six hundred miles in length. While our navy is in this shattered condition, and entirely unable to afford the necessary protection to our commerce, the Mexicans have found means to make such additions to their own naval strength as will enable them to hold an entire control over the Gulf....

Whether they will attempt another campaign against us remains to be solved by time. But every consideration of pride and interest will compel them to the undertaking, and while we have every assurance from that Government that the conquest of Texas will not be given up, it becomes us at least to be as well prepared for the worst as the exigencies of our country will allow, and even on the score of economy it appears to me that the interest of our country will be most promoted by adopting measures to secure the command of the Gulf, to protect our commerce and defend our most important points on the Gulf. We should then obviate the necessity of a large number of troops, which must be required to guard the shore, in the event of a weak and inefficient navy. By this means an expenditure of near half a million dollars might be avoided by a reduction of the number of troops required to keep up the different military posts along the coast....

But the necessity of a navy, great at all times, will be imperious in case of another invasion by the Mexicans. With the sea closed against our commerce, the crops of our enterprising planters, either destroyed or rendered valueless, and our country invaded by a large army, you may readily calculate the embarrassed situation of all classes of the community. Contemptible as we view the paltry nation who are annoying us, it is nevertheless part of wisdom to be prepared for the worst.

Shepherd's pleas fell on deaf ears. The president's November 21, 1837, message to Congress paid lip service to the need for a new fleet, but expended most of its rhetorical energy on a lamentation of the Republic's "embarrassed" financial state. No new ships would be purchased for the officers, and the next year and a half was devoted to administrative, personnel, financial, and disciplinary matters, none of which protected Texas from invasion. Meaningless appropriations bills were passed, Houston refused to pay naval expenses, and Captain Wheelwright began to get himself into trouble with the general through his liberal leave policy and his stubborn refusal to take the oath of office. On April 15, 1838, Houston, irritated as always with his naval officers, dismissed Wheelwright, and despite a Senate request for his reinstatement, Houston refused to take him back into the service. Houston, citing Wheelwright's refusal to take the oath, his overspending, and his disrespectful attitude to Secretary Shepherd, summed up his distrust of his military commanders:

Unless officers employed in the service of their country obey and respect those whom the law has placed over them, there can be no guarantee for the performance of any duty; and when acts of disobedience the most flagrant, and disrespect the most palpable, are permitted, it must always have the effect of destroying discipline and promoting sedition in every grade of the Army or Navy.... Heretofore, the greatest calamities to our service, have arisen from disobedience and insubordination. The fall of the Alamo—the massacre of Fannin and his men . . . and the destruction of our navy, have all resulted from disobedience.

With Wheelwright's dismissal, command of the Navy devolved to a favorite of Secretary Shepherd, Lt. John Taylor, the officer who surrendered *Independence* to Commodore Lopez's squadron. Taylor ambled around the Yard in an oversized, second-hand coat made for a major general of the militia. Its twenty buttons ("more than his rank entitles him to," grumbled one purser) and its gaudy gingerbread braid gave Taylor a somewhat farcical appearance, and his fellow officers soon dubbed the ostentatious lieutenant "Major General Boots." Soon "General Boots," seeing no real purpose to his idle station, fell into the fog of alcoholism that so often claims unfulfilled men. After repeated warnings against drunkenness on duty, Secretary Shepherd confined Taylor to the Yard and forbade anyone to give him liquor. It didn't work. Purser Fleming T. Wells complained, "There is nothing he will not descend to get spirits, though he knows he is under arrest and charges against him for drunkenness. . . . He will even go round to the Marines and Sailors in the Yard and beg their rations. I would sooner expect to see a resurrection of the buried, as to see him a reformed man."

It was painfully apparent that the Texas government had more officers than it needed or could hope to employ in the near future. President Houston conceded the obvious by ordering his acting navy secretary, George W. Hockley, his artillery commander from San Jacinto, to disband the officers and seamen until Texas acquired ships that could use their talents, excepting only enough to man *Potomac* and administer the Navy Yard. Based on John Tod's audit, officers were furloughed and men were discharged, and the Navy was soon down to one lieutenant, two midshipmen, a doctor, two pursers, and two seamen (both deserters from the U.S. war schooner *Grampus*). "Mexico" Thompson was also discharged, lingering in Galveston until late 1841, when he went back into the commercial trade. That year he met his end during a drunken assault on a local cantina in Tampico, in which the violent sailor met a like-minded bartender whose shotgun, unlike Thompson's pistol, did not misfire. Shepherd, upon his return to the new capital of Houston, protested that it was unfair to discharge loyal, dedicated officers and men without providing some kind of severance pay. Shepherd proposed three months' salary, but nothing ever came of his recommendation.

The Texas Navy was becalmed in still waters, and until new ships arrived, Texas's coastline and, by extension, its economy, would be at the mercy of Mexico.

CHAPTER FIFTEEN

Vive la France!

Nothing could be more gratifying to my feelings than to be considered as one of you, gentlemen, whose industry and energy I do so much admire. Be assured that I would vastly prefer being the humblest member of a well regulated and thriving community, like yours, than to moving in the sphere of wealth and power in a corrupt and decaying society.
—French Adm. Charles Baudin to the Citizens of Galveston, May 1838

AS SECRETARY SHEPHERD APTLY POINTED OUT, "every consideration of pride and interest" compelled Mexico to reconquer Texas. Its burning desire to avenge a national humiliation and roll back the tide of "Yanqui" imperialism continued unabated, and from time to time one politician or another would use the "*Cuestión de Tejas*" to promote himself while furthering national interests. To the north, the United States's rejection of Houston's 1837 proposal to annex Texas sent a clear message to the world that the U.S. was not ready to tie itself to the Lone Star Republic until the painful issue of slavery in the West was resolved. With a hostile power on its southern border, Texas was on its own.

Why, then, did Mexico not pounce upon Texas while its coasts lay unprotected? The answer was preoccupation. Between 1837 and 1839, the centralist government was besieged by a series of political, military, economic, and environmental crises that distracted its government until the early 1840s. After the loss of Texas, Mexico's civil wars and the effects of an international depression drained its treasury of the funds needed to finance a second invasion. Political instability in northern Mexico, Tabasco, Yucatán and other regions tied down large numbers of centralist troops, drawing them deeper into Mexico's interior and further from staging areas for an invasion of the north.

But the biggest setback to invasion was dealt by a fleet flying the Tricolor, not the Lone Star. During the 1830s, relations between the Mexican and

French republics had soured over, among other things, Mexico's debts to France and the seizure of a pantryful of chocolate éclairs from a French baker. In 1837, the French government presented President Bustamente with claims exceeding $600,000, and when this demand went ignored, the Tuileries dispatched a squadron to impose a blockade of the heavily guarded port of Veracruz, the home base of the Mexican Navy.

Failing to get Bustamente's attention, on March 21, 1838, France presented an ultimatum to the Mexican government. When the ultimatum went unanswered, France sent a larger fleet under Adm. Charles Baudin to force Mexico into submission. Baudin's flagship *Neride*, backed by a fleet of twenty-six battleships, sailed into Mexican waters in early November 1838.

Admiral Baudin, a one-armed veteran of Trafalgar, concentrated his fleet off Veracruz near the fortress of San Juan de Ullúa, the "Gibraltar of America." The debonair commander brought some of France's finest ships of the line, the large, heavy warships that had dominated European seas since the time of the Spanish Armada, but were rarely, if ever, seen in the Gulf. Baudin reiterated the French demand for $600,000, plus another $200,000 to pay for the cost of the expedition; he warned the government that if his demands were not met by November 27, he would level the vaunted Mexican fortress.

On November 27, as promised, Baudin's 104 heavy guns opened up on the ancient castle. San Juan de Ullúa, which had withstood the pounding of Spanish guns, began crumbling around its garrison as missile after missile crashed into its stone walls. By nightfall, all defending guns fell silent, and the old walls were breached in several places. Soon the castle was in French hands. Veracruz's commanding generals jointly agreed to evacuate the city, but President Bustamente, running for political cover, demanded an expedition to drive the occupying French back to the sea.

Santa Anna, recalled to the colors in his country's time of crisis, rode to Veracruz and took command of a Mexican force of five thousand. As they approached, the small French holding party evacuated the fort, but a night attack by fifteen hundred French marines drove the Mexicans out; the Frenchmen captured Gen. Mariano Arista and forced Santa Anna to flee into the fog clad only in his underwear. Rallying his men for a counterattack, Santa Anna was hit in the leg by a volley of grapeshot as the French rowed back to their armada. His leg had to be amputated (and was buried with full honors in the National Capital), but the loss of a limb breathed new life into Santa Anna's political career.

The capture of San Juan d'Ullúa gave the French the Mexican Navy's entire Atlantic squadron, which had been built up at great expense by Secretary Tornel. Baudin's staff recorded a haul that included the twenty-four-gun corvette *Iguala*, three brigs, and two schooners, all fresh from their Baltimore shipyards and in exceptional condition. Baudin then revoked the blockade of any ports that fell into federalist hands, reinvigorating federalist revolts north of Tampico and setting the stage for a federalist buffer zone between Texas and centralist-controlled Mexico City.

In March 1839, a treaty mediated by Great Britain resolved the dispute. France received its $600,000, and its fleet sailed home. On his way, Admiral Baudin paid a courtesy call on Galveston, which owed France an inestimable debt of thanks. Baudin was given a grand welcome by Galveston officials, and the aldermen presented the distinguished admiral with the keys to the city. With a gracious letter to Galveston's citizens and a thirteen-gun salute from *Neride*, Charles Baudin left the Gulf coast secured against the Mexican fleet, playing a critical if largely overlooked role in the life of the Republic of Texas.

ACT THREE

The Second Texas Navy
(1839–1846)

CHAPTER SIXTEEN

Houston, Lamar, and Shifting Political Currents

Mexico has set us an example: with impoverished coffers, she has through her energy put afloat an efficient fleet built by the most experienced workmen, and vessels which are not surpassed by any in the world; and shall we not profit from this example?
—Report to President-Elect Mirabeau B. Lamar

IT TOOK THE DISASTERS OF 1837 to force the Texas Congress to think seriously about rebuilding the Navy. In November 1836, when *Brutus* and *Invincible* had abandoned the Texas coast for New York, Congress passed a law calling for the purchase of a twenty-four-gun sloop, a ten-gun steamer, and two eleven-gun schooners. But without funds to buy the ships, the law was dead on arrival. By September 1837, the Texas Navy was whittled down to virtually nothing.

The battle off Galveston, the destruction of Racer's Storm, and the death of Commander Thompson breathed new life into the Navy's fortunes, galvanizing support in the Second Congress for a newer, better fleet. The ever-faithful *Telegraph* prodded Congress, warning, "The thunder of Mexican cannon pealing along our coast may announce to [Congress] the startling fact that *title to the lands of Texas is not yet secured.*" The rumored purchase of a twenty-two-gun brig by Mexico moved the *Telegraph*'s editor to concede, "President Bustamente is evidently entitled to much credit for energetic and efficient measures which he has taken to place the Mexican navy on a respectable basis."

Secretary Shepherd's report to Houston in September 1837 requesting naval appropriations was well-timed to add momentum to the pro-Navy movement, and in October the Committee on Naval Affairs drafted a resolution to send a naval agent to buy Texas a twenty-four-gun corvette, two ten-gun brigs and two "substantial" schooners. This recommendation was refined to authorize the purchase of a 500-ton sloop-of-war mounting eighteen guns, two 300-ton twelve-gun brigs, and three 130-ton schooners mounting five or seven guns apiece. The resolution sped through Congress, and on November 4, 1837, Houston signed the bill into law.

In December 1837 Houston appointed Peter Grayson, the former attorney general, as naval agent to the United States to acquire the needed warships. To provide Grayson with maritime expertise, "so the Navy be made respectable," Houston asked the enterprising John Grant Tod to accompany Grayson, and gave Tod a letter of introduction to U.S. President Martin Van Buren.

Grayson did not last. He resigned his post in early 1838 to throw his hat into the presidential election ring, and soon afterwards, in a fit of drunken depression, he put a bullet in his brain. Houston then offered the job to Dr. Anson Jones, but changed his mind and instead made Jones Texas's minister to the United States. Ultimately, Houston appointed Samuel May Williams, the financier of the first Texas Navy, to replace Grayson. With his family connections to the Baltimore shipbuilding and financial industries, Williams had been the logical choice from the beginning, but better late than never. As the sun was setting on Houston's administration in the fall of 1838, Williams packed his trunk for Baltimore to see his brother Henry about buying Texas a new fleet of warships.

Williams set up headquarters at a hotel in Philadelphia, to evade the Republic's creditors in Baltimore, and soon he and his brother found a shipbuilder who would construct the appropriate warships and was not scared off by Texas's miserable credit rating. Henry's connections in Baltimore and New York lent credibility to the venture, and soon the two brothers negotiated a contract with Frederick Dawson & Sons. Dawson agreed to build six warships for $280,000 in Texas bonds, with a 100 percent penalty to be paid, also in bonds, in the event of default. (It does not appear to have occurred to Dawson that if Texas were unable to pay him $280,000 for his work, it could not pay him $560,000, either.) An elated Williams signed the contract in Baltimore, penned a quick note to his wife relating the momentous news, and left Baltimore for New York, satisfied that he had once again secured a navy for his adopted country.

While Williams was up north, another Texas agent, James Hamilton, located a fine, sturdy steamboat off the Carolina coast. The steamer *Charleston*, a double side-wheeler built in Philadelphia for the Charleston and Philadelphia Steam Packet Company, demonstrated her mettle by surviving a deadly gale off Cape Hatteras in October 1837. Driven aground at Cape Lookout, she managed to limp into Beaufort, South Carolina for comparatively minor repairs before getting back to her regular Charleston–Philadelphia route.

Charleston, although a civilian packet, was almost perfectly suited for naval work. She was a stout, heavily timbered vessel, solid enough to carry a battery, and her two "walking beam" steam engines were reliable enough to weather the high seas of the Atlantic and Gulf coasts. She was nearly 211 feet long, 569 tons burthen, and with reasonable alterations, she could serve Texas as a passenger and mail steamer in peacetime, a towing vessel for Texas harbors or a warship. As the rough steamboat *Laura* demonstrated in her fight with *Correo Mejicano* in 1835, an armed steamer could fight independently, or could tow sailing ships into firing position in adverse winds.

Charleston, freshly repaired after the Hatteras storm, fit the bill nicely. At peak performance, she could make nine knots between New Orleans and Galveston—a mere forty-two-hour trip for the splendid steamer. Her price tag of $120,000 was substantial, but she could be paid for over ten years at five percent interest. Given the naïve optimism that seduced the Texas government, the price was considered negligible; the Republic's great natural wealth and solid economic prospects would surely enable it to make good its commitment. By October 24, 1838, a deal was struck, and the Texas Congress quickly approved the transaction. *Charleston*'s captain, James Pennoyer, began recruiting engineers, firemen, and seamen from the steamship *Rochester* to get the vessel underway, then headed for Texas.

While agents were working abroad to convince investors that Texas could repay its debts, a new administration with a very different agenda took office. On December 10, 1838, Mirabeau Buonaparte Lamar of Milledgeville, Georgia—Sam Houston's vice-president and an outspoken critic of Houston's policies—leapt onto the saddle of the broken-down nag that was Texas's government and prepared to gallop southwest in search of an empire.

For nearly everything Sam Houston supported, Lamar represented the opposing view. Houston opposed a strong standing military force; Lamar favored one. Houston sought peace with the Indians and Mexico through rapprochement; Lamar believed peace must be forced on those peoples with the barrel of a gun. Houston was fiscally conservative; Lamar favored a "print and spend" policy that would have made the Weimar Republic blush.

But most of all, Sam Houston, whose dreams were bigger than Texas could ever hope to be, favored annexation to his beloved United States. Lamar, by contrast, wrote, spoke, and lived for an empire of the Lone Star stretching from the Sabine River to the Pacific Ocean. Lamar spoke out bitterly against the United States's brusque treatment of Texas when it requested admission in 1836, and stressed Texas's need to triumph over adversity on its own.

By supporting policies of relocation or extermination towards the great Indian tribes and "peace through strength" towards Mexico, Lamar created (or at least amplified) a need for a large, robust army and navy. He told Congress that the military "could not, compatible with safety, be either small or inactive," and, echoing the U.S. Second Amendment, he declared, "a well regulated militia is the strongest and surest bulwark of liberty." His administration, he promised, would "foster a spirit of military pride and emulation among the people," and to spread this spirit among his Texians, he pledged to build up a formidable fleet that would protect the Texas banner "from insult and depredation on the high seas." In response, Congress appropriated $250,000 for the Navy for the year 1839.

Cleaning house, Lamar swept away all remnants of the Houston administration that might hold back his naval programme. First, he replaced Secretary Shepherd with Memucan Hunt, a thirty-one-year-old North Carolinian who had been Texas's minister to the United States. Next, he replaced Samuel May Williams with James Hamilton of South Carolina, a move that angered the Houstonites in Congress. It appears that Lamar's move was driven by heavy support for Lamar's opponent during the presidential election from Williams' business partner, Thomas F. McKinney. McKinney, outspoken as ever, wrote to Williams of one senator's reaction: "Bob White became so excited on the subject of Hamilton that he realy ran crazy and called on God to damn a Senate who were so Submissive as to confirm his nomination to the Exclusion of S.M.W. and refused to make any apology for the insult to the Senate and added more and was expelled but the universal feelings of the people are in his favor and although he deserved expulsion he will be returned I think beyond a doubt. . . ." (A resolution was passed thanking Williams for his efforts, and anti-Houstonite William Wharton magnanimously challenged his fellow patriots to name one man who had done more for Texas than Samuel May Williams.)

One Houston appointee Lamar could not easily replace was his naval liaison to the United States, John Grant Tod. The fair-haired Tod was born in 1807, a native of Lexington, Kentucky, who left the Bluegrass State at the age of seventeen on a Mississippi flatboat bound for New Orleans. He applied for a midshipman's appointment to the U.S. Navy, but hearing nothing for some time, he enlisted in the Mexican Navy as a midshipman under Commodore Porter. Through the influence of Sen. Henry Clay, he obtained a midshipman's appointment in the United States Navy in 1828, and Porter discharged him to pursue a career in the States. He served aboard the receiving ship *Alert*, then aboard the USS *North Carolina* off the Virginia coast before being transferred to the West Indies Squadron aboard the sloops *Erie* and *St. Louis*. Tod was a dutiful seaman, but not a good student; he repeatedly missed his Passed Midshipman's examinations, and in June 1836, after missing his third examination, he was "permitted" to resign.

In early 1837, rumors that Texas was building an impressive new fleet reached Tod's ears, and he toyed with the idea of offering to help Texas procure the proper ships. Dropping the names of high-ranking U.S. Army and Navy officers, Tod offered his services to then-Secretary Fisher, without success, and asked army surgeon-turned-congressman George Washington Hill to use his influence to get Tod an appointment to procure a warship in the United States, "a subject," Tod asserted, "that the Hon. Secretary of the Navy alone appears to view in rather an indifferent light."

In the spring, Tod later claimed, Fisher had asked him to provide recommendations on the site for a future naval depot, and Tod took some preliminary steps towards a plan for a navy yard. After Fisher's dismissal, Tod had advised Sam Houston to charter a vessel to watch the Mexican coastline for signs of hostile movement, and reiterated his offer to the influential Hill. "I would be happy to see the [Texas Navy], Phoenix-like, to raise again, whether I have any thing to do with it or not.... I feel from my acquaintance with some of the Senior Officers as well as the Naval Constructors of the U.S. Navy, that I could, with great propriety, make a good use of their knowledge and experience in forming a contract for the building of a vessel."

After the Naval Act of 1837 was passed, President Houston, impressed with Tod's credentials, gave him an unofficial position as technical advisor to Commissioner Grayson. Grayson implied, or perhaps promised, that Tod would become second-in-command of the Texas Navy and would be given his own vessel if he were successful in obtaining a fleet. Grayson's resignation and death in 1838 derailed these plans, and Tod began worrying aloud that President Lamar, to spite Houston, might reinstate Captain Wheelwright as second-in-command, moving Tod down to the third spot. A subsequent rumor, that Navy Clerk Peter Humphreys would become the second officer, sent Tod into yet another panicked frenzy, and soon Tod began seeing, in the incoming Lamar administration, conspiracies against him and other Houston appointees. But once the Dawson contract was signed, Tod's work overseeing the construction of the fleet at Baltimore's Schott and Whitney shipyards made him an indispensable part of the new navy.

The most important field position had yet to be filled. The last man to hold unquestioned command over the Navy was Captain Wheelwright, but he had been sacked by Houston in April 1838. Wheelwright was succeeded by "Major General Boots" and, in rapid succession, other lieutenants whose claim to command was based solely on the seniority of their lieutenants' commissions, not their rank. A new navy would require a post captain who could bring energy, creativity, and an indomitable will to the post. He would have to be experienced enough to command the respect of veteran officers, many of whom had battle records. And most of all, the new commander would have to share Lamar's vision of a world-class fleet to protect the seagoing interests of a world-class nation. Lamar found all these qualities, and much more, in one of the brightest young lieutenants in the United States Navy.

Edwin Ward Moore was born on July 15, 1810, to one of the great families of Virginia. His grandfather and great-uncle had been distinguished Revolutionary War officers, the former being wounded at Brandywine. Moore had another relative who sailed for the Virginia Navy, while another uncle, Alexander Moore (a distant relative of George Washington), fought in defense of Washington, D.C., during the War of 1812. As a lad, Moore attended Alexandria Academy, a school founded by his grandfather, among others, and one of his boyhood schoolmates was a young man from Stratford Hall named Robert Edward Lee.

Answering the call of the sea in 1824, the fourteen-year-old Moore entered the U.S. Navy as a midshipman. He excelled at his post, and eagerly soaked up whatever knowledge of naval technology and tactics he could acquire. His first seaside assignment came in August 1825, when he was posted to the USS *Hornet*, and after a brief leave of absence to recover from a bout of malaria, he served aboard the warships *Fairfield* and *Delaware* along the Atlantic Coast and in the Mediterranean.

In 1830 he was assigned to the Norfolk Navy Yard in southern Virginia, where he learned a great deal about naval logistics, construction, funding and ship repair. After passing his midshipman's exam in 1831, he was reassigned to *Fairfield* as her acting sailing master, where he sailed with the West Indies Squadron until he was again stricken with tropical fever. The next year Moore was assigned to the USS *Vincennes*, but his orders were soon revoked on account of his recurring health problems, and he would not receive a shipboard assignment until after his promotion to lieutenant in March of 1835. Moore was assigned to his squadron's flagship, the sloop-of-war *Boston*, and he began his service in the Gulf of Mexico on July 1, 1836.

As an officer, Moore was known for his coolness under pressure. In July 1836, a West Indies hurricane hit *Boston*'s patrol zone, and the ship began floundering. Moore asked his commander for permission to cast overboard 150 thirty-two-pound cannonballs and scuttle the berth deck to allow water to drain from the spar and quarterdecks to the bilge, from which it could be pumped overboard. Permission was granted, and Moore's quick thinking saved the drowning *Boston*. Moore also proved his courage under fire by leading a landing party against Indians in the Seminole War.

But Moore was not simply brave. An expert swimmer, fluent in Spanish, a born diplomat, an amateur inventor, a good spinner of yarns, and most of all, intellectually curious, Moore would make a fine leader for Texas's small, up-and-coming navy. As John Tod later wrote to a friend, Moore was "as gallant and intrepid an officer as ever stepped on the plank of a vessel. He is a good seaman, and an accomplished gentleman, just the person required to bring the Navy of Texas, to what you, and every other friend of the country would like to see it."

Moore was aboard *Boston* when he first met Texians at sea. In September 1836 the ship captured the privateer *Terrible* off the coast of New Orleans and sent her into Pensacola on piracy charges, although there is no record of what Moore thought or did when he first encountered seafarers of the Lone Star. When Mexico declared a blockade of Texas in early 1837, Moore's *Boston* spent the spring escorting New Orleans vessels to Texas ports.

News then, as today, traveled fast through the tight-knit maritime community and, during one of *Boston*'s visits to Galveston, Moore very likely learned that Texas was buying a new, state-of-the-art fleet. No records describe the meeting in which Moore presented himself to President Lamar, but both men must have sized each other up with the wariness of two business partners about to embark on a risky venture. Moore stood a scant five feet eight inches tall, but his stocky build, his sharp blue eyes and his confident, genial nature marked him as a patrician who was not intimidated by men of power. Moore's eagerness for combat and his reputation as an outstanding officer put him high on Lamar's short list to command the Navy. Moore beat out several naval veterans for the job, and he was offered the position sometime in March of 1839.

Moore had good reasons for giving up a promising career in the United States Navy. Promotion in any peacetime force is slow, and this was especially true in the U.S. Navy of the early nineteenth century. Many commanders of the War of 1812 still held the quarterdeck at the time Moore was offered the Texas post, and with peacetime retrenchment, few of Moore's vintage would command capital ships until the Civil War. Additionally, the U.S. Navy was technologically stagnant, refusing to embrace steam power, which ran against Moore's progressive philosophy of naval innovation. (In 1839, the United States had only one steam-powered warship in its fleet, the *Fulton II*, and would not expand its inventory of war steamers until it commissioned the battleships *Missouri* and *Mississippi* in 1842.) In Texas, by contrast, Moore would have a freer hand to push for improvements in steam power, naval ordnance, small arms and small boat technology.

Another advantage of coming to Texas was that the pay was theoretically better. The U.S. Navy placed many of its officers on leave with half-pay unless they were actively serving aboard ships or in the Navy Yard. As a result, many fine junior officers had to support themselves through other means until recalled to active duty. Some became lawyers, writers, or merchant captains or went back to their family farms until duty called. Some simply became poor. Because Moore had been with the U.S. Navy since he was fourteen, he had no other readily marketable skill, and was thus at the mercy of the secretary of the navy for his livelihood. In Texas, by contrast, Moore would not only be guaranteed full-time employment, but he would be paid at the higher rate of a post captain. Moreover, the Texas Navy had decent prospects of taking rich prizes that would be shared by captain and crew; while the U.S. government did not abolish the practice of awarding prize money until 1899, the American fleet would not actively hunt prizes on any significant scale until the Civil War.

Thus, power, riches, and prestige were to be had in the new Republic. But in the end, it seems that Moore was just one of those restless souls who wandered from challenge to challenge, seeking new ways to prove himself to the world; the task of organizing a navy from virtually nothing was irresistible to the young, ambitious lieutenant. The downside, of course, was that if Moore were ever captured by the Mexican Navy, he might be hanged as a pirate. But Moore had no intention of being captured, and after spending half his twenty-eight year life in a peacetime navy, he was itching to command a combat vessel. From the date of his commission, issued three years later, it appears that Moore officially accepted the post around April 21, 1839. His rank was that of post captain, but as commander in chief of the naval forces of Texas, he would be known to the world as Commodore Moore.

Regardless of the exact date of his acceptance, it apparently preceded his resignation from the U.S. Navy, and this caused problems. The United States government did not take kindly to its officers serving concurrently in foreign navies, and President Jackson's concern with the appearance of neutrality carried over to the Van Buren administration. With the U.S. Navy in a retrenching mode, the Navy Department was acutely sensitive to officers who took capable subordinates with them into foreign service, as Commodore Porter had done with Charles Hawkins, Alex Thompson, John Tod, and others in the mid-1820s. When Moore was absent from *Boston* without leave, the Navy Department demanded an explanation. Rumors circulated in southern newspapers, claiming Moore had been appointed the new commander in chief of the Texas Navy, and in a letter to Moore in late April, U.S. Navy Secretary James Paulding demanded to know whether the rumors were true.

As Moore was pondering his reply, Commodore Charles Ridgley of the Brooklyn Navy Yard informed Paulding that Alex Moore, Edwin Moore's cousin, had let slip that the Moores were recruiting officers for Texas, and that Alex was to receive a commission in the Texas Navy. Word on the docks was that Lt. Moore was shipping eighty members of *Boston*'s crew to Baltimore to man the new warships Texas was building. Secretary Paulding put Moore on leave while he began quietly gathering information for a court-martial. One of the key witnesses was a boy who had served under Moore aboard the sloop *Boston*, and was reportedly leaving for Texas to become Moore's steward. (The boy, Samuel Edgerton, did in fact come to Texas as Moore's steward, and served aboard Moore's flagship until the lad's death in 1840.)

In June 1839, Moore assured Paulding that he had neither recruited sailors nor shipped sailors to Baltimore. He claimed he had nothing to do with any vessel the Texians might have been building there. Paulding shot back a reply: Moore's denial was not explicit enough; had Moore used others to recruit U.S. officers or sailors for Texas? In his correspondence, Paulding did his best to appear reasonable at what must have been an infuriating situation. "It is far from the slightest wish or intention of the Department to place the slightest obstacle in the way of any officer of the American Navy when he wishes to change his colours for higher rank or more liberal wages. But he can not be permitted to serve two missions at the same time, and his resignation of one commission should precede any final or even preliminary engagements to accept another."

Moore, knowing time was running out, submitted his resignation to Secretary Paulding on July 8, 1839. Paulding inadvertently accepted it eight days later, then tried to rescind it when he realized who he had just discharged. But it was too late: Moore was a private citizen, outside the jurisdiction of the United States Navy, and he was free to accept whatever office Texas might offer him.

With Lamar in command and Moore at the helm, the Texas Navy had the two things it needed most: competent leadership and solid presidential support. Its assignment for the remainder of 1839 would be to complete its warships, recruit men, and prepare for operations against Mexico.

CHAPTER SEVENTEEN

Phoenix of the Sea

[The men of war] are, in the opinion of the Naval officers, and of all the professional men who have examined them, perfect models of naval architecture; their construction is excellent in every respect— for speed, as well as for strength and durability.
—Secretary of the Navy Louis P. Cooke, November 1839

1839 WAS A GLORIOUS YEAR for the Texas Navy. By the end of the year, the hard work of Commodore Moore, John Tod, Memucan Hunt, and others would bear fruit, giving Texas the promise of military power at sea that it could never hope to wield on dry land. One South Texas doctor wrote to his brother of the Navy's expansion, "Our Navy will be extended, and as we do not anticipate further operations by land either offensive or defensive, we look for the coercion of recognition to the Navy alone. Every arrival tells strongly of our increasing preparations."

Galveston, that rough but growing seaport, was the center of it all. Midshipman Cornelius C. Cox described Texas's principal port of entry a half-century later:

> The city of Galveston was not the attractive place that it is 50 years later. The population probably didn't exceed 2000, the Houses were plain wooden structures ranging from the little 10 x 12 shanty to the somewhat pretentious storehouse, and here & there a respectable-looking dwelling and of course the indispensable Hotels which were ample for the needs of Town. The wharves which in later years have formed a bulwark for the city from the storms and waves that come down from the North, had not been built—and on the occasion of my first visit, the steamer ran head on to the shore—or as near as the water would allow—and the passengers disembarked on staging from the Boat to the Shore. The storm which had swept over the Island in '37, had left many reminders of the visit. . . . But our new Navy rode at anchor in the harbour and made cheerful the otherwise gloomy prospect.

That new navy came to be when the elegant steamboat *Charleston* paddled her way up Galveston's East Pass under an American flag in mid-March of 1839. In her hold, she carried her dismounted cannon, designated as "merchandise" to evade U.S. neutrality laws. On March 22, she was re-registered as a Texas vessel and commissioned as the Steam Ship *Zavala*, after the Republic's *ad interim* vice-president, the late Lorenzo de Zavala.

Her first commander, Addison C. Hinton, was given the task of overhauling the steam packet as a warship. Commander Hinton and the Navy Yard's erstwhile commander, Lieutenant Taylor, assembled a team of carpenters, engineers and shipwrights to renovate the vessel and prepare her for a battery of eighteen-pounder guns. This small army crawled over the beached vessel, replacing paddle-wheel arms and paddles, shoring up decking, and making any repairs that could be done at Galveston's rudimentary shipyard.

In May, Commander Hinton suggested a number of improvements to Louis P. Cooke, who succeeded an increasingly uninterested Memucan Hunt in May 1839. Hinton requested permission (and a large budget) to step up three masts, which would allow her to conserve coal by using wind power on favorable days. He also asked to modify her decks, take off the steamer's saloon, build poop and forecastle decks, and reinforce her planking so that she could bear her battery more comfortably. Until she left for New Orleans in November to complete more extensive modifications, *Zavala* served as a tangible reminder to Galveston's citizens of the nation's commitment to its coastal defense.

Near the end of June, the first of the Dawson Contract vessels arrived. She was the sharp five-gun schooner *Viper*, bearing five sailors and passengers Samuel May Williams, Anson Jones, and Moses Austin Bryan, among others. Subsequently rechristened *San Jacinto*, she was assigned to Moore's most talented subordinate, Commander John T. K. Lothrop, a Massachusetts pilgrim's son who had worked his way up from the midshipman's ranks aboard *Brutus* and *Independence*. Once in port, *San Jacinto* was assigned a full complement of thirteen officers and sixty-nine sailors and marines.

On August 7, *San Jacinto* was joined by a second schooner, evidently named *Scorpion* but subsequently rechristened *San Antonio*. Built to the same specifications as her sister ship, she carried six twelve-pounders and a pivot gun. At the end of the month, the last of the three sisters, the schooner *Asp*—an exact copy of *San Antonio*—sailed into Galveston's harbor. According to the *Telegraph*, *Asp* was "represented as being a beautiful specimen of Naval architecture and highly creditable to the builders." She was soon renamed *San Bernard*, and with those four warships, the half-finished *Potomac* and the barely seaworthy harbor vessel *Louisville*, which was acquired the following month, Texas had the beginnings of a real fleet.

In early 1839, Lamar and Moore addressed the dearth of officers and sailors for the new fleet. A memorandum sent to Lamar sometime around the end of 1838 estimated that the new navy would require one post captain, a signal officer, six commanders, two commanding lieutenants, twenty-five lieutenants, seven sailing masters, eight pursers, seven surgeons, twelve master's mates, fifty-two midshipmen, eight gunners, eight boatswains, eight carpenters, eight sailmakers, ninety-nine petty officers, 355 able seamen, 305 ordinary seamen and 205 landsmen and boys. The memorandum pointed out that the United States was the best place to recruit these crewmen, although doing so would be a gross violation of U.S. law. From the seven officers and two sailors the Navy had at the beginning of 1838, Moore and Lamar had a long way to go.

But word of the beautiful new warships generated plenty of talk among the would-be admirals back east. Even before Lamar's inauguration, Texas agents began receiving applications for officers' commissions. They came from all over, seeking pay, prize money and opportunities for promotion. But for most of them, the greatest lure was sheer adventure, the chance to smell burning powder, to hear the roar of Neptune's thunder and to watch enemy ships strike their colors. These opportunities were denied men in the all-too-static fleets of Britain, France, and the United States, and gave the Texas Navy a way of standing out among the larger, better-established fleets of the day.

The proposals from these applicants all stressed an eagerness to serve the young republic that had arrested the imagination of her older cousin:

From N. T. Rosseter of Hudson, New York: "I am desirous, sir, of obtaining a warrant as Midshipman in the Texan Navy. . . . I have been informed through the Texan Minister that the Government is about purchasing several vessels for the Navy, and should be most happy to join the first that shall be sent to Texas."

William Howard of Brunswick, Georgia: "Having noticed in the Public Prints the non-acceptance of the Commission of Commander in Chief of the Navy of Texas, by Lieut Moore, I take the liberty of offering my Services to the Republic in that capacity."

J. P. Fisher of New York City: "I had, in the US Navy, participated in the Scenes of the late War, with Great Britain. . . . I have been from early life regularly bred in Neptunes School and desirous of becoming Your fellow Citizen. . . ."

William Bowers, Providence, Rhode Island: "Sir: Will you please inform me, as soon as your convenience will admit, what officers are wanted in the Texican Navy as commanders. . . ."

Most of the applicants never received any response, as the Navy needed good sailors far more than it needed amateur commanders. Because New Orleans was the logical recruiting ground, Moore quickly sent Commander Lothrop to the Mississippi mouth to recruit men and purchase supplies.

The close of the Third Congress in early 1839 gave President Lamar the opportunity to appoint naval officers on an interim basis without seeking the immediate consent of the Senate. Partly out of necessity, and partly in hope that the Senate would approve his appointments when Congress resumed, Lamar began appointing officers in March 1839. By the next session of Congress in November, Lamar had appointed one post captain, four commanders, twenty-five lieutenants, forty-four midshipmen, and twenty petty and warrant officers. These men hailed from many countries, states, and navies, and the final roster indicates that Lamar granted commissions based on merit, as best he could determine. Midshipmen and junior lieutenants of the U.S. Navy provided the best source of new recruits, although a number of officers had carried over from the original Texas Navy.

As officers began mustering into the service, Secretary Hunt began acquiring supplies for his new recruits. One of the first items on his lethal shopping list was a new type of pistol being manufactured by a hard-pressed inventor from Connecticut named Samuel Colt. In late March 1839, Hunt heard of a new five-shot revolving pistol through John Fuller, proprietor of a Washington, D.C., hotel whose son had just joined the Texas Navy. Fuller, who had picked up a "Paterson" model revolver from a New York arms dealer, extolled the virtues of the new weapon to President Lamar, War Secretary Albert Sidney Johnston, and Col. George W. Hockley, Johnston's predecessor. Hockley, a firm believer in "flint and steel," was dead-set against the newfangled percussion weapon, but Hunt evidently liked what he saw. At the end of April, Hunt ordered Post Captain Moore to purchase 180 of Colt's revolving carbines and a like number of his Number Five Model Paterson revolving pistols for the Navy's use. The Paterson revolver, the precursor to the "Gun that Won the West," was thus introduced to Texas through the foresight of the secretary of the navy, and the Navy's large order (filled the following August) temporarily saved Colt's company from financial ruin. These Patersons, along with cutlasses, Roman-style short swords, Bowie knives, tomahawks, pikes, muskets, and even battle axes, made up the small arms selection for men who would have to use them in close-in fighting.

Small arms, cannon, and sail are the most obvious items of necessity to a war fleet, but it should be remembered that the Texas Navy was establishing itself from the ground up. The Revolution's naval officers and department heads were long on courage, but short on organizational skills—at least, the kind necessary to make the transition from a revolutionary expedient to a well-regulated military establishment. Like a business that struggles to wrest itself from its "founders' mentality" and become a perpetual, working institution, the Texas Navy needed the tools for regulating its conduct on an intra-organizational basis. So the new Secretary of the Navy, Louis P. Cooke, authorized the purchase of treatises on courts-martial and maritime laws, blank ships's logs and midshipmen's journals, invoices, books on marine surveying, and clerical supplies ranging from writing papers to preprinted inventory forms. He purchased uniforms for his sailors and marines (frequently using U.S. military surplus), regulated officers' uniforms (one epaulet for a lieutenant, two for a commander or captain), and ensured that the Navy's regulations reflected established practices in the U.S. and British navies. Proving that all is fair in war, if not love, each vessel was also equipped with a set of "flags of all nations." Humble as it may have been, the Texas Navy was President Lamar's first step in obtaining international recognition of Texas as a regional, if not world power, and Secretary Cooke was determined to outfit the Navy in a respectable if not especially grand style.

Modern warships, particularly capital ships such as battleships and aircraft carriers, have been aptly described as "cities on the sea." While these vessels operate on a scale unimagined in Commodore Moore's day, the warships of the Age of Sail still required extensive planning and provisioning before they could weigh anchor. In the Texas Navy's great shopping spree of 1839, all vessels' department chiefs were kept busy loading, signing for, and storing the items entrusted to their care. Indeed, a great deal of an officer's time in those days was spent accounting for each item given to him, since lost items were, in theory, replaced out of the officer's paycheck. (In practice, Texas officers were rarely paid by their cash-strapped government, so charges against their salaries were generally meaningless.)

Supplies issued to the schooner *San Antonio*, Texas's smallest class of warship, illustrate the administrative, storage, and inventory chores performed by a ship's department heads in late 1839. On a single day in November, the master's department of the *San Antonio* was issued one barometer, one hanging compass, one thermometer, one sextant, one quadrant, one copy of Blount's *Coast Pilot*, nautical almanacs for the years 1839 and 1840, one chart of the Gulf of Mexico, one twenty-eight-second glass, two fourteen-second glasses, one chronometer, two Bowdiche's Navigators, one case of mathematical instruments and two spyglasses. That same day the gunner's department received ten Colt's revolving carbines, twelve cap primers, five hundred percussion caps, and twelve loading levers. The boatswain's department, for its part, was issued twenty-six-and-a-half pounds of marlin line, a like amount of hawseline, and one-half hank of sewing twine. And the purser's department, which was responsible for clothes, food, and sundry items, received seventeen jackets, thirty-four flannel shirts, and twelve pair of brogan shoes. The sixty-foot craft also received two-and-a-half cords of wood and 750 gallons of water from the transport schooner *Louisville* (nicknamed "*Striped Pig*"). It was these mundane items, not the thrill of battle, which occupied the vast majority of a ship's officer's time.

Spending the summer in New York and Baltimore, Commodore Moore returned to Texas aboard the steamship *Columbia*, arriving in Galveston on October 4. He met briefly with his officer corps for the first time, impressing even the pious purser Fleming Wells as "a man without ostentation or vanity and [who] wishes to seem no more than he is." From Galveston, Moore rode to Austin, which was about to be officially declared the new seat of government. He spent long hours with Secretary Cooke, working at the Navy Department's new headquarters on the west side of Austin's Congress Avenue, preparing for recruiting operations.

On October 18, the day after the new government arrived in Austin, the next Dawson warship, the 400-ton brig *Brazos* sailed into Galveston Bay, her sixteen medium eighteen-pounders jutting proudly from her gun portals. She carried a complement of nineteen officers and 112 men, and sported five fine boats lashed tightly to her 110-foot hull. Upon her arrival, she became the largest sailing vessel Texas owned. To mark her as Lamar's trophy—not Houston's—*Brazos*, named for the river on which Sam Houston's first capital stood, was soon rechristened *Colorado*, for the river on which Lamar's capital stood.

During the fall of 1839, Lamar, Cooke, Moore, Tod, and Hinton worked hard to get the fledgling navy in shape, although they encountered serious financial and political obstacles. Lamar, who had spent the summer appointing scores of naval officers, came under attack by the pro-Houston faction in Congress for making these recess appointments. His appointments had not become the *fait accompli* he had hoped, and he quickly withdrew his requests for commissions for the time being, hoping to let the political heat die down while the officers carried out their duties in unofficial capacities.

It was not to be. Ex-president Sam Houston, now a representative from San Augustine County, attacked Lamar's nationalist policies in the House, while Houston's supporters in the Senate raised a ruckus over Lamar's naval appointments. When Lamar responded to the Senate's inquiries about his appointments on January 3, he only made matters worse. The Senate's Committee on Naval Affairs investigated the matter, and Chairman Oliver Jones of Austin, an ardent Houstonite, wrote a vociferous minority opinion castigating Lamar for hiring far more officers (a total of ninety-six) than were needed for the sailors and marines they commanded (a total of ninety-nine).

The view that Lamar was encumbering his economy with a burdensome military establishment was taking root even among moderate politicians. Texas's U.S. ambassador, Anson Jones, quipped, "Texas is overwhelmed with Army & Navy officers—there are enough for Russia and poor Texas is without means to support them many weeks longer." When the Senate Committee recommended laying up the larger vessels "in ordinary"—partially dismantled for long-term storage until the need arose or funds were found—the ball began rolling on a defense bill that would lay up most of the Navy, throwing a wrench into Lamar's "peace through strength" strategy with Mexico.

With the attack on Lamar's naval appointments and other political initiatives (such as the continuing debate over moving the Texas capital from Houston to Austin), the battle for the future of Texas was joined. For the next three years, Sam Houston would fight a guerilla war from the opposition benches to quietly maneuver Texas into the arms of the United States, while Lamar held fast to his imperialist agenda. Since the Texas Army was all but disbanded during Houston's administration, the Texas Navy became the centerpiece of Lamar's foreign and military policies, making the Navy a lightning rod for anti-Lamar sentiments.

As the political skirmish lines erupted, Secretary Cooke faced opposition on a more practical level. The Senate began pressing him for progress reports on his survey of the harbors and coasts of Texas, a task never completed due to lack of funds. Cooke, meanwhile, lobbied vainly for additional funds for his department (an estimated $516,039.59 for the year 1840), and asked the Texas Congress to establish a liaison between the fleet and the Navy Department to supply the secretary, a landlubber, with technical information about his fleet's needs. These recommendations, like virtually all others, fell on deaf ears, or at least impoverished ones; the Republic had spent everything it had or would ever have on its seven shiny new ships, leaving nothing for the officers and civilians who ran them.

John Grant Tod's problems began exactly three minutes after his meeting with Lamar's first navy secretary, Memucan Hunt. Hunt was evidently under the impression that Tod was to be appointed a lieutenant aboard *Zavala* under Commander Hinton. Hunt told Tod to report to Hinton for orders until Tod could be sent to Baltimore to succeed Henry Williams as naval agent. The orders—and the implication that he would be junior to men less capable than himself—infuriated Tod, whose name had been bandied about previously as a possible secretary of the navy. Tod openly fretted that the old "cider-ant officers" of the original navy would outrank him. During a heated argument, Tod defiantly told Hunt that he would never accept a lieutenant's commission, since his services entitled him to a rank just below Commodore Moore, as he had been promised by the late commissioner Peter Grayson. He would just as soon take a lowly midshipman's warrant as serve under a Wheelwright or a Hinton, he declared.

The two men stormed out of their meeting, but Moore and James Hamilton managed to calm Tod by assuring him that he would have an active role in the command of the fleet. Apparently mollified, Tod came to his senses. He wrote a conciliatory letter to Hunt the next day, declaring that he would accept whatever duties his country required of him. Believing that he would indeed receive the number two spot, he wrote to his friend, Rep. George W. Hill, a week later. "I understand that I am to be second in command of the Navy! And rather than be driven from the field under such flattering prospects, I am quite reconciled to swallowing a bitter pill. . . ." Tod received his commission as commander in mid-1839, but the bitterness this pill left in Tod's stomach was, however, to grow stronger and more painful as the years passed.

Moore, as a Lamar appointee, soon became the natural focus of the embryonic wrath of Tod and Samuel May Williams, both Houston men, notwithstanding that both men respected Moore when he joined the Texas cause. Tod, never one to keep silent about his feelings, began complaining to Williams about Moore's "interference" with his work as naval agent. Williams confidently replied that Moore's actions were beginning to spawn enemies in government, and that should Moore go on a cruise against Mexico, opposition at home would rise up against him. This budding enmity would one day create major problems for Moore at a time when he most needed friends in government.

After Commander Hinton completed those upgrades he could make on *Zavala* in Galveston, Secretary Cooke sent him to New Orleans with detailed instructions to make additional renovations: reroute boiler pipes, alter the bulkheads, enlarge the hold, install throttle valves, and so on. In addition, Cooke ordered Hinton to recruit as many seamen, landsmen, and boys as his funds would allow, "being at the same time very cautious that you do not violate the neutrality of the United States." To fulfill these tasks, Hinton was given $9,000 through the account of Navy Agent William T. Brannum, which would be provided to *Zavala*'s purser upon Brannum's arrival in New Orleans. Of the $9,000 provided to Hinton, $1,000 was earmarked for the enlistment of marines, and another $2,200 was to be used for recruiting sailors, leaving him $5,800 to upfit *Zavala*. Hinton was also to purchase 576 rations and 1,000 barrels of coal for the Navy Yard, and send home some additional stationery for the clerks back in Galveston. After Hinton arrived in the Crescent City on November 20, he learned that Brannum had already spent $1,500 of the $5,800 repair allowance on other items, leaving only $4,300 to repair the ship and purchase rations, coal, and supplies. In December, Commodore Moore, writing from his flagship *Colorado*, ordered Hinton to overhaul *Zavala* on a scale much larger than that envisioned by Secretary Cooke.

It must have been apparent to Hinton that he could not possibly accomplish his mission with the funds provided by the Department, but he persevered. When *Zavala*'s chief engineer, George Beatty, requested new wheel arms, paddle buckets and other materials, Hinton got them. When new copper plating was needed for the ship's hull, Hinton found the materials. When contractors pointed out additional work that was needed, Hinton approved it. His secret was simple: he ignored his budget. When the cash ran out, he used the government's credit.

Unfortunately, Hinton's men could not extend credit to their government; contractors may forego payment for a month or two, but men cannot forego food or clothing with the same alacrity. By late November, *Zavala*'s officers were owed $3,000, but Brannum had only $500 to pay them. In a letter to Secretary Cooke, Hinton estimated that his expenses would exceed his budget by $4,000.

Cooke replied to Hinton with a cold warning more characteristic of a minister appointed by Sam Houston than Mirabeau Lamar. "You appear to have forgotten the very first principle of naval discipline, to wit: that *the first duty of an officer, as well as a seaman, consists in obeying orders.* If you have so far transcended yours, as to purchase *anything* for which you can not show definite orders, be assured that you will be held responsible; and you furthermore are strictly forbidden from incurring, under any pretext whatever, any liabilities against the Government for repairs. . . ."

On January 11, 1840, Commander Hinton began hearing rumblings from Galveston that the government was going to hold him accountable for exceeding his budgetary authority; bad feelings between Hinton and *San Antonio*'s commander, Lt. Francis Wright, did not help Hinton's cause. It was no surprise, then, that when Hinton's estimated cost overrun climbed to $7,000, and ultimately to $14,000, the Navy Department dismissed him. On February 6, 1840, Cooke persuaded President Lamar to revoke Hinton's commission and dismiss him from the service.

An embittered Hinton returned to Galveston and wrote to President Lamar, asking for an explanation. When his letter went unanswered, he penned an indignant letter to Secretary Cooke. "I hereby call upon the Navy Department for a 'Court of Enquiry' upon my conduct, touching the cause of my dismissal in New Orleans, no reason as yet having been assigned for it, in contradistinction to which, even a Midshipman has been dismissed from the Navy, on a Home Station, to whom reason were courteously assigned, why that officer was dismissed."

This letter, too, went unanswered, so Hinton petitioned Congress for reinstatement. Congress ultimately passed a law declaring, "It shall not hereafter be lawful to deprive any officer in the Military or Naval service of this Republic, for any misconduct in office of his commission, unless by sentence of a court martial." The law was not retroactive, so it did not help Hinton, but Congress did pass a separate resolution directing the Secretary of the Navy to organize a court-martial to try formal charges against the Commander.

Hinton ultimately was acquitted of any wrongdoing, but justice, as so often happens, arrived too late to do much good. In early 1842, Congress passed a resolution clearing Hinton of "any act of misconduct reflecting upon him as an officer or gentleman whilst a commander in the Navy of this Republic," but it did not reinstate him.

Hinton was sacrificed for *Zavala*'s refitting, but he could take some pleasure in knowing that he helped build the finest ship in the Texas fleet, and the most advanced warship in the western hemisphere. Before his dismissal, Hinton was able to report to the Department that the steamer's hull was "extraordinarily strong," and she could make twelve to sixteen knots in fair weather with all three boilers fired and pumping. With a load of good Pittsburgh coal, she could keep a head of steam for twenty-five days if necessary. Secretary Cooke in turn reported candidly to President Lamar, "[O]n the return of the Zavala to Galveston, her natural efficiency was found to be very much increased, and I have no hesitation in saying that the unauthorized repairs were essentially needed, and they would have been suggested by the proper authority, except for the consciousness of inability to pay for them." If properly managed, Cooke predicted, the eight-gun *Zavala* "will be of a much greater national advantage to this Government than both the Brigs contemplated by the act of Congress." Cooke's pronouncements were not the usual political puffery; his opinion of the war steamer was consistent with that of every officer who served aboard her, from Commodore Moore down to the lowly middies.

CHAPTER EIGHTEEN

Wintertime in New York

If any new and well founded complaints are made against any Naval officer in the service of your Government the President will deem it his duty to exclude the vessels of war to which they belong from the waters of the United States.
—U.S. Secretary of State John Forsyth to Texas Minister Richard Dunlap

WHILE COMMANDER HINTON WAS DOING HIS BEST to execute impossible orders, Commodore Moore took up residence aboard the brig *Colorado*, raising the broad blue pennant of a squadron commander atop the vessel's mainmast, signifying its status as the Texas flagship. From Galveston, he dispatched Lt. Francis Wright and Marine Capt. John Parker to New Orleans aboard the schooner *San Antonio* to pick up men recruited by Commander Hinton and his officers.

San Antonio's brief errand was wracked by desertions, the theft of the schooner's boats, and tall stacks of unpaid bills. Commander Hinton, who held a grudge against Wright, grumbled to Secretary Cooke, "Her bills unsettled, the Sheriff with numbers of writs against her commander for private debts. Since his arrival Mr. Wright literally playing hide and go seek to avoid the bailiff & last left them unpaid; and almost every body with curses in their mouths, some against the whole Navy, others against Mr. Wright especially." Because Hinton lacked sufficient funds to provide proper recruiting bonuses, the harvest of recruits there was quite disappointing.

Lacking enough men to put the fleet to sea, Commodore Moore prepared for a recruiting call of his own at the Port of New York. Moore selected New York on the recommendation of Gen. Richard Dunlap, Texas's minister to the United States. Although it would be a gross violation of the Neutrality Act of 1818 to recruit sailors on U.S. soil, Dunlap reasoned that in such a great harbor a small naval brig would not attract much attention, and the large number of merchant sailors and former U.S. Navy men there would provide fine prospects for the Lone Star's recruiters. Taking what little bonus money he could scrape together, Moore picked the best men from his subordinate vessels, and made sure they were outfitted in exceptionally fine uniforms when they presented themselves to potential recruits.

After a brief stop in New Orleans, Moore's *Colorado* sailed to New York, arriving at the harbor on December 9, 1839, after a remarkably short voyage. *Colorado* rounded the southern tip of the island and anchored so that the Battery stood between Moore's flagship and the Brooklyn Navy Yard. This exposed *Colorado* to chunks of ice floating down the Hudson River, but it shielded Moore and his officers from prying eyes in the Navy Yard, some belonging to officers who vividly recalled Moore's earlier attempts to lure good men away from United States service.

Following accepted protocol, the Navy Yard's commandant, Commodore James Renshaw, sent Moore a written greeting. "I have directed the gunners at Ellis Island to receive your Powder for temporary safe keeping and shall take pleasure in extending you such other facilities as are in my power." Moore sent his powder ashore, commenced overhauling the ship's empty magazines, and began purchasing small arms and supplies for the Navy with his $40,000 budget.

While Moore was going about the city, buying goods for his ships and men, his officers haunted the taverns, dockyards, and boarding houses of Manhattan, looking for more than a few good men. Clad in their sharp new uniforms, carrying shiny new swords and newfangled Colt sidearms, they must have exuded the kind of cutting-edge confidence President Lamar wished to project upon the world.

They set up clandestine meetings ashore with sailors who wanted to sail for Texas. The rations, pay, and conditions were the same as the U.S. Navy the officers promised, but since Texas was at war with Mexico, recruits would see action and adventure, capture enemy ships, and collect prize money. These opportunities, combined with the reputation of the new Texian commander and the twenty-dollar enlistment bonus, sealed the deal for 157 sailors and midshipmen. They signed statements claiming to be free men "hailing from Texas and calling themselves Texians," and came aboard *Colorado* for life in the Texas Navy.

The fine haul of seamen came to an abrupt end at the close of December. On December 30, 1839, Lt. Charles Hunter of the USS *North Carolina* filed an affidavit in federal court averring that Commodore Moore was recruiting on United States soil. The next day, Moore and four local accomplices were arrested and charged with Neutrality Act violations. Texas agents, who had anticipated such a move, came to Moore's rescue; he was released on $1,000 bail, and a lawyer was retained to refute the charges against him, at least until he could get clear of U.S. territory. Moore's officers continued their work for a few more days, but Moore could not obtain any more receipts for the $3,000 in enlistment bonuses and shipping costs he paid, since the enlistments officially never happened.

Moore's stay in New York might have been prolonged, but the recurring neutrality violations came to the attention of Secretary of State John

Forsyth—the same beleaguered official who had wrangled with Mexican and Texian officials over the *Correo* and *Pocket* affairs. Although Richard Dunlap assured Forsyth that Moore was under strict orders to abstain from recruiting on U.S. soil, a nonplussed Forsyth replied that if Moore's activities continued, he would bar all Texian war vessels from U.S. ports, a threat that effectively ended Moore's recruiting trip.

On January 3, Moore retrieved his powder from the Brooklyn magazine and prepared to weigh anchor for home. He tarried for several more days, enduring harsh newspaper reports of Texian press gangs, complaints to the local marshal's office, and charges by the British consul that Moore was holding a British subject aboard *Colorado* against his will. Blandly assuring Dunlap that he had never violated U.S. neutrality laws, Moore headed into the Atlantic on January 20, his brig loaded with plenty of new faces to man his fine fleet.

When *Colorado* pulled into Galveston Harbor nineteen days later, Moore must have grinned from ear to ear at the sight that awaited him. In addition to the eight-gun *Zavala* and the three nimble schooners of war, he saw for the first time his new flagship, the 600-ton sloop of war *Texas*. This fine flush-deck sloop had three tall masts fully rigged with billowing square sails, which propelled the ship and her battery across the waves with the grace and speed of a clipper. Her Georgia pine decks easily bore the weight of eighteen medium twenty-four-pounder guns and two medium eighteens. About the size of Moore's former sloops, *Boston, Fairfield,* and *Hornet*, the new flagship could carry a full complement of 60 officers, 226 sailors, and 26 marines. Her spacious holds could accommodate hundreds of pounds of black powder, 8,000 gallons of water, and 20,000 pounds of sea biscuit, in addition to spirits, navigational equipment, slops (clothing and sundries), small arms, tools, and other items necessary for life at sea. At her stern she had a spacious commodore's cabin with two swinging cots, eight staterooms for her lieutenants, surgeon, and purser, and hammock space for the men. To shuttle her crew about, she carried a twenty-six foot launch and four smaller boats. She was the only fighting ship Texas ever owned (the rest were technically vessels), but she was a beauty. If Moore needed anything more to impress his new recruits, or his adopted government, *Texas* certainly gave it to him.

By the time *Colorado* eased into her moorings at Galveston Harbor, Moore, Lamar, Cooke, and Tod had created a navy in every sense of the word. From six officers and two derelict sailors, the Texas Navy had acquired ships and men and an organization. It had everything a navy needs to sustain itself, except for a tradition of honor, glory, and great deeds of arms under its proud ensign. And Moore was determined to make sure that those last items were won at the expense of Mexico, none too soon.

CHAPTER NINETEEN

The Seafaring Life

Life at sea is, no doubt, a beautiful mode of existence to a poetic soul allied with a cast-iron or bronze stomach; but to an individual who regards the comforts of life, the continuous shocks to his nervous system, and the complete overthrow of gravitation, are annoyances that can only be balanced by the delightful convictions that at least he cannot be worried by a mad bull. . . .

—Lt. Alfred G. Gray, 1854

MANY OF THE OFFICERS AND SAILORS Moore harvested from New Orleans and New York were an experienced lot, but they had never worked together before. Few knew how their comrades would perform while battling the enemy or the sea, so each man's instinct was to work and fight as an individual, not as a team. Many had served in other navies, but the green recruits—notwithstanding that they claimed to "hail from Texas and call themselves Texians"—had little or no idea of what Texas asked of them. (Several, in fact, believed that they were signing on to build public roads, not sail ships.)

The recruits needed regulations, they needed training, they needed inspiration. They needed that *esprit de corps* that makes sailors cheer when their captain asks them to take to battle, when all rational instincts should drive them away from the possibility of a violent, horrible death. Commodore Moore spent the spring of 1840 imparting these qualities to his men.

The first order of business was to distribute the coveted command assignments. Working from a ramshackle office in Galveston's Navy Yard, Moore assigned Lt. William Postell, a former midshipman from the U.S. sloop *Grampus*, temporary command of the flagship. Lt. James O'Shaunessy, a former midshipman from the U.S. sloop *Concord*, was to command the schooner *San Antonio*, and Lt. William S. Williamson was given *San Bernard*. Commander J. T. K. Lothrop took charge of the steamer *Zavala*, while Lt. James Gibbons was assigned to *San Jacinto*. The brig *Colorado* went to Captain Wheelwright, whom Lamar had rehired, apparently to spite Houston. Lt. Downing H. Crisp, a Royal Navy midshipman who had served aboard *Brutus*, commanded the dilapidated receiving brig *Potomac*, while Lt. Thurston M. Taylor, a former purser from the *Grampus*, commanded the Navy Yard. The vessels were assigned subordinate officers and men, while Moore revised naval regulations and conferred with Secretary Cooke on matters of naval policy.

It was in these spirited, fair-weathered days of the Texas Navy that shipboard routines began to take hold. The white-jacketed sailors were mustered into divisions and assigned tasks commensurate with their experience and talents. The petty officers drilled the sailors, the warrant officers organized their departments, and the lieutenants, assisted by midshipmen, supervised the lot of them. The marines practiced with small arms and learned the basic duties of landsmen. Slowly, these clumsy, frustrated men began to master their routines, and as they did, a slow yet ultimately impressive transformation took place, like a new ball team as it progresses through its inaugural season, or a band of musicians playing together for the first time. These men became a crew.

The process was not without its snags, and snags usually brought beatings, often with a cat-o'-mine-tails or a "colt," a knotted length of rope. "Some of our men were real land lubbers," Midshipman Cox recalled of Gibbons's *San Jacinto*, "and of course had to be drilled in the duties of the ship—but to run up the rigging and out on the yard arms, and swing yourself like a monkey by one hand or balance yourself on a foot rope 40 feet in the air and furl and unfurl sails like an old Tar was just what the recruit could not do, but the Liet had great faith in the 'Colt' and for every blunder, poor Jack would have to come down—and lay himself across the gun and receive a dozen from the Boatswain's mate." *Colorado*'s crew proved almost incapable of maneuvering the nimble brig into her moorings the first time she entered Galveston's harbor, and Moore's officers, never better than passed midshipmen in the U.S. Navy, were unable to rig their own ships. If the crews were going to war, they had many lessons to learn.

Moore and Cooke made great strides that winter, addressing the Navy's many personnel and equipment problems as best they could. Moore dispatched a team of veteran sailors to inspect each ship, overhaul its rigging, and fix faulty equipment. He then sent his warships out into the Gulf, one or two at a time, short distances from Galveston to get the crews on their sea legs. At a higher level, Secretary Cooke finally swept away the last remnants of the old navy commanders, cashiering the besotted "General Boots" and the equally inebriated Lt. Francis Wright.

When the Age of Sail drew to a close, it put an end to shipboard routines that had been established, more or less, for the last hundred years. The typical day would go something like this: Just before four in the morning, the drum and fife play "reveille" to rouse the sleepy, muttering sailors from their hammocks. At that time, the end of the midwatch (which runs from midnight until four in the morning) is signaled by eight rings of the ship's bell—one for every half hour—followed by the cry of, "All hands—Up all hammocks!" The midshipman of the watch scurries down to steerage, where the midshipmen sleep, rudely shakes his sleeping successor, and bawls into the dazed midshipman's ear, "Eight bells! I'll thank you to relieve me!"

As the bleary-eyed watchman stumbles up the ladders to the deck, he passes sailors scurrying topside with their hammocks, which are rolled up and lashed to the hammock rail under the watchful eye of the quartermaster. The sailors fetch buckets of water, pails of sand, and soft, abrasive sandstones called holystones, and the crew scrubs down the pine decks, pushing away the excess water with a large leather hoe called a squilgee. By the time the process is finished, the deck is clean enough to eat from; Midshipman George Fuller would later reminisce, "There was nothing on earth so clean as an old sailing man-o' war."

With the deck thoroughly scrubbed, the crew's attention turns to the running rigging and sails. The running rigging is the system of lines, blocks and tackles that the crew adjusts to maneuver the yardarms and sails, which in turn regulate the ship's speed. (The standing rigging, by contrast, is the pitch-covered network of lines more or less permanently affixed to the masts and hull, keeping the masts upright; these include the ladder-like ratlines one sees men climbing up and down to get to the upper reaches of the masts.) The running rigging is "flemished," or laid out in flat mat-like coils on the deck for the quartermaster's inspection. As the morning watch ends, the night pennant is hauled down, the Texas jack runs up the gaff, and the commodore's broad blue pennant is raised atop the main masthead.

Assuming no problems, the process of cleaning the ship and ensuring that its rigging is satisfactory takes about four hours, and just before eight a.m., at the end of the morning watch, the quartermaster checks the ship's hourglass. The quartermaster of the watch touches his hat towards the midshipman and reports, "Eight bells, sir." The midshipman reports this to the officer of the deck, who nods and orders, "Report it to the commodore, sir." The midshipman scurries down to the commodore's cabin and reports eight bells, to which the commodore replies, "Make it so, sir, and pipe to breakfast." The midshipman runs back to the quartermaster, who strikes the bell eight times, and the boatswain blows his fife to signal breakfast, followed by the eagerly awaited call, "Grog!"

Grog, that immortal drink so essential to the well being and morale of the men, is served just before breakfast and dinner. In the Royal Navy, grog consisted of one part brandy or rum watered down with one to four parts water, usually mixed with lemon or lime juice and brown sugar. In the Texas Navy, the active ingredient would be whiskey near Texas or Louisiana ports, local rum on an extended cruise. At 8:00 a.m., the men of the watch line up while the purser's steward hauls the grog-tub and three tin cups up the port gangway. Under the watchful eye of the master's mate, each man files past the purser, drains his tin cup dry, and moves along for breakfast.

Breakfast—as well as dinner and supper—is poor by civilian standards, but it keeps the men going. Each man is allotted, in theory, something over a pound of beef or pork each day except Friday, as well as a ration of cheese, rice, beans, raisins, or molasses, depending on the day of the week. Bread, either in loaves or crackers, was issued at the rate of twelve ounces per day, and hot tea, coffee, tobacco, and, of course, grog was issued throughout the week. This is the theoretical ration; however, allowances have to be made for food that became rancid, worm-eaten, or inedible for any of a host of reasons stemming from the way victuals are stored at sea in the nineteenth century. Midshipman Cox later recalled the Navy's standard fare:

> Texas was poor in that day and could not furnish her pantrys with many delicasys. Salt Beef, Salt pork Beans Tea and "hard tack" were the staples. Our crackers were nearly always old musty and full of worms. The worms were easily disposed of by heating the bread and then knocking them out—or soaking the crackers in hot tea, they are easy Killed and I never discovered any difference in the taste of the worms and the Bread.

Occasionally, however, Jack Tar finds that better fare can be had. Turtles can be captured and kept aboard ship as a source of fresh meat, and resting points such as the Arcas Islands provide a supply of fresh birds and eggs for the grateful tars. Additionally, when a naval vessel makes its way into port, it is usually set upon by a flotilla of merchant boats purveying all the comforts and conveniences denied at sea. The prices were usually high. As Lt. Alfred Gray, a former midshipman of the *Grampus*, wrote of one visit to Sisal, "We were scarcely anchored when our ship was surrounded by shore-boats loaded with tropical fruit, and an immense trade was carried on for a short time with the most unmitigated set of yellow-faced land sharks that ever attacked a ship's crew. Absurd ideas of the relative value of Mexican and American coin on the part of these descendants of the Caciques, told fearfully on our finances, and a board of Wall Street brokers might have acquired some valuable hints upon foreign exchange sharing our experience."

After breakfast, the men drill at the great guns or small arms, while the idlers—specialists such as carpenters, cooks, and sailmakers, who are not part of the watch—go about their duties. (In the days when powder was expensive and hard to store aboard a ship at sea, gun drills generally included all movements of the gun crews except actually firing their piece; since the object of all warships since Nelson's day had been to close with the enemy before firing, long-range target practice was virtually unheard of.)

If punishment was to be meted out, it would generally be carried out in the morning. Lesser offenses, such as insolence to a minor officer or negligent performance, could warrant double-duty, heavily watered grog, or confinement to cabin. Graver offenses, such as theft or falling asleep on duty, could result in confinement in irons or flogging. The death penalty, carried out by hanging from the foreyard, was available for a number of crimes, including sleeping while on watch, sodomy, mutiny, desertion, and murder. The ultimate sentence was only officially imposed on one occasion, as we shall see, but it appears that during the Texas Revolution's early days, at least one commander, Captain Hurd of the schooner *Brutus,* had two men summarily shot for attempted mutiny.

For commissioned officers, penalties such as flogging were forbidden, except by sentence of court-martial. But to the midshipmen, sailors and marines, the awful threat of corporal punishment depended entirely on the personality of the ship's commander. Commodore Moore, it appears, was fairly lenient with his use of the "cats," or cat-o'-nine-tails, a leather whip with nine knotted rawhide strips. Other commanders, such as Captain Hurd or *San Jacinto*'s Lieutenant Gibbons, favored liberal use of the cats. Gibbons in particular was recalled by one midshipman as "the most tiranical officer that I have ever Known in either the navy or army," although *San Jacinto*'s deck logs indicated that under later, more compassionate commanders, the somber order "All hands to witness punishment" was virtually never called out.

When a sentence of flogging was executed, the unfortunate seaman was led by the master-at-arms to the vessels' side, stripped to the waist. His hands were tied to the standing rigging, his back to the deck, and his feet were secured to a bilge grate on which he stood. The ship's marines were lined up, arms shouldered, and the culprit was flanked by the boatswain and the physician. At six bells (11:00 a.m.), all hands were summoned by divisions to witness the punishment, and the articles of war were read aloud. The boatswain then began his work while the lashes were counted. Midshipman Cox recalled the sight. "At each stroke of the lash the solemn count, 1-2-3 & so on was proclaimed aloud and the poor criminal would cringe & grunt at every blow—by the time the 3 doz, the usual compliment, were given, the fellow's bare back was varagated with the colors read black blue & white—and the blood running in little rivers at his feet." The surgeon, checking the victim's pulse throughout his ordeal, was authorized to suspend, but not commute, the punishment if he felt the prisoner might expire. The bloody pulp of a sailor was then carried back to the sickbay, where his flayed, open back was treated until he was fit to return to duty.

Dinner, the sailors' main meal, was piped at the beginning of the afternoon watch (12 to 4 p.m.), preceded by the obligatory grog. After dinner, men who were not on duty were free to pursue their personal chores and pastimes. Sailors would mend clothing, gather and talk, exercise or find other ways to fend off the monotony of life at sea. Midshipman Cox recalled, "I made myself a straw hat—and one pair of pants while in the service & had my arms tattooed as all old sailors do."

Another ancient tradition was singing old sailors' songs. Lieutenant Gray found particular amusement in these afternoon pursuits. "There is one feature in a briny transit through the world, especially as seen on board a man-of-war, that is perfectly delightful to one of a keen perception of the ludicrous and the humorous," he wrote, "and that is the impromptu concerts of the sailors in the dog-watches. To quietly establish oneself in the vicinity of some 20 or 30 old bearded tars, to watch the contortions of features when modestly and bashfully declining to sing, and the transfer of the invitation to the mess-mate; and when the blushing circle have all refused, to be startled by the sudden outburst of a preparatory note from the most inflexible one—suggesting an astonished hippopotamus, and to listen to the interminable verses which sing the deeds of some impossible pirate . . . is one of the most delightful of entertainments, especially if the nautical gentleman adds to the touching sentiment of the verse the charm of a voice which blends a bass with a falsetto, and is given to trills and shakes, and original roulades."

At four in the afternoon come the "dog watches," two-hour evening shifts from four to six, and six to eight, that split the day into seven watches, not six, so that the crews take turns taking the middle watch (eight to midnight) and morning watch (midnight to four). This alternating routine governs the sailors, boys, and marines, as well as midshipmen and junior lieutenants who were assigned to oversee them.

For young midshipmen, in particular, it was a hard life; as Midshipman Cox wrote, "a boy of the age of 14 & 15 has not physical capacity to perform the regular watch on shipboard—4 hours on duty and eight off—with 2 'dog watches'—4 to 6 & 6 to 8 P.M. each day . . ." Cox recalled, "On one occasion tired nature dropped me into the arm of Morphius—when I should have been walking the deck—this was death by the regulations—Liut Gibbons commuted the punishment to double duty for 2 weeks—In discharging the sentence I forfeited my life several times—but as it was necessary to discover the offense before inflicting the punishment I escaped hanging, always by timely warning."

Officers, by contrast, lived the life of gentlemen, at least in theory. They dined together on special food they purchased with loans or advances on their pay and were free from the threat of flogging, or worse, in the absence of a formal court-martial. They purchased their own uniforms, which were patterned after those of the Royal Navy, although several months of hard use and poverty generally wore their fine threads to rags.

The crews did retain a few traditions reflecting their frontier heritage. From time to time, the men or midshipmen would petition their commander in the manner of a volunteer militia for the redress of grievances, generally lack of pay or adequate clothing. They also wore their hair long, in a manner that disgusted one British diplomat. "The schooners are pretty vessels but I can't say the same for the others neither can I for the *officers of the Texas*

Navy generally speaking," snorted British consul Francis C. Sheridan. "These take a delight, after the effeminate fashion of the French, in allowing the hair to grow down the back, which of all the damnable fooleries ever introduced is the most damnable. It is neither cleanly or becoming, and is infinitely more ridiculous than if they were to turn it up behind and stick a large tortoise shell comb with gold knobs on it, after the manner of women. But if it is bad when there is no artificial or natural curl, what is it when there is no curl at all and when their hair hangs down like the matted ends of a wet swab—and this is generally the case with these officers." Whether Her Majesty's consul held the same opinion of the long-shanked Lord Nelson, England's greatest naval hero, is not recorded.

While the fleet was in training, President Lamar suffered a string of political setbacks. The Fourth Congress passed a bill that effectively disbanded the army, and there was growing opposition to Lamar's plans for comprehensive public education. On February 5, 1840, Congress went one step further, laying up nearly the entire fleet unless Mexico again threatened the Texas coast.

With disasters rolling in from Congress, Commodore Moore spent a portion of the spring shoring up the Navy's political support. He frequented the Navy Department headquarters in Austin to confer with Cooke and Lamar, and by early April his relationship with Lamar was solid enough that he was frequently able to bypass Secretary Cooke and take orders directly from the commander in chief. Moore also courted the opposition, inviting Representative Houston and his retinue aboard *Colorado* in late February, giving the former president a seventeen-gun salute. He repeated this gesture in early March, inviting Houston to visit the flagship *Texas*, this time giving him an eighteen-gun salute. When Houston saw the first-rate shape of the officers, men, and ships of Moore's fleet, he remarked to Francis Moore, editor of the *Telegraph* (no relation to the commodore) that he was pleasantly surprised by the outstanding quality of the reborn navy. "Gen. Houston," Moore wrote to Lamar, "says he did not know that the navy was so well fitted for service and has quite changed his opinion. He thinks the vessels ought to be sent to sea immediately, and regrets that he made any opposition to the 'navy bill.'" In mid-April, Commodore Moore hosted an elegant ball aboard his flagship, "said to excel any thing of the kind that was ever given in Texas," to advance public support for the service. But it was too little, too late. The naval retrenchment law of February 5, 1840, straitjacketed the Navy, and with the return of John Grant Tod from Baltimore, life was about to get more complicated.

In the spring of 1840, Commander John Tod was wrapping up his business in Baltimore. As naval agent to the United States, Tod had overseen the construction of six magnificent warships, and he developed a lasting friendship with the corpulent, gregarious Frederick Dawson, the contractor who built the fleet. With the arrival of the brig *Dolphin* in Galveston on April 25, 1840, Dawson's part of the contract was completed, and Tod went to great lengths to praise the ships Dawson had built. "I feel it is a duty," said Tod in a letter to Dawson, "as well as a pleasure to express to you the satisfaction I have in testifying to the very creditable and liberal manner in which the contract has been fulfilled on your part."

Tod went out of his way to laud Dawson's work because it reflected well on the man who oversaw the construction. He evidently felt he would need this credit when he lobbied for a sea assignment as second-in-command of the Navy. On May 9, 1840, Tod left New York with his slave, Perry Marshal, and Marshal's free wife Francis, who worked as Tod's personal cook. Upon his arrival in Galveston on the first of June, Tod was welcomed by a delegation of the city's elders, including navy stalwart Thomas McKinney, and a public dinner was offered in his honor at the Tremont Hotel, the Republic's grandest establishment. Tod declined, citing the urgent press of public business, but he penned a letter of thanks to the delegation, crediting Henry Williams of Baltimore and several officers of the U.S. Navy with providing valuable assistance to the project. Tod quickly made his way to Austin, where he presented voluminous reports to Secretary Cooke highlighting Dawson's fine work and faith in the Texas government to pay him when the time came.

Had he been appointed to the post, as some had predicted, Tod might have been the greatest navy secretary the Republic of Texas ever produced. He certainly had more knowledge of ship construction and naval operations than any other naval secretary did, and unlike Commodore Moore, he possessed an uncanny ability to maneuver seamlessly between the military and civilian establishments.

But Tod, like most officers, did not see himself commanding a desk; he wanted a ship. He wanted adventure. He wanted a showcase for his bravery and tactical skill. His appointment as commander of the Navy Yard in 1840 no doubt disappointed him—a desk assignment was no way to win laurels and springboard into the top spot. Tod's unrequited ambition, and budding problems that could be traced to Dawson's workmanship, would soon put him into conflict with Commodore Moore.

While Congress was moving to place the Navy in ordinary, President Lamar took an apparently spontaneous moment to address one last matter of civilian housekeeping: renaming the Dawson contract ships. On April 20, as Moore busied himself in Secretary Cooke's Congress Avenue office, Lamar burst in and announced that he wanted the larger vessels' names changed. The brig *Dolphin*, which had been renamed *Brazos*, was to become *Branch*

T. Archer, after Lamar's secretary of war, while her sister ship, *Colorado,* became *Wharton,* after the two notable Texas diplomats. The sloop-of-war *Texas,* meanwhile, was renamed *Austin,* joining the three Dawson schooners—*Viper, Scorpion,* and *Asp*—which had been previously rechristened *San Jacinto, San Antonio,* and *San Bernard.* Secretary Cooke, unaware of the name changes, groused in a letter to Gen. Albert Sidney Johnston afterwards, "In this matter I have not been the least consulted—Gen. came in to the office whilst I was out and instructed Comd're Moore to make the changes. The Austin City Gazette is giving hell to the administration and Lamar. The Colorado people are much displeased at it."

These warships, plus *Zavala,* still being overhauled in New Orleans, would constitute the mightiest fleet Texas ever possessed, and these Texians were about to make their debut on the world stage.

CHAPTER TWENTY

Gunboat Diplomacy

> *Should you receive a despatch from Mr. Treat informing you that he has failed in his negotiations, you will in that event be authorized to cruise against the Mexican vessels, and make prizes of them.*
> —President Lamar to Commodore Moore, June 20, 1840

IN THE LATE SPRING OF 1840, Commodore Moore was putting the finishing touches on his fleet training. Though ostensibly limited by Congressionally mandated personnel reductions, Moore, encouraged by Lamar, drilled his full complement of men until they acquitted themselves well in both appearance and performance. As the summer of 1840 crept over the calendar's horizon, the men were in high spirits. There were still problems from time to time—a marine was shot in the act of desertion, the Navy Yard's office was broken into and ransacked, and three deserters made off with *Austin*'s gig—but by and large the men, the officers, and especially the commander, were ready to show the world what they could do.

The adjournment of the Fourth Texas Congress in the spring of 1840 provided President Lamar with more or less a free hand to conduct foreign policy as he wished, without legislative interference. Since 1838, Lamar had taken the position that "The protection of our maritime frontier . . . is a public duty," and in late 1840, Lamar would defend his failure to lay the Navy in ordinary by claiming, "It was confidently asserted in the papers of the United States, and as confidently believed here, that the Mexican Government had made a contract in Europe for the purchase of several vessels of war, and that she had actually procured an armed steam ship from a commercial house in England, with a view of making a descent upon the coast of Texas."

For all Lamar's tendencies to generalize and disparage based on race, he recognized that not all Mexicans could be considered enemies of Texas. The United States of Mexico had for centuries been home to a large number of diverse cultures, including Spanish *peninsulares*, native Mexicans (such as Tlascalan, Aztec, and Chichimeca), native Texans (for instance, Comanche,

Waco, and Karankawa), Mayans and Toltecs, plus a small number of Anglo-Americans, Creoles, and non-Spanish Europeans. Over hundreds of years, many of these groups intermarried to become *mestizos*, people of mixed race, while others retained their original genetic, ethnic, or cultural structures.

The cultural and geographic diversity within Mexico's empire, ranging from Northern California to Yucatán, frustrated Mexico City's efforts to govern effectively and plagued the struggling republic long after Texas left its ranks. Yucatán and Campeche on the peninsula, Tabasco in the swampy south, and the Rio Grande region in the north presented particular problems for the central government, and at one time or another, all sought an alliance with Texas. In February 1840, Yucatán declared for federalism, which was tantamount to a revolt against the central government. *Federalistas* drove centralist forces out of most of Yucatán, and in June the last centralist stronghold on the peninsula, the garrisoned port of Campeche, surrendered to the federalists. Soon afterwards, Yucatán sent feelers to Texas with the idea of an eventual military alliance against Mexico. Similar uprisings in the Rio Grande region and Tabasco tied down other government troops in the principal cities of those regions.

If Lamar could keep Mexico preoccupied with any of these dissenting provinces, he reasoned that Mexico would be unable to turn its considerable resources against Texas. This need to find a federalist ally thus became the great exception to Lamar's implacable hostility to the Mexican people.

Yucatán, in particular, seemed a promising choice. Lamar explained Yucatán's position to Congress: ". . . instead of unifying with the benighted, the corrupt, the Priest-ridden portions of Mexico, for our extermination, they are themselves at war with the very power that withholds our rights, and seeks our distruction. . . . Every blow that they deal upon the bigotry and tyranny of Mexico, is as beneficial to us as it is to them." To Lamar, active support of Yucatán seemed to be the greatest assurance of the safety of the Republic.

Balanced against Lamar's efforts to keep Mexico in a perpetual state of instability was his desire for recognition by the great European powers of the world, particularly Great Britain, the greatest maritime power of the age. The United States formally recognized the Republic of Texas in March 1837, but soundly rejected its request to join the Union the following August, and rejected it again in 1838. In 1836 President Jackson had personally favored annexation, but the Whig Party vociferously opposed any extension of slavery, which Texas annexation would entail, while southern Democrats were unwilling to fight the political battles necessary to override opponents of annexation. The issue would be revisited between 1837 and 1845 during the administrations of Martin Van Buren, John Tyler, and James K. Polk, but for the moment, Texas had to swallow the rebuff and go it alone.

Her Britannic Majesty's Foreign Minister Lord Palmerston had rejected the Texians' application for recognition during Sam Houston's administration, in part due to the slavery question. The mere fact that Texas permitted indentured servitude was obnoxious enough to British popular opinion (and injurious to the competitiveness of Britain's West Indies plantations), but tolerance of the international slave *trade*—an industry reviled throughout Western Europe—presented political problems no prime minister wanted.

On the other hand, the cornerstone of England's Texas policy was to prevent its annexation to the United States, which would greatly magnify U.S. influence in the western hemisphere at a time when the U.S. and Britain were drawing closer to a third war over the U.S.-Canadian border. As British Consul-General William Kennedy warned British Foreign Minister Lord Aberdeen in 1841: "...unless English influence be employed in raising up a stable independent power on the South-Western and North Western frontiers of the [Mexican] Union, a very few years will suffice to place the whole of the territory they covet under the Sovereignty of the United States. *There* lies the danger to the Maritime and Commercial supremacy of Great Britain." One way to keep Texas out of the arms of the United States, Kennedy felt, was to grant formal recognition of Texas, or at least dangle that possibility in front of the young Republic.

Other nations of Europe were slowly beginning to come around, particularly as they became convinced that Mexico could not, or would not, reconquer its breakaway province. In 1839, on the heels of the Pastry War with Mexico, France became the first European power to recognize the Republic of Texas, while Holland and Belgium granted recognition the following year.

Taking into account these competing strategic goals, President Lamar felt the best approach to Mexico was a carrot-and-stick method backed up by his new fleet. In February 1839, Lamar sent envoy Barnard E. Bee to Mexico to negotiate Texas recognition from the central government, which was then hard-pressed by Gen. Antonio Canales's federalist revolt in the north. The government, however, refused to allow Bee to set foot on Mexican soil. In November, as the fleet was concentrating in Galveston, Lamar made a second attempt, dispatching James Treat, a dual citizen of Texas and the United States. This time Mexico accepted the delegate, but talks were doomed by Texas's insistence upon the Rio Grande as the border between the two countries, its push to run its southwestern border from El Paso to California, and the political climate under President Bustamente, which had hardened against recognition. As talks dragged on for months with no signs of progress, Lamar and Secretary of State Abner Lipscomb concluded that Mexico's negotiations with Treat were simply a ruse to keep the Texas Navy off the Mexican coast until Mexico could rebuild its forces after the disastrous Pastry War. Lamar decided the time was right to back Treat with what Theodore Roosevelt would later call a "big stick."

On June 3, 1840, President Lamar and his suite paid their respects to the flagship *Austin*, which saluted the president with twenty-two guns. Two days later, Secretary Lipscomb paid a similar visit, and was received with seventeen guns. The timing of these visits was not coincidental. Lamar was preparing orders to terminate Treat's negotiations within ten days unless Mexico City agreed to recognize Texas; by this time, Lamar undoubtedly had instructed Commodore Moore to begin preparations in earnest for a cruise along the Mexican coast, and to determine the order of battle for the fleet that would accompany him.

Things moved quickly from there. On June 20, Lipscomb prepared sealed orders for Lamar's signature instructing Commodore Moore to take as many ships as he could to the Mexican coast off Veracruz and find a safe anchorage. Moore was to take the "ten day ultimatum" instructions to Treat via the British consulate, then wait thirteen days for Treat's reply, which should be relayed to Galveston with all possible speed. "Should you receive a despatch from Mr. Treat informing you that he has failed in his negotiations," his orders stated, "you will in that event be authorised to cruise against the Mexican vessels, and make prizes of them, taking care to avoid all collision with neutral powers, always respecting the principle, that a Neutral Flag protects the cargo. You will be particular to avoid all offensive means, and not shew yourself before Vera-Cruz or any other Mexican Port, until after you have heard from Mr. Treat. . . . If you should be attacked, you will of course be at liberty to defend yourself, and the honor of the Flag, by destroying, or capturing the enemy's vessels, whether public or merchantman." While waiting for Treat's reply, Moore was to dispatch another vessel to deliver a letter from General Canales, the northern rebel leader, to Gen. Juan Pablo Anaya in Yucatán, and reciprocate any friendly act by the Yucatecos.

Although he did not know the precise nature of his assignment at the time, it was clear to Moore that he had the orders he had been craving for nearly a year. He quickly scribbled off an order to *Wharton*'s Captain Wheelwright, directing Wheelwright to man and provision his brig and prepare her for action. For now, Moore would take with him the indispensable *Zavala*, commanded by his most capable subordinate, Commander J. T. K. Lothrop. The squadron would also include the three battle schooners: Lt. William Williamson's *San Bernard*, Lt. Alex Moore's *San Antonio*, and Lt. William Postell's *San Jacinto*, while Moore would personally command the big sloop *Austin*. *Zavala* would be of great value to the fleet in case of adverse or calm winds, while the schooners would maintain communications between the main fleet and Texas. They would also be a useful part of the net Moore intended to spread along the Mexican coastline when the inevitable order to blockade Mexico was issued. When all was ready, Moore set a course for New Orleans, arriving there with the mightiest fleet Texas had ever fielded.

Initially, Commodore Moore planned to take *Austin* and *San Bernard* to Yucatán to ascertain the intentions of that state. Simultaneously, Commander Lothrop was to take *Zavala* to Sisal—the Yucatán port into which *Invincible* had fired less than three years earlier—where Lothrop would deliver the despatch from General Canales to General Anaya. *San Antonio* would lie off Galveston as a communications vessel, while *San Jacinto* was to sail to Point

Mariandrea, some thirty-five miles off Veracruz. There *San Jacinto* would deliver Treat's dispatches to Sir Richard Packenham, England's minister plenipotentiary to Mexico for delivery to Treat, and wait thirteen days for Treat's reply.

Moore also hoped the eighteen-gun *Wharton* would rendezvous with the fleet off Galveston, to provide greater firepower and another link in the chain he would run along the Mexican coast. What he did not know was that seaworthiness concerns and supply problems prevented Wheelwright from getting *Wharton* to sea. In Austin, Secretary Cooke ordered the brig partly dismantled and placed in ordinary, while the fleet's other vessels—the undermanned brig *Archer* and the receiving ship *Potomac*—were to remain at Galveston as a backstop against any Mexican cruiser that managed to slip past Moore's net.

It was high tide for the Texas Navy, and as the fleet prepared to leave New Orleans, its commander looked every inch the mighty captain that he was. The daughter of one prominent New Orleans family recalled her first and only meeting with Commodore Moore nearly seventy years later. "With his imposing uniform and huge gilt star on his breast, a sword at his side, and a rather fierce mustache (mustaches were little worn then), he looked as if he were capable of doing mighty deeds of daring, for the enterprising new republic on our border."

The fleet sailed from the mouth of the Mississippi beginning on July 22, *Zavala* leading the way. To the rural citizens of the poor frontier republic, the pride and treasure of Texas was about to sail onto the world stage in a terrific show of force. There were certainly larger fleets on the seas, and there were more advanced ones. But the five men-of-war that left New Orleans under the command of Edwin Ward Moore that day represented the very best the young, bankrupt republic could offer. A half-century before Roosevelt's Great White Fleet and Britain's HMS *Dreadnought*, the flotilla that Commodore Moore led into the Gulf represented the hopes and aspirations of the young republic and the idealistic president who led her.

CHAPTER TWENTY-ONE

At Sea

Every Mexican Vessel can be captured that dare put to sea, and their whole Sea Coast be kept in a perfect state of fear and trembling; why then should we temporize any longer with them, when, if they had the power they would annihilate every male Inhabitant of Texas and spread devastation and ruin throughout our devoted Country. . . . Now is the time to push them for they never were so prostrate!
—Commodore Edwin W. Moore, August 18, 1840

COMMANDER LOTHROP'S *ZAVALA* LEFT the Mississippi mouth around July 22, and arrived off Sisal three days later with the letter for Yucatán's General Anaya. Sisal's port commandant spoke of Anaya in very harsh terms, and Lothrop worried that his dispatch would not arrive safely if he simply left it with the port authorities. He kept the letter with him and proceeded west to the Arcas Islands.

Las Arcas are actually a small triangle of three tiny coral islands some fifty miles northwest of the Campeche coast. The islands protected a relatively safe anchorage of beautifully clear water that ran to forty feet of depth, and the system was home to an ample supply of birds, fish, and turtles. Its highest point was only twenty-one feet above sea level, but it was dry, and compared to Veracruz and the Yucatán mainland, it had few disease-carrying mosquitoes. The coral cluster lay off the usual trade routes, making desertion impossible, so the Arcas made a perfect rest stop for a sailing fleet in the Gulf. Pirate Jean Lafitte had used the islands in the early part of the century as a safe haven, and two decades later, Captain Rafael Semmes of the Confederate Navy would do the same. Being only 250 miles east of Veracruz (some 373 miles closer than Galveston), the Arcas were the perfect forward base for the Texas Navy, and Commodore Moore intended to use them as a rendezvous point for his fleet.

On July 26, *San Jacinto* cleared the Southwest Pass off New Orleans, bound for Veracruz with dispatches for Treat and Packenham. The next day *Austin* and

San Bernard sailed down the Mississippi for Sisal. Out in the Gulf *Austin* boarded the Mexican merchant schooner *Picalina* and let her go, taking aboard five large turtles offered by her friendly federalist captain, but the four-day voyage to Sisal was otherwise uneventful. On the last day of July, *Austin* and *San Bernard* arrived off Sisal under American colors and signaled for a boat. A Yucatan officer rowed out to the visitors and informed Commodore Moore of *Zavala*'s recent visit, stating that the Yucatán government at Merida had directed port authorities to offer every courtesy to arriving Texian vessels.

Encouraged by this reception, Moore ordered the Texas ensign hoisted aloft, and the two ships proceeded south to the port city of Campeche to meet with General Anaya in person. They arrived at Campeche two days later, where they were met eight miles out to sea by a five-gun schooner bearing General Anaya and his retinue. Welcoming the federalist general aboard the flagship, Moore sent *San Bernard*, with Anaya's personal secretary, back to Sisal to find *Zavala* and General Canales's letter and bring both to Campeche. Anaya spent the day aboard *Austin* in cordial meetings with Commodore Moore, and the two men parted as friends.

On August 4, Moore met with Yucatán's governor-elect Santiago Mendez to discuss relations between Texas and Yucatán. Moore reported that Mendez claimed he "disliked to see his country cut up into small republics; that it was not the intention of the state of Yucatan to separate from the other states, but that she wanted to see the Federal Constitution re-established, when a convention of states would be proposed, and that the proposition would extend to and include Texas, which she might decline with perfect freedom! And he seemed to have no idea that she would do otherwise." Mendez was, wrote Moore, "most anxious that the most friendly relations should be established at an early period, and assured me that the ports of the State of Yucatán were opened to any Texian Vessel." By the end of these meetings, Yucatán had moved closer to the Texian orbit.

Moore had passed his first test as an ambassador for Texas. In the midst of these uncharted waters, this meeting between Moore and Yucatán's chief executive was to set the stage for an extraordinary relationship that would change Moore's life forever and affect the history of the two states.

While Commodore Moore was laying the groundwork for an alliance between Yucatán and the Republic of Texas, Lieutenant Postell's *San Jacinto* arrived off Port Mariandrea near Veracruz with Lamar's dispatches for James Treat. The letters ordered Treat to break off negotiations within ten days unless Mexico indicated a willingness to recognize Texas independence. In that event, Treat would inform Commodore Moore that he was free to prey upon any merchant ships his squadron encountered. True to his instructions, Postell delivered the letters to the ubiquitous Royal Navy, which in turn forwarded them to Lord Packenham for delivery to Treat. Postell proceeded to wait the requisite thirteen days for Treat's response.

The last thing Great Britain needed, however, was war between Mexico and Texas, two of England's trading partners. So British diplomats, aware of the contents, held on to the letters for thirteen days after *San Jacinto* dropped them off, preventing Treat from giving Commodore Moore timely permission to commence hostilities. Lieutenant Postell was thus kept in a state of limbo, unable to take any positive orders back to Galveston or Commodore Moore.

Lying at anchor off Campeche, Moore was puzzled. *Zavala* had not delivered the letter as planned, and there was no word yet from *San Jacinto*. On August 7, he ordered *Austin* to sail for Point Mariandrea, to rendezvous with *San Jacinto* and see what the good Mr. Treat had to say. On the way, *Austin* detoured to Las Arcas where Moore found *Zavala* at anchor, running low on fuel and provisions. He accepted Commander Lothrop's explanation for not delivering General Canales's letter to General Anaya at Sisal ("Under the same circumstances I would have retained the letter myself," he remarked), and had his men supply *Zavala* with provisions and water. He gave the crews a restful day of swimming, and spent a happy afternoon on August 10 diving off *Zavala*'s deck into the cool, deep water of the Arcas harbor—proving that he could backstroke as fast as any other sailor could swim freestyle. After a day of relaxation, Moore sailed back to Campeche with Canales's letter, leaving *Zavala* to wait for additional fuel from Galveston or New Orleans.

Arriving at Campeche on the thirteenth, Moore delivered the letter to Anaya, and met again with governor-elect Mendez, who relayed the incumbent governor's assurances that Yucatán would remain friendly to Texas. Scanning the critical port, Moore noted that "the naval force of the State of Yucatán consists of *one* small brig and *two* schooners," and upon further inquiry, Moore determined that the town was garrisoned by "not more than four hundred men, a number having marched to relieve the City of Tabasco, which had declared for the Federalists, but the castle still being in the possession of the Centralists."

To the federalists of Yucatán, Tabasco, that swampy, malaria-infested state at the southernmost point of Mexico's Gulf coast, was a tough nut to crack, but cracked it had to be. If the centralists were driven out of Tabasco, Yucatán would have an impassable buffer state between itself and the centralists' strongholds, which would preserve its own safety. For the moment, this was Yucatán's problem, not Moore's. But it would soon present the Texas Navy with an opportunity that would lead to bigger things.

On August 14, *San Bernard* breezed into Campeche, and the following day the schooner and her flagship weighed anchor for the one-day trip back to the Arcas Islands. Moore would have loved to pick up *Zavala* and take her back to Point Mariandrea for a real show of force, but the steamer simply could not afford to consume any more fuel until she had a reserve supply.

Between New Orleans and Las Arcas, she burned about one-third of the 1,700 barrels of low-quality coal that the government had supplied, and until more arrived from Texas, she had to stay right where she was. Moore transferred *San Bernard's* injured Lt. Armstrong I. Lewis to *Zavala* (he had broken his leg in a careless fall from the schooner's trunk), and the two sailing ships left for Point Mariandrea to see what news *San Jacinto's* Lieutenant Postell had for them.

Arriving off Point Mariandrea on August 18, Moore was disappointed to learn that nothing had been received from James Treat. Moore was also undoubtedly vexed by the silence from *San Antonio* and *Wharton*, both of which should have been somewhere between the Point and Campeche by then. The warships off Veracruz—*Austin, San Jacinto,* and *San Bernard*—sat idly at anchor for three days while Moore pondered his next move.

On August 22, Moore sent a landing party ashore in two of *Austin's* cutters to procure beef from the locals. It seems the lessons Secretary Fisher had taught the coastal inhabitants in 1837 had not been forgotten, as the five villagers who stumbled upon the landing party "viewed us as savages," Moore reported, "and begged us most imploringly 'not to molest the women.'" He recalled: "On being assured that they would not be, and that we only wanted some fresh beef, they were really astonished. The men were formed on the beach, and the Mexicans soon had three beeves down, and we were under way again at dark." From here until the end of his cruises, Commodore Moore took great care to respect the personal property of Mexican civilians, trying hard to erase the impression among Mexicans and Europeans alike that the Texas Navy was nothing more than a government-sponsored pirate fleet.

On August 23, Moore lifted for Veracruz under American colors, intending to board any Mexican vessels departing from the centralist port. He later explained to Secretary Cooke that his goal was to find out whether Mr. Treat had left Mexico "and have a look at their shipping." Within two days *Austin* boarded three merchant vessels, and spotted seven or eight more, but with no definitive word from Treat, Moore let every vessel under his guns sail away in peace.

On the morning of August 25, the British sloop *Penguin* worked her way alongside *Austin* and delivered four letters from James Treat—one addressed to President Lamar, one to Moore, and two to Secretary of State Lipscomb. *Penguin's* senior officers, exchanging pleasantries with those of the *Austin*, told the Texians that Mexico had no warships at Veracruz, but they expected the new sloop-of-war *Iguala* to arrive from France any day, and that centralists were trying to buy another French vessel then in port. The steamer *Argyle*, a troopship, was also said to be somewhere north of Veracruz chugging away in Mexican service. *Penguin's* commander was evidently impressed with the professionalism of Moore's squadron, and "appeared much pleased with the bold manner in which Lieut. Postell stood down for him," according to Moore.

After bidding the Brits a good day, Moore read Treat's message. Treat felt that Moore's presence off the Mexican coast was interfering with his efforts to win recognition from the centralists. Even though Treat's policy of negotiation with no backing force had achieved nothing, the amateur diplomat pointedly told Moore that he had "not hesitated to assure [Mexico] in the most *positive manner* that your instructions were certainly of a pacific character *so long* as negotiations with the government were *open* and *pending*."

In his reply, an exasperated Moore assured Treat that he had no intention of capturing Mexican vessels so long as negotiations were "open and pending." To give Treat some backbone, however, he emphasized, "I can anchor this Ship within four miles of Vera Cruz without the 'protection' or 'hospitality' of the Mexican Government, but in defiance of their whole force!" Moore's subsequent claim that *Austin* also could have captured "seven or eight" Mexican ships off Veracruz is supported by the journal of Midshipman James Mabry, which recorded a number of spottings by *Austin*'s lookouts. Moore was thus far, on the surface at least, playing the part of the dutiful officer carrying out his orders with delicacy and finesse.

Inwardly, however, Moore must have been incredulous. Did Treat not see that he was being played like a fiddle by the centralists? That Mexico's only interest was in prolonging negotiations until the balance of naval power shifted back to Mexico? He fretted to Secretary Lipscomb, "With all due deference, I cannot refrain from the expression of the opinion that we have temporized too long already; and if we let them see that we really are in earnest, by capturing their Vessels and annoying their Sea Coast; which we can do with our Naval force, to at least some extent, I cannot but believe that they will very soon come to terms. I have no faith in their promises, unless they *feel* that they can be forced to keep them;—The whole history of their negotiations is strong proof of this position." Firmly convinced that the centralists were in no position to retaliate, Moore somewhat impertinently concluded, "You may keep *Treating* with them until the expiration of your administration and will, in all probability leave for your successor, whoever he may be, to reap all the advantages of your efforts; now is the time to push them for they never were so prostrate!"

Moore was right, although it would take Lamar until the end of his term to admit it publicly. In the summer of 1840, Mexico had nothing to throw against the five cruisers prowling off its coast. Mexican newspapers reported the presence of "three Texan vessels of war laying off our port at the distance of five leagues," and screamed for action. "We are in a moment blockaded by the Texians, and although pirates, they will not be permitted, with impunity, to molest the vessels of other nations. This we confess, makes our blood boil; we cannot view it with serenity; it makes us desperate." The Jalapa *Conciliador* decried the Texas menace to Mexican commerce, while another newspaper, *El Censor*, warned that Texas was becoming "more robust each day. Supreme Government, awake! A little longer and it will be too late."

If Mexico was truly helpless, why did Lamar not press his advantage at the time? For one thing, he had a number of tightropes to walk. Neither the British nor the Americans wanted an all-out war between Texas and Mexico, and without the support of these two giants, Lamar had to tread most carefully. Moreover, hopelessly optimistic messages from Treat repeatedly assured Lamar and Lipscomb that recognition, or at least a permanent truce, was just around the corner. Finally, Lamar was still stinging from the bitter Congressional rebuke of his naval appointments made during the legislative recess; how much more incensed would the legislators be if Lamar commenced a war without seeking their advice and consent?

The end of August found an uncertain Commodore Moore plodding north in company with *San Jacinto*, leaving *San Bernard* to monitor events off Veracruz. In his August 28 report to Secretary Cooke, he expressed concern about the absence of *Wharton* and *San Antonio*, and predicted that the fleet would be out of supplies by the first of December if not restocked. Some of the sailors' enlistment terms would also be up in November and December, he noted, and Moore remarked, "I hope that money will be placed in the hands of the Navy Agent to pay them off." Moore also reiterated his conviction that a show of force would break the stalemate of the Treat negotiations. He suggested that the fleet be permitted to board every vessel coming out of Veracruz, foreign or otherwise, so that Treat could leave Mexico aboard any vessel he could find or send dispatches aboard any outbound craft and be assured that they would reach their destination.

As they approached the mouth of the Rio Grande, *Austin* signaled for *San Jacinto* to proceed north to Galveston, while the flagship came to anchor about a mile and a half offshore, just north of the Mexican military outpost at Brazos de Santiago. Moore's motives for lingering so close to Mexican troops were never recorded, but they are easily inferred. Moore knew Lamar wanted an excuse to raise the level of heat in Mexico City, and his orders made it clear that, if fired upon, Moore would have *carte blanche* to commence a blockade. Moore also knew that the hard-pressed federalists of the Rio Grande region could use some relief, and that the appearance of the Texas flagship off Brazos de Santiago would draw troops away from General Canales's rebels along the interior. Moore was baiting the centralist troops.

As it turned out, the three to five hundred soldiers that the Matamoros commander rushed to the beaches wisely refrained from firing on *Austin*, a tempting target a mere thousand yards from shore. The commodore's move gave Canales a brief respite, however, and four days later *Austin* weighed anchor and sailed back to Point Mariandrea.

The month of September was a dull one, as cruises in enemy waters go. The fleet ferried more messages to James Treat, one vessel had a tense run-in with the Spanish corvette *Guerro*, and *San Antonio* brought out some badly-needed provisions. But for the most part, the officers and men experienced few adventures, and bad luck that was to plague them for the rest of their careers began to visit them regularly. George Wheelwright, the former commodore, was finally relieved of command, apparently due in part to embarrassment he had caused the Department by recruiting sailors for particular ships and granting them the right to refuse transfer to other vessels where they were more urgently needed. Moore's ablest lieutenant, *San Jacinto*'s William Postell, was forced to resign by Secretary Cooke, who believed he had violated naval regulations. Moore could find no credible evidence to support any charges, and at least once he went over Cooke's head to ask Lamar to rescind orders to arrest Postell. But for the moment, Postell was out.

Postell's command was taken over by Lt. James O'Shaunessy, who would remain until *Austin*'s Lt. Thurston M. Taylor could assume command. This change in command would become a serious blow to the young navy's fortunes. Lieutenant O'Shaunessy—who in early 1840 had nearly resigned with a group of midshipmen in a harebrained scheme to found a Texas colony on Cozumel—was easily the worst commander in Moore's officer corps; he would be responsible for the loss of more equipment during the next year than the Mexican Navy would cause for the rest of the Texas Republic's life.

The squadron as a whole was deteriorating. Scurvy ravaged the flagship, which had a dozen serious cases, and many mild cases that would become serious if nothing was done. *Zavala*'s Commander Lothrop left a handwritten plea for food and fuel in a locked box on the Arcas Islands, then sailed to Yucatán, while *Wharton* remained at anchor off Galveston for reasons Moore could not fathom. Moore split up the fleet, sending *San Antonio* to Tampico to monitor events on the north coast and anchoring *Austin* off Lobos Island, some sixty miles southeast of Tampico. He dispatched *San Bernard* to Las Arcas to resupply the famished *Zavala*, and ordered *San Jacinto* back to Galveston with more useless messages from James Treat. For all this activity, there was no glory, there were no prizes, there was nothing that Moore and his men could lay their hands on as a spoil of war.

In October, nature added to the fleet's woes. Between late August and late November, as the earth tilts on its axis to cool off the northern hemisphere, Gulf weather becomes unpredictable. Hurricanes and tropical storms plow through the Gulf, while sporadic northers—those winds from the North Pole that usher in a cacophony of gusts—strike with little or no warning. When they hit the middle of the Atlantic, they can cause great danger to sailing ships. When they strike along the shallows of the Gulf, where the Texas Navy did its work, they create titanic breaker waves that devour vessel and village alike.

One such beast struck the fleet on the third day of October. At the time it descended, the fuel-starved *Zavala* was two miles off the mouth of the Tabasco River, today called Rio Grijalvo, having arrived when the tides were too low to allow it to cross the bar safely. A midshipman recalled that when night fell, "the sea was quite smooth the sky clear and not a breath of wind." But whatever calm may have settled into the mind of the ship's commander, John Lothrop, broke up quickly as the Gulf's glassy waters were overtaken by growing, remorseless rolls. As the steamboat began to roll, Commander Lothrop ordered his men to drop the vessel's heavy anchor into the mud to ride out what he hoped would be a very short storm.

Instead, the storm hovered above the Tabasco mouth, smashing *Zavala* for the next three days. Like a huge, grunting bull battering against a rickety wooden gate, the storm surge shoved the steamer closer and closer to the Tabasco bar, where she would inevitably be stranded, knocked over by the waves, then dashed to pieces.

This was war in every sense of the word; *Zavala* was fighting for her life against one of nature's grand killers. Lothrop ordered his officers to weigh anchor and get *Zavala*'s boilers up so they could back the ship away from the dangerous bar. But before his men could carry out these orders, huge waves lashed at the steamer, bouncing her on her anchor cable like an inverted yo-yo. The current ripped *Zavala*'s rudder off her pintles, making navigation impossible. The lives of *Zavala*'s terrified men now depended upon her anchor gripping the muddy bottom of the Tabasco River bed. And still the waves came.

Commander Lothrop was not about to let nature have her way with his beautiful ship. At least, not without a fight. When an attempt to safely cross the Tabasco bar failed, the resourceful commander ordered the men to rig a makeshift rudder with a spar and hawser, then cast 400 eighteen-pound cannonballs overboard to lighten the vessel and reduce the strain on the anchor cables.

But the waves still came.

Canister and grapeshot followed the balls overboard. The ship's anchor began to drag. *Zavala* rolled in the trough of the sea, and a dreaded thumping sound rang through the lower decks—the sound of a boat bottoming out on a rock or sandbar. Lothrop had the ship's guns lashed to long ropes and thrown overboard to serve as additional anchors. Then he ran her engines as hard as he could against the force of the smashing tides, desperately trying to keep *Zavala* off the shallows. At one point, a giant wave dumped so much water into *Zavala*'s weather beam that she listed hard enough to pull her opposing paddle wheel out of the water.

And the waves still came.

Time was running out for what had once seemed an impregnable ship. Hardened sailors began vomiting from sea sickness, and as the nights turned into days with no break in the storm's punishment, *Zavala*'s dazed men could do nothing but stay below decks in the damp, suffocating heat, or lash themselves to something solid if above, and pray that the steamer would hold together one more night while Neptune slashed at the boat with his watery cat-'o-nine tails.

When *Zavala*'s coal ran out, the crew used the ship's meager supply of firewood to keep the engines running against the tide. The storm refused to let up. When the firewood was gone, a desperate Lothrop ordered his men to demolish the boat's upper structures and burn spars, walls, doors, and furniture—anything made of wood except the hull—to keep the engines alive and give the battered ship's anchors some relief.

The topsail yards were taken down and burned. Then the topmast. Then the mainmast. Then the saloon. Midshipman Cox later described those three dark days. "Our Coal gave out, for we had steam up all the time—and all the bulkheads and available parts of the interior of the ship was cut out to make fuel—in all these days & nights the vessel rolled like a log—first one Wheelhouse, then the other under water, it was unsafe to be on deck without fastening yourself to something. Every moment it looked as if the next would upset the ship or nock her to pieces. I was dreadful sea sick and felt quite indifferent to the danger."

Terror, being an emotion, cannot sustain itself indefinitely, even for the fury of the dark, overpowering sea. It will eventually give way to exhaustion, or perhaps resignation. With well-disciplined men, it will give way to instincts drummed into their subconscious during training. It is a testament to the training of the officers and men of the Texas Navy that her crew wrestled the rolling hydra for three violent days. As the steamboat pitched and rolled, the disoriented men somehow managed to chop up enough furniture, doors, and deck structures to keep the engines running long enough to survive the storm. The men would live to fight another day.

As the seas grudgingly subsided, *Zavala* limped into the town of Frontera, some five miles up the Tabasco River, and anchored to assess the damage. The men had cut apart the masts, yards, saloon, wardroom, steerage deck, and berth deck for fuel. They had thrown every cannon overboard, along with all their shot. They sailed on an improvised rudder, and barely had enough deck planking to walk from bow to stern.

But they survived, and so did the most basic parts of their ship. When they drifted into the safety of Frontera, Lt. Tennison optimistically recorded, "we came in here all well and hearty on the 7th October. The Hull of the Vessel and engines being not at all hurt." Lothrop's men repaired their rudder as best they could, affixing a makeshift rudder to the hull with cannon eyebolts and chains. They pumped water out of the paddle cowlings and began felling trees for fuel. Soon they cut enough timber to get the pathetic-looking steamer to sea, where they could recover their guns. Amazingly, the men suffered no loss of life—or at least, they did not care to record any.

The maelstrom was not one *Zavala* should have survived. Commodore Moore wrote to Secretary Cooke, "No person on shore thought it possible that she could ride it out, the gale was so violent, and the sea so high that it broke in ten fathoms water." Rumors of the steamer's death made the Texas newspapers; the Galveston *Courier*, for example, reported in December that the warship had been lost. The embarrassed editors retracted the article upon the miraculous news of *Zavala*'s survival, and the *Texas Sentinel* reported with pleasure the following January, "The Zavala, we learn, was got off the bar of Tobasco with little difficulty, and is now in good repair."

One ship that was not so lucky was the Mexican brig *Segunda Fama*, of Veracruz. Commodore Moore reported that on the afternoon of October 3, the second day of the storm, *Austin,* safely anchored off Isla de Lobos near Tampico, spotted a distress signal from the Blanquilla Reef along the north end of the island. The norther had blown a brig into the reef, and she was in danger of breaking up. Moore sent a lifeboat to the island to see if anyone could pilot a rescue boat out to the stranded passengers, but the storm, having pounded the island for nearly two days, squelched any brave impulses of the weary inhabitants, and Moore's boat returned with no hope of assistance. As night was falling, Moore sent a boat to shore to build a fire as a beacon to the stranded brig, but apparently helpless, it did not budge while waves slammed her against the reefs.

Realizing that the brig could not move, Moore sent Lt. Downing Crisp in a lifeboat for a nighttime rescue mission, and dispatched a launch and *Austin*'s second cutter to accompany the rescuers. The launch and second cutter were driven back by the heavy head seas and returned to the sloop, but Crisp and his men soldiered on, heaving against the black, undulating waves.

With some much-needed luck, Crisp's sailors managed to row their pitching lifeboat over the waves' crests to the trapped brig. Pulling himself onto the listing deck, Lieutenant Crisp was met by twenty-five huddled refugees who were about to abandon ship in a makeshift raft. Crisp could see that they would be dashed to pieces on the reef, or washed overboard, and he persuaded the passengers and crew to stay with the stranded brig.

Crisp's men were exhausted, having pulled against the raging waters for over an hour, but the thought of spending the night aboard the dying wreck held no appeal, either. Ultimately, Crisp decided to stay with the passengers of the stricken vessel until morning, when *Austin* might be able to send help.

Next morning, in heavy swells, Lieutenant Crisp shoved off in his lifeboat with some of the brig's passengers, while Capt. Pablo Alcedan followed closely in *Segunda Fama*'s lifeboat with other passengers and crewmen. By now the wet, bedraggled civilians were more afraid of the churning waves than the "pirates" and "cut-throats" of the Texas Navy. As they were hauled up to *Austin*'s deck, Commodore Moore reassured the brig's passengers and crew that they were safe, and would remain under his personal protection.

After an unsuccessful effort to row *Austin*'s launch over to the crippled *Fama*, a lifeboat and cutter managed to make it across the reef to the vessel and take away the remaining passengers and crew. The passengers shuttled their personal belongings over to *Austin*'s hold, and Moore's men brought aboard a portion of the brig's cargo of flour, coffee, vermicelli, and some equipment before giving up on the sinking ship.

Thus loaded, *Austin* ferried *Fama*'s refugees and the Navy's worst scurvy cases to Isla de Lobos, leaving them under the temporary care of Lt. Thurston Taylor. There Moore and his ship's surgeon, Dr. John Burrows Gardiner, provided an unconventional treatment for the scurvy victims: they were buried up to their necks in the island's sand. Dr. Gardiner put his physician's imprimatur on the unconventional treatment, writing in *Austin*'s medical journal, "I have no hesitation...in recommending strongly in all cases, where any report of the Squadron may have bad cases of scurvy on board, that she would if practicable proceed to some land, where the Scurvy cases can be buried for several hours each day. The mode is very simple and should never be continued longer than two hours, and another interval of four hours should elapse between each internment, as if continued longer it will produce violent delusion."

It was an absurd prescription, given the relationship we now know scurvy bore to the crew's diet, which lacked citrus fruits, but Dr. Gardiner never mentioned the possibility that the limes growing wild on the island might be connected with the remission of the disease. On the other hand, Gardiner did correctly postulate that stagnant water from Lobos and the Tabasco River were the primary carriers of diseases that began striking the squadron with a vengeance the following month.

As Lieutenant Taylor's men scouted the island and picked through the wreckage of *Segunda Fama*, they were surprised to run into another group of refugees. Pedro Lemus, a famous federalist commander who languished for fourteen months in a Matamoros prison, had escaped from his centralist captors in Tampico aboard the Campecheano schooner *Conchita*. Lemus had boarded *Conchita* with his brother, a Yucatán colonel, and his wife and six children, and the group was on its way to Campeche when the storm grounded them. Seeing the Texians, the old general begged for their protection, and presented them with a letter of support from John McGregor, the United States consul at Campeche. Moore reported, "The gray haired and lame old man . . . seized, and in the most emphatic, and ardent manner, implored the protection of our Flag, stating that it was the only chance of life, and which I could not refuse." Lemus was an important figure in the Yucatán revolutionary movement, and Moore was only too happy to show both compassion and respect for the old war-horse. He took the Lemus family aboard *Austin*, then set a course for Tampico to drop off the *Segunda Fama* refugees.

Commodore Moore must have felt pleased with himself as he sailed into Tampico under American colors. Slowly, steadily, he was salvaging the Texas Navy's reputation; no longer were they considered pirates by the vessels they encountered. Men-of-war of the U.S. and European navies rendered Texas fighting ships the same courtesies and respect they offered to the other great naval powers of the world. Moore came to Texas and found a navy regarded by the world as barbarians, "cut-throats," and worse; what he gave Texas was a marine service that was a model of professionalism, run by gentlemen of the seas.

On the afternoon of October 16, Moore stood in for the Tampico bar, clewing up his topsails, hauling down his jib, and dropping his port anchor under U.S. colors. At three o'clock the pilot boat came out to guide the American-flagged sloop into port and was surprised to find Texas officers delivering Mexican passengers to safety. The pilot boat took *Segunda Fama*'s captain to the port, and an hour later a launch sent by the port authorities picked up the remaining passengers, crew, and baggage, sailing back in company with the *Fama*'s boat. The next day, Tampico's commanding general, Dr. Joachim Rivas, sent a grateful letter of thanks to Moore for the "timely and efficient exertion" of *Austin*'s crew in saving the twenty-six souls aboard *Segunda Fama*. Her captain, Pablo Alcedan, sent an eloquent letter of thanks to Commodore Moore, which was undoubtedly appreciated by Moore's officers—but not as appreciated as the demijohn of brandy, the loaf of sugar, and the rice and beef that accompanied Alcedan's letter, especially since the men had run out of spirit rations in September.

Much pleased with his reception and certain that the port authorities would not fire on his men, Moore ordered *Austin*'s launch out a mile and a half off Tampico to gather fresh water. What they found was somewhat salty, but it was the best that could be had without going close to Mexican soil, which was out of the question, notwithstanding the goodwill Moore had bought by rescuing the *Fama*'s passengers. While *Austin* was procuring water, the English sloop *Racer* pulled alongside, trimmed her sails respectfully, and sent her captain aboard *Austin* for a pleasant pre-dinner visit to Commodore Moore's suite.

While Moore was busy rescuing *Segunda Fama*, and *Zavala* was drying out at Frontera, the schooners *San Bernard* and *San Jacinto* were having troubles of their own. Moore had ordered *San Bernard*'s Lt. William Williamson to Las Arcas with five weeks' provisions for *Zavala* in September, but late September calms and then the October 3 norther kept Williamson close to the mainland. When *San Bernard* arrived at Las Arcas on October 9, she grounded for four hours on the reefs while entering the harbor, losing several sheets of copper sheathing that protected her hull from wood-eating parasites. Sickness had also taken its toll; Williamson had but three men fit for duty, so he lingered at the islands for nearly a month, while two of his crewmen died. Lieutenant O'Shaunessy's *San Jacinto* sailed from Galveston in late September, delivering dispatches to *San Antonio* off Point Mariandrea on October 20, then proceeding, without orders, to the Arcas to replenish the schooner's water supply. *San Jacinto* arrived there two days later, bucking heavy head seas and northerly winds. It would not be long before O'Shaunessy's failings as a mariner doomed his warship to the Gulf's dark depths.

For all his activity in Mexican waters, Moore was not happy with the strategic situation. He wrote time and again to the heads of the Navy and State Departments, arguing that Treat's mission was pointless, that the Mexicans were prolonging negotiations to keep Texas from attacking them while they quietly rebuilt their fleet. But orders were orders. Moore was not permitted to take a vessel flying the Eagle and Snake, no matter how tempting she might be, until hostilities were opened. And they would not be opened unless the centralist troops were stupid enough to fire upon them, or James Treat's unlimited patience ran out.

Then, on October 20, the situation changed. While *Austin*'s second cutter made its way close to Tampico to collect fresh water, the nearby fort opened fire on the boat, sending three cannonballs close enough to splash the sailors with sea spray. *Austin*'s signal flags instantly ran up, recalling the cutter, and Moore ordered a gun fired at the fort. Moore's shot had to fight a headwind, and the ball fell harmlessly short. Since he would not be able to hit the fort unless he sailed dangerously close to the bar, Moore simply backed off and waited for the cutter to return.

Moore now had his wish—his July 20 orders specified that he could commence offensive operations if he were attacked. And feeble though it had been, the cannon volley directed at his cutter was an attack. The crew's indignation at being fired upon soon gave way to the delightful realization that they could now consider themselves at war. Glory! Prizes! Action! This, not obscenely dull diplomatic missions, was what they had signed up for, and this was what they would have.

The excitement that took hold of his crew that afternoon left a deep impression on Moore. Two months later, he recalled the moment when smoke billowed from the guns of Tampico and sent his men scurrying back to their ship. "From that moment," he wrote, "fresh life and vigor was apparent in the countenances of all on board, for we all felt that we could now do something for the country, the Navy and ourselves." Moore's only regret was that the Mexicans had not fired on him sooner. "If this circumstance had occurred in the early part of the cruise," he grumbled to Secretary Cooke, "I could have captured with this Ship alone, Mexican vessels, which with their cargoes would have brought at least two hundred thousand dollars in specie." But, he consoled himself, "it is not yet too late for the Navy to pay for itself, and yield something to the country." With a breath of fresh air, the revived crew weighed anchor and set their sights for Point Mariandrea, now carrying orders to attack the enemy.

Moore rounded up his fleet to prepare them for action. After sailing through a bitter squall that flung one topgallant yardman to his death, *Austin* found *San Antonio* in the western Gulf, where Moore received supplemental orders from Secretary Cooke and dispatches for Packenham in Mexico City. Moore set off promptly with *San Antonio* for Veracruz, where he would inform James Treat that hostilities had commenced, deliver his letters, and impose a blockade in earnest.

Arriving off Veracruz on October 29, Moore informed Treat that his negotiations were no longer relevant. "I am fully authorized, in the event of a shot being fired at our Flag, to commence active hostilities," he wrote, "and if your negotiations are broken off in consequence, you will find a Vessel off Point Mariandrea to convey you to Texas, for from this day any Mexican Vessel that I fall in with, will be captured."

Leaving *San Antonio* behind to pick up Treat, Moore delivered Packenham's letters to the English brig *Sappho*, then headed north to the Rio Grande to support a rumored invasion of Matamoros by General Canales. As he approached Brazos de Santiago after dark, he nearly fell victim to an old mariner's trick. "The inhuman wretches lit only the lower tier of Lanterns in the Light House, to deceive me in the distances so that the ship might be lost on the Reefs forming the Harbour, which they knew we had to stand in for again," he fumed. Moore was, however, able to back his ship off the reefs far enough so that when a swirling norther hit that night, it did not drive his vessel against the rocks.

Rumors of invasion proved to be exaggerated, as most were, but the fierce night of October 30 brought the first loss to the reborn Texas Navy on the other side of the Gulf. Being short of water and worried about a rotten foremast, Lieutenant O'Shaunessy ordered *San Jacinto* back to the Arcas Islands, where she arrived too late on the afternoon of October 29 to wind her way safely through the maze of jagged coral shoals. The next day, she obtained a pilot from *San Bernard*, which was anchored safely in the delicate harbor, and *San Jacinto* worked her way off the port beam of her sister ship. This simple maneuver proved beyond O'Shaunessy's abilities. *San Jacinto* dropped anchor dangerously close to her sister, so O'Shaunessy had to back her up, tethering her port bow gun to the deck to throw overboard as an anchor, if necessary. A boat sent from *San Bernard* to assist O'Shaunessy capsized, injuring two men, and *San Jacinto* had to retreat almost as far as the harbor's entrance, where she anchored dangerously close to the toothy reefs.

As the evening wore on, the skies darkened and the waters began to swirl rapidly around the schooners. While winds and rain lashed his ship with increasing force, O'Shaunessy imprudently decided to go ashore, leaving Lt. Alfred Gray in command. The gale grew fiercer, hitting *San Jacinto* hard, and Gray dropped his kedge anchor to keep the vessel's stern off the rocks. The anchor was too light and the ground too hard to catch the anchor; the schooner began dragging. Gray then dropped a stern gun as a makeshift anchor, but *San Jacinto* continued to drag, and when the kedge anchor finally did catch, it broke off at the shank.

By one in the morning, it was clear that *San Jacinto* would be doomed if she stayed in the rocky harbor. In desperation, Lieutenant Gray decided to shoot his vessel past the harbor's mouth by setting the jib sail, then cutting the line to the stern gun, praying his ship would clear the mouth before the cross-current smashed her against the reef. The gamble almost worked. At Gray's command, *San Jacinto* shot forward, and nearly cleared the harbor's mouth. But her stern struck, and with a sickening crunch, she heeled around so that her bow struck. The waves forced *San Jacinto* clockwise against the rocks, punching a hole in her starboard bow while she wallowed in several feet of water. The sea began pouring in, and Lieutenant Gray quickly realized the fight was hopeless. He gave the order to abandon ship, and by 4:00 a.m. not a soul was left on board. She lay on the rocks lifeless, aground on her starboard side in several feet of water, while *San Bernard*'s Lieutenant Williamson frantically organized salvage operations.

Two days later, *Austin*'s faint outline appeared over the horizon. Commodore Moore sailed to the islands' outer perimeter, where he found *San Bernard* sitting at anchor, collecting provisions from her sister's carcass. *San Jacinto* lay on her starboard side with a hole half the size of his cabin. Anchoring nearby, he summoned Lieutenant Williamson, the ranking officer, for an explanation. Hearing Williamson's story, Moore relieved him of command for disobedience to his orders to assist the stricken *Zavala*, and replaced him with *Austin*'s Lt. Thurston Taylor.

Moore decided to survey *San Jacinto* himself, to see what could be done. On the morning of November 3, he brought *Austin* around to the south end of the islands and anchored near the wreck. *San Jacinto* was a mess, but Moore thought she could be saved. He was jealous of his tiny fleet, and he was not about to let the monstrous gulf have its way with his year-old schooner. Not without a fight.

Moore's salvage effort was creative and determined, just like the commodore himself. He ordered seamen to man the schooner's two small pumps and had a bucket brigade bail water. He had two large auxiliary pumps constructed, and as he gained on the waters, he prepared to flip the schooner over onto her good side. Taking anchors and cables salvaged from *Segunda Fama*, he had his men heave on the cables for two days until, inch by inch, the stricken vessel flopped over so that she was listing on her port side. With the gaping hole now on top, the flow of water stopped, and it could be pumped out more efficiently. A swarm of sailors crawled over the vessel and patched the hole with oakum and wood, caulked her from the inside, then pumped her down to fourteen inches of water.

His men righted the stricken ship. She floated, but she would not be seaworthy until further repairs were made—repairs that could not be made without planks or spikes, neither of which were available on the islands.

Moore therefore had *San Jacinto* dragged closer to the beach to protect her from the seas, and set a course for Campeche to find supplies and, God willing, his other ships. He left *Austin*'s first cutter, one launch, 445 gallons of water, some coffee, flour, and vermicelli for Lieutenant O'Shaunessy and *San Jacinto*'s crew. He sent *San Bernard* off to find Commander Lothrop's *Zavala*, and on November 6 he filed away for Campeche with the federalist General Lemus.

Four days before Commodore Moore left Las Arcas, his cousin, *San Antonio*'s commander Lt. Alex Moore, spotted what would be the Texas Navy's first prize of the 1840 campaign. As the 90-ton Mexican schooner *Ana Maria* appeared over the horizon off Point Mariandrea, *San Antonio* hoisted U.S. colors. When *Ana Maria* ran up her Mexican ensign, Lieutenant Moore ordered the Lone Star run to the maintop, whereupon *Ana Maria* bore all sail and made a run for it.

After a brief chase, *Ana Maria* surrendered peacefully. On board she carried a rich cargo of flour, coffee, and dry goods, with a value sufficient to keep the Navy running for another month. Lieutenant Moore put a prize crew aboard her under the command of Lt. Charles Fuller then sent *Ana Maria* speeding away for Galveston.

Unfortunately for Lieutenant Moore, *Ana Maria* belonged to a friend of Texas, American consul John McGregor. When *San Antonio* arrived in Galveston on December 8, bearing the remains of James Treat (who died aboard *San Antonio* on November 30 after a lengthy illness), Lieutenant Moore began feeling political heat over the affair. The criticism the lieutenant took for his capture soon passed his very shallow breaking point, and Alex Moore disgraced his cousin by becoming one of two commanding officers to desert the service.

While *Ana Maria* was heading to Galveston as a prize of war, Commodore Moore sailed for Campeche to drop off General Lemus and his family. During the trip, he and Lemus must have discussed the idea of Texas-Yucatán military cooperation, and Moore knew that his safe delivery of the prominent federalist general would add yet one more strand to the growing bond of trust between the two governments. Arriving off Campeche on November 8, a very pleased Commodore Moore sent his guests ashore, and set about procuring supplies to repair the stricken *San Jacinto*. Worried about the destitute condition of his men, Moore also bought clothing and other necessary personal items from Consul McGregor, at a cost of $430. Moore pointedly noted in his report to Secretary Cooke that he had to use his personal finances to buy the supplies, as McGregor was unwilling to accept a draft on the name of the notoriously bankrupt Texas government. While in port, Moore heard the worrisome news that *Zavala* had been heavily damaged in a bad norther off the Tabasco bar and was stranded in Frontera, just up the Tabasco River.

Moore rushed to Frontera to assist Commander Lothrop. *San Bernard* arrived there first, on November 13, bearing much-needed provisions. Three days later, *Austin* hove in sight and prepared to cross the Tabasco bar.

In an incident uncharacteristic of Commodore Moore, *Austin* grounded not once, but twice. Midshipman James Mabry reported in his journal for November 16, "At 5 grounded on Tobasco bar in 9 feet of water; backed her off and stood north. At 10, fired a gun and hoisted Jack for a pilot." The next day Moore made another attempt, and grounded a second time until a sea breeze drove the ship over the bar. Mabry noted on November 17, "At 4 grounded on the bar in 9-1/2 feet of water. Carried out kedge and at 5,30 hauled over. At 6,30 came to in 4-1/2 fathoms of water with 25 fathoms of chain. At 9/30 sent a second cutter down to the bar to weight the kedge. At 11,40 got under way and proceeded up the river."

After coming to anchor, Moore summoned his commanders to learn the disposition of their crews. *San Bernard*'s crew was holding its own for the moment, but *Zavala*'s men were barely hanging together. After landing at Frontera, Commander Lothrop, virtually penniless, had put his men to work chopping wood and forging metal to make their own replacement parts. His tired, famished men had quickly succumbed to an outbreak of tropical fever, and at least two had died during their stay. Lothrop had been able to obtain a few supplies from sympathetic Tabascan merchants, but the men were low on food and nearly out of fuel. The sight of their comrades, and the supplies they brought with them, must have seemed a gift from God.

While Moore was assisting *Zavala*, federalist General Anaya came aboard for an interview with the commodore. Anaya informed Moore that Yucatán was holding a convention at Merida, its capital, to declare its independence. He proposed a joint venture between the Texas fleet and the rebels, suggesting that with the Texas Navy's help, the federalists could recapture the Tabasco capital of Villahermosa de San Juan Bautista, which a strong force of centralists was holding. With several naval batteries to help the small group of besieging federalists, Anaya believed that the town could be easily captured. To drive his point home, Anaya showed Commodore Moore a letter from the centralist commander, General Gutierrez, which indicated that the centralists were ready to surrender should Anaya be able to muster a force large enough to allow the centralists to quit the town honorably.

Anaya's request put the Navy in uncharted waters. In effect, he wanted to borrow the Texas Navy.

Moore agreed—for a price. After considerable haggling between the *generalissimo* and the Virginian, Moore promised to send his squadron up the Tabasco River with a Yucatán brig in tow, and force the centralists out for $25,000. Anaya promised to pay $10,000 up front and the rest as soon as it could be raised, which he estimated to be in fifteen to twenty days.

With the bargain struck, Commodore Moore ordered his three-ship squadron to sail up the slow, swampy, tree-lined river in the company of the federalist brig. On November 19, Moore ordered *Zavala* to raise steam for towing the other ships upriver. At 1:00 the next morning, *Zavala* dutifully chugged alongside *Austin*, and the squadron left Frontera on a day-long excursion, carrying General Anaya, his secretary, and French consul Eugene Elys. Like the forlorn travelers in Conrad's *Heart of Darkness*, the further the squadron plodded, the more dismal the jungle became. *San Bernard* lost her topsail in a tree limb, and *Zavala* had to fight the current to pull the three sailing ships upriver. But after an eighteen-hour voyage, the squadron reached the outskirts of Villahermosa de San Juan Bautista.

The city the conquistadors had named for John the Baptist was home to about ten thousand inhabitants at the time. Dominated by the Tabasco River, it was cut off from the rest of the world by a thick collage of forests and swamps, and it relied upon the river for news, trade, and—of critical importance to its military commandant—reinforcements. Control of the river meant control of the city. Since the outbreak of rebellion, the city had been in the hands of about 600 centralist troops under General Gutierrez, who held the city against a motley collection of roughly 125 federalist rebels. That would change with the arrival of the Texas Navy.

When the squadron's scouts entered the city's outskirts, they were greeted by a courier who informed them that the centralists had evacuated. Moore, not surprised at the centralist withdrawal, anchored his ships at dusk, and at sunrise on November 21, he moved up to the town's harborage. A rebel officer came aboard and informed Moore that the city had been quiet for days; General Gutierrez had evacuated the town once the centralists learned through a friendly priest that the Texas Navy had managed to cross the Tabasco bar in strength.

Upon landing Moore wrote, "Salutes were fired immediately after our arrival, from the Federal Brig, the Fort, and by the Artillery in the Square, to Gen'l Anaya, he was on board the Ship. And on his disembarking, I saluted him, and the French consul; both Salutes were returned from the Fort, and the next day I saluted the town twenty one guns which was returned." On December 3, Commodore Moore threw a ball for the citizens of Tabasco, which was "numerously attended," according to one midshipman. The federal brig departed three days later, hoisting the Texas ensign to her foremast and firing a seventeen-gun salute to the Texas fleet, which the Texians promptly returned.

Relations between the Texians and the celebrating federalists were "most amicable," according to the *Telegraph*, until the issue of payment came up. The first $10,000 was delivered as promised, and a portion was divided among Moore's impoverished men; the rest went to pay for future provisions and for supplies already purchased at Campeche and Frontera. It was the remaining $15,000 that proved problematic. After two weeks of excuses and obfuscation by General Anaya, who probably felt the Texians had not earned their fee, Moore prepared to collect the remaining debt with powder and iron. "I told him," an indignant Moore wrote, "that unless the pledges made by him were fulfilled, the good feeling between the Federalists of Tabasco, and the Government of Texas would at once be at an end, for I would protect and secure myself; after which I left him, proceeded immediately on board and had the Guns loaded with round and grape, and primed." That afternoon, Moore received a message from the provisional governor expressing regrets that anything should have affected the harmony between Texas and Yucatán. Moore nonetheless politely but firmly threatened to blockade the Tabasco River and its tributaries, starving the town and its federalist garrison into submission. Moore put his threat in writing to General Anaya, and in his words, "got underway and dropped below the town, stern foremost, so as to keep the broadside of the Ship presented to the Town and Battery." On December 15, he began menacing river traffic between Frontera and San Juan Bautista, boarding the merchant vessel *Elizabeth* to underscore his position. That was enough for the federalists; additional money was pledged by Yucatán, and Moore was eventually paid in full.

The issue of money caused other problems, as some of *Austin*'s underpaid crew, seeing a hoard of silver hauled aboard, sensed a vague opportunity for personal enrichment. On the night of November 20, foretop captain Edward Thornton got thoroughly drunk and disclosed that a mutiny was afoot and that he was involved. When word of Thornton's admission reached the commodore's ears, he had Thornton clapped in irons and taken below decks. Moore ordered his officers to convene a court-martial against Thornton, which commenced aboard *Zavala* on November 23 under the chairmanship of Commander Lothrop.

After eight days of proceedings, the court pronounced Thornton guilty and sentenced him to death with a recommendation that, in view of his previous good conduct, his sentence should be commuted to 200 lashes with the cats. Moore forwarded the trial transcript to the Navy Department for further instructions, but on January 4, the hapless Thornton died of congestive fever before the sentence could be executed. A stickler for judicial protocol, Moore ordered the sentence of the court read over Thornton's body in front of the assembled crew before committing Thornton to his eternal sleep on the Tabasco shore.

For all the damage the October and November squalls wrought on the Texas fleet, the rains did provide one important benefit. The commodore had, with great foresight, set the crew to work putting out rainwater collection barrels, which yielded some five thousand gallons of the precious liquid. *Austin*'s surgeon, Dr. Gardiner, later commented that the fresh water the thirsty men collected kept the crew healthy while it lasted, which was not long enough.

As November gave way to December, Fate again turned its back on the intrepid sailors. In early December, the fleet was visited by the dreaded tropical fever, that imprecise name for a host of serious ailments common around the Tropic of Cancer, the most feared of these being yellow fever, or "black vomit," as the Yucatecos called it. In December, pestilence hit the Navy hard. "During the month of November," Dr. Gardiner wrote in his medical journal, "there were but ten new cases, and but of little importance. At the close of the month, officers & men were all healthy, and the sick list continued clear, until the 5th of December, when sickness broke out suddenly and with great violence."

Austin's crew, closely-packed aboard ship, was stricken with twenty-two cases of fever and eighty-six cases of various kinds of influenza, including sixty-seven cases of intestinal flu. With cold impartiality, debilitating sickness struck landsmen, marines, lieutenants, pursers, carpenters, sailmakers, and surgeons. As the squadron drifted peacefully down the fetid Tabasco River, death picked off crewmembers with the deliberation of an enemy sniper. Purser Norman Hurd noted the regularity of the afterlife's call on *Austin*'s crew: seaman James Duffus, December 16; marine Charles Hoyt, December 17; seaman Michael Clark, December 19; landsman Henry Rowan, December 20; commodore's steward Samuel Edgerton, December 21. And the list went on. Aboard the smaller *San Bernard*, disease claimed two marines, a boatswain, a seaman, and the ship's steward.

The fleet's surgeons, Doctors Gardiner, Thomas P. Anderson and R. M. Clark, conferred in late December, and throughout the month did what they could to stem the dank tide of death. But primitive medicines such as sulfur drugs, castor oil, and ammonia potions did little to help. Burials at sea and on foreign shores were becoming regular rituals, and they would continue unabated through the first two months of 1841. As the weary crew sailed on, they saw many a good man sewn into canvas, round shot at his feet, the designated "chaplain" standing over him with a weathered Bible as the crew committed his body to the bosom of the sea.

Doctor Gardiner, writing in his spindly physician's hand, in fact felt fortunate that more men did not succumb to disease. "When the constitutions of the crew and their frequent previous attacks of illness are taken into consideration," Gardiner wrote, "I feel surprised that thirty or forty did not fall victim to the disease, which was a combination of the worst forms of fever that occur in a Southern Climate. Had it occurred in N. Orleans when Y. Fever pervaded, it would have been called by that name." Gardiner attributed the crew's wretched condition in part to the stagnant water at Isla de Lobos and in the Tabasco River, and recommended that the Navy Department order iron casks to replace the vessels' slimy wooden water barrels. Like virtually every other constructive suggestion made to the Department, this one was ignored.

When Yucatán paid the bulk of the Tabasco fee in late December 1840, Moore's business there was concluded. He ordered *San Bernard* back to Galveston, and by the time she arrived there, she had only four men fit for duty. Soon afterwards, Moore called all hands to weigh anchor, and *Austin* proceeded down the Tabasco River in the company of *Zavala*, which was almost completely repaired from the devastation of the October storm.

Moore needed to return to Galveston, and he also had to pick up O'Shaunessy's marooned crew from the Arcas Islands. *San Jacinto* had been wrecked by a storm shortly after Moore's departure from Frontera, but her crewmen were in surprisingly fine spirits during their stay on the accommodating little island. On Christmas Day, midshipman Alfred Walke exulted in his journal, "Spent this day very pleasantly indeed, quite a Paradise in the Dear Arcas. I shall never forget it. At 3 Oc'k set down o'er a kid of very good Egg Nogg. Drank all my absent friends healths and retired at 10.30 in a perfect state of happiness. Hurrah for the Arcas!"

Moore reached Las Arcas shortly after New Year's Day, picked up the stranded crew, and by February 1, 1841, he was back in Galveston, at home for the first time in seven months. Moore and his band of argonauts had survived storms, disease, and fire from Mexican shore batteries, but they were about to face an even greater threat, this time from the government they served.

Sam Houston, commander of the Texas Army (1835–1836), president of the Republic of Texas (1837–1838, 1841–1844), and U.S. senator (1846–1859), pictured around the time of Texas annexation. *Texas State Library and Archives Commission*

Antonio Lopez de Santa Anna, seen here during his rise to power, was the Texas Republic's most implacable foe, but he had little understanding of naval tactics until it was too late. *Benson Latin American Collection, University of Texas at Austin*

Texas's first Navy secretary, Robert Potter, was a bitter enemy of Sam Houston. *Courtesy of the Daughters of the Republic of Texas Library*

As seen in this period advertisement, Sam Colt paid tribute to the Texas Navy by engraving a scene from the Battle of Campeche on one of his most successful military revolvers of all time, the 1851 "Navy" model.

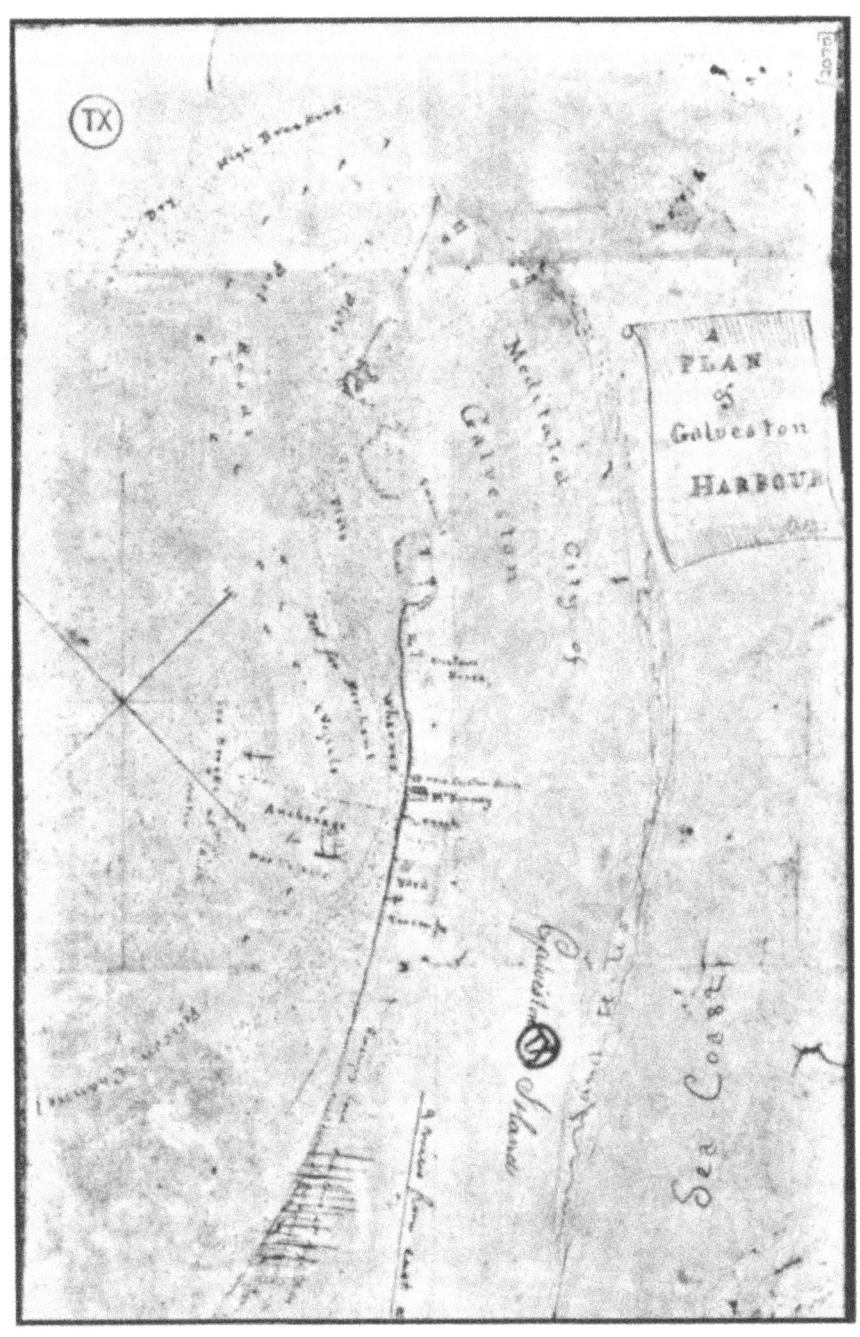

Plot of Galveston showing the site of the Navy Yard and anchorage, evidently a plan made around 1836. *Texas State Library and Archives Commission*

Texas *ad interim* President David G. Burnet was the Texas Navy's civilian commander from March to October 1836. *Texas State Library and Archives Commission*

Gen. Vicente Filisola, Santa Anna's Italian-born second-in-command, outnumbered Sam Houston's force but evacuated Texas when his army's supplies began running out. *Benson Latin American Collection, University of Texas at Austin*

Samuel May Williams, financier of two Texas Navies. *Courtesy of the Rosenberg Library, Galveston*

The fiery Galveston shipping tycoon Thomas F. McKinney financed the Texas Navy with his business partner, Samuel May Williams. *Courtesy of the Rosenberg Library, Galveston*

As president of the Republic of Texas, Sam Houston commanded the Texas Navy from this two-room shack that was the Executive Mansion in Houston from 1837 to 1838. *Texas State Library and Archives Commission*

Navy Secretary Samuel Rhoads Fisher defied President Houston in 1837 by sending the Texas Navy on an attack along the Mexican coast. *William Fisher IV*

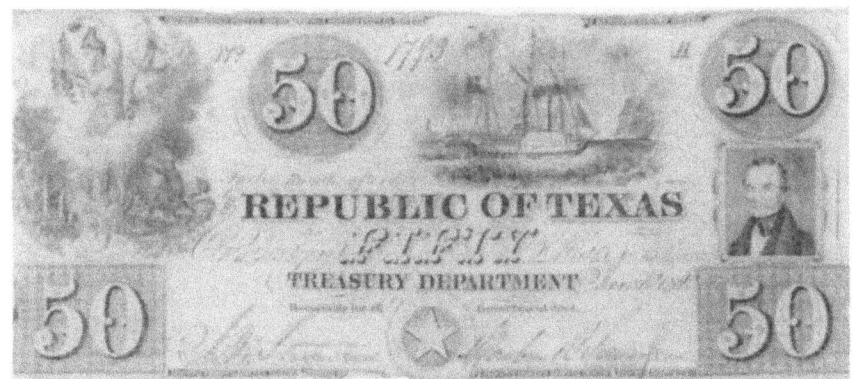

Texas paid tribute to its warships on its "Redbacks," paper currency issued during the Lamar administration. *Author's collection*

The Texas Navy's strongest supporter, Texas President Mirabeau B. Lamar. *Texas State Library and Archives Commission*

Memucan Hunt introduced the Colt revolver to Texas during his brief tenure as Navy Secretary. *Courtesy of the Rosenberg Library, Galveston*

Sketch of the Galveston Navy Yard, made by an English traveler in 1840. On the extreme left is the brig-of-war *Archer*, while the Navy Yard offices lie on the extreme right.

Commodore Edwin Ward Moore, commander of the Texas Navy from 1839 to 1843. *Naval Historical Center*

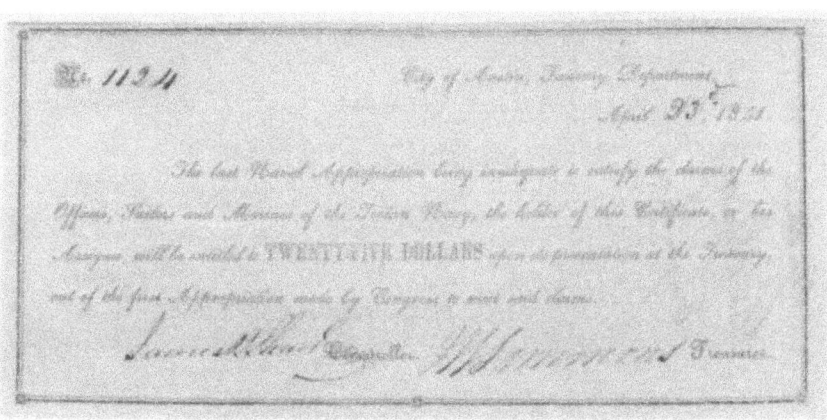

In 1841, the bankrupt Texas government paid its naval officers in promissory notes, issued by President Lamar. These notes were repudiated by President Houston after he took office in 1841. *Author's collection*

John Grant Tod, naval agent, Navy Yard commander, and acting navy secretary. *Star of the Republic Museum, Washington-on-the Brazos, Texas*

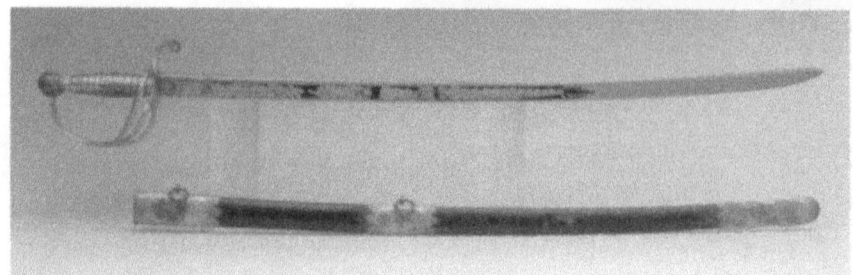

Officer's sword worn by Commander Tod, Texas Navy.
The San Jacinto Museum of History, Houston

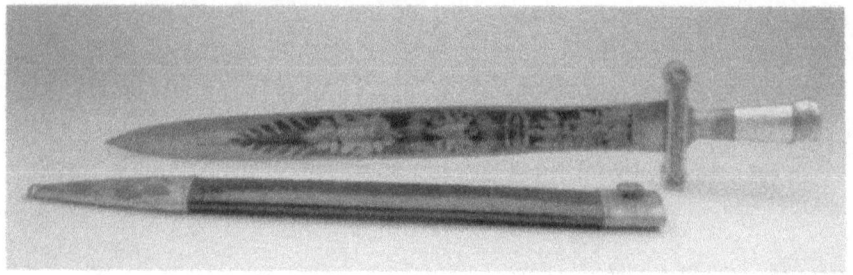

Roman-style boarding sword owned by Commander Tod.
The San Jacinto Museum of History, Houston

The Texas Navy's flagship from 1840 to 1846, the sloop-of-war *Austin*.
Naval Historical Center

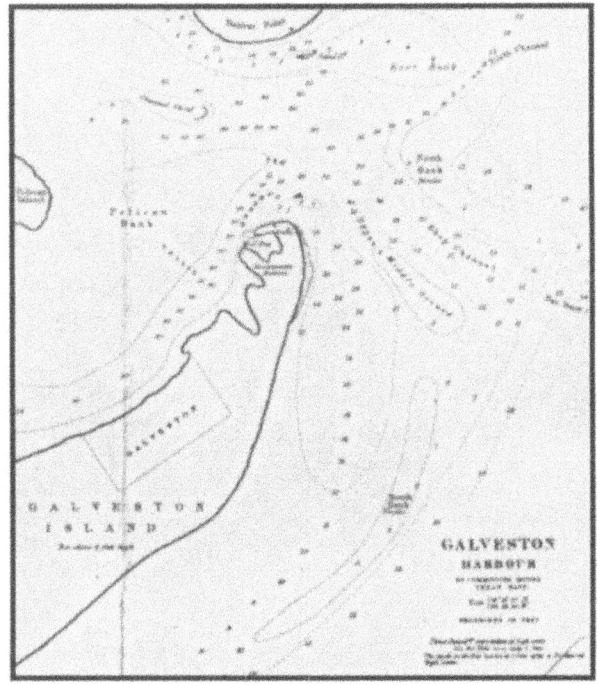

Commodore Moore surveyed the coast of Texas in the summer of 1841. *Texas State Library and Archives Commission*

One of the few surviving contemporary sketches of the Texas Navy in squadron strength, made sometime in 1840. *The Newberry Library, Chicago*

Contemporary watercolor of a cutter and brig by Texas Navy Midshipman Alfred Walke. *Texas State Library and Archives Commission*

José Maria Tornel y Mendivil, Santa Anna's longtime secretary of war and marine, rebuilt the Mexican Navy after the disasters of 1836 and 1838. *Benson Latin American Collection, University of Texas at Austin*

Texas's fastest warship, the schooner *San Antonio*, mysteriously disappeared in 1842 while on a mission to Yucatán. *Center for American History, University of Texas at Austin*

In 1842, the world's most powerful steamer was the Mexican frigate *Guadalupe*.
From Moore, Sir Alan. Sailing Ships of War 1800–1860

The Texas Navy's coastal survey included this chart of the Matagorda Bay area. *Texas State Library and Archives Commission*

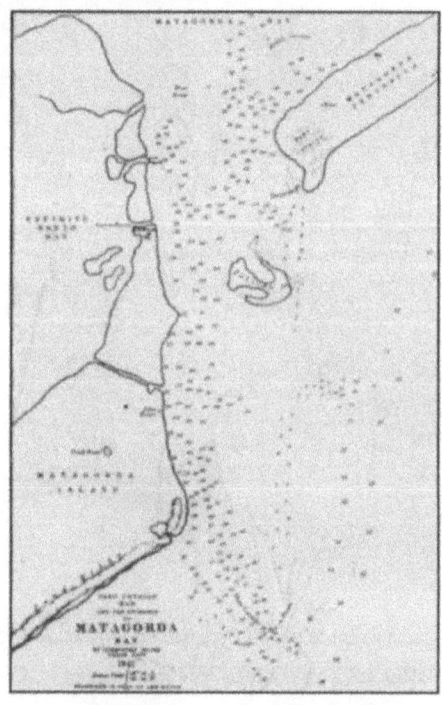

James Morgan, pictured here later in life, authorized Commodore Moore to battle the Mexican fleet off the coast of Yucatán in 1843. *Courtesy of the Rosenberg Library, Galveston*

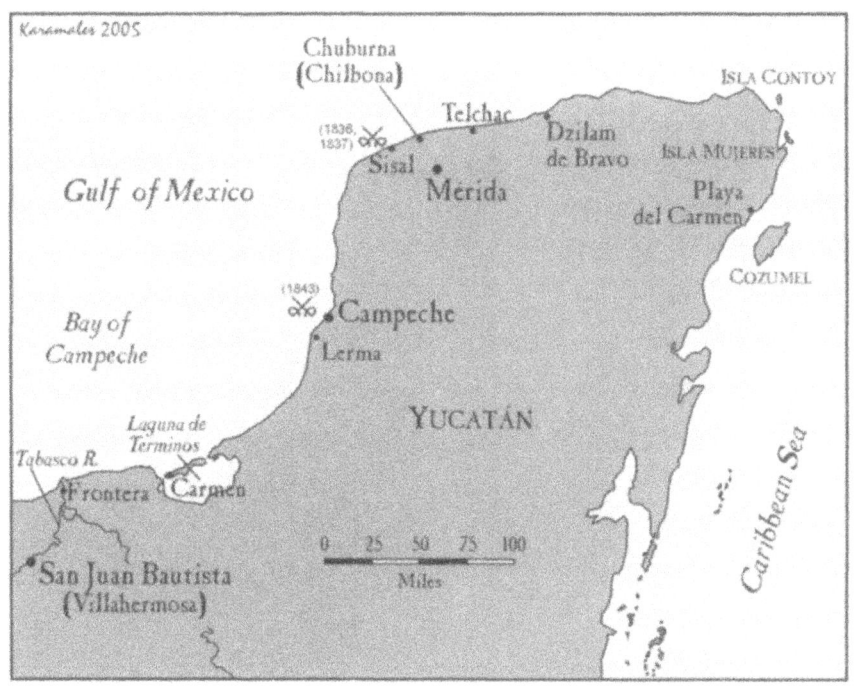

Mexico's Yucatán peninsula was the theater of many of the Texas Navy's operations between 1836 and 1843. *Jay Karamales*

An auction notice that appeared in the *Telegraph and Texas Register* in 1843. *Author's collection*

In late 1843, Commodore Moore published "To the People of Texas," a vigorous defense against charges brought by Sam Houston. *Author's collection*

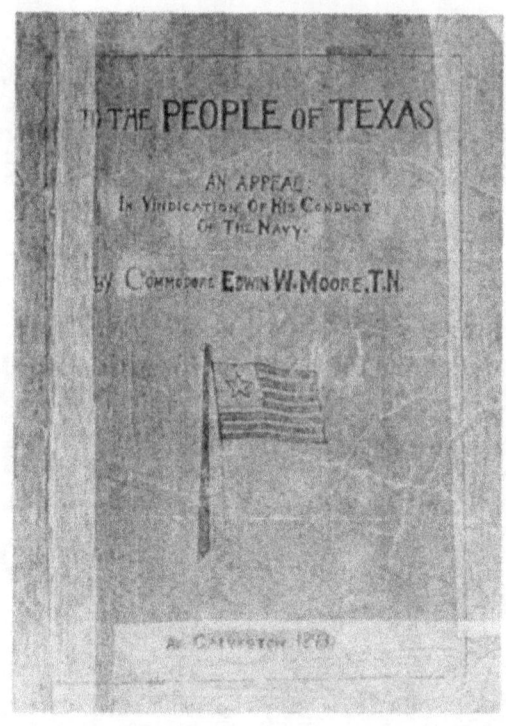

CHAPTER TWENTY-TWO

Second Thoughts

The navy which has cost this government so dearly, is the right arm of its defence, and whenever it is mutilated and destroyed, the strength of our capacities for defensive or offensive operations will be shorn, and Texas left a prey to her enemies.
—Navy Secretary Louis P. Cooke, November 4, 1840

IN THE FALL OF 1840, AS Commodore Moore's squadron blanketed the Mexican coast, James Hamilton, President Lamar's minister to London, began thumping the Republic's Big Stick upon the inlaid cherry-wood conference tables of the Court of St. James. It was Hamilton's job to win official recognition from Great Britain, and if possible, to secure Britain's pledge to force Mexico to recognize Texas.

Hamilton, unlike James Treat, knew the advantages of negotiating from a position of strength, and quickly perceived Britain's pressure points. First, Britain wanted to avoid a Texas blockade of the Mexican coast, which would imperil Britain's lucrative trade with Mexico and threaten British holders of Mexican bonds. Second, Britain sought a reliable supplier of high-quality cotton to compete with the United States, and Texas was the logical alternative. Third, and most critically, Britain wished to avoid driving Texas into the arms of the United States, with whom war over the disputed Oregon territory was becoming more likely with each passing year. Clearly perceiving British objectives, Hamilton used the Texas Navy's dominance of the Gulf as his lead card.

On October 14, Hamilton notified British Foreign Minister Lord Palmerston that if recognition was not secured within sixty days, "Vera Cruz, Tampico & Matamoras will be blockaded by the Texian Squadron, which consists of one Corvette, two Brigs, three Schooners & one naval Steamer, now off the Coast of Mexico, while Mexico is destitute of all naval force whatsoever." The Texas Navy, he warned, might also levy heavy duties from ships sailing under flags of nations that did not recognize Texas. Hamilton further cautioned that if Britain did not recognize Texas, the Republic would have no choice but to align itself with other great powers (a veiled reference to the

United States) as well as with the growing assortment of Mexican states that were in open rebellion.

Hamilton's approach worked. In mid-November, Palmerston and Hamilton signed three treaties, subject to ratification by the Texas government within six months. The first treaty recognized Texas and opened commerce between the two countries. With this treaty came British assurances that it would act as mediator between Mexico and Texas, with the aim of securing Mexico's recognition of her former province. The second treaty required Texas to assume one million pounds of Mexican debt, while the third treaty, designed to appease Britain's abolitionist sentiments, called for the navies of Texas and Great Britain to jointly patrol water traffic between Texas and West Africa to suppress the slave trade. With British recognition, diplomatic momentum had clearly shifted in favor of Texas; Hamilton's diplomatic triumph was arguably the high point of the Lamar administration.

During the fall of 1840, the guns of *Austin* and her sisters also made their presence known in Mexico City, where President Bustamente was feeling a great deal of political heat. On one hand, Texas naval operations forced Bustamente to continue negotiating with James Treat, lest Treat go home and the Texas Navy shut down Mexico's entire eastern seaboard. Dragging out negotiations with Treat would keep Commodore Moore at bay until Bustamente could obtain new warships from the United States and England. On the other hand, negotiations of any kind with the Texians were highly unpopular; the militant centralist press railed against the government for not chasing the Texas pirates back to Galveston. And waiting in the wings, ready to take power at any sign of weakness, was the self-styled Cincinnatus of Mexico, Antonio López de Santa Anna.

What hamstrung Bustamente militarily was cooperation between the Texas Navy and Yucatán. Without Yucatán's ships and ports—indeed, with Yucatán sheltering the Texas fleet—he could not retake Texas. But Bustamente could not conquer Yucatán while the Texas Navy controlled the Gulf, as the mosquito-ridden swamplands of Tabasco blocked the overland movement and supply of troops from central Mexico to the Yucatán Peninsula. As the Bustamente regime began to totter, *el presidente* did his best to improve Mexico's strategic options, principally by laying the groundwork for a large, effective navy that could someday wrest control of the Gulf of Mexico from Commodore Moore.

Given these diplomatic and political results, the Texas Navy could be pleased with the fruits of its labors. What it could not predict, however, was how nearly it came to putting itself out of a job.

As Commodore Moore was picking his way along the Mexican coast, an immense political storm broke out in Austin. Congress was furious at

President Lamar for ordering warships to sea in the face of a law requiring the fleet to be placed in ordinary. As the opposition saw it, this was the second time Lamar had defied Congress while it was out of session. Lamar had first used the congressional recess of 1839 to evade laws limiting the number of naval officers. To rein in Lamar, Congress had ordered the Navy to be placed in ordinary unless Mexico made threatening moves against Texas. Lamar then used the summer 1840 recess to evade this second law by invoking the "Mexican threat" loophole when Mexico possessed no warships. Congress, led by Lamar's implacable foe, Sam Houston, was determined to bring the adventure-loving president to heel at all costs.

Part of the Navy's problems stemmed from James Hamilton's success in winning British recognition of Texas. As many Texians saw it, Mexico's influential trading partner, the most powerful maritime power in the world, would not allow Mexico to bully Texas into the arms of the United States. By January 1841, Texas confidence in Britain's aegis was so high that peace with Mexico was taken for granted, and many considered the Navy almost irrelevant—a relic of Texas's "cold war era." The Texas *Sentinel* opined that month, "It is almost a matter of regret that the probable intervention of an armistice between Mexico and Texas, will render the further test of the efficiency of our little fleet unnecessary."

Another problem was, as always, money. Everyone knew the Republic's small, fragile economy would sink under the weight of the new fleet. As anti-Houston activist James Love had warned John Grant Tod a year before, "[Texas] cannot for herself be a military power, and never a Naval one, the expense of a Navy can never be borne by us to any great extent." A British diplomat reached the same conclusion in 1840.

> One great fault of the Texians is that [they] try to do everything at once, & having done very little & that badly, they imagine they have succeeded—they contract a great debt for a navy, & having disgusted the officers they have seduced from other services by irregularity of pay, and inactivity as regards service they lay it up, together with the officers.

Bills for the Navy began to mount. By the end of January, a very worried Frederick Dawson made a personal trip to Austin to cajole Congress into paying him the $280,000 it owed for his warships. In Galveston, the brig *Potomac* sprang a leak and sank up to her berth deck for want of repairs. To most, the financial state of the Republic provided ample justification for cutting the naval budget, and when the Fifth Texas Congress went to work in early 1841, most observers knew where the budget ax would fall.

Lamar tried to deflect congressional wrath by justifying his failure to comply with the spirit of the 1840 law that required the Navy to be laid up unless Mexico threatened the Republic. "It was confidently asserted in the papers of the United States, and as confidently believed here," Lamar told Congress, "that the Mexican government had made a contract in Europe for the purchase of several vessels of war, and that she had actually procured an armed steam ship from a commercial house in England, with a view of making a descent upon the coast of Texas, and of cutting off our commerce with foreign nations; and during the prevalence of that opinion, the executive would have been violating the evident intention and spirit of the act of congress, instead of carrying it into effect, had he caused the seamen already in service to be disbanded, and the vessels to be laid up in ordinary." Lamar warned that personnel cutbacks would destroy the Navy for all time, as naval officers could not easily be recalled or replaced. "Competent officers and soldiers [who] constitute an army, may at any time be selected from the body of the population, but seamen and efficient naval officers are not to be found among a rural people, they belong to the element on which they serve, and are nurtured only on the ocean waves. To have disbanded the accomplished and gallant officers who have embarked in our naval service, at the moment when we had reason to believe our enemy was preparing a naval armament for our coast, would, in the opinion of the executive, have not only been indiscreet and impolitic, but would, as he believes, have been contrary to the true intention and meaning of congress, as expressed in the act of the last session. It is true it might have saved us some expenditure, but it is equally true, that it might have involved the country in great disaster, and an irreparable loss of reputation."

Secretary Cooke worked with Lamar to head off the decimation of his department, issuing a lengthy report on November 4, 1840. While Congress might see disbanding most of the Navy as the immediate solution, Cooke observed, it would cost Texas more in the long run if officers and men were needed to repel an invasion from Mexico. "Sailors are not to be procured with the facility of soldiers," Cooke warned, "nor are competent and honorable naval officers to be obtained whenever they are needed. So many changes have taken place in our navy, that if it had been disbanded . . . it would have been impossible on any occasion, however much the interest of security of the country required it, to procure them again." In other words, given Texas's history of broken promises, the current navy was the last Texas would ever have; if it were broken up, no one would seriously consider signing up to sail for Texas again, no matter how dire the situation might be.

It was an uphill battle. The day Cooke's report was issued, the Austin *City Gazette* published an estimate of $571,879.59 for the upkeep of the Navy over the following year. Pointing out Texas's dilemma the *Gazette* reported, "Though this estimate was at a very low rate, the amount was still sufficient to deter Congress from making the appropriation, while no greater necessity existed of keeping up a large naval establishment than did or does now."

Shortly after finishing his report, Secretary Cooke left the seat of government, leaving John Tod behind as acting secretary of the navy, which fit in nicely with Tod's ambitions. It was during this time that Tod began the process of dismantling the service, starting with the Galveston Navy Yard, now commanded by John C. Clark. After Clark finished a number of improvements to the Yard's fence, storeroom and kitchen, Tod suggested that he discharge any men not so deeply in debt that they could not leave Galveston. *San Antonio* was next: Tod ordered Lt. Alfred Waite to strip the schooner of her masts, powder, sails, rigging, and gun tackle and transfer these items to the Navy Yard for storage. To cap the reductions, Tod also suggested the abolition of the Department of the Navy, which could be folded into the War Department as a subsidiary bureau.

In November 1840, Congress—frustrated with Lamar's expensive adventures and mindful that Texas was essentially bankrupt—went to work on legislation to scale back the Republic's government. On January 18, 1841, the Texas Congress passed a law cutting the military establishment to a size that would have made even Thomas Jefferson shudder. The Navy Department was absorbed into the War Department under a secretary of war and navy. As Tod suggested, the Navy Department became a bureau within the Department of War and Navy, to be led by a chief clerk, Augustus Seegar. The posts of naval storekeeper and navy agent were eliminated, those duties devolving to the Navy's commander in chief, who was at that time hundreds of miles away managing operations against Mexico. Ironically, one of the members of the Senate Naval Committee who presided over the abolition of the post of Secretary of the Navy was Texas' first naval secretary, Robert Potter.

Another provision of the reorganization law drastically limited the number of naval officers: "*Be it enacted, &c.,*" the statute read, "That the naval establishment of this republic shall be composed of one captain, one master commandant, eight lieutenants, ten midshipmen, with such other warrant and petty officers as may be necessary for the establishment, upon the scale provided for by this act, with sixty seamen and marines, and one lieutenant of marines, one surgeon, one assistant surgeon, and two pursers."

Tod no doubt believed he would be elevated to the position of "master commandant," making him a bigger fish in a smaller pond, and he vigorously lobbied President Lamar for the job. His commission, delivered to him in 1839, had never been submitted to the Senate. But Tod was disappointed, for he was dismissed from the service by the personnel cuts he initiated; the number two spot instead went to the able Commander Lothrop. Tod, relieved of command of both the Navy Yard and the vessels in ordinary, was relegated to the role of unofficial naval agent, and to make matters worse, the Republic's auditor, Charles Mason, called Tod's accounts into question in April, surmising that Tod had attempted to claim some of Commodore Moore's vouchers as his own during the recruiting trip to New York—a conclusion affirmed by other Texas officials. The accusation set off a war of letters between Tod, Moore, and the government that was to put a further strain on the two men's relations.

As mentioned previously, a seemingly minor law, passed in reaction to the high-handed dismissal of *Zavala*'s Commander Hinton, provided, "It shall not hereafter be lawful to deprive an officer in the military or naval service of the republic, for any misconduct in office, of his commission, unless by the sentence of a court martial."This law was to play a big part in the final act of the Texas Navy's stormy political life.

As Commodore Moore was learning of the political disasters of early 1841, President Lamar was authorizing another diplomatic mission to Mexico. In London, Her Britannic Majesty's ministers, anxious to avoid all-out war in the Gulf, agreed to mediate the Texas-Mexico dispute, and in late January the Navy Bureau ordered Lieutenant O'Shaunessy to take *San Bernard* to Veracruz and distribute copies of the Anglo–Texas recognition treaty to the British squadron. After sailing around the Gulf flagging down British warships, *San Bernard* headed down the Mexican coast to Laguna de Terminos, off the Tabasco-Campeche coast. There, the schooner's crew noticed that her foremast was sprung. The crew struck her foretopyards to relieve the strain on the mast and shaped a course for Frontera to replace it.

In early March, while *San Bernard* was at Frontera, her commander deserted. The bizarre disappearance of the erratic Lieutenant O'Shaunessy was apparently part of a scheme to steal the vessel's revolvers and sell them to the locals. It seems the Yucatecos were as enamored of Sam Colt's newfangled five-shooters as were the Texians, and while *San Bernard* was moored at Laguna de Terminos, O'Shaunessy and Captain's clerk H. A. Goldsborough sold "25 or 30 Colt's pistols and other arms" belonging to the ship. Other officers, including Lt. Thurston Taylor and *Wharton*'s commander, Lt. J. P. Lansing, may also have been part of the theft ring, and ultimately their nonexistent paychecks would be docked for the cost of these firearms. The schooner's bewildered first lieutenant, Armstrong Irving Lewis, took the helm, then sailed his understaffed warship for Veracruz to carry dispatches from Lord Palmerston to the British consul in Mexico.

When *San Bernard* was spotted off the coast of Veracruz, she caused an uproar among the local command. Fearing that the schooner was the vanguard of a Texas invasion, the region's commandant transferred 800 men to the coastal sectors and brought up four heavy guns opposite *San Bernard*'s anchorage. Lieutenant Lewis hoisted a flag of truce and came alongside the British sloop *Comus*, soliciting the protection of the British flag. Lewis asked the sloop's commander to sell him enough supplies on credit to enable him to get his vessel home. The British commander replied that he could not spare any supplies for the Texas warship, so Lewis spent the night alongside the man-of-war. The next day, a Mexican officer came aboard *Comus* with a message for *San Bernard*'s commander: if the Texian did not leave the harbor by 9:00 a.m., the shore batteries would open fire.

Lieutenant Lewis undoubtedly would have preferred to move his warship out to sea, but shortly after 9 a.m., heavy gales forced Lewis to anchor on the lee side of Isla de Sacrificios, with few able men and almost no water. The Mexicans held their fire. Eventually the nervous British commander loaned Lewis enough men and supplies to get him out to open sea. A norther crashed into the Mexican coast, keeping *San Bernard* in port for four more days, but on March 12, she was able to limp out to sea and head for Galveston, where she arrived on March 18. In the final analysis, the only lasting result of *San Bernard*'s diplomatic mission was the loss of some thirty expensive revolvers and the waste of a great many pesos on an unnecessary (and by some accounts, fraudulent) Veracruz defense effort.

When Commodore Moore arrived at Galveston on February 1, 1841, it looked as though his days with Texas, and those of the Navy itself, were numbered. Austin's *Texas Sentinel* lamented on February 19, "Commodore Moore and several of his officers are said to be in ill health. Much regret would be felt at the resignation of the commodore, which is said to be highly probable when his active services are no longer required."

To add insult to injury, Moore was given the unhappy task of furloughing officers and discharging sailors without the means to pay them for their services. When the angry men demanded back pay and clothing due them, Moore issued what shoes and trousers he could from naval stores, but he had little else to give them. To deepen Moore's humiliation, on March 22 his cousin, Lt. Alex Moore, returned to Galveston, two months after deserting the Navy. Moore forced him to resign at once.

In late March, Moore rode from Galveston to Austin to meet with Lamar and Secretary of War and Navy Branch T. Archer. The main topics at these meetings were the disposition of the fleet's ships, back pay for the men and officers, and a survey of the Texas coast, ordered by Congress the previous year. During his twenty-five-day visit, Moore and Archer decided to keep *Austin* in commission, albeit under skeleton crew, while *San Bernard* would take former U.S. District Judge James Webb to Mexico on yet another diplomatic mission. *San Antonio* would survey the Texas coast under Commodore Moore's command. The brigs would be placed in ordinary, but no firm conclusions were reached about *Zavala*, which was still at Yucatán, retrieving the last payment from the Tabasco raid. The government could not provide any money for Moore's men, but it did give Moore $100,000 in promissory notes that entitled the bearers to the next unencumbered funds that Congress might happen upon.

Moore returned to Galveston in late April, having replaced *San Bernard*'s acting commander, Lt. A. I. Lewis, with Lt. Downing Crisp, *Austin*'s first lieutenant. *Zavala* returned to Galveston with over $8,400 in Yucatán silver, but this was a small fraction of what the government owed its sailors, officers, and suppliers. In early May, a government auditor ordered Moore to return the nearly worthless promissory notes he had been given while he was in Austin, but Moore refused, informing the auditor that he already had distributed the certificates to his impoverished, hungry men. In a final cost-cutting measure, on May 2 Commodore Moore formally relieved John Tod of his duties as naval agent, commander of the Navy Yard and commander of the fleet in ordinary, fulfilling the wishes of Congress, but creating another political enemy.

For Moore and his men, there was little to do but bide their time. Their government had no intention of calling upon their combat skills for the foreseeable future, but Moore could both keep his men in shape and serve his nation by completing the coastal survey project. This project, first ordered by President Houston in 1837 and mandated by Congress in January 1839, had been held up by the Navy's other commitments and a lack of surveying equipment, which had been loaned to a commission working to formalize the boundary between Texas and the United States. By April 1841, the government turned over some of the $20,000 originally appropriated for the project, and Moore began buying maps and specialized surveying tools. He spent the months of May and June shipping men and readying *San Antonio* for her special assignment. On July 4, 1841, *San Antonio*, flying the broad blue pennant of a squadron commander, shoved off for Lake Sabine on the Texas–U.S. border.

An accurate survey of the Texas coastline was long overdue. Navigation charts of the Texas coast were as much as seventy-five miles off for important landmarks like Galveston Island or the Sabine Pass. One British diplomat complained that four of the sixteen British vessels that visited Galveston between 1841 and 1842 were lost on the coast because of poor navigation charts. The U.S. sloop *Warren*, which had captured *Invincible* in 1836, ran aground in July 1842 because of poor nautical charts that depicted the Texas shoreline sixty miles off its actual position. The true depths of the harbor bars were as much as four feet shallower than those shown on some earlier, more optimistic charts. The cumulative effect of these navigation hazards was to restrict foreign trade and inflate insurance rates to a prohibitive level.

Commodore Moore, suffering from congestive fever as his schooner left Galveston, took *San Antonio* to the Sabine Pass, and began taking soundings along the river mouth and lake. Moore charted the pass, and on July 14 he turned westward, taking careful measurements down the coast to Galveston, the Brazos mouth, Matagorda Bay and Paso Cavallo. His survey kept him at sea until mid-October, which was fortunate; for a man like Moore, being anywhere at sea was immensely preferable to rotting away with his fellow officers at the Galveston Navy Yard. Moore's labors would bear fruit late the following year, when nautical charts based on his measurements would be published in New York and by the British Admiralty in England. These maps provided navigators with a much more reliable picture of the Texas coast, which in turn reduced the costs of shipping and insurance considerably over the following years.

Judge Webb's mission to Mexico was a diplomatic necessity for President Lamar and a precondition to further military action; now that Lamar had invoked the aid of the British government in settling matters with Mexico, he could hardly declare war without making a diplomatic gesture. But no one, including Lamar, thought that Mexico would willingly recognize Texas. For this reason, Lamar ordered Moore to have *San Bernard* take Webb to Yucatán if he was rebuffed by the central Mexican government to negotiate a treaty of alliance with the federalists.

On May 14, Moore ordered Lieutenant Crisp to take *San Bernard* and Judge Webb to the coast of Veracruz. By May 30, the war schooner arrived off Sacrificios Island and fell in with the U.S. sloop *Warren* and the British sloop *Comus*. Crisp, an Englishman by birth, desperately wanted to consort with his brother officers aboard the foreign vessels, but by 1841 his fine lieutenant's uniform had worn away to rags, and his embarrassment over his appearance discouraged him from making any personal visits. Thus limited, he had to content himself with exchanging civilities by signal and letter.

Sending Judge Webb's credentials to the local authorities, Crisp sailed north to Lobos Island to await a response from the Mexican government. For two weeks, Crisp's men helped themselves to the island's abundance of turtles, fish, and limes while they recaulked the ship and waited for a reply. On June 16, the French frigate *Sabine* informed the Texians that Mexico had rejected Webb's credentials, effectively closing the last diplomatic door. The next day, *San Bernard* weighed anchor for Yucatán.

The winds that began favorably for *San Bernard* soon turned foul, and on June 19 the schooner's foremast snapped about a foot below its crosstrees, leaving a huge repair project for Crisp's men at the closest shore. Upon inspection, the core of the foremast proved to be rotten, a sign of defective materials. Crisp saved a sample of the mast for the Commodore's inspection, and after conferring with Judge Webb, he rerouted his ship to Galveston, arriving there on June 28.

Judge Webb was no James Treat, and he quickly understood that the political climate in Mexico City would never allow an administration to concede the *Cuestión de Tejas* without a fight. On June 29 he wrote to Lamar, giving advice nearly identical to that urged by Commodore Moore six months earlier.

Let Texas enter into arrangements at once with Yucatán and Tobasco, and each party mutually recognize the Independence of the other, and let them conjointly renew and prosecute the War until the Central Government shall be forced into terms.... Texas would only be expected to furnish her navy.... The federalists of Yucatán and Tobasco have now everything that is necessary to carry on the War successfully, but a Navy.... Without a Navy they can make no effectual impression upon the [centralist] seaports, and that is the most essential object to be obtained.

Late in the summer of 1841, most observers concluded that Mexico would never negotiate in good faith with Texas. The uproar among the centralists, and the sticky question of the land between the Rio Grande and Nueces Rivers (which both sides claimed) ruled out a negotiated solution for President Bustamente or his immediate successor. Furthermore, on June 19, 1841, President Lamar launched his ill-fated Santa Fe Expedition against Mexico's New Mexico territory, killing any hopes for resuming talks in the near future. The rapid failure of the Santa Fe Expedition, and the failures of previous Mexican incursions into Texas, proved that the two countries were at an impasse, each powerless to coerce the other into submission.

Evan Napian, commander of the British sloop *Comus*, summed up the views of many neutral observers in a letter to his squadron commander.

I have been given to understand that Mr. Packenham has been ordered to act as Mediator between the parties, but I fear hitherto with little or no success. It is very certain, that Mexico has great reason to feel indignant, at the bad faith and total want of honesty on the part of the Texians in the first instance, but as these people are now become a free and independent Republic and recognized as such by the great powers of Europe, it is folly to contend any longer against the state of things which is totally out of the power of Mexico to remedy.

France's King Louis Philippe made the point more bluntly to Mexico's minister to Paris, Máximo Garro. "To describe the kind of obstinacy that prevents one from seeing what is evident, we have a word in French that is very easy to translate into Spanish—*infatuation*. This *infatuation* prevents you from recognizing what everybody else sees; that is, you have lost Texas irrevocably."

It appeared that Mexico's strategy was to rebuild its navy to support an invasion of Yucatán, then turn its eyes back upon Texas. The government purchased a Spanish brig and mounted an eighteen-gun battery on her decks, then sent Commander Tomás Marín to the United States to buy two five-gun schooners, to be delivered by September 1841. Conscripts were drafted and trained for a landing in Yucatán in late fall. And, pointedly, the government ordered two ultra-modern steam warships from Great Britain, to be delivered in early 1842—too late to arrive for operations in Yucatán, but perfectly timed for a spring invasion of the Lone Star Republic. It appears that by the summer of 1841, the Mexican government had fully realized that pacification of Yucatán, with her large shipping industry, strategic placement, and military resources, was key to the conquest of Texas.

In Austin, Webb's June 29 message drove this point home to Lamar. Efforts by Barnard Bee and Richard Packenham in 1839, James Treat's efforts in 1840, and now Webb's efforts in the spring of 1841 had all come to naught. With no other options, Lamar threw in his lot with Yucatán. Three weeks after Judge Webb wrote his report, President Lamar sent Yucatán's governor a proposal for a treaty of friendship and a de facto military alliance against Mexico. On August 24, Yucatán's Gov. Miguel Barbachano dispatched Col. Martín Peraza to Austin with the authority to conclude an agreement with Texas. Reciprocating Lamar's warm tone, Barbachano replied, "Yucatán wishes to draw closer its relations with the people of Texas, and unite with them to sustain the cause of liberty which has been proclaimed against the oppressive Government of Mexico." With this letter, a most unconventional era in Texas's diplomatic relations began.

CHAPTER TWENTY-THREE

The Great Game

It was in the month of July of that year that the Texas Navy was subsidized to Yucatan, an integral part of the Republic of Mexico.... This was done without any authority or sanction of the Congress or Senate of the Republic of Texas. It was a mere act of grace or will on the part of the President.
—Senator Sam Houston to the U.S. Senate, 1853

On September 5, Colonel Peraza stepped ashore in Galveston from the Yucatán schooner *Campecheano* with six bags and one strongbox stuffed with money, which he deposited at the customs house for safekeeping. He then proceeded to Austin with his secretary, Donanciano Rejón, nephew of Yucatán's secretary of state. Clattering into the capital six days later, he called upon Secretary of State Samuel Roberts, and asked Roberts to arrange an appointment with Lamar.

The next day, Peraza was ushered in to Lamar's office, to meet with the president and Secretary Roberts. Peraza informed Lamar that Yucatán had scheduled a convention for October in which it would declare its independence, and suggested the immediate need for a security agreement with Texas. Correctly surmising the biggest obstacle for Texas, Peraza stressed that money was no object for Yucatán. They went through elaborate diplomatic motions, but Lamar and Peraza knew they needed each other, and a bargain was a foregone conclusion.

Since Yucatán was not yet an independent nation, a treaty was inappropriate; Lamar therefore agreed to an executive order providing naval support to Yucatán under terms to be worked out between Roberts and Peraza—a treaty by any other name. On September 13, Peraza sent Roberts a communiqué addressing "relations of Amity, Navigation & Commerce," in which he conceded that Yucatán's navy was too small to throw back a Mexican invasion. Given the immediacy of the crisis, he wrote, "I am fully authorized by my Government to contribute to the removal of any pecuniary obstacles which might perhaps for the moment embarrass that of Texas in putting her vessels in action." As a first course of action, Peraza suggested, "Texas and Yucatan should agree upon the expediency of laying a formal blockade upon the ports of Mexico, or of making maritime reprisals, the product of this will be divisible between the two Governments in proportion to the expences that they may have effectively incurred."

Roberts, not wanting to let the moment pass, replied the next day. "When therefore you tell us that you have reason to apprehend that the same despotism which for a time waged so savage and relentless a war against us, is preparing to attack the newly established liberties of your country, we can not hesitate to cooperate with you in preparing to repel the premeditated attack by sending such a portion of our Naval force to sea as may be deemed adequate to the service required of it." The diplomats agreed that Texas would send at least three warships to aid Yucatán for $8,000 per month, for as long as Yucatán felt the need for Texas support. Any prizes would be divided equally between Yucatán and Texas after deducting the expenses of the enterprise. Captures made by Texas vessels would be towed to Texas ports for condemnation, and Yucatán captures would likewise be sent to Yucatán. By the afternoon of September 17, Peraza accepted Roberts's terms, writing, "Being conformable to the spirit of my instructions, they are sanctioned on my part in the name of my government, which is pledged to their most punctual and religious observance."

The next day Roberts affirmed that a bargain had been struck. "The President has this day given orders, in conformity with the stipulations and agreements which have been mutually made between the two governments, for three or more vessels to proceed with as little delay as possible to the port of Sisal, when it is expected the Government of Yucatán will furnish the Commander of the Squadron with such information as will enable him to operate to the advantage of Yucatán," he wrote. "It is hoped the action of Commodore Moore, who will personally command the squadron, will be such as to give entire satisfaction to the government of Yucatán. His orders have been made in strict conformity with the agreement which has been entered into between the two governments."

The day the pact was signed, a great ball was announced to celebrate the alliance. War Secretary Archer introduced the representatives of Yucatán from the speaker's platform in the Texas Senate chamber, while Yucatán and Lone Star flags brightened the state ballroom. The same day, the Department of War and Navy ordered Commodore Moore to return from his coastal survey and prepare to sail for Yucatán.

On September 20, Lieutenant Crisp's *San Bernard* ran down the coast to find Moore and bring him home. Moore, commanding *San Antonio* near Matagorda Bay, immediately sailed back to ready his ships for a short trip to New Orleans, where he could buy provisions and recruit sailors with Yucatán's hard currency.

Commodore Moore was undoubtedly thrilled at the prospect of putting his squadron to sea. His only cause for regret was that the nearly indispensable *Zavala* would be unable to join them, because she had never been properly repaired after her last turbulent cruise. Another problem was the fact that the Navy's men had not been paid in hard currency in quite some time, which would not help recruiting. But the cash infusion from Yucatán would, at least, provide bonus money to recruit new sailors who had not yet been disillusioned by the Texas government. With luck, captured prizes and the $8,000 monthly rent would provide an ample source of payment.

On October 13, Moore received two sets of orders from the War Department—one commanding him to prepare for an upcoming cruise, and another, sealed set to be opened once he put to sea. Moore's general orders, dated September 18, 1841, cautioned him not to accept any money from Yucatán if he could not commence operations on an $8,000 budget. Fortunately for Moore, Peraza generously advanced an additional $6,000 over the next month, to prime the warships for operations.

Moore knew time was short. The isolated government of Yucatán was feeling intense pressure to return to the centralist fold. And while the balance of forces in the Gulf favored Texas momentarily, Mexico was rebuilding its fleet. It had already acquired one armed brig and had shipped sailors from New Orleans to man her. If it deployed a second brig, then Mexico's two men-of-war would be able to pick off any Texas vessels that strayed from the squadron. And Mexico's order for two large English steamers would throw the balance of power decisively to Mexico if the ships arrived and could be fitted out under Mexican command.

But most worrisome of all, Sam Houston had been elected president of the Republic for a second term. His inauguration, set for December 13, would undoubtedly mark another period of retrenchment for the Texas Navy; if Moore was not at sea by the time Houston was sworn in, the Navy might never leave port again.

For the next two months, Moore worked feverishly to ready the fleet for an attack on the Mexican coast. He requested, and received, appointments for new officers, and had his lieutenants scour harbors and seaports for recruits. With his limited budget, Moore carefully chose three warships that would accompany him. Since Mexico was reportedly buying a sloop of war, Moore selected *Austin* as his flagship and ordered her out of reduced commission. *San Bernard* and *San Antonio* were in full commission already, so he took them as well. The rest of the fleet would have to stay behind. *Zavala*'s repair bill would have consumed a quarter of Moore's $14,000 budget, *Wharton* had no crew, and the stripped-down *Archer*, which had never left port, had a foot of water in her bilges.

Unfortunately for Moore's recruiting efforts, *San Antonio* and *San Bernard* arrived in New Orleans during an outbreak of tropical fever, and Moore, who was prone to bouts of malaria, came down with a severe case himself. After only two days, though, the sweat-soaked, shivering captain hauled himself up out of bed, well aware of the huge workload that duty commanded him to manage. First on his list was ammunition. He ordered two thousand rounds of twenty-four-pound shot, which he later had to send back because the cannonballs were made to army dimensions, which failed to account for a layer of sea rust that would build up on the balls. Moore also sent Lt. William Seeger's *San Antonio* to Yucatán to pick up the November installment of silver. When Seeger returned with $6,000 in late November, Moore paid the Navy's supply and recruiting bills, then returned to Galveston aboard the merchant ship *Neptune* with supplies for *Austin*. When *Neptune* arrived off the Galveston Bar on December 4, Moore ordered *Austin* towed out to meet her, so that *Austin* would not have to cross the shallow bar while loaded down with a bellyful of supplies. To Moore's horror, *Austin* bumped the bar fifteen or twenty times nonetheless, probably shedding some of her protective copper sheathing in the process. Moore was certain that his beloved flagship would never weather another such crossing.

As November gave way to December, Moore worked like a man possessed, keeping supplies flowing from New Orleans to Galveston via *San Antonio*. From Galveston, Moore ordered furniture, paint, and supplies for *Austin* and *Wharton*, which he still hoped might put to sea in due course. He assigned crews to painting, loading, and rigging on a frenetic schedule. While not on these specialized duties, the officers drilled the men in shipboard tasks until the fleet could be safely taken to sea.

The hard work paid off with the fleet's departure just before Houston's inauguration day. On December 9, four days before the inauguration, Lt. William Seeger's *San Antonio* lifted anchor for Sisal, while Lieutenant Crisp's *San Bernard* sailed away to the rendezvous point at Sisal via a reconnaissance trip to Tampico and Veracruz. On December 13, 1841, the day the Republic swore in its new commander in chief, the flagship *Austin* bade goodbye to her home port and disappeared over the horizon to the south.

As Moore would find out, his suspicions about President Houston were right.

CHAPTER TWENTY-FOUR

Red Skies in Morning

Our navy has not yet started, and if it could be of any use to us I would be glad that it should not go. If it should sail, you may rely upon it that it will be the last of our navy. That it will be in the hands of Santa Anna in ninety days, I would be willing to wager a trifle.
—Sam Houston, November 10, 1841

IN 1841, SAM HOUSTON CAMPAIGNED for a second presidential term on an anti-Lamar platform. He was anti-imperialist, fiscally tight, and privately, at least, still a believer in annexation to the United States, notwithstanding the rebuffs of the late 1830s by the Jackson and Van Buren administrations. Although he rarely expressed it publicly, Houston was also anti-navy, now more than ever.

Much of Houston's ill will towards the fleet stemmed from its cost, a very reasonable consideration given the sorry state of the Republic's treasury. As a congressman from San Augustine, Houston lamented in 1840, "The finances of this nation have been destroyed by the excessive issue of treasury notes," referring to Lamar's "redbacks," the paper currency that, among other things, financed the Navy. During his first administration, Houston had decried the continued expense of maintaining the Navy Yard, which further drained the Republic's budget. In 1841, a campaigning Houston wrote to the *Austin City Gazette*, "Our motto ought to be, *fewer officers and more cornfields!*"

A second, deeper reason for Houston's mistrust lay with the insubordination of his naval commanders during his first term. In 1836, the commanders of *Brutus* and *Invincible* had sailed to New York against President Burnet's orders and had gotten themselves so deep into debt that they could not obey orders to return. In 1837, Secretary Fisher and Commander Thompson had defied Houston by cruising against Mexico—an adventure that cost the Republic its best fighting ship and created diplomatic havoc with England. In 1838, the Navy's commander, George Wheelwright, had refused to take the oath of office and was dismissed, while in 1839, Commander Hinton had overspent his prescribed budget, and was also dismissed, that time by Lamar. Houston attributed the Revolution's greatest disasters—the fall of the Alamo and the massacre of Fannin's men—to insubordination by headstrong army officers, and he undoubtedly felt his naval commanders were cut from the same cloth.

Houston's ambivalence toward the Navy only increased over time, although he had to be careful not to assault the institution publicly. In a letter to Capt. John Hall shortly before he took office in 1841, Houston privately expressed skepticism over Lamar's naval alliance with Yucatán:

> I would not be surprised if it would turn out that the whole revolution in Yucatán was set on foot by Santa Anna with a view to inveigle Lamar and get the navy in possession. The revolution was a bloodless one and soon ended. Moreover, Santa Anna has a great contempt for Lamar and would be quite delighted to play a trick upon him. Besides, it would furnish Mexico with a navy, which she is not able to purchase, and have our whole coast at her mercy. We will see.

After he was sworn in for his second term, Houston hinted at his distrust of Commodore Moore in a letter to his wife Maggie. "Now my dear, I will respond to you on the subject of politicks. I have ordered the Navy in to port some days since, but kept it a secrete, as I do not wish to alarm their fears while at sea or until I can get them within my control! You will take the hint. There are some in command that I would not like to trust, if they saw their advantage lay on the other hand."

Houston was not alone in his views. A significant faction in Congress believed that Lamar's pact with Yucatán was an elaborate trap set by Santa Anna's agents, while others supported the concept of a navy but were alarmed at the financial straits in which Lamar had placed Texas. The Yucatán expedition would cost an estimated $40,000 for a three-month cruise, while Yucatán would only be obliged to contribute $24,000 for the same period of time, or at most, $32,000, even if Yucatán viewed the October payment as a "sunk" cost. Still others, like former Secretary of State Anson Jones, felt that Mexico should be left alone entirely as a matter of sound foreign policy.

By the fall of 1841, the capricious political tide, which had been set so strongly against Houston at the end of his first administration, had turned with equal force against Lamar. On September 6, Houston easily defeated Lamar's chosen successor, former interim president David Burnet, and the Houston faction mounted up for one last assault on Lamar before he left office on December 13.

On November 19, the House Committee on Naval Affairs issued a report which concluded that Lamar had violated the 1841 law by not placing the Navy in ordinary. Four days later, Lamar informed the Sixth Texas Congress that he had ordered the fleet to sea in support of Yucatán, but offered to recall the expedition if Congress passed a resolution expressing its disapproval. The Houston faction launched a withering three-week attack on President Lamar, linking the Yucatán venture with the disastrous Santa Fe Expedition. The radical Houstonites drafted a resolution to recall the fleet, but they made the classic political mistake of overkill. The preamble to the resolution excoriated the president in the most abusive language the Houston faction could use publicly, and when the resolution was unveiled, Houston's moderate supporters were repelled. They urged their party to tone down the invective, but the Houston stalwarts and the pro-Lamar faction, for opposing reasons, would not allow the offensive language to be softened. The moderates thus sided with Lamar in the interest of governmental dignity, and the bill was defeated on December 14 by a vote of twenty to eighteen.

The resolution was a perfectly wasteful exercise, since everyone knew that Houston would recall the fleet once he was in office, and such a resolution could only dash the newfound morale of the Navy and its officers. Commodore Moore, following events from his flagship off Galveston, wrote bitterly to his friend, Gen. Albert Sidney Johnston, that he was well aware of the attacks that would be made in Congress after his fleet left Texas waters, and would resign rather than see his service suffer a public humiliation. Moore warned, "If the Navy is ordered back I will be humbugged no longer but will quit, and if I do not one Officer will remain and if our Navy is again laid up it will be impossible to keep the Officers in Service any longer and our Ports will be blockaded and Galveston battered down."

As expected, Houston called Moore home. On December 15, the newly-appointed secretary of war and navy, George W. Hockley, sat down at his desk and penned the following terse orders: "Sir—I am directed by His Excellency the President to order that the squadron under your command return forthwith to the port of Galveston, and there await further orders." Hockley's orders were sent to Galveston, but they did not reach the port collector, Gail Borden, until December 28. Since the fleet had already left, Borden forwarded the orders to New Orleans, and wrote Hockley back, offering to hire a boat to take the orders to Yucatán if a receipt was required. Of course, the Republic had no money to hire a boat for such a small errand, so the recall orders sat in New Orleans until a merchant ship bound for Yucatán could be found. In a speech before the U.S. Senate some twelve years later, Sen. Sam Houston attributed the delay in dispatching his orders "to peculiar influences at Galveston."

CHAPTER TWENTY-FIVE

The Wooden Aegis

> *If it be the wish of His Excellency the President to coerce Mexico to acknowledge our Independence, I can at once blockade all the ports of entry... if I had the steamer Zavala to co-operate with the Squadron, I could levy contributions on several of their towns to a greater amount than the entire cost of the Navy.*
> —Commodore Moore to Secretary Hockley, January 31, 1842

ONCE *AUSTIN* CLEARED THE GALVESTON BAR, Commodore Moore summoned Lieutenant Alfred Gray, Purser Norman Hurd, and Dr. William Richardson to his cabin and opened his sealed orders. The orders contained no surprises; they included copies of the Roberts-Peraza-Lamar correspondence and reiterated the main points of the September 18 pact. War Secretary Archer permitted Moore to levy contributions on seaside cities and towns, and to destroy those that refused, "[t]he effect of which will be to give the Central Government active employment at home for all their available forces, to cut off the revenue derived from their Custom Houses, and to strike a terror among the inhabitants, which may be very useful to us should it again be thought advisable to enter into negotiations for peace."

Thus clothed in official sanction, Moore sailed for Tampico in late December, to see what kinds of targets he could set his canvas against. He stopped two ships, which being friendly, he promptly released: the Yucatán vessel *Fortune*, and a Belgian galliot whose captain was very ill. Moore sent his chief surgeon, Dr. Anderson, to tend to the captain, and gave the Belgian skipper a complimentary chart of the Gulf.

Sailing east, Moore rejoined *San Antonio* and *San Bernard* at a rendezvous point forty miles west of Sisal. The next day, January 6, the Texas squadron entered the harbor with great ceremony, firing off a salute to the port castle, which was respectfully returned. Moore's only recorded business at Sisal was his receipt of $2,000 in funds from the port collector, but he probably also sent forth pursers to bargain for supplies from local merchants, as his midshipmen were nearly all in need of new pants, shoes, and buttons.

On January 8, Commodore Moore dispatched the schooners to Isla Mujeres, near modern-day Cancún, to collect water, as fresh water was scarce on the peninsula during the dry season. Leaving 1st Lt. Alfred Gray in command of the flagship, he and Lt. William Seeger came ashore and proceeded southeast to Merida, Yucatán's capital. Arriving there that night, Moore penned a short letter to Yucatán's secretary of war and marine, Pedro Lemus, announcing, "I am ready to carry out the spirit of the agreement on the part of the Government of Texas." Lemus, whom Moore had rescued after his escape from the centralists in 1840, welcomed the commodore with open arms, and promptly arranged an interview with Yucatán's governor.

The Yucatán newspapers, however, gave the Texians a nasty shock, which was confirmed at Moore's brief interview with the governor the next morning: Yucatán, far from declaring independence at its October convention, as Colonel Peraza had promised, had instead decided to negotiate a return to centralist Mexico. The central government had sent the highly respected Yucatán patriot, Andréas Quintana Roo, to negotiate terms of accession, and on December 28—one week before *Austin* arrived off Sisal—a pact was signed. Under the proposed treaty, Yucatán would retain all her recently-enacted reforms and would have complete autonomy over her customs and finances. Taxes would only fund state programs, and federal conscription would not apply to Yucatán. Pending ratification, an armistice would be observed on both sides. From the Texian point of view, it was a complete diplomatic victory for Mexico.

Moore was flabbergasted. All his work for the last three months was for nothing! He immediately fired off a stern letter to Joaquin Rejón, Yucatán's secretary of state, expressing his dismay at crossing the Gulf of Mexico only to be turned away. Texas, he declared, would never have negotiated with Yucatán had it believed that Yucatán lay within the political sphere of the Central Government of Mexico.

Rejón was unimpressed. He pointed out that Yucatán had not given up her right to negotiate reentry into the Mexican union, and the September 18 agreement specifically provided that either party could cancel the pact on short notice. Nevertheless, Rejón recognized the threat the Texas Navy posed to Yucatán's coast—and the implied threat to the centralists if Mexico City refused to ratify the treaty—so he assured Moore that, until the central government formally ratified the December 28 treaty, the governor would consider Mexico as Yucatán's enemy, and until that time, Moore's ships would be paid their $8,000 monthly fee and be welcome in Yucatán's ports.

Moore, somewhat mollified, replied, "You will oblige me by giving His Excellency the Governor my assurances that he may rely on my continued exertions to strengthen that Friendship and Amity which at present exists between the two Governments." Here Moore was walking a diplomatic tightrope: push the Yucatán government too hard—or not enough—and it would revert back to the centralist sphere, leaving Texas without an ally in the Gulf.

Moore's delicate balance was nearly disrupted by the well-meaning but illtimed actions of Lieutenant Gray, whom Moore had left in command of *Austin* back at Sisal. For two days after Moore and Seeger left for Merida, Gray continued to receive reports of Yucatán's impending reunion with Mexico. Newspaper articles, casual conversations with government officials and port rumors stated that commissioners from Mexico City were about to depart with a treaty of reconciliation. No doubt the rumors also exaggerated the potential hostility to Texas, at least to Texian ears. Gray's level of alarm reached its peak on January 12, when he discovered that the American barque *Louisa*, anchored near *Austin*, was taking aboard Mexican treaty commissioners, who were expected to depart shortly.

Fearing for the lives of Commodore Moore and Lieutenant Seeger at the hands of the treacherous Yucatecos, Gray sent lieutenants Armstrong Lewis and Cyrus Cummings to *Louisa* with a detachment of marines. They notified the barque's master that the Texians were bringing the Mexican delegation aboard *Austin* pending Commodore Moore's safe return.

Over the loud and profane objections of the barque's captain (a "blustering blackguard," Moore called him), Cummings brought back a coterie of federalist and centralist diplomats, including Col. José Lemus, Andréas Quintana Roo, Gen. Juan Pablo Anaya, and several Mexican commissioners. After informing the diplomats politely but firmly that they would not be allowed to leave the ship, Lieutenant Gray promptly sent the Yucatán delegation's secretary back to Merida with a report to Commodore Moore.

Shortly before two o'clock the next morning, Moore was roused from his bed with the news that Gray had taken Mexican and Yucatán envoys hostage. Shaking off his sleep, he read Gray's letter and quickly penned a reply, assuring him, "I am perfectly safe here ... there is not the least possibility that the people or government of Yucatan" would act in a treacherous manner. Certainly, Moore was unhappy with Gray's interference with Texas's already questionable relations with Yucatán, but inwardly, he must have been pleased with the initiative shown by his capable subordinate, who had already proved himself resourceful while fighting the seas aboard *San Jacinto* in October of 1840. Gray's actions also subtly underscored the Texas Navy's power along the Yucatán coastline, which did not hurt, either.

Hurriedly buttoning his blue dress uniform, Moore quickly strode across the darkened Plaza de Armas to the governor's residence, where he announced himself and assured the governor that he had not been behind Gray's actions at Sisal, and had ordered the commissioners' immediate release. Setting things right with the governor, he returned to his quarters, and was greeted the next day with an obligatory letter of outrage from Secretary Rejón. Explaining Gray's actions as the result of the widespread rumors of reconciliation with Mexico, Moore replied that he had ordered

Gray to allow his guests to leave his ship immediately, and the matter ended there with evidently no hard feelings among the Yucatecos. Rejón affirmed Yucatán's commitment to the September 18 pact, and informed Commodore Moore that the government had established a special signal to distinguish Yucatecan warships from those of Mexico: a blue flag at the foremast. With mutual expressions of friendship and support, Moore left his hosts at Merida to resume command of his ship at Sisal.

Moore spent several days at Sisal—completing calculations for his chart of the Texas coast, buying limes and other essential fruits for his crews, and tending to his ship—until the afternoon of January 24, when news reached Sisal that the American schooner *Sylph* was in peril at the rocky Alacranes. Ordering his men to lift anchor at once, Moore sped seventy-five miles northwest to the islands through a fierce norther. Through the biting gale he found *Sylph* and her crew trying to save some of the stricken vessel's cargo with the help of local fishermen. Sending out salvage parties, Moore's boats managed to get *Sylph*'s captain, passengers, crewmen, and some cargo safely aboard before the schooner went to pieces. By January 27, Moore headed back to Sisal, where he transferred his guests to *San Antonio*. The American captain's letters to newspapers and U.S. Secretary of State Daniel Webster thanking the Texas Navy for saving his crew more than offset the bad publicity that would arise from Lieutenant Gray's temporary detention of *Louisa*'s passengers. The rescue of the *Sylph* and *Segunda Fama* passengers, and Moore's new charts of the Texas coast, helped build an aura of respectability around the Texas fleet that would pay important dividends soon enough.

In Moore's report to the government on January 31, he faithfully reported the events that had transpired, knowing full well that they would only fuel President Houston's distrust of the Yucatecos and their government. He did, however, emphasize positive developments; because of the Yucatán subsidy, he told the cost-conscious administration, "I will be able to keep at sea until the 1st May, without calling on the government for one dollar." He warned that Mexico had ordered two warships from New York, and recommended that the government order a complete blockade of the Mexican coast, which would extend to any foreign vessel carrying contraband of war into Mexican ports. Even the schooners' long watering trip bode well for offensive operations: they returned, not only well supplied with drinking water, but also with a chart of the coast and a report of plentiful wood and water at Mujeres Harbor. Moore clearly had not given up on the possibility that Sam Houston could be persuaded that Texas's interests lay with an aggressive naval policy backing up its diplomatic efforts.

Still unaware that he had been recalled home, Moore informed the Department that he would depart for Campeche, and thence to Veracruz. "Off the latter place," Moore mused, "I will cruize sometime." Bidding farewell to Secretary Rejón, on February 1 Moore sent *San Antonio* to Galveston with his report and copies of public proclamations from Yucatán, and then sailed with *San Bernard* to Veracruz, to have a look at what the nascent Mexican Navy was doing.

Because *Zavala* was deteriorating in Galveston, Moore was unable to get too close to the harbor at Veracruz; a sudden gust from the Gulf's belly could easily blow him against the rocky shore, or into range of the guns of Castle San Juan d'Ullua. Even so, by February 5 he was able to inch close enough to the harbor to spot one of two warships that Mexico had ordered from New York. Later that day, *Austin* took her first prize, the 180-ton brig *Progreso*, sailing from Veracruz to Matamoros. Running her down easily, Moore sent a detachment of marines to search the ship, which yielded a rich haul of sugar, coffee, and flour, as well as a Mexican artillery lieutenant, who tore off his epaulette and stuffed it in his pocket when he realized that *Progreso* was about to be taken. Moore wrote of the lieutenant, "I intend keeping him, as I will all other officers of the government who fall into my hands, until I can hear something definite of the Santa Fe expedition." Moore sent the brig to Galveston under Lieutenant Tennison and Midshipman Robert Clements, and *Progreso*'s arrival was heralded along the coast as a badly-needed victory for Texas.

Near Veracruz, *Austin* and *San Bernard* continued to prowl Mexican waters in search of prizes and information, but violent north winds, the same sorts of gusts that splintered *Zavala* and *San Jacinto*, shook the two warships so badly that Moore could only get close enough to spy on the port three times over two and a half weeks. Finally, on February 17, the storms let up. Moving up to the harbor under a U.S. flag, Moore was greeted by a local pilot, whom Moore detained and asked about recent developments. The pilot reported that the reconciliation treaty with Yucatán almost certainly would not be ratified by the centralist government, and that Mexico had received one of its two new war schooners, the *Aguila* of New York. She sat in the harbor, still flying the Stars and Stripes. Another schooner, *Libertad*, had wrecked off the Florida reefs as she sailed for her new home.

A third vessel, the dirty old steamer *City of Dublin*, now renamed *Regenerador*, sat under the guns of the castle, having paddled into Veracruz three days before. Moore must have known that the steamboat was a very bad sign of things to come; such a vessel, while unarmed for the moment, would give Mexico's armed sailing ships mobility in adverse winds, something Moore's squadron—lacking *Zavala*—did not have. (*Regenerador* would later mount six medium eighteen-pounders and a long eighteen pivot.) The good news, for the moment, was that the two ironclad steamers being constructed in England for Mexico had been delayed due to Mexico's financial problems and the timely interference of Ashbel Smith, Houston's feisty minister to the Court of St. James.

After paroling the captured Mexican lieutenant and setting him ashore near Veracruz, Moore sailed east to report his findings to the Yucatán government and collect the Navy's monthly fee. Arriving at Sisal on the twenty-fifth, he sent a friendly request for payment to Secretary Lemus. Upon receipt of the $8,000, Moore fired off a twenty-one gun salute to Yucatán, then sailed for the Arcas Islands to meet *San Antonio*. Not finding her there, Moore left a letter at the island ordering her to join *Austin* at the port of Carmen, at Laguna de Terminos, in the province of Campeche.

It was at Campeche that Commodore Moore once again had to reassure the federalists of Texas's continued loyalty to her ally. As he dropped anchor at Campeche Bay, he learned that an American brig had brought a New York newspaper publishing a letter from Galveston dated January 30. This letter claimed that the sloop *Washington* had been dispatched with orders for Commodore Moore directing him to capture any Yucatán vessels of war he encountered. Given Yucatán's concerns over Lieutenant Gray's detention of their diplomats in mid-January, it was not surprising that the news sent shock waves through the Yucatán state and defense ministries.

Moore quickly sent letters to the military commandant of Campeche and Captain Juan Celarayn, commander of the Yucatán squadron, to assure them "that the good feeling which existed when I left Texas, between us and the Government of Yucatan, still exists on my part, and on the part of my Government, and that nothing is more foreign from my intentions or my instructions than hostile acts against the vessels or people of Yucatan." With similarly reassuring replies of friendship from the Yucatán commanders, Moore sent another letter to Secretary Lemus, blaming the unfounded reports on "a certain set of men in Texas whose interests I have clashed with in the proper execution of my duty." With this cryptic message, the Yucatán government's vague feeling that Texas spoke with two voices was confirmed; Commodore Moore and the Lamar faction still stood by the peninsular states, while the Houston administration doggedly opposed intervention on Yucatán's behalf.

With things set straight in Campeche for the moment, Commodore Moore sailed for Carmen via Las Arcas on March 6, and the following day, *San Antonio* hove in sight. The schooner bore the December 15 orders from the War Department ordering Moore to return home.

Moore was discouraged by the orders, but not altogether surprised. The likelihood that Houston would recall the fleet was, after all, the reason for Moore's hasty departure from Galveston on December 13. Time had simply run out for the Navy's adventure. What gave the commodore particular annoyance, however, was *San Antonio*'s tardiness in returning to Yucatán as ordered.

The explanation, when he heard it, must have shocked Moore and his senior commanders: *San Antonio*'s crew had mutinied; one officer was dead, and two others were wounded.

CHAPTER TWENTY-SIX

Mutiny on the San Antonio

I will mete out to the rascals the uttermost penalties of the law.
—Commodore Moore, March 8, 1842

BY EARLY 1842, THE OFFICERS OF the Texas navy had their hands full. Their men were bored, destitute, and homesick. They had watched their ragged comrades desert, succumb to disease, faint under the lash, and fall from the rigging, but they had only the captures of the slow, unarmed merchantmen *Ana Maria* and *Progreso* to call victories. The fact that the Texas Navy forced Mexico City to negotiate seriously with Yucatán meant nothing to them. The men had signed up to fight, get paid, and capture prizes. Since leaving Galveston in December 1841, they had done damned little of any of these.

On the first of February, Commodore Moore ordered Lt. William Seeger to take *San Antonio* from Yucatán to Galveston, drop off the crew of the wrecked *Sylph*, and pick up additional orders from the War and Navy Department. From Galveston she was to sail to New Orleans, where she would use some of the Yucatán silver to buy provisions for the fleet before returning to the Yucatán coast.

Seeger made quick work of the voyage. Touching briefly in Galveston, he sailed to New Orleans, anchoring off Slaughterhouse Point on February 10, some distance from the harbor's busy slips.

It was no mystery why Lieutenant Seeger chose to anchor on the right bank of the Mississippi River, rather than in one of the French Quarter's crowded slips. Seeger knew that many of his seamen would desert at the first chance they saw, and swimming from an isolated ship in the middle of the Mississippi River was much harder than swimming from a vessel nestled among American merchantmen off the Vieux Carré. Additionally, liquor, that bane of shipboard discipline, would be harder to smuggle aboard the schooner if there were fewer tenders, pilot boats, cutters, and dinghies scurrying back and forth along *San Antonio*'s hull.

On February 11, 1842, Lieutenant Seeger took his first lieutenant, Alfred Waite, and rowed across the Mississippi to a nearby landing to bargain for supplies. Seeger left the schooner in the capable hands of Lt. Charles F. Fuller, the son of John Fuller, the Washington hotel proprietor who introduced the Colt revolver to the Texas government in 1839.

Fuller knew he would have his hands full until Seeger returned and the vessel left New Orleans. The men, ragged, hungry, and tired of the rigors of sea life, would be sorely tempted by the sights and sounds of the Crescent City. Disturbing reports of unrest among the crew from a seaman named William Barrington had also reached the commander's ears. Seeger did not have to tell Fuller that desertion plots were afoot, and when Fuller posted Sailing Master M. H. Dearborn as officer of the deck for the eight-to-midnight watch, he warned Dearborn to be on the lookout for trouble.

Trouble had been brewing on *San Antonio*'s forecastle for some time. In January, crewmen from *San Antonio* and *San Bernard* began plotting a joint mutiny while the vessels were off the Yucatán coast. The plan was to put the officers aboard *San Bernard* and take *San Antonio* to Mexico, where the conspirators would sell the schooner and divide up the money. If the officers resisted, they would be put to death. Circumstances forced a postponement of the plot until the schooners reached Sisal, but arriving there, they found *Austin* lying at anchor. Not wishing to cross guns with the biggest warship in Mexican waters, the uprising was postponed until February, when *San Antonio* arrived off New Orleans.

About an hour into his shift, Dearborn saw a loud and apparently drunken group of seamen and marines approaching his station. One of the number, an intoxicated marine sergeant named Seymour Oswald, loudly demanded permission to go ashore. Dearborn calmly replied that no one was allowed to leave the ship, but that Oswald could take his request to Lieutenant Fuller if he wished. Dearborn and other officers on deck became nervous, as the group was louder and angrier than most (evidently having run out of liquor) and worst of all, the insubordinates included some marines.

Hearing a commotion on the darkened deck, Lieutenant Fuller clambered up the gangway to the disturbance, where he overheard loud demands for shore leave from the small mob. Surveying the scene quickly, he undoubtedly responded the way he had been taught: *Maintain a sense of authority. Stay calm. Show no fear. Call out the marine guard.*

It will never be known if Lieutenant Fuller knew that marines were among the ringleaders. Surely, Fuller would not have ordered the very men who defied him to arm themselves. On the other hand, it was a classic leadership ploy to order some members of a cabal to disarm and arrest their co-conspirators. Whatever his reasoning, Fuller gave word to arm the marines, and Sergeant Oswald and the others quickly obeyed, returning with a mob of seamen and marines brandishing muskets, pistols, tomahawks, and cutlasses. Oswald had blood on his mind.

As Oswald approached his officers, he slashed at Fuller with his tomahawk; the blow missed. Fuller went for his pistol, but he never had a chance against the heavily armed marines. Several shots rang out, and a ball from marine Pvt. Benjamin Pompilly's pistol ripped through Fuller's chest, lodging in his lung. The lieutenant crumpled to the deck, mortally wounded. As he fell, other mutineers joined in the carnage, hacking at Fuller's body with cutlasses and beating him with their musket butts. Two midshipmen, William Allen and T. H. Odell, tried to rescue their stricken commander. Allen was hit in the foot by a bullet. Pvt. Antonio Landois, who broke off the tip of his bayonet in Fuller's body, turned his weapon against Allen; Landois was shoved back by boatswain Frederick Shepherd, and Allen scrambled to safety. Midshipman Odell was hit in the thigh by a pistol ball and the officers, including Sailing Master Dearborn, were dragged back to the cabin hatch, thrown below decks and locked inside. With the foredeck awash in blood, the mutineers—Oswald, Landois, Pompilly, Shepherd, Cpl. William Simpson, cook Edward Keenan, and Seamen William Barrington, John Williams and Thomas Rowan—ran past Fuller's body, lowered two of *San Antonio*'s launches and rowed frantically towards the harbor.

The shouts and gunfire aboard *San Antonio* quickly attracted the attention of other vessels, including the U.S. revenue cutter *Jackson*. Sending out boats to intercept the fleeing boatmen, *Jackson*'s crew spread the alarm to those ashore, where New Orleans police and U.S. marines captured six of the fugitives. Three more—the remaining mutineers except Landois, who was captured in a Louisiana swamp six months later—were arrested the following day.

The mutineers were thrown into an Orleans Parish jail. *San Antonio*'s officers managed to find Lieutenant Seeger, who rushed back to his vessel to lock down the crew and see that all was quiet. The next morning he lamented that had he the foresight to shoot one or two of the ringleaders earlier, Lieutenant Fuller's murder might have been prevented.

Fuller's mangled body was carried ashore and buried in the Girod Street Cemetery (now covered by the Louisiana Superdome parking lot), in a ceremony attended by officers of his ship and the USS *Jackson*. It was an early irony of Texas's gunslinging tradition that Fuller was killed by one of the Colt revolvers his father had introduced to Texas.

Within a few weeks, *San Antonio* was provisioned and ready to leave New Orleans. Lieutenant Seeger sailed for Campeche, taking the two conspirators charged with mutiny but not murder, Boatswain Frederick Shepherd and Seaman Thomas Rowan, and leaving the others—held under state murder charges—to rot in jail for the time being. News of the mutiny preceded *San Antonio*'s arrival, and Commodore Moore mourned the loss of "one of the most promising officers whom I have ever known." Angry and grief-stricken, he vowed to avenge the young lieutenant's death to the utmost limits of the law.

Hearing of the mutiny, Commodore Moore left instructions for Seeger to meet him at Isla del Carmen, at the mouth of Laguna de Terminos in southern Campeche. Shoving off for Carmen on March 8, Moore took steps to ensure that no sailor would try a repeat of the *San Antonio* uprising. Upon reports of insolent language by two crewmen, Moore had one placed in double irons and the other discharged. He locked all firearms in the wardroom, posted a guard, and called all hands to quarters. With the grim righteousness of a Puritan minister, he read the Articles of War to the crew, informed them of the mutiny aboard *San Antonio*, and told them of the deadly consequences of the heinous crime. Then, he waited for *San Antonio* to return.

While waiting at Laguna, Moore convened courts-martial on unrelated charges for Seaman William Beatts (who was acquitted), Midshipman John Postell (who was shipped back to Galveston in disgrace), and three crewmen who attempted to desert the flagship. Shortly after *San Antonio*'s arrival on March 10, a court-martial convicted Seaman Rowan of complicity in the mutiny, sentencing him to one hundred lashes with the cats. Boatswain Shepherd also stood trial, although Moore granted Shepherd a continuance to allow him to gather evidence from his alleged co-conspirators in New Orleans.

Even senior officers were not immune from the Commodore's renewed efforts at discipline. Moore reported Purser J. F. Stephens to Secretary Hockley for making a false return. He also charged Lt. Thurston M. Taylor with illegally selling some of *San Bernard*'s slops, giving away one of *San Bernard*'s Colt revolvers, and failing to keep adequate property records for his vessel. In the end, these measures had the desired effect: for the time being, incidents of insubordination disappeared.

While Moore saw the need to root out and repress mutinous urges, he also realized that his dispirited men needed a rest. Tarrying at Carmen, he allowed a number of *Austin*'s crewmen to take limited shore leave in town, in hopes of burning off some pent-up frustration. The sea dogs promptly got themselves drunk, and not surprisingly, fights broke out between Texas sailors, the townsfolk, and the local militia. Lt. Cyrus Cummings went out on the ship's second cutter to see what was the matter, but Cummings, for all his strictness aboard his vessel, turned a blind eye to whatever ruckus he found.

Returning to the flagship to report, "All quiet, sir," the officers were startled by a pistol shot fired from a boat that darted back into the black lagoon night. Setting off in pursuit in the ship's cutter, Cummings returned empty-handed about the time that Lt. J. P. Lansing and Lt. Alfred Waite, having rowed back from town, delivered breathless reports of riots and injuries to sailors and civilians.

Commodore Moore characteristically took charge of the situation. In classic "one riot, one ranger" fashion, Moore came ashore and waded into the fray. Knocking seamen aside, the captain's roar rose above the din. He ordered his men to stand down, and threatened to burn the town if the locals did not disperse at once. A bellowing Moore cursed and kicked his dazed, drunken men back into their launches, where they returned to their vessels licking their wounds and mourning the death of a *San Bernard* sailor who was killed in the fray. Moore managed to smooth things over with the local *alcalde* the next day, and his men prepared to shove off.

One letter *San Antonio* brought from Galveston was Secretary Hockley's December 15 order to return home. But Moore knew that to return home would be to risk the dismemberment of the Navy at a time when Mexico was as vulnerable as she would ever be. He also had to collect hard currency from Yucatán, and he was down to a three-day supply of water. So after filling up with 5,000 gallons of water and picking up $6,000 of the Navy's fee from the port collector, Moore left for Veracruz on March 28, later writing of Hockley's directive, "although a peremptory order, I was compelled to disobey it."

At Veracruz, Moore ran in close to port off the Isle of Sacrificios, sending a boat to greet the USS *Warren*, which he had seen passing at Carmen a few days before. Surveying the harbor carefully, Moore soon discovered the steamer *Regenerador* raising steam alongside the armed schooner *Aguila*, and he ordered his men to general quarters so that the Texians could "give them a warm reception." Running just outside the range of the castle's guns, Moore hovered off the harbor, passing in and out of its reefs, daring the Mexican commander to come to grips with him in open sea. But a schooner is no match for a sloop-of-war, and the outgunned Mexicans wisely declined the invitation.

Warren's officers confirmed reports that the Santa Fe Expedition had ended in complete disaster, the survivors being sent to three Mexican dungeons. They did report, however, that one fugitive from the expedition, Thomas Lubbock, was waiting to rendezvous with the Navy at Laguna, and Moore sent *San Antonio* to verify the report.

Standing out to sea in company with *San Bernard*, Moore's luck improved. On April 1, *San Bernard* ran down and captured the merchant vessel *Doric*, and sent her to Galveston. Two days later, *Austin* and *San Bernard*, hunting as a pack, overhauled the Mexican merchant schooner *Doloritas* out of Matamoros. She was close to land, and the schooner's crew fled in the vessel's lifeboat, leaving only the captain, his mate, and a young boy on board; Moore landed the trio of unfortunates ashore off Point Delgado, treating his prisoners and their personal property with strict and measured respect. The next day, the two warships captured the schooner *Dos Amigos* a few miles off Tuspan in central Mexico, laden with a cargo of salt. Sending Lieutenant Cummings aboard as her prize officer, *Austin* and *San Bernard* took their captive vessel to nearby Lobos Island to regroup.

At Lobos, Moore completed his report to Secretary Hockley, warning that when he arrived back in Galveston, he would be out of money and provisions, and that the terms of service for nearly all his crewmen would be up. He pleaded for hard currency, stating, "it must be known by the sailors in New Orleans that we pay our men in money, and not in certificates." He recommended a blockade of Mexico's eastern ports, arguing, "Without the speedy return of our navy on this coast, the navy of Yucatan will be captured or join that of Central Mexico, through fear, if nothing else." He also requested state-of-the-art weaponry for his squadron: "I hope that some steps have been taken to procure two bomb cannon for this ship, and one for each of the schrs., if not, I hope that Cochran's Repeating Cannon will be procured as early as possible, they being, in my opinion, decidedly preferable to the 'Paixhan Cannon.' Twenty-four pounders for this ship and eighteen pounders for the schrs., are as heavy as they ought to have mounted on them."

Moore also advocated a continued alliance with Yucatán. He tried to allay the fears of the Houston faction, asserting, "it is my firm conviction that the Government of Yucatan will remain our friends unless we give them cause to change their ground, not that they have any feelings in common with the people of Texas, for they are Mexicans, but because it is in their interest to keep on terms with us." To preempt the usual plea of poverty, Moore made it clear that "to effect this object, I do not want from the Government *one dollar*," since Yucatán funding and prize money from captures would keep the fleet at sea indefinitely. Finally, without referring to the department's orders to return his warships to Galveston, Moore commented, "Agreeably to my recommendation they are all laying at Campeache, where I wish them to remain, at least for the present."

Moore got his wish, thanks to events occurring far from the Gulf's waters. On March 5, 1842, Gen. Rafael Vásquez led some 600 Mexican regulars into San Antonio, capturing the city, then withdrawing below the Rio Grande. Smaller numbers of Mexican troops seized Goliad, the site of the 1836 massacre of Fannin's soldiers, and Refugio, which General Urrea had occupied during that horrific campaign. Like the main body, they quickly withdrew into Mexican territory.

The shocked Texas government declared another blockade of Mexican ports on March 26, and when *San Bernard*'s dispatches were placed on Secretary Hockley's desk on April 13, Hockley immediately ordered Moore to bring his squadron to New Orleans via Galveston in preparation for a cruise off the Mexican coast. He directed Moore to disembark at Galveston and meet with the president in Houston for personal instructions, assuring Moore, "Your proceedings personally, and of Courts Martials, specially, are approved, and the latter confirmed." Hockley's orders were sent back aboard

San Bernard, and the brig *Wharton* was dispatched to Sisal under Lieutenant Seeger with Houston's official proclamation of a blockade against Mexico.

At that point, however, Moore was in another bind. He had orders to go on the offensive, and Mexican traders were obviously worried about the energetic and hostile Texas sharks circling the waters. ("Mexican vessels are now nearly as scarce as sperm whales within the Gulf," one newspaper commented.) But at just the wrong moment, the Yucatán government decided to cut off its monthly subsidy. On the day Moore arrived off Sisal, a messenger came with letters from Secretary of War Pedro Lemus. The old general, friendly as ever, counseled Moore that Merida viewed a Mexican invasion as unlikely for the time being, "and that if they do invade at all it will not be for eight months or a year, for reason of the want of resources and the embarrassed position in which Gen. Santa Anna finds himself." A letter from Secretary of State Rejón confirmed that the April installment of silver would be the last, at least until the centralists menaced Yucatán again. Worse yet, since Yucatán was short on cash at the moment, it would also have to pay $4,000 of the last installment with a thirty-day note.

It did not soothe Moore's sense of frustration that within five days of his arrival at Sisal, he had *Austin*, *Wharton*, *San Bernard*, and *San Antonio*—fifty guns in all—with orders to take the war to the Mexican coast. Even so, Moore took pains to assure Secretary Lemus and the commandant of Campeche that the Texas government wished only the best for Yucatán, although Houston's blockade of centralist ports would necessarily include Yucatán goods being transported in centralist ships.

The persistent Moore made one last effort to get Yucatán to reconsider, stressing his belief that Mexico City would never ratify the Yucatán reconciliation treaty. "I will in my communication with my Government consider as you state the matter only suspended," he wrote to Lemus, "and express the hope that next time I will have the pleasure of hearing from you (which will be from Sisal, in about five weeks) that Yucatan will have taken her stand among the nations of the world. The people have taken that stand against oppression and they are determined to maintain it at all hazard!!!"

With that, Commodore Moore took his fleet home, getting underway at one o'clock in the morning on April 26, touching at Las Arcas, and arriving at Galveston on May 1.

CHAPTER TWENTY-SEVEN

The Horse Latitudes

If the Angel of the Book of Revelation was to make his appearance in Texas at present, as he did to the Apostle John at the Island of Patmos, He no doubt would take up the same cry of "woe, woe to the inhabitants of the land." For verily these be the days of tribulation & disappointment to all those who have looked to Government or Congress for just and equitable claims.
—Acting Navy Secretary John Grant Tod, January 5, 1842

To SAM HOUSTON, THE NAVY, that source of horrendous expenditure and disgraceful insubordination, was a prime target for dismemberment. But two realities Houston could not alter made the Navy a necessary evil—for the moment. The first was the political climate. Houston could lament the expense of a fleet all he wanted, but the Texas Navy had become a source of pride for the Republic's citizens, particularly in the coastal regions where the squadron was the main line of defense. As he took office, Houston could not forget that his faction had recently been defeated on an attempt to recall the Navy, though this was due to political bungling in committee rather than broad support for Lamar's policies.

The second factor was Mexico. Houston had heard rumors that Mexico was preparing for an invasion of Texas, possibly preceded by the reconquest of Yucatán, and in late 1841 the rumors appeared to have more truth than usual. Seventeen days after his inauguration, Houston addressed the House of Representatives, declaring, "there can be no doubt that some movements against Texas are in preparation. Mexico, in my opinion (relying on the current intelligence of the day) has, at no time since 1836, been in a situation so favorable for *annoying* our country as at the present moment." Houston prophesied, ironically, that Mexico "will not decide to invade us, unless they are assured they possess decided naval superiority."

So for the moment, the Texas Navy would be permitted to exist.

On December 22, 1841, Secretary Hockley issued his report on the state of the Navy and the balance of power in the Gulf. He summarized accurate intelligence reports from the United States that claimed, "the Mexican Government have now building at New York two Brig Schooners of about 170 tons burthen and to carry seven guns each (and in England two Iron Steamers), these vessels will no doubt carry one or more Bomb Cannon or Paixhan Guns." Hockley, to his credit, advocated the immediate repair of the Navy's sturdy steamer, noting, "The Government of Yucatan have offered to furnish the means for fitting out the Zavalla, and the dry dock at New Orleans can be procured for the purposes of our hauling her." He further remarked that the 1841 government reorganization law making Commodore Moore the navy agent and naval store keeper, as well as commander of the navy, was hopelessly unrealistic; Moore could not command the fleet in the Gulf and at the same time purchase goods in New Orleans and keep an eye on naval stores in Galveston.

Hockley obligingly took up the cause of the officers and men, noting that they had not been paid since April 1841. In fact, the "pay" the officers and men received in the spring of 1841 came in the form of promissory notes that would only become payable when the Republic had unencumbered money in its treasury—a weak prospect, at best. Irregular pay had been a very public source of problems since 1840, when a visiting British diplomat wrote, "As most of the officers were originally in the American Navy and quitted that service, where at least they were certain of good pay, for the inducements held out by the Texians, it certainly does appear most unjust to turn them adrift in the cavalier way proposed." The diplomat Francis C. Sheridan conceded that "when the wretched poverty of the republic is taken into consideration—a Treasury without a shilling & the country without credit—the keeping up a naval armament in active service even if in the power of the Gov't, which I doubt, would be a farce."

Unfortunately for the Navy, Houston remained unmoved by Hockley's arguments. He refused Yucatán's offer to pay for *Zavala*'s refit on grounds that he did not wish to become entangled in the Mexico-Yucatán conflict, and did not trust the Yucatán government. He vetoed a resolution to provide sailors of the Revolution with land bounties, which were given without hesitation to all who had served in the Texas Army. (Houston protested that Texas's sailors, if they could be located, had no interest in land and would likely end up losing their lands to prostitutes and sutlers, "to whom seamen usually become indebted.") He also ordered the Treasury Department to dishonor the "Naval Scrip" issued by Lamar to seamen and officers the previous spring; ignored a Treasury Department report that concluded that Commodore Moore was entitled to reimbursement for personal expenses in the amount of $2,000; and vetoed a January 1842 resolution thanking John Grant Tod for his energetic work on the Baltimore ship construction project.

It was only in this last action that Houston had any real grounds for objection; the Baltimore ships were not that well constructed, and a government cannot single out for special praise every employee who simply does his job well. But Congress disagreed, and in a frivolous waste of political energy, it overrode Houston's veto on January 31. The resolution, drafted with the help of someone familiar with naval procedure (someone like Tod), required Commodore Moore to have the vote of thanks read before all officers and men of every vessel and of the Navy Yard, and to enter the resolution into the ships' log books. (Moore, still fuming over serious problems caused by defective anchors and foremasts, evidently ignored this order.)

In a supplemental report in January 1842, Hockley described the fleet as decrepit in nearly all respects. Of *Austin*, he wrote, "the hull of the ship has been found rotten in many parts." Of *Zavala*, it would "require from 15 to 20,000 Dollars to repair, and an additional amount (to be regulated by the number of men furnished) to send her to sea." *Wharton* he described as "probably in want of running rigging—with men and provisions, she can be ready for service in a short time." And he wrote that the brig *Archer* "has four guns unfit for service, and has been lying exposed since she has been turned over to the government, without an officer or man on board and subject to the depredation of any boat or person passing at night.... I am informed that she has a foot of water in her magazine, and that some stores, probably powder, have been lost."

The Navy Yard was falling apart. Hockley reported that the Yard "requires much repair—the Magazine is badly constructed—without ventilators the powder is constantly subject to injury—situated upon the immediate action of salt air." He continued, "The Navy Yard is now open and subject to the distruction incident to the range of cattle and all other depredations—the appropriation, some time since made for erecting a fence around it—has been expended by the late Navy Agent William Brannum for other purposes. ...The shore opposite the Yard is shoal and level, and except at high tide, the boats approaching it receive considerable injury." Boats had been exposed and warped beyond repair from the want of a shed, blacksmith tools had been appropriated by ships' crews, and the yard's muster rolls "show the small force now on duty there, is wholly incompetent for the duty of the yard and protection of the property." *San Bernard* and *San Antonio* were in good order, but "discontent prevails amongst the officers of the Navy, in relation to the relative rank of Lieutenants and other subordinate officers under the Command of Commodore Moore."

Houston, acknowledging deficiencies in the Republic's fleet, made a halfhearted effort to drum up congressional funding. On January 4, he lamented *Zavala*'s condition, blaming her sorry state on unspecified government officials. "The necessity for making some provision for the preservation of our vessels of war," he wrote to Congress on January 22, "is too obvious to need argument; without suitable means afforded by the Honorable Congress for that purpose they must inevitably go to decay and destruction."

Since the Sixth Texas Congress had repudiated Lamar's "Redback" notes, replacing them with more limited "exchequer bills," Houston knew that he would get little from Congress. He requested an appropriation of $20,000, which even he admitted would fall at least $17,000 short of what was needed to keep the Navy in ordinary. On February 3 Congress complied, although it again reduced the pay and number of naval officers.

Houston's anemic support for the Navy was diminishing rapidly, and by February 1842 he ordered Secretary Hockley to reiterate his recall orders to the fleet, still off Yucatán, on February 17. He made no effort to disburse the $20,000 appropriated for the Navy, and was content to sit idly by as Congress passed an act providing that the Dawson contract ships would be returned to Frederick Dawson in full satisfaction of Texas's debts. This last provision was of course subject to Dawson's agreement, and no one, least of all Dawson, believed that five worn-out, battered vessels were worth the $280,000 Texas owed when it took possession of the six new men 'o war. Fortunately for the Navy, nothing came of this ludicrous proposition.

To Houston, the Navy was bankrupt, it was a drain on the nation's treasury, and it was difficult to control once deployed. Should it somehow become effective, through Yucatán financing or otherwise, it would only entangle Texas in Mexico's internal matters, contrary to Houston's foreign policy goals, and it would prop up the myth of Texas independence at the expense of annexation to the United States. Houston, therefore, would only permit the Republic's navy to exist until its widespread political and popular support subsided, as surely it would.

Sam Houston's attitude changed somewhat in March 1842, as war clouds between Mexico and Texas began to darken. From Mexico's standpoint, the lingering issue of Texas had to be resolved, both to preclude Texas independence from becoming a *fait accompli* and to discourage future raids like the Santa Fe Expedition. Santa Anna, who had regained power in 1841, wrote about it to Texas plenipotentiary Barnard Bee in February 1842."I fully appreciate the problematic conditions of Texas; and I have before me seen the entire series of its consequences. I believe war to be necessary. I believe it a measure indispensable to the salvation of Mexico, and that her government will not faithfully perform her duties, if she does not strain her resources to the utmost, boldly to enforce a full confession of her justice."

War came, though only briefly, on March 5, 1842, when troops under General Vásquez occupied San Antonio briefly before retreating back across the Rio Grande. Although the event was more a demonstration of force than an invasion, it seemed to be a harbinger of grave danger to come—especially in light of rumors that Santa Anna had collected thirty thousand men to help him restore Mexican sovereignty over Texas.

The Vásquez raid sent shock waves through Austin, which lay only eighty miles from San Antonio. Congress and the public demanded that Houston do something. Reluctant to take any action that would trigger a full-scale war with Mexico, Houston called out the Galveston Coast Guards, or "Sea Fencibles," as they were known, and sent a detachment to Corpus Christi aboard the steamer *Lafitte* and the sloop *Washington*. He chartered the schooner *Colonel Hanson* to ship military supplies from Galveston to Aransas Bay, pressed the captured *Dos Amigos* into government service, and ordered James Boylan, former commander of the warship *Brutus*, to charter the hermaphrodite brig *Retrieve* to transport troops from Galveston to Live Oak Point off Aransas Bay. (The Sea Fencibles' only victories were the capture of the American schooner *Mary Elizabeth*—which caused the same sort of outrage as the earlier captures of *Eliza Russell* and *Pocket*—and the arrest of a lone Mexican herder, who promptly escaped astride a borrowed mule.)

Houston's plan for defending the Texas coast was as ill-defined as his original plan for the San Jacinto campaign. He asked Congress to appropriate funds for erecting shore batteries—using the very Paixhan guns Commodore Moore wanted for his warships—at Galveston and Matagorda, where local militia could use them to blast an invading force to pieces. The problem, of course, was that with hundreds of miles of coastline, an amphibious invasion could take place at points other than the two where Houston happened to have his guns sited. Besides, Paixhan cannon are not hunting rifles, and Houston's reliance upon untrained militia to direct sophisticated artillery at ships a mile or more away was an obvious recipe for disaster. The Texas Congress refused to endorse Houston's questionable proposal. To scrape together a makeshift coastal defense, Houston ordered the eighteen-pounders from *Archer* moved ashore to augment Galveston's land batteries, and had *Zavala* moved to the east end of the island.

Notwithstanding the judgments of Houston and the Texas Congress, the only promising offensive option was, as usual, a naval one. While Houston was wedded to a shore-based solution, he occasionally awoke to the value of concentrated naval power along Mexico's coast. In an excited letter to Commodore Moore on March 11, a week after the Vásquez raid, Houston wrote, "The enemy have invaded us at last. It appears to be formidable, and our coast is exposed to the enemy at every point." Houston told Moore he wanted to cut off Mexico's trade and supply lines, and expressed the hope that Moore would be able to attack Mexico before summer. In the letter, which Moore would not receive until June 25, Houston conceded, "my acquaintance is less with [the Navy] than that of any other Department." Notwithstanding his lack of familiarity, Houston assured Moore that while Congress had not provided much in the way of funding, "we find the citizens disposed to do every thing in their power to sustain the Navy." In other words, Moore would find plenty of farmers, tradesmen and merchants ready to lend a hand, even though these unskilled lubbers were no more useful to the Navy than to Houston's phantom shore batteries.

On March 26, 1842, Houston declared a blockade of Mexican ports. He also made sure that when Commodore Moore returned from Yucatán at the end of April, Secretary Hockley was waiting for him with orders to that effect. A second, inconsistent order—allowing the captured *Progreso* to depart New Orleans and proceed to Mexico unmolested (allegedly carrying some 400 kegs of gunpowder)—was a slap in the Navy's face and a bizarre exception to the blockade. But at least Houston was moving in a more aggressive direction. Moore had every reason to feel hopeful.

Moore's officers were not so sanguine. On May 7, virtually every officer of the Texas Navy handed in his resignation. Moore forwarded their complaints to Secretary Hockley, stating, "None of them have received *one* dollar from the Government for twelve months, and they all have nearly two years pay due them." Moore hardly needed to remind the secretary that officer salaries were overdue, since Hockley had pointed out this fact to the president some five months earlier. But Hockley, however reluctantly, was Houston's man, and he sent Moore two terse letters ordering the commodore to accept the resignations, if the Navy's regulations so required. If the men chose to leave, the squadron was to return to Galveston. "The Department have always been under the impression that the situation of our country was known to them," he coldly stated, and made it clear that if the officers chose to resign, they would be blamed for whatever ills befell Texas that summer.

Moore could not have been more frustrated. On the one hand, he was ordered to commence the blockade he had been advocating since December. On the other hand, Houston would not lift a finger to obtain the funds the Navy needed to pay its men for past services, much less fund the mission contemplated by Houston's new orders. Now his officers were in revolt, and with honest cause. Moore had promised them that they would be paid out of the remaining proceeds of the Yucatán adventure, and assured Secretary Hockley that he would sail for the mouth of the Mississippi as soon as his launch returned with sufficient drinking water.

In his report to Hockley, Commodore Moore began to express disgust at the Republic's neglect of its seagoing servants. "The steps taken by the officers on this occasion is what I have feared for a long time they would do," Moore wrote. "No other officers of the Government have borne *one twentieth* that officers of the Navy have. Since I took command of the Navy in October 1839 the officers of the Navy have actually received pay from the government but *three times,* viz: in November 1839, May 1840 and May 1841—neither of which times did they get what was due them, even in Texas Treasury notes, while the other officers of the Government have received their pay almost every month. . . . [A]t this time their stock of clothing is nearly worn out, and the prospect of their going to the United States without having in their power to make even a decent appearance, many of them are going at this time without a pair of decent shoes. . . ." The officers, Moore pleaded, "are willing now, as many of them have stated to me, to serve the country during the present emergency without pay, but they all have, or nearly all, incurred debts here and in the United States which they expected to pay with the money due them from the Government."

Moore knew that he could no longer depend on the Republic to finance its little fleet, and on the day his officers resigned, he reported to Secretary Hockley that he and another gentleman, Lewis M. H. Washington, had purchased the steamer *Patrick Henry*, and offered her to the government free of charge until Moore needed her. Perhaps *Patrick Henry*, later rechristened *Merchant*, could generate enough capital to keep the Texas Navy afloat, or at least help stave off the ignominious fate that befell the original navy's *Liberty*. If *Zavala* became worm-eaten and sank, as it seemed she probably would, *Merchant* could in a pinch fulfill the same motive function that *Regenerador* was handling for the Mexican Navy.

Sam Houston took no official note of the resignation of his entire naval officer corps during a declared national emergency, but he did mention the incident in a letter to his wife Maggie. "A few malcontents have attempted to destroy the hopes of an army, and even to create mutiny in the Navy by circulating false reports about pay. The fact was discovered and plans, I hope defeated! They are few in number, but true to their mischievous purposes. They are such spirits, as would rather reign in hell than serve in Heaven! They will not dim the star of Texas. They try to obscure its lustre, but it will be in vain, and they will receive the execrations of all friends to human liberty and regulated government." Old Sam did not mention who the "malcontents" might be, but he was clearly unwilling to consider the possibility that his failure to provide the officers with regular pay had anything to do with their resignations.

In any event, Moore had his orders, even if he lacked the means to effectuate them. Around May 8, Moore shoved off for the Southwest Pass, arriving at New Orleans a few days later, so the squadron there consisted of *Austin*, *San Bernard*, and *San Antonio*. For the time being, Moore kept the fleet in port, unable to do more than keep enough men to guard the ships from disgruntled former sailors who might help themselves to the vessels' supplies by night. Despite Sam Houston's high rhetoric, it would be a long, frustrating summer for the Texas Navy.

The Horse Latitudes are two belts of dull, light winds that span the globe, running through the Gulf of Mexico to the north and across sub-Saharan Africa to the south. The fatally slow breezes that ply these regions are the result of air that heats up high over the equator, and loses altitude rapidly as it approaches the north and south poles. To sailors lacking the benefit of steam power, the Horse Latitudes carried great danger. They could leave an entire fleet becalmed in still waters, unaided by wind or currents. According to legend, stranded sailors who slaughtered or threw their horses overboard to conserve precious drinking water gave this feared region its name.

To the officers of the Texas Navy, the year 1842 was like sailing through the Horse Latitudes. The fair winds of the Lamar administration had come to an abrupt end in April, and spread before the sailors was a vast sea of calm, where they would receive nothing—no food, no water, no necessities of life—from their government. Marooned in the bustling city of New Orleans, the men had no money to buy food, clothe themselves, or even move to another town, assuming they were qualified to do anything other than sail the seas in the service of their employer. These mariners would be prisoners of their government.

When *Austin* arrived in New Orleans in early May, Commodore Moore knew the Navy was more or less on its own. *San Bernard* and *San Antonio* went to Mobile to pick up supplies from the Texas consul, and to ferry Army volunteers from Alabama to Corpus Christi. Moore would have been very surprised to receive any appreciable help from Texas's agents in Mobile, and as it turned out, he was not surprised. In late May, Moore traveled to Mobile with Lamar's secretary of war, Branch Archer, to whip up support for the cause at pro-Texas banquets and other fundraising events. The rallies provided some assistance, but unfortunately, most of the funds were consumed chartering the steamer *Tom Salmon* to transport volunteers to South Texas for a battle that would never take place. In desperation, on May 26 Moore sent Lieutenant Seeger and *San Antonio* back to Yucatán to collect the remaining $4,000 owed for the last month of his previous cruise. With his request for payment, Moore reiterated that he could put his fleet to sea immediately if Yucatán would send more money.

Returning to New Orleans on May 29, Moore found, to no one's surprise, that President Houston had not released the $20,000 in exchequer bills Congress had appropriated that February. Houston's written pledge to release the funds as soon as they were printed could not be cashed anywhere in the United States. Men were beginning to desert, and neither merchants nor sailors took the Republic's official promises seriously. An exasperated Moore complained to Hockley, "I find myself cramped at almost every town by the failures heretofore of the officers of the Government to meet their liabilities."

Moore's financial plight was made worse by the arrival of Commander Lothrop's *Wharton* on June 6, fresh off the Mexican coast. Having been undermanned to begin with, the brig was now down to nine sailors, no provisions, and no ammunition. She did, however, bear orders from Hockley to include her in the blockade of the Mexican coast. At any other time Moore would have been thrilled to see the big warship, with her formidable battery of sixteen guns. But without the $6,000 it would take to provision and man her, she was just another useless hulk that had to be guarded by his dwindling group of ragged officers. And the officers had to be fed, even if they were not paid.

On June 11, Moore made another attempt to release the money Congress had appropriated the Navy. He sent his brother, Ship's Clerk James W. Moore, to find Houston and obtain half of the $20,000 appropriation, promising

Secretary Hockley that even with half of the exchequer bills appropriated (which were being traded at fifty percent of face value), Moore could put *Austin* and *Wharton* to sea. Anticipating the government's objections, Moore assured the secretary that the exchequer bills would not be spent, but would only be used as collateral to entice credit from local merchants, who would be paid with prize money once his fleet put to sea. "Not *one dollar* of this amount do I contemplate throwing into circulation," promised Moore, "but if I had it I would be able to raise a sufficient amount here on my own paper, using the Exchequer bills as collateral security, and if I succeed in my operations, which I am now endeavoring to get through, I will not use the Exchequer bills at all."

Feeling confident that the Republic would show at least this much support—the money having been appropriated by Congress and promised by the very man who ordered the blockade—Moore procured some of what he needed, recruiting 230 sailors and putting down contracts for provisions. When James arrived with the exchequer bills, he would deposit them, take the supplies aboard, and shove off for Veracruz.

But James returned empty-handed. President Houston, Hockley wrote, had publicly pledged not to circulate any exchequer bills until the next session of Congress. Instead of money, such as it was, Commodore Moore would have to negotiate Houston's personal promise to have the bills issued by the Texas treasury in the near future.

When Moore received this news on June 23, he was bitterly disappointed. Houston's promise was considered worthless even in New Orleans, the city most sympathetic to Texas. Men began deserting in droves, officers became disheartened, and suppliers refused to deliver food, supplies, and ammunition on credit. Instead of heading to sea, a heartbroken Moore was even more hopelessly stuck in port.

Still, Moore refused to let his dream of an offensive against Mexico die. As he later wrote, "I believe the natural promptings in most bosoms would have been to abandon the service in disgust, at the failure of my Government to redeem its pledges, thereby involving me in its breach of faith. But I still hoped to redeem the enterprise from failure, which was so important to the very salvation of my country, and on the success of which I had been induced by my Government to stake my property, credit, character and life." Of the adjectives used to describe the Texas commander, the words "determined," "tenacious" and "stubborn" appear with great frequency. Mexico's consul in New Orleans reported to his superiors that Moore "is an active and resolute man. It is said that as soon as a steamer of war hoists the Mexican flag in Veracruz he will capture her."

Of course, without funds from Texas, Moore was going nowhere for the moment. But that did not stop him from trying. He continued to press the government for money for provisions and for *Zavala*'s repair, and he informed Hockley that he had perfected a new type of cheap exploding shell, "to be thrown out of every gun in the navy with efficiency and safety . . . with these the efficiency of our navy will be increased *ten fold.*" And he never stopped dreaming of a renewed alliance with Yucatán.

It might be wondered how the Texas Navy obtained anything, given Houston's refusal to aid the service. The principal source of funding in 1842 was Commodore Moore's personal credit, which for all its embarrassment over broken government promises, was still adequate to keep his men from starving. Moore assigned backpay owed to him by the Republic to local vendors, prevailed upon friends for loans, and mortgaged one-half of all prize money he collected during his upcoming voyage. He ran his steamboat *Merchant* as a charter vessel between New Orleans and Galveston, and through these efforts, he was able to raise $34,700 for the upkeep of the fleet during its time in the wilderness. Junior officers also managed to get by, partly by prevailing on old friends in the United States, and partly by living off the generosity of locals, who felt sorry for these impoverished public servants. At one time, for instance, the sheriff of Galveston County gave the forlorn crew of the brig *Archer* two quarters of beef, for sheltering an unpopular young man "from the summary jurisdiction of Judge Lynch" behind the brig's guns until the man could quit the county safely.

When his brother James returned from Texas with another patently false promise, Commodore Moore decided to make a personal appeal to President Houston. Surely, Moore believed, he could convince the president that sound foreign policy, as well as humanitarian considerations, required some funding for the Navy at a time when Houston himself had ordered a blockade against Mexico. Writing from Houston on July 5, Moore sent Hockley a lengthy plea on the usual matters—pay for the men and officers, *Zavala*'s repair—as well as old issues that had been long neglected, such as the lack of formal commissions for naval officers. (This last item was more than just a mere formality for nineteenth century naval officers, since a commission, as "Mexico" Thompson learned, could make the difference between a legitimate capture and a trial for piracy.)

In late June, Commodore Moore paid the thirty-dollar boat fare and took passage to Galveston, leaving the reliable John Lothrop in command of the squadron. From there he would ride to the City of Houston in time for a special summer session of Congress convening there.

A daunting task lay ahead. While the sympathetic Hockley asked Galveston's port collector, Gail Borden, for funds to feed *Zavala*'s skeleton crew (knowing that Borden, like every other government official, had no money at his disposal), Hockley confided to Borden that he fully expected Congress to order the steamer sold, consistent with his reluctant recommendation. From Houston, of course, Moore could expect nothing but empty promises and public posturing for the hawks in Congress, although the tone of Houston's recent anti-Mexico rhetoric was strident enough to convince a few naval officers that he would do something soon. Moore again wrote to

Hockley on July 19, pleading for $10,800 to provide men, provisions, clothing, and ammunition for his vessels; this, when combined with the money that Yucatán owed, would be enough to get to sea.

To buttress the Navy's prospects in the special session of Congress, Moore met with a number of legislators and persuaded them that real funding was needed to keep Mexican gunboats from having free reign of the Gulf. The pro-war faction needed no convincing; a bill to authorize an offensive against Mexico quickly passed. The bill, however, granted Houston the discretion to do nothing, and Houston vetoed even that limited measure by claiming that the March 26 blockade had been induced by assurances from the Navy that it could put to sea. A minor breakthrough came on July 20, when twenty-three officers of the Texas Navy, including Commodore Moore, finally had their commissions approved by the Senate. That same day, President Houston sanctioned a request by Hockley to have *Archer* rescued from its sinking condition, although both men knew that there was little that could be done without government funds.

The Navy's real payoff came on the last day of the session, when Congress, over Houston's objection, passed a resolution appropriating $15,000 for *Zavala*'s repair, plus another $25,000 for provisions, to "be paid out of the first money in the Treasury, or at the disposition of the Executive." (This last phrase was intended to keep President Houston from sitting on the money, as he did with the $20,000 authorized during the previous session.) Another $28,231.00 was appropriated for back pay due through July 1, 1842, plus another $29,428.50 for future pay for the coming six months. Officers also got modest raises, and Moore was no longer required to act as fleet commander, storekeeper and navy agent, all at the same time. Sam Houston, having publicly affirmed the need for a navy, could hardly veto the measure, and he signed the law promptly.

On the day Congress voted its appropriation, Commodore Moore called on President Houston at his Houston office, at the corner of Texas and Main. A very pleased Houston informed Moore that he had just signed a new bill appropriating $97,659.50 for the Navy, and asked Moore, "When will you leave for New Orleans?" Moore, to Houston's chagrin, replied, "it is useless for me to leave without raising money to sustain the Navy," and repeated his request for the $20,000 appropriated during the *previous* session of Congress, which he would use to get to sea. Houston, in his typical indirect manner, refused, offering instead a bond to use in raising the money.

This was another obvious ruse, and Moore finally lost his temper. In an exchange that obliterated any civil feelings between the two men forever, Moore charged that, given the worthlessness of Houston's last two promises, it was clear that Houston was "trifling" with a matter that disparaged Moore's reputation as well as that of the Navy. Fully convinced that Houston's true aim was to break up the Texas Navy as it lay in a foreign port, Moore recalled his tirade on that hot Houston afternoon: "I had already tried fruitlessly to negotiate similar bonds, as I had before stated to him, and that he need not try to *humbug* me with another bond or power of attorney, for I would not be *humbugged* by him—That a power of attorney from the President of Texas for *one million dollars* would not bring in New Orleans *one hundred dollars*! ...That as to his inquiry of when I would leave for New Orleans, I had to inform him that the steamer Merchant was waiting at Galveston for me, to which place I would repair the next day, and on my arrival in New Orleans, I would disband the Navy and leave the vessels to rot in a foreign port, as officers and men could not be kept on board without rations."

Moore was perfectly accurate in his complaints, and his frustration is understandable in light of what he and his officers had endured. But he overplayed his hand. Sam Houston, president of the Republic of Texas and Moore's commander in chief, was not a man to be taken to task. In the words of Moses Austin Bryan, Houston was by nature "excessively vain, a flatterer, and loved to be flattered." He would not take Moore's upbraiding lightly. Houston was also no doubt incensed by Moore's threat to disband the Navy, since that prerogative (and apparently that objective) belonged to Houston alone. And at this stage in his life, in the midst of sagging personal popularity, a deep vein of vindictiveness had begun to mark Sam Houston's political character, becoming noticeable to those even casually familiar with the man. As Commodore Moore left Houston's office with a companion who knew Houston well, the companion warned Moore that he would be persecuted in unimaginable ways for his insolence. And as Moore learned over the next twelve months, when it came to persecuting enemies, Sam Houston had no equal in the Lone Star Republic.

The next day, as he was about to board *Merchant* for New Orleans, Moore again wrote Hockley. He reiterated that he and Lothrop had used up all their personal credit, and would be compelled to discharge their seamen within a few days, or let the men discharge themselves in the dark of night. He warned that yellow fever season was approaching New Orleans, and if he did not get the fleet out soon, there would be too few sailors to man the ships until winter. He again asked for the Sixth Congress's $20,000 appropriation (now reduced to $18,812), writing, "it is now barely possible that I can get to sea with the whole appropriation."

As Moore's letter made its way to President Houston, Old Sam decided how he would entrap his now-immutable enemy. The day after Moore wrote "it is now barely possible that I can get to sea with the whole appropriation," Secretary Hockley stopped him, vowing that he would bring the signed exchequer bills the next day. On July 27, Hockley handed Commodore Moore a packet of exchequer bills and an order directing Moore to open additional "sealed orders" once he arrived in New Orleans.

The sealed orders put Moore in an impossible situation. Moore was required to sustain a tight four-month blockade against the Mexican coast on an $18,812 budget, "the Department understanding clearly, from your estimate of the expense necessary for the accomplishment of that object, that the hypothecation of the above sum will enable you to do so." This "clear understanding" came from one of Moore's earlier letters stating that he could hypothecate the bills rather than spend them. Moore's claim that he could do so, however, was made at a time when the fleet was lacking only a few more provisions for *Austin* and *Wharton*. By late July, sailors had deserted, provisions had been consumed, and the credit of the Texas government had slipped even further. At this point, Moore would not be able to get to sea by simply pledging the exchequer bills as collateral for naval loans, a pledge that had proved worthless twice before.

When he arrived at New Orleans on July 31, a despondent Commodore Moore knew that his fleet might well never sail again. The schooners were now preoccupied with ferrying volunteers from Galveston to Corpus Christi, in preparation for a farcical punitive invasion of Mexico. In Galveston, *Archer* was sinking, and the leaking *Zavala* had been run aground on the island's north shore to prevent her loss. Her hull was rotting, and another month or so among the barnacles and worms would seal her fate. In New Orleans, *Wharton* was in desperate need of repairs, particularly on her mainyard and fore topyard, and most alarming, *Austin* was taking on water at the rate of seventy-three inches a day—probably the result of Gulf shrimp picking away the caulking in places where her copper sheathing had become loose or broken. The leaks, unfortunately, rendered 500 pounds of black powder useless, and Commander Lothrop ordered them thrown overboard after a survey revealed the propellant to be useless.

Using the exchequer bills as collateral and whatever ragged credit of his was left, Moore had *Austin* dry-docked so her leak could be recaulked and her hull recoppered. While *Austin* was being repaired, he asked the mayor of New Orleans to release the *San Antonio* mutineers into his custody. (Moore's request was refused, as the authorities told him a special demand would have to be made upon the governor of Louisiana by President Houston.)

Within three days *Austin*'s hull was repaired, and the replacement yards for the ship and brig were ready for delivery. But Texas promissory notes were nearly worthless in New Orleans markets, and Moore's inability to pledge the few notes Houston had given him made it impossible for him to obtain adequate food, supplies, and ammunition. Besides, the stream of disappointed army volunteers trickling back from South Texas in the wake of Houston's war bill veto made recruiting next to impossible. Moore described the scene the following year.

> When I first reached New Orleans, in May, 1842, the city was healthy, shipping abundant, and seamen plenty.... Choice sailors were readily shipped, and I needed but small assistance from my government to put to sea well manned and provisioned. But the means were withheld, and mark the consequences—the course pursued toward volunteers, and the vacillating policy of the Executive,

changed the enthusiasm into contempt. The seamen, believing that their treatment would be of the same ungenerous character as that pursued towards the volunteers, deserted daily. . . . Texas became a by-word for bad faith and ingratitude. What wonder then, that I should find it difficult to man the vessels.

It was not just ships that were becoming rotten from maltreatment and disuse. To an alarming degree, discipline was slipping among the restless officers. In late August, Purser Fleming Wells reported Lt. Armstrong Lewis for ordering the storeroom opened and liquor distributed without the consent of the purser, a violation of naval regulations. On land, Midshipmen Calender I. Fayssoux and Peyton Middleton met in the shrouded mists of the Mississippi's banks for an "interview" over a matter of gentlemanly honor. The men chose pistols for this occasion, and both being good shots and full of hot blood, it was widely believed that both would fall dead at the first round. As it happened, Fayssoux fired first, and the ball struck the hammer of Middleton's pistol, glancing off the weapon and shattering Middleton's cheekbone. The impact of the bullet threw off Middleton's timing, and his bullet hit the rim of Fayssoux's cap, creasing Fayssoux's hair as it blew through his chapeau. *Austin*'s surgeon, Dr. Gardiner, also exchanged letters with another officer in preparation for a duel, while another midshipman, Andrew Jackson Bryant, was written up frequently for insolence to his superiors and disobedience of orders.

Moore's hopes were sinking faster than the *Archer*, and he had to act quickly. He ordered Lieutenant Crisp to bring *San Bernard* to Galveston for maintenance; repairs on *Austin* and *Wharton* were completed, although they still lacked sailors to get the ships to sea. With the few dollars he had left, Moore transferred the bulk of his men to his fastest vessel, *San Antonio*, and sent her under Lt. William Seeger to Merida on August 27 to see if he could breathe new life into the defunct Texas-Yucatán agreement.

After *San Antonio* cleared the Southwest Pass, there was little else Moore could do for the moment. His men settled down to an uncertain fate. They continued to make small repairs on their vessels' masts, spars, and rigging, and they performed their civic duty by voting in the September 1842 elections. But until money came in from either Texas or Yucatán, the officers had to sit tight and let events take their course.

As it happened, remorseless tides in Texas were again breaking against the Navy. Secretary Hockley tried to help out by asking President Houston for permission to sell *Zavala*'s engines for money to get the fleet to sea, since it was obvious that the sturdy steamer would never leave port again. Houston disingenuously refused on the grounds that he would never take any action without the specific approval of Congress. When compared with his refusal to disburse appropriations specified in laws passed in two separate sessions of Congress, Houston's strict compliance with the will of the legislature seemed selective at best, and Hockley took exception to Houston's political gamesmanship.

Relations between Sam Houston and George Hockley had been strained for some time. Hockley, Houston's chief-of-staff during the Revolution, had known Houston since their days in Washington, D.C., when Houston was a congressman from Tennessee, and Hockley was a young War Department clerk. During his first term, President Houston appointed Hockley war secretary and, briefly, acting navy secretary, and in his second term, Houston made Hockley his secretary of war and navy. But being Sam Houston's senior military advisor was a thankless task. Houston may have been the Hero of San Jacinto, but his aversion to a standing army or navy rendered the secretary's position all but irrelevant. Hockley, on the other hand, took a genuine interest in the welfare of the Republic's military servants, only to see his recommendations ignored by President Houston time and again. Most irritating to Hockley was Houston's frequent derision of his naval officers as "pirates," and his legal double standard, whereby Houston could act as commander in chief whenever he pleased, but would not lift a finger to help the Navy without specific direction from Congress, as in the case of the dying *Zavala*. As Houston effectively disbanded the Army in the summer of 1842 and then turned his attention to the Navy, friction between the two men disrupted their ability to serve in the same administration.

The breaking point came in late August 1842, when Houston took Hockley to task in public, prompting Hockley's resignation on September 1. In his resignation letter, Hockley accused Houston of allowing *Zavala*'s destruction, recounting how Houston had publicly acknowledged that the Navy would "sink and rot before he would lift a finger for its preservation." Houston's reply characteristically obfuscated the point, and convinced no one that he foresaw any use for a navy or any other standing national arm of defense.

With Hockley's departure, the last voice of opposition within the administration was silenced. Hockley's clerk, Morgan C. Hamilton, succeeded Hockley as acting secretary of war and navy, and Houston made it perfectly clear to Hamilton that he would brook no contrary opinions on military matters. From September 1842 until its last voyage, the Texas Navy never had another advocate in the executive branch. It was truly on its own.

Throughout September, the Texas Navy's fortunes sank lower and lower. Congestive fever gripped New Orleans, and seamen who had not yet deserted were stricken down with appalling regularity; between September 12 and 15, the Navy incurred expenses for the funerals of four seamen. To compensate for the Navy's poverty, Moore amended the table of rations, cutting back on cheese and other non-staples, so that a seaman's fare cost only $1.40 per week. And on September 26, Moore received orders from Acting Secretary Hamilton rescinding the blockade of Mexico, in light of the scheduled mediation under the auspices of Great Britain.

The orders did not, however, let Moore off the hook: he was still required to cruise the Gulf. Of the proclamation rescinding the blockade, Hamilton informed Moore, "You will not, however, relax your exertions in consequence of it, nor will your activity on the Gulf be in the smallest degree impeded thereby." In other words, Moore was still obligated to go to sea with obviously inadequate funding, blockade or no.

Houston had Moore boxed in, and he was not about to let him go. Moore, for his part, gave up trying to follow the spirit of any orders issued by Houston or the War Department. Mexico's consul in New Orleans, aware of the now-public rift, wrote to his superior at the *Departamento de Relaciones Exteriores*: "Houston is a mortal enemy of Moore's. Moore never again will obey Houston's orders, but will act as appears best to him."

In mid-September, a hurricane struck the gulf coast, drenching New Orleans and lashing Galveston in a spectacular show of Neptune's fury. When *San Bernard*'s commander, Lieutenant Crisp, saw his barometer dropping precipitously on the evening of September 17, he knew that the schooner was in for a long night. He scattered his officers about the vessel, stripping down the yards and unstepping masts so that gusts would have the smallest amount of surface area to grab. As the winds began to howl, the sea swells rocked the schooner so hard that she stood on her beam ends, swaying between her fore and aft anchor cables from starboard to port. The force of the storm surge eventually parted the schooner's cable and pushed her stern into Commodore Moore's *Merchant* before blowing the warship ashore, smashing her starboard quarter-boat in the process. *Merchant*'s captain, meanwhile, ran his vessel aground to allow his passengers to abandon ship, although several aboard drowned in the churning swells of the hurricane. *Merchant* soon went to pieces, and with it went Moore's only hope of a steamer to aid him against Mexico's *Regenerador* and other steamers on order from Great Britain.

After *San Bernard* and her crew had dried out, Crisp inspected the damage. The hull's copper was ragged, and the upper section was full of holes, allowing worms to get at the wood beneath. In some places it was hard to tell whether the schooner's injuries were due to the storm or neglect. "She leaks freely, but she did the same when ashore here before, and I do not think has sustained any fresh damage," Crisp wryly noted in a report to

Commodore Moore four days later. Lieutenant Crisp attempted to repair the damage, but the Navy's credit in Galveston was worthless, and it was all he could do to feed his twenty men and coax some spare rope from the equally impoverished port collector, Gail Borden.

In New Orleans, October was even worse. The month opened with a duel between *Wharton*'s midshipmen Fielding R. Culp and George White, in which the former suffered a mortal wound to his torso, dying three days later. Culp was buried ashore and laid to rest in a small mausoleum alongside *San Antonio*'s murdered commander, Lieutenant Fuller. Three days later, Moore's marine commander, Capt. Robert Oliver, also died, a victim of congestive fever. He joined Fuller and Culp in their increasingly crowded crypt.

The news from Lieutenant Crisp was perhaps most discouraging of all. The former Royal Navy midshipman was an excellent mariner, described by one Englishman as "one of the finest specimens of a gentleman it was ever my lot to meet on salt water," notwithstanding that, "a somewhat protracted mingling with Yankees had tainted him with some of their bad habits." But with *San Bernard* stranded in two feet of water, leaking badly, and with no hope of rescue, in mid-October Crisp ordered his men to transfer her equipment and rigging to the brig *Archer*, which was itself a leaking, dismasted hulk. On October 17, Crisp wrote to Moore from the helpless brig, "My provisions are nearly out—I have written to the Department for instructions [on] how to obtain more." On October 24 he reiterated that "my provisions will last about three days more, and then unless I hear something from the department I shall be obliged to discharge my men. The Navy appears to be *hard up*, and I think we are finished." He signed the letter, but a few days later he added a postscript. "Tuesday morning. Having but one ration of meat left on board I have discharged all the men except two, and two boys. The officers can now live about ten days, meanwhile they must of course endeavor to provide for themselves." On November 2, he again wrote Moore. "Since writing you I have received a letter from the department informing me he could do nothing, and I must do the best I can. . . . The Secretary said something of action of Congress; I can't see what they can do—some believe they will lay the Navy up—I think it is the best thing they can do—no one can stand this kind of life."

Despite disappointment after disappointment, Moore kept trying to bring the War Department to its senses. "I have used every effort to get money without success," Moore wrote to Hamilton on October 14, "and unless the citizens of the country do something to get the Navy to sea, I feel confident that a descent will be made upon our coast and Galveston be destroyed." His entreaty was answered only with icy venom from his civilian commanders. Acting Secretary Hamilton replied, "His Excellency the President . . . directs me to inquire why the instructions of the Department have been violated, and the President's verbal instructions disregarded." A second letter was more specific: "[You] have never advised the Department whether the Exchequer bills in your hands had been hypothecated or sold, nor the probable sum that could be claimed upon them. It was presumed, however, that you had disposed of at least a part of them in some way. . . . If these statements were true, the instructions to you have been disregarded." In other words, Moore was supposed to have put up the notes as collateral for loans, not spent them.

Moore denied violating orders. He only hypothecated the bills, he protested, putting them up as collateral for notes that became due in mid-October and late November. As he later explained, until November 8, he had not sold a dollar of exchequer bills, and it was not until November 24 that he sold the remainder, some $8,700, under duress from creditors who were threatening to sequester the vessels. Moore claimed he had done nothing wrong. But the communiqués from the War Department made it clear that Houston's mind was made up: there was to be no expedition, no funding, no Navy. On November 19, Moore received a letter from Secretary Hamilton, instructing him in no uncertain terms to hold the exchequer bills, unless they were specifically needed to fulfill a previous commitment.

Reflecting an intention to gather the fleet at Galveston, where it could be brought under Houston's control, Hamilton gave Moore another impossible order in mid-October: "If you cannot with the means at your command, prepare the squadron for sea, you will immediately sail for the port of Galveston, and on your arrival there, make a special report of the disposition made of the money placed in your hands, and also of the condition of the vessels, number of officers, seamen and marines, stores, &c., on hand...." In November, Moore received a second letter from Hamilton, ordering him to comply with previous instructions to return to Galveston if he could not put the fleet to sea.

As if Commodore Moore did not have enough to worry about, he had not received word from *San Antonio* since she left New Orleans on August 27, not long before a hurricane swept the Gulf. His hopes of her safe return were darkened by Lieutenant Crisp's pessimistic letter of October 24. "I hope we may hear something from the 'San Antonio' by the next arrival. I much fear that the gale which drove me ashore capsized her—with my yards down it laid me on my beam ends, and I believe would have capsized me if she had not driven ashore." Secretary Hamilton's correspondence of November 5 seconded Crisp's apprehensions. "I much fear that *San Bernard* is lost to the Government, and from accounts there is much reason to fear that the San Antonio is also lost, with those on board." As the months went by, Moore reluctantly concluded that the darkest fears of the naval community had been realized: *San Antonio*, with Lieutenant Seeger and a fine crew, was gone.

As the months went by, *San Antonio* became one of those ghost ships that haunt the choppy waters of the eastern Gulf. Some said she became a pirate ship cruising off the Isle of Pines, a notorious buccaneer haven off the Cuban coast. The captain of a vessel who hailed a phantom ship in a heavy gale "was led to believe that he was entering on board a Texian man-of-war; that she is armed with a long 32-pounder amidships on a pivot, six carronades, and a crew of 80 men—appendages unusual for a slaver." The *Houston Morning Star* lamented, "There is too much reason to fear that Lieut. Seeger has been murdered, and this fine vessel is now freighted with as base a crew of cut throats and villains as ever infested the ocean." The *Houston Press* later published an item from Nassau dated March 1843. "The Boxer fell in with a vessel near the Isle of Pines which answers the description of the San Antonio. The captain thinks it was her. The master says he is sure he has seen her at Galveston and does not think he can be mistaken. . . . The Boxer first run a French flag; the signal not being returned, the American ensign was run up and a fire opened on the schooner, the captain hoping to disable her. . . . The chase continued for two days but the winds were too light for the Boxer. . . . Her Britannic Majesty's frigate Illustrious was sent in search of her, but the cruise was in vain."

If *Boxer* did indeed encounter *San Antonio*, it was the last recorded time mortal men ever saw her. With the loss of the fast schooner went Commodore Moore's last hope for a revival of the pact with Yucatán.

On November 15, 1842, Acting Secretary Hamilton penned a report to President Houston that drove the final nail into the Navy's coffin. Commodore Moore, he wrote, had been ordered to return to Galveston to explain his use of the exchequer bills to the War Department, but had not yet complied. As for the warships, *Austin* and *Wharton* were well provisioned but lacked enough sailors to get to sea. *San Antonio* was lost. *San Bernard* was not heavily damaged, but she would require expensive dry docking to make her seaworthy again. *Zavala* was beyond salvation—her engines could have been sold for $25,000 previously, but by November 1842 they would be lucky to command $10,000. *Archer*, Hamilton reported, "is securely moored, and doing well. She is however, stripp'd of her Guns, Rigging and Sails, and indeed almost everything that could be removed." It would take ten thousand dollars to refit her, and until then, the hulk would serve as a shelter for *San Bernard*'s officers. Hamilton made no mention of the Navy Yard, which by this time had evidently been abandoned.

The winter of 1842–43 was to the Texas Navy as the winter of 1776–77 was to the Continental Army of George Washington. Stuck fast in New Orleans, Commodore Moore was down to two warships, which together could not muster enough seamen to put even one to sea. His officers must have believed that both government and Fate had turned their backs on the little navy—and not in equal measure, since government neglect had claimed more vessels than the raging Gulf. It was a minor miracle that during the long, impoverished months in port, any officers remained with Moore to see the adventure through to its end.

On December 2, Moore complained to an unsympathetic Hamilton, "I have been compelled to discharge within the last month about *thirty men*, whose term of service have expired, and had not *one dollar* to pay them off... on the 14th inst. There are not more than *six* men in both vessels whose term of service will not have expired." "Under this state of things," he continued, "the department will see the utter impossibility of moving the vessels from their present anchorage without means to ship seamen, and not one will ship until those who are in the city (and they are running after me whenever I am on shore for their pay) are paid off."

Moore also told Hamilton that he had dispatched *San Antonio* to Yucatán to reconnoiter the coast, "and in the event of the people of that country holding out against the troops of Santa Anna, Lieu't Com'g Seeger was to communicate with the Governor and endeavor to obtain funds to fit out the Navy." However, he conceded, "I fear that nothing can be expected from that quarter, for the enemy are on them both by sea and land." Always the fighter, Commodore Moore concluded his letter by reiterating that, given the poor quality of the Mexican Navy blockading Campeche, "I would not hesitate attacking them with this ship and the brig Wharton—every officer in the service is anxious, exceedingly anxious, to get off."

Back in Galveston, the anxious officers finally reached the end of their patience. By December 1842, the forlorn crew of the grounded *San Bernard*, now living aboard *Archer*, consisted of Lieutenant Crisp, two other lieutenants, two midshipmen, a captain's clerk, a cook named Hussy, and Lieutenant Crisp's pet pig, who "roamed about, lord of the deck," as one visitor put it, rooting through the men's personal effects and chewing holes in the few spare pieces of underwear the officers possessed. Not a stick perched upright on *Archer*'s hull, but masts, yards, rigging and spare equipment from *San Bernard* and *Archer* lined the spar deck in a disorganized mess. Her seams were loose enough to stick one's finger through, and with any more neglect, she would meet *Zavala*'s fate. She carried on board *San Bernard*'s armament—eight eighteen-pounders and one long gun, as the visitor recalled—but almost no food, coffee, or whiskey, none of which sailors can do without for long.

By Christmas Day, even Crisp's sacred pig was gone—the victim of a mutiny of sorts. After a pig-sized hole appeared in the lieutenant's undress uniform, the exasperated Englishman blurted out, "I wish someone would kill that pig," clearly not intending that anyone would act upon his utterance. To Crisp's dismay, this particular order was carried out that night with astonishing swiftness and efficiency. Crisp's outrage upon learning of the crime the next morning was, however, quickly assuaged by the delectable qualities of the victim.

The crew continued to live on the pig and other donated food until sometime in January, when the officers decided that the Texas Republic was bankrupt, and they, being creditors of the government, were entitled to foreclose on *Archer*'s equipment in lieu of payment. Soon sails, ropes, chronometers, azimuths, compasses, and other items began disappearing, the proceeds filling the officers' bellies in the process.

After living off *Archer*'s bounty for several weeks, most of the officers rowed ashore, discarded their commissions, and left. Crisp informed Commodore Moore that he had obtained a six-month leave from President Houston. He transferred his pathetic little command to Lt. Charles B. Snow, who in turn left his post for New Orleans in March to join his commander, taking with him the muskets, carbines, pistols, pikes, and cutlasses from *San Bernard* for future use aboard *Wharton*.

If Commodore Moore felt that things could not get any worse, he was wrong. As 1842 drew to a close, he received confirmation that Mexico had enough ships to take back the Gulf. The *New Orleans Tropic,* ignorant of the true state of the Texas Navy's affairs, published a report on the balance of forces in the Gulf of Mexico. Mexico was nearly ready to deploy three well-armed steamers—*Moctezuma* (mounting two sixty-eight-pounders and six forty-two-pounders, all shell-firing Paixhan guns), *Guadalupe* (two sixty-eight-pounder Paixhans and two long-range thirty-twos, and *Regenerador* (one long thirty-two and two long nines)—plus four sailing ships, including the seven-gun schooner *Aguila*, the three-gun schooner *Sisaleno*, the seventeen-gun brig *Yucateco*, and the nine-gun brig *Iman,* for a total of fifty-one heavy guns. To counter this fleet, the Republic of Texas possessed six warships the paper described as being in active service—*Austin, Wharton, Zavala, Archer, San Bernard,* and *San Antonio*. In reality, however, four of these warships would never sail again, and the two Texas vessels remotely capable of action—*Wharton* and *Austin*—could muster just thirty-six guns, not one larger than a twenty-four pounder.

Like many pro-Texas publicists, the *Tropic* resorted to sweeping claims of innate Anglo-Texian superiority to overcome Mexico's advantage in guns and technology. Each of the Texas Navy's officers, the *Tropic* claimed, "by natural capability, by education and by experience is worth the whole squalid and heaven-abandoned herd of Mexicans afloat on the Gulf. They received their principles and spirit from too noble a source to prove unfaithful to their trusts. The Texian vessels, moreover, are manned by seamen of a race in whose veins never flowed the blood of cowards. They are generally true samples of the genuine Yankee tars who have made the naval history of the United States a simple history of the most brilliant achievements ever witnessed upon the ocean. According to all accounts," continued the report, "the Mexican officers are in a sad state, lacking in all the essential requisites of good seamen. Such a crowd stands no chance against the perfect discipline of the Texian navy. In an action, they will probably injure each other about as much as they are injured by the enemy."

Moore knew better. Two of Mexico's steamers, built at Birkenhead, near Liverpool, were monsters by the standards of the day. *Guadalupe*, the world's first iron-plated steam warship, displaced approximately 842 tons, but she held a shallow draft—nine feet when loaded with ten days' coal—making her perfectly suited for the Gulf's shallow harbors. She was 183 feet long, 30 feet abeam, and boasted a hull covered with iron plates. Equipped with a 180-horsepower Forrester engine, she could chug along at nine knots, her two sixty-eight-pounder Paixhan guns spitting explosive shells "as large as good-sized pumpkins." Her hull was constructed with watertight compartments, to reduce the risk of sinking in case a Texian ball somehow managed to penetrate her iron sides. Like all steamers of the time, she also carried a complement of sails to take advantage of whatever the wind offered.

Britain's Royal Navy, still clinging to the glory days of the Age of Sail, had not embraced steam power fully. In 1842, *Guadalupe* was the largest iron vessel ever built, and the most advanced warship in the world, and Mexico quickly snapped her up. When she arrived at Veracruz on July 24, 1842, *Guadalupe* became the first steam-powered warship to cross the Atlantic Ocean. In addition to her imposing armament and defensive plating, *Guadalupe* was led by Commander E. P. Charleswood, a Royal Navy officer on furlough, with a crew of about eighty British sailors on leave.

Guadalupe's companion, the 1,100-ton *Moctezuma*, was almost as imposing. Her 203-foot heavily timbered hull sported two 68-pounder Paixhans and six long-range 42-pounders, giving her the heaviest battery of any belligerent in the Gulf. Like *Guadalupe*, she was manned by Englishmen: Commander Richard Cleaveland, junior officers, 150 sailors, and a dozen marines. Even without Cleaveland's experienced leadership, *Moctezuma*, like *Guadalupe*, was more than a match for Commodore Moore's two smaller, thinner, wind-driven vessels. Notwithstanding the efforts of Texas's minister to the Court of St. James, Ashbel Smith, to block the sale through diplomatic and clandestine channels, *Guadalupe* lifted anchor for Veracruz in the late spring of 1842, while *Moctezuma* followed her in early September.

By December 19—four days before Moore informed the War Department that he had "definite information that the Mexican steamer Montezuma is on her way to Vera Cruz"—Secretary Hamilton ordered Moore to report to the Department in Galveston. On January 2, 1843, Hamilton reiterated his order, conveying Houston's crocodile tears at the condition of the Navy: "His Excellency the President. . . . has deplored the misfortune as much as any citizen of the Republic, but these evils do exist, and there is no present remedy for them. You will therefore report in conformity (if practicable) with your previous orders at Galveston." Given the Navy's poverty, another trip to Galveston appeared to be decidedly impracticable.

The sad truth was, by the beginning of 1843, Texas had no navy. President Houston had not released a penny of the $97,000 that Congress had appropriated for the Navy's use, principally because, from Houston's view, the funds did not exist. *Austin* and *Wharton* were stranded in New Orleans, the latter with but five crewmen and fourteen officers. *Archer* sat idle in Galveston's harbor, *Zavala* and *San Bernard* were grounded on Galveston Island, and *San Antonio* had disappeared without a trace. The snorting, bucking warhorse that was the Texas Navy in 1840 had fallen victim to starvation and neglect, its heartbeat growing fainter by the day. Buried within *Austin*'s wooden carcass was only a forlorn, dying flicker of hope, meticulously nurtured by a captain who had virtually no crew, a soldier whose country had forsaken him. In effect, the Texas Navy was down to one man.

But what a resourceful man he was. His mission—to sail for the glory of his country—had now become a personal obsession. He would let no obstacle, not even a six-foot two-inch giant named Sam Houston, stand in the way of what he saw as his duty to save the Lone Star Republic. His anger and impatience towards the government seemed to work him into a frenzy, and he thrashed out verbally at an enemy he could not yet fight. Like an enraged lion in a wooden cage, he fumed to Gen. Albert Sidney Johnston from the confines of his cabin, "My firm conviction is that before the War is terminated every Mexican Officer who is captured will have to be shot or hung; the World will justify the course, and the sooner it is begun the better for Texas."

Moore's frustration and anxiety were noticeable even to passing acquaintances. An English traveler likewise wrote of her meeting with Moore around that time. "All the Commodore wanted was money, and that seemed very scarce with him just then; had he but possessed that necessary article, he 'would go to sea, take the Montezuma and Guadaloupe, and whip the Mexicans all around!' And so he very likely would, for he enjoys the reputation of being a good officer, and a very fighting one . . . he certainly appeared ready to do any thing, (as the schoolboys say 'from pitch and toss to manslaughter') for his country."

How right she would be.

CHAPTER TWENTY-EIGHT

The Plan

[Our intelligence] indicates to the Executive in the most authentic and impressive terms, that Mexico, in the event of being successful against Yucatán, will immediately invade Texas with a formidable force both by land and sea.
—Sam Houston to Texas Congress, January 10, 1843

IN EARLY 1843, SAM HOUSTON was indulging in what Kipling would call "the Great Game" in the Gulf of Mexico. He was, in his own Byzantine way, aiming to pit Great Britain's interests against those of Mexico and the United States.

The first piece of Houston's diplomatic puzzle—the United States—was torn between the Whigs of the northeast, who adamantly opposed annexation because it would extend slavery, and the Democrats of the south and west, whose cries for annexation were growing louder every month. The second puzzle piece—Great Britain—was also conflicted. Britain abhorred Texas's slavery practices, and had strong economic ties to Mexico, but she desperately wanted to avoid giving Texas and the United States cause to unite, particularly at a time of rising hostility between the U.S. and Britain over the Pacific boundary with Canada. Queen Victoria's ministers also saw in Texas another western market for its manufactured goods, "without having to climb over the United States tariff," as Lord Aberdeen put it. Furthermore, Britain had an interest in cultivating an alternative source of high-quality cotton, to reduce its dependency upon U.S. exports.

President Houston, recognizing these competing interests, encouraged Britain, possibly in hopes of nudging the leading suitor, the United States, closer to annexation. In late 1842, Great Britain sent Houston a new diplomatic chief, Royal Navy Captain Charles Elliot. While privately deriding Texas as "this flotsam or derelict of the Prairies," Elliot played the game well, convincing the old general to withdraw his March 26 blockade against Mexico on September 10,—the day before Mexican Gen. Adrian Woll marched into Texas and captured San Antonio. Elliot also persuaded Houston that the sales of *Guadalupe* and *Moctezuma* were legal commercial transactions, along identical lines to the Dawson contract for Texas's ships. In this regard, Elliott was so successful that Houston apologized to Elliott for Ashbel Smith's energetic efforts to prevent the warships from steaming to Mexico, and admonished Smith, "when your hand is in the lion's mouth it is safest to withdraw it quietly without slapping the lion on his nose."

From Houston's standpoint, such kowtowing to Queen Victoria may have been a ploy to interest Washington in annexation. However, Houston had the war hawks in Congress to think of, and his actions during the fall of 1842 were inconsistent with a purely pacifist approach. He authorized two punitive expeditions against Mexico as a political expedient, but refused to provide any support for them, and pressed his acting secretary of state to convince the United States, Britain, and France to sponsor a treaty ending the Texas–Mexican border raids.

Mexico was, of course, unswayed by Sam Houston's diplomatic maneuvering, and proceeded to roll back the revolutionary tide. After rebuffing the treaty Andréas Quintana Roo negotiated with Yucatán in early 1842, Mexico City launched a war against the peninsular states to return them to the centralist fold once and for all. On July 5, Commander Tomás Marín of the Mexican Navy took fifty-seven men aboard the merchant schooner *Margarita* and captured the seventeen-gun brig *Yucateco* in a daring night raid. Two months later, the resourceful Marín struck again, capturing the nine-gun schooner *Iman*, the three-gun schooner *Campecheano*, and the pilot boat *Sisaleno* when the key port of Carmen at Laguna de Terminos fell to centralist troops. Having established complete naval supremacy in the Gulf, Mexico began landing soldiers in the states of Yucatán and Campeche. By the fall, some 3,000 soldiers and a brigade of artillery under Mexican Gen. Pedro de Ampudia had been transported by sea to the peninsula, and on December 1 Mexico proclaimed a blockade of Campeche.

The port of Campeche was the key to the reconquest of the Yucatán peninsula. The city, built by the Spaniards, was home to around 70,000 inhabitants. Surrounded by a forty-foot stone wall built in the 1600s as a defense against such pirates as Henry Morgan and Francis Drake, Campeche was one of the few truly fortified cities in the Americas. Situated in the shark-infested Bay of Campeche, it had no protective harbor, only an open roadstead. Its anchorage facilitated heavy commerce, even though offloading was limited by the long shallows that gradually meandered up to dry land.

Unfortunately for its citizens, Campeche's walls were designed to defeat a seventeenth-century enemy; its battery of long eighteen-pounders was no match for the heavy Paixhan guns of the Mexican Navy, or for the field artillery General Ampudia would unlimber in the suburbs of Eminencia and San Romans. When the Mexican blockade commenced, the U.S. consul there openly fretted that the city would not hold out for long.

By late 1842, British diplomats were predicting Yucatán's defeat, and the British foreign ministry noted a buildup of troops earmarked for an invasion of Texas. It did not take long before Ashbel Smith, Houston's envoy to England, concluded that Santa Anna's peremptory rejection of British mediation, Secretary Tornel's comments to Sir Richard Packenham, and Mexico's enlistment of Spanish assistance left "no room to doubt that Mexico was in savage earnest to subjugate Texas." Albert Sidney Johnston also heard rumors (possibly from Commodore Moore) that Mexico planned to invade Texas early in the spring, and these rumors were confirmed by the British ambassador to Mexico. General Woll's occupation of San Antonio on September 11, 1842, produced a "very great excitement" along the coasts, according to a doctor from Liberty, who warned a colleague, "We are looking out for an attack on Galveston by water." The dogs of war may not have been unleashed yet, but they were awake and growling with impatience.

In January 1843, even Sam Houston believed an invasion of Texas would take place once Yucatán was returned to centralist control. The invasion, he predicted, would be launched in the spring, and because the Great Powers would not tolerate a long and bloody war of occupation by Mexico, "it may be supposed, that all her available energies will be called into action and employed with the greatest efficiency." Houston predicted that the invading force would incorporate two divisions. The first would occupy San Antonio and proceed north to Austin, while the second would land near Victoria, "and advance along the seaboard in cooperation with the fleet destined for Galveston." In such a case, the invaders "would thus have the entire command of our waters, and the gulf, and could sustain themselves, receiving supplies by water."

Strangely enough, Houston's defense plans did not include the Navy. Most likely, he believed that the Republic's poverty had already condemned that branch to oblivion. Perhaps he was also enamored of the British envoys, who assured him that English mediation would bring Mexico to her senses. He may have thought that Mexico would leave Texas alone if she were incapable of giving offense, even on the high seas. Or perhaps he was deliberately weakening Texas' defenses to draw in the United States, for the same reasons he believed that a retreat to the Sabine River in April 1836 might bring the U.S. Army galloping to the rescue. Regardless of his state of mind, Houston's failure to align Texas with Yucatán or support the Navy in the face of Mexico's acknowledged threats struck many of his contemporaries as supremely irresponsible, or even criminally negligent.

With the fate of Texas growing more uncertain by the day, Commodore Moore sent another appeal to the governor of Yucatán, offering once again to renew the 1841 alliance. The terms would be nearly identical to those observed the year before: Yucatán would contribute $8,000 per month for the Navy's upkeep, and Moore would sweep Mexico's warships from the Yucatán coast, placing Laguna de Terminos back in Yucatán's possession and breaking the blockade of Campeche. Moore wrote that the failure of General Lemus, who had since defected to the centralists, to renew the agreement in October had been "the *sole* cause of the enemy not having been driven ere from your territory and sea coast."

Yucatán's reply came quickly. On January 25, two days before Moore's letter arrived, Yucatán's acting governor, Miguel Barbachano, dispatched Colonel Peraza, Lorenzo de Zavala, Jr. (son of the former Texas vice-president), and Secretary Rejón to New Orleans to renew the alliance. On January 31, Barbachano confirmed the new alliance and informed Moore that four days earlier, *Moctezuma*, with a crew of only sixty men, had anchored off Sisal and opened fire on the town. The military commandant of Campeche reported that the Mexicans now had *Guadalupe, Moctezuma, Regenerador, Yucateco* (rechristened *Mexicano*), *Iman, Aguila*, and *Campecheano* stationed off the coast, easily hemming in Yucatán's eight tiny gunboats. Barbachano suggested that if Moore could not take on the entire Mexican squadron, he might be able to capture the enemy garrison at Laguna de Terminos, "where they have a place of deposit of arms, ammunitions and provisions, and in the Customshouse, there should be a large amount of money." Such a bold step in southern Campeche might persuade the governor of neighboring Tabasco to side with the federalists, as he already was privately inclined to do.

Back in New Orleans, Moore's hands were full just keeping his officers and ships together. One group of sailors, furious that they had been discharged without pay, threatened to return to the docks and burn the ships, until some of Moore's friends loaned him $3,000 to pacify the mob. Moore's officers were also a problem, itching either to get into the fight off Yucatán, or to leave the service entirely. *Austin* midshipman Andrew Jackson Bryant wrote to his mother on January 8: "We have been here a long time whereas we ought to go Down the Coast whooping the Mexicans." He continued, "We have got a Bad reputation in the world as long as we have Been Laying here to long." On February 8, *Wharton's* midshipmen, destitute and barely clothed, submitted their resignations to Commodore Moore, who rejected them out of hand. A week later, they submitted a resolution to Moore listing their numerous grievances, and requested that he either accept their resignations or provide them with adequate winter clothing and food. Moore ignored this resolution, partly because he had no means to satisfy the men, and partly because he had other things on his mind.

These other things included the signing of a new compact with Colonel Peraza, the architect of the 1841 agreement. On February 7, Peraza landed at the Crescent City's wharves, and four days later, he and Moore executed a new agreement for the Texas Navy's services. Working quickly, Moore sent word to Captain James Boylan, the former Texas officer who now commanded the Yucatán Navy, announcing his pending assistance, and on February 24, Commodore Moore advised Yucatán's Gov. Santiago Mendez that he would coordinate with Boylan to attack the Mexican squadron first.

Moore worked feverishly. Using Yucatán silver to buy provisions, ammunition, sailors, and supplies, he prepared to avenge the wrongs done to Yucatán, cover the Texas Navy in glory, and stop a bloody invasion before it ever reached Texas soil. Like William Barrett Travis at the Alamo, Moore's moment in history had finally come, and nothing could stop the Texas Navy from carrying out a mission that it had yearned to tackle for three disappointing years.

Until two men delivered news that stopped Moore dead in his tracks.

CHAPTER TWENTY-NINE

Amateurs in Command

Good God! Did the President think I was going to run away with the vessels or turn pirate?
—Commodore Moore, April 5, 1843

AFTER READING SECRETARY HAMILTON'S REPORT in November 1842, Sam Houston decided to sell the Navy. Evidently he felt that by selling the vessels and equipment, he could generate some badly needed currency to fund the nucleus of an army, to be led by the invincible Hero of San Jacinto. Besides, without new funds, the Navy was not going anywhere, according to Commodore Moore. Since Houston had rebuffed Yucatán's invitation to refit *Zavala* in 1842, and had ignored two letters from Governor Barbachano on the subject, he was reasonably certain that the embattled federalists would not trust Texas to come to their aid. And neither did he trust the federalists.

Calling members of the Seventh Texas Congress to meet in secret session in January 1843, three weeks before the regular session convened, Houston delivered a secret message that painted a dismal picture of the Texas Navy. It began, "No reference was made to the Navy in the annual message for the reason it was deemed unwise to present to the world the deplorable condition of that branch of the public service." Implying that Moore was incompetent for failing to get to sea on the $20,000 allotted him by the Sixth Congress, Houston faulted his impertinent, disloyal, embezzling naval commander for holding the fleet hostage in New Orleans for nine months without so much as lifting an anchor to defend Texas. "Every assistance which the government thought advisable under the circumstances in which it was placed, had been afforded in accordance with the views of its commander," the message ran. Moore, in violation of direct orders, took $18,000 worth of exchequer bills and immediately put them into circulation. The Navy, Houston claimed, would cost $300,000 a year to maintain, and Moore, evidently lining his pockets with public funds, would never go to sea.

Houston then revealed what many had long suspected. He told the body, "It is for the Honorable Congress to determine the question, whether Texas is in a situation to accomplish the object of keeping our Navy longer afloat, or whether a good policy does not require us to abandon that arm of defense and make sale or such other disposition of the vessels as will relieve the nation from a burden which it is so utterly unable to sustain." Houston's proposed solution was simple: he would mount cannon at Galveston, Velasco, and Matagorda and call out the local militia to defend Texas. (Houston had, strangely enough, rejected an offer by James Hamilton to sell a battery of Paixhan guns to the Republic less than one month earlier, citing lack of funds.)

Soon afterwards, President Houston again addressed Congress, this time more forcefully. He complained of the state of the Navy and Moore's lack of financial accountability. Noting Moore's requests for even a small part of the $97,000 appropriated the previous summer, Houston callously remarked, "He appears to rely upon an appropriation made at the called session in July last, to enable him to extricate himself from his present difficulties, although he must be fully aware that the appropriation has not been and is not now available." Houston claimed the Navy would cost the bankrupt republic two hundred dollars per day, and with no hope of getting the vessels to sea, he again urged Congress to sell off the ships, or return them to their builder for credit.

Heeding the President's advice, Congress passed a secret act on January 16, 1843, which read as follows:

An Act to provide for the Sale of the Navy of Texas.

Sect. 1. Be it enacted by the Senate and House of Representatives of the Republic of Texas in Congress assembled, That the President be and he is hereby authorized and required [as] soon as practicable, consistent with the public interest, to dispose of the vessels comprising the Navy of Texas, to wit, The Ship Austin the Brig Wharton at the highest price which can be obtained either by sale or in exchange for and in redemption of the entire liabilities of the Government contracted in the purchase of said vessels, and the Brig Archer and the Schooner San Bernard together with the Steamship Zavalla her tackle, furniture and apparel, also the property of the Navy Yard with all the Naval Stores be sold for cash or credit as the President may deem proper, and the proceeds from the sale from the Archer, San Bernard and Zavalla with the public property at the Navy Yard, shall be disbursed in the following manner, to wit, fifteen thousand dollars for the payment of claims due the present or former officers, seamen and marines of the Navy in proportion to the time they have served and the amount which may be due, and the balance to be paid into the Treasury of the Republic.

Sect. 2. Be it further enacted That the President be and he is hereby authorized to appoint some trustworthy and suitable person or persons, to act as agent or agents, in affecting at as early a period as practicable the object of this act.

Sect. 3. Be it further enacted That this act take effect from and after its passage.

N. H. Darnell
Speaker of the House of Representatives
J. A. Greer
President Pro. Tem. of the Senate,
Approved 16th Jany 1843
Sam Houston

Houston's new secretary of war and navy, George Washington Hill, moved quickly to dispose of the Navy. On January 23, Hill sent James Morgan, William Bryan, and Samuel May Williams confidential letters appointing them as commissioners to carry out the provisions of the new law. That same day, Hill sent another letter to Frederick Dawson, offering to return *Austin* and *Wharton* in exchange for cancellation of the $560,000 debt owed by the Republic. Whether anyone seriously expected Dawson to accept two used, worn-out vessels in return for a contracted half-million dollar obligation is unknown, but perhaps Houston assumed that Dawson would take the ships back, since Texas had nothing else to offer. Four days later, Secretary Hill ordered Purser J. F. Stephens to report to Galveston for "Extra duty to Messrs. William Bryan, James Morgan and Samuel M. Williams, Commissioners appointed by His Excellency the President, to carry into effect a secret act of Congress in reference to the Navy, and act as Secretary to the Commission until the business is closed." He also instructed Galveston's Gail Borden to provide whatever information the commissioners needed.

Samuel May Williams, financier of the Texas Navy since its earliest days, declined to preside over the demise of the fleet he helped build. James Morgan, the militia colonel who led the defense of Galveston Island in 1836, had grave doubts about the wisdom of denuding the coast in the face of Mexican threats, but he accepted the commission, hoping that Mexico was no more able to invade Texas in 1843 than it had been in 1837. William Bryan, the junior commissioner, was a former Texas agent in New Orleans, and would serve as its consul there until annexation in 1846. These two civilians, Morgan and Bryan, would be the Navy's new commanders in chief.

When the commissioners left for New Orleans in late February, President Houston and Secretary Hill had every reason to think that the Navy was as good as sold. On January 22, Hill had ordered Commodore Moore to leave his vessels in the care of the next senior officer and return to Galveston to report to the Department. The reason, Hill explained, was that Moore's presence was required before an act of Congress was passed in relation to the Navy. This was a ruse, of course, since the act he referred to had been passed six days before. That same day, Hill ordered "Commander J. T. K. Lothrop, Or officer in command of Navy" to report to the commissioners, and to take all further orders from them. The intent was clear: Hill wanted to get Commodore

Moore out of the way, so that the commissioners would be able to deal with the presumably more pliable Commander Lothrop.

Unfortunately for the Houston cabal, Hill's letters were coincidentally delayed, and both arrived the very day the commissioners did. Moore, sensing what the commissioners were up to, greeted the two men on the afternoon of February 25 at the Texas consulate. Going straight to the point, he said, "Well Gentlemen, I understand you have come for the vessels under my command." The commissioners were taken aback by the Commodore's abruptness, but they quickly settled in for a pleasant conversation about the state of the vessels and Moore's plans for them. Assuring Morgan and Bryan that he would comply with any orders from the Department had he the means to do so, Moore took his leave for the evening. As he was walking out with James Morgan, a messenger ran up to him with his orders dated January 22, requiring him to leave for Galveston. Moore read the orders in Morgan's presence, then returned to his ship.

The following Monday, February 27, Commodore Moore prepared a written report to the commissioners on the status of his squadron. The vessels were provisioned for a three month cruise, and he had managed to recruit half the men needed to put to sea. "We have a full complement of officers," Moore wrote, "who are eager to get to sea and convince the Government what great injustice and neglect they have met at its hands undeservedly." Not entirely satisfied with this reply, the commissioners wrote Moore back the next day, asking for a direct response to their most pressing question: Would he turn over the squadron to the commissioners? Moore replied, politely and correctly, "As commander of the Navy, I as a matter of course am bound to obey no order except those issued by the head of the Navy Department. If Congress in their wisdom have thought proper to alter the existing laws by which I have been heretofore governed, I must of course be informed, not only of the passage of such laws, but must be furnished with a certified copy by the head of the Department of War and Marine, before I can be expected to obey, or even know the existence of such laws." Moore's polite objection sent Morgan and Bryan to an attorney they knew, a friend of Houston's named William Christy. On Christy's advice, the commissioners sent Bryan back to Texas for further instructions, taking with him Moore's report to the Department outlining his plans to attack the Mexican fleet off Campeche.

This delay gave Moore his chance. James Morgan, who had lived near the shameful wrecks of *Zavala, San Bernard,* and *Archer* off Galveston, expected to find *Austin* and *Wharton* in the same miserable shape. Instead, he found the vessels well supplied, fully manned and in fighting trim. The officers, flush with prospects of action, had a high level of *esprit de corps*, and Yucatán's silver allowed Moore not only to silence the grousers who had been discharged without pay, but also to recruit the best sailors on the New

Orleans wharves. Moore had funds, warships, ammunition, men, and best of all, a good reason to fight; a victory off Yucatán would spare Texas a second invasion—one guaranteed to be larger and more dangerous than the first.

Moore's arguments rang true for Morgan, who held personal misgivings about the wisdom of Houston's naval policy. Over the next few weeks, Moore spent many hours with Morgan, discussing the state of the fleet and its capabilities, and relaying unsettling reports of centralist forces closing in on Campeche. So by the time William Bryan returned from Texas, James Morgan fully supported Moore as the one man with a workable plan to save the Republic.

Back in Texas, reports from New Orleans set off a firestorm in the Houston administration. Moore's March 10 report to Secretary Hill explained that the Navy had received funds from Yucatán, which would enable the squadron to attack the Mexican Navy off Campeche. The report also noted that since the Act of Congress referred to in Hill's January 22 message had already been passed, there was no need for him to return to Galveston. Besides, Moore protested, he could not afford to do so, having already run up $1,800 in unreimbursed travel expenses for previous trips to the seat of government.

When Houston read this, he erupted with fury. It was almost as if Secretary Fisher's insubordination of 1837 was repeating itself, except it was not one, but several orders that the fleet commander was violating. This time, Houston was not going to leave Moore any room for argument or obfuscation: he immediately suspended Commodore Moore from command. Acting Secretary M. C. Hamilton, returning to torment Commodore Moore, delivered instructions charging Moore with "repeated disobedience of orders" by entering into the Yucatán agreement, "without even the knowledge of the Government." (Here Hamilton overlooked Moore's December 2 report, which stated that he had sent *San Antonio* to do just that).

Moore was finished. "You are hereby suspended from all command," Hamilton concluded, "and will report forthwith, in arrest, to the Department in person. Any interference on your part with the command, or with those who have been directed to assume it, will be regarded by the Government as mutiny and sedition, and punished accordingly."

To spur the commissioners to decisive action, Houston personally instructed them to "employ all proper and legal means to get possession of the national vessels," and hold them subject to further orders from the War Department. Houston further informed the commissioners that Moore had no authority to ship men or marines, appoint officers, or do anything other than sail to Galveston, or turn over his command to the next ranking officer and return to Texas. Accusing Moore of treason, Houston warned that any resistance to his orders would be considered "mutiny," and persistence in dereliction would be "piracy."

To keep Moore in line, Houston gave the commissioners a signed but unpublished proclamation that declared that Moore and his officers were pirates. The proclamation called upon "the Naval Powers of Christendom" to arrest the officers and deliver them up to the Texas government for trial. Should Moore fail to comply with the commissioners' orders, they were to publish the proclamation in New Orleans, and forward copies to Texas ministers in Washington, London, and Paris.

Houston's latest round of orders was handed to Commodore Moore by James Morgan on April 3. Moore knew he was at a crossroads. His labors over the last three years had brought him to the point where a single decision could deliver Texas from Santa Anna's armies. Or it could doom the Texas Navy. The power to make that decision rested with a civilian who had never held a naval command; in effect, amateurs would determine the fate of Texas.

Commodore Moore was playing a dangerous game of political chess with Sam Houston, a master at the game, and had to consider his next move very carefully. After pondering his orders and thinking through the president's likely next move, he visited James Morgan at his hotel. "You see the situation I am now placed in," Moore pleaded. "I have been at a vast expense to get these vessels fitted out and ready for sea; you know in what situation the vessels are now. I entered into a contract with the Yucatán Government, which I felt myself legally authorized to do, and am now suspended from command of the vessels by this order. If I obey this order and leave the vessels in the port of New Orleans, every officer under me will resign. The vessels will be left at the mercy of the sailors, who will be sure to mutiny and destroy them—which they threatened to do once before when I could not pay them off."

Morgan was sympathetic, but resolute. He replied, "The orders the commissioners have now received, are painful to me, I assure you. I accepted this commission with a great deal of reluctance, but I mean to execute the orders, regardless of consequences."

Moore then asked whether Morgan had other orders for Lothrop or any other officer. "I had another communication for Captain Lothrop, to take charge of the vessels." Upon learning that Morgan had given Lothrop's orders to Purser J. F. Stephens for delivery, Moore reiterated his pleas to keep the vessels from being abandoned and vandalized. Morgan wouldn't budge.

At last, Moore accepted his fate. Or rather, he took a calculated risk, offering Morgan a bargain: if Morgan would withdraw his orders to Lothrop, Moore would take the warships back to Galveston, bring Morgan along, and report to President Houston personally to prove to him that he had done nothing to compromise the nation's honor. This would avoid the certainty that the officers would resign, that the sailors would loot the vessels, and that the ships would die a slow, agonizing death in New Orleans.

Morgan, to Moore's relief, agreed. "That is exactly what I want done with the vessels," he said. "If Captain Lothrop has not received and read the communication I have sent him by Mr. Stephens this evening, the arrangement proposed shall be made, and you shall continue in command of the vessels until our arrival in Galveston."

Morgan scurried off to find Stephens, fully aware that if Moore resigned, the vessels would never see Galveston. On his way, he ran into Commander Lothrop. Morgan inquired, "Captain Lothrop, if you do receive a communication from Mr. Stephens, I would be glad if you would not break the seal, but return it to me with the seal unbroken."

Lothrop dug into his jacket pocket, and pulled out a sealed envelope. "Is this it?" he asked. Morgan nodded. It was orders from the Department of War and Navy, he explained. Lothrop handed back the envelope, dutifully replying that all communications from the Department should be given to him through his superior, Commodore Moore. Morgan agreed, and the two men parted for the night.

Rushing back to Moore, Morgan sealed the bargain. "I have got the communication from Captain Lothrop, and he had not broken the seal; and the understanding between us now, is that you will continue in command of the vessels until we get them to Galveston, where we are to proceed immediately."

Moore nodded. "Yes, I pledge to you my honor that there shall be no delay, and we will go immediately to Galveston."

"As it will be saving the Government some expense," continued Morgan, "I will take passage with you if you have no objection."

"I should be happy for your company," the commodore replied.

Next morning, Morgan informed William Bryan of the arrangement. Bryan, seeing the wisdom of retaining Moore until the ships were safely anchored off Galveston, concurred with Morgan's decision. That same day, Commodore Moore memorialized their agreement in a letter to Morgan and Bryan, adding, "In order to preserve the Navy (now in ready for sea, with the exception of a few seamen) and save my own reputation, it is absolutely necessary that the tenor of the communication referred to above, should not be known to *anyone* until we arrive at Galveston."

At last, Morgan had Moore's promise in writing. Moore, for his part, remained in command and had a few more days to persuade Morgan to disregard Houston's orders to return to Galveston. Or at least, to permit the Navy one slight detour on the way home—a detour to Yucatán. To keep the sailors from stripping the vessels and deserting, he told them that they would touch at Galveston before heading back to the Mexican coast.

A few days later, Colonel Morgan remarked to Commodore Moore, "I feel particularly gratified that matters have taken the turn between us that they have, for if you had been obstinate or disposed to act incorrectly in any way with the vessels, I had a paper that would have controlled you."

Smiling, Moore wondered aloud what that could be. Morgan told him to come to his hotel room at any time, and he would be glad to show it to Moore. The next day Moore knocked on Morgan's door and asked to see the mystery document. Morgan showed him Houston's proclamation.

Moore's jaw dropped. "Good God!" he said in disbelief. "Did the President think I was going to run away with the vessels or turn pirate?"

The question needed no reply. James Morgan was no one's fool. He had been wrestling with his conscience over scuttling the Texas Navy when Mexico was publicizing its plans to reconquer Texas. Morgan had accepted Houston's appointment because he had convinced himself that Mexico lacked the means to invade Texas a second time. Now, faced with news of ironclad warships and veteran armies closing in on Yucatán, he had to think long and hard about whether he was willing to put his home town of Galveston on the front lines of an invasion that would claim even more lives than the last one. With the fate of Texas resting on his decision, keeping Moore temporarily in command seemed a safer course than betting on the incompetence of Mexico or the effectiveness of England's diplomacy. Besides, should Moore take one step out of line, Morgan could publish Houston's proclamation declaring Moore and his officers pirates. On April 8, the commissioners wrote to Secretary Hill that they would return to Galveston with Moore and his warships.

Commodore Moore almost had James Morgan convinced that Yucatán, not Galveston, was the squadron's proper destination. But not quite. Orders were orders, and the Navy would sail west, not south. It was a shame to return to Texas, now that Moore had one of the finest crews ever to clamber up *Austin's* rigging, but the game was over: the Texas Navy was coming home.

Using a request Houston penned the previous fall, Moore took into custody the remaining *San Antonio* mutineers from the New Orleans jail. The ringleader, Seymour Oswald, had escaped, and private Benjamin Pompilly died in his cell, confessing to Lieutenant Fuller's murder on his deathbed, but the rest were brought aboard the flagship. On the evening of April 15, with a heavy heart, Moore welcomed Colonel Morgan aboard *Austin* for her final voyage to Galveston.

The ship had slumbered off New Orleans for the better part of a year, and when the time came to go, the crew seemed unfamiliar with the process of moving it. At a word from Lt. Alfred Gray, the boatswain piped, "All hands up anchor!" which, as Gray remembered a decade later, "was followed by the tramping of feet, as men ran around to the capstan to the tortured melody of a fife. . . . As that piece of crooked iron had been buried in the mud of the Mississippi River for some ten months," he continued, "and as it had been supposed that the bed of the father of waters had foreclosed the mortgage, my astonishment at this unexpected demand was no doubt obvious to the gentleman with the speaking trumpet." Some of the men, having been frequently disappointed before, harbored doubts as to whether they were really going. But these doubts, said the lieutenant, were "speedily dispelled by the appearance of an exceedingly disreputable looking tow boat, which seized us and bore us up the river."

Austin's departure ended an eternity of silence for the flagship, during which time Commodore Moore and his officers had made many friends in New Orleans. As the steamer *Lion* came alongside to guide *Austin* and *Wharton* into the pass that leads to the Gulf, the onlooking crew of the USS *Ontario* crowded the sloop's decks and yards; they gave three hearty cheers to their Texas comrades, which were returned by the Texians with equal gusto.

With that, the crew bade farewell to the lights of New Orleans, a bittersweet time that would stand out in the memories of those who were there. Lieutenant Gray wrote of this moment, "[T]he steamer rounding, we passed down the river, took one last long look at the glorious Crescent City, and were fairly underway for a cruise which was destined to be the last one—the final appearance on the waters of the flag of the young Republic."

The trip from New Orleans to the Northeast Pass took some time, and when the ships arrived at the Pass, a dense fog set in and the winds died down, becalming both vessels. The next few windless days were anything but calm, though, for the Texas sailors. Moore ran a tight ship, and it was tighter on this voyage than any other, particularly since he was carrying nine mutineers and a naval commissioner. During the lull, he exercised his men at the guns twice a day, test-fired his new explosive shells, and saw to it that shipboard discipline was strict for both officers and men. "The conduct of Com. Moore on board of the Austin," Morgan later remarked, "was such as I should have expected from the commander of a fleet, rather more perfect than I should have expected for a man of his age."

The next item of business was the *San Antonio* mutineers. At one in the afternoon on April 16, Commander Lothrop convened a court-martial for the nine defendants. The panel that was to decide their fate consisted of Lothrop, as president, Lt. Alfred Gray, Lt. J. P. Lansing, Lt. Cyrus Cummings, and Lt. D. C. Wilbur. The ship's surgeon, Dr. Thomas Anderson, served as judge advocate. The prisoners were charged with murder and attempted murder, mutiny, and desertion.

The prosecution was hampered by a significant loss of evidence, as most of the witnesses had vanished along with *San Antonio* the previous September. After some undoubtedly hard negotiating, Seaman Joseph Shepherd was persuaded to testify with the promise of a pardon. The court took testimony from several witnesses, and adjourned until the next day.

The verdict was mixed, indicating that the court took account of the individual defendants' various degrees of culpability. "In discharge of the painful duty and awful responsibilities imposed upon us, we have endeavored to confine ourselves strictly to the law governing courts-martial, and to the evidence that has been brought before us," read the court's April 18 verdict. Boatswain Frederick Shepherd was found not guilty. Seaman John Williams and cook Edward Keenan were sentenced to fifty lashes with the cats, although the court recommended mercy to Williams. Seaman William Barrington, the court found, was deeply implicated in the mutiny. But because he informed his officers of the conspiracy at the last minute, he was sentenced to one hundred lashes with the cats. Then came the heavy sentences. "Of the prisoners Antonio Landois, James Hudgins, Isaac Allen and William Simpson, we have only to say that we deem the evidence elicited at the trial of each and every one of them sufficiently clear and distinct to convict them of the various charges and specifications preferred against them, and have therefore sentenced them to death."

CHAPTER THIRTY

"To Save the Republic"

This Ship and the brig have excellent men on board, and the officers and men are all eager for the contest—We will go to make one desperate struggle to turn the tide of ill luck that has so long been running against Texas.

—Commodore Moore, April 19, 1843

WHILE THE COURT-MARTIAL WAS handing down its verdicts, some electrifying news reached New Orleans, changing everything. As the squadron lay at anchor in the Northeast Pass, three men from the schooner *Rosario*, fresh from Yucatán, arrived with news of Mexico's war against Yucatán. That state, tired of waiting for Texas, was on the verge of making peace with Mexico. They had beaten back centralist troops from the very gates of Mérida, the capital, but surviving centralist units under Generals Matias de la Peña y Barragan and Pedro Lemus were waiting to be picked up by *Moctezuma* at Telchac, under generous terms that allowed the units to quit the country within twelve days. From there, the soldiers would await orders for an invasion of Texas.

Further south, the war was going badly for the federalists. Governor Mendez, besieged in Campeche, had nearly succumbed to claims of Texas faithlessness by General Ampudia's centralists, and was on the verge of siding with Santa Anna against the treacherous Texians, who had promised to come to his aid three months before. Ampudia, with two thousand troops, had set up operations in Campeche's suburbs, establishing a mortar battery on a little eminence commanding the town, and put two or three batteries on the beach to create an effective cross-fire against the old city. With these, Lieutenant Gray wrote, "he poured in all the uncomfortable projectiles which the Mexican finances were able to furnish him with." A fierce battle for the suburb of San Roman ensued, and when Ampudia's infantry assault proved ineffective, the two sides settled down to a protracted siege while Ampudia attempted to negotiate an end to the fighting. *Moctezuma*, Moore's informants claimed, was alone off Telchac, a target ripe for the picking, and the Mexican steamers were badly manned, being heavily dependent upon underpaid English soldiers, who were on the brink of mutiny.

To Commodore Moore, this was splendid news. With a little push from the winds, he could easily close with *Moctezuma* and outgun her; if she capitulated, he would have a fine warship and, more importantly, steam power to move his ship and brig into fighting position.

But as long as Colonel Morgan was in command, he dared not issue this order.

Morgan was at first skeptical of the merchants' stories. He questioned *Rosario*'s men at length, but he eventually concluded that the reports were genuine. "If our two vessels were to proceed to Telchac," he reasoned, "we would find [*Moctezuma*] there alone and might easily capture her; by which means the balance of the Mexican fleet would easily fall into our hands." Having wrestled with his doubts, Morgan recalled how Houston had assured him during the winter, "there was to be a formidable invasion of the country; that it was gone and out of his power to save it; that it would cease to be a Republic in six months." Morgan also undoubtedly heard another rumor making the rounds in New Orleans, that Mexico and Great Britain had reached a secret deal whereby, if Mexico could not retake Texas by May 15, Mexico would at last recognize the independence of her former province.

Observers in the United States and Great Britain substantiated rumors of an invasion upon the capitulation of Yucatán, although Morgan and Moore did not know of these details at the time. On the seventh anniversary of the Battle of San Jacinto, Texas's minister to the United States, Isaac Van Zandt, claimed U.S. Sen. Daniel Webster had predicted that "the favorable or unfavorable termination of that campaign [in Yucatán] would determine the ability or inability of Mexico to reinvade Texas." Captain G. B. Elliot of the HMS *Spartan* wrote on April 25, "Campeche will very shortly have to surrender and leave the squadron free to engage in operations against Texas." And Percy Doyle, Britain's new envoy to Mexico, wrote to London's foreign office on April 24 that upon rumors of Mérida's fall, Santa Anna was "so elated with the successes his troops have met with in Yucatán that he had declared his intention of sending at once from thence an Expedition to Galveston, and of marching troops through the Interior to attack Texas on the other side." Mexico's foreign minister also warned British and French diplomats that during the upcoming invasion of Texas, foreign diplomats would be considered merely foreigners squatting on Mexican soil.

Surely, Morgan thought, if President Houston knew of the fine state of his vessels and the dangerous situation unfolding in Yucatán, he would have reached the same conclusion—the Navy must go to Campeche. Morgan later testified, "[A]ll these circumstances taken together, with information so fully confirmed, that the enemy intended to make descent upon the coast, I was induced to hazard the responsibility of suggesting to Com. Moore, to take Telchac and the coast of Yucatan, on our way to Galveston, 'To save the Republic,' if I could."

The high state of the Navy's professionalism played no small part in Morgan's decision, as he conceded in a letter the following month. "I felt fully justified in taking the Coast of Yucatan on our way. The fact was, I found our vessels in such apple pie order—the officers so anxious to proceed on the Cruise—such bully crews: and knowing if the vessels did go into Galveston Harbor they would never come out again as *Texas* vessels—if at all. . . . For these & other *still more cogent* reasons, I concluded to stretch my authority as Commissioner, a little, and authorize Com. Moore to go ahead: believing we could visit the Coast of Yucatan & accomplish every object we had in view, in 20 or 30 days, at fartherist."

Morgan offered the suggestion Moore had been waiting for. Should not the squadron return to Galveston by way of Yucatán?

Moore was thrilled at the suggestion, but also wary. After all, he had been accused of treason, piracy, disobedience, and every other charge Sam Houston could muster. He was not about to do anything without clear, specific orders from his superior. Moore later wrote, "[Morgan] informed me that he had the power, as Commissioner, to take the responsibility, and that he would not only advise me to proceed to Galveston by the way of the coast of Yucatán, but that he would accompany me and risk his life and reputation in order to save Texas from the charge, by Yucatán, of *bad faith*, and to see justice done to me." Morgan confirmed that he had instigated the detour to Yucatán, testifying before a court-martial the following year, "I felt assured that Com. Moore, had not the least intention of going anywhere but to Galveston when I suggested it to him."

So the decision was made. Morgan wrote to his fellow commissioner back in Texas, cautioning Bryan not to tell Houston or Hill anything for the moment, since Morgan might change his mind and proceed to Galveston. Whether Morgan's request was a ruse to prevent Bryan from heading straight to Houston is unknown.

On the evening of April 19, *Austin*'s drummer beat "to quarters," the men shotted their guns and made sail in the company of *Wharton*. A few hours later, on "a moonless night, as black as a crow's wing," *Austin* plowed into salt water. Commodore Moore knew that President Houston would probably declare him an outlaw, even though he was following orders from the commissioner who was officially in command of the Navy. In a bit of political damage control, Moore wrote a letter to the editor of Galveston's *Texas Times*. The plain-spoken missive reveals Moore's devotion to his adopted country.

In the event of my being declared by Proclamation of the President as a Pirate, or outlaw; you will please state over my signature that I go down to attack the Mexican Squadron, with the *consent* and *full concurrence* of Col. James Morgan, who is on board this Ship as one of the Commissioners to carry into effect the secret act of Congress, in relation to the Navy, and who is going with me, believing as he does that it is the best thing that could be done for the country.

This Ship and the brig have excellent men on board, and the officers and men are all eager for the contest—We will go to make *one desperate struggle* to turn the tide of *ill luck* that has so long been running against Texas.

You shall hear from me again as soon as possible.

Very soon, all the world would indeed hear of Commodore Moore. Very soon.

CHAPTER THIRTY-ONE

The Last Hurrah

I could not imagine more coolness & determination than was displayed by the Officers & crew in the fight—all appeared delighted & the young middys & powder boys made a perfect Jubilee of the affair! For my own part I had much rather been at a feast—For d—- me if I saw any fun in it!

—James Morgan, May 11, 1843

UPON REACHING THE GULF, Commodore Moore opened his sealed orders from Secretary Hamilton, dated September 26, 1842. The orders, written long before Houston ordered the Navy sold, directed Moore to cruise along the Mexican coast, capturing "both armed and merchantmen," levying contributions on cities within his guns' reach. No doubt Moore took great pleasure reading Hamilton's words, "The Department having great confidence in your capacity and discretion as well as your knowledge of international law, deems it unnecessary to give more detailed or particular instructions."

Unfortunately, these orders had been revoked, sort of: Houston countermanded Moore's sealed orders on March 21, but he also had placed the commissioners in command. And the lead commissioner was telling him to go to Yucatán. So to Yucatán they would go.

Splitting up with *Wharton* briefly, Commodore Moore had one solemn bit of business to attend to—the sentences of the mutineers. At 10:30 on the morning of April 21, Moore ordered all hands on deck to hear the sentences of the court-martial. The officers came up first; then the marines filed in under arms, bayonets fixed. Finally, the sailors took their appointed stations, and all stood at attention while their captain read the Articles of War and naval regulations concerning mutiny, murder, and desertion. He then read the sentences of the court-martial for Shepherd, Williams, and Barrington. Frederick Shepherd, being acquitted, was released. John Williams, who was sentenced to fifty lashes, was also released. Seaman William Barrington would receive his sentence of one hundred lashes the next day.

On April 22 at 11:00 a.m., all hands were called to witness Barrington's punishment. Years later, Midshipman George Fuller recalled the gory scene:

> The man was served up at the gangway, naked to the waist. The boatswain gave the first blow with the "cat," with its nine cords; a reddish tinge appeared as the cat was raised for the second stroke; the marks on the back assumed, as the punishment continued, a purple hue; then the blood flowed. The surgeon stood by with his hand on the culprit's wrist. At the end of fifty lashes he made a sign that signaled, "The man can bear no more," which caused his release. A shirt was thrown over his back, and he was led forward. He did not, at any time afterwards, receive the other fifty lashes, nor did the other mutineer receive one. Perhaps the commodore judged that the lesson to the crew was quite sufficient.

The next two days were fairly routine. The commodore put his crew through intense battle drills while the light winds pushed *Austin* along very slowly. Then, on April 25, Moore again assembled the men, and with great care he read aloud the sentences of marine Pvt. Antonio Landois, Seaman James Hudgins, Seaman Isaac Allen, and Cpl. William Simpson. James Morgan recalled, "He then stated to those who were condemned to be hanged, that they had been fairly tried by a court martial selected for the purpose, and had able counsel assigned to defend them; that after a patient investigation of the whole affair, they were condemned to the punishment of death, which he, as the officer in command, was bound by his oath, and the laws of his country, to see executed; that it was the first time in his life he had ever to do anything of the sort, and he hoped to God it would be the last." He turned to the four condemned men and gave them until noon the next day to prepare themselves for death. The crew were piped down, and the four mutineers were locked in irons behind the Number Nine gun.

On the morning of April 26, the flagship hove to, furled all sails and anchored in a light sea. The officers, wearing their side arms, took their places on deck, as did the marines. On command, the foretopmen laid the fore topsail to the mast and hoisted the colors.

Even before the crew was piped up and the prisoners brought forward, the occasion was greeted with reluctance. Midshipman Fuller recalled the scene.

> Preparatory to carrying out the execution of the decree four lines were suspended from the foreyard after the foresail had been furled. There was not a man of the whole crew on board from the boatswain down who knew how to make a hangman's knot, which of course was affected ignorance. Gray, the first lieutenant, who was a thoroughly marlinspike sailor, exclaimed in a mildly sarcastic tone, "I'll show you how to make a hangman's knot!" which he did.

The four lines from the weather and lee *yard arms*, led through blocks to the deck, were "married" together and passed through leading blocks aft and to and around the main mast and forward to a point under the yard. One half of the crew were to walk aft with the line, the other half to walk forward.

At 11:45, all hands were summoned on deck to execute the sentence. Commodore Moore spoke briefly to the crew on the subject of mutiny, then a marine detachment escorted the condemned men under the foreyard. The nooses were placed around their necks. As Midshipman Alfred Walke wrote in his journal that night, "Until this time they appeared to believe they would be pardoned & did not evince much fear but now the truth flashed upon them & they knew they had to pay the Penalty of their crimes & commenced praying eagerly & piteously for Pardon." The crewmen lined up dutifully along the two main ropes, and a shot from the ship's bow gun commenced the death march. Fuller noted, "The four culprits were raised to the yard arm, and must have strangled in the ascent; for they neither struggled nor made the slightest motion."

The bodies were left hanging for an hour as the men were piped to lunch, then the corpses were lowered and given over to their messes for burial. An hour later, all hands were again called on deck to bury the dead mutineers. Dr. Anderson read the funeral service rites, and prayers were said over each of the bodies as it was committed to the deep.

The sentence was severe, even by nineteenth-century naval standards, but it was considered by most to be necessary. Fuller was circumspect about it many years later.

> This melancholy but necessary act of justice had a depressing effect on every man and boy aboard. But the crime of mutiny accompanied with murder cannot possibly be condoned. It is discipline that ensures the safety of the officers, that enables them to control the crew which outnumbers them so greatly—twenty officers to perhaps three hundred and fifty sailors.

New Orleans newspapers, learning of the sentences, predicted the executions would "exercise a most beneficial effect in preserving the discipline of the Navy of Texas." Commodore Moore, for his part, wrote that while he had never seen a hanging before, "there was never a crew that performed the *awful, painful* but *sacred duty* with better decorum and discipline."

The winds were light, and the warships ambled much more slowly than their masters would have liked. Had he known that the Mexican consul in New Orleans had warned Commodore Francisco de Paula López of the vessels' sailing, Moore would have been even more impatient. But try as he might, the obstinate headwinds slowed *Austin* such that the voyage to Telchac on Yucatán's north coast took a frustrating eight days.

Commodore López, not wishing to lose *Moctezuma* to the northern ruffians, immediately dispatched a vessel to recall his big steamer and her escort, the schooner *Aguila*. By the time *Austin* arrived off Telchac on the afternoon of April 27, *Moctezuma* and *Aguila* had retreated south to Campeche to rejoin the Mexican fleet. In Lieutenant Gray's words, "[S]ome three or four days after leaving the Balise one bright morning we made the little town of Truxillo, but too late for our scheme of conquest—the birds had flown. The enemy's steamers, which we had been informed were out of coal and waiting at this point for that very essential article in the internal arrangements of a steamer, had received their supply the day previous, and had steamed off for Campeche without leaving their regrets."

When *Wharton* pulled alongside the flagship the next morning, Commodore Moore ordered the squadron to make all sail to overtake *Moctezuma* and *Aguila* before they could rejoin Commodore López's main body. Hugging the Yucatán coast, the two warships came in sight of Sisal on the afternoon of April 28. A friendly messenger rowed out from the harbor and shouted that the Mexican squadron had pulled south for Campeche. Losing no time, Commodore Moore dashed off a note to Acting Governor Barbachano announcing his arrival and immediately sailed for Campeche.

For once, the winds were excellent, and Moore ordered his canvas shortened so that *Austin*, running only under topsails, jibsails and spenser, would arrive off Campeche in the morning, and not at night, to avoid being surprised by the Mexicans' greater numbers. Concerned that *Austin* was still moving too fast, Moore strode on deck and asked the midshipman of the watch, "What is she making?"

"Eleven, six," came the reply.

"A mistake, sir. Try again," ordered Moore.

The speed log was heaved over the stern, and the readings were again taken. Same result. The ship was under short sail and making over eleven knots, astonishing speed. But it was too fast. At seven that evening, Moore hove to and anchored some fifteen miles off Lerma, the Mexican fleet's anchorage just south of Campeche.

Austin moved out at four in the morning of April 30. The crew was piped on deck, hammocks were stowed, and the order "All hands up anchor!" sent the men scurrying to the capstan to begin the short trip to meet the enemy fleet. "The process of getting a man-of-war under way is at all times a rapid one," Lieutenant Gray recalled, "but on this occasion one had scarcely time to draw a long breath before the anchors were at the cat-head, and both vessels with royals set standing down towards the enemy." Commissioner Morgan later testified that Commodore Moore also ordered the ship's magazines prepared for demolition: if he were defeated, he would go down with his flagship rather than dangle from the yardarm of a Mexican warship as a pirate captain.

As the first rays of light touched the verdant forests of Campeche, the Mexican fleet came in to sight. *Moctezuma* and *Guadalupe* formed the backbone of López's force. Accompanying them were two brigs, the seventeen-gun *Mexicano* and the nine-gun *Iman*, as well as the seven-gun schooner *Aguila* and the three-gun *Campecheano*. The forty-eight heavy guns of the Mexican Navy outnumbered those aboard Moore's two ships by a dozen, but worse yet was the presence of the heavy, long-range Paixhans mounted on the two steamships. Spread out before Moore was the most powerful, technologically advanced battle squadron ever assembled on the Gulf of Mexico.

Seeing his flagship outdistancing the slower *Wharton*, Moore brought in his main topsail to let Lothrop catch up. The two warships skillfully placed themselves between the Mexican fleet and the harbor; the town's guns could not reach the steamers' heavy guns, so they could be of no help, but Moore's position would allow the small vessels of the Yucatán Navy to sally forth to assist him.

By 6:40 a.m., Moore was ready. Taking advantage of the morning land breeze, he worked his way towards López's fleet, attempting to get the weather gage on the enemy. At 7:05, he ordered his colors hoisted—the Texas ensign at the mizzen, his broad blue pennant at the mainmast, and the British and American flags at the foremast. With the gauntlet thrown down, the crews of both warships gave three cheers, and the men got down to the bloody business ahead.

Moore must have been in fine spirits that beautiful April morning. The sun was shining, the winds were fair, and the water sparkled as it splashed against the prows of the wooden vessels. Best of all, the enemy was straight ahead. Just then, the lookout's cry went out: *Moctezuma* appeared to be aground. Moore ran towards the stranded steamer, while Captain Boylan's Yucatán squadron—the schooners *Independencia* and *Sisaleno*, and five tiny gunboats, all sporting small-caliber long guns—rallied behind him in support. Before Moore could get within firing range, however, *Moctezuma* extricated herself, and the Mexican ships maneuvered south to regroup.

Fifteen minutes later, Commodore López gave the order to attack, and the Mexican squadron came on in full strength. *Austin*'s men lined the crowded deck, watching silently as the enemy frigates approached from the weather side. At 7:35, flashes from Mexico's steamers announced the opening salvos from three miles out. Shells and balls rained down on the Texas squadron, missing their marks each time. "As they were yet a long distance out of range of our guns, no reply was made to this bit of politeness," Lieutenant Gray commented.

At 7:50, Moore ordered his port battery to open fire, and *Austin* exchanged five broadsides with the steamers. He then ordered *Austin* to charge into the enemy's formation, heading north with the steamers off his port bow and the sailing ships to starboard. In response, the steamers pulled back. "They don't intend to let us get any nearer to them," he snarled to his officers, "they are paddling off stern foremost, faster than we can come up to them. Keep her away a little, so our broadside can bear, and damn them, give it to them!"

Aguila, Mexicano, Campecheano, and *Iman* hovered cautiously off the squadron's starboard bow. Moore ordered his staysails hove in, and sent gun crews scurrying to the starboard battery. A heavy broadside from *Austin*'s starboard guns sent the sailing vessels scurrying for cover, keeping them out of range for the rest of the battle, while Moore turned to concentrate on the steamers.

At 8:00, *Wharton* passed near *Austin*'s lee quarter, and Commodore Moore signaled for Commander Lothrop to keep *Wharton* close behind him, mimicking *Austin*'s every move. Ten minutes later, as the squadron crept closer to the steamers, Moore decided to have another go at them. He ordered his battery to open fire, and sent three more broadsides at *Guadalupe*. He scanned the water with his spyglass, looking for telltale splashes that would show how close his shells were falling. As the action continued, rolling billows of white smoke briefly obscured the view, sending the familiar sulfuric stench of burned black powder wafting along *Austin*'s gun deck. The gunners, their hands and faces coated with oily black residue, swabbed, searched and shotted their guns, then squinted into the distance to make out the effect of their blasts.

To Commissioner Morgan, the thrill of battle was tempered with the dread of the Mexican great guns. "I summoned up courage enough to keep on deck during the action to be sure & like a frightened child who will make a noise to keep fear away—I huzzaed for Texas most of the time as loud as I could howl; but I could not help bowing instinctively to the enemy's 68 lb shot as they came over my head."

Unfortunately for the Texians, *Austin*'s medium-range twenty-four-pounders could not hit the steamers from such a distance, while the long-range sixty-eights from *Moctezuma* and *Guadalupe* could certainly reach Moore's wooden ships. "The enemy," wrote Lieutenant Gray, "finding that they had us under the range of their guns, and calculating that they were still out of range of our twenty-fours, went about and commenced a game of long bowls, in which we were not able to participate with any degree of satisfaction. In fact, a few trials of our batteries showed that no effect could be produced." The Texians had to wait while the enemy fired at them with impunity.

The Mexican shells, ranged against the flagship, sailed harmlessly overhead, although the effect was still unnerving. Gray wrote of one terrifying salvo from *Guadalupe*, "Soon a shot from the Mexican Admiral passed over us; and not having yet learned to judge the direction of the ball by its whistle, as we afterwards had abundant reason to do, it seemed to me to be directed with remarkable skill on a line with the necks of the whole crew, and I must confess my astonishment when I saw from the plunge into the water astern that it must have passed over us as high as the to'gallant mast-head."

The Mexican sailing ships moved south, passing astern of the Texas squadron, while the steamers paddled in the same direction to join forces. After some fifteen minutes of ineffective salvos, Moore ordered his outranged gunners to conserve their ammunition and cease fire.

At 8:35, the squadron heard three hearty cheers from Captain Boylan's Yucatán squadron, which the Texians returned. Boylan's small vessels fell in with Moore's ships, but the now-consolidated Mexican squadron had had enough for the moment. Five minutes later, as the land breeze was fading, Moore knew the winds would not sustain another charge. He ordered his vessels to sail back to the harbor, and his tired men were piped to a well-earned grog. The squadron dropped anchor in two fathoms of water—about as close as the ships could safely get to Campeche—and, securing the vessel, Moore ordered the crew to breakfast.

The two fleets sat there sullenly, the Mexicans off *Austin*'s starboard beam, *Wharton* off her port beam, the Yucatecos idling off the port quarter. The Bay of Campeche remained silent for nearly two hours when the resurgence of black smoke from the two steamers' stacks signaled that the action was about to resume. Moore ordered his crew to battle stations, and as the men quietly scrambled about the deck, finding their designated positions, the steamers opened fire for a second time. Moore ordered *Austin* to wear around to bring the ship's starboard battery into play.

Watching the weather closely, Moore had set his sails to catch a light breeze that puffed its way along the coast. An obedient *Austin* lunged forward and began trading shots in earnest. "[D]uring the whole of the engagement," James Morgan observed, "the Commodore kept cool and collected, and managed his ship with great skill, so I thought." But after a few shots, the English gunners found *Austin*'s range. One shell, lobbed from *Guadalupe*, sailed through *Austin*'s mizzen after-shroud some eight feet above the deadeye; it flew right at Commodore Moore and Lieutenant Gray, and would have killed them both had they not leaped aside. The shell passed clean through the poop deck into the cabin, exiting through the ship's stern a few feet above the transom.

By 11:40 a.m., finding the steamers to be well out of *Austin*'s range, Moore again ordered his men to cease firing. The Mexican fleet was upwind from the allied vessels, and Moore's men, having been at battle stations since four in the morning, were exhausted. The Texas ships moved closer to Campeche, the Yucatán squadron following close behind. Commander Boylan sent a pilot aboard, and by noon the vessels were making their way through the shallow, treacherous approaches to the city.

Just after noon, while moving in, *Austin* struck ground, heeling over slightly. The enemy steamers, sensing *Austin*'s predicament, moved in closer and lobbed several more shells at *Austin*. As explosive shells fell around Moore's ship, Lothrop's brig came alongside. Lothrop hailed his commander, "Shall I heave to?" Moore replied, "No, sir, keep on to your anchorage." One midshipman later recalled that Commodore Moore's cool contempt for his formidable enemy astonished the officers of both Texian vessels.

Moore, as always, returned fire, but a few shots at maximum elevation told him that *Austin*'s medium twenty-fours were helpless against the long-range Paixhans, so Moore again ordered his batteries to cease fire. Now it was Boylan's turn to strike. According to Lieutenant Gray, the steamers' "pleasant amusement was, before long, most impertinently interfered with. A cloud of new white sails made their appearance, and running down before us the Campeche gunboats with their long eighteens opened so warm a fire upon the steamers that they soon paddled off for their anchorage." A fresh breeze pushed the struggling *Austin* over the shoal, and the Mexican vessels pulled away to the southeast towards Lerma. The battle was over.

Regrouping off Campeche's anchorage, the allied ships took stock. Most of the fire was directed at the Texas vessels, and the only casualties apparently took place there. *Austin* received one hit, but because the shell passed through the ship's stern before exploding, no one was hurt. *Wharton*, also taking a hit, was less fortunate; it reported two killed and four wounded during the engagement.

On the Mexican side, Midshipman Walke noted in his journal reports of seven killed and a large number injured aboard *Guadalupe*, while *Moctezuma* lost her captain and fourteen men. Another thirty were said to be wounded, a report attested to by James Morgan's sources. Undoubtedly, these reports were exaggerated, as they apparently included casualties of tropical diseases. (*Moctezuma*'s Captain Cleaveland, in fact, had died of yellow fever the previous day, while a number of his fellow Limeys also had been incapacitated by the "black vomit" since their arrival off the Yucatán coast.) Texas sources were unable to get a definitive report on the effect of their salvos, but Morgan did report that the Mexican fleet's carpenters were kept busy at Lerma repairing shot holes.

In the short run, the battle had done the Texas cause enormous good, most of all by demonstrating that the Texians would fight. One English lieutenant fighting for Mexico afterwards complained to Thomas Jefferson Green about the lack of support from the Mexican officers and crewmen, and predicted, "had the breeze lasted for Commodore Moore to come to close quarters at that time, the Mexican Navy would have fallen an easy prey." *Guadalupe*'s Captain Charlesswood resigned soon afterwards, and a number of his brother officers and crewmen, many of whom had not been paid in months, also decided that they did not need to risk death from Texas round shot or "black vomit." Commodore López also lost many of his own tired, underpaid but vital crewmen, who had lived off a mosquito coast in wartime conditions too long to be effective any longer.

For their part, the Texians' blood was up; their confidence in themselves and their commander was at an all-time high. One officer aboard *Wharton* wrote, "All our officers are in the finest health and spirits, and anxiously desire 'a fair fight and no favor.'" A reporter for the New Orleans *Tropic* confirmed the high morale of the Texians, writing on May 5, "As for the crews, it appeared to be a perfect frolic for them—while it was a perfect jubilee for the young middys and powder boys."

The engagement was a disaster for Mexico. Traffic into Campeche was now open from the sea, and Mexican warships could no longer pour fire into the city. General Ampudia, besieging Campeche from the landward side, was out of contact with the fleet, and his soldiers, lacking food and proper medical treatment, were deserting in droves. To the north, the two thousand troops under Generals Barragan and Lemus, who promised to be out of the country by May 13, were now stranded and in danger of having to surrender.

The strategic picture was even worse. Having shattered the blockade of Campeche and threatened General Ampudia with starvation, Campeche's Governor Mendez haughtily rejected centralist peace overtures and began shelling Ampudia's positions in earnest. Midshipman Alfred Walke wrote in his journal, "When we first appeared off the City they were about to make a treaty for an Armistice, but no sooner than our Flag was seen than one universal shout of joy was heard throughout the City and the stipulations for the Treaty rejected by the Governor of Campeche with scorn. . . ." James Morgan, who had a good grasp of the relative troop strengths of Yucatán and Mexico, concluded, "[B]y the visit of our two vessels to this coast, we have prevented the Mexican government from subjugating Yucatan and invading Texas, with the same forces to have been transported thither by her steamers and transports, and have upset the arrangements of the Mexican Government in regard to Texas and Yucatan altogether." As Morgan put it, "The fact is, we have done more to humble the pride of Mexico in this expedition, and have caused her more real injury, than any and every expedition thrust against her before—besides breaking the charm of the great humbug *Paixhans*!"

On May 20, after receiving reports from the peninsula, the *Houston Morning Star* agreed with Morgan, offering an assessment that was a far cry from Sam Houston's prediction in December that the Republic would not survive another six months.

> If our little Navy had not arrived at that opportune moment, Gov. Mendez might have been compelled by necessity to have acceded to the propositions of Ampudia, and when once the Mexicans had gained the ascendancy they would probably have thrown off the mask in conformity with the policy of Santa Anna, as declared in the City of Mexico, they would have driven thousands of unwilling soldiers from Yucatan to fight against Texas. Now however the scale is turned.

The paper concluded: "It seems as if an over-ruling Providence directed the movements of our little Navy for the welfare and possibly the salvation of the Republic. . . . We have injured Mexico in this expedition more than she has been injured since the battle of San Jacinto."

CHAPTER THIRTY-TWO

Cat and Mouse

Give us a good wind, and our word for it, the Texian Navy will prove itself true to the core—we await only the favours of fortune, due to strike who diligently seek them.
—Officer of the *Wharton*, May 10, 1843

ADMIRAL LÓPEZ COULD NOT survive this kind of setback; the stakes for Mexico were simply too high. The aging commander had also made many enemies in the Department of War and Marine, and had been accused of timidity as far back as the David Porter era of 1826. While commanding the northern squadron at Matamoros, it was whispered, López had turned a blind eye to the escape of Commodore Wheelwright, Dr. Levy, and Lieutenant "Mexico" Thompson. The star of the aggressive Tomás Marín, by contrast, had risen steadily after his capture of the Yucatán warships the previous summer, and a movement was afoot in Mexico City to replace the old sea lion. López's failure to break the Texas-Yucatán squadron was the last straw; his government recalled him, and the gentleman commander was court-martialed for being driven off by a numerically inferior force. On May 7, López's pennant was hauled down *Guadalupe*'s mainmast, while Commodore Tomás Marín took charge of the fleet.

For all his daring and abilities, Commodore Marín knew that his crews were strained, and he was careful to keep expectations in Mexico City low. He immediately complained of poor morale, conscripted sailors, sick engineers, and the dismal state of his warships. His men had been off the Yucatán coast for several months, while the Texians had arrived fresh from New Orleans. *Moctezuma*'s crewmen, particularly the English, were dying at a rate of three to four men per day, while many, many others lay sweating, shivering, vomiting, and praying in their soaked hammocks as they struggled to survive a lethal medley of tropical viruses. Marín's fleet would need to shift personnel, and that would probably mean the loss of crucial warships. And worse yet, the reorganization would cost him time—time for the Texas pirates to grow bolder, time for Campeche to grow stronger, time for his manpower to diminish further.

Anchoring off Campeche on April 30, Commodore Moore suggested that James Morgan go ashore in *Austin*'s launch to meet with Governor Mendez, while *Wharton*'s wounded were sent ashore to a nearby hospital. Morgan did so, and checked into the seaside American Hotel, a small two-story, flat-roofed house which served up some "villainous lime punch" to its guests, but offered a good view of the *Bahia de Campeche*, where the allied squadron lay at anchor.

For the officers and the crewmen, May 1 was a day of rest from the ardors of battle. The midshipmen supervised the preparation of shot wads and other battle stores, while the off-duty watches rested. Every eye on the standing watches was fixed on the distant Mexican fleet, anchored some five miles off Campeche and now reinforced by the arrival of the old steamer *Regenerador*.

At four o'clock on the morning of May 2, the men were summoned to quarters, and the ships weighed anchor. Catching a morning land breeze, the allied fleet maneuvered swiftly through the maze of sandbars that frame the Campeche anchorage, then stood out for the Mexican squadron. The Mexican vessels pulled back, drawing the vanguard further out into open waters. But the land breeze soon died away, and the allied vessels were forced to return to their anchorage, and wait for another of the fickle tropical winds.

The dance repeated itself over the next several days. On the morning of May 3, the breeze blew long enough for the Texas warships to exchange a few shots with the enemy, and one officer aboard *Wharton* believed that one of its balls did considerable damage. But by and large, nothing came of it. "The only object of the Mexicans, as we plainly understand, is to induce us to leave our anchorage with the morning breeze—and as the calm usually comes on a little before mid-day, they hope to catch us forward, and to use us up by the aid of steam, in the most summary manner. To this operation, as you may well imagine, we all object," wrote the officer. Commodore Moore, for his part, lamented to the editor of the *New Orleans Tropic*, "If I had a steamer here, I would give *ten years* of my life, as with *one*, I could get to close action at once, and decide the fate of Texas."

It was obvious that Moore, with his Trafalgar-era medium-range guns, was unlikely to close with the Mexican steamers, which would use their steam power to stay out of range of the Texas cannon while their own long-range Paixhans shelled Moore's forces with impunity. Moore needed long-range guns, and he got them from the cooperative Campeche government. On May 3, Campeche's governor offered Moore the use of two long eighteen-pounders for *Austin* and one long twelve-pounder for *Wharton*. Moore graciously accepted the loan, sending his officers ashore to remove the guns from Campeche's ramparts and have the eighteens mounted on two vacant twenty-four-pounder carriages in the port and starboard Number Seven positions. "Now," one of *Austin*'s officers remarked, "if our Mexican brothers want to play a game at long bowls we can take a hand."

For Moore's junior officers, Campeche was a welcome sight. Its harbor—not so much a harbor as a long, unbroken roadstead exposed to the elements—sloped so gradually that *Austin* could not get within three miles of the city. While sailors were generally not allowed on shore leave at this critical point, a number of officers were permitted to row ashore and fraternize with the natives, and what they found there delighted them. The memoirs of 1st Lt. Alfred Gray read like a travelogue brochure: "Campeche is one of the oldest towns on the American continent built by Europeans, dating back almost to the discovery and conquest of the country. The City proper is completely enclosed by high walls armed with long brass guns 'en barbette' but incomplete as a fortified work from its having no ditch, and from the curtains not being flanked by bastions or other projecting works. . . . The City itself is like most of the Spanish-American towns—narrow streets, stone built houses with projecting balconies, defended by ornamental wooden gratings presenting a quaint and picturesque appearance." A party of officers dispatched to reconnoiter the city, recalled Gray, "passed out of the Almeida and making a fruit garden right ahead hove to, and bargained for the sacking of the same at a rate of a *real* a head—a degree of liberality on the part of the proprietor in happy contrast to the avaricious vendors of bananas and pineapples who attacked us on the water." After touring the suburb of San Roman, which had been battered in the fierce fighting, the party found itself at "the square of the suburb of St. Ana, gravely inspecting a review of Campeche soldiers. . . . The square, however, possessed other attractions in the shape of pretty women, with a few ugly ones, attracted thither by the military spectacle." Midshipman George Fuller later wrote that the fleet received "a hearty welcome in Campeche, and the Mexicans, as if in a satirical mood, commenced bombarding the city, which they kept up for three days and nights. . . . [Midshipmen] Walker, Clements and I passed a cheerful hour on the ramparts, working a 42-pounder." The bombardment, and the centralist reinforcements, did not seem to bother the Texas officers. "The Campecheanos expect reinforcements from Merida every hour and whether these expectations are fulfilled or not they will unquestionably be able to hold out against the enemy," wrote one officer of the brig *Wharton*.

At sunrise on May 7, Moore took advantage of the morning land breeze to test his new guns. He sailed close enough to the enemy to fire his long eighteens while the Campecheano gunboats shelled the centralist-held port of Lerma to the south. Unfortunately for Moore, the easterly winds again died down, and the allies were forced to scurry back to their protective anchorage.

As frustrating as the picture was for Commodore Moore, his counterpart was having an even tougher time. *Mexicano*'s crew had to be transferred to fill out the steamers, so she was sent to Carmen on water duty with a skeleton crew. Another brig in the same condition was also put on water duty, while the schooner *Libertador* was sent away for refitting. The schooner *Aguila* was in better shape, although her mainmast was damaged, while *Regenerador* was shoddy in both crew and hull, so Marín sent her north to Telchac. The Mexican fleet at Campeche had thus been reduced to the still-formidable *Guadalupe*, *Moctezuma,* and *Aguila*.

During the lull between May 7 and 16, Commodore Moore kept busy attending to his duties and preparing for battle. He wrote out a full report to the War Department, and sent a second letter to Secretary Hill, vainly trying to explain how his actions had been misinterpreted by President Houston and Moore's opponents in the government. "I have never intended to disobey any order, but have been required to do that which I could not execute. . . . The whole matter has arisen from a misconception on the part of His Excellency, the President, as to my *intentions*; which I again repeat have always been for the interest of Texas." Morgan more realistically wrote, "I expect 'Old Sam' will 'hang me'—for I have travelled out of the course his instructions dictated. But—we have played h-ll with the enemys arrangements and calculations in this quarter."

Through it all, Moore drilled his men with the firm conviction that their best efforts would be needed soon. On May 10, when all was ready, he wrote to the *New Orleans Tropic*'s editor, "I am waiting for a good breeze, when I shall go out and attack them."

That breeze, it would turn out, would blow six days later.

CHAPTER THIRTY-THREE

The Showdown

A curious experience is that which comes by being shot at from a long distance. One sees the flash of the gun, then hears the whistling of the ball, and then the report, the ball out-travelling the sound.
—Midshipman George Fuller

COMMODORE MARÍN WAS BEING pushed from two sides. At home, Admiral López's court-martial underscored his government's displeasure at seeing its timetable for the conquests of Yucatán and Texas thwarted by two creaky wooden ships. It had gone to great lengths to acquire the most technologically advanced fleet in the world, and it wanted the Texians swept aside and the blockade of Campeche reinstated immediately. On the peninsula, General Ampudia, bivouacked at Lerma, also pressed Marín for action; his desperately sick men were dying or deserting in droves, and if he were to force Yucatán to come to terms, he would have to reduce Campeche, thereby isolating the capital of Mérida.

Moore wanted a battle as well, but would not risk stranding his small squadron in the open seas where fickle winds could leave him at the mercy of the enemy's steam power and long-range guns. Like Julius Caesar on the plains of Pharsalus, Moore had to be content to draw up for battle each morning, then decline Marín's invitations to fight under patently unfavorable conditions. And so, the two sides stared at each other, making tentative feints each morning, each daring the other to charge, returning to their anchorages in time for the afternoon siesta.

In mid-May, General Ampudia launched an offensive with his pen, not his howitzers. On May 15, he publicly challenged Commodore Moore to come out in three fathoms of water for a fair fight with Mexico's schooner and frigates. He sent his message to the Texas commander by the American schooner *Fanny*, and to underscore the challenge, General Ampudia published *Boletín Oficial No. 1*, in which he repeated the challenge for all Yucatán to read.

Fanny was to arrive in Campeche the morning of May 16, but by then Moore was already out to sea. At 4:30 a.m. the familiar order, "Up all hammocks!" was piped, and the men hustled up to stow their sleeping gear and prepare for combat. Fifteen minutes later the command "Up anchor!" was given, and by five a.m. the crew had set *Austin*'s topsails to catch an unusually strong morning breeze.

Signaling the Yucatán squadron and *Wharton* to get underway, Moore set his topgallants and had his drummer beat "to quarters" while the men cleared the decks for action. Unnecessary items were hastily stowed, protective netting was thrown up into the rigging to keep falling yards and blocks away from the crew, and sand was spread on the decks to soak up the expected blood. With a lively easterly breeze floating over the jungle and out to sea, the Texas flagship gracefully knifed through the dark rolling waters as she sailed to meet her foe.

Commodore Moore looked aft. *Wharton* was pressing ahead, about a quarter mile behind his stern, but Boylan's gunboats had not left their anchorages. What was the matter with them? Moore hove to, and sent another signal out, calling the gunboats to arms. Still no reaction. The wind might not last long enough to get the entire fleet launched, so Moore was faced with a dilemma. He could charge ahead, outnumbered three to two, or wait for the Campecheanos, and possibly lose an opportunity to bring the enemy to battle. To other officers, this might have been a difficult choice; to Moore, it was no choice at all. He would fight.

Commodore Marín, anchored off Lerma to the south, was just as alert that morning. As *Austin*'s canvas began to drop from her yardarms, Marín hustled his engineers to quarters and began firing up *Guadalupe*'s engines. Signaling to *Moctezuma* and *Aguila*, he chugged downwind, hoping the fickle easterly winds would die off and leave the Texians stranded in the middle of the bay.

Moore got within two-and-a-half miles of the enemy when it became clear that Marín, heading west-southwest with his squadron, was not going to let him close. Moore ordered the men to stand down, and piped them to breakfast.

Dawn spread across Campeche, and spectators began lining the walls and rooftops of the old city. One guest at the American Hotel, James Morgan, opened his windows to a hopeful sight. "Soon after daylight on the 16th," he wrote, "I discovered from the hotel where I boarded on shore, the ship Austin and brig Wharton, under way standing out of the harbor, and the two Mexican steamers standing out from Lerma, to sea, under a press of steam, and a schooner in company. . . . I could perceive the ship, brig, and gun boats, and the two Mexican steamers and the schooner Eagle; the steamers under way under a press of steam, running out to sea; Commodore Moore and his squadron in pursuit of them."

At 8:00 a.m., as the winds began to die, Moore threw down a silent challenge to Marín by hoisting the Texas ensign to his peak and his broad blue pennant to the mainmast. The two squadrons sat there, scowling at each other across two and a half miles of sea. The waiting game resumed.

By 10:00 a.m., Marín was through waiting. His men cleared the decks, stoked the boilers and prepared to meet the foe. At 10:40, *Guadalupe* hoisted the Mexican ensign at the peak, and—in a nod to the ancestry of a large portion of her crew—ran the Union Jack up the foremast. In reply, Moore had Old Glory and the Union Jack run from his foremast while the Texas Navy colors rippled proudly from his gaff. *Moctezuma*, with a more heterogeneous crew, ran up the English ensign at the fore and the Spanish jack at the main. Belching thick black smoke from her stacks, *Moctezuma's* twin paddles began churning, and she joined *Guadalupe* and *Aguila* on their charge into history.

At 10:55, when the Mexican squadron was off *Austin's* port bow, observers reported flashes from *Guadalupe's* fearsome guns. Faint whistles told the crew that the heavy shells would miss, and the sixty-eight pound shells splashed down well ahead of *Austin's* bow, launching tall geysers of salt water on their way to the bottom.

Heading southwest, with *Wharton* a quarter-mile back, Commodore Moore ordered a general broadside. *Austin's* guns boomed, echoed by fire and smoke from *Wharton's* gunports. As before, Moore's bucking twenty-fours could not reach the enemy, and he ordered his men to cease fire, except for the long eighteen on loan from Campeche.

At 11:18 a.m., *Wharton's* second broadside got lucky, slicing through *Guadalupe's* flagstaff and sending its ensign over the side. The Texans, seeing a great omen in this shot, gave three hearty cheers as Marín's men ran a replacement flag up the main gaff. As the crews were cheering, the daring *Aguila* darted forward and sent a thirty-two pound shot into *Austin* over the Number 6 gun, which took a large bite out of a sailor's heel and wounded two other men as it bounced off the steerage hatch, skipped across the deck and passed out the opposite Number 7 gunport. This shot would be her last for the day, as she was quickly driven off by the blazing twenty-fours of *Austin's* battery. "After this bit of mischief," recalled Lieutenant Gray, "the Eagle, fearing to be blown out of the water as a reward for her temerity, went rapidly about, and disappeared from the action."

Unfortunately for *Austin*, *Guadalupe's* gunners found their range just as the breeze died down. The Paixhans flashed, the dreaded whistles grew louder, and two sixty-eight-pound shots sliced through *Austin's* starboard rigging, splintering some of her yards. Moore described the sporadic hail of incoming shells. "Those 68-pound balls are tremendous missiles, and the way they did whistle or rather hum over our heads was a caution, I tell you. They fired a great many over the poop where I was standing, and several of them were disposed to be rather too intimate."

The enemy steamers focused on *Austin*, *Moctezuma* hovering off the sloop's port bow while *Guadalupe* blasted away at her port quarter. Moore was a sitting duck, but his seaman's instincts told him there was one good breath left in the sky, and he meant to ride it all the way to the frigates' gunwales. He braced his yards, close-hauled his sails, and shotted both batteries. Then he waited patiently while hot Mexican shells splashed around his precious ship.

At 12:20 p.m., Moore got his wish. A light breeze blew over the waters and snagged *Austin*'s topgallants, then topsails, then mainsails, and thrust the flagship forward, propelling her between the enemy steamers. At last—Moore had them where he wanted them!

At mid-range (one and three quarters miles), *Austin*'s batteries blazed away on both sides, against *Moctezuma* on her starboard beam, *Guadalupe* to port. Along both sides of the gun deck, carriages bucked violently through thick clouds of white smoke as they launched round after iron round towards the enemy. Grimy gun crews, soaked with sweat and blackish mop water, ran their guns in and out of the portals—mop, search, powder, wadding, shot, wadding, prime—while gun captains bellowed orders and squinted over the rudimentary sights, touching off another round, sending breathless crews through their choreographed steps once again. Powder boys clambered up from the bowels of the ship's magazine, shuttling ammunition to the great guns, while Moore and his officers stood aft with their spyglasses, watching the steamers intently for hits and planning their next move.

Aguila, witnessing the battering her larger consorts were taking, immediately made all sail and fled south, permanently out of the contest. Commander Lothrop, caught unawares by the wind, squandered the breeze, and *Wharton* was left stranded on the landward side of the fray, too far back to be of any use. Marín's frigates paddled off to the north, firing as they went; a few shots sliced through *Austin*'s rigging, but most flew harmlessly overhead.

Soon afterwards, *Wharton* took her only casualty. As a gunner rammed home an iron ball, the gun captain carelessly triggered the lock at the gun's vent. One of the brig's officers described this bit of wartime negligence. The gunner "was ramming home the cartridge and the captain of the gun not seeing him at the muzzle fired, and he was blown to pieces." Another hazard of shipboard life.

At 12:50, a sixty-eight pound shot from *Guadalupe* screamed down onto *Austin*'s deck, blew through the hammock netting, skirted the top of the Number 7 gun, and passed out the opposite side, carrying away a support beam on the Number 9 port. For another hour, *Austin* traded blasts with the two steam frigates, which ignored *Wharton* and her single long twelve-pounder.

By 1:42, the Paixhan gunners had again found their range, and *Austin* paid the price. A sixty-eight pound shot cut through the main-brace, followed by another shot through the lower rigging. At two o'clock a shell exploded over the deck, gouging the main-royal mast and sending a shower of shrapnel that cut through the ship's rigging. *Austin*'s real punishment was about to begin.

Ten minutes later, a shell from *Moctezuma* struck home just ahead of *Austin*'s Number 9 gun on the starboard side, throwing off a quiver of wooden splinters that cut down two seamen. The shot blasted through deck into the wardroom, through the Number 3 and Purser's staterooms, and lodged in the armory. Seaman John Norris, nicked in the elbow by this shot, hurried to Doc Anderson to have his wounds dressed. He quickly returned to his station, only to have his left arm carried away a few minutes later by a shell that barreled through the ship's hull.

At 2:24, a shell from *Guadalupe* ripped through *Austin*'s ensign, and a minute later another round smashed a gaping hole in the edge of the sloop's copper under the Number 1 gun, causing a severe leak that the ship's carpenters scrambled to plug. One minute later, another sixty-eight-pound shell cut away more of *Austin*'s rigging, mostly on the starboard side, putting a strain on her starboard rigging.

At 2:34, another shell from *Guadalupe* struck home at the Number 7 gun, killing one sailor and wounding seven others. The gun crew was flattened on the deck; Midshipman Bryant lost a portion of his right hand and thigh, spraying the deck with blood from a severed artery. At the same time, Lieutenant D. C. Wilbur and five other crewmen—a clerk and four sailors—were thrown about the deck, permanently out of this fight.

A minute later, another shell screamed onto the deck, hitting the sill of the Number 5 gun port, ripping apart three feet of planking, and hurling wooden splinters like a sheaf of throwing knives into the crew. The shot killed the gun captain and wounded four of his men. A few minutes later another man was killed and four more were wounded, this time at the Number 6 gun. Another hit cut away the main topsail's backing, and two minutes later another iron missile shredded the starboard mizzen rigging, the mast's topgallant sail, some halyards and the main brace. A simultaneous hit blew through the starboard bulwark just behind the Number 9 gun above the pinrail, wounding two men as it flew across the deck and out the opposite gun port.

As *Austin* was being savaged by the steamers, the Yucatán force kept to their anchorages, for the most part. As Midshipman Fuller recalled, "The most unaccountable mystery connected with this fight in which a superior force, more than three to one, fled from their adversaries, was the inaction of the Yucatan gunboats, which obstinately remained at anchor defying all signals made by Moore for them to make sail." At the last minute, one of the gunboats—evidently *Sisaleno*, commanded by a Frenchman, Captain LeRoy—sailed south towards the enemy base at Lerma and exchanged several shots with the shore batteries.

By three o'clock, the battling crews were exhausted. *Austin*'s hot guns had fired 530 rounds at the Mexican steamers, and *Wharton*'s long twelve-pounder had fired sixty-five shots. The steamers, low on ammunition, began to back off, but Commodore Moore was too worried about the flagship's shattered rigging to give chase. The starboard side had been cut to ribbons, so he wore his ship around to present the port battery to the enemy and take some of the strain off the starboard rigging. Unfortunately, when the wind blew from the port side, the starboard side heeled over, and the hole "between wind and water" under the Number 1 starboard gun began leaking dangerously.

As much as Moore hated to admit it, the battle was over. With large portions of his rigging shredded, one gun disabled, little ammunition and his magazine flooding, Moore reluctantly signaled for *Wharton* to follow the flagship back to Campeche, picking up *Guadalupe*'s severed flagstaff on the way as a war trophy. The brig threw a parting broadside at the enemy, then followed in the flagship's wake. Lieutenant Gray summed up Moore's predicament: "After a cannonade of two or three hours, and a run which sunk the City of Campeche below the horizon when twenty of our crew had been put 'hors de combat,' one gun dismounted, bulwarks torn to pieces, and a shot between wind and water which brought an uncomfortable allowance of the latter article into our hold, the Commodore reluctantly wore round and stood back for the anchorage followed for a short distance by the enemy, who at last ran down for their anchorage off Llerma."

By 5:30 p.m., the ship was safely anchored off Campeche, sails were furled, and the men piped down to supper. Dead and wounded lined the deck as Dr. Anderson frantically plied his gory trade—tourniquets, amputations, sulfur powder and other wartime expedients—and his efforts were such that only eight men required hospitalization in Campeche the next day.

Commodore Moore's last task of the day was to summon Commodore Boylan for an accounting of his failure to join the battle. Midshipman Fuller later recalled the scene. "The commander of the gunboats, an American by the name of Bowie or Bowen, came on board when we anchored, looking frightened and deadly pale. What kind of rating he received from Moore we never knew." (Moore evidently accepted, publicly at least, Boylan's explanation, and repudiated public criticism of Boylan by Texas officers.)

As dawn broke on May 17, the Texians took stock of where they were. Three men died aboard *Austin* during the battle, and twenty-one were wounded—about one sixth of the ship's complement. The dead lined Dr. Anderson's sick bay along with the more seriously injured. Boatswain's Mate Frederick Shepherd, acquitted of wrongdoing in the *San Antonio* mutiny, lay lifeless, his bare chest a purplish mass of bruises. What killed Shepherd was not his grotesque chest trauma, but a tiny wooden splinter that had been driven inconspicuously through his hairline into his brain. Joining Shepherd in death were Landsman George Barton and Seaman William West, both killed at their guns.

Among the injured were Seaman John Norris, whose arm was torn off at the shoulder; boy Dick Streachout, whose left arm was ripped off at the elbow; boy Thomas Barnett, with one arm avulsed at the elbow and another arm, apparently injured from an exploding powder bag and requiring amputation. Marine George Stephens, whose lower left leg was shattered, with part of his foot torn off; Landsman Owen Timothy, who suffered the surgeon's saw above his left knee, and Marine Asa Wheeler. These men were classified "wounded dangerously" by Dr. Anderson. "Wounded severely" included 4th Lt. D. C. Wilbur, Midshipman A. J. Bryant (who was in danger of losing his right hand), Seaman Thomas Adkins, and Landsman George Frier. All told, *Austin* sustained twenty-five casualties, most of whom were able to return to duty within four days. *Wharton* lost only one man, the victim of the gun captain's carelessness.

Austin was heavily damaged, but a few days of repairs would have her back in reasonable shape. During the fight, she took twelve hits from Mexican guns, all but one from the heavy sixty-eights. Lieutenant Gray recalled, "I had an opportunity of looking around and observing the effects produced by the heavy batteries of the frigates. The quarter-deck and part of the main deck were completely covered with splinters, the bulwarks in part riddled and in part torn to pieces, one of the main deck guns dismounted. . . ." The Number 5 gun had been completely unshipped by a Mexican shell, and the hole beneath the Number 1 gun had to be patched and caulked before the sloop could sail. The rigging was a devilish mess; fallen blocks, rigging, and spars had become tangled up in the protective nets, and some debris had made its way down to the deck to join the mess of blood, sand, splinters, balls and equipment that lined *Austin*'s deck.

Mexican losses were harder to pin down, partly because so many of the participants were serving as mercenaries rather than personnel of the Mexican Navy. The *Houston Morning Star* reprinted a letter from Commodore Marín to his government that stated, "The enemy succeeded in striking the Montezuma four times and the Guadaloup six times, doing but trifling damage to either vessel and not wounding even any person on board." Moore stated shortly afterwards that a fisherman who had been alongside *Guadalupe* reported forty-seven killed and thirty wounded aboard that ship, while one English deserter told the Texians that *Guadalupe* suffered forty-seven killed, thirty-two amputations, and sixty-four serious injuries. (The same sailor claimed that *Moctezuma* lost her captain and forty other combatants, although he apparently included casualties from the original April 30 engagement and losses to tropical disease.) Most of the Texas officers appear to have accepted claims of one or more deserters that Marín's fleet sustained at least sixty casualties. Whatever losses were taken by Marín's frigates probably took place during Commodore Moore's noon charge between the ships.

Much worse than the direct losses to Mexico was the breakdown of discipline and morale in the Mexican squadron. Soon after the battle, the schooner *Charlotte* brought news to Texas that "Eighty-three English seamen belonging to the crews of the Guadaloupe and Montezuma had left the steamers and sailed on a vessel to Vera Cruz. Their term of service had expired, and they refused to enlist again under the Mexican officers."

Who won the Battle of Campeche? Mexico claimed victory, striking a medal in honor of the engagement bearing the motto, "Through Courage Defeated the Texas Squadron," while Commodore Marín's report to his superiors emphasized Moore's retreat to the safety of shallow waters near the guns of Campeche. But the fact remained that Campeche's blockade had been broken. Supplies came pouring in, and as they did, General Ampudia's position became more and more untenable. Because *Austin* and *Wharton* could outgun Marín's steamers at close range, Moore could defend any spot in the bay he chose, so long as he was aggressive—and he certainly was that. Ampudia had stressed the need to keep the blockade tight around Campeche, to prevent Yucatán gunboats from shelling his positions from the shore near Lerma. Now, those gunboats—and virtually all other federalist or Texas vessels—could operate practically at will along the Yucatán coast.

Over the next ten days, Commodore Moore prepared to break the back of the Mexican squadron. He knew that the moment his fleet sailed away, the blockade would resume; the Mexican government could not afford to allow Yucatán, a Texas ally, to tie down men and harass its sea routes if the reconquest of Texas were to succeed. For the rest of the month, Moore's carpenters, sailmakers, and armorers worked to repair damage sustained in the action of May 16, in order to resume the battle with a decisive attack on the remaining enemy ships. But while Moore's flagship was gradually brought back to fighting shape, he still faced a crippling lack of gunpowder, which kept him close to shore.

During this lull, the resourceful Moore harassed Mexican forces by sending Yucatán warships out under the command of Lieutenants Gray and Lewis. Campeche's Governor Mendez ordered the commander of the brig *Independencia*, Antonio Hernandez, to remove her crew, stores, and small arms and loan the vessel to the Texians. On May 22, two gunboats under Texas officers intended to sail to the windward side of some transports evacuating Mexican soldiers, but returned that same day, "the Mexican part of the Crew being too Cowardly to proceed," according to a Texas midshipman. The next day Lieutenant Gray took out the sturdy *Independencia*, returning four days later escorting the American schooner *Glide* past the Mexican warships. *Independencia* then sailed to intercept a vessel from New Orleans loaded with ammunition for the centralist forces; Moore also hoped to capture

General Barragan, who might be exchanged for some prisoners of Houston's disastrous Mier Expedition. He requested, and received, fifty twelve-pound cannon balls for *Wharton*, and two hundred eighteen-pound balls for *Austin*'s borrowed long gun. Governor Mendez agreed to a renewed offensive, provided it was not a long one, and proposed a joint expedition to liberate Carmen and roll back the centralist grip on the southern peninsula. By June 1, Ampudia had proposed an armistice with Yucatán, under which he would quit the peninsula peaceably.

Back in Texas, word of the fleet's victory electrified Galveston. News arrived on the steamer *Lady Byron* on May 17, sparking frenzied celebrations in the city that knew it was marked for invasion. "We learn that the citizens of Galveston celebrated the late achievements of the Navy in becoming style," wrote the Houston *Morning Star*. "Salutes were fired, a procession formed and every demonstration of public joy was made as for a national jubilee. The citizens of this place also celebrated the event by firing a national salute. Governments may be ungrateful; but the people appreciate and reward merit."

Two days later, Capt. Charles Cox's gunboat *Republicano* left Galveston for Campeche, loaded with twenty or thirty adventurers who had been moved to offer their services to the Yucatán cause. On May 20, a "large and general meeting of citizens of Galveston" was held at Shaw's Hotel on Galveston's Strand. Chaired by Mayor John Allen, the citizens praised Moore's conduct and passed a resolution "that the late chivalrous conduct, and almost reckless self-devotion of Commodore E.W. Moore and the brave officers and men under his command on the coast of Yucatan, in a conflict with a greatly superior naval force of Mexico; while it is calculated to elevate our national character abroad, has justly entitled him and them to the fullest measure of the nation's gratitude."

Twenty days later, when word had filtered through South Texas, the citizens of Matagorda held their own meeting, tendering to Moore the Republic's thanks "for his daring gallantry." The resolution proclaimed him to be "a soldier without fear, and a man without reproach, whose achievements have already adorned the annals of his country.... Long may he live to wear the laurels he has so nobly won." A rumor even circulated that *Archer* and *San Bernard* were to be refitted for service and sent to join the victorious squadron off Yucatán.

This outpouring of national gratitude was not unexpected. So imagine Commodore Moore's surprise to find that, at his moment of triumph, President Houston had publicly branded Moore a pirate, a traitor, and a murderer!

CHAPTER THIRTY-FOUR

The Pirate Navy

We hear but one opinion expressed in relation to Sam Houston's recent proclamation and that is deep indignation and merited rebuke. The opinion obtains alike, in this city as well as in Texas, and the President is universally pronounced either as a black-hearted traitor to his country or a mad man.

—New Orleans Picayune

AFTER COMMODORE MOORE dressed down Houston in July of 1842, the naval commander became one of those few men who stirred such rage within Houston's breast that Old Sam's generally astute political senses abandoned him. To Houston, Moore symbolized the insolence inherent in the Republic's navy, from its infancy in early 1836—when William Brown refused to turn over *Liberty* to its duly-appointed captain—to the spring of 1843, when Moore ignored Houston's explicit orders to return to Galveston under arrest. To Houston, any naval captain who disobeyed his commander in chief was a pirate and a traitor, and during the spring of 1843, Houston's tirades against Moore grew more violent and emotional.

March 26:

By all means have the Commodore 'yoked' and manacled, if possible. The law has appropriated the suitable punishment to mutiny, treason and piracy. All three offenses are embraced in the conduct of Post Captain Moore.... Examples must be made.... The doctor must be the rope, and hanging the cure.

Early May:

[O]ur navy has gone to sea. In doing so, I can only say that the commander has committed the most flagrant outrage possible upon his country and the law of nations.

May 7:

By the papers, I learn (for there is no official report to the Department) that [Moore] has adorned the catalog of his crimes with murder, and under piratical circumstances.... What has now been done? A lie given to the action of the Government—the laws trampled upon and contumely heaped upon the Executive by a traitor ... my indignation is *called* into action by acts of outrage, piracy, and murder added to mutiny and sedition!

May 13:

You speak of that miserable Col'el Moore. The poor soul will fall by his own poison, or rather he will be strangled with his own venom! If it were not that he injures my country I would not regard all his slanders. He is like the bloated maggot, can only live in his own corruption. A healthy atmosphere would destroy him at once! He is heaping up wrath against the day of wrath, and the righteous judgement of the wicked. I do regard him as the cause of our brave fellows languishing in the loathsome prison of Mexico—as well as *Moores* late Treason, & Piracy! How he will answer to his country for such heinous offenses, time must tell!

The same day:

Poor, poor Texas!!! I think it is probably the [sic.] our Commodore Moore, will make the best of his way to the "Isle of Pines" or sell out our Navy to Santa Anna!

July 21:

I have *"dishonorably discharged E. W. Moore, from the naval service of the Republic"* for his various acts of contumacy, and crime... !

Houston's blind rage against Moore would burn brightly for many years. Two years later, he cursed Moore at a gathering of polite company as "the damnedest scoundrel on the face of the earth, the damnedest villain unhung."

Houston's bitterness toward Commodore Moore was compounded by two other factors. The first was his personal unpopularity in Galveston and the Gulf Coast area, the region that supported the highly critical *Telegraph and Texas Register*, that applauded Secretary Fisher's defiance of Houston's orders, that lionized the useless Texas Navy and its treacherous commander.

The second factor was more substantive, although it was a problem of Houston's own making. In early 1843, Sam Houston's strategy of playing off the United States against Great Britain was reaching its climax. Houston had told Britain's *chargé d'affaires*, Capt. Charles Elliott, that Texas would consider reentry into the Mexican union as an autonomous state; in the meantime, a mediated peace would ensure Britain of a client state on the United States' southwestern border. To the United States, however, Houston sent different signals. If annexation were again refused, he asserted, Texas would have no choice but to align with Great Britain for protection, which would check U.S. expansion to the southwest. To pull off his strategy, Houston needed to convince both sides that Texas could not stand alone, for a Texas that could resist Mexican integration needed neither annexation nor Great Britain's protection. A strong Texas therefore would not force the United States to make a play for annexation to parry British influence on its southwestern border.

But a strong Texas was exactly what a naval victory over Mexico would project to the world. Accordingly, Houston assured Her Britannic Majesty's ministers that, so long as negotiations with Santa Anna were pending, Texas would not attack Mexico. It mattered little that all intelligence from Mexico, Great Britain, and the United States pointed to only one conclusion: Mexico was determined to invade Texas, and would do so as soon as the Yucatán campaign was complete.

When Commodore Moore struck the Mexican fleet at Campeche, then, Houston's credibility with both Britain and Mexico, with whom Texas was still negotiating, was put into question. A furious Houston wrote to Elliott shortly afterward.

> *The ink is scarcely dry upon the assurance that no aggressive action would take place on the part of this government against Mexico, beyond our avowed limits, unless it should be rendered necessary by the acts of Mexico towards Texas.* In [going to sea], I can only say that the commander has committed the most flagrant outrage possible upon his country and the law of nations.... The crime is one of great atrocity, and I have availed myself of the first moment to apply the only corrective in my power.

The "corrective," as it turned out, was the unpublished proclamation that Houston had written for James Morgan and William Bryan. The proclamation was originally given to the commissioners to keep Commodore Moore in line, but Houston had not anticipated that Morgan might fall under Moore's spell, go with him to Yucatán, and decline to publish the proclamation. So, in light of Morgan's "abduction," as Houston called it, President Houston discharged Morgan and publicly denounced his navy to the world. The proclamation, published on May 6, left no ambiguity.

PROCLAMATION
BY THE PRESIDENT OF THE REPUBLIC OF TEXAS

Whereas, E.W. Moore, a Post Captain commanding the Navy of Texas, was, on the 29th day of October, 1842, by the acting Secretary of War and Marine, under the direction of the President, ordered to leave the port of New Orleans, in the United States, and sail with all vessels under his command, to the port of Galveston, in Texas; . . . and, whereas, the said Post Captain, E. W. Moore, has disobeyed, and continues to disobey, all orders of this government, and has refused, and continues to refuse, to deliver over said vessels to the said commissioners in accordance with law; but on the contrary, declares a disregard of the orders of this government, and avows his intention to proceed to sea under the flag of Texas, and in a direct violation of said orders, and cruize upon the high seas with armed vessels, contrary to the laws of this Republic and of nations; . . . and for the purpose of according due respect to the safety of commerce and the maintenance of those most essential rules of subordination which have not heretofore been so flagrantly violated by the subaltern officers of any organized government, known to the present age, it has become necessary and proper to make public these various acts of disobedience, contumacy and mutiny, on the part of the said Post Captain, E. W. Moore; Therefore: I, Sam Houston, President, and Commander-in-Chief of the Army and Navy of the Republic of Texas, do, by these presents, declare and proclaim, that he, the aforesaid Post Captain, E. W. Moore, is suspended from all command in the Navy of the Republic, and that all orders "sealed" or otherwise, which were issued to the said Post Captain, E. W. Moore, previous to the 29th October, 1842, are hereby revoked and declared null and void, and he is hereby commanded to obey his subsequent orders, and report forthwith in person to the Head of the Department of War and Marine of this Government.

And I do further declare and proclaim, on failure of obedience to this command, or on his having gone to sea, contrary to orders, that this Government will no longer hold itself responsible for his acts upon the high seas; but in such case, requests all the governments in treaty, or on terms of amity with this government, and all naval officers on the high seas or in ports foreign to this country, to seize the said Post Captain, E. W. Moore, the ship Austin and the brig Wharton, with their crews, and bring them, or any of them, into the port of Galveston, that the vessels may be secured to the Republic, and the culprit or culprits arraigned and punished by the sentence of a legal tribunal.

The Naval Powers of Christendom will not permit such a flagrant and unexampled outrage, by a commander of public vessels of war, upon the right of his nation and upon his official oath and duty, to pass unrebuked; for such would be to destroy all civil rule and establish a precedent which would jeopardize the commerce on the ocean and render encouragement and sanction to piracy.

In testimony whereof, I have hereunto set my hand and caused the great seal of the Republic to be affixed.

Signed,   SAM HOUSTON

Most Texians, particularly along the coast, read Houston's proclamation with dismay. Galveston's *Texas Times* condemned the "demonic malice" that drove Houston's treatment of the Texas Navy. The *Morning Star*, published in the city that bore the President's name, gave its initial, perplexed response on May 11, giving Houston a backhanded benefit of some very grave doubts. "We publish to-day the proclamation of President Houston relative to the Navy. It has excited a general feeling of astonishment and indignation in this section . . . so long as Gen. Houston holds the reigns of government even if *insane*, his legal orders should be respected."

News of the Navy's victory at Campeche changed "astonishment and indignation" to disgust, both at home and abroad. On May 23, when news of the battle reached Texas, a "large and respectable meeting" of Galveston's citizens convened at the harbor to pass a resolution denouncing Houston's proclamation as "ill-timed," "useless" and the product of "the imbecility of the President." Four days later, the *Morning Star* described popular reaction in New Orleans.

> The Proclamation of [the] President against Com. Moore has been received in the United States with a general burst of indignation. The editors of New Orleans papers denounce it in the strongest terms. They consider it one of the most disgraceful public documents that has ever emanated from any Executive officer of a free and intelligent people—They do not hesitate to declare, that it must have been dictated by insanity, or something worse.

The *Morning Star*'s observations were not simply anti-Houston hyperbole. The *New Orleans Commercial Bulletin*, a strong supporter of the Texas cause going back to 1836, opined, "[T]he proclamation of Houston is not only without warrant of law and unsupported by precedent, or by those general and implied powers that grow necessarily out of a Chief Magistry; but it is of no legal effect, because, by fair legal construction, the President of Texas is *insane*—is not *compos mentis*." The *Picayune* was even harsher.

> We have little fear that the promulgation of the infamous proclamation against Com. Moore will affect that officer, certainly not in the eyes of his friends here nor of those of Texas. But, in common with all, we feel mortified and chagrined that any such paper should have been published in the world. All look upon it as an emanation, either from an arch fiend or traitor, jealous of every other man who may in any way signalize himself and reap a harvest of renown—in other words fearful that there may be some other man in Texas than Sam Houston, or else the act of a wild lunatic—a man beside himself.

The proclamation may have been illegal, an act of insanity, or simply a bad political move. But when *Independencia* brought back word of it to Campeche on May 30, Commodore Moore and James Morgan quickly agreed that the squadron had to retire to Galveston as soon as it had enough powder to shoot its way through any Mexican ships that came out to greet them. The officers and men had no prior knowledge of the proclamation or Houston's views, and Moore, as Morgan reported, "evinced some anxiety lest the crew should get hold of the Proclamation, and seeing themselves outlawed, might mutiny and take possession of the vessels." Furthermore, Moore knew that if he and his men were captured by Mexico after Houston had branded his men pirates, they could expect to be summarily hanged.

On June 4, the schooner *Republic* arrived off Campeche fresh from Galveston, bringing more volunteers and a few Texas newspapers. Midshipman Walke noted in his journal, "We also received a copy of Resolutions expressive of their gratitude & esteem and a Handsome Badge for each of the officers from the Ladies of Galveston." How Moore handled his crew when news of Houston's proclamation spread is not recorded, but it is a tribute to his leadership that no unusual reports of discipline surfaced between the *Republic*'s arrival and June 16, when the schooner *Charlotte* arrived from New Orleans with sixty kegs of gunpowder ordered by Governor Mendez for Moore's vessels. As Moore wrote, "It is wonderful that the weary days and nights of inaction and indignation which ensued, were characterized by no act of insubordination on the part of daring crews, having a *license* under the seal of the Executive of Texas for any enormity they might see proper to commit against the officers." Since the English sailors quit the Mexican service around June 10, Moore was hopeful that he could launch another attack against the disorganized squadron before it could man its vessels properly, notwithstanding its reinforcement by *Regenerador* and *Iman* on May 19. The officers, however, did not conceal their disgust with President Houston and the Texas government, and expressed an unwillingness to fight Mexico, except in self-defense. So the campaign off Yucatán's coast came to an ambiguous and inglorious conclusion.

Once the gunpowder had been rolled aboard and stowed in the warships' magazines, Commodore Moore prepared to sail home, undoubtedly for the last time. He stocked *Austin*'s larders with food, settled his accounts with Governor Mendez, and prepared to ship out. Logistical delays pushed back the departure date to June 26, and a fierce storm damaged *Austin*'s foremast, keeping the squadron in port for repairs an additional three days.

On the twenty-ninth of June, the Mexican fleet left Campeche. When word went out that the Texians were leaving, Commodore Marín publicly declared that Moore would never leave Campeche's harbor alive. But the next day, according to Lieutenant Gray, "the morning light shone on the waters of the Bay, but touched not upon the spars of the enemy's ships."

Marín had sailed home to Veracruz to receive the *Cruz de Honor*, and Mexico declared victory. But the blockade of Campeche was broken, the Yucatán people were secure, and Santa Anna's troops would not invade Texas. On June 22, Ampudia's troops had embarked for central Mexico, leaving the federalists in complete control of the peninsula. The *Morning Star* later observed, "The relinquishment of the siege of the city so soon after the engagement of the 16th is the best commentary in favor of the Texian Navy."

Mexico's strategy, which required a favorable result in Yucatán before invading Texas, was a complete failure. The loss of Yucatán and the specter of Texas annexation to the United States undoubtedly influenced Santa Anna's willingness to consider terms with the Lone Star Republic, and on June 14, 1843, less than one month after the Battle of Campeche, Mexico entered into an armistice, effectively resigning itself to the permanent loss of Texas. Mexican conservatives would criticize Santa Anna for squandering men in Yucatán who should have been fighting the *norteamericanos*, and given Houston's refusal to extend Lamar's military alliance with Yucatán, this criticism may have some merit.

On June 29, amid victory celebrations in Campeche and Mérida, *Austin* and *Wharton* weighed anchor at Campeche for the last time. Upon his departure, Moore informed Acting Governor Miguel Barbachano that he would touch at Sisal the next day to collect the remaining amounts due him, and assured the governor, "in the event your unpleasant difficulties with Mexico not being settled . . . it will afford me great pleasure to lend my feeble aid to your just cause." The next day, the two ships anchored at Sisal, sending Commodore Moore's brother James to Mérida to collect the Yucatán government subsidy. Barbachano dutifully paid the last $1,700 on July 6, and tendered Moore the thanks of his country, wishing "a happy result in the difficulty raised against you by President Houston." With that, the Texians sailed from Yucatán, never to see the shores of the peninsula again.

The next day the squadron touched at Las Alacranes one last time, to replenish the men's supply of sea turtles, and at 5:30 p.m. on July 10, the two ships unfurled their canvas on a final course for Galveston, over a year after they last saw Texas.

CHAPTER THIRTY-FIVE

The War at Home

> [W]hether Captain Moore was guilty of treason, murder, and piracy, or not, it forms no justification . . . for the violation of a positive statute dishonorably dismissing him from the service without a trial, or an opportunity of defending a reputation acquired by severe toils, privations and hardships, in sustaining the honor and glory of the flag under which he sailed and fought.
> —House Naval Affairs Committee 1844

NEAR MIDNIGHT OF JULY 14, the lights of Galveston could be seen twinkling some six miles in the distance as the two warships came to anchor for the night. As dawn broke the next day, the homesick crews could make out the wharves, houses and hotels of Galveston's shore even before a local pilot came out to escort the two vessels across the bar.

It didn't take long for word of the returning heroes to spread across the island, and the Texas Navy was in for a grand welcome. The *Morning Star* reported the squadron's reception.

> The event was celebrated as a national jubilee. . . . When the vessels were first seen in the offing in the morning the joyful news was soon communicated throughout the city, and the people gathered in crowds to welcome home the gallant tars that had so recently weathered the terrible storms of battle. The cannon in the city were soon prepared and a national salute was fired, to which the gallant Commodore immediately responded, firing his heavy cannon at regular intervals as the vessels slowly advanced into port.

As the cannons drummed their booming tribute, a small boat rowed out to *Austin* with a note from Mayor Allen, informing Commodore Moore that the citizens and local militia wished to give him a proper welcome. He asked if the hour of Moore's arrival could be set for 4:00 p.m., "to receive the testimony of [the Citizens and Military of Galveston] of their friendly feelings, at Menard's wharf." Moore was undoubtedly flattered, but he informed His Honor that he had no intention of leaving his vessel except to turn himself over to local law enforcement authorities for arrest. He promptly sent ashore a letter to H. M. Smythe, Sheriff of Galveston County, stating, "Having been proclaimed by the President of Texas an outlaw and a pirate, and all the nations of Christendom in amity with Texas having been called upon to seize and bring me to this port for trial, I herewith inform you that I have voluntarily returned here, and surrender myself to you, for the purpose of meeting the penalties of the law."

Sheriff Smythe was nobody's fool and probably held Sam Houston in as much contempt as the rest of his fellow Galvestonians did. He wrote back, "Much as I admire a disposition of submission to the legal tribunals of your country, so manifested, I am not aware, nor do I conceive that it is incumbent on me in my official capacity, to take cognizance of the matter. . . ." With that, Moore came ashore a free man, to the thunderous applause of the crowds that turned out at Menard's Wharf to greet the returning heroes. The citizens of Galveston threw a sumptuous banquet, local politicians made speeches (of course), and a number of self-appointed welcoming committees passed flowery resolutions in the Navy's honor.

The reception was a hopeful sign. Moore, emboldened by his welcome, sent a full report to Secretary Hill on July 21, concluding, "The vessels are safe in the harbor of Galveston, and I am not only ready, but anxious to appear before that tribunal which His Excellency, the President, has expressed so much solicitude to the world to have me brought before." If the government in Washington-on-the-Brazos held the Texas Navy in one-tenth the esteem of its citizens along the coast, or could be moved by their insistent voices, then things would work out just fine.

But it didn't. On July 25, 1843, commissioner William Bryan and James Morgan's replacement, William Brashear, handed Commodore Moore a note informing him of Morgan's discharge and enclosing a letter from Secretary Hill dated July 9 dishonorably discharging him from the service. Hill's letter was every bit as vitriolic as Houston's rhetoric, accusing Moore of murder, treason and piracy. It claimed Moore had entered into an alliance with Yucatán "without the sanction or knowledge of the authorities of this government" (which was untrue, as Moore had informed the department of his intentions in December 1842). It claimed that Moore, while under suspension and arrest, had "assumed to exercise the functions of commander of the Navy of Texas," which amounted to "piracy" (also untrue, since a legally authorized commissioner had retained Moore in command of the squadron, then ordered him to Yucatán). Finally, Hill's letter accused Commodore Moore of murder for the hanging of the *San Antonio* mutineers, overlooking the War Department's approval of the 1842 court-martial of accused mutineer Thomas Rowan, and ignoring Sam Houston's letter to Louisiana's Governor Roman asking the state's officials to release the remaining mutineers into Moore's custody.

Whatever the fallacies of Hill's claims, it was clear that the administration was going to break Moore, regardless of the facts. Hill's letter was followed up by a similar missive to Commander Lothrop, discharging him for "disobedience to orders, delinquency in the discharge of your duty and contempt for your superiors." (Hill either did not know, or did not care, that Lothrop had never seen the orders, which Lothrop had handed back to Commissioner James Morgan unopened at Morgan's request.) Bryan and Brashear ordered Lothrop to turn command of his brig to Lieut. William A. Tennison, a more politically reliable officer. Lieut. Charles Snow, the Navy Yard commander who had been starved out by an uncaring administration, was also cashiered for taking small arms and other equipment from Galveston to New Orleans to be used against Mexico with the Texas squadron. Sam Houston had declared war on his naval officers.

Edwin Moore's temper had grown short over the years, perhaps understandably, given the persecution and neglect he received at the hands of President Houston. His temper, however, caused him to overplay his hand with other powerful men, which deprived him of several potential allies. The day he arrived in Galveston, he pointedly and rudely snubbed Samuel May Williams, the founder of both Texas fleets, over a matter related to Moore's disposition of the exchequer bills to Williams' brother-in-law in 1842. As a result, the two men began exchanging correspondence characteristic of gentlemen who intend to resolve their affairs at the muzzle of a dueling pistol. Ultimately, mutual friends interceded, and Moore claimed satisfaction with Williams' explanations. But Williams was an influential Galvestonian, one who had refused Houston's appointment as commissioner to sell the Texas Navy, and was dead-set against annexation. Commodore Moore lost a strong potential ally at a time when he would be fighting for his commission, his reputation, and quite possibly, his life. In a similar vein, he insulted legislator and fiery Houston-hater James Love to the point where arrangements were again made for a gentlemanly "interview." Once again, the *Code Duello* was not invoked, but the affair cost the Texas Navy another potential ally.

The day after their dismissal, Galveston's *Telegraph and Texas Register* published letters written by Morgan and Moore after their return, explaining their actions to the public. Morgan's letter stated, "I had just as much authority from my instructions to touch on the coast of Yucatan with the vessels, as I had to proceed direct to Galveston with them, and that I had no instructions to do either!" While Morgan could not disclose everything due to the injunction of the "Secret Act" of January 16, he did state unequivocally that Commodore Moore was blameless of insubordination in taking the war to Yucatán, and that there were sound tactical reasons for ordering Moore to proceed to Campeche in April of 1843. He also informed the public that if Houston's orders had been obeyed and Commodore Moore dismissed, the vessels undoubtedly would have been looted and burned in New Orleans by their crews. His most important conclusion, however, was buried near the end of his lengthy message. "By the timely move made by said Vessels after receipt of the news at the Balize, we put a stop to the contemplated invasion of Galveston *in the Spring* altogether; saved that place from falling into the hands of the enemy or being destroyed."

Commodore Moore's letter, entitled "To the Public of Texas," was an impassioned defense of his conduct, and an accounting of funds placed at his disposal, which had become the basis of another charge by Secretary Hill. "A great number of my countrymen have been led to believe that the Navy appropriation (of $97,659.50) . . . passed during the extra session of July 1842, was paid over to me, and I am aware that some of the members of this Congress who acted in the 'secret session' were fully impressed with this belief. Not *one dollar* of that appropriation has ever reached me." Moore insisted that his conduct had been proper according to his orders, and the right course of action for Texas.

Popular support for Commodore Moore remained strong throughout 1843. The *Telegraph*'s editor credited the Texas Navy with saving the Republic from invasion.

> That our fleet induced the Mexican government to send the propositions for armistice may be inferred from the following facts . . . the engagements of the 30th April and 16th May ensued. On the 9th of June succeeding, the Scylla arrived at Galveston from Vera Cruz, bearing the propositions of Santa Anna for armistice! . . . While the Navy is efficient, the country is safe. The very salvation of Texas, like that of Athens in former days, may depend on "wooden walls," and we hope no stupid, *blockhead* policy will deprive our country of its best resource.

On July 26, the Navy's officers and men were officially notified of their commanders' dismissals. At four o'clock in the afternoon, Commodore Moore turned command of the ship over to Lieutenant Gray, bade farewell to his officers, and walked down the gangplank to his waiting launch. As his men rowed him to shore, he heard the crew bellow out three heartfelt cheers, followed by the familiar boom of one of *Austin*'s big twenty-fours. Then another. Then another. On pealed the thunder, echoing over the waters, until thirteen guns had paid tribute to the ship's unflagging leader as he walked into civilian life. As a mark of respect to Commander Lothrop, *Wharton*'s new commander, Lt. W. T. Lewis, ordered three cheers and an eight-gun salute as Lothrop departed his brig, never to return.

As Houston and Hill could have predicted, the dismissal of Moore and Lothrop sealed the Navy's fate. Secretary Hill reported on the event to Houston:

> The Officers of the Ship Austin abandoned the vessel, went on shore, and forwarded to the Department their resignations as Officers in the Naval service of the Republic. Their resignations were not accepted, but furloughs for the Officers whose services were not required, were forwarded to the Commissioners, with instructions to furlough or discharge such of the crews as were not actually necessary. . . .

The last entry in Midshipman Alfred Walke's naval journal, dated July 27, 1843, stated events more succinctly. "All the officers in the Service excepting Lt. Tennison & Sailing Master Dan'l Lloyd, resigned on this day & left the vessels. The End."

Moore and Lothrop were unwilling to go without a fight. On July 25, the two men informed the commissioners that they would submit their grievances to Congress. Three days later, Lothrop protested the "gross injustice and inequality of this summary action on the part of His Excellency" and the Department's refusal to provide "a fair and impartial hearing for the charges brought against me." He concluded, "as His Excellency and the Department have not thought proper to render me that common justice I shall at the proper time appeal to a higher tribunal."

As he waited for the Eighth Congress to assemble at the capital of Washington-on-the-Brazos, Commodore Moore's standing in coastal Texas remained high. He kept his cause before the press by occasionally writing letters to various newspapers, always calling for a public trial to test Houston's charges against him. His heaviest broadside was unleashed on September 21, 1843, when he published a 201-page pamphlet entitled *To the People of Texas: An Appeal in Vindication of His Conduct of the Navy*. Moore's pamphlet, which contained copies of every significant piece of correspondence to and from the naval commanders between late 1841 and Moore's dismissal, set off another wave of public indignation directed at Houston. One of the *Telegraph*'s subscribers, signing his name "A friend of the Navy," went so far as to advocate Galveston's secession from Texas, electing Moore as president and Lothrop vice-president, or, "in case we prefer a monarchial form of Government, we can elect the first King and the Latter Prime Minister."

Commodore Moore spent the early part of 1844 persuading Congress to force the War Department to convene a court-martial, to try the charges raised by Houston and Hill. On January 11, Moore brought his case before Congress. The Committee on Naval Affairs, keenly aware of the "Commander Hinton" law prohibiting the president from dismissing a commanding officer without a court-martial, came down unequivocally in Moore's favor. Noting that Houston lacked any constitutional or statutory authority for summarily dismissing Moore, the committee concluded, "So direct and palpable a violation of the positive provisions of a statute well known to the Executive at the time he gave the order, cannot be justified." The committee found "abundant evidence" that Moore spent more on the Navy than he was charged with receiving, prompting the conclusion that Hill's intimations of embezzlement were groundless. The committee opined that Houston had violated the law by withholding naval appropriations, while Houston's charge of piracy must have been a reference to a "new and singular species of piracy—a species which seems to have escaped the knowledge of most, if not all, the elementary writers on international law." But these political conclusions were largely academic anyway, since even if Moore were guilty on all counts, under the law of February 4, 1841, Houston could not dismiss him without a fair trial.

The Naval Affairs Committee's report was returned to Congress with a resolution decreeing, "It is due to Post Captain E. W. Moore, to have a full, fair and impartial investigation of the charges." The resolution provided that a court-martial would be convened as soon as was practical. With no naval officers left, the court-martial would be presided over by the major general of the militia, at least two brigadier generals, and other officers of succeeding rank. The resolution passed both houses on February 5, 1844. Because it so plainly followed established law, Houston had little choice but to approve the resolution, no doubt confident that among military men subject to Houston's orders, Moore would be found guilty.

Houston's case against Edwin Moore was arguably the most dramatic of Sam Houston's many political vendettas. Moore's activities kept him in the public eye, and he was fêted with banquets and dinners along the Gulf Coast region. As the *New Orleans Bulletin* reported in late 1844, the citizens of Houston, Texas, "without the distinction of party," gave a huge dinner in his honor, and many glasses were raised to Moore and Commander Lothrop.

The court-martial began its work on May 20, 1844, under the chairmanship of Maj. Gen. Sidney Sherman, Texas's ranking military commander. Joining Sherman were Brig. Gen. Alexander Somervell, commander of the Texas expedition that bore his name; Brig. Gen. Edwin Morehouse; Col. James Reily; and Col. Thomas Seypert. Thomas "Ramrod" Johnson, a Houston stalwart who edited the *Texian and Brazos Farmer*, a pro-Houston newspaper, was appointed judge advocate for the tribunal.

The court had no need to deal with Commander Lothrop, the Navy's popular cavalier. After his dismissal, Lothrop took a job as master of the steam packet *Neptune* until April 1844, when his trial date came up, and he dutifully reported to the seat of government for trial. On May 29, however, Secretary Hill abruptly dropped the charges, and Lothrop was restored to his rank as commander in the Texas Navy.

The gallant commander did not have long to enjoy his vindication. Yellow fever descended on the Texas coast when an infected French sailor arrived aboard the frigate *Brilliante*. In the ensuing outbreak, an estimated ten percent of Galveston's population died, and Commander Lothrop succumbed to the disease on August 14, the same month the plague claimed Lt. Downing Crisp, who had ventured back from Europe to assume command of *Austin* in January 1844. The thirty-year-old Lothrop was buried in Washington, Texas, with full military honors, a sword on his breast. His estate was entrusted to the care of his best friend, Edwin Ward Moore.

The court took up the case against Lt. Charles Snow, accused of deserting *San Bernard* and having taken her gear to New Orleans for use with Moore's squadron. Since Moore had ordered Snow to do exactly that on January 31, 1843, it was not a difficult case to decide. Snow was acquitted and, like Lothrop, he was reinstated by an unhappy Houston.

On May 20, the court got down to the business of trying the case against Commodore Moore. The charge of piracy was so ludicrous that it was thrown out without further proceedings. Based on the court's understanding of Houston's remaining allegations, Commodore Moore was charged with six counts of neglect of duty, three counts of embezzlement and fraud, six counts of disobedience to orders, five counts of contempt and defiance of laws and authority, one count of treason and one count of murder.

Moore hired James Mayfield, a die-hard Houston opponent, as his trial counsel. Mayfield's defense was to attack every aspect of Houston's naval policy, and at that he was masterful—so much so that one of the judges, Colonel Reily, later told Anson Jones that if he needed a trial lawyer, he would rather have Mayfield than anyone else. Witnesses for both the prosecution and defense included Purser Fleming T. Wells, Commissioner William Brashear, Lieutenant Snow, Commissioner Bryan, Sailing Master Daniel Lloyd, Lieutenant Tennison, Commander Lothrop, Moore's brother James, and James Morgan, among others.

When it came time for the defense to present its case, Commodore Moore conducted himself like a veteran political operator, playing an active role in the proceedings and staying in close personal contact with members of the court. As he made the traditional presentation of his sword to the tribunal, he solemnly declared,

> I place in your keeping, Mr. President, and gentlemen of this court, my sword, which I have worn in this and my native country upwards of nineteen years, and in this country of my adoption for nearly five years, and which I can safely say I have always used to the utmost of my ability, with prudence, firmness, discretion and humanity. . . . From the intelligence of this court I confidently believe that after a full investigation of the charges and specifications, I will receive at your hands an impartial verdict, which is all I ask.

The trial plodded along for seventy exhausting days. Long before it was over, Texas and New Orleans newspapers confidently predicted Moore would be acquitted. They were not disappointed. The court summarily dismissed the charges of treason and murder. Treason, after all, meant making war *against* Texas, not in defense of it. As to murder, Moore had clearly been given the authority to punish the *San Antonio* mutineers by a duly authorized commissioner, so he was not a murderer.

The remaining charges were thoroughly examined, and in all but four instances, the findings came down solidly in favor of the commodore. The court found Moore guilty of four charges—disobedience to specific orders—but expressly found that the orders implicated were either conditional and thus arguably complied with, or were impossible to obey. No punishment of any kind was recommended. On December 7, 1844, a fuming "Ramrod" Johnson wrote Moore a letter in his capacity as judge advocate, informing him that the court had rendered its verdict, and that he would be informed of the result through proper channels.

Since the court-martial had been mandated by Congress, not the War Department, Secretary Hill ordered General Sherman to seal the court's findings and hold them until the House elected its speaker. The speaker, in turn, broke the court's seals but forwarded the findings to Houston rather than make them public.

We have no record of the reactions of Houston, Hill, or Hill's naval bureau chief, M. C. Hamilton, upon learning of the court's verdict. But we do know that the House of Representatives passed a resolution demanding Hamilton's dismissal for using "indecorous language" to the House in relation to Commodore Moore's court-martial. And we do have a record of Sam Houston's endorsement of the court's findings, in the words, "The President disapproves the proceedings of the court in toto, as he is assured by undoubted evidence of the guilt of the accused." It was clear that Houston was so incensed by his naval commander that he was now willing to dispense with due process of law—due process insisted upon by Congress—in order to rid himself of the troublesome commodore.

Houston could not keep the court's exoneration of Moore under wraps forever, of course. On January 6, 1845, the House of Representatives passed a resolution requesting that Houston transmit the court's proceedings to the House. Giving up this battle, Houston permitted General Sherman and the other members of the court to publish their findings, "to relieve the general anxiety as to the result of the investigations."

Congress was outraged at Houston's flagrant disregard of the judicial process, and Moore and Snow were the beneficiaries of this indignation. In January 1845, the House of Representatives passed a bill for the officers' relief, restoring them to their former ranks. Texas's new president, Anson Jones, vetoed both resolutions ("to gratify Houston," Moore grumbled), bemoaning the fate of the poor murderers whom Moore had hanged from the foreyard. Jones' veto message protested that the Executive, not Congress, was legally permitted to pardon someone, but ignored the fact that Moore had never been convicted of any crime that carried a sentence. In Moore's place, President Jones appointed John Grant Tod, backdating his commission to June 1840. Privately, James Morgan chalked up Moore's legislative defeat to Moore's "inordinate vanity," and his unwillingness to take advice to moderate his attacks against Houston and his henchmen.

The day after President Jones's veto, Congress reacted again with indignation. The Texas Senate passed a resolution declaring that Commodore Moore's court-martial was "final and conclusive," and that same day the House passed two more resolutions, one reinstating Moore as naval commander, and another giving Moore the thanks of the House and the Republic for his services. Unfortunately for Commodore Moore, these flowery resolutions did not have the force of law, and Moore was out of the Navy for good.

It was an ignominious end to the brilliant career of Texas's greatest naval commander, and it would parallel the sad tidings that fate had in store for the remainder of the Texas Navy.

CHAPTER THIRTY-SIX

A Slow Death

We think the Navy of Texas (even though dismantled and advertised for sale), while still in our possession is the best guarantee we have at present, against Mexican treachery.
—Houston *Morning Star,* October 7, 1843

IN THE SUMMER OF 1843, Commissioners Bryan and Brashear had one duty as co-commanders of the Texas Navy: they were to close it down for good. After the shock of the officer corps resignations had worn off, they settled into the sad business of liquidating the Navy in a methodical fashion. On July 27, they ordered Lt. William Tennison to take command of *Austin*, and placed John Clark, onetime *Wharton* commander, in charge of *Austin*'s cutter. Four days later, they ordered Purser Fleming Wells to furnish copies of muster rolls and other paperwork, so they could figure out exactly what the Navy had that could be sold. When Wells voiced his dismay at the treatment he and his fellow officers received from an ungrateful government, Secretary Hill chided him. "It is [the Department's] province to direct, and expect obedience, and no murmurs and protests from its subordinate officers. There has been too great a want of discipline and subordination in the service already. . . ." As for Wells' request for funds to travel from Galveston to the seat of government to convey his returns, Hill dryly added, "I must inform you that the Dep't cannot command a single dollar at this time."

Lieutenant Tennison, now effectively commander of the fleet, began placing the vessels in ordinary without much hope that they would ever sail again. He had the ships dismasted and securely moored in Galveston Harbor, sent ashore the flagship's small arms and powder, and discharged the crews, except for a "very small number" who would be paid on a monthly basis. These were little more than unskilled watchmen, occasionally rousing themselves to fire a salute for visiting dignitaries or foreign vessels, drag leaking warships into shallower water, and break down the vessels' rigging and equipment. Despite Commodore Moore's plea for the veteran amputees who lived aboard *Austin* with no family to help them and no means to earn a living, Secretary Hill reported that throughout 1843, a number of men were forced to live aboard the ship until they could find a way back to their families or friends. Hill acknowledged, "These men are in a destitute condition, and the means necessary to enable them to visit their friends, would relieve many of their present inconveniences."

The arrangement could not last long. Regardless of whether Texas wanted to put its navy to sea, the remaining crewmen wanted to be paid, and the government had no means to compensate them. Discipline began breaking down, and Tennison had to discharge a number of agitators (those who did not desert first), giving one a dozen lashes for insolent and threatening language. On October 2, Commissioner Brashear came aboard and addressed the near-mutinous crew, pleading that he could not pay them any wages until the middle of October, which prompted another round of heated demands for discharge.

Hearkening back to the January 16, 1843 law, the commissioners's next order of business was to sell the warships. A contractor was hired to remove *Zavala*'s engines from her rotten, mud-encased hull, and see if she could be raised. The engines were pulled out and hauled up on the beach, but *Zavala*'s stubborn carcass would not budge. Other men were put to work making repairs on the now-sunken *San Bernard* and the dismasted *Archer*, which had never put to sea after her maiden voyage, the most useless warship Texas ever owned.

As repairs were being made, strange advertisements began turning up in coastal newspapers. The notices read as follows.

VESSELS AT AUCTION

In accordance with an Act of Congress of the Republic of Texas, approved 16th January 1843 and instructions from the Hon. G.W. Hill, Secretary of War and Marine, the undersigned will proceed to sell, at public auction, on Saturday the 14th of October next, in the city of Galveston, the following property belonging to the Government of Texas, to wit:

The brig Archer and Schooner San Bernard, now lying in the Harbor of Galveston, together with their rigging, tackle, apparel and furniture. The brig is about 450 tons capacity and the schooner 140 tons. These vessels were built in Baltimore, of good materials for the Texas naval service, in 1839, coppered and copper fastened and are now being thoroughly repaired and fitted as merchant vessels and are in every respect well found and in good condition.

Also at the same time and place the two low-pressure Engines of the Steamer Zavala, of 150 horse power, each nearly new and in good order.

Terms of sale—One half cash and the balance in approved endorsed paper at 60 days from the day of sale and botomry security on the vessels.

WM. BRYAN
WM. C. BRASHEAR,
Navy Commissioners.

The commissioners also advertised the sale of "Two large Cisterns, water Casks, one Iron Safe, Chairs, Tables, Settees &c., the houses and fixtures at the Navy Yard with sundry other articles."

As the commissioners could have predicted, the sale was not well received in Galveston. Galveston would be the most likely invasion beachhead if Santa Anna broke his promised armistice, and Santa Anna had given everyone ample reason to be skeptical of his promises. The citizens of Texas's largest port had little faith in Houston's plans to call out a "sea militia" or turn back an invasion fleet with small coastal guns manned by untrained civilians. The sale no doubt would have been held somewhere else—at Matagorda, or even New Orleans—had there been anyone left to sail the ships out of the harbor.

As the auction date approached, the good citizens of Galveston determined in advance that no bona fide bidders would be permitted anywhere near the warships, so they would stay right where they were. Two days before the sale, a petition with over two hundred signatures circulated throughout the city, declaring, "[W]e recognize no such power as SECRET LEGISLATION; that it never was conceded, nor ever by implication can it have been intended by this FREE PEOPLE, to concede the *tyrannical* privilege of forming SECRET LAWS. We therefore solemnly *protest* against the act styled Secret Act of the 16th January last, and against all action upon it." Another circular, this time with about a hundred signatures, went even further, pledging to oppose the sale of the Texas Navy by forcible means if necessary.

On the morning of the sale, Secretary Hill rode into Galveston and was greeted by a committee of Galveston's citizens begging him to cancel the auction. When he refused, a committee of one hundred was appointed to take such measures as they deemed best for the Republic and Galveston. The gathering mob grew ugly, and Hill foresaw a riot if the vessels were sold out of the port. To pacify the menacing crowd, he eventually agreed to allow one of the citizens to make a bid on behalf of the Texas government.

When the vigilantes showed up at the pier at auction time, they came heavily armed, determined to allow no one to outbid their "government agents." One Galveston resident later described the tense scene.

> All kinds of dire threats were made against any nation or individuals who should have the temerity to bid on the vessels. As the time drew near things waxed to the boiling point. Companies were organized and armed for battle to protect the country from the outrage to be perpetrated on it. At last the day of the sale arrived, the city was full of excited people, and Captain Howe was on hand with his battalion all in uniform and armed to the teeth. At about 11 a.m. an officer of the Republic appeared at the place of sale and announced the property for sale to the highest bidder. The people waited in breathless anxiety and with thumping hearts to see who was going to offer to buy.

Judge Benjamin Franklin, the private who had rowed up to *Invincible* with news of the victory at San Jacinto, bid one thousand dollars for *San Bernard* on behalf of the citizens of Galveston, while Thomas McKinney, the former owner of *San Felipe, William Robbins,* and *Invincible*, bid $1,100 "for the Republic of Texas." *Archer* was similarly "sold" for an unacceptably low bid of $1,500, and the agitators returned home with no further incident. One witness later wrote, "You can imagine the effect of dropping a piece of ice on a white-hot iron. The temperature went down like when a blue norther strikes the country. I venture to say that the warlike spirit of Galveston has never been at so high a pitch, nor never been cooled off so suddenly since." The Houston *Morning Star*, alluding to a violent feud over the Republic's archives the year before, concluded, "The affair fortunately has neither resulted in a violation of the laws nor in the sale of the National vessels; enough however has been done to convince the officer of government, that it will be as difficult to sell the Navy before peace is secured, as to remove the archives from Austin."

The sale was evidently attempted a second time, but with the same result. The Navy, bare and helpless though it was, had survived another assassination attempt by President Houston.

Secretary Hill recorded the auction succinctly, noting in his November 1843 report, "The amount offered for the vessels and engines, being nominal, compared with their true value, they remain the property of the Republic." Sam Houston, foiled yet again in his quest to rid his country of a naval service, disclaimed responsibility in a speech in November. "There was a blow-up at Galveston the other day about the Navy. Galveston cut herself right off. They would not let the President execute the law. (He didn't happen to be present.) Why? Because the Mexicans might come and take them!—They were now fitting out a secret expedition—destined for Galveston! . . . What interest has the President, my friends, to sell the Navy? He is only the Executive of the law."

With all efforts to sell the Navy blocked by patriots in Galveston, commissioners Bryan and Brashear had little else to do. On November 22, Secretary Hill ordered them to settle their accounts with the government, leaving Tennison in nominal command of the squadron. Plans had to be made for keeping the ships in ordinary, at least until the question of Texas's future—annexation or independence—could be resolved once and for all. On November 30, Secretary Hill forwarded his annual report to Houston, concluding, "A Navy well appointed, and furnished with ample means of sustenance is one of the most powerful means a nation can possess, of resisting an enemy and enforcing her just requirements; deprive the establishment of these prerequisites and none is more expensive and of less utility." It was an odd statement from a man whose administration did more than any other to deprive the Texas Navy of its "means of sustenance." Hill also noted that the skeleton crew needed food and pay, and that if the vessels could not be sold, Congress must find some funds to repair them in such a way that they would not rot, flood, and sink.

Congress was also concerned. In December 1843, both houses of Congress passed concurrent resolutions asking President Houston to estimate the amount necessary to refit the squadron and keep it in operation, as well as the amount needed to mothball the ships. In early January Lieutenant Crisp, who had returned from furlough in Europe, joined Lieutenant Taylor, Purser Wells and Purser Stephens in asking Congress to pay one third of the salaries due the Texas Navy's officers. They noted that the last time they had been paid by the government was May 1841, nearly three years before, and that large but ineffective appropriations from the Sixth and Seventh Congresses had resulted in nothing for the men who ran the ships. Lieutenant Crisp would be struck dead by yellow fever shortly after his petition, and nothing for the time being came of the officers' request.

The Committee on Naval Affairs did request and receive a list of seamen disabled during the Navy's most recent cruise, which President Houston forwarded with the comment, "They are recommended by E. W. Moore, late in command of the Texas Navy, to the liberality of the present Congress, as richly deserving of a pension. Their claims are respectfully submitted for such action as the Honorable Congress may think merit. Humanity, at least, pleads in their favor, and though they have thus become disabled and dependent by the acts of others, they must now live upon the bounty of a generous people or endure that want which their unhappy necessities impose." Before the end of January 1844, Charles Mason, the Republic's auditor, concluded that back pay due the officers totaled about $46,000.

Help was on the way, or so it would seem. In January 1844, the Texas Congress passed a bill "making an appropriation to pay in part the officers of the navy." Not surprisingly, the measure was vetoed by President Houston, still smarting from the near-riot over the sale of the Navy the previous October. Houston piously claimed, "None can feel a more lively interest for, nor a more ardent desire to see compensation afforded to all those who have rendered the country faithful service, than the Executive." But since the Republic had no money to pay anyone, Houston asserted that it would simply raise unrealistic hopes for many veterans who would flock to the seat of government in vain efforts to collect their pay. "Could the navy have been sold, as provided for by law, some sixty or seventy thousand dollars might have been placed at the disposition of the Government for the payment of the claims of both officers and seamen. As it is, however, the Government is wholly unable to do so." An attempt to override the veto was pressed by the anti-Houston faction, but it failed by a vote of five to seven.

With no money to operate the fleet, the Texas Congress passed a bill to keep the Navy in ordinary, and Houston signed it. The law called for a contractor to maintain *Austin, Wharton, Archer,* and *San Bernard* for one year, and officially repealed the act of January 1843 that required the sale of the warships.

With few exceptions, the remainder of the Texas Navy's operational life was spent discharging employees, gathering up property, and selling it off wherever possible. On February 24, 1844, General Order Number 3 honorably discharged all officers, sailors, and marines not necessary for the minimal upkeep of the Texas fleet, although in 1844 several gentlemen were appointed as officers, evidently for political reasons. That same month, the Navy's Colt pistols were turned over to Capt. Jack Hays of the Texas Rangers, who galloped off to lasting fame with them by turning back a large war party of Comanches at the Perdenales River that summer.

The ships themselves were in a horrendous state. On New Year's Day, 1844, Secretary Hill described them to President Houston. In some cases, the hulls were "entirely eaten through by worms where the copper was off, by which they are rendered unsafe as slight injuries may produce free and dangerous leaks." Although the ships were not five years old, "their timbers have decayed and are still decaying much more rapidly than vessels built of the best materials." *Austin* and *Wharton* still bore holes punched by Mexican cannon, which had not been properly fixed. "Laying them in ordinary will not preserve them," he warned. "I beg leave here to state, that I am in daily expectation of the receipt of intelligence, that the vessels are abandoned for want of means to maintain a crew on board." As for the Navy Yard, it was in such decrepit state that a military survey of the forts, harbors, and posts of Galveston taken two years later by the U.S. Army did not even bother to mention the Navy's home base.

In truth, however, Texas no longer needed a navy. Annexation talks with the United States had re-opened, thanks to support from President John Tyler in the fall of 1843. The U.S. had every intention of preventing Mexican intervention so long as the possibility of annexation remained. U.S. Secretary of State Abel Upshur gave Texas ambassador Isaac Van Zandt vague assurances of defensive assistance, and William Murphy, Washington's *chargé d'affaires* in Texas, made more explicit promises of protection. In early 1844, President Tyler went further, ordering U.S. Navy Secretary George Bancroft to dispatch a squadron to the Gulf of Mexico to intercept any hostile Mexican warships. With a strong United States squadron defending Texas, the Mexican Navy became irrelevant as an invasion spearhead, and *Moctezuma* and *Guadalupe* paddled off to New York for extensive repairs.

As annexation talks dragged on between the United States and Texas from late 1844 to the middle of 1845, the forlorn fleet continued its precipitous decline. In September 1844, Lieutenant Tennison reported that *Austin* was heavily damaged: her rotten foremast had snapped in the middle, and she was taking water below decks. The worm-eaten *Zavala*, once the sturdiest steamer on the Gulf, lay rotting on the beach, while *Wharton*, leaking badly, began sinking beneath Galveston's waves. On September 23, Secretary Hill demoted Lieutenant Tennison, placing commissioner William Brashear, now holding the rank of commander, in charge of the fleet in ordinary.

In November 1844, Brashear hired a carpenter to repair *Wharton*'s hull in a belated effort to save her, but the brig was a lost cause; her sixteen guns, boats and other possessions were transferred to *Archer*, and the battle-scarred brig slipped below the water's surface. By May 1845, the Texas Navy was effectively no longer a Texas problem anyway, as a joint resolution of the United States Congress provided that upon annexation, Texas would cede to the U.S. "all public edifices, fortifications, barracks, ports and harbours, navy and navy-yards, docks, magazines, arms, armaments and all other property and means pertaining to the public defense."

As the waters claimed the vessels, inch by inch, former officers shuffled forward to claim meaningless commissions. In most cases, they wanted to parlay their Texas commissions into employment with the United States. President Anson Jones's war secretary, William G. Cooke, dismissed Brashear in March 1845, but John Grant Tod successfully lobbied for his long-awaited captain's commission, which President Jones backdated to June 23, 1840. By January 1846, the Texas Navy consisted of six commissioned officers, two midshipmen, and about two dozen unskilled laborers.

The drive for annexation moved quickly during 1845, and the U.S. Navy stepped up operations to cover coastal areas once defended by the Texas fleet. A squadron under Commodore Robert F. Stockton arrived at Galveston in May 1845, and on June 2, U.S. Navy Secretary George Bancroft ordered Commodore Stockton to patrol the Texas coast, being careful to avoid hostilities with Mexico while annexation was being negotiated. The following month, Bancroft informed Commodore David Conner that once Conner determined that the Texas annexation convention had voted to join the Union, he would be charged with defending Texas as he would any other part of the United States. For this mission, he could call upon the services of the forty-four-gun frigate *Potomac*, the twenty-gun sloops *Saratoga* and *St. Mary's*, the eighteen-gun *Falmouth*, the twelve-gun brig *Somers* and the ten-gun *Lawrence*. His squadron would soon be augmented by the steam frigates *Mississippi* and *Princeton*, as well as the sloop *John Adams* and the brig *Porpoise*. Conner would not be permitted to attack Mexico or dislodge forces north of the Rio Grande, but if Mexico declared war, he would be ordered to take Tampico and, if sufficiently strong, to capture San Juan d'Ullua, as the French had during the Pastry War of 1838.

All this meant that the Texas Navy would never again defend her homeland, and after Texas accepted the U.S. resolution annexing Texas on July 4, 1845, both the Texas War Department and the U.S. Department of the Navy made preparations to transfer the warships to the United States. On January 30, 1846, the Navy Secretary dispatched an engineer from the Bureau of Construction, Equipment & Repairs to inspect the Texas vessels in Galveston, and U.S. naval vessels took up anchorage off that strategic Texas port.

On February 19, 1846, the Republic lowered its national flag one last time in a bittersweet ceremony outside the log-hewn capital in Austin. With a flourish, President Anson Jones announced to the world, "The final act in this great drama is performed. The Republic of Texas is no more!" With his announcement, war with Mexico became a virtual certainty. The U.S. Navy began building a forward base in Texas for possible operations against Mexico.

On April 21, Commander Victor Randolph was dispatched to Galveston to assume command of Texas' naval assets. One of his first duties was to ascertain the cost of maintaining the warships and the best mode for disposing of them. Four days later, Gov. J. Pinckney Henderson ordered Lieutenant Tennison, "Comd'g Navy in ordinary," to turn everything over to Mr. Hiram G. Runnels, Galveston's port collector, who would act as agent for the United States government. This was the last executive order to the Texas Navy stated.

> Sir: — You will upon the receipt of this be informed that the Honorable H.G. Runnels is authorized on the part of the United States Government to secure all public property connected with the Navy of the Republic of Texas. You are therefore hereby required to hand over to him all vessels arms stores the Navy Yard and all buildings and other property connected with the Naval Service of our later Republic and take an inventory & his receipt for the same which you will return to this officer as soon as practicable.

Upon receipt of his orders, Lieutenant Tennison prepared a list of officers attached to the Texas Navy, evidently to facilitate their payment by the United States government. This handwritten roster included the following stalwarts:

John G. Tod	Post-Captain
Wm. C. Brashear	Commander
A.I. Lewis	Lieutenant
George C. Bunner	do.
Wm. A. Tennison	Lieut Comdg
J.F. Stephens	Purser
H.L. Garlick	Midshipman
C.I. Fayssoux	do.
Richmond Price (negro)	Steward
John Lewis (do.)	Boy

The final act of the Texas Navy played itself out on May 11, 1846, when Lieutenant Tennison officially transferred command of *Austin, Wharton, Archer,* and *San Bernard* to Mr. Runnels in a virtually unheralded ceremony. The *Telegraph and Texas Register*, the Texas Navy's most vocal supporter for ten years, scarcely took note of the event, remarking in passing on May 20, "On the morning of the 11th inst. the vessels of the Texian navy were delivered to the U.S. Commissioners, and at 12 M. the banner of the Lone Star was lowered, and the flag of the Union was hoisted to their mast heads." Commodore Moore was absent for this milestone, but in his 1853 letter to Senator James Pearce of Maryland, he recalled that a salute was fired by *Austin*'s battery, the Texas flag was run down, and the United States colors were hauled up in its place.

The warships were a sorry lot. A survey taken by the U.S. Navy's Bureau of Construction, Equipment and Repair recorded that *Wharton* was sunk in ten to twelve feet of water; it contained no reference to *Archer*'s armament, although she apparently strained under the weight of *Wharton*'s entire battery and six medium twelves transferred from *San Bernard*. On July 31, Commander Randolph wrote to Secretary Bancroft. "*Wharton* and *Archer* are utterly worthless (*Wharton* worm eaten and sunk) *Archer* rotten totally. Schooner *San Bernard* is but little better—very slightly built and much decayed. If sold they will yield, 'tis true, but little to the government but on the other hand if kept, they are now and they will continue to be a heavy expense to the country." *Austin* was the lone exception, passable for the moment, still mounting twenty guns, small arms, and the bulk of the Navy's possessions, according to Lieutenant Tennison's final inventory.

Charles Morris, chief of the Construction, Equipment and Repairs Bureau, advised Navy Secretary Bancroft to sell all the Texas warships. Bancroft concurred, except in the case of *Austin*, which was towed to Pensacola as a receiving ship at the end of June 1846. Commander Randolph promptly dismissed the bulk of the crew, keeping Garlick, Fayssoux and seven unidentified laborers as "ship keepers" from August 1 to December 1.

In all, it was a shameful end to a once-promising squadron. Most comparable warships lived much longer and fuller lives than those of Texas, due to the better care they received. Commodore Moore's former sloop *Boston* served in commission for twenty years; *Warren*, the sloop that seized *Invincible* in 1836, held her commission for nineteen; and *Ontario*, the sloop whose crew cheered the Texas squadron onward to Yucatán in 1843, served in the War of 1812 and completed her service in 1844, after serving twenty-nine years. By contrast, *Austin* was barely serviceable after four years, and by December 1846 she was probably no longer seaworthy. *Archer* went unused after her maiden voyage, and *Zavala* survived only one cruise. Only two ships of the Navy's 1840 fleet—*San Antonio* and *San Jacinto*—had been lost to causes other than neglect.

In September 1846, Secretary Bancroft's successor, John Mason, threw in the towel. He asked President Polk for permission to sell the crumbling carcasses of *Archer, Wharton,* and *San Bernard*. He wrote to Commander Randolph on September 19, "Your letter of the 5th inst. relative to the property of the late Navy of Texas now under your charge has been received, and application has been made to the President of the U.S. for authority to sell the vessels." On October 9, Polk approved Mason's request, and three days later, Mason ordered Randolph to remove all guns from the three vessels and sell them.

On November 30, the three former warships were sold at auction. *Archer*, still afloat, sold for $450, and *San Bernard*, which caused so much alarm in Veracruz in 1840, went for $150. The submerged *Wharton*, which with *Austin* threw back the most advanced warships in the world, fetched a mere fifty-five dollars.

The last trace of *Austin*—the pride of a nation—is found in two memoranda buried in the dusty files of the U.S. Navy's archives. The Pensacola station's commandant, William Latimer, reported that his early hopes for *Austin*'s use as a receiving ship had come to naught; she was leaking so badly that she could no longer be of service to her new government. The flagship's fate was recorded simply by the Navy Secretary, in his report to President Tyler dated November 1, 1848, in these words, "The sloop *Austin* has been broken up, being unworthy of repairs."

CHAPTER THIRTY-SEVEN

Flotsam and Jetsam

I ask [Senator Houston] to pause and consider whether he is not striking a fatal blow at some of [Texas'] most glorious achievements.
—Tennessee Senator James Jones, August 2, 1854

THE LEGACY THE REPUBLIC OF TEXAS LEFT for its naval officers was one of bitterness and despair. The full weight of frustration fell on ex-Commodore Moore, who began his struggle for vindication even before his court-martial, beginning with a thorough audit of his official and personal accounts. In April 1844, auditor Charles Mason reported to the government that Moore owed the Republic $50,875.36, assuming that the near-worthless exchequer notes Houston gave him in July 1842 were actually worth their face value, and disallowing "informal" vouchers such as third-party receipts used to avoid legal problems when recruiting in New York.

Given Commodore Moore's personal financing of the Republic's navy during its long, disheartening stay in New Orleans, he was unwilling to accept this patently erroneous conclusion. Shortly after annexation, he pressed the State of Texas to review his accounts, and in May 1846, the legislature passed a resolution requiring the Texas Comptroller to settle Moore's accounts once and for all. A committee of the state's House of Representatives reviewed the 1844 audit and concluded that the state owed Moore $11,398.54 for personal expenditures incurred on behalf of the Texas Navy, and another $11,725.54 in back pay from April 1839 to June 1843. The committee reported, "Far from censuring as extravagant the conduct of the commodore in supplying the navy with all the necessary means of bringing to an honorable conclusion the contest he was about engaging in, your committee are more disposed to applaud his efforts and admire the zeal manifested by that officer, directed, as it was, to the promotion of the country's glory." When all accounts were settled, the committee recommended that the Texas Legislature appropriate $26,510.41 to settle Moore's claims against the former Republic.

Further action had to wait until 1848, when a joint resolution approved in January reimbursed Commodore Moore in the amount of $11,398.36-1/2 for supplies he had purchased for the Navy, plus $15,202.06 to release Moore from creditors who supplied the Texas fleet. Another resolution in February gave Moore an additional $3,575.39 in backpay, and in April 1849 he received $9,190.17 in past salary, bringing his paycheck current through January 1, 1844. A final allowance of $5,290 was granted to Moore, but not until February 2, 1856—nearly thirteen years after his dismissal—"Provided the said Moore shall first file with the treasurer a full and final release against the Republic and the State of Texas for all demands."

While Commodore Moore was lobbying the Texas legislature for sums earned by him years earlier, he and a number of Texas Navy officers pressed the United States government to recognize them as officers in the U.S. Navy. Because the treaty of annexation called for the United States to acquire Texas's barracks, warships, armaments, and "means pertaining to the public defense" of the Republic, they reasoned that not only the war vessels, but the officers as well, should assume their rightful place in the navy of the United States.

Commander William Brashear filed a lawsuit, asking the courts to require Navy Secretary John Mason to compensate him as a U.S. Navy officer. The U.S. Supreme Court, in its 1848 decision *Brashear v. Mason*, concluded that the language of the May 1, 1845, law annexing Texas covered only property, not people, so that Brashear was not entitled to a job with the U.S. Navy. Besides, the court observed, Brashear's lawsuit was improperly directed against the Secretary of the Navy, who had no legal authority to pay anyone—that was the exclusive province of the secretary of the treasury.

Commodore Moore and others took the legislative route, petitioning Congress to induct them into the U.S. Navy at the ranks they held in Texas. Public opinion was generally favorable; the *New York Mirror* editorialized,

> For our part, we know and like the young Commodore, and should be pleased to see him enjoying his well earned rank in our navy. He has done brave service to Texas, and should we have fighting to do, would, we doubt not, keep his laurels green among the veteran commodores of our navy.

Despite the ironic support of Senator Sam Houston of Texas, who still despised Moore but was persuaded to help other Texas officers, such bills came and went between 1846 and 1849 with no result. All the while, Moore kept up a vigorous defense of his conduct as Texas's naval commander, producing a thirty-two-page pamphlet with the cumbersome title *A Brief Synopsis of the doings of the Texas Navy under the command of Com. E.W. Moore: together with his controversy with Gen. Sam Houston, President of* the *Republic of Texas; In which He Was Sustained by the Congress of That Country Three Different Sessions; by the Convention to form a State Constitution; and by the State Legislature, Unanimously.* Moore's *Brief Synopsis*, like *To the People of Texas*, was primarily a defense of his professional reputation and an attack on Sam Houston, both personally and politically, claiming among other things that Houston had "prostituted the high office which he filled."

In 1850, another petition signed by Moore and other Texas officers asked the House to admit them into the United States Navy at their respective ranks. The House Naval Affairs Committee supported the Texians, stating, "The spirit of this union, fairly embodied, would entitle the officers of the Texas navy to equal privileges with those of our own, and at the same time would subject them, in equal degree."

The committee report was as close as the former officers ever got to holding United States commissions. The U.S. officer corps, spurred into action by the committee report, fretted that inducted foreign officers would claim seniority in an already crowded ladder of advancement. A committee of three officers—Commanders Franklin Buchanan, Stephen Dupont, and George Magruder—led the charge against the western interlopers by publishing a forty-three-page pamphlet entitled *In Relation to the Claims of the Officers of the late Texas Navy*. Responsive pamphlets published by the Texas commanders and Commodore Moore only served to turn the discourse into a disjointed argument over Moore's performance as the Texian commander, and did little to further either side's cause.

By the early 1850s, Moore had become very bitter over the matter. His tirades against Sam Houston were intensely personal and contained so many veiled invitations to duels that the *New York Mirror* regretted that Moore "indulges in some bitter invectives against the ex-President, and seems savagely intent upon inciting that person to 'deeds of arms' which apparently, can alone satisfy his 'great revenge.'" Moore's editorials, pamphlets and letters denounced Houston as a criminal who has "violated almost every law, human and divine," and "has neither honor, courage or morality." He castigated Houston as "a man false to his country, false to his domestic relations, and false to his friends ... whose life has been a lie; a living deceit upon the worlds, corrupt and tainted in morals and body ... a man who has continued to be the recipient of honors he never won, of dangers he never shared, and of fame he never earned." In one letter to Houston, Moore tried to taunt the old warrior into a duel, writing, "I would willingly adopt another course, and demand of you that redress which one gentleman has a right to expect from another who has abused, vilified, and misrepresented him, as you have me on so many occasions, in public barrooms, in the streets, and even in the presence of ladies, but for the well-known fact that you have refused to render satisfaction to General Lamar, Judge Burnett, and Doctor Archer, for gross and flagrant acts of injustice which you have done to them."

Houston, for his part, ignored Moore's tirades, publicly at least, until 1854, when a published letter from Moore to Senator James Pearce of Maryland finally got his goat. The livid Houston rose on the Senate floor and delivered a lengthy speech "clarifying" some of Moore's "misstatements," savagely attacking his character and conduct. Claiming that Moore was guilty of embezzlement, fraud, insubordination, murder and treason, he trained his gift for sarcasm on the well-known incident at Campeche where Moore and Lieutenant Gray had ducked to escape a sixty-eight-pound Paixhan shell fired from *Guadalupe*. "It all resolves itself," he explained, "into dodging that sixty-two pound Paixhan shot. That is his most memorable exploit—the only one of note performed by him."

To the amusement of the Senate, he chortled, "Why, sir, Nelson had not half the address, or he never would have lost his arm; he never would have been presented to the world mutilated after the action of Trafalgar. He continued, "So, too, Charles XII of Sweden might have survived. Why, sir, he would have conquered Russia if he had possessed half the tact of the Texas commodore to perceive a Paixhan shot, and dodge it." Referring to Moore's offer of a duel, Houston mockingly protested, "Why, sir, for me to depreciate such a gallant gentleman in the presence of ladies, after his great feat of dodging cannon balls, would not be exactly clever on my part."

Houston's speech went on for thirteen pages of Senate transcript, accusing Moore of defrauding the widows of Commander Lothrop, Lieutenant Wilbur and Purser Wells; of cowardice before the Mexican Navy at Campeche; of serving Yucatán at the expense of Texas; and leaving the coast of Texas unprotected. In all of these things, Houston ignored key facts: that Yucatán had offered to pay for *Zavala*'s repairs; that a conquest of Yucatán was a prerequisite to an invasion of Texas in 1843; that Moore had informed the War Department in December 1842 that he was pursuing a renewed alliance with Yucatán; and that no Mexican warships had been sighted off the Texas coast while Moore was in New Orleans and Yucatán.

Never content to let someone else have the last word, Moore turned to Senator James Jones of Tennessee, who rose in Moore's defense two weeks later on the Senate floor. Drawing extensively from sources provided by Moore, Senator Jones refuted Houston's charges of embezzlement, fraud, and murder. Jones, apparently disgusted with what other senators must have viewed as a petty squabble over the two men's places in history, concluded, "It is true, sir, that the gallant conduct of the commodore may not have equaled the grandeur and the splendor of Sincinius; it is true that he may not have his untold fleets in his wake; but I am prepared to say that for his deeds of gallantry, and nobleness, and daring, by the witness of the honorable Senator himself, he stands vindicated before the world." At the end of the day, all that the personal vendetta between Texas's greatest army commander and Texas's greatest naval commander accomplished was the derailment of the move to incorporate Texas Navy officers into U.S. service.

The squabbling over the officers's fate went on for two more years. The Texas Legislature repeatedly urged its representatives in Washington to support incorporation of naval officers, who dwindled in number as the years went by. In 1857, Congress settled the matter once and for all, passing a measure on March 3 that awarded the officers five years' pay at the salaries of corresponding U.S. Navy officers, in return for "a full relinquishment and renunciation of all claims" of further compensation or position in the United States Navy. In other words, each of the three branches of the federal government had spent enough time considering the issue; Texas Navy officers would get five years' pay, and that was the end of it.

Only a few officers benefited from this legislation, including Commodore Moore, whom Houston had lobbied hard to exclude; Lieutenants Gray, Cummings, Tennison, Snow, and Oliver; pursers Stephens and Hurd; and the widow of Lieutenant Lewis, who died before his claims were settled. Midshipmen, who hung on into the next century, evidently were not covered by this act, although one middie, George Fuller, did prosecute a claim under the 1857 act in the early twentieth century.

As the post-Republic years wore on, a veil of obscurity began to cast a shadow over the once-mighty naval officers. A few went on to adventures elsewhere. Calender I. Fayssoux, the last midshipman of the Texas Navy, joined William Walker's filibuster army in Nicaragua. He became the commander of the Nicaraguan Navy—blowing up the entire Costa Rican Navy, which consisted of a single brig—and saw action off Cuba. Lieutenant Armstrong I. Lewis also joined the filibusterers, commanding a vessel, the *Creole*, on an expedition to Cuba. Lieutenant William Ross Postell worked briefly in the slave trade, then became the first mate of the Confederate privateer *Jefferson Davis* during the Civil War.

Several former officers served the United States government, although none commanded a man-of-war. Lieutenant Alfred Gray piloted transport vessels for the Union during the Civil War. Lieutenant Charles Snow joined the U.S. Coastal Survey, while Lieutenant Tennison went into the U.S. Revenue Service, the precursor of the Coast Guard. *San Bernard's* Midshipman Matthew Kintzing, who had left Texas service in 1841, became an officer in the United States Marine Corps, retiring in 1879 at the rank of colonel.

A number of officers went into civilian pursuits. John Grant Tod and Gen. Sidney Sherman founded the Buffalo Bayou, Brazos & Colorado Railway Company, Texas's first railroad. Tod also helped construct the Galveston customs house just before the Civil War, and ran a beef-packing business that supplied food to the Confederate Army. He died in 1877 in Harrisburg, Texas, leaving a son who later served as Texas's secretary of state, and assisted Dr. Alex Dienst at the turn of the century in compiling the first comprehensive history of the Texas Navy.

Purser Norman Hurd, whose sword may be seen at the Rosenberg Library in Galveston, became a customs officer at Galveston, dying in 1870 at the ripe old age of eighty-five. His son, Lt. James Gardner Hurd of the schooner *Brutus*, went on to become Galveston's manager for the Morgan Lines, a Galveston city councilman, and the inspector for the port of Galveston until his death in 1893.

Two civilian associates developed notable businesses of their own. Commissioner James Morgan became a wealthy land developer, cattle rancher and promoter of the Houston Ship Channel, dying in 1866. Port Collector Gail Borden, the man Sam Houston repeatedly ordered to support the Navy without giving him funds to do so, drew up fanciful plans to air condition the City of Galveston to eradicate yellow fever, then went on to form the condensed milk company that bears his name to this day.

But most of the Texas Navy's band of brothers simply lived and died with little or no record of their lives after leaving the remarkable navy they once served.

An exception, of course, was Edwin Ward Moore, whose exploits ensured that he would never go unnoticed. After his court-martial, Commodore Moore courted Emma Matilda Stockton Cox, the widow of a U.S. Navy lieutenant, and a distant cousin of Commodore Robert Stockton. The two were married in Philadelphia in 1849, and spent their years traveling between Washington, New York, and Philadelphia. Moore also spent a good deal of time in Austin, where he lobbied for legislative support for his claims, and in Galveston, where he and partner C. B. Cluskey contracted to build a customs house, the city's first federal building. (Never one to leave a grudge behind, Senator Houston lobbied against Moore's getting the contract.)

While work on the customs house dragged on for years, Moore spent many days and nights in Galveston as a local celebrity, shooting billiards, smoking cigars, and regaling visitors with stories of his adventures at sea. One can imagine Moore in these later years strolling down Galveston's Strand. Pausing, hands in his pockets tucked beneath a growing belly, chomping on a fat cigar as he squinted out at the old navy's anchorage. On a clear day, he must have felt as old as the sea when he stood in the warm gulf breeze, looking out at the harbor he surveyed, lived on, and defended during those heady days when Texas was a country, a sovereign nation, whose pride shone like a star through the dirty beggar's cloak it wore for ten eventful years.

For all his gentlemanly challenges, the only duel the feisty Moore fought was not with Sam Houston, but with a relative of his former benefactor, President Mirabeau Lamar. Lamar, it seems, had a cousin, C. A. L. Lamar, who ran a brisk slave trade from his sloop *Wanderer*. When Moore was called to testify against the younger Lamar on charges of importing slaves, the infuriated cousin publicly insulted Moore, who challenged the man to a duel. Their "interview" took place on May 24, 1860, at Screven's Ferry, just outside of Savannah, Georgia. Both men missed, a not uncommon occurrence in the age of dueling, and both men agreed that gentlemanly honor had been satisfied.

During the Civil War, Commodore Moore apparently lived in the north and took no part in the conflict, notwithstanding his family's Virginia roots. Emma's family lived in Charlottesville, at a farmhouse that would become Gen. George Custer's headquarters during Sheridan's Shenandoah raid in 1864.

In his last years, Commodore Moore's creative urges struggled for expression. The man who improvised explosive shells, water pumps, and countless shipboard expedients passed his time working on a revolutionary steam engine that would represent the next leap forward in motive efficiency. Having outlived Sam Houston, who died in 1863, Moore now seemed happier; the demon from Texas was no more.

Moore's last invention, begun in New York, was never completed. On Wednesday, October 4, 1865, he left his beloved Emma for work, announcing as he bade her good-bye, "Next week we expect to astonish the world." In the afternoon, he was brought home by some friends, speechless, the victim of apoplexy. He died the next day, and was taken to the cemetery of First Presbyterian Church of Germantown, Pennsylvania, for burial. The *New York Herald* eulogized the fallen commander. "He was a stranger to fear, and modest and unpretending, as all brave men are."

CHAPTER THIRTY-EIGHT

Ghosts and Graves

If I had a boat/I'd go out on the ocean.
—Lyle Lovett, 1987

IN NOVEMBER 1986 THE EARTH grudgingly surrendered the corpse of the Texas Navy's most advanced fighting ship. The National Underwater & Marine Agency (NUMA), a non-profit nautical archeology group founded by bestselling novelist Clive Cussler, located the hull and boilers of the steamship *Zavala* in the last place a person would look for a shipwreck—under a parking lot on Galveston Island.

The story of *Zavala*'s recovery, which formed a chapter of Cussler's 1996 book *The Sea Hunters*, is an object lesson: where the Texas Navy is concerned, things are rarely as they seem. We last left *Zavala* rotting on the beach on Galveston Island—her stacks broken, her engines stripped—offered for sale towards the end of 1843. In the following years, the ship sank deeper into the mud alongside Bean's Wharf on the north side of the island, just off what is now Twenty-ninth Street. By 1862, as the battle for the U.S.S. *Harriet Lane* raged on Galveston's waters, *Zavala* had sunk below the surface, a single smokestack warning vessels of her resting place. The great hurricane that struck Galveston in 1900, along with the natural buildup of sand on Galveston's lee shore, extended the shoreline so that by the late twentieth century, *Zavala* lay deep beneath dry ground.

Most local historians had long since written off *Zavala* as lost to the ages, but in the mid-1980s, researchers from NUMA managed to pinpoint *Zavala*'s location from an old drawing of the battle for *Harriet Lane*. Superimposing old harbor surveys upon modern street maps, Cussler and his team tentatively identified *Zavala*'s grave under a parking lot for a grain elevator on Twenty-ninth Street. Using a gradiometer, a core drill, and a great deal of patience, the team tapped core samples from the ground beneath the parking lot. On the thirty-seventh try, the volunteers recovered a sample containing seventeen inches of wood covered with copper plate.

This finding, along with samples of coal from a steamer's bunker, sent a wave of excitement through the NUMA crew. After obtaining permission from J. Barto Arnold III, the Texas antiquities commissioner, Cussler's volunteers unearthed the grave of *Zavala*'s hull and boilers. The site was photographed, marked, and filled in to prevent damage to the old warship until it can be properly removed and studied. (Even on land, Nature would not permit *Zavala*'s tomb to be disturbed without the obligatory soaking of her hunters; the location and excavation phases were marked by heavy, cold rains.) A number of abortive attempts to raise funds to exhume *Zavala* have been made, but none have been successful enough to finance a proper recovery, and the steamer lies underground to this day.

Zavala has been the only vessel recovered from the legendary Texas Navy. But others are out there, and investigators are getting close.

Brutus's last trip was a short one, as she limped home from the Galveston Bar in 1837 after a failed attempt to assist the besieged *Invincible*. Her broken rudder and broken commanders kept her stuck in port until Racer's Storm swept over in October, two months later, throwing her onto the beach near Williams Wharf.

NUMA researchers believe they have pinpointed *Brutus*'s final resting place. Researcher Mike Davis of the Nineteenth Century Living History Association discovered an 1884 report describing a harbor-dredging near Williams Wharf that allegedly uncovered two of the schooner's guns and a section of her frame. According to Davis, *Brutus*'s wreckage now waits for future archeologists at the foot of Twenty-fourth Street, at the end of Pier 23, under a warehouse. In 1967 one of the two cannon, a long eighteen-pounder, was recovered; the gun is now on display at Galveston's Texas Seaport Museum.

The grave of *Invincible*, for its part, remains a mystery, but divers are getting closer. Cussler and a NUMA team first began searching for her on the Galveston shore between 1986 and 1988, locating several possible wrecks, but no positive results. Undaunted, NUMA surveyed the waters off Galveston repeatedly between 1994 and September 1996, using divers, helicopters, boats, and a sophisticated array of scanning equipment. The archeologists found a number of wreckage sites buried underwater on a giant clay shelf that encompasses the Galveston shore, but the closest match is probably a clipper from a later period, according to one of the dive masters on the surveys. Another wreck, located in 1998, turned up only a small number of objects that have been recovered, and may provide some answers in the future. Presently, NUMA is planning a more tightly focused survey of the most promising wrecks.

Undoubtedly, the salvage efforts that Commander Boylan, Lieutenant Wright, and others undertook unwittingly robbed present-day divers of at least some clues to the wreck's location, although researchers disagree as to the scope of the salvage operation. Archeologists today debate the exact location of the wreck, but as underwater scanning technology progresses, the recovery of *Invincible* is only a matter of time.

At this writing, researchers have only cold trails for four other vessels. *Austin* was last seen at the Pensacola Navy Yard, having been broken up in 1848. *San Jacinto* lies off the shoals of Las Arcas, although she was probably too thoroughly salvaged by the marooned crew over the next three months to be recognizable. *Independence* last sailed to Mexico, having joined the Mexican squadron after her capture in April 1837. Mexican naval records may provide clues to her final end, although these have not yet been located, and the loss of valuable naval records at Mexico City's national archives during the 1985 earthquake makes the search for her fate a daunting one. *Liberty*, formerly the privateer *William Robbins*, was sold to her creditors in the summer of 1836, and was probably put back into merchant service; her trail undoubtedly will be picked up someday by other enterprising researchers, but where that trail will lead is anybody's guess.

San Bernard, *Wharton*, and *Archer* will probably never be found. These three vessels were most likely salvaged for their timbers, although the submerged *Wharton* may have been left where she lay. The fate of the receiving brig *Potomac* was never recorded, even by Texas's secretary of the navy, who had only *Potomac* to oversee for nearly two years, and who had plenty of time for making reports and keeping records. Similarly, the last record of the harbor boat *Louisville*, or *Striped Pig*, was that one of her masts was sunk off the eastern end of Galveston Island as a marker for passing vessels. Thus, the corpses of these five Republic of Texas vessels may be lost to the ages. But the patient determination of nautical archeologists from NUMA, Texas A&M University at Galveston, and other underwater research centers should not be underestimated. Vessels written off as lost for all time may yet, like *Zavala*, be found where we least expect them.

EPILOGUE

The Verdict

The [Texas Navy] had done so much to secure and maintain [Texas] independence, and to elevate the character of the country at home and abroad....

—Texas Governor P. H. Bell, 1850

How has history treated the navy of the Republic of Texas? Much like the old steamer *Zavala*, the Texas Navy was lauded by its advocates as strategically vital and ridiculed by its detractors as a farcical waste of money. But as the years went by, the Navy, like the once-proud steamer, sank slowly into the mud of fading memories and confused and biased reminiscences. Today, the Texas Navy is little more than an obscure bit of trivia from the Gilbert & Sullivan-like comic opera that was the Republic of Texas.

But the accomplishments of these two little fleets made their contemporaries take notice. Lt. Raphael Semmes of the U.S. Navy, who would go on to become the Confederacy's greatest sea captain, wrote in his 1854 work *Service Afloat and Ashore in the Mexican War*,

> History will bear me out, when I affirm, that next to General Houston, the hero of San Jacinto, Texas owes more to Commodore Moore than to any other man who has figured in the drama of her revolution.... He maintained a discipline in his squadron, which none but a man of firmness and courage could have maintained, and caused the flag of Texas not only to be feared by its enemies, but respected by neutrals.

Another tribute came from a gathering of society women of the City of Galveston, who in 1845 passed the following quaint but heartfelt resolution of thanks.

> Although we feel it does not become us to meddle, in any manner, in public affairs, yielding to the "lords of creation" the right to applaud or censure the

wisdom or folly of political management, we yet claim it as our peculiar prerogative to bestow thanks and applause on the gallant and brave.... The bravery and gallantry of the Commodore, his officers and men, and the wise and prompt action of Colonel Morgan in sanctioning the sailing of *two vessels* to the coast of Yucatan, deserve and have our most deepest and lasting gratitude.

Perhaps the most widely-distributed tribute of the nineteenth century came from a grateful Sam Colt, whose struggling firearms business was helped immeasurably by an order of 180 new Patent Revolving pistols and a like number of carbines in 1839. Colt had a scene from the Battle of Campeche engraved onto the cylinder of one of his most successful revolvers of all time. This weapon, which was manufactured in the thousands and used extensively by both armies during the Civil War, became known to history as the Colt 1851 "Navy model."

In 1876, the Texas legislature honored three of the Texas Navy's leaders by naming three newly-formed counties in the Texas Panhandle after Edwin Moore, Robert Potter, and S. Rhoads Fisher. Texas historian Billy Bob Crim has remarked that it is one of the ironies of Texas history that the counties named for leaders of the Texas Navy should be placed about as far away from the Gulf of Mexico as Texas's wide borders will permit.

In later years, historians have generally been kind, particularly those with a first-hand appreciation of military operations. Brig. Gen. Theodore Roosevelt, Jr., son of president, assistant navy secretary, and naval historian Teddy Roosevelt, wrote

> [S]ome of history's greatest achievements are not given due credit for their influence on events because the spotlight was playing on some [other] actors at the moment. The halfback who tears down the field with the football tucked under his arm and makes the touchdown gets the headlines. The guard who opens up the hole which makes the run possible never gets a sentence. This has been the facts of the Texas Navy.... Without it, there would probably have been no Lone Star Republic and possibly the State of Texas would still be part of Mexico.

Adm. Chester W. Nimitz, commander of the U.S. Pacific Fleet during World War II, frequently wore the "anchor and star" buttons of the Texas Navy on his admiral's uniform, and remarked in 1944 that with the help of *Independence, Invincible,* and *Brutus,* Commodore Hawkins "controlled the sea approaches to Texas, blocked reinforcements to Santa Anna, and contributed in large part to the many victories which beset the Mexican Army in its long overland march to the Alamo, Goliad, and San Jacinto Battles of 1836.

So it was that Texas established a naval tradition to stand alongside its brilliant military record achieved on land."

During the twentieth century, works by Alex Dienst (1909), Jim Dan Hill (1936), and Tom Henderson Wells (1960) have formed the bedrock of serious scholarship on the Texas Navy's history. The modern U.S. Navy also paid homage to Texas's naval tradition with a transport vessel named *Austin*, a missile frigate and a light carrier both christened *San Jacinto*, an aircraft escort vessel named *Archer*, and the World War II Liberty ship SS *Edwin W. Moore*. On land, the Texas Navy Association, established by Gov. Price Daniel in 1958, has kept the memory of the Republic's seafarers alive through its award-winning website and its educational programs.

Aside from these fleeting references, the Texas Navy was mostly forgotten. It was never as large as the fleets of the other western powers, and it was a source of financial drain and frequent political embarrassment for the Republic. It also was the target of wrathful politicians who tried to starve out the "pirate navy" while it was alive and contemptuously ignored it after it died.

But another, more fundamental reason for its obscurity is discernable through the shifting haze of history. The Texas Navy was a victim of its own success. An invasion arrested hundreds of miles away commands no immediate attention, and deprives its actors of the "backs to the wall" drama that begets legends. If the Japanese Navy's task force had been crippled by U.S. submarines in November 1941, America would have chalked up the engagement as a victory—and an act of war—but the battle would not have been forever burned into the American psyche as a turning point in our nation's destiny. If foreign terrorists had been apprehended at airports on September 11, 2001, the country would have taken notice, but the nation would not have been galvanized into aggressive action.

In the same vein, neither the Texas Navy's defeat of centralist forces in Yucatán in May 1843 nor the *Invincible*'s attack on Mexico's relief operation in April 1836 involved any heroic "last stand" gallantry that the Texas public could easily perceive and appreciate. The Navy ignored this axiom of drama, and as a result could claim no Alamo (a glorious defeat), or San Jacinto (a glorious victory). Instead, the Navy, at a minimal cost to its nation, won the kind of strategic victory that makes these more colorful deeds of arms unnecessary.

The price of such economy, such decisiveness, and such professionalism, is glory. And so the Texas Navy, for all it did to shape the history of Texas, and thereby the American West, may never share in the laurels worn by its fellow patriots.

APPENDIX A

The Texas Navy and The San Jacinto Campaign

THE MINOR ENGAGEMENT OFF the Rio Grande mouth on April 3, 1836, received little official note during the Texas Revolution; only four fleeting references to it appear in the *Papers of the Texas Revolution* (three Texian and one Mexican), and fewer than a dozen articles in contemporary Mexican, Texas, and New Orleans newspapers refer to the incident. But regardless of how important *Invincible*'s brush with *Bravo, Correo Segundo,* and *Pocket* was viewed at the time, it very likely prevented the Mexican Army from continuing its drive into East Texas—a campaign that would probably have driven the Texians at least as far as the Neches River, if not across the Sabine into Louisiana, and snuffed out the forty-five-day-old republic.

Two weeks after the *Bravo* engagement, the forward elements of the Mexican Army were defeated at San Jacinto. But Sam Houston's triumph was militarily no more decisive than the Mexican victory at the Alamo; a second San Jacinto, had there been one, probably would have ended in a Mexican victory, and with it, the destruction of the Republic. According to José Enrique de la Peña, a staff officer in Santa Anna's army, after San Jacinto, Gen. Vicente Filisola had 1,500 men under his direct command, including four cannon, while Gen. Antonio Gaona commanded 900 men plus the sapper battalion, additional pickets, and sixty to eighty horses. (De la Peña 135-36) Gaona's men, on the road to Nacogdoches, had already been recalled, and joined Filisola around April 23. (Filisola to Tornel, April 28, 1836, in Filisola, *Evacuation*, 37-38; Dimmick 49) Gen. José Urrea had 200 infantry, four guns and 150 horses at Columbia, all within an easy two-day march of Filisola's camp. (De la Peña 135-36) Indeed, the only significant Mexican force not within easy reach of the San Jacinto theater was the 1,000-man garrison under Gen. Juan Andrade at San Antonio. (De la Peña, 135) All told, Filisola could have mustered at least 2,810 men, eight guns, and some 200 horses, to Houston's roughly 900 men, sixty horses, and three cannon (the "Twin Sisters" and Santa Anna's captured brass eight-pounder). (Hardin 209) Other sources place as many as 3,315 Mexican troops at Filisola's disposal, including 1,400 men, five guns, and 87 horses in Filisola's main body; 700 men under Gaona, and 1,165 men, three guns and 220 horses under Urrea at Columbia. (Dimmick 8, 34-35,

49, 62, 86) Houston's strength also would have been reduced by the number necessary to guard some 600 prisoners taken at San Jacinto, a minimum of fifty men. (Rusk to Houston, 23 April 1836, quoted in Haley 154) Even ignoring the need to guard 600 prisoners, on April 25 Filisola held a 3-to-1 advantage over Houston in overall strength, an 8-to-3 advantage in artillery, and a 3-to-1 advantage in cavalry. (Once the battle was over, Mexico's 200 lancers would have been employed running down the retreating Texians to prevent them from regrouping). The Mexican regulars also had a qualitative edge over their Texas counterparts in terms of discipline and experience. (Hardin and Pohl 275-76) Filisola's soldiers, of course, were at some disadvantage in terms of morale, given the long march and the capture of their leader, but in battle this kind of loss can be turned into a rallying point; at San Jacinto, the loss of the popular Fannin, Travis, Bowie, and Crockett soon gave way to cries of "Remember Goliad!" and "Remember the Alamo!"

Now, how did the Texas Navy affect the balance of power after San Jacinto?

If the planned relief expedition from Matamoros had been successful, Filisola would have received at least another couple hundred fresh men, plus food, equipment, maps, and officers crammed aboard the *Pocket, John M. Bandel, New Castle,* and to a lesser extent, the warships *Bravo* and *Correo Segundo*. Had these vessels landed near Galveston (an option denied by the Texas Navy's presence there), or even at the mouth of the Brazos, the ratio of Mexican to Texian forces would have exceeded 3-to-1, which was probably enough to drive back Houston's force and march upon the civilian leadership at Galveston. To be sure, Houston's men were in high spirits after their victory; they were, on balance, better marksmen, and they were receiving small numbers of reinforcements from the United States almost daily. (Haley 156-58) But using De la Peña's numbers, a six-day rest by Filisola would have allowed Filisola to concentrate his troops in overwhelming strength, and there is little reason to believe that the surprise Houston achieved at San Jacinto (the exclusive result of Santa Anna's personal carelessness and overconfidence) would have repeated itself with Filisola, who was now on notice that the Texians were not to be underestimated.

Why, then, did Filisola not attack? His writings, and those of his contemporaries, provide three explanations. First, he lacked the food and supplies to continue the offensive. Filisola makes a great deal of his army's tired, underfed condition in his dispatches and memoirs. These explanations have been debated by De la Peña, General Urrea, and others, and it appears that at least Urrea's troops at Columbia may have obtained adequate food from the inhabitants of the town. (Filisola to Tornel, 14 May 1836, in *Evacuation*, 40, 44; De la Peña 141-42; Dimmick 52, 61-62; Hardin 216) But if Filisola's assessment of the condition of his main force is to be believed (or more to the point, if Filisola believed it at the time), then the appearance of *Bravo, Correo Segundo, John M. Bandel, New Castle,* and *Pocket* in mid to late April, loaded down with food, fresh troops, and supplies, should have easily given him the necessary means to march the relatively short distance from the Brazos to the Louisiana border. As it happened, the surviving Mexican ships were delayed by easterly winds, and were therefore not ready to sail until after April 28, three days after Filisola began his retreat from east Texas (Tornel to Santa Anna, 28 April 1836, PTR) *Pocket*, with its supplies, maps, officers familiar with Texas, and other intelligence, was of course out of the picture entirely *Invincible* thus affected the strategic picture on land by depriving Filisola of these reinforcements and supplies, and by giving him political cover for returning to Mexico.

A second possible explanation for Filisola's retreat is that he may have overestimated the size of Houston's army. After all, he would not expect undisciplined colonists to overcome 1,200 soldiers led by the "Napoleon of the West" unless they were present in overwhelming numbers. (Dimmick 17, noting exaggerated reports of Houston's strength) But this rationale breaks down if additional forces were placed unjder Filisola's command east of the Brazos. Assuming Filisola feared that he was facing not nine hundred insurgents, or even twice that number, but two thousand men, he still would hold a nearly 1.5-to-1 advantage if his 2,800-man force had been increased by a few hundred, to say nothing of the fact that a number of Houston's men would be preoccupied guarding and moving six hundred Mexican prisoners. Furthermore, Filisola knew from interrogations of Texas prisoners that Houston had somewhere around 800 men, and that the whole of the opposition forces in Texas did not exceed 1,200. (De la Peña 136) In either case, the addition of fresh men from Matamoros would have given Filisola an impetus to fight a second Battle of San Jacinto.

A related factor weighing on Filisola's mind was Texas naval supremacy in the campaign theater. In his May 14 dispatch to Mexico City, he noted that the three steamers and several schooners the Texians fielded could have easily carried troops up the Brazos River, attacked his army's right flank and rear guard, and defeated the small detachments at Copano, Goliad, and Matagorda. At the time, these latter detachments were isolated, since the swollen Brazos and Colorado Rivers would have made communications with the main army impossible. (Filisola to Tornel, 14 May 1836, in Filisola, *Evacuation*, 41)

Finally, Filisola may have evacuated out of concern for Santa Anna's safety. De la Peña rightly points out that the better way to rescue the former commander would have been to march against Houston and, at a minimum, negotiate from a position of strength, rather than abandon Santa Anna, Cós, Almonte, and the rest to their fates. (De la Peña 137) Any number of historians have also pointed out that Santa Anna's orders to retreat did not legally bind Filisola after April 21, since time-honored military tradition (well understood by Santa Anna, Sam Houston, President Burnet, and President Jackson) dictates that a general's authority ceases once he is taken prisoner. Certainly Filisola was under no illusion that Santa Anna's orders were effective when issued from behind Texas lines.

The most likely conclusion is that Filisola's decision to retreat to San Antonio, and thence to the Rio Grande, was a combination of underconfidence in his army, an exaggerated view of Houston's forces, and a reluctance to jeopardize Mexico's chief magistrate. At a minimum, the first two excuses for departing Texas could have been addressed by timely reinforcements and supplies from Matamoros, and these reinforcements could very well have given Generals Ramirez y Sesma, Gaona, Woll, Urrea, and others—many of whom expressed their disgust with the retreat—the courage to demand that Filisola press forward when they met in Filisola's headquarters tent on the night of April 25. This would leave Filisola with only one reason for quitting Texas—Santa Anna's safety—and this rationale was so unpersuasive that Filisola abandoned it as a legitimate justification for bringing his army home.

If Filisola had attacked Houston and had driven him from the field, the question then becomes whether the United States would have underwritten the success of the Texas Revolution with its army. President Jackson had long coveted Texas, and had, albeit without conviction, pressed a claim to Texas lands as far as the Neches River, a tributary of Lake Sabine, on the basis of an alleged scrivener's error in the Florida Treaty of 1819. By the eve of the Texas Revolution, Jackson considered the land between the Neches and Sabine Rivers to be "neutral territory," and Houston believed Old Hickory would defend the "Neches Strip." (Barker, "Jackson's Neches Claim," 259-60, 266-67) On April 25, 1836, Jackson authorized Gen. Edmund P. Gaines, commander of the U.S. forces in the southwest, to march into Texas as far as Nacogdoches, if necessary, to protect U.S. territory against "Indian depredations" or violations of United States territory by either belligerent. (Garrison 88) General Gaines, for his part, appeared to Texians at the time to be perfectly content to march into Texas on terms favoring the settlers. (Barker, "Jackson's Neches Claim," 267; Hardin 177; Haley 156-57) Gaines called out state forces from Louisiana, Tennessee, Mississippi, and Alabama, and actually marched some of his men to Nacogdoches in June 1836, over a month after Filisola recrossed the Rio Nueces. (Gaines to Governors, 8 April 1836, in H.R. Exec. Docs., 25th Cong., No. 351, 771)

However, moving into "neutral" territory between the Sabine and Neches Rivers was one thing; invading what was by all accounts Mexican territory in April 1836 was entirely different, and it was unlikely that President Jackson would have authorized a naked territory grab for Texas, no matter what his personal feelings of Manifest Destiny. In his comprehensive biography of Andrew Jackson, Professor Robert V. Remini recounts Jackson's unwillingness to acquire Texas through any means that smacked of illegality. He repeatedly counseled his ambassador to Mexico, Col. Anthony Butler, to avoid bribery or other unsavory means when seeking a treaty of annexation. Remini also describes Jackson's uncharacteristic concern with world opinion, and the verdict of history over the Texas issue if he dared violate the Treaty of Florida by crossing the Sabine/Neches. (R. Jones to Gaines, 11 April 1836, in H. R. Exec. Docs., 25th Cong., 2nd Sess., 351, 766; Remini 354-55, 359) To underscore his caution, Jackson's orders to Gaines expressly forbade him from capturing Mexican territory. (Fehrenbach 237; Remini 351) Jackson prepared orders to Gaines allowing more aggressive action on April 25, but whether these orders would have reached Gaines in time to influence events is questionable. (Barker, "Jackson's Neches Claim," 270) Jackson had good political reasons for trepidation: the abolitionist North, led by John Quincy Adams, was ardently opposed to any extension of slavery through territorial expansion in the southwest, and even southern Democrats as a whole were reluctant to stir up a hornet's nest when the issue was put before them in 1837. (Remini 360-61) Jackson therefore would have been unlikely to force the divisive issue upon the Union in early 1836 and potentially split the country asunder, or at least cripple the Democrats' hold on the country during an election year.

Furthermore, as a military matter, the United States lacked the forces to drive deep into Texas, at least at the outset. It should be remembered that the entire U.S. Army consisted of only 8,000 men on the eve of war with Mexico in 1846, and in June 1836 General Gaines commanded only 1,600 men, spread out in the territory south of the Arkansas River, with no cavalry to provide vital reconnaissance. (Gaines to Secretary of War, 7 June 1836, in H. R. Exec. Docs., 25th Cong., 351, 788) Even to muster this small number, Gaines would have had to send orders to strip the territory of all soldiers—including those areas subject to Indian incursions—and concentrate them in Natchitoches, Louisiana, before crossing the Sabine into Texas. This clearly could not be done before Filisola had forced a battle that either defeated Houston or drove him to Galveston or western Louisiana. Over the next several months, Camp Sabine's numbers swelled to a full infantry regiment (the Seventh), twelve companies of infantry from the Third and Sixth regiments, three companies of the First Dragoons, and an artillery train, but those would not be in place until November. (Crimmins 298) While the United States probably would have defeated Mexico in a full-scale, drawn-out war, and undoubtedly would have swallowed up more than just the land east of the Neches, the balance of forces in late April 1836 would have favored Mexico's *Ejercito de Operaciones* if she were reinforced with the troops marshaled at Matamoros, at least long enough to drive the Texians out of the country and make it much more difficult to justify invading what was in theory and in fact part of Mexico.

Given the political volatility of 1836, it is also unlikely that Gaines's force would have become a tripwire to a Mexican-American War of 1836. When Gaines marched into Nacogdoches briefly in June, he was severely reprimanded by President Jackson, who for political reasons derided the Texians' Declaration of Independence as "a rash and premature act," the following December, adding, "Our neutrality must be faithfully maintained." (Fehrenbach 237; Barker 805; Remini 359-60) Even in 1846, with Manifest Destiny pressing against the southwest like a surging tide, only the Mexican movements into Texas—bona fide U.S. territory by this time—presented a *casus belli* sufficient to send Gen. Winfield Scott into Mexico.

Of course, this is all speculative. There was no second battle of San Jacinto, and the Republic of Texas muddled on for nearly ten years, annexing itself to the United States and triggering a war that bequeathed the United States the land between the Sabine River and San Francisco Bay. But in 1836, Texas was in such a precarious position that the history of Texas and, by extension, that of the United States, could have been dramatically altered had an obscure Rhode Island sea captain not fired on the warship *Bravo* that bright April morning of 1836.

APPENDIX B

Glossary of Selected Naval Terms

NAUTICAL TERMINOLOGY FROM the nineteenth century is frequently hard to fathom (no pun intended), and the following terms are provided for the benefit of those twenty-first century lubbers who understandably could not tell a "spanker" from a "cathead" or know where to go to find "abaft."

Historians of the Age of Sail may quibble with some of the definitions listed here. More than likely, this is because generally accepted English and American terms became "Texanized" when used by the Lone Star's naval officers, just as American "English" sounds at times foreign to inhabitants of the British Isles (and vice-versa). It is also because authorities disagree on the exact meaning of words such as "hermaphrodite brig," and these terms evolved and mutated over the three centuries of "modern" sailing navies.

This appendix is not intended to be an exhaustive glossary—it is simply my best shot at defining some of the terms used in this book, to add a bit of convenience. For something comprehensive, refer to works such as Dean King's *Sea of Words* or, for purists, William Falconer's *Universal Dictionary of the Marine*.

Aft: The rear portion of a vessel. If you are going towards the rear of a ship, then you are going **abaft**. (If the ship is moving backwards, it is going **aback**.)

Amidships: The middle section of the ship.

Athwart: Across a vessel, perpendicular to the *keel*.

Barque (or **bark**): A sailing vessel with three or more *masts*, the *aft* mast being *fore-and-aft rigged* and the other *masts* being *square-rigged*. A barque is technically a *ship*. If the *sloop-of-war Austin* had a *fore-and-aft rigged mizzenmast*, she would be a barque.

Beam: Timbers running perpendicular to the length of a vessel. Also, the width of the vessel at its greatest point. Also, the portion of the hull *amidships*. A ship off the *San Jacinto*'s *starboard* beam would be a ship that a sailor could spot by going foreward to the middle of the ship and looking to the right.

Bow: The foremost portion of a vessel's hull.

Bowsprit: The long, mast-like *spar* that angles forward from the *bow* of a vessel. The bowsprit holds *fore-and-aft rigged* sails such as the *jib* and *fore* staysail.

Brig: A vessel, smaller than a ship, with two *masts*, both of which are *square-rigged*. It also has a *fore-and-aft rigged* sail extending from the *mainmast* behind a *square-rigged* mainsail. Not to be confused with a **brigantine**, which also carries two masts but carries a *fore-and-aft rigged* mainsail. (A close cousin of the brigantine is the **hermaphrodite brig**, which has all *foremast* sails *square-rigged* and all *mainmast* sails—both *topsail* and *mainsail—fore-and-aft* rigged.) Brigs, which typically carried up to sixteen guns, were used extensively by the Mexican Navy, in contrast to the Texas Navy, which tended to rely upon *schooners*. The sixteen-gun Mexican brig *Libertador* and the sixteen-gun Texas brig *Wharton* were typical brigs-of-war.

Brig-rigging: See *square-rigging*.

Burthen: A measure of tonnage, or approximate size of a vessel. It was, more or less, the length of the *keel* multiplied by the *beam* multiplied by the depth of hold, divided by ninety-four. Other methods of measuring ship size included Builders Old Measurement (a complex formula employed between 1667 and 1873), and displacement, a modern measurement of the weight of water displaced by a vessel. In the days of the Texas Navy, measurement of a vessel was generally stated in tons burthen.

Canister: A shotgun-like antipersonnel projectile fired from a cannon, much like *grape shot*, except that the projectile is a disintegrating can of musket balls instead of a sack of one- or two-inch balls.

Carronade: A short-barreled cannon capable of firing a very heavy projectile at short range. The advantage of a carronade is that it packed a tremendous wallop, but did not weigh so much that it would strain the ship's deck or slow it down intolerably much. At long range, however, a carronade was worthless.

Colors: A ship's flag, or ensign, indicating her nationality. A modified form of the national flag was also called a **jack** (*e.g.*, the Union Jack). To **strike one's colors** was to surrender. Many vessels, including those of Texas, regularly flew false colors, running up their true colors just before an attack.

Commander: A rank above *lieutenant* and below *post captain*, originally called **master and commander**.

Commodore: A commander of a squadron. Not an actual rank.

Cutter: A small, single-masted sailing vessel with more than one *jib sail* used as a scout ship, frequently belonging to a warship. However, schooners such as the U.S. Navy's *Ingham* and the Mexican *Correo Mejicano* were frequently, if imprecisely, referred to as **revenue cutters.**

Draft (or **draught**): The depth of water that a vessel requires to stay afloat. The schooner *Invincible* drew about eight feet before adding the weight of her guns, so she had trouble crossing the Galveston Bar at low tide. (For an illustration of what happens when a captain ignores draft considerations, see chapter twelve.)

Fathom: A measurement of six feet, most commonly used to measure depth of water.

Fore: The front portion of a vessel, at or near the *bow*.

Fore-and-aft rigging: Rigging that allowed a ship to carry sails running parallel with the ship's *keel*. *Schooners's* principal sails were rigged fore-and-aft, while *brigs's* principal sails were *square-rigged*.

Forecastle (or **fo'c'sle**): Originally a raised portion of the upper deck at the *bow* of a vessel from which archers could shoot (hence the term "fore castle"). By the nineteenth century, the general term for the upper deck in front of the *foremast*.

Foremast: See *mast*.

Gaff: A *spar* running *aft* from a mast, from which a *fore-and-aft* sail is suspended. A schooner's *mainsail* hangs from a *mainmast* gaff and is secured at the bottom by another *spar* called a **boom**.

Grapeshot (or **grape**): A cannon projectile consisting of a net bag holding iron balls weighing one to three pounds each. Essentially, a giant shotgun. Very useful against enemy sailors and sails at close range, but useless at long range.

Grog: A drink of whiskey or rum, mixed one part spirits to three parts water, fortified with lemon juice and brown sugar. Grog was used to help ward off scurvy and low morale, and could be diluted as punishment for minor offenses.

Hawser: A thick rope or cable, usually more than five inches in diameter, used to moor a vessel to its harbor.

Heel: To lean to one side, as a ship does in the wind.

Jib: A triangular sail running between the *bowsprit* and the *foremast*.

Kedge anchor: A small anchor used for **kedging** (moving a vessel by hauling out the anchor in a rowboat, dropping it, and hauling the anchor's line in).

Keel: The main structural member of a ship's hull, on which all other portions of the hull rest. Falconer compared the keel to the backbone of a human skeleton. The **kelson** (or more correctly, the **keelson**) is the innermost layer of the keel. Because the keel lies at the very bottom of the hull, if a vessel grounded, it was usually the keel that hit ground first.

Knot: A measure of speed, usually the number of nautical miles a ship is traveling per hour. In its trip to Yucatán in 1843, the flagship *Austin* made eleven knots, which was incredibly good speed for a sailing vessel. The steamer *Zavala* could make nine knots between New Orleans and Galveston.

Larboard: The left, or **port** side of a ship. Opposite of *starboard*. The term "larboard" was replaced by the term "port" after commanders realized that "larboard" sounds a lot like "starboard" in the middle of a storm or battle. The name change to "port" prevented many embarrassing mistakes, although crusty old tars still used the term "larboard" even in the days of the Texas Navy.

Lee: The side protected from the wind, such as the lee *beam* or lee *quarter*.

Letter of Marque and Reprisal: A certificate issued by a government allowing a private vessel, or **privateer**, to capture enemy *prize* vessels, usually with a portion of the booty being given to the issuing government. Basically, a limited license to commit what would otherwise be piracy. The provisional Texas government authorized eleven letters of marque in late 1835, but few were actually used.

Luff: To steer a ship towards the direction of the wind, as when a ship *tacks*.

Magazine: The portion of a ship designed to carry gunpowder. The magazine was located deep within the hull for protection, and was generally lined with lead or wood, as iron or steel could create sparks, with disastrous results. During combat, boys called **powder-monkeys** would scurry into the magazine and bring out lead boxes of powder for the guns. Just before the engagement of April 30, 1843, Commodore Moore ordered his magazines prepared for demolition in case of capture.

Mainmast: See *mast*.

Mast: The vertical *spar* rising from the hull that holds the *yards* that carry the sails. All sailing ships have them, and most early steamers, such as the *Zavala*, carried them to conserve fuel. The mast closest to the *bow* is the **foremast**. On a *schooner* or *brig*, which has two masts, the *aft* mast is the **mainmast**. On a sloop-of-war such as the *Austin*, the middle mast is the mainmast and the *aft* mast is the **mizzenmast**.

Master: The navigation officer of a ship. When the master held a rank above lieutenant and below *post captain*, he was called a **master and commander**, or more commonly, a *commander.*

Midshipmen: Non-commissioned officers, generally young teenagers, who assisted the commissioned officers in their duties. Basically, lieutenants in training.

Mizzenmast: See *mast.*

Ordinary (or **in ordinary**): Partly dismantled for long-term storage; "mothballed." Vessels placed in ordinary were run by skeleton crews whose main job was to keep each other (and passers-by) from stealing the vessel's equipment. All *spars* and rigging were taken down and stored, usually in the Navy Yard, portals were closed, and the guns were covered against the elements. After 1842, the Texas brig *Archer* was placed in ordinary, while after November 1843 the entire fleet was placed in ordinary.

Paixhan (or **Paixhan gun**): A shell-firing gun designed by French colonel Henri Paixhans in 1822. The shells were designed to explode above or within a ship, improving the attacker's destructive force, but problems with fuses and lack of accuracy limited the usefulness of these shells. At the battles off Campeche on April 30 and August 16, 1843, the Mexican steam frigates *Guadalupe* and *Moctezuma* fired sixty-eight-pound Paixhan shells at the Texas squadron, and while they did considerable damage to the *Austin*, none exploded on impact.

Poop (or **poop deck**): The aftermost portion of the upper deck, over the captain's cabin, usually found only in very large ships, although crewmen aboard the *Austin* referred to the *Austin*'s poop deck being damaged by a Mexican shell in 1843. Despite the name, the poop deck was not the location of the crew's seats of ease, which would undoubtedly have spoiled the captain's majestic view from his cabin windows. (The crew's facilities, or head, was located amidships and near the bow.) A ship would be "pooped" when waves were large enough to crest over the poop deck.

Port: See *larboard.*

Post Captain: A commissioned officer commanding a "post ship," which was a ship carrying more than twenty guns. Also, a formal rank, replaced by the term **captain** in the Royal Navy beginning in 1824. The term *captain,* like *commodore* and *commander*, was used fairly loosely in reference to the Texas Navy after 1843, particularly during the scramble for employment with the U.S. Navy in the wake of Texas's annexation.

Pounder: A measurement of cannon size, indicating the weight of a given gun's cannonball. *Schooners* and *brigs* of the Texas Navy generally carried guns between six and eighteen pounders, although smaller guns, such as four pounders and one pounders, were often used as antipersonnel weapons. The *sloop-of-war Austin* carried twenty-four pounders, while the *Guadalupe* had two sixty-eight pounders. Any of these guns could be designed for short-, medium- or long-range firing. Long-range guns, which had to withstand the explosive force of large powder charges, were very heavy and could not be carried in large numbers, so these "long toms," such as that on the *Brutus,* would usually be mounted *amidships* on a pivot to fire forward or to either side.

Prize: A vessel and its cargo legally captured by a warship or privateer. Prizes were usually enemy vessels or neutral merchant vessels carrying contraband of war to an enemy port. Prizes would be brought to admiralty courts, and when adjudicated as lawfully captured, they would be ordered sold, and the proceeds would be distributed to the government, officers, and crew according to a detailed formula contracted for by the crew (in the case of privateers), or as set forth in government regulations.

Quarter: The *aft* portion of the ship, roughly the last quarter or third of the hull.

Quarterdeck: The deck at the ship's *stern quarter.* The quarterdeck is traditionally the raised deck from which the ship's commander directs the vessel's activities.

Officers: See chapter six for an explanation of the various commissioned, noncommissioned, and petty officers aboard warships.

Round (or round shot): The classic round cannon ball, used for doing structural damage to an enemy vessel, and the only effective shot at long range.

Schooner: A two-masted vessel, rigged with two equal-sized *fore-and-aft rigged* sails, the rear sail being generally referred to as a **gaff sail** or **spanker**. A *brigantine* is also a type of schooner, despite its name. Typical Texas Navy schooners such as the *San Antonio* also had *square-rigged* topsails on each *mast*, and were sometimes referred to as **topsail schooners.**

Ship: An oceangoing vessel larger than a boat, bearing three *square-rigged masts.* *Austin* was a ship, and *Zavala* was a steam ship.

Sloop: In naval parlance, an unrated vessel directed by a *commander*. Sloops include *brigs, schooners,* and other small warships. Not to be confused with the modern sloop, which is a single masted *fore-and-aft rigged* vessel. A **sloop-of-war** is generally a three-masted ship with fewer than twenty-four guns (fewer than eighteen in the Royal Navy).

Spar: Any wood above the hull, such as *masts, yards, bowsprits,* booms, or *gaffs.*

Square-rigging: Rigging in which most sails run perpendicular to the ship's *keel.* Most of the large sails on the USS *Constitution* are of this type, as were most sails on the Texas flagship *Austin.*

Starboard: The right side of a ship, opposite the *larboard,* or *port* side.

Stern: The *aft*-most portion of a vessel; opposite the *bow.*

Tack: To turn a ship's *bow* into the wind.

Wear or wear around: To turn the *bow* away from the wind, opposite of *tack.*

Weather: The side against which the wind is blowing, such as the weather *beam* or weather *quarter.* Opposite the *lee* side. Firing the weather battery would mean firing guns into the wind.

Weather gage: A position between the oncoming wind and the enemy. The ship that gets the weather gage on an opponent has an easy time charging against or chasing the enemy, but a hard time fleeing.

Yard (or yardarm): A horizontal *spar* that is affixed to a *mast*, from which the sails are suspended. On a typical three-masted *square-rigger* such as the flagship *Austin*, the lowest yard was called the **foreyard, mainyard,** or **crossjack**, depending on whether it was attached to the *foremast, mainmast,* or *mizzenmast.* The next lowest yard was called the **foretopmast yard, maintopsail yard** or **mizzen-topsail yard**, again depending on the mast to which it was affixed. The next yard up would be the **foretopgallant yard, maintopgallant yard,** or **mizzen-topgallant yard.** The highest yards would be the **fore royal yard, main royal yard,** or **mizzen royal yard.** The *bowsprit* had its own yard, a **spritsail yard.** Smaller vessels, or *fore-and-aft rigged* vessels, had a different scheme.

NOTES

Abbreviations used frequently in the source descriptions are listed here:

BCHM: Brazoria County History Museum, Angleton, Texas
CAH: Center for American History, University of Texas, Austin, Texas
Diario: *Diario del Gobierno*
Dienst Collection (including Tennison documents): Alex Dienst Papers, CAH
DRT: Daughters of the Republic of Texas Library, San Antonio, Texas
GLO: Texas General Land Office
Handbook: Handbook of Texas Online
Houston: *The Writings of Sam Houston*
Moore: Edwin W. Moore, *To the People of Texas*
NARA: National Archives and Records Administration
NHC: Naval Historical Center
Official Correspondence: Binkley, *Official Correspondence of the Texas Revolution*
PTR: *Papers of the Texas Revolution*
Rosenberg JGT: Rosenberg Library, John Grant Tod Collection
Rosenberg JM: Rosenberg Library, James Morgan Collection
Rosenberg SMW: Rosenberg Library, Samuel May Williams Collection
Rosenberg TNC: Rosenberg Library, Texas Navy Collection
ROT Claims: Claims File, Republic of Texas, TSLA
SMW: Samuel May Williams Collection
SRM: Star of the Republic Museum, Washington-on-the-Brazos, Texas
Telegraph: *Telegraph and Texas Register*
TSLA: Texas State Library and Archives (Navy Papers unless otherwise noted)
Tulane ASJ: Tulane University, Albert Sidney Johnston Papers

ONE: THE TROUBLED TEXAS WATERS

The cultural, economic, and political friction that erupted into revolution in 1835 has been described in great detail by many of its participants, including Manuel de Mier y Terán 2, 31-38, 104-05, 133, 180-84, 209, 225-36, 234; Vicente Filisola, *Memoirs*, 46-51, 62-88; Santa Anna 49-50; and Tornel, in Castañeda 359-60, on the Mexican side, and in widely circulated accounts by David G. Burnet, Sam Houston, and Stephen F. Austin on the Anglo side. The best modern summaries of the cultural, economic, and political differences between Texians and mainstream Mexicans are found in Fehrenbach 81-173; Lack 3-37; Tijerina 113-144; and Haley, *Texas*, 22-30. The French comment on Texian temperament comes from Gaillardet 73 (dispatch dated July 24, 1839).

The 1832 uprising at Anáhuac was recounted by Henson, *Juan Davis Bradburn*, 97-98, 120-145 (quoting Bradburn to Terán); Kokernot 273-75; Filisola, *Memoirs*, 78, 90; Looscan 24; Haley 27-28; Fehrenbach 170; Francaviglia 106; Guthrie 2: 12-13; Barker, *Difficulties of a Mexican Revenue Officer,* 199; Vázquez, "Causes of the War with the United States," in Francaviglia and Richmond 45; and Lack 6-7. Maritime trading in 1833-35 is sketched in Powell 16-17.

The Mexican Navy during Mexico's years of independence, empire, and republic is best described in Hererra, *Memoria*; Tornel, *Memoria*, 1835, 36-38; Hill 21; Bidwell 407-410; Borgens 47-48; and most thoroughly, Cardenas de la Peña 1:92-106. The University of Michigan currently maintains an excellent Web site on Mexico's Adm. David Porter, which contains useful information about the Mexican Navy taken from the Porter family papers. Reports of antismuggling operations by the Mexican Navy along Texas waters between 1830 and 1835 are found in Thomas M. Thompson's report, July 5, 1830, et seq. (Bexar Archives).

The *Martha* incident was reported in William B. Travis to David G. Burnet, May 21, 1835 (Lack 24); John Forsyth to Powtahan Ellis on June 20, 1836 (PTR 7:498); Hill 23-24; Francaviglia 107; Lack 24; and Bidwell 409.

TWO: DRAWING BLOOD

Unease and frustration among Mexican commanders in mid-1835 was described in Col. Domingo de Ugartechea to Capt. Antonio Tenorio, June 20, 1835 (PTR 1:156). The Travis uprising at Anáhuac in the summer of 1835 is recounted in William B. Travis to Henry G. Smith, July 6, 1835 (Looscan 24); Dienst 1:66; Fehrenbach 185; Barker, *Difficulties of a Mexican Revenue Officer*, 200; and Lack 25. The Texas reaction is recounted by Dienst 1:166, Lack 26 and Fehrenbach 185, while the Mexican government's official reaction is recorded in *Diario*, July 6, 1835.

Descriptions of the *Correo Mejicano* can be found in Yoakum 1:356, Cardenas de la Peña 1:93, Powell 17; and Douglas 12. Details of "Mexico" Thompson's life are drawn from Thomas M. Thompson to Editor (*Telegraph*, October 18, 1837); Thompson, Reports, July 5, 1830, et seq. (Bexar Archives); and Winthop 17. Thompson's tenure in Texas is recounted in Thompson to Francisco de Paula López (*Diario*, November 2, 1835); Declaration of Carlos Ocampo, September 21, 1835 (PTR 1:473) (the "Ocampo Declaration"); Hooten 17; and depositions of Cpl. Lino Perez, Edwardo Cumpa, and other crewmen of the *Correo* taken on September 3, 1835 (Bexar Archives) (the "*Correo* Investigation"). Texian opinion of Thompson in the summer of 1835 can be found in the sworn statements of A. J. Yates, I. N. Moreland and Augustus C. Allen (*Texas Republican*, September 19, 1835); Thomas J. Rusk to James Morgan, March 29, 1836 (PTR 5:236); and David Thomas to Sam Houston, April 8, 1836 (PTR 5:391-93). Thompson's correspondence to Capt. Tenorio, dated July 25, 1835, as well as Tenorio's reply three days later, can also be found in the Bexar Archives, while his "Proclamation to the Citizens of Anahuac, &c." was published in the *Texas Republican*, September 19, 1835. The reaction of Texians at the time can be found in an unsigned letter from Lynchburg dated September 8, 1835 (PTR 1:430); Burnet 165; and Nacogdoches Resolutions, August 15, 1835 (*Austin Papers* 3:100). Ugartechea's disapproval of Thompson's tactics is found in Ugartechea to Stephen F. Austin, October 4, 1835 (*Austin Papers* 3:155). Early historians' accounts, which are scarcely more sympathetic to Thompson than those of the participants themselves, include Newell 45, Burnet 165, and Kennedy 2:94.

Details of the *San Felipe* are found at Cardenas de la Peña 93; Dienst 1:169; Winthrop 11; and McKinney 10. Captain Hurd is described in Franklin, *Harris Memoirs*, 243.

The events of September 1 and 2, 1835, are recounted in great detail by the *Correo* Investigation (depositions of Lino Perez, Eduardo Cumpa, Felipe Antonio Jiminez, Daniel London, Demetrio Alvarez, Manuel Cruz, Alvino Lorenzo, and Tomas Casanova); Ocampo Declaration; Winthrop (testimony of Washington Stiles, Captain Hurd, Mr. Scott, A. C. Allen and Capt. Grayson); *Texas Republican*, September 19, 1835; *Telegraph*, October 10, 1835; and *Commercial Bulletin*, January 18, 1836. Shearer (63) and Francaviglia (108) attempt to piece together what Thompson was doing at the mouth of the Brazos on September 1, while Bryan (108) discusses Austin's passage home aboard *San Felipe*. The battle is also described by early historians such as Newell (45); Bancroft (2:162), Yoakum (2:132), and Dienst (1:169-70), and more recently in Powell 28-30.

The diplomatic fallout between the U.S. and Mexico can be traced through the correspondence of Mexican consul Francisco Pizzaro Martinez to District Attorney Henry Carleton, September 16, 1835 (PTR 1:449); Carleton to Martinez, September 17, 1835 (PTR 1:452-53); J. M. Castillo y Lanzas to Ashbury Dickens, October 6, 1835 (H. Exec. Docs., 25th Cong., 2nd Sess., Doc. 351 708); Dickens to Castillo y Lanzas, October 10, 1835 (*id.* 710-11); U.S. Secretary of State John Forsyth to Castillo y Lanzas, October 21, 1835 (*id.* 713-15); Castillo y Lanzas to Forsyth, October 29, 1835 (*id.* 714-15 and *Telegraph*, August 18, 1836); Forsyth to Castillo y Lanzas, October 27, 1835 (*id.* 715); José Maria Ortíz Monasterio to Forsyth, November 19, 1835 (*id.* 720-21); Forsyth to Castillo y Lanzas, December 8, 1835 (*id.* 721-22); Castillo y Lanzas to Forsyth, December 11, 1835 (*id.* 722-23); Castillo y Lanzas to Forsyth, February 4, 1836 (PTR 4:253); Castillo y Lanzas to Forsyth, February 14, 1836 (*id.* 731-32); and Castillo y Lanzas to Forsyth, February 15, 1836 (*id.* 713-15).

The Mexican reaction to the *Correo* incident was described in *Diario*, November 2, 1835, and privately in letters from Gen. Martín Perfecto de Cós to Ugartechea, September 28, 1835 (PTR 1:499), Ugartechea to Cós, September 30, 1835 (PTR 1:515; and Powell 33-34. It was also summarized well by Mexican Secretary of War and Marine José Maria Tornel (Castenada 359-60). In Texas, we find word of the *Veracruzana*'s approach from Edward Gritten to Capt. Wylie Martin, September 18, 1835 (PTR 1:458); R. R. Royall to Austin, September 30, 1835 (PTR 1:510); James Fannin to David Mills, September 18, 1835 (TSLA Domestic Correspondence); McKinney to Royall, October 29, 1835 (McKinney Papers, CAH); James Herr to Austin, September 28, 1835 (TSLA Domestic Correspondence); and in Powell 39.

"Mexico"Thompson's trial was recounted in detail by Winthrop, as well as the *New Orleans Courier*, January 14, 16, and 18, 1836. The fates of *San Felipe*, *Laura*, and *Correo de Mejico* are described by the *Telegraph*, October 17 and 26, 1835 (*San Felipe*) and February 20, 1836 (*Laura*); and by Cardenas de la Peña (94; *Correo*). The life of Thompson's attorney, Pierre Soulé, was sketched out in Gaillardet 132-50.

THREE: THE INFLUENCE OF NAVAL POWER ON THE TEXAS REVOLUTION

The topography of Texas Naval and its influence upon the land campaigns of 1835 and 1836, are described at Filisola, *Evacuation*, 60; Hogan 53-57, 66-80; and Fehrenbach 201. Excellent surveys of the military campaign are provided by Hardin; Pohl and Hardin; and Barker, *The San Jacinto Campaign*. The logistical challenges facing Mexico were described in Vicente Filisola to José Maria Tornel y Mendevil, May 31, 1836 (PTR 7:435-36); José Urrea to Antonio Lopez de Santa Anna, March 21, 1836 (PTR 5:156-57); Santa Anna to Filisola, December 17, 1835 (PTR 3:353); and Santa Anna to Filisola, March 29, 1836 (PTR 5:237). The commentary on Napoleon comes from Chandler (162, 384).

Lieutenant Wright's letter to Austin and Houston is found at *Official Correspondence* 1:47. The importance of New Orleans to the Texas cause was described in, among other places, Stephen F. Austin to R. R. Royall and S. Rhoads Fisher, January 7, 1836 (PTR 3:434); Thomas J. Rusk to James Morgan, March 29, 1836 (PTR 5:237); and James F. Perry, et al. to Provisional Government, November 29, 1835 (PTR 3:32-33). James Fannin's opinions are described in his letters to Francis Belton, August 27, 1835 (PTR 1:372), and James Robinson and the General Council, February 16, 1836 (PTR 7:424-26). The partisanship of New Orleans' citizens during the early days of the Texas Revolution was described in Miller; Denham, *Charles E. Hawkins*, (94); and Denham, *New Orleans* (511-16).

The Mexican perspective on the naval theater is described in Filisola to Secretary of War and Marine, May 31 and June 10, 1836 (Filisola, *Evacuation*, 48, 54); William

Bryan to Governor and Council, February 6, 1836 (*Official Correspondence* 1:398); —— Vallejo to José Maria Ortíz Monasterio, January 12, 1836 (PTR 3:500); *Diario*, July 2, 1835, March 23 and 30, 1836, and April 9, 1836; D.C. Barrett and A. Houston to General Council, November 15, 1835 (*Proceedings of the General Council* 8); Edward Hall to Governor Smith and the General Council, December 8, 1835 (PTR 3:132); William Bryan to Henry Smith, January 31, 1836 (*Official Correspondence*, 1:369); Stephen F. Austin to Thomas F. McKinney, January 16, 1836 (PTR 4:38-39); Austin to Houston, January 16, 1826 (PTR 4:38); and McKinney to Royall, October 29, 1835 (McKinney Papers, CAH).

The land campaign of 1835 was described generally at Pohl and Hardin 274-306; Hardin 5-92; Burke 48-53; Vázquez 313-48; and Fehrenbach 220. The disposition of the Mexican Army at the beginning of the war was recorded by Nofi 203-05.

FOUR: A WAR OF PRIVATEERS

Initial observations on the chaos of the Consultation and the formation of the Provisional Government are made, among other places, at Fehrenbach 199; Lack 38-52; and Denham, *New Orleans*, 511-12.

The history of the privateer acts, and their ultimate repeal, comes from *Journals of the Consultation* 25-26 (November 18, 1835 entry); Thomas F. McKinney to R. R. Royall, October 29, 1835 (McKinney Papers, CAH); D. C. Barrett and A. Houston to the General Council, November 15, 1835 (*Proceedings of the General Council* 8); Dienst 1:175-181; Gammel 1:52-54 (November 25, 1835 resolution) (Dienst copy, CAH); George Fisher to General Council, November 4, 1835 (TSLA Domestic Correspondence); Denham, *New Orleans*, 529-30; *Proceedings of the General Council*, 25-27, 31-32, 37-38, 44-45, 51-52, 53, 55, 73-76, 114, 275, and 286; Gray to Public, November 7, 1835, PTR 2:348-49; Proclamation dated Harrisburg, March 25, 1836 (*Telegraph*, April 14, 1836); Silas Dinsmore to Royall, November 30, 1835 (TSLA Domestic Correspondence); Robert Potter to General Council, December 1, 1835 (PTR 3:69); Ira R. Lewis to Government, December 5, 1835 (TSLA Domestic Correspondence); *Telegraph*, September 16, 1843; Unnamed newspaper clipping dated December 21, 1835 (Rosenberg TNC); Steen 28-29; Gammel 1:942; and Fehrenbach 225.

San Felipe's short career as a privateer was recounted in the *Telegraph and Texas Register*, October 17 and 26, 1835; *Diario*, November 2 and December 21, 1835; "Sea Letter" dated November 1, 1835 (Rosenberg TNC); McKinney to General Council, November 9, 1835 (*Proceedings of the General Council* 10); McKinney to President of the Council, November 11, 1835 (*Official Correspondence* 1:65); James Welsh to Royall, November 9, 1835 (*Official Correspondence* 1:63); William Hall to Austin, November 23, 1835 (*Austin Papers* 3:264-65); McKinney & Williams to Branch T. Archer, November 15, 1835 (*Official Correspondence* 1:82); Steen (31); *Proceedings of the General Council* (346); and Borgens (49-50).

The story of *William Robbins* was taken from Deposition of Edward Morehouse, February 5, 1839 (TSLA); Ira R. Lewis to General Council, December 5, 1835 (PTR 3:98); James W. Robinson to McKinney, December 17, 1835 (PTR 3:235); S. Rhoads Fisher to Provisional Government of Texas, December 17, 1835 (PTR 3:218); Edward Hall to Stephen F. Austin, November 23, 1835 (Dienst 1:184); Depositions of Joseph C. Beckford, William Reed, and Isaac F. Sheles, December 29, 1835 (PTR 3:357); Depositions of Thomas Pugh, Edward Scrugham, Alonzo Marsh, and William S. Brown, December 27, 1835 (PTR 3:336); James Fannin to Henry Smith, December 11, 1835 (PTR 3:159-60); *Proceedings of the General Council* (9, 168, 172-73, 193, 197, 215, 249, 251, 254 and 271); *Diario*, December 21, 1835; Daniel W. Smith to Commandant of Tamaulipas, December 12, 1835 (PTR 3:173); J. M. Guerra to Daniel W. Smith, December 14, 1835 (PTR 3:188-89); Smith to Guerra, December 15, 1835 (PTR 3:206-07); Thomas Barnett to Henry Smith, January 2, 1836 (Dienst collection, CAH);

Affidavit of Peter Kinsey and S. Rhoads Fisher, February 16, 1836 (Rosenberg TNC); Petition of James W. Fannin, et al., December 12, 1835 (Rosenberg TNC); and Gammel 1:52-54. The commission's file was transmitted by Barnett to Governor Smith on January 2, 1836 (Dienst collection, CAH). Early histories include Bancroft 2:271; and Yoakum 2:38-39. Modern sources include Ellenberger (354, 366-67); Dienst 1:168, (184-85); Steen (30); Denham 516 n. 16; and Borgens 50-51.

The story of *Flash* and the plight of the Galveston refugees was told by Clopper 128, 130, 134; Samuel P. Carson to James Morgan, April 1, 1836 (Rosenberg TNC); Edward Hall to Bailey Hardeman, June 18, 1836 (Rosenberg TNC); Alex Huston to Daniel Pittman, April 8, 1836 (PTR 5:381); S. Rhoads Fisher to A. S. Thruston, April 15, 1837 (Rosenberg TNC); William P. Harris to "Friend Hanks," January 19, 1836 (PTR 4:72); Fisher to Sam Houston, November 12, 1836 (TSLA); Crimmins' *Army and Navy Chronicle*, November 17, 1836; Dienst 1:193-94 (citing *Texas Almanac 1865;* Galveston *News*, October 8, 1899; *National Intelligencer*, May 30, 1837; and Thrall 521); and Fischer 88-91 (citing John J. Linn, *Reminiscences of Fifty Years in Texas* (New York: D&J Sodlieb, 1883; reprinted by Steck Co., (Austin, 1935)).

Yellow Stone's history was taken from the following sources: George H. T. French, "The Yellow Stone" (DRT); Jackie L. Pruett, "Texas Sampler: The Yellow Stone," *Texan Express*, November 14, 1874; Garland Roark, "Famous Ships of Texas," Houston *Chronicle*, October 1, 1961; Crimmins; Goldthwaite (33, 36); Turner (44-45); Francaviglia (133) (citing Texas Maritime Museum Photograph Collection and Donald Jackson's *Voyages of the Steam Boat* Yellow Stone (NY: Tiknor and Fields 1985)); Powell 17; and Fischer (89).

Descriptions of other vessels and their exploits come from Bancroft 2:271; H. D. Ripley to Gen. E. W. Ripley, November 27, 1835 (PTR 2:13) (*Julius Caesar*); Bancroft 2:271 and Yoakum 2:212 (*Champion*); *Proceedings of the General Council* 6 (*Mary Jane*); Report of John Buchanan, November 3, 1836 (TSLA); Harkort p. 367; William P. Harris to "Friend Hanks," January 19, 1836 (PTR 4:73); D.C. Barrett et al. to James W. Robinson, January 22, 1836 (PTR 4:111); Crimmins; Dienst 1:201; Shearer p. 66; Fischer pp. 87-88 (*Cayuga*); Clopper p. 130; and John A. Wharton and W. L. Brown, Certificate, March 22, 1836 (Rosenberg TNC) (*Durango*); *Telegraph and Texas Register*, January 26, 1836 (*Bounty*); *Telegraph*, October 31, 1835 (*Columbus*); Harkort, May 20, 1836 (*San Jacinto*); Edward Hall to Governor Smith and the General Council, December 9, 1835 (PTR 3:132) (*Pennsylvania* and *Santiago*); David G. Burnet to James Morgan, April 21, 1836 (PTR 6:5) (*Congress*); James W. Fannin to James W. Robinson, January 21, 1836 (PTR 4:103), and Dienst 2:251 (citing *Commercial Bulletin*, May 23, 1836) (*Flora*); Kerr to Austin, September 30, 1835 (PTR 1:508-09) (*Laura*).

Public reaction in New Orleans to the use of privateers was described at Denham, *New Orleans*, 532 (quoting *Bee*, August 27, 1836), and William Bryan to Henry Smith, January 28, 1836 (PTR 4:162-63); and Miller 126.

FIVE: THE FLEET THAT SANK ITS GOVERNMENT

The legislative history of Texas's first naval legislation is told in *Proceedings of the General Council* 25-27; Henry Smith to Stephen F. Austin, William H. Wharton, and Branch T. Archer, December 7, 1835 (PTR 3:114); Austin and Wharton to Edward Hall, January 14, 1836 (PTR 4:5); Henry Austin to Asa Brigham and J. S. D. Byrom, March 31, 1836 (*Austin Papers* 3:321); *Telegraph*, January 2, 1836; and Gammel 1:182-84. Modern sources include Dienst 1:193 (citing Gammel 1:588, 593); Nichols (299); and Steen (30). Additional background on Samuel May Williams can be found in Moses Austin Bryan (170).

The acquisition and equippage of *Liberty* was described at Gammel 1:182-84; Steen at p. 29; Cushing 147; Dienst 1:189; and Powell 52. The schooner's trip to New Orleans and her foreclosure sale was noted at Thomas F. McKinney to Austin, December 17, 1835 (*Austin Papers* 3:286); McKinney 10; Austin to Francis W. Johnson, et al., December 22, 1835 (*Austin Papers* 3:289); Denham 511 (citing *New Orleans Bee*, January 4, 1836); Archer, Austin, and Wharton to Henry Smith, January 10, 1836 (PTR 3:462); Henry M. Morfit to John Forsyth, August 13, 1836 (H.R. Exec. Docs., 24th Cong., 2nd Sess. 5); Smith to General Council, January 7, 1836 (Rosenberg TNC); *Proceedings of the General Council* 277-78; Steen 30, 33; Gammel 1:750; and F. Y. Alden to William H. Wharton et al., January 12, 1836 (PTR 4:480). *Liberty's* description comes from Capt. Jeremiah Brown to Henry Smith, January 27, 1836 (*Official Correspondence* 1:342); Edwin Ward Moore, "Statement of Texas's Naval Force in 1843" (*Lamar Papers* 4:25-26) (hereinafter, "Moore, *Statement*"); and John A. Wharton to Smith, January 26, 1836 (*Official Correspondence* 1:341), as well as in two early Texas histories, Bancroft 2:271, and Yoakum 2:192. Austin's cautionary statement to Henry Smith comes from his letter of January 20, 1836 (PTR 4:79).

Invincible's register was reprinted on McKee p. 6 and Oertling 1997 p. 5. Other contemporary descriptions come from Henry L. Thompson to Navy Department, August 29, 1837 (TSLA); Jeremiah Brown to Smith, March 6, 1836 (*Official Correspondence* 1:483); John A. Robb, Carpenter's Certificate, October 28, 1835 (Oertling 1997 p. 3); Clopper (128); William P. Harris to James W. Robinson, January 19, 1836 (PTR 4:74); Henry M. Morfit to John Forsyth, August 13, 1836 (H. R. Exec. Docs., 24th Cong., 5); Moore, *Statement*; and Allen. More modern accounts can be found at Denham, *New Orleans*, 516 n. 16; Hill 44; and Dienst 1:202. *Invincible*'s purchase was described in Asa Brigham and H. G. Hudson to Thomas F. McKinney, n.d. (*Telegraph*, September 18, 1836, and *Official Correspondence* 2:936); McKinney & Williams Loan Documents, February 24, 1836 (Rosenberg TNC); McKinney (13); Hall (12-18); and in the more recent works of Dienst 1:202; Dienst 2:253; and Denham, *New Orleans*, 516 n.16. The legislative brawl over *Invincible*'s purchase was documented in *Proceedings of the General Council* (250-52, 252, 286, 290-92); Gammel 1:1031-33; Advisory Committee to James W. Robinson, February 1, 1836 (*Official Correspondence* 1:376); John A. Wharton to Smith, January 26, 1836 (*Official Correspondence* 1:341); Smith to General Council, January 6, 1836 (*Proceedings of the General Council* 266); General Council to the People of Texas, January 12, 1836 (PTR 3:473); Smith to Thomas R. Jackson, January 24, 1836 (Rosenberg TNC). *Invincible*'s early manpower problems were discussed in Jeremiah Brown to Smith, January 27, 1836 (*Official Correspondence* 1:342).

Independence, originally the U.S. revenue cutter *Ingham*, was described at Denham 516 n.16; Dienst 1:202; Francaviglia 118; Silverstone 83; and Oertling 1992 3. Her armament was variously described in Moore, *Statement*; George W. Wheelwright to William M. Shepherd, April 20, 1838 (TSLA); Charles E. Hawkins to Branch T. Archer et al., January 14, 1836 (Rosenberg TNC); Gregory Byrne to William H. Wharton, et al., January 14, 1836 (PTR 4:5); Morfit to Forsyth, August 13, 1836 (H. R. Exec. Docs., 24th Cong., 2nd Sess. 5); and John Wharton to Smith, January 26, 1836 (*Official Correspondence* 1:340). The description of her purchase comes from Gregory Byrne to William H. Wharton et al., January 14, 1836 (PTR 4:5); Hawkins to Austin and Archer, January 18, 1836 (PTR 4:57); Austin to Smith, January 20, 1836 (PTR 4:78); Hall (10); Financial Report of Stephen F. Austin, n.d. (PTR 4:99); and Edward Hall to Bailey Hardeman, June 18, 1836 (Rosenberg TNC).

The fourth warship, *Brutus*, was described by Denham, *New Orleans*, 516 n.16; Dienst 1:202; and Hill 44. Her armament was reckoned by Yoakum 2:192 and Hill 55 and was noted by U.S. *charge d'affaires* Alcée LaBranche to R. A. Irion, November 29, 1837 (Garrison, *Diplomatic Correspondence*, 2:270-71). Her armament's original inclusion of six-pounders was noted in the Deposition of Edward Hall, January 4, 1836 (PTR 3:486); and Morfit to Forsyth, August 13, 1836 (H. R. Exec. Docs., 24th Cong., 5). Her purchase was discussed by Denham in *New Orleans*, (521, citing A. C. Allen to William Bryan, January 22, 1836 (PTR 4:110)); Bryan to Smith, January 28,

1836 (*Official Correspondence* 1:353); and James G. Hurd to Texas Auditor, December 2, 1870 (ROT Claims). Her legal problems are documented in Henry Carleton to Forsyth, January 21, 1836 (PTR 4:102); *Diario*, February 10, 1836; John A. Mirle & Co. et al. to Carleton, December 26, 1835 (PTR 3:331); Carleton to Cuculla et al., December 28, 1835 (PTR 3:341); Carleton to Forsyth, January 21, 1836 (PTR 4:102); Carleton to Judge Gallien Preval, n.d. (PTR 4:480); Deposition of Edward Hall, January 4, 1836 (PTR 4:486); Deposition of William Bryan, January 4, 1836 (PTR 3:487); Deposition of R. M. Carter, January 4, 1836 (PTR 3:485); Advisory Committee to Robinson, February 15, 1836 (*Official Correspondence* 1:437) (noting that *Brutus* was not involved in trade); George M. Collinsworth to General Council, January 24, 1836 (*Official Correspondence* 1:336); and Deposition of New Orleans Port Collector J. W. Breedlove, January 5, 1836 (PTR 4:488). Her voyage to Texas with the Alabama Red Rovers was recounted in Deposition of Levi Charles Harby, November 21, 1870 (GLO). Her transfer to Texas on February 12, 1836, was documented by Denham in *New Orleans*, p. 512, although McKinney claims she was at the Southwest Pass in February 1836 waiting for a crew (McKinney 6).

SIX: IRON MEN FOR WOODEN SHIPS

The Texas government's efforts to recruit officers are described by the Provisional Government's Committee on Naval Affairs, January 3, 1836 (*Proceedings of the General Council* 183) and Advisory Committee to James W. Robinson, February 1, 1836 (*Official Correspondence* 1:375).

The organization of the navy of the nineteenth century was taken from the following sources: Anonymous, "Remarks Upon the Texas Navy" (*Lamar Papers* 2:233); Fuller (224); and Texas Navy Regulations (*Laws of the Republic of Texas* 122-24). Modern sources, which describe Britain's Royal Navy as the typical naval structure, include King (340) (naval command structure); Sullivan (25-28) (Texas marines); and *Houston Post*, December 16, 1934. Details of the uniforms worn by the various ranks can be found in Marshall (15-20, 22, 75-76, 78-79); and the Scovill Manufacturing Company Collection, 1836-1837 (DRT).

Biographical information on Robert Potter can be found at the *Handbook of Texas Online* (entry for "Potter, Robert") and in Fischer and Shearer's biographies of this controversial North Carolinian. Material about Washington-on-the-Brazos comes from *Capitols of Texas* 8-10.

A general list of commissioned officers appointed between March 12 and October 1, 1836, can be found in John Buchanan, "Expose of Naval officers appointed and commissioned by the Convention of March; and Subsequently by the Government 'ad interim'," November 3, 1836 (TSLA A. J. Houston Collection) (hereinafter, "Buchanan Expose"). Sources on Commodore Charles E. Hawkins are Lewis Miles Hobbs Washington, "Eulogy on Commodore Charles Hawkins, Delivered at Richmond, August 9th, 1838," (L. M. H. Washington Papers, CAH); Hawkins to Sam Houston, December 9, 1835 (PTR 3:133); Houston to Stephen F. Austin et al., December 18, 1835 (PTR 3:256); Henry Smith to Austin et al., December 20, 1835 (quoted by Dienst 2:270); Harris Diaries (243); William Bryan to Governor and Council, February 26, 1836 (*Official Correspondence* 1:458-59); Edward Hall to Bailey Hardeman, June 18, 1836 (Rosenberg TNC); John Wharton to Smith, January 26, 1836 (*Official Correspondence* 1:341); Bryan to Governor and Council, February 6, 1836 (*Official Correspondence* 1:458); *Proceedings of the General Convention* 71 (Dienst copy); *Journal of the First Congress, House of Representatives* 15; Gammel 1:890-92; Dienst 1:201; Denham, *Charles E. Hawkins*; Abstract of Service, Charles E. Hawkins (NHC); Denham, *New Orleans* (515); Powell 48-51; and Dienst 2:269.

Background sources on Capt. William S. Brown include Bryan to Smith, January 28, 1836 (*Official Correspondence* 1:354); *Journal of the First Congress, House of Representatives* 17-18; Gammel 1:890-92; and Powell 45-46.

Background sources on William A. Hurd include Cushing pp. 50-51 and Dienst 1:184-85.

Jeremiah Brown was described in the research paper "Velasco: Captain Jeremiah Brown Residence, ca. 1838, Block, 13, Lot 10," Velasco vertical file (Brazoria County History Museum Papers); *Texas Republican*, July 4, 1835; Jeremiah Brown, Account, March 23, 1837 (ROT Claims, Jeremiah Brown); Branch T. Archer et al. to Smith, January 10, 1836 (PTR 3:462); Wharton to Smith, January 26, 1836 (*Official Correspondence* 1:342); Jeremiah Brown to Smith, March 6, 1836 (*Official Correspondence* 1:483) and Powell 38-39.

Sam Houston's orders to Secretary S. Rhoads Fisher, April 5, 1837, illustrate the great latitude given to naval ministers in the early nineteenth century (Houston 4:28-29). James Robinson's recommendation of the formation of a marine corps was noted at *Proceedings of the General Council* 319. Arthur Robertson's commission as "Lieutenant" of marines comes from Buchanan Expose.

SEVEN: THE REVOLUTION AT SEA

The initial tasks assigned to the Texas Navy—escorting troop and supply convoys—were discussed in John A. Wharton to Henry Smith, January 26, 1836 (*Official Correspondence* 1:341); Jeremiah Brown to Smith, January 27, 1836 (*Official Correspondence* 1:342); William Bryan to Governor and Council, February 15, 1836 (*Official Correspondence* 1:431-32); Betsey L. Higgins to Texas Auditor, August 22, 1851 (Rosenberg TNC); Bryan to Governor and Council, February 15, 1836 (*Official Correspondence* 1:431); Bryan to Governor and Council, March 8, 1836 (*Official Correspondence* 1:488); and *Telegraph*, March 12, 1836. Mexican reports of the Texas naval buildup come from *Diario*, January 10, 25, and 27, 1836, and February 10, 1836.

The capture of the *Pelicano* and related adventures of the schooner *Liberty* are detailed in *Telegraph*, February 20, 1836, and August 18, 1838; *Diario*, January 11, 15, and May 19, 1836; E. L. Holmes, Report of the House Judiciary Committee (*Journal of the Third Texas Congress, House of Representatives* 114); William S. Brown to Editor (*True American*, May 8, 1836); Sam Houston, Proclamation to the People East of Brazos, March 31, 1836 (PTR 5:253); T. A. Sawyer to Judge Franklin, April 12, 1838, BCHM; Henry Austin to Asa Brigham and J. S. D. Byrom, March 31, 1836 (*Austin Papers* 3:332-33); Bryan to Governor and Convention, March 29, 1836 (*Official Correspondence* 2:960); "Abstract of the Log of the Schr Liberty on her cruise to Sisal, &c," dated entries February 13-April 25, 1836, www.dsloan.com/auctions/A6/Lots_81-90.html (hard copy on file with author); Cushing (22-23); Senate Finance Committee Report; January 4, 1842 (*Journals of the Sixth Texas Congress* 1:195); Clearance Pass for *Pelicano*, February 24, 1835 (TSLA Domestic Correspondence); Deposition of Edwin Morehouse, February 5, 1836 (TSLA). Modern sources include Powell (67-68); Denham, *New Orleans* (522-25); Hill (48-49); Borgens (52); and Dienst 2:249-51 (citing *Commercial Advertiser*, April 25, 1836).

Details of the Mexican relief expedition at Matamoros in early April 1836 were compiled by Hill (50) and Dienst (2:252), and documented by Francisco Vital Fernandez to Secretaria de Guerra y Marina, April 4, 1836 (*Diario*, April 30, 1836); José Maria Espino to Fernandez, April 3, 1836 (two letters, one citing report of 1st Lieut. Fernando R. Davis) (*Diario*, April 30, 1836). Yoakum 2:124, citing reports of David Thomas, Acting Secretary of War dated April 7 and 8, 1836, states that Mexican authorities intended to land one thousand men at Galveston Island. Evidently Thomas's reports were based on information obtained from those aboard *Pocket*. Samuel Ellis's letter to the editor of the *Bee*, May 20, 1836, states that Captain Howes of the *Pocket* admitted that he was chartered to transport Mexican troops from Matamoros to Texas upon his arrival, which supports Thomas's reports.

The engagement between *Invincible* and *General Bravo* was described in *Diario*, April 23, 26, and 30, 1836 (reprinting reports of José Maria Espino and Fernando R.

Davis dated April 3, 1836); Vicente Filisola to José Maria Tornel y Mendivil, May 31, 1836 (PTR 7:435);Tornel to José Urrea, May 31, 1836 (PTR 7:443); and Tornel to Santa Anna, April 28, 1836 (PTR 6:114-15). Historical references include Yoakum 2:124, Reuben Potter, "The Prisoners of Matamoros," *Magazine of American History* (May 1879) 273-94, quoted in Powell 77-78; Miller 167, and Cardenas de la Peña 94. "Mexico" Thompson's involvement was discussed in *Diario*, April 18 and 23, 1836. Commodore Hawkins lated learned that one of *Bravo*'s guns was transferred to *John M. Bandel* (Charles E. Hawkins to James Morgan, May 11, 1836 (Rosenberg JM).

The capture of the brig *Pocket* is recounted in the following contemporary sources: Austin to Asa Brigham and J. S. D. Byrom, March 31, 1836 (PTR 5:248); *Bee*, May 20, 21, and 24, 1836; *Diario*, April 18 and June 17, 1836; Robert Potter to David G. Burnet, May 12, 1836 (PTR 6:246); Burnet to George M. Collinsworth, April 12, 1836 (quoted in Neu 282); Jeremiah Brown to James Morgan, April 7, 1836 (*Official Correspondence* 2:605); Morgan to Thomas J. Rusk, April 8, 1836 (PTR 5:384-85); William H. Wharton to Government, April 9, 1836 (*Diplomatic Correspondence* 1:82); Bryan to Burnet, April 18, 1836 (quoted in Neu 284); Thomas to Houston, April 8, 1836 (PTR 5:392); Robert Triplett to Burnet, April 9, 1836 (*Official Correspondence* 2:615); Jeremiah Brown to Morgan, April 7, 1836 (Rosenberg JM); Morgan to Hawkins, April 8, 1836 (Rosenberg JM); and on Harkort p. 345. Zacharie & Co.'s cancellation of future shipments because of *Pocket*'s capture was noted in Filisola to Secretary of War and Marine, May 31, 1836 (Filisola, *Evacuation*, 48). *Pocket*'s use as a storage ship and sick bay comes from Rick Cochran to Morgan, July 17, 1836 (Rosenberg JM). Neu's "The Case of the Brig *Pocket*" provides an excellent overview of the brig's seizure and the legal and political repercussions of the incident.

The military analysis of the effect of the *Bravo* incident derives from the sources cited in Appendix A and from Santa Anna to Tornel, February 16, 1836 (PTR 4:357-58); Fehrenbach (205-06); and Pohl and Hardin (306).The impact of theTexas Revolution on the United States' expansion into the west is discussed extensively at Vázquez, "Causes of the War with the United States" (Francaviglia and Richmond 42-43, 50-57); Sam W. Haynes, "But What Will England Say?" (*id.* 20-26); Miguel Al González, "The War Between the United States and Mexico" (*id.* 91-93); Robert W. Johansen, "Young America and War with Mexico" (*id.* 160-63); Stephenson 185; Eisenhower, *Winfield Scott*, 215-16, 219-23; Christensen 25 (quoting Tornel in 1836); Eisenhower, *So Far From God*, xix-xxi and 22-26; and DeVoto 131-35, 188-91.

The presence of the *Independence* was reported in the *Telegraph*, March 12, 1836. Documents from Lt. William A. Tennison (Dienst Collection, CAH) flesh out some of the details of this period, as does *Handbook of Texas Online*, "Hawkins, Charles E." (citing Francis W. Johnson), and Powell 71-76.

The defense of Galveston Island during the Revolution's darkest days can be pieced together from first-hand accounts, including Thomas to Houston, April 8, 1836 (PTR 5:391); Lt. W. C. Ogilvie to Morgan, April 15, 1836 (*Official Correspondence* 2:635); Proclamation of David G. Burnet, April 21, 1836 (PTR 6:5-6); Burnet to Potter, April 20, 1836 (*Official Correspondence* 2:641); Proclamation of David G. Burnet, April 25, 1836 (PTR 6:52); Harris Diaries p. 243;Yoakum 2:124; Dienst 2:266-67; and Cartwright p. 66.A short but excellent description of the Battle of San Jacinto is provided at Fehrenbach 229-33, and, in more detail, at Barker, "The San Jacinto Campaign"; Hardin 208-17; and Haley 147-51. Judge Calder's delivery of news of the Texians' victory was recorded by Thrall (519-21), from an interview with Calder.

EIGHT: DEFENDING THE LONE STAR

General Filisola's lack of supplies is documented in Filisola's letter to Secretary Tornel, May 14, 1836 (PTR 6:258-66), and Filisola to Tornel, May 31, 1836 (Filisola, *Evacuation*, 48). Mexico's desire and efforts to renew the war are found in Tornel to Filisola, May 15 and 19, 1836 (Filisola, *Evacuation*, 56, 63); Tornel's writings

(Casteneda pp. 356-57); and Vázquez (314). *Vencedor*'s acquisition and movements are described by Captain Ribeaud in a letter dated May 1, 1836 (*Commercial Bulletin*, May 19, 1836); *Commercial Bulletin*, July 9, 1836; and Tornel to Santa Anna, April 28, 1836 (PTR 6:112-13). Rumors of invasion during the summer of 1836 are found at Charles E. Hawkins to James Morgan, May 11, 1836 (Rosenberg JM) (report on schooner *New Castle*, 2 short guns, 25 sailors, 30 marines, Commander Thompson; schooner *J.M. Bandel*, 1 long gun taken from *Bravo*, 2 gunnades, 36 men, Commander Davis; brig *Paragon*, 12 short guns); Hogan 13; Harkort 374 (June 29, 1836 entry); T. Morgan to A. Briscoe, September 30, 1836 (PTR 9:31-32); *Commercial Bulletin*, June 29, 1836; William Bryan to David G. Burnet, June 20, 1836 (PTR 7:205); George Hammeken to Austin, July 18, 1836 (PTR 7:482); Thomas J. Rusk to Sam Houston, July 6, 1836 (PTR 7:370-71); Burnet to Memucan Hunt, July 1, 1836 (PTR 7:327); Thomas Toby & Brother to Burnet, July 11, 12, and 16, 1836 (PTR 7:424-25, 436, and 467); Captain Bridges to ——, July 21, 1836 (PTR 7:510).

Liberty's loss was recounted in Dienst 2:251 (citing *Telegraph*, August 18, 1836); "Notes and references taken from documents on file in the Navy Department," November 3, 1836 (TSLA A. J. Houston Collection); Denham, *New Orleans* (523, citing *Bee*, May 8, 1836); Fischer (127); *Commercial Bulletin*, May 23, 1836; Cushing (50-51); Bryan to Burnet, June 1, 1836 (*Official Correspondence* 2:734-35); Toby & Brother to Burnet, June 20 and July 11 and 12, 1836 (PTR 7:320, 424 and 436); Requisition of Robert Potter, June 3, 1836 (Rosenberg TNC); Robert Triplett to President and Cabinet, June 2, 1836 (Rosenberg TNC); Bryan to Burnet, June 9, 1836 (*Official Correspondence* 2:765); Burnet to Toby & Brother, September 3, 1836 (*Official Correspondence* 2:979); Toby & Brother to Burnet, September 22, 1836 (*Official Correspondence* 2:1033); Dienst 2:251 (citing Henry W. Morfit, Report, August 13, 1836, in *Senate Documents*, 24th Cong., 2nd Sess., Document 20, 5). Evidently there is some conflicting evidence on the exact location of Sam Houston's injury; Houston's "left ankle" injury conclusion is based on an interview with preeminent Houston biographer James L. Haley.

The trial of *Invincible*'s crew, and the diplomatic fallout over the seizure of the *Pocket* was recounted at *Diario*, June 17, 1836 (citing *Louisiana Advertiser*); Neu 284-85, 291 (citing *Bee*, May 6, 7, 10 and 16, 1836, *True American*, May 5, 1836, and F. A. Sawyer to Secretary of State, December 21, 1837); Burnet to Benjamin C. Franklin, June 15, 1836 (TSLA Executive Records Book 119); Bryan to Burnet, April 28 and May 14, 1836 (PTR 4:101-02 and 6:255-56); *Bee*, May 7, 1836; *Commercial Bulletin*, May 3, 4, 5, 7, 10, 11, and 12, 1836; *True American*, May 2, 3, 6, 9, 10, 12, 1836; Statement of Jorge H. Vaustavren, May 7, 1836 (*Diario*, May 19, 1836); Bryan to Burnet, May 9, 1836 (PTR 6:191-92); J. K. West to Burnet, May 16, 1836, and William H. Jack to J. K. West, June 4, 1836 (TSLA Department of State Records, Book 34, 31, and 257); R. A. Irion to Bryan, October 27, 1837 (TSLA Department of State Records, Book 36 17); Burnet to Congress (*Proceedings of the First Texas Congress* 17-18); Public Notice, May 4, 1836 (PTR 6:170); Thomas J. Green et al. to Randall Hunt et al., May 7, 1836 (PTR 6:181); Thomas Urquhart et al. to A. J. Dallas, May 9, 1836 (PTR 6:199-200); Dallas to Urquhart et al. May 16, 1836 (*Commercial Bulletin*, May 19, 1836); Irion to Alcée LaBranche, December 30, 1837 (Garrison, *Diplomatic Correspondence*, 1:275); Statement of William Christy, May 10, 1836 (PTR 6:202-03); Thomas Toby to Burnet, September 1, 1836 (*Official Correspondence* 2:977); James Reed to James Morgan, May 12, 1836 (Rosenberg JM); Samuel Ellis to Secretary of the Treasury, June 10, 1836 (*Official Correspondence* 2:769-70); U.S. District Court Records, Case No. 3798, Department of State Records (cited in Neu p. 287); and Miller 167. Brown's subsequent arrest and the resulting lawsuit was documented by the *Commercial Bulletin*, May 23, 1836; *Diario*, June 17, 1836 (citing *National Intelligencer*); Neu (on pp. 288, 292, quoting Bryan to Secretary of State, February 28, 1839, in Department of State Records, Book

34, 15l; and Bryan to Burnet, May 21, 1836, *id.*; and citing minute entries, U.S. District Court, 1839-1841); Request for Production, *Louisiana State Marine and Fire Insurance Company v. Brown*, Case No. 3789 (TSLA). U.S. claims against Texas were documented by M. Dickerson to Bryan, July 8, 1836 (PTR 7:394); Bryan to Dallas, May 25, 1836 (abstract in PTR 7:386); Catlett to Irion, June 22 and July 7, 1838 (quoted by Neu (294)). Filisola's complaint was documented by Filisola to Tornel, May 31, 1836 (PTR 6:439).

Commodore Hawkins's campaign against the "Tories" was documented by Charles E. Hawkins to C. Gallagher, May 15, 1836 (Rosenberg TNC); Statement of Captain W. S. Brown, n.d. (TSLA); *Telegraph*, August 18, 1836 (evidently eulogy for W. S. Brown written by L. M. H. Washington), and Dienst 2:251. The nine-pounder acquisition for *Independence* was mentioned in *Diario*, May 11, 1837 (quoting *Mercurio del Matamoros*). Hawkins's activities over the summer of 1836 were documented by Hawkins to Acting Secretary of Navy, May 19, 1836 (PTR 7:337); George Fisher to Hawkins, May 27, 1836 (PTR 7:385).

Invincible's run-in with her sister ship *Brutus* was documented in Duval on pp. 22-23; Reports of Lieutenant F. Johnson, May 30, 1836, Surgeon O. P. Kelton, June 1, 1836, and Quartermaster Seward P. Morse, May 30, 1836 (TSLA); Jeremiah Brown to Burnet, June 1, 1836 (*Official Correspondence* 2:731). Identification of Francis Johnson as First Lieutenant of the *Brutus* also comes from John Grant Tod, Report, n.d. (Rosenberg JGT).

Santa Anna's stay aboard *Invincible* and the activities of *Ocean* and her volunteers are documented at Green 484; Harkort 367, n.53; Dienst 1:195 (citing *El Correo Atlantico*, June 20, 1836); Dienst 2:256; McKee 17-18; Memucan Hunt to President and Cabinet, June 3, 1836 (PTR 6:512); and —— to —— (fragment dated *Invincible*, June 26, 1836) (PTR 7:276-77). Santa Anna's return to the U.S. was noted at Fehrenbach 244-46 and Weems 109.

The "Horse Marines" episode was documented by Thomas Toby to Burnet, September 22, 1836 (*Official Correspondence*, 2:1031); *Telegraph*, August 2, 1836 (dating the capture of *Comanche* and *Fanny Butler* June 18); Bryan to Burnet, June 20, 1836 (PTR, 7:205); Toby & Bro. to Burnet, July 23, 1836 (PTR, 8:24-25); B.E. Johnson to Houston and Rusk, June 24, 1836 (PTR 7:241); I.W. Burton, n.d., in (Rosenberg TNC); Filisola to Tornel, May 31, 1836 (PTR 6:435); Francisco V. Fernandez to Commander-in-Chief, May 31, 1836 (PTR 6:433); Dienst 2:256; A. Houston to Pinkney Caldwell, July 12, 1836 (PTR 7:430-31); A. Houston to Burnet, June 25, 1836 (PTR 7:255-56); Harkort (374); Hiram Marks to J. E. Rees, July 2, 1836 (PTR 7:341); Henry H. Moffit to John Forsyth, September 14, 1836 (PTR 8:474); *Telegraph*, August 2, 1836; Yoakum 2:160; I.W. Burton, July 11, 1836, (Rosenberg TNC); Dienst 2:256 n. 6; and Hill (60).

Secretary Potter's absence from his post is inferred mainly by the absence of evidence of orders or official correspondence, but it is also found mainly in Bailey Hardeman, "Acting Secretary of the Navy," commission (Rosenberg TNC); Frederick A. Sawyer, "Acting Sec. Of War," to James D. Boylan, August 28, 1836 (TSLA) (ordering Boylan to take charge of the schooner *Passaic*); A. Somervell, "Acting Sec.," to David L. Kokernot, June 30, 1836 (PTR 7:318); and Fisher 245 n.23 (citing Andrew Forest Muir, "The Municipality of Harrisburg," *Southwestern Historical Quarterly* (July 1952)). Fischer, on p. 147, states that Potter never formally resigned, but drew a salary until October 22, 1836. Details of his romantic interests are at Handbook, "Ames, Harriet Moore Page Potter" and Fischer 245 n.23.

Burnet's orders and doings of the *Vencedor, Invincible, Brutus, Viper, Independence,* and *Union* during the summer of 1836 are found at Toby to Burnet, July 27, 1836 (PTR 8:49); *Commercial Bulletin*, May 25, June 7 and 14, July 18, and August 3, 1836 (reprinting Thomas Jefferson Green to William Christy, May 22, 1836);

Telegraph, August 16, 1836 (*Invincible* and *Vencedor*); Green to William A. Hurd and Jeremiah Brown (*Commercial Bulletin*, May 25, June 7, 14, August 4, 1836); "Lisle" to Editor (*Commercial Bulletin*, May 27, 1836); Dienst 1:195; Dienst 2:251, 256 (citing *Louisiana Advertiser*, July 14, 1836), 257, 262-63 (quoting *Bee*), and 268; William S. Brown to James Morgan, August 8, 1836 (Rosenberg JM); Burnet to Jeremiah Brown, June 20, 1836 (*Commercial Bulletin*, June 29, 1836); Burnet to Jeremiah Brown, July 6, 1836 (PTR 7:370); John R. Jones Sr. to John R. Jones Jr., July 17, 1836 (PTR 7:470); Burnet to Toby, June 28, 1836 (PTR 7:297-98); Burnet to Morgan, June 27, 1836 (PTR 7:281); *Diario*, August 8, 1836; Hill 63 (citing *Diario*, August 5, 1836), 64 (citing *Memoria de la Guerra y Marina*, 1839, 25); George Fisher to Austin, August 4, 1836 (PTR 8:118); Austin to Lamar, July 8, 1836 (PTR 7:385); Toby to Burnet, July 11, 1836 (PTR 7:424-26); Haugh 378 (quoting New York *Journal of Commerce*, September 13, 1836); Toby to Burnet, September 22, 1836 (*Official Correspondence* 2:1031); Morgan to A. Briscoe, September 30, 1836 (PTR 9:32); Toby to Burnet, October 15, 1836 (PTR 9:100); and James D. Boylan, "Due to James D. Boylan commander of the National Schooner Viper," September 12, 1841 (ROT Claims).

Terrible's adventures are found in Burnet to Jeremiah Brown, June 29, 1836 (Rosenberg TNC); Navy Department Report, November 3, 1836 (TSLA) (hereinafter, "Navy Report, 1836"); *Telegraph*, August 16, 1836; *Commercial Bulletin*, August 16, 1836; Denham, *New Orleans* (530, citing *Ship Registers and Enrollments* 3:141); Dienst 2:268-69; and Dienst Collection document 326 (CAH). The trial of the privateer and her crew were recounted by Denham in *New Orleans* on pp. 530-31 (citing Mobile *Commercial Register*, August 19 and September 18, 1836, and *Bee*, August 27 and October 8, 1836); Dienst 1:190-91; and Crimmins on p. 397.

The New York sojourn for *Invincible* and *Brutus*, and its repercussions in Texas, are found at Burnet to Senate, October 24, 1836 (PTR 9:141); S. Rhoads Fisher to Houston, November 12, 1836 (TSLA, A. J. Houston Papers); Burnet to Toby, August 10, 1836 (TSLA); Haugh 378 (citing New York *Journal of Commerce*, August 21 and September 1 and 12, 1836); Dienst 2:268 (citing *Commercial Bulletin*, August 4, 1836) and 269; Broome County (N.Y.) *Republican*, September 8, 1836; Burnet to Toby, September 12, 1836 (*Official Correspondence* 2:995); Toby to Burnet, September 1 and 22, 1836 (*Official Correspondence*, 2:974, 995); invoices for *Brutus* purchases, December 15, 24 and 31, 1836 (TSLA); Promissory Note, W.A. Hurd, September 15, 1836 (TSLA); Jeremiah Brown to Williams, October 17, 1836 (TSLA); Charles Sayre to Williams, October 16, 1836 (TSLA); Jeremiah Brown to Williams, October 17, 1836 (TSLA); Samuel Swartwout to Williams, March 30 and April 4, 1837 (TSLA); Fleming T. Wells to J. M. L. and W. H. Scovill, December 8, 1836 (DRT); and McKee 18.

The final actions of the Burnet administration were documented in Peter W. Grayson to William H. Jack, July 30, 1836, and August 11, 1836 (Garrison, *Diplomatic Correspondence*, 2:114-16 and 2:121-22); Burnet to Congress, October 4, 1836 (*House Journal, First Texas Congress*, 14-15); Lewis M. H. Washington, Eulogy for W. S. Brown, n.d. (*Telegraph*, August 18, 1838); W.S. Brown to James Morgan, August 8, 1836 (Rosenberg JM); M. D. McLeod to James D. Boylan, September 24, 1836 (TSLA); John A. Wharton to Boylan, October 1, 1836 (*Official Correspondence*, 2:1049); Frederick A. Sawyer to Boylan, September 3, 1836 (Rosenberg TNC); Sawyer to Rusk, September 6, 1836 (PTR 8:407); Navy Report, 1836; Boylan to Rusk, June 22, 1836 (PTR 7:224); Crimmins (397, quoting *Army and Navy Chronicle*, November 17, 1836); Alex Huston to Boylan, September 21, 1836 (*Official Correspondence* 2:1027); "List of Officers Bearing Commissions of Letters of Marque and Reprisal," November 3, 1836 (TSLA); Buchanan Expose; "Notes and references taken from documents on file in the Navy Department," November 3, 1836 (TSLA A. J. Houston Collection; R. J. Love to J. H. Kipp, June 10, 1903 (Dienst collection, CAH); Harkort (363) (May 20, 1836 entry); *Commercial Bulletin*, August 18 and November 2, 1836; Dienst 1:192; Burnet to Francis B. Wright and Officers of *Independence*, September 13, 1836 (Rosenberg TNC); Hawkins to Wright, September 21, 1836 (TSLA); and Burnet to Toby, July 2, 1836 (PTR 7:335).

NINE: THE GENERAL AT THE HELM

Background on Sam Houston comes from numerous works, notably Haley and James, Fehrenbach pp. 223-24, and Roberts pp. 101-02. The Velasco *Herald* quote comes from the *Courier*, April 24, 1837. Houston's early thinking on naval strategy is revealed in his address to the Texas Congress, May 5, 1837 (*Telegraph*, May 9, 1837 and Houston 2:85-86); Bollaert (36, quoting Houston); and Houston's veto of the *Independence* resolution, discussed later in the chapter. Houston's election is documented at Fehrenbach 245-46; Winfrey 185-86; Haley 164; and Connor 28. Background on S. Rhoads Fisher comes from Houston 1:457-58 n.2; Fisher to Austin, January 10, 1831 (Winkler (106-08)); and Sons of DeWitt Colony web site. Fisher's initial report to Houston is found in Fisher to Houston, November 12, 1836 (TSLA A.J. Houston Collection).

The October 26 committee report, naval appropriations bill, and Houston's early orders to the Navy Department, are found at Gammel 1:1132 and 1146-68 and 2:30; Houston to Toby, October 26 and 27, 1836 (Houston 1:459, 461-62); Denham, *New Orleans* 533 (citing Mobile *Commercial Register*, November 28, 1836); Fisher to Algernon S. Thruston, January 21, 1837 (Rosenberg TNC); Benjamin S. Grayson to Thruston, February 9, 1837 (TSLA); Thruston to Fisher, February 11, 1837 (TSLA); Houston to Senate, December 9, 1836 (Houston 1:499); Certificate of John Duncan, n.d. (TSLA); Hill (66, citing Gouge, *Fiscal History of Texas* 54-55); and Navy Report, 1836.

The adventures of *Thomas Toby* were documented at Denham, *New Orleans* 530, n.65 (citing *Ship Registers and Enrollments* 3:59 and *Bee*, November 3, 1836); Borgens 188 (citing Buchanan); *Commercial Bulletin*, November 3, 1836; Francis Wright, survey, September 20, 1837 (TSLA); Robert Potter, letter, April 4, 1836 (Rosenberg TNC); Thomas W. Grayson to Texas auditor (TSLA); Crimmins 397 (quoting *Army and Navy Chronicle*, November 17, 1836); "List of Officers Bearing Commissions of Letters of Marque and Reprisal," November 3, 1836 (TSLA); Dienst Collection document 334 (CAH); and Dienst 1:191 (citing *National Intelligencer*, February 25, 1837), 193 (quoting William G. Cook to Toby, December 3, 1836).

The release of *Brutus* and *Invincible* from their New York creditors is documented in Houston to Toby, October 27, 1836 (Houston 1:461-62); Schroeder (148); Handbook of Texas Online, "Swartwout, Samuel"; Charles Sayre to Williams, October 27, November 29, and December 20, 1836 (TSLA); Haugh (378, quoting *Journal of Commerce*, November 22, 1836, and 379, quoting *Journal of Commerce*, January 9 and March 1, 1837); Jeremiah Brown to Williams, November 30, 1836 (TSLA); records of the Court of Common Pleas, December 31, 1836 (TSLA); Order to Show Cause, December 16, 1836 (TSLA); I.M. Wolfe to Williams, February 25, 1837 (TSLA).

Commodore Hawkins's travels between Texas and New Orleans and his death were recounted in General Land Office Certificate No. 202, January 21, 1838 (GLO); Charles E. Hawkins, receipt, December 3, 1836 (ROT Claims, Charles E. Hawkins); Thruston to Fisher, February 11, 1837 (Rosenberg TNC); Lewis M. H. Washington, Eulogy for Charles E. Hawkins, August 9, 1838 (L. M. H. Washington Papers, CAH); Stone (34-35, quoting *Telegraph*); *Courier*, February 13, 1837; and Dienst 2:269.

The return of *Brutus* and *Invincible* to Texas, Captain Wheelwright's succession of Hawkins, the Mexican naval buildup, the dismissals of Captains Brown and Hurd, the blockade of 1837, Commodore López, Mexico's hostility towards Texas, and the Texas response are documented in Thruston to George Wheelwright, February 9,

1837 (TSLA); Dienst 2:270 (citing Tennison document 314); *Plaindealer*, April 15, 1837 (citing article from the *Mobile Register*); *Bee*, May 1 and 13, 1837; Fisher to Thruston, February 26, March 28, and April 15, 1837 (Rosenberg TNC);Thruston to Fisher, February 17 and 26, 1837 (TSLA); *Telegraph*, August 2, 1836 (background on Boylan); Gen. Nicholas Bravo to U.S. Consul Daniel W. Smith,April 12, 1837 (H. R. Exec Docs., No. 75, 6); Adm. Francisco de Paula López to Judge,April 1, 1837 (H. R. Exec. Docs., 25th Cong., 2nd Sess., No. 75, 24); Lopez to Sr. Juez,April 1, 1837 (*id.* 19); R. Delgado, Statement, April 26, 1837 (*id.*); Fisher to Messrs. Shreeves and Grayson, March 3, 1837 (Rosenberg TNC);Thruston to Fisher, March 17, 1837 (Rosenberg TNC); contract between Benjamin S. Grayson and Thruston, April 8, 1837 (TSLA); *Commercial Bulletin*, February 10 and March 13, 1837; statement of Downing H. Crisp, n.d. (Newberry Library,Ames Collection) (hereinafter,"Crisp Statement"); *Secret Journals* 49 (May 18, 1837 entry); Handbook of Texas Online,"Brown, Jeremiah" (citing *Telegraph*, October 20, 1838); *Houston Morning Star*,August 29, 1843; Memucan Hunt,"To the Heirs of William A. Hurd, dec'd." March 30, 1839 (ROT Claims,William A. Hurd); Memucan Hunt,"To the Curator of H. L.Thompson, Dec'd.,"April 28, 1839 (ROT Claims, H. L.Thompson);Thomas M.Thompson to Editor, *Telegraph*,August 16, 1836 and October 18, 1837; Houston to Congress, May 5, 1837 (*Telegraph*, May 9, 1837 and Houston 2:86); *New York Times*,June 1, 1837 (quoting *Mobile Commercial Register*, May 25, 1837); Houston to Fisher,April 5, 1837 (Houston 4:28-29); Fisher to Thruston, April 15, 1837 (Rosenberg TNC); *Bee*,April 24 and May 13, 1837; Hill (69, citing Lopez to District Judge of Nuevo Leon,April 1837, in H. R. Exec. Doc. 75, 25th Cong., 2nd Sess., 24; and 70); *True American*,April 24 and 27, 1837; Hill (69, citing Nicholas Bravo to D.W. Smith, April 13, 1837, in H. R. Exec. Doc. 75, 24); Albert Levy to Editor (*Telegraph*, June 8, 1837); Jose M. Espino to Secretary of War and Marine, April 21, 1837 (*Diario*,June 2, 1837); *Courier*, February 9, 1837; and Vázquez 316-17.

TEN: A CLASH OF FLAGSHIPS

The final voyage of the Texas flagship *Independence* was documented in Tennison documents 314, 316;Anonymous,"Remarks Upon the Texas Navy," n.d. (*Lamar Papers* 2:229); John W.Taylor to S. Rhoads Fisher,April 21, 1837 (*Telegraph*,June 8, 1837); José Espino to Secretary of War and Marine, April 21, 1837 (*Diario*,June 3, 1837); *Diario*, May 11, 1837; Moore, *Statement*; Hill (80, quoting *Diario*, May 11, 1837); Dimmick 31, n.1.

The treatment of the *Independence* prisoners was documented at Tennison document 316 (Dienst collection, CAH); José Espino to Secretary of War and Marine,April 30, 1837 (*Diario*, June 4, 1837); account of J.W. Taylor, n.d. (*Diario*, July 26, 1837); Dienst 2:274 (citing *Commercial Bulletin*,July 12, 1837, *Gazeta de Tampico*,April 29, 1837, and *Mercurio de Matamoros*,April 21, 1837); *Telegraph*, May 26,June 8,July 15, September 2 and 9 and December 2, 1837; Hill 71-72, 78 (quoting William H.Wharton to Houston, April 22, 1837 and *New York Times*, June 15, 1837); Albert M. Levy to *Telegraph*,June 8, 1837; *New York Times*, June 1, 1837 (quoting Mobile *Commercial Register*, May 25, 1837); Fischer 131; Handbook of Texas Online,"Levy,Albert Moses"; *Texas Almanac for 1860*, 164; Cardenas De la Peña 145.

The legislative response to *Invincible*'s capture is found in Gammel 1:1329, 1398-99; *House Journal, First Congress, 2nd Session* 70, 84-87 (quoting Houston to Texas Congress, May 31, 1837); Joint Resolution, vetoed June 1, 1837 (Dienst collection, CAH); and Houston to Congress, November 21, 1837 (*Telegraph*, November 25, 1837).

ELEVEN: MISTER FISHER'S REVENGE

Popular reaction to *Independence*'s surrender is found in *Telegraph*,June 8, 1837, and Tennison documents 345-46 (Dienst Collection, CAH). News of the Mexican buildup is found in James Tongue to A. S.Thruston,April 30, 1837 (Rosenberg TNC); S.

Rhoads Fisher to Thruston, May 6, 1837 (Rosenberg TNC); Fisher to Thruston, May 18, 1837 (TSLA); and Thruston to Commodore W. B. Taylor, May 26, 1837 (TSLA).

The description of Commander Thompson's idiosyncrasies derives from the sworn statements of J. G. Dunn, Fleming T. Wells, Corneilus Hoit, and Daniel Lloyd (TSLA). Fisher's preparatory orders for the summer cruise are found in Fisher to Henry L. Thompson, May 23, 1837 (TSLA). Houston's opposition to the expedition and Fisher's response are documented in Memucan Hunt to Sam Houston, June 1, 1837 (R.A. Irion Papers, UTA); Fisher to *Telegraph*, September 16, 1837; Speech of Sen. Sam Houston of Texas, July 15, 1854; and Hutton (40).

Thomas Toby's activities are recounted in Nathaniel Hoyt to "R. S. Fisher," April 27, 1837 (TSLA); Thruston to Fisher, April 4, 1837 (TSLA); Thompson to Navy Department, August 29, 1837 (TSLA) (hereinafter, "Thompson Report"); *Diario*, June 18, 1837; Hill (95); and Dienst 1:192 (quoting *Telegraph*).

The 1837 cruise is documented at Thompson to Navy Department, August 29, 1837 (TSLA); report of James D. Boylan, September 1, 1837 (TSLA) (hereinafter, "Boylan Report"); Hutton 40 (quoting Houston to Senate, November 2, 1837, in St. Pius X Library, Incarnate Word College, San Antonio); Fisher to Dr. Bartlett, June 18, 1837 (*Telegraph*, September 9, 1837); P. W. Humphreys to Thompson, September 24, 1837 (TSLA); Forrest Moreau to "My dear old Lady," August 20, 1837 (Rosenberg TNC); Crisp Statement; Worley 6 (citing Charles Elliott to G. W. Terrell, December 13, 1842); Tennison document 328 (quoting unnamed newspaper which cites report of Midshipman Robert Foster); charges and specifications of James S. Simons, Cornelius Hoyt, Lt. Davis, Fleming T. Wells, and Daniel Lloyd (TSLA); *Telegraph*, August 22, 1837; Wells to William M. Shepherd, March 20, 1838 (TSLA); *Diario*, March 24, 1836 (background on *Telegrafo*); Thompson to Humphreys, September 20, 1837 (TSLA); Thompson to Navy Department, September 20, 1837 (TSLA); George Fisher to Anson Jones, April 25, 1842 (TSLA); Survey by Thomas F. McKinney, October 24, 1837 (TSLA); affidavit of John Marks, March 4, 1839 (TSLA); Hill 87 (citing depositions of Pablo Canesa and Antonio Corral, August 18, 1837, Mexican archives); and Cardenas de la Peña 97. The landing at Dzilam de Bravo was documented in the Boylan Report and the statements of Francisco Sota, Juan Pablo Pacheco, Domingo Sansores, Apolinario Lisama, trans. Richard Saiser and Sandra L. Myres (Rosenberg TNC).

TWELVE: DEATH OF A NAVY

The battle between *Libertador, Iturbide,* and *Invincible* was described in the Boylan Report; Thompson to Navy Department, August 29, 1837 (TSLA) charges and specifications of James S. Simons and statements of Fleming T. Wells and Cornelius Hoit (TLSA); *Telegraph*, September 2 and 9, 1837; P.W. Humphreys to Henry L. Thompson, September 24, 1837 (TSLA); José de Aldana to Ministeria de Guerra y Marina, September 7, 1837 (*Diario*, September 11, 1837); Aldana to Commandant, Department of Yucatán, August 19 and 21, 1837, (*Diario*, September 11, 1837); Oertling 1992 (12-14, citing Dienst papers, quoting Charges of Midshipmen Cyrus Cummings, Alfred A. Waite and Sam M. Wybrants); Francis B. Wright to S. Rhoads Fisher, September 20, 1837 (Dienst collection, CAH); Thomas F. McKinney, letter, September 8, 1837 (Dienst collection, CAH); Crisp Statement; James D. Boylan to William M. Shepherd, September 19, 1837 (TLSA); and Boylan to William L. Sawyer, December 14, 1837 (TSLA, reprinted in Oertling, 1997, 7).

"Racer's Storm" and the destruction of *Brutus* were recorded at Boylan to Shepherd, September 19, 1837 (TSLA); Wright to Navy Secretary, October 9, 1837 (TSLA); Bancroft 2:283; Turner 46; Anonymous 9; Anonymous, "Remarks Upon the Texas Navy" (*Lamar Papers* 2:235); Fisher to Shreeves and Grayson, March 1, 1837 (Rosenberg TNC); Cox 119-20; and Hogan 92 (quoting Mary Austin Holley to Mrs. William A. Brand, December 19, 1837, in Holley Papers, CAH).

THIRTEEN: HELL TO PAY

Popular reaction to the 1837 cruise was recounted in the *Telegraph*, September 2 and October 7, 1837; and Dr. Moreau Forest to his wife, September 28, 1837 (Rosenberg TNC). Background on Shepherd comes from the Handbook of Texas Online, "Shepherd, William M." The statute requiring cabinet officers to remain at the seat of government is documented at Gammel 1:1137.

Court-martial proceedings against Commander Thompson, and his subsequent death, were recorded in Memucan Hunt, "To the Curator of H. L. Thompson, Dec'd.," April 29, 1839 (ROT Claims, Henry L. Thompson); Dienst 2:264-65 (citing *House Journal, Second Texas Congress* 170); Charges of James S. Simons and Oscar Davis, September 16, 1837 (TSLA); Oertling 1992 (12-13); Henry L. Thompson to Navy Department, September 20, 1837 (TSLA); Navy Department to Thompson, September 24, 1837 (TSLA); Thompson to P. W. Humphreys, September 30, 1837 (TSLA); *Telegraph*, November 4, 1837; *Senate Journal, Second Texas Congress* (42); and James D. Boylan, Invoice, September 12, 1841 (ROT Claims, James D. Boylan).

Secretary Fisher's dismissal, trial and death were described in Tennison document 328; Fisher to John Birdsall et al. September 4, 1837 (*Telegraph*, September 9, 1837); Fisher to Friends and Fellow Citizens (*Telegraph*, September 9, 1837); Constitution of the Republic of Texas, Art. VI, sec. 10; Fisher to Hon. Chairman, House Committee on Naval Affairs, September 20, 1837 (TSLA); Houston to Senate, October 6, 1837 (Houston 4:37); *Secret Journals* (73, 80-83, 87, 89-90); Houston to Senate, November 7 and December 5, 1837 (Houston 2:146, 164); Houston to Anna Raguet, December 4, 1837 (Houston 2:162) (referring to "Dr. Shippers"); Anonymous, "S. R. Fisher's Case," (*Lamar Papers* 1:584-87); *Telegraph*, November 25, 1837; *Senate Journal, Second Texas Congress*, (72-73, 90) (Dienst copy, CAH); Fowler (80); George Wheelwright to Mirabeau B. Lamar, August 24, 1838 (*Lamar Papers*); *Capitols of Texas* (61); and Sons of DeWitt Colony website.

FOURTEEN: MANAGING A GHOST FLEET

Secretary Shepherd's efforts to rebuild the fleet and administer the naval service were documented by William M. Shepherd to Sam Houston, October 20, 1838 (TSLA); Houston to Senate, December 5, 1837 (Houston 2:163-64); Shepherd to George Wheelwright, December 30, 1837, and April 3, 1838 (TSLA); Wheelwright to Shepherd, April 2, 9, 15, and 18, 1838 (TSLA); Report of the Secretary of the Navy, October 4, 1838 (*House Journal, Third Texas Congress, Regular Session* 15-16; John W. Taylor to ——, May 31, 1839 (TSLA); John Grant Tod, Report on *Potomac*, n.d. (Rosenberg JGT); affidavit of Francis B. Wright, March 20, 1839 (TSLA); Account of Prize Agent Thomas M. Duke, October 30, 1839 (TSLA); Schedule of Prize Schooner *Correo*, October 24, 1837 (TSLA); Thompson to Navy Department, August 29, 1837 (TSLA); Francis B. Wright, Report, September 20, 1837 (TSLA); J. W. Niles to Shepherd, January 4, 1838 (TSLA); Shepherd to Niles, January 16, 1838 (TSLA); George Wheelwright to ——, February 6 and April 3, 1838 (TSLA); Anonymous 8-9; letter from Thomas W. Grayson, n.d. (TSLA); Gammel 1:1353-54 and 1392; *Telegraph*, September 16, 1837; *Plaindealer*, April 15, 1837 (citing article from *Mobile Register*); Gammel 1:1450-51; Cartwright (72-74); Turner (46); Dienst 1:192 (citing Tennison document 332, Dienst Collection CAH), 2:275, 3:2 (citing Shepherd to Houston, September 30, 1837 (*House Journal, Second Texas Congress, 1st and 2nd Sessions*, 166-72)) and 3:4-5 (quoting Report of the Secretary of the Navy, November 4, 1840, in *House Journal, Fifth Texas Congress, First Session* at 185-96 (hereinafter, "Navy Department Report, 1840")); Houston to Congress, November 21, 1837 (*House Journal, Second Texas Congress, Regular Session*, 151-57); Houston to Senate, April 30, 1838 (Houston 4:46-51); Executive Act, May 17, 1838 (Rosenberg TNC); Shepherd to Houston, April 20, 1838 (TSLA); Wheelwright to Shepherd, April 2, 1838 (TSLA);

Joint Resolution, May 23, 1838 (Gammel 1:1495-96, Dienst copy); Houston to George W. Hockley, April 15, 1838 (TSLA); George Wheelwright to Secretary of Navy, April 18 and 19, 1838 (TSLA); Vázquez 315, 318, and 321; Hockley to John W. Taylor, April 16, 1838 (Rosenberg TNC); Louis P. Cooke to Mirabeau B. Lamar, December 28, 1839 (*Journals of the Fourth Texas Congress* 1:202); Taylor to Lamar, December 9, 1838 (*Lamar Papers* 2:315); Houston to Hockley, July 2, 1838 (Rosenberg TNC); Hockley, pay voucher, September 1, 1838 (Rosenberg TNC); Connors (18); and Hogan (99, re: Texas finances).

Management of the Navy Yard under Secretary Shepherd is found in John Grant Tod to Fisher, May 22, 1837 (Rosenberg JGT); Fisher to A. S. Thruston, March 20, 1837 (Rosenberg TNC); Navy Department to Alex Thompson, September 15, 1837 (TSLA); Alex Thompson to ——, October 5, 1837 (TSLA); Thomas M. Thompson to Tod, May 18, 1838 (Rosenberg TNC); Wheelwright to Thomas M. Thompson, February 2, 1838 (Rosenberg JGT); Shepherd to Thomas M. Thompson, February 28, 1838 (Rosenberg JGT); Wheelwright to Shepherd, April 2, 1838 (TSLA); James S. Gillet, letter re: James Boylan, March 1, 1854 (ROT Claims, James D. Boylan); Handbook of Texas Online, "Thompson, Thomas M."; Shepherd to Tod, April 29, 1838 (Rosenberg JGT); Houston to Tod, May 2, 1838 (Rosenberg JGT); Sheridan (12-13); and Houston, Memorandum to Departments, May 26, 1838 (Rosenberg JGT).

The prize controversy was documented by District Judge Shelby Corrigan, Orders, September 23 and October 12, 1837 (TSLA); R. A. Irion to Shepherd, April 26 and May 1, 1838 (TSLA); Shepherd to Irion, May 1, 1838 (TSLA); Hoolen (17); Thomas M. League to Shepherd, January 4, 1838 (TSLA); Account of Prize Agent Thomas M. Duke, October 30, 1837 (TSLA); Gammel 1:1495-96 and 2:246; P. W. Humphreys to Henry L. Thompson, September 24, 1837 (TSLA); Asa Brigham to Gail Borden, Jr., August 23, 1837 (Rosenberg TNC); Gail Borden, Jr. to Joseph Russell, August 29, 1837 (TSLA); Worley (5, 7, citing Ashbel Smith to Charles Elliott, February 22, 1845); Dienst 2:259; and Samuel B. Shaw, Treasury Warrant, March 9, 1844 (Rosenberg TNC).

FIFTEEN: VIVE LA FRANCE!

Federalist disturbances, the French campaign of 1838-39, and related events were recounted at Hill 97-102, 113 (citing Luis G. Cuevas, *Exposicion del ex-Ministerio sobre las Differences con Francia* (Mexico City 1839)); Bancroft, *History of Mexico* 5:197 and notes of Lt. De Vaisseau E. Maissin, in P. Blanchard and A. Dauzats, *San Juan de Ulloa* (Paris: M. E. Maissan 1839) 519-20; Hogan 13, 92 (quoting Ashbel Smith to Charles Fisher, May 24, 1839 (Ashbel Smith Papers, CAH)); Vázquez 321-22; Gaillardet dispatch dated July 24, 1839 (Gaillardet 72, n. 7); Dienst 3:6; Cartwright 79; and A. C. Hinton to Louis P. Cooke, May 18, 1839 (Annual Report of the Secretary of the Navy, November 1839 (*Journals of the Fourth Texas Congress* 3:117) (hereinafter "Navy Department Report, 1839") 30). Admiral Baudin's calls on Texas were described in Gaillardet, dispatch dated May 23, 1839, and Baudin to Mayor and Aldermen of Galveston, May 13, 1839 (Gaillardet 10-12); Certificate of Galveston City, San Jacinto Museum, Houston, Texas.

SIXTEEN: HOUSTON, LAMAR, AND SHIFTING POLITICAL CURRENTS

Legislative and popular support for a new navy in late 1837 was documented in Gammel 1:1090 ("Act Providing for an Increase of the Navy," approved November 18, 1836) and 2:129 (act approved January 26, 1839); *Telegraph*, October 11, 14, and 28, 1837; and Dienst 3:3.

The mission to Baltimore and negotiations for the Dawson ships can be found in John Grant Tod to Gustavus A. Parker, December 11, 1844 (Rosenberg JGT); Sam Houston to William M. Shepherd, June 9, 1838 (Rosenberg JGT); Shepherd to Tod, June 10, 1838 (Rosenberg JGT); Houston to Martin van Buren, June 13, 1838 (Rosenberg

JGT);Thomas F. McKinney to Samuel May Williams, August 21, 1838 (Rosenberg SMW); Williams to Tod, September 11, 1838 (Rosenberg JGT); "Reprimand Delivered by the President of the Senate to Hon. Robert Wilson, by order of the Senate, January 13, 1839"; Houston to Anson Jones, June 12, 1838 (on Jones pp. 132-33); J. P. Henderson to Jones, October 6, 1838 (on Jones p. 133); Henson, SMW 100; Shepherd to Houston, October 30, 1838; George W. Hockley to Tod, August 2 and 6, 1838 (Rosenberg JGT); Williams to Shepherd, October 9, 1838 (TSLA); contract between Samuel May Williams and Frederick W. Dawson, November 13, 1838 (TSLA); Williams to Mrs. Williams, November 13, 1838 (Rosenberg SMW); Dawson to Williams, November 24, 1838 (Rosenberg SMW); Dienst 3:3; Hill at 105; and Connor at 19.

The acquisition and history of the steamer *Charleston*, and her trip to Texas, was found on Arnold pp. 105 and 107 (citing passenger account and William A. Baker, *Commercial Shipping and Shipbuilding in the Delaware Valley*, paper presented at Society of Naval Architects and Marine Engineers, June 2-5,1976); John Grant Tod, "Memorandum of Service," (NARA); Baldwin p. 11; Log of *San Bernard*, May 6, 1840; Williams to Shepherd, October 9, 1838 (TSLA); Navy Department Report, 1839; Silverstone p. 88; Francaviglia pp. 90-91, 98-103; A. J. Yates to Stephen F. Austin et al. January 14, 1836 (PTR 4:28); William P. Harris to "Friend" Hanks, January 19, 1836 (PTR 4:73); James Pennoyer to Williams, October 23, 1838 (Rosenberg SMW); James Hamilton to Secretary of the Navy, November 3, 1838 (TSLA); Henson, SMW p. 101 (citing Hamilton to Williams, October 27, 1838, Hamilton to Lamar, November 2, 1838, and James Treat to Williams, November 28, 1838); and contract between James Hamilton and James Holford, October 24, 1838 (TSLA).

The events, policies and personnel changes attendant to the incoming Lamar administration can be found at Schroeder 147; Lamar, Message to Congress, December 21, 1838 (*Lamar Papers* 2:368); Winfrey 186-88, 190-91; Roach 156 (citing Lamar to Lewis Cass, December 22, 1858); Lamar to Congress, November 12, 1839 (*Lamar Papers* 3:164, 167); Lamar, Inaugural Address, November 10, 1838 (*Lamar Papers* 2:319); McKinney to Williams, January 1, 1839 (Rosenberg SMW); Senate Resolution, December 2, 1838 (*Senate Journal, Third Texas Congress, First Session* 72-73); Gammel 2:129-30 (act approved January 26, 1839); Hogan 81-82, 99-100; Fehrenbach 253; Gaillardet 58; and Henson 102.

Background and events concerning John Grant Tod can be found at the USN Early History Files, Midshipman John G. Tod (NHC); Petition of John Grant Tod to Senate and House of Representatives of Texas, n.d. (circa 1852) (ROT Claims, John Grant Tod); Dienst 3:9 nn. 4 and 10; Tod to G.W. Hill, May 25 and 30, September 6 and 25, and December 4, 1837 (Rosenberg JGT); Tod to Houston, December 22, 1837 (Rosenberg JGT); Tod to Shepherd, December 20, 1837 (Rosenberg JGT); Tod to Andrew J. Donelson, April 4, 1846 (Rosenberg JGT); Henson SMW, 102 (citing Tod to Williams, January 22, 1839); Hill (109); Navy Department Report, 1839; Louis P. Cooke to Musgrove Evans, October 24, 1839 (TSLA); and Tod, "Memorandum of Service," (NARA).

Background on Edwin Ward Moore and events surrounding his resignation from the U.S. Navy and appointment to command the Texas Navy can be found at the USN Early History Files, Lt. Edwin W. Moore (NHC) (citing Charles G. Ridgley to James K. Paulding, May 30, 1839; Paulding to Ridgley, June 1, 1839; Ridgley to Paulding, June 3, 1839; Ridgley to Paulding, June 4, 1839, and Paulding to Moore, June 14, 1839); on Wells p. 6 (citing Moore to Secretary of the Navy, March 19, 1825), 7 (citing Moore to Levi Woodbury, February 6, 1833, and Letter to Passed Midshipman E. W. Moore, September 4, 1832), 8 (citing log of sloop *Boston*, September 20, 1836 entry), 9 (citing George Bancroft to Moore, February 28, 1848), 10 (citing James K. Paulding to Moore, April 29, 1838; Paulding to Commodore Jacob Jones, June 24, 1839; Moore to Paulding, June 14, 1839; Moore to Paulding, July 8, 1839; and Texas General Land Office Records, certificate dated February 1838), and 12 (citing Hockley to Moore, July 21, 1842); Smith, *Grant and Lee* (21); Dienst 3:13 and 3:15 (quoting Midshipman

George F. Fuller to Dienst, October 27, 1904); Cox (126); Speech of Sen. Sam Houston of Texas, July 15, 1854; Ramsay (114); Houstoun 1:58, 1:139; Tod to Hill, April 6 and September 6, 1839 (Rosenberg JGT); *Telegraph*, July 15, 1837; Hill (110, citing A.C. Howard to Lamar, June 17, 1839 (*Lamar Papers* 5:295)); Moore to Charles Mason, August 1, 1841 (TSLA); Koury (29, citing Memucan Hunt to Moore, April 29, 1839); and Tod to Lamar, December 2, 1840 (Rosenberg JGT).

SEVENTEEN: PHOENIX OF THE SEA

The description of Galveston comes from Cox p. 113. The arrival and fitting out of *Zavala* and the Dawson ships was recounted in Navy Department Report, 1839; *Telegraph*, June 26 and August 7, 1839 (arrival of *Viper* and *Asp;* command of *San Jacinto* given to Lt. Lothrop); Edwin W. Moore to John Grant Tod, August 1839 (Rosenberg JGT) (noting travel of Colt's representative to Texas aboard *Scorpion*); Memucan Hunt to Mirabeau Lamar, May 1, 1839 (SRM); Dr. J.W. Copes to Joseph S. Copes, May 6, 1839 (Tulane, Copes Papers); Tod, "Memorandum of Service" (NARA); James Love to Albert Sidney Johnston, June 21, 1839 (Tulane, ASJ Papers); deck log, *San Bernard*, summer 1839; Samuel May Williams to James Hamilton, January 23, 1839 (Rosenberg SMW); warranty deed, James Holford to Republic of Texas (TSLA); Addison C. Hinton to Navy Department, February 3, 1839 (TSLA); John W. Taylor to J.F. Stephens, February 19, 1839 (TSLA); Moore to Hamilton, March 6, 1851 (Rosenberg TNC); Tennison document 350 (Dienst collection, CAH); Baldwin at 12; Houston to House of Representatives, January 7, 1842 (Houston 2:423); Hinton to Louis P. Cooke, May 18, 1839 (1839 Report 32); Cooke to Tod, May 18, 1839 (San Jacinto Museum Library, John G. Tod at Papers); Nichols at 203 (citing Gambrel, *Anson Jones*, 167); Stephens to ——, May 24, 1840 (TSLA); Moore, *Statement*; Norman Hurd to Tod, July 13, 1839 (Rosenberg JGT); January 4, 1840 Report of the Chairman of the Committee on Naval Affairs (*Journal of the Fourth Texas Congress,* 1:245-48); Dienst 3:10; conract between Samuel May Williams and Frederick W. Dawson, November 13, 1838 (TSLA); Wells at 11-12 (citing Nelson J. Maynard to William T. Brannum, June 24, 1840); Handbook of Texas Online, "Brannum, William T." *Zavala*'s armament is subject to some question. In early 1842, it appears she mounted four 18-pounders and a long 18 pivot. Thurston M. Taylor, "Memorandum of the Present Condition of the Navy of Texas," n.d. (c. January 15, 1842) (TSLA).

Recruiting efforts were documented at Anonymous, "Remarks Upon the Texas Navy," (*Lamar Papers* 2:230-33); N.T. Rossetter to Williams, September 18, 1838 (Rosenberg SMW); William A. Howard to Lamar, June 18, 1839 (*Lamar Papers* 5:295); J. P. Fisher to Williams, December 16, 1838 (Rosenberg SMW); William R. Bowers to Williams, December 27, 1838 (Rosenberg SMW); C. F. Duerr Papers, 144-47 (CAH) (Lothrop eulogy from *National Vindicator*); Thomas F. McKinney to Johnston, June 18, 1839 (Tulane, ASJ Papers); Willis Roberts to Lamar, June 20, 1839 (*Lamar Papers* 6:296); Hurd to Tod, July 26, 1839 (Rosenberg JGT); Hill (112, citing *Secret Journals* 137).

Purchases of weapons and supplies were documented at Koury 29, 34; January 1840 Navy Yard returns (TSLA); Tod to Cooke, June 23, 1840 (in Navy Department Report, 1840, CAH); Journal of Midshipman James Mabry, October 27, November 4 and November 9, 1839 and June 9, 1840 (in *Galveston News,* January 9, 1893) (hereinafter, "Mabry Journal"); Navy Department Report, 1839; Marshall 18; and requisitions dated May 28 to August 14, 1840 (Rosenberg TNC). Naval regulations for 1839 are reprinted in Marshall (75-76).

Moore's arrival in Texas was reported in the *Telegraph*, October 9, 1839. Early efforts to organize the reconstituted navy are found in Mabry Journal, October 27, 1839 (*Galveston News,* January 9, 1893); Tod to Hill, September 6, 1839 (Rosenberg TNC); Fleming T. Wells to Tod, October 7, 1839 (Rosenberg JGT); Yoakum 2:271; Navy Department Report, 1839; Report of the Chairman of the Committee on Naval Affairs, January 13, 1840 (*Journal of the Fourth Texas Congress* 1:245-48); Fuller (223);

Dienst 3:8-9 (citing Gammel 2:129-30); Wells (11); and Connor (86). The reference to the brig name "*Brazos*" comes from Tod to Hill, September 8, 1839 (Rosenberg JGT).

Political challenges faced by Lamar and Cooke were documented in *Journals of the Fourth Texas Congress* 2:157, 183; Cooke to Senate Committee on Naval Affairs, December 16, 1839, and Cooke to Senate, December 20, 1839 (*Journals of the Fourth Texas Congress* 2:145, 150, 187, 188, 205); Lamar to Senate, January 3, 1840 (*Journals of the Fourth Texas Congress* 1:200); Majority Report, Naval Affairs Committee (*Journals of the Fourth Texas Congress* 1:251-53); Gambrell (169, 172); Naval General Orders, March 13, 1838 (CAH); Hill (117-18); Wells (19); and Ramsay (114).

Problems faced by John Grant Tod were documented by Hunt to Tod, February and March 23 and 25, 1839 (Rosenberg JGT); Hunt to Tod, March 24, 1839 (Rosenberg JM); Taylor to Tod, May 27, 1839 (Rosenberg JGT); Tod to G.W. Hill, April 6 and September 6 and 9, 1839 (Rosenberg JGT); Tod to Hunt, March 25, 1839 (Rosenberg JGT); Cooke to Tod, July 13, 1839, (San Jacinto Museum Library, John G. Tod papers); Love to Tod, October 2, 1839 (Rosenberg JGT); and Williams to Tod, September 14, 1839 (Rosenberg JGT).

Hinton's efforts to fit out *Zavala*, his financial constraints and his ultimate dismissal, were documented in Cooke to Hinton, October 25, 1839 (TSLA); Hinton to Cooke December 18, 1839 (TSLA); Moore to Hinton, November 1839 (TLSA); Hinton to Cooke, November 20 and 29, 1839 (TSLA); George Beatty, Requisition, November 4, 1839 (Rosenberg TNC); Hinton to Cooke, January 7 and 11, and May 11, 1840 (TSLA); Cooke to Hinton, December 21, 1839 (*House Journal, Fifth Texas Congress, First Session* 238); Navy Department Report, 1840; Dienst 3:7-8 (citing *House Journal, Fifth Texas Congress, First Session* pp. 187, 221-22) and 15-16; Lamar to Cooke, January 28, 1840 (TSLA); Hinton to Lamar, March 1, 1840 (*Journals of the Sixth Texas Congress* 2:347); Gammel 2:609 (Joint Resolution approved February 4, 1841) (Dienst Copy); Hinton to Cooke, May 18, 1839 (Navy Department Report, 1839, 31-32); Moore to Cooke, August 28, 1840 (*House Journal, Fifth Texas Congress, First Session*, Appendix 232-37); Navy Department Report, 1840; Cox on p. 123; and Wells on pp. 16, 17 (citing *House Journal, Fifth Texas Congress, First Session* 238), 18.

EIGHTEEN: WINTERTIME IN NEW YORK

San Antonio's recruiting trip to New Orleans was documented in Edwin W. Moore to A.C. Hinton, November 1839 (Rosenberg TNC); and Moore to William T. Brannum, November 12, 1839 (TSLA); Mabry Journal, December 12 and 16, 1839; Hinton to Louis P. Cooke, December 18, 1839 (TSLA); and deck log, *San Bernard*, December 9 and 30, 1839 (NARA).

Moore's recruiting trip to New York was documented in Hinton to Cooke, December 18, 1839 (TSLA); Wells at 15 (citing Garrison, *Diplomatic Correspondence* 2:410), 21 (citing Moore to Albert S. Johnston, December 9, 1841), 29; *House Journal, Third Texas Congress* 15-20 (Dienst copy, CAH); Haugh at 380 (citing New York *Journal of Commerce*, December 10, 1839 and *New York Evening Post*, December 10, 1839), 381 (citing *Journal of Commerce*, January 6 and 7, 1840 and Garrison, *Diplomatic Correspondence* 3:885-86), and 382 (quoting Moore to Richard G. Dunlap, January 20, 1840); James Renshaw to Moore, December 12, 1839 (TSLA); Navy Department Report, 1839; Moore to George Wheelwright, June 26, 1840 (*Lamar Papers* 3:414); Moore, "List of Sundries Purchased by E.W. Moore in New York, 1839-1840," January 20, 1840 (Rosenberg TNC); Moore, *Statement*; Receipt dated January 9, 1840 (TSLA); Auditor's Records, Texas Navy (TSLA); "Shipping Articles" for brig *Wharton* (*Lamar Papers* 3:443); Affidavit of Charles S. Hunter (TSLA); Dunlap to David G. Burnet, January 27, 1840 (Garrison, *Diplomatic Correspondence*, 1:436); John Forsyth to Dunlap, January 15, 1840 (Garrison, *Diplomatic Correspondence* 2:437); Deposit of F. T. Wells, January 2, 1840 (TSLA); Receipt of J. Prescott Hall, December 31, 1839 (TSLA); Moore to Renshaw, January 3, 1840 (TSLA); F.T. Wells to

Tod, February 24, 1840 (Rosenberg JGT); Houstoun 1:139; Anonymous, "Remarks Upon the Texas Navy" (*Lamar Papers* 2;228, 234); Sullivan at 29 (citing *Journals of the Fourth Texas Congress* 3:143-51); and Fuller at 223.

NINETEEN: THE SEAFARING LIFE

Initial command assignments were documented in Fleming T. Wells to John Grant Tod, February 24, 1840 (Rosenberg JGT); Edwin W. Moore to William R. Postell, William S. Williamson and James E. Gibbons, February 14, 1840 (TSLA); Postell, Williamson and Gibbons to Moore, February 15, 1840 (TSLA); Moore, *Statement*; and Thurston M. Taylor to Moore, February 20, 1840 (TSLA).

Life in the Texas Navy was documented by Fuller at 224-29; Cox at 120-27; Wells to Tod, February 24, 1840 (Rosenberg JGT); Norman Hurd to Tod, July 25, 1839 (Rosenberg JGT); Navy Yard Stores, January 1840 (TSLA); Moore, Order Regarding Rations, September 28, 1842 (TSLA); Journal of Midshipman Alfred Walke (TSLA) (hereinafter, "Walke Journal"), Mabry Journal, January 20, 1840 (*Galveston News*, January 9, 1893); Robert Oliver, "Account of quantities of Provisions saved by the Company of the Texas Schooner 'San Jacinto' out of their daily allowances between the 1st day of July 1840 and the 17th of January 1841," January 17, 1841 (Rosenberg TNC); Gray (4-6); Sheridan (77-78); Blake (105); and Wells (27-28).

Political problems faced by the Navy are documented in Cooke to Lamar, April 5, 1840 (*Lamar Papers* 3:363); Mabry Journal, February 23 and March 29, 1840 (*Galveston News*, January 9, 1893); Gammel 2:364; Francis Moore to Lamar, March 9, 1840 (*Lamar Papers* 3:349); *San Bernard* log, January 13, 1840. The reference to Lieutenant Wright's inebriation comes from Francis Wright to James Morgan, November 22, 1841 (Rosenberg JM).

Tod's activities during this time were recounted in Moore to Sen. James A. Pearce, March 28, 1853 (CAH); Moore, *Statement*; Dienst 3:11 (citing Navy Department Report, 1840); Tod to Frederick Dawson, March 19, 1840 (TSLA); Dawson to Tod, March 19, 1840 (TSLA); Gray (5); Moore to Tod, June 28, 1840 (Rosenberg JGT); Tod to Cooke, June 4 and 23, 1840 (TSLA); affidavit of John Grant Tod, March 20, 1852 (TSLA); Tennison document 356 (Dienst collection CAH); Tod to R. A. Irion, January 22, 1838 (R.A. Irion Family Papers, UTA); Tod, receipt, August 15, 1840 (Rosenberg TNC); Moore to Albert Sidney Johnston, December 9, 1841 (Tulane ASJ Papers); and Moore to Wheelwright, June 26, 1840 (*Lamar Papers* 3:414).

The vessel names were discussed in Moore to Wheelwright, June 26, 1840 (*Lamar Papers* 3:414); Fuller (223); Nathan Smith, Naval Store Keeper, "Receipt from Norman Hurd," March 13, 1840 (Mrs. Floyd Williams, ed., "Research Notes on the Ships of the Texas Navy," Chambers County, Texas Historical Commission (Sam Houston Regional Library and Research Center, TSLA); receipt from Hurd to Smith, April 25, 1840 (*id.*); Cooke to Johnston, April 4, 1840 (Barrett Collection, Tulane); note dated August 6, 1839 re: schooner *Asp* (TSLA); William A. Tennison, "Inventory," May 16, 1846 (NARA) (listing five medium eighteens and three medium sixes from *Archer*); Wells to Tod, October 7, 1840 (Rosenberg JGT); Moore, *Statement*.

TWENTY: GUNBOAT DIPLOMACY

Affairs in Galveston were reported by Thurston M. Taylor, May 20, 1840 (TSLA); Mabry Journal, May 10, 1840 (*Galveston News*, January 9, 1893); *San Bernard* log, March 4, 1840; and "Account of Sales of Clothing Belonging to Thomas Ramsay who Deserted from the Texas Schooner of War San Jacinto on May 9th, 1840" (Mrs. Floyd Williams, ed., "Research Notes on the Ships of the Texas Navy," Chambers County, Texas Historical Commission (Sam Houston Regional Library and Research Center, TSLA)).

The diplomatic situation facing Lamar, and Lamar's naval policies, were documented by Mirabeau B. Lamar to Edwin W. Moore, June 20, 1840 (TSLA and *Lamar Papers*);

Baldwin (11); Navy Department Report, 1839;A.C. Hinton to Louis P. Cooke, May 18, 1839 (Navy Department Report, 1839, 33); Hill on p. 122 (citing David G. Burnet to James Treat,August 9, 1839) and 124-25 (citing S. Baqueiro, *Ensayo Historico sobre las Revoluciones de Yucatan* 1:15, 35-38); Lamar to Texas Congress, November 3, 1841 (*Journal of the Sixth Texas Congress* 1:9); Adams on p. 223 (citing Garrison, *Diplomatic Correspondence* 3:218 and 239), 225 (citing Sheridan to Garraway, July 12,1840), 226 n. 1, and 245 (quoting Kennedy to Aberdeen,August 4,1841); Schroeder (132, 141-43, 146); Holt (168-69); Schlesinger (428-32); Fehrenbach (253-54); Tijerina (9);Vázquez (328, 330); Cartwright (79); and Worley (11, 16-19).

Preparation for the June 1840 cruise was documented in Mabry Journal,June 5, 1840 (*Galveston News*, January 9, 1893); Requisition of James O'Shaunessy, June 19, 1840 (RosenbergTNC);Abner Lipscomb to Treat,June 13, 1840 (*Diplomatic Correspondence* 2:645); Lamar to Moore,June 20, 1840 (TSLA); Dienst 3:20 n.1; Cooke to Lamar,June 2, 1840 (*Lamar Papers* 3:406); Moore to Lamar, June 26, 1840 (*Lamar Papers* 3:414); Moore to George Wheelwright,June 26, 1840 (*Lamar Papers*); Moore to Cooke,August 28, 1840 (*House Journal, Fifth Texas Congress, First Session*,Appendix, 232-37) (hereinafter,"Moore's August 28, 1840 Report"); Lamar to Wheelwright,June 25, 1840 (TSLA); Navy Department Report, 1840; Moore, *Reply*; and Wells (29-32).

TWENTY-ONE: AT SEA

The fleet's cruise from June to September 1840 was documented in *San Bernard* log, June 28, 1840 (NARA); Alex Moore to John Grant Tod, July 23, 1840 (Rosenberg JGT); Moore's August 28, 1840 report; on Wells p. 32 (citing Raphael Semmes, *Memoirs of Service Afloat During the War Between the States* 568), 33-34, 36, 38; Cox on p. 126; Mabry Journal, September 19, 1840 (*Galveston News*, January 16, 1893); Hill on p. 125 (citing Abner Lipscomb to James Treat, June 13, 1840), 126-27; Moore to Treat,August 25, 1840 (TSLA);Treat to Moore,August 21,1840 (TSLA); Lamar to Congress, November 3, 1841 (*Journal of the Sixth Texas Congress* 1:7-8);Tennison document 368 (Dienst collection, CAH); *Wharton* log,August 6,7,14,15, and 21, 1840 (NARA); Moore to Cooke, December 24, 1840 (TSLA) (hereinafter,"Moore's December 24, 1840 Report");W. S. Williamson to Moore, September 26 and November 3, 1840, in Moore's December 24, 1840 Report; James S. O'Shaunessy to Moore, November 2, 1840, in Moore's December 24, 1840, Report;William A.Wyse to Tod,January 18, 1842 (Rosenberg JGT); Cooke to Moore, September 16,1840 (*Lamar Papers* 3:448); Moore to Lamar,June 10,1840 (*Lamar Papers* 3:409); Cooke to William R. Postell, September 17, 1840 (*Lamar Papers* 3:449-50); Postell to Cooke, September 17, 1840 (*Lamar Papers* 3:449); and Fleming T. Wells to Tod, February 24, 1840 (Rosenberg JGT).

The progress of the cruise during October and November was recounted in Moore's December 24, 1840, report; J. T. K. Lothrop to Moore, November 23, 1840 (*Journals of the Sixth Texas Congress* 3:390); *San Bernard* log, October 31 and November 1-3, 7 and 8, 1840 (NARA); *Wharton* log, November 18, 1840 (NARA); Nance 278 (quoting Jalapa *Conciliador*, October 18, 1840 and *El Censor*, October 22, 1840); Cox (123-24); Dienst 3:125; Norman Hurd's personnel ledger (*Galveston News*, February 13, 1893); *Texas Sentinel*, January 28, 1841; Wells (40-43, 52-53); *Brutus* personnel records (TSLA); Mabry Journal, October 4-7, 17 (quoting Joachim Rivas to Moore and Pablo Alcedan to Moore, October 17, 1840), 18-21 (*Galveston News*,January 16, 1893) and November 4, 16-18, 1840 (*Galveston News*,January 23, 1893); John Burrows Gardiner,"Abstract of the Medical Journal of the Sloop of War *Austin*," October 1 to December 31, 1840 (DRT Library, San Antonio) (hereinafter, "Burrows' Medical Journal"); Galveston *Courier*, November 19, 1840 (reprinted in Augusta [Ga.] *Chronicle* and *Sentinel*, December 1,1840); report of James O'Shaunessy, 1840 (Dienst copy, Dienst collection, CAH); Moore, *Statement*;Wyse to Tod, March 30, 1841 (Rosenberg JGT); Norman Hurd, "Amount due men who died on Board the

Texian Sloop of War Austin in 1840 & 1841," (Research Notes) (hereinafter, "Hurd, *Austin Deaths*"); Moore to Treat, October 29, 1840 (TSLA Diplomatic Correspondence); Alex Moore, Power of Attorney, March 23, 1841 (ROT Claims, Alex Moore); Alex Moore to John C. Clark, December 8, 1840 (Rosenberg JGT); Augustus Seegar, Report, October 21, 1841 (TSLA); libel complaint against *Ana Maria*, November 18, 1840, First Judicial District, Judge A. B. Shelby (TSLA); Charles F. Fuller to Clark, November 18, 1840 (Rosenberg TNC); Deposition of Pietro Divescovi, November 18, 1840 (Rosenberg TNC); Bill of Sale, *Ana Maria* (Rosenberg TNC); William T. Brannum to Cooke, November 19, 1840 (Rosenberg TNC); Augustus Seegar to Branch T. Archer, October 1, 1841 (TSLA); Alex Moore to Tod, November 5, 1840 (Rosenberg JGT); Fuller to Tod, November 18, 1840 (Rosenberg JGT); Deposition of Predencio Tenorio, February 6, 1841 (Rosenberg TNC); Clark to Tod, December 8, 1840 (Rosenberg JGT); Tennison document 352 (Dienst collection, CAH); and Tod to William Seeger, April 12, 1841 (Rosenberg JGT).

The adventure at Tabasco was documented at Moore's December 24, 1840, report; Augustus Seegar to Archer, October 1, 1841 (TSLA); Wells 44-45 (citing *Journals of the Sixth Texas Congress* at 376); Cox 124; *San Bernard* log, November 21-22 and December 9-13, 1840 (NARA); *New York Daily Tribune*, March 17, 1846 (SRM); Mabry Journal, November 21, 23, and 27, and December 3, 6, 15, 22, and 25, 1840 (*Galveston News*, January 23, 1893); Mabry Journal, January 5, 1841 (*Galveston News*, February 13, 1893); Dienst 3:26 (quoting *Telegraph*, January 13, 1841); and Hurd, *Austin Deaths*.

Health problems for the Texas crews were documented in Gardiner's Medical Journal; Hurd, *Austin Deaths*; Mabry Journal, December 11, 17, and 22, 1840 (*Galveston News*, January 23, 1893); Purser J. F. Stephens, "A List of Men who died on board the Schr. San Bernard," (TSLA); Thomas P. Anderson to William C. Brashear, July 30, 1842 (TSLA); and at Cox 125. Other difficulties that beset *San Bernard* were recounted in "Statement of Thurston M. Taylor, A. I. Lewis and William A. Tennison, December 28, 1840," in *San Bernard* log, December 28, 1840 (NARA).

The fleet's return to Galveston in early 1841 was documented at *Wharton* log, February 2 and 26, 1841 (NARA); Tennison document 372 (Dienst collection, CAH); Thurston M. Taylor to Tod, January 7, 1841 (Rosenberg JGT); Dienst 3:26 (quoting *Telegraph*, January 13, 1841); Walke Journal (December 25, 1840); Moore's *Reply* 19; Purser's Records (TSLA); and Wells 45-48.

TWENTY-TWO: SECOND THOUGHTS

Diplomatic relations between Texas and Great Britain were documented at Adams 201-63; Worley 1-39; Wells 48 (citing James Hamilton to Lord Palmerston, October 14, 1840); and Hill 135-40. Texas's relations with Mexico were documented at Hill 138-40. Congressional and popular reluctance to provide financial support for the Navy was documented at *Texas Sentinel*, January 28 and 30, 1841 (TSLA); James Love to John Grant Tod, January 1, 1840 (Rosenberg JGT); Sheridan 113; Margaret L. Houston to Sam Houston, January 27, 1841 (Houston, *Personal Correspondence*, 81); Lambert S. Norwood to David G. Burnet, January 27, 1841 (TSLA); Dienst 3:16-18 (quoting Mirabeau Lamar to Congress, November 1840); Navy Department Report, 1840, 9-12; *Austin City Gazette*, November 4, 1840.

Events at home during John Grant Tod's tenure as Acting Secretary and in the wake of the 1841 reorganization law are found in U.S. House Committee Report, Committee on Foreign Relations, November 23, 1857 (Dienst copy, CAH); Tod, "Memorandum of Service" (NARA); Petition of Tod to Senate and House of Representatives of Texas, n.d. (circa 1852) (ROT Claims, John Grant Tod); Lamar to Tod, November 18, 1840 (Rosenberg JGT); Lieutenant John Appleman to Tod, March 10, 1841 (ROT Claims, John Grant Tod); *Journal of the Sixth Texas Congress* 2:31; Appleman to Tod, December 4, 1840 (Rosenberg JGT); Tod to John C. Clark, October

17, 1840 (Rosenberg JGT); *San Bernard* log, April 24 and May 19, 1841 (NARA); Tod to Edwin W. Moore, May 3, 1841 (NARA); Moore to Tod, May 2, 1841 (NARA); Tod to Alfred A. Waite, December 28, 1840 (Rosenberg JGT); *Senate Journal, Fifth Texas Congress, First Session,* 22; Christian (250, citing Gammel 2:569); *Wharton* log, November 23, 1840 (NARA); Augustus Seegar to Branch T. Archer, October 21, 1841 (TSLA); Seegar to Tod, April 20, 1841 (NARA); Moore to Tod, May 3, 1841 (NARA); Joint Committee Report, January 12, 1842 (NARA); Tod to Burnet, December 31, 1840 (Rosenberg JGT); Speech of Senator Jones of Tennessee, August 2, 1854 (9, citing Committee Report, December 20, 1847); Moore to Sen. James A. Pearce, March 28, 1853 (CAH); Wells (50, citing *Journals of the Sixth Texas Congress* 1:280 and 54, citing Moore to Tod, May 2, 1841) (NARA); Seegar to William Sevey, January 12, 1841 (TSLA); Tod to Lamar, December 2, 1840 (*Lamar Papers*); Tod to George W. Hill, September 6, 1839 (Rosenberg JGT); Tod to Lamar, March 26 and May 20, 1841 (Rosenberg JGT); Seegar to Tod, June 23, 1841 (Rosenberg JGT); Charles S. Mason to Tod (Rosenberg JGT); Moore to E.& G.W. Blunt, May 26, 1841 (TSLA); Moore to N. P. Hossack, May 26, 1841 (TSLA); Moore to Cruger, July 3, 1841 (TSLA); Cruger to Moore, September 20, 1841 (Rosenberg JGT); Musgrove Evans to Moore, October 30, 1841 (TSLA); Joint Committee Report, January 10, 1842 (Rosenberg JGT); Houston to Senate, January 31, 1842 (Rosenberg JGT); Tod to William E. Jones, January 31, 1842 (Rosenberg JGT); Bill for the Relief of George Wheelwright, February 4, 1841 (TSLA); Wheelwright to Sec. of Navy, December 21, 1841 (TSLA); Act of Congress, February 5, 1841 (Moore's March 28, 1853, letter to Sen. James A. Pearce); and Charles F. Fuller to Clark, November 18, 1840 (Rosenberg TNC).

San Bernard's diplomatic mission off Veracruz is documented in the *Texas Sentinel*, January 28, 1841; Tennison document 371 (Dienst collection, CAH); Wells (50-51, citing "Special Report of the Secretary of War and Marine," January 4, 1845 in *Journals of the Ninth Texas Congress,* Appendix 75-90, and Naval Returns, June 15, 1842), 52 (citing Evan Napian to Peter John Douglas, July 24, 1841); *San Bernard* log, January 15 and February 7, 1841 (NARA); *Wharton* log, March 18, 1841 (NARA); George Bunner to Thurston M. Taylor, February 24, 1844 (TSLA); and M.C. Hamilton to Mason, February 29, 1844 (TSLA).

The Navy's financial and political difficulties in early 1841, and naval cutbacks, were documented in *Texas Sentinel,* February 19, 1841; Dienst 3:27 (quoting *Austin City Gazette,* April 21, 1841); *Wharton* log, February 19 and 24, 1841 (NARA); promissory note, April 23, 1841 (author's collection); Moore to Charles Watson, May 10, 1841 (TSLA); Alex Moore, "On Account With the Texas Schooner San Antonio," n.d. (ROT Claims, Alex Moore); and Moore to Tod, May 2, 1841 (TSLA). The act prohibiting an officer's dismissal without the benefit of court-martial is found in Gammel 2:609 (act approved February 4, 1841); and Wells (50-55).

Moore's survey of the Texas coast was documented in Archer to Senate, February 2, 1841 (TSLA); Moore to Samuel A. Roberts, June 8, 1841 (TSLA); Abstract of Claims Against the Texas Navy, May 23, 1846 (TSLA); Moore to Blunt, May 26, 1841 (TSLA); Tennison document 372 (Dienst collection, CAH); Dienst 3:29 (quoting *Telegraph,* July 14, 1841); Wells on p. 55 (citing William Kennedy to Bidwell, January 9, 1844, and Texas Treasury Papers), 56; Moore to Department of War and Navy, July 14, 1841 (TSLA); Norman Hurd to Moore, July 2, 1841 (TSLA); Mason, Regulations for Texas Navy Pursers, September 24, 1841 (TSLA); at Moore, *Reply* 19; and at Ramsay 116.

San Bernard's second diplomatic mission under Lieutenant Crisp and the political situation with Mexico in the late spring of 1841 were discussed in Lamar to Congress (*Journal of the Sixth Texas Congress* 1:8); Downing H. Crisp to Moore, June 28, 1841 (TSLA); *San Bernard* log, January 22 and 30, February 1-22, March 5, 10, and 13, March 30-31 and June 2, 8-12, 20, and 28, 1841 (NARA); Archer, extract of report, September

1841 (Houston 2:456); Report of the Secretary of War & Navy, September 30, 1841 (*Journal of the Sixth Texas Congress* 3:358 et seq.); Christensen (48, quoting King Louis Philippe to Maximo Garro); John D. Morris to Roberts, September 20, 1841 (*Journal of the Sixth Texas Congress* 3:262); James Webb to Lamar, June 29, 1841 (*Diplomatic Correspondence* 2:762-63); Adams 241, 242 (quoting Napian to Douglas, July 24, 1841); Miguel Barbachano to Lamar, August 24, 1841 (TSLA, Diplomatic Correspondence); Wells (53-54, 58, citing Juan de Dios Boniooa, *Apuentes para la historia de la Marina Nacional* (Mexico: D. F. 1946) and Garrison, *Diplomatic Correspondence*, 2:529-30)); Hill (141, citing Comacho to Packenham, June 8, 1841); Dienst 3:30 (quoting Sen. Sam Houston speech in the U.S. Senate); and Ramsay (116-17).

TWENTY-THREE: THE GREAT GAME
The situation with Mexico and negotiations with Yucatán were documented at Martín F. Peraza to Samuel A. Roberts, September 16, 1841 (TSLA Diplomatic Correspondence); Wells 58 (citing Garrison, *Diplomatic Correspondence*, 2:529-30), 59; John D. Morris to Roberts, September 20, 1841 (*Journal of the Sixth Texas Congress* 3:262); Report of the Secretary of War & Navy, September 30, 1841 (*Journal of the Sixth Texas Congress*, 358 (CAH); Ramsay 116-17; Dienst 3:30, n.1 (quoting Sen. Sam Houston, 1853), 32; Miguel Barbachano to Mirabeau B. Lamar, August 24, 1841 (TSLA Diplomatic Correspondence); introductory letter of Peraza, September 11, 1841 (TSLA Diplomatic Correspondence); Roberts to Peraza, September 17, 1841 (TSLA Diplomatic Correspondence); Peraza to Roberts, September 17, 1841 (TSLA Diplomatic Correspondence); and Roberts to Peraza, September 18, 1841 (TSLA Diplomatic Correspondence).

Moore's orders to sail in support of Yucatán and his preparations for the December 1841 cruise were discussed at Moore to Charles Sayre, October 13, 1841 (Rosenberg TNC); Augustus Seegar to Branch T. Archer, October 1, 1841 (TSLA); *San Bernard* log, September 20, November 4, and December 19, 1841 (NARA); Moore to Pedro Lemus, January 13, 1842 (TSLA Diplomatic Correspondence); Archer to Moore, September 18, 1841 (Moore 12-13); abstract of Claims Against the Texas Navy, May 23, 1846 (TSLA); Moore to Mason, October 5, 18, and 19, 1841 (Rosenberg TNC); Moore to Albert Sidney Johnston, October 19 and December 9, 1841 (Tulane ASJ); "E.W. Moore on account with the Government of Yucatan," n.d. (ROT Claims, Edwin Ward Moore); Vázquez 334; Tennison documents 372 and 374 (Dienst collection, CAH); Dienst 3:32-33; Wells 60-62; and Sullivan 29 (citing *Secret Journals of the Republic of Texas*, 207-08).

TWENTY-FOUR: RED SKIES IN MORNING
The Houston faction's antipathy towards the Navy was documented by Sam Houston to Texas Senate, April 20, 1838 (Houston 4:49-52); Houston to *Austin City Gazette*, August 10, 1841 (at Haley 223 and Houston 2:372-73); Houston to John L. Hall, November 10, 1841 (Houston, *Personal Correspondence*, 106); Houston to Margaret Houston, December 24, 1841 (Houston, *Personal Correspondence*, 144); Wells on p. 64; Tennison document 374 (Dienst collection, CAH); Anson Jones, Memoranda, November 6, 1838 and December 22, 1841 (Jones 30-31, 124); and by Hill (146).

The bill to recall the fleet was documented at Lamar to Congress, November 3, 1841 (*Journal of the Sixth Texas Congress* 1:7); Report of the Minority of the Committee on Naval Affairs (*Journal of the Sixth Texas Congress* 2:56-59); *Journal of the Sixth Texas Congress* 2:28, 99, 123-25; Edwin W. Moore to Albert Sidney Johnston, December 9, 1841 (Tulane ASJ); and Wells 63-64.

The orders recalling the fleet were documented in George W. Hockley to Moore, December 15, 1841 (Moore 42); Wells (64, citing Gail Borden to Hockley, December 28, 1841).

TWENTY-FIVE: THE WOODEN AEGIS

Commodore Moore's orders to proceed to Yucatán and his initial report are found at Branch T. Archer to Edwin W. Moore, September 18, 1841 (Moore 14); and Moore to Department of War and Navy, January 31, 1842 (Moore 21-25). Activities and events of the squadron's voyage until March 1842 are documented by Moore to Department of War, January 31, 1842 (Moore 21-25); Moore to Pedro Lemus, January 8, 1842 (Moore 25); Lemus to Moore, January 8 and 12 and April 8, 1842 (TSLA, Diplomatic Correspondence); *San Bernard* log, December 29-31, 1841 and January 6 and 12, 27 and 31, 1842 (NARA); Wells 66-74 (citing logs of *Austin* and *San Bernard*, Garrison, *Diplomatic Correspondence* 2:555, and Letter of William A. Tennison (*Telegraph*, March 2, 1842)); Moore, Requisition Approval, January 3, 1842 (Rosenberg TNC); Charles G. Bryant to Andrew Jackson Bryant, February 27, 1842 (Bryant Papers, CAH); Abstract of Claims Against the Texas Navy, May 23, 1846 (TSLA); Joaquin G. Rejon to Moore, January 18, 1842 (at Moore 34-35, quoting Decree of Santiago Mendez, Governor of Yucatán, October 25, 1841); resolution dated October 25, 1841 (TSLA, Diplomatic Correspondence); treaty dated December 28, 1841, (TSLA, Diplomatic Correspondence); Hill 147, 148 (citing Tratados de 28 de Diciembre de 1841); Moore to Rejon, January 10, 12, 15, and 31, 1842 (Moore 26, 29, 32-33, 35); Moore to Rejon, January 14 and 18, 1842 (TSLA, Diplomatic Correspondence); Rejon to Moore, January 12 and 18, 1842 (Moore 27-29, 32, 34); Alfred G. Gray to Moore, January 12, 1842 (at Moore 30); *Daily Picayune*, February 11, 1842; Gray to "Gentlemen," January 12, 1842 (at Moore 31); A. I. Lewis to Gray, January 12, 1842 (TSLA, Diplomatic Correspondence); Gray to Lewis, January 12, 1842 (TSLA, Diplomatic Correspondence); Moore to Gray, January 13, 1842 (at Moore 31); "E.W. Moore on account with the Government of Yucatan," n.d. (ROT Claims, Edwin Ward Moore); and Moore to Secretary of War and Navy, February 6, 1842 (at Moore 36). The description of the *City of Dublin* comes from the *Telegraph*, March 2, 1842, quoted in Nance on p. 530 (noting armament, two 60-hp engines, schooner-rigged).

TWENTY-SIX: MUTINY ON THE *SAN ANTONIO*

Events surrounding the mutiny aboard *San Antonio* and the death of Lieutenant Fuller are recorded at the *Commercial Bulletin*, February 11, 12, 14, and 17, 1842; *Picayune*, February 13, 1842; *Daily Picayune*, February 16, 1842; Report of the Court Martial, April 18, 1843 (Dienst collection, CAH); Moore 41-42; Dienst 4:85, 86 (citing *Bee*, February 12, 1842), 89-90 (citing testimony of J. F. Shepherd and summary of testimony by Moore dated May 10, 1843); Charles S. Mason to James B. Shaw, April 25, 1844 (ROT Claims, Edwin Ward Moore); Tennison document 382 (Dienst collection, CAH); Abstract of Claims Against the Texas Navy, May 23, 1846 (TSLA); Wells 78 (citing Leslie Combs to Albert Sidney Johnston, February 12, 1842), 79-80; Carroll 126-27; Pedro Lemus to Edwin W. Moore, March 8, 1842 (Moore 41-42); and Hill 152 (citing Moore's *Reply*); *The Texian*, January 3, 1955 (DRT Library); and Beaumont, Texas, *Sunday Enterprise*, January 16, 1955 (DRT Library).

The remaining events of the fleet's winter 1842 cruise can be found in Moore to George W. Hockley, April 4 and May 1, 1842 (Moore 46-50, 60-61); Hockley to Moore, December 15, 1841, and April 14, 1842 (Moore 42, 50-51); Moore to Hockley, April 5, 1842 (Rosenberg TNC); Hockley to Sam Houston, n.d. (c. January 15, 1842) (TSLA); Moore to Lemus, March 8 and 28 and April 19 and 26, 1842 (at Moore 41-42, 52-55, 59); Lemus to Moore, March 29 and April 22, 1842 (at Moore 53, 55); Lemus to Moore, April 8, 1842 (TSLA, Diplomatic Correspondence); Wells 80-83 (citing Journal of Midshipman Edward Johns, March 28, 1842 and Mexican military report dated April 6, 1842), 85 (citing Downing H. Crisp to Purser, April 1, 1842 and Johns Journal, April 3, 1842); Joachim G. Rejon to Moore, April 9, 1842 (TSLA Diplomatic Correspondence); receipt for *San Bernard*, March 21, 1842 (Rosenberg TNC); Tennison document 390

(Dienst collection, CAH); Moore to José Cardenas, April 25, 1842 (Moore 58); George Fisher to Anson Jones, May 3, 1842 (Jones 195); and "E.W. Moore on account with the Government of Yucatan," n.d. (ROT Claims, Edwin Ward Moore).

TWENTY-SEVEN: THE HORSE LATITUDES

Sam Houston's views on the Navy, his reasons therefor, and naval administration under Secretary George W. Hockley early in Houston's second term were recounted in John Grant Tod to Fleming T. Wells, January 5, 1842 (Rosenberg JGT); *Texas Sentinel*, March 5, 1840; Mariano Arista to John Morris and C. Van Ness, August 18, 1841 (*Journal of the Sixth Texas Congress* 3:263); Houston to Congress, December 20, 1841 (Houston 2:401); Houston to House of Representatives, December 30, 1841 (*Journal of the Sixth Texas Congress* 1:173 and Houston 2:415); Houston, *Personal Correspondence*, 144; George W. Hockley to Houston, December 22, 1841 (Rosenberg TNC); Sheridan (78-79); Wells (64-65, citing *Journals of the Sixth Texas Congress* 2:237), 89; Houston to Texas Senate, January 31, 1842 (Houston 2:453-54, 457-58); Houston to Texas Congress, October 24, 1837 (Houston 2:145); Houston to E. Lawrence Stickney, December 18, 1841 (Houston 2:399); Charles S. Mason, credit memorandum, January 14, 1842 (Rosenberg TNC); senate resolution (*Journals of the Sixth Texas Congress* 2:139) (Dienst copy); and Dienst 4:123 (citing *Journals of the Sixth Texas Congress* 195, 198).

The decline of the Navy during the first half of 1842 and Houston's efforts to obtain funding from the summer 1842 session of Congress were documented in Hockley to Houston, January 1, 1842 (TSLA); Houston to House of Representatives, January 4, 1842 (*Journals of the Sixth Texas Congress* 2:278); Houston to Texas Congress, January 22, 1842 (Houston 2:438-39); Houston to House of Representatives, January 7 and 27, 1842 (Houston 2:415, 446); Hockley to Moore, February 17, 1842 (on Moore p. 45); Act Establishing the Pay of Officers of the Texas Navy, approved February 3, 1842 (Rosenberg TNC); Moore to Hockley, May 8 and July 4, 1842 (on Moore pp. 66, 78); Fleming T. Wells to Hockley, March 30, 1842 (TSLA); Wells (90-91, citing Moore to Albert Sidney Johnston, December 9, 1841, 162).

The threatened war with Mexico in early 1842, Houston's interest in naval protection of the Texas coast, and Moore's efforts to obtain funding for operations are documented at Dienst 4:90 (quoting Santa Anna to Barnard E. Bee, February 6, 1842 and Sam Houston to People of Texas, April 4, 1842); Fehrenbach 261; Adrian Woll to Juan Almonte (*Diplomatic Correspondence of the United States* 12:254); Marshall 25 (citing William Bollaert, *William Bollaert's Texas* (Norman: University Oklahoma Press 1856), 45-51); Houston to James E. Haviland, March 11, 1842 (Houston 2:498); Cardenas de la Peña 99; Charter, *Colonel Hanson*, April 2, 1842 (TSLA); Houston to James D. Boylan, June 17, 1842 (Houston 3:70); Hockley to Boylan, April 3 and May 9, 1842 (ROT Claims, James D. Boylan); permanent register, *Mary Elizabeth*, January 9, 1842 (Rosenberg TNC); newspaper clipping, unnamed, n.d. (Rosenberg TNC); James H. Causten to John M. Swisher, March 12, 1851 (Rosenberg TNC); statement of Causten, March 12, 1851 (Rosenberg TNC); St. John 265; Houston to Moore, March 11, 1842 (at Moore 68-69 and Houston 2:497-98); Houston to John Wade, March 11, 1842 (Houston 2:498-99); Hockley to Moore, May 3, 1842 (at Moore 61-63); Moore to Hockley, May 7 and 8, 1842 (at Moore 61-63, 66); Hockley to Moore, May 7, 1842 (at Moore 63-65); Houston to Margaret Houston, May 11, 1842 (Houston, *Personal Correspondence*, 224); *Newark Daily Advertiser*, April 2, 1842; Worley 21; and Weems 215.

Commodore Moore's efforts to fund the Navy during the summer of 1842 were documented in Moore to Hockley, May 7, 1842 (Moore p. 64); contract between L. H. M. Hitchcock, Jr., as agent for Edwin W. Moore, Hamilton Washington and L. J. Wilson, May 30, 1842 (TLSA); Hockley to Moore, July 27, 1842 (TSLA) (note appended by Moore); "List of Supplies by L. M. Hitchcock for 'Zavalla' approved April 27, 1842 (ROT

Claims, Edwin Ward Moore); Moore (66-74, 82); Hockley to Moore, May 3, 1842 (Moore 63); Wells (100-01, citing *Mobile Register and Journal*, May 23, 1842), (102, citing Francisco Arrangoiz to Ministerio de Relaciones Exteriores, June 21, 1842); Moore to Pedro Lemus, May 26, 1842 (at Moore 76); Moore to Hockley, June 1, 1842 (at Moore 69);Abstract of Claims Against the Texas Navy, May 23, 1846 (TSLA); Hockley to Moore, June 19, 1842 (at Moore 72); Proclamation of President, June 18, 1842 (at Moore 73); Moore to Hockley, June 11 and July 2 and 5, 1842 (at Moore 71, 75-76, 79); Moore to M.C. Hamilton, December 2, 1842 (Moore 113); J. F. Stephens, Auditor's Note, February 17, 1844 (TSLA); Moore, mortgage certificate, October 10, 1842 (TSLA); William C. Brashear to D. F. Thornton, July 4, 1842 (Rosenberg TNC); "E.W. Moore on account with the Government of Yucatan," n.d. (ROT Claims, Edwin Ward Moore); and St. John (265-67).

The circumstances surrounding Moore's trip to Austin in the summer of 1842, the summer session of Congress, and Moore's rupture with Houston, were documented in Brashear to Thornton, July 4, 1842 (Rosenberg TNC); Abstract of Claims Against the Texas Navy, May 23, 1846 (TSLA); "Republic of Texas, in account with James W. Moore" (ROT Claims, James W. Moore); J.T.K. Lothrop to Alfred G. Gray, n.d. (TLSA); Maggie Houston to Houston, July 5, 1842 (TSLA); Moore, "List of Naval Officers confirmed by the Senate on 20 July 1842," (NARA); Hockley to Gail Borden, Jr., June 1 and 23, 1842 (TSLA); Houston to Congress, June 27 and July 22, 1842 (Houston 3:75, 118); Wells 106-107; Moore to Hockley, July 19, 1842 (TSLA); Dienst 3:93, 125 (citing Gammel 2:813); Houston to Texas Senate, July 19, 1842 (Houston 3:109); Hockley to Borden, July 20, 1842 (Houston 3:114); Joint Resolution Making Appropriations for the Support of the Navy, July 23, 1842 (on Moore pp. 80-81); Moses Austin Bryan (165, Houston's desire for flattery); Andrew Jackson to Houston, August 17, 1842 (Houston 3:121 n.2) (supporting Houston's refusal to authorize an invasion of Mexico); Houston to House of Representatives, July 22, 1842 (Houston 3:118, 121); Hockley, "Naval Appointments Confirmed by the Senate on 20 July 1842," (NARA); Hamilton to Houston, November 15, 1842 (TSLA); Moore (74-75, 82-83); and Connor (93).

Houston's orders to Moore after their clash are documented in Moore to Hockley, July 24, 1842 (at Moore 83-84); Hockley to Moore, July 27, 1842 (at Moore 85); and on Moore pp. 87-88.

The state of the Navy in late summer and early fall 1842 was documented in Tennison document 390 (Dienst collection, CAH); Moore to Hockley, August 3 and 19 and September 7, 1842 (Moore 90-91, 93); Moore to Hamilton, December 2, 1842 (Moore 114); Lothrop to Moore, August 16, 1842 (Rosenberg TNC); survey by Lts. Lewis, Cummings, and Oliver, July 6, 1842 (TSLA); Fleming T. Wells to Lothrop, August 23, 1842 (TSLA); A. Irving Lewis to Wells, March 1844 (TSLA); Lewis, Daniel Lloyd, and Norman Hurd to Lothrop, September 5, 1842 (TSLA); Fuller (223-25); Charles G. Bryant to Andrew Jackson Bryant, September 14, 1842 (Bryant papers, CAH); *New York Observer*, October 15, 1842; Abstract of Claims Against the Navy, May 23, 1846 (TSLA); Moore to Dennis Prieur, August 12, 1842 (CAH); Moore (91-92); and Wells (111, 112, citing Francisco Arrangoiz to Ministerio de Relaciones Exteriores, August 23, 1842).

Houston's opposition to the Navy in late 1842 is documented at Wells 113 (citing Hockley to Houston, September 1, 1842); and Moore to James Hamilton, March 6, 1851 (Rosenberg 233). Hockley's resignation was detailed in Hockley to William G. Cooke, March 28, 1846 (Rosenberg TNC); Hockley to Houston, September 1, 1842 (Sam Houston Library, Burch Collection); Houston to Hockley, September 3, 1842 (Houston 3:153).

The Navy's condition at the end of 1842 was described in Moore to Secretary of War and Marine, October 14, 1842 (at Moore 100); "Muster Roll of the Brig of War Wharton," December 18, 1842 (Dienst collection, CAH) (*Wharton* down to five crewmen and fourteen officers); Moore, Amended Ration Table, September 28, 1842 (TSLA); Downing H. Crisp to James F. Stephens, October 1, 1842 (TSLA); Houston, Proclamation,

September 12, 1842 (at Moore 101); Fehrenbach 261 (re: Woll's invasion); Wells 105 (citing Arrangoiz to Ministerio de Relaciones Exteriores, June 29, 1842); Crisp to Moore, September 22, 1842 (Moore 108-09); J.T. S. to Editor, *New Orleans Tropic,* October 7, 1842 (reprinted in Augusta *Chronicle and Sentinel,* October 14, 1842) [loss of Merchant]; Crisp to Moore, January 20, 1843 (TSLA); Carroll 126-27; Lothrop to Moore, October 8, 1842 (Rosenberg TNC); *The Texian,* January 3, 1955 (DRT); San Antonio *Express News,* September 11, 1954 (DRT); *Beaumont Sunday Enterprise,* January 16, 1955 (DRT) (burial of Culp and Oliver); St. John 265, 267-68, and 424; Charles S. Mason to James B. Shaw, April 25, 1844 (ROT Claims, Edwin Ward Moore); Oscar Fansh, affidavit, October 4, 1848 (ROT Claims, William O. Oliver); Crisp to Moore, October 17 and 24 and November 2, 1842 (at Moore 109-111); Hamilton to Moore, September 15 and 23, October 29 and November 5 and 19, 1842 (Moore 95, 98, 101, 104, 106-07, 111-12); Hamilton to Houston, November 15 and December 13, 1842 (TSLA); Moore to Hamilton, December 2, 1842 (at Moore 114); Henson, SMW, 121-22 (citing David Read to William H. Wharton, July 26, 1857); Wells 130 (citing receipt dated January 21, 1843); George W. Hill to George C. Bunner, May 14, 1843 (at Moore 190-91); Houston to Crisp, January 27, 1843 (Houston 3:303); Moore to Charles B. Snow, January 31, 1843 (at Moore 188); Houston, *Morning Star,* June 1, 1843; Moore 108; and Handbook of Texas Online, "Brannum, William T." and "Brashear, William C." entries.

The Mexican naval rearmament of 1842 was documented by *Houston Press,* June 16, 1843 (quoting *New Orleans Tropic,* November 5, 1842); Ellis (453-54); Wells 118-19 (quoting Garrison, *Diplomatic Correspondence* 2:986 and citing James Phinney Baxter, *Introduction of the Ironclad Warship* 34, Ashbel Smith to Sam Houston, September 1, 1842, and William S. Murphy to Earl of Aberdeen, August 19 and 20, 1842; 120, citing José Maria Tornel, "Report," January 17, 1842); Alan Moore (55-56); Cardenas de la Peña (99 and n. 163); Hill (173, citing M. P. Russell to Ashbel Smith, June 2 and 4, 1842; Pringle to Smith, June 29, 1842; Smith to Aberdeen, September 14, 1842, Smith to Anson Jones, September 19, 1842; and Aberdeen to Smith, September 28, 1842); Ashbel Smith, "Reiminscences of the Texas Republic, December 15, 1875 (Sons of DeWitt Colony website); Moore to Albert Sidney Johnston, October 6, 1842 (Tulane, ASJ Papers); *Niles' National Register,* March 11, 1843 (SRM); Moore to Hamilton, December 19, 1842 (at Moore 116-17); *New York Observer,* October 15, 1842; and Worley (22).

Moore's orders to return to Galveston are found in Hamilton to Moore, December 14, 1842, and January 2, 1843 (at Moore 116, 117); and in Wells on pp. 131-32 (quoting Houston 155-56).

TWENTY-EIGHT: THE PLAN

The diplomatic situation facing Texas in late 1842 and early 1843 was documented in Moore, *Brief Synopsis,* p. 13; Sam W. Haynes, "But What Will England Say?" (at Francaviglia and Richmond 20-21); Ashbel Smith, *Reminiscences;* Sam Houston to Charles Elliott, May 11 and 13, 1843 (Houston 3:385, 387-88); in Adams pp. 201-63; Wells pp. 120-21 (citing Elliott to Lord Aberdeen, November 15, 1841), 122 (citing Houston to Alexander Somervell, October 3, 1842 and Webster to Van Zandt, 1842 in Garrison, *Diplomatic Correspondence* 2:152); and Worley pp. 3-4, 22.

The revolt in Yucatán, and the Mexican response, was documented at Wells 120 (citing Tomás y Carbó Aznar, *El Estadeo de Campeche* (Campeche 1955) and report, August 30, 1842 (AGN, Mexico City)), 120 (citing British Consul at Veracruz to Lord Packenham, October 20, 1842 and U.S. Consul, Campeche, to Secretary of State, December 1, 1842); *Niles' National Register,* March 11, 1843; Fuller 231; Walke Journal, May 1-16 entry; Hill 171 (citing Serapio Baqueiro, *Ensayo Historico sobre las Revoluciones de Yucatan desde el ano 1840* (1878) 1:70); Martín F. Peraza and Edwin W. Moore, Agreement, February 11, 1842 (in Moore p. 125).

Renewed threats of invasion in early 1843 were documented on Wells p. 120 (citing British Consul at Veracruz to Lord Packenham, October 20, 1842, and Packenham to Aberdeen, September 10, 1842) and 126 (quoting Houston to Congress, January 10, 1843); George W. Terrell to Sam Houston, May 5, 1843 (Catholic Diocese Archives, Austin, Texas); Houston to Congress, December 1, 1842 (*Niles' National Register,* March 11, 1843 (SRM)); Dr. B. Townsend to Dr. Joseph S. Copes, October 12, 1842 (Tulane, J. S. Copes Papers); Moore to Johnston, October 6, 1842 (Tulane ASJ Papers); and Smith, *Reminiscences.*

Moore's attempts to renew negotiations with Yucatán and other activities that took place around this time were documented in Moore to Governor of Yucatan, January 17, 1843 (at Moore 120); Moore to José Cardenas, January 16, 1843 (at Moore 121); Miguel Barbachano to Moore, January 31, 1843 (at Moore 122); Cardenas to Moore, February 5, 1843 (at Moore 124); Moore to James Morgan and William Bryan, February 27, 1843 (Moore 134); Santiago Mendez to Moore, February 3, 1843 (at Moore 122-233); Moore, *Brief Synopsis,* 8; Andrew Jackson Bryant to Mother, January 8, 1843 (Bryant papers, CAH); Resolution of Steerage Officers, February 15, 1843 (TSLA); and Peraza and Moore, Agreement, February 11, 1843 (at Moore 125-26).

TWENTY-NINE: AMATEURS IN COMMAND

Houston's efforts to bring home and sell the Navy are documented in Sam Houston to Congress, December 22, 1842, and January 3, 1843 (Houston 3:241-42 and 261); on Wells pp. 124, 127 (citing *Secret Journals of the* Senate 316), 129-30 (citing *Secret Journals of the Senate,* 275, and Manning, *Diplomatic Correspondence of the U.S.* 12:254); Moore (125); Houston to George W. Hockley, January 18, 1843 (Houston 4:154); George W. Hill to Samuel May Williams, January 23, 1843 (Rosenberg SMW); Charles S. Mason to M.C. Hamilton, December 16, 1842 (TSLA); Hill to Frederick Dawson, January 23, 1843 (TSLA); Hill to Fleming T. Wells, January 27, 1843 (TSLA); Houston to Gail Borden, Jr., January 25, 1843 (Houston 3:307); Hamilton to William Bryan, December 23, 1842 (Dienst Collection, CAH); and James Morgan to Samuel Swartwout, February 20, 1843 (Rosenberg JM); Houston 2:454-55 n. 3 (re Frederick Dawson); and Nance (527, citing *Journal of the Sixth Texas Congress* 1:215).

The commissioners' backgrounds and activities in New Orleans were documented by Hill to Moore, January 22, 1843 (at Moore 130); Hill to Lothrop, or Officer in Command of Navy, January 22, 1843 (at Moore 131); Moore to Hill, March 10 and May 10, 1843 (at Moore 137, 151); Ashbel Smith to Morgan, June 9, 1842 (Rosenberg JM); Moore to Morgan and Bryan, February 27, March 2 and April 4, 1843 (at Moore 134, 136 and 140-41); Morgan to Hill (Moore, *Brief Synopsis* 16) (Dienst copy); Morgan and Bryan to Moore, February 28, 1843 (at Moore 135); Moore (130-31); Dienst 4:102; Wells 133 (citing *Telegraph,* August 28, 1844), 135 (citing Morgan, *To the Public,* 2, and Arrangoiz to Ministerio de Relaciones Exteriores, March 20, 1843); Abstract of Claims Against the Texas Navy, May 23, 1846 (TSLA); Hamilton to Moore, March 22, 1843 (at Moore 140); Houston to Morgan and Bryan, March 22, 1843 (Houston, July 15, 1854 speech); Report of the Secretary of War and Navy, November 30, 1843 (TSLA) (hereafter, "War Department Report, 1843"); Sen. James Jones to Senate, August 2, 1854, 15; Moore, *Brief Synopsis* 10, 13, 20.

The vessels' planned return to Galveston was documented in Moore's *Brief Synopsis* on p. 14 (citing testimony of James Morgan); Fuller p. 223; Gray 3; Walke Journal, April 16, 1843 entry; Moore p. 145; and Tennison folio 396. The court-martial of the mutineers was documented in Dienst document 406, dated May 10, 1843 (Dienst collection, CAH); Lothrop, et al., Report of the Court Martial, April 18, 1843 (Jones's August 2, 1854 speech and Moore, *Reply,* 27); and Boston *Daily Times,* April 22, 1843 (quoting *New Orleans Bulletin* (SRM)).

THIRTY: "TO SAVE THE REPUBLIC"

News of the Mexican fleet's presence off Yucatán, as well as the precarious situation of the federalist rebels, was documented at Moore 145-46; Gray 7-8; James Morgan to Department of War and Marine, May 9, 1843 (in Moore, *Brief Synopsis* pp. 18-19) (Dienst copy); Edwin W. Moore to F. Pinckard, May 10, 1843 (*Houston Morning Star*, May 23, 1843); *Niles' National Register,* March 11, 1843 (in Wells pp. 140-41); Dienst 4:106 (citing Moore, *Brief Synopsis* pp. 12-13); *Houston Morning Star*, May 18 and 23, 1843.

Reports of an invasion of Texas upon the pacification of Yucatán come from Isaac Van Zandt, April 21, 1843 (Garrison, *Diplomatic Correspondence*, 2:168); *Houston Morning Star*, May 18, 1843; and Wells p. 144 (quoting G. B. Elliott to Sir Charles Adam, April 25, 1843 and Percy Doyle to Adam, April 24, 1843). Reports to Houston include George W. Terrell to Sam Houston, May 5, 1843 (Catholic Diocese Archives, Austin, Texas).

Morgan's decision to authorize Moore to proceed to Yucatán was documented by James Morgan (at Moore, *Brief Synopsis* 13); Morgan to Moore, June 10, 1843 (at Moore 172); *Houston Morning Star*, May 20, 1843; Morgan to James Reed, May 11, 1843 (Rosenberg JM); and Moore to Pinckard, May 10, 1843 (*Houston Morning Star*, May 23, 1843).

The vessels' lifting for Yucatán was documented in Fuller on p. 227; and Moore to Pinckard, May 10, 1843 (*Morning Star*, May 23, 1843).

THIRTY-ONE: THE LAST HURRAH

Moore's stale orders and his departure of U.S. waters were documented in James Morgan to James Reed, May 11, 1843 (Rosenberg JM); M. C. Hamilton to Edwin W. Moore, September 15, 1842, and March 21, 1843, (Moore 98 and 139-40); and Moore to Morgan and William Bryan, April 4, 1843 (Moore 141).

The punishment of the *San Antonio* mutineers and the crew's reaction was described in Testimony of James Morgan (Moore, *Brief Synopsis* pp. 14-15, and Sen. Jones's August 2, 1854 speech); Walke Journal, April 21-26, 1843; Wells p. 142 (citing Moore, *Brief Synopsis*); Moore to George W. Hill, May 10, 1843 (at Moore 149); in Fuller pp. 227-28; Moore to New Orleans *Tropic*, May 5, 1843 (*Houston Morning Star*, May 20, 1843); Tennison document 396 (Dienst Collection, CAH).

The Texas squadron's arrival off Yucatán and preparations to battle the Mexican fleet were documented at Moore to *New Orleans Tropic*, May 5, 1843 (*Houston Morning Star*, May 20, 1843); Moore 147; Walke Journal, April 28-May 1, 1843; Gray 5; Moore to Miguel Barbachano, April 28, 1843 (Moore 148); Wells 144 (citing Peña y Barragan to Minister of War, May 16, 1843); Morgan to Hill, May 9, 1843 (Sen. Jones August 2, 1854 speech, 15); Moore to Hill, May 10, 1843 (Moore 149); James Morgan Testimony (at Moore, *Brief Synopsis* 17); James W. Moore, Minutes of Engagement, April 30, 1843 (at Moore 151); and Cardenas de la Peña 100.

The engagement of April 30, 1843 was documented in Walke Journal, May 1, 1843; James W. Moore, Minutes of Engagement, April 30, 1843 (at Moore 151); Morgan to Department of War and Marine, May 10, 1843 (at Moore, *Brief Synopsis* 17-18); Gray (5-6); Moore (162); Fuller (229-30); Morgan to Hill, May 9, 1843 (Jones August 2, 1854 speech 15); Morgan to James Reed, May 11, 1843 (Rosenberg JM); Morgan Testimony (at Moore, *Brief Synopsis* 15); and Cardenas de la Peña 103.

The casualty and damage estimates of the April 30 engagement come from Morgan for Department of War and Marine, May 10, 1843 (at Moore, *Brief Synopsis* 18); *Houston Morning Star*, May 18, 1843 (citing *New Orleans Tropic*, May 5, 1843); Walke Journal, April 30, 1843; Dienst collection document 408 (Dienst collection, CAH) (May 10, 1843 letter of anonymous officer of *Wharton*); Cardenas de la Peña 101 (quoting report of Tomas Marín); Moore p. 157; and at Wells p. 148.

The repercussions of the April 30 battle were documented by Morgan for Department of War and Marine, May 10, 1843 (Moore, *Brief Synopsis* 18-19); *Houston Morning Star*, May 18, 1843 (citing *New Orleans Tropic*, May 5, 1843); Anonymous officer of *Wharton,* May 10, 1843 (Dienst Document 408 (CAH)); Walke Journal, May 1, 1843; and at Wells 140.

THIRTY-TWO: CAT AND MOUSE

The reorganization and disposition of Commodore Marín's naval forces was documented by Cardenas de la Peña (101-102 and n. 45, citing Commandant of Veracruz to Minister of War, June 8, 1843); Edwin W. Moore to F. Pinckard, May 10, 1843 (*Houston Morning Star,* May 23, 1843); and Wells (148, citing Santa Anna to Pedro Ampudia, May 5, 1843 and Tómas Marín to Pedro Ampudia, May 5, 1843).

The movements of the Texas vessels, their commanders, and their crews from May 1 to May 10 were detailed in Morgan Testimony (Jones's August 2, 1843 speech); at Gray 7-9; Walke Journal, May 1-16, 1843; Moore to Pinckard, May 10, 1843 (*Houston Morning Star,* May 23, 1843); at Fuller 231; Dienst document 408 (letter dated May 10, 1843); Moore to Hill, May 10, 1843 (at Moore 149-51); James Morgan to James Reed, May 11, 1843 (Rosenberg JM); and Moore to Charles S. Mason, May 10, 1843 (TSLA).

The description of Campeche and the surrounding environs comes from Gray pp. 7-9, Fuller pp. 230-31, and Dienst document 408 (May 10, 1843 letter) (Dienst collection, CAH).

The politico-military situation in which the Texas sailors found themselves was documented in Walke Journal, May 1-16, 1843; Miguel Barbachano to Moore, May 1, 1843 (at Moore 148); Santiago Mendez to Pedro Ampudia, May 1, 1843 (at Moore 155-56); *Houston Morning Star,* May 20, 1843; and Cardenas de la Peña (101-02, citing Marín to Ampudia, May 5, 1843). Moore's and Morgan's forebodings about Houston's reaction are documented in Moore to Hill, May 10, 1843 (in Moore pp. 149-50); and Morgan to Reed, May 11, 1843 (Rosenberg JM).

THIRTY-THREE: THE SHOWDOWN

The battle of May 16, 1843, was described in Walke Journal, May 16, 1843; in Gray p. 10; Fuller on pp. 231-33; James W. Moore, Minutes of the second action with the Mexican Squadron, May 16, 1843 (at Moore 160); James Morgan, testimony (at Moore, *Brief Synopsis* 15-16) (Dienst copy); extract of report of Surgeon Thomas P. Anderson, May 20, 1843 (TSLA); Dienst document 410 (Dienst collection, CAH) (letter from *Wharton* officer, May 17, 1843); *Houston Morning Star,* July 15, 1843 (citing Boylan); and in Wells p. 150 (citing Boletín Oficial Numero 1, May 15, 1843), and 153 (citing Tómas Marín to Secretary of War, May 19, 1843).

The descriptions of casualties and damage to the Texas vessels come from Fuller p. 233; Dienst documents 410 and 428 (Dienst collection, CAH) (James Moore, "Return of Killed and Wounded"); Walke Journal, May 16, 1843; Mr. Bryant to Sarah Bryant, June 8, 1843 (Bryant collection, CAH); extract of report of Surgeon Thomas P. Anderson, May 20, 1843 (TSLA); M. C. Hamilton, "Extract of Captain Edwin W. Moore's Report, July 21, 1843" (TSLA); Wells p. 153 (citing enclosure, Charles Elliott to Lord Aberdeen, May 29, 1843); *Telegraph,* September 25, 1844; and from Cardenas de la Peña pp. 102-03.

Mexican losses were described at Gray 10; Moore, letter dated May 19, 1843 (reprinted in *New Orleans Tropic,* May 27, 1843), Moore 175; Walke Journal, May 16, 1843; *Houston Morning Star,* July 15, 1843; Hill 188 (citing Marín to Comandancia General Esquadra del Mar del Norte, May 17, 1843).

Early assessments by both sides over the effect of the battle are found in *Houston Morning Star,* July 15, 1843; Wells 153 (with photograph of medal at 102); Hill 188 (citing Marín to Comandancia General, May 17, 1843); John Lloyd Stephens, quoted in Douglas W. Richmond, "A View of the Periphery," (on Francaviglia and Richmond pp. 129-30); and Ampudia to Marín, April 17, 1843 (*Houston Morning Star,* May 12, 1843). The aftermath of the battle is described in *New Orleans Tropic,* June 10, 1843, and Anonymous (evidently Lt. Lewis), letter from "Texian Schr. of War Independence," to editors, *New Orleans Tropic*, May 28, 1843 (reprinted in Augusta *Chronicle and Sentinel*, June 17, 1843); and J. D. Boylan to Editors, *New Orleans Tropic*, June 22, 1843, and Anonymous, letter from "Sloop-of-War Austin" to editor, *New Orleans Tropic*, June 5, 1843 (both reprinted in Augusta *Chronicle and Sentinel*, July 13, 1843).

THIRTY-FOUR: THE PIRATE NAVY

Sam Houston's views towards Commodore Moore in particular, and the Navy in general, were documented in Sam Houston to John D. Andrews, March 24, 1842 (Houston 4:174-75); Houston to William Christy, May 7, 1843 (Houston 4:198-99); Anson Jones, *Memoranda and Official Correspondence* 39, 241 (journal entry December 31, 1843); Houston to James Morgan, March 26, 1843 (Houston 4:175-76); Houston to Thomas M. Bagby, May 13, 1843 (Houston 3:382-83); Houston to Charles Elliott, May 11 and 13, 1843 (Houston 3:377-78, 379 n.2, 385-86); Houston to Ashbel Smith, July 21, 1843 (Houston 3:418); in Wells p. 156 (citing Elliott to Lord Aberdeen, April 14, 1843, U.S. Consul at Veracruz to Secretary of State, March 8, 1843), 177 (citing Callender I. Fayssoux Collection of William Walker Papers, Tulane); Ashbel Smith, *Reminiscences*; William Bryan and William C. Brashear to Edwin W. Moore, July 25, 1843 (Moore 131). Houston's awareness of the threat of invasion was documented in George W. Terrell to Houston, May 5, 1843 (Catholic Diocese Archives, Austin, Texas).

Published public reaction to Houston's May 6 proclamation was recounted in the *Houston Morning Star*, May 11, 23, 25, and 27 and July 18, 1843; *Houston Morning Star*, May 27, 1843 (quoting *Commercial Bulletin*); *Seminario Politico*, July 13, 1843 (SRM); and the *New Orleans Picayune* (reprinted in *Morning Star*, May 27, 1843).

The Texas fleet's departure from Yucatán was documented by Walke Journal, May 17-31, June 4, 16, and 26 and July 1, 7, 9, and 10, 1843; Morgan testimony (at Moore *Brief Synopsis* 19); Moore to Morgan, June 2 and 4, 1843 (at Moore 170-71, 173); Moore to Miguel Barbachano, June 20, 28, 1843 (at Moore 177); Barbachano to Moore, July 6, 1843 (at Moore 178); Morgan to Moore, June 3, 1843 (Moore 171-72); Fleming T. Wells to Jones, August 3, 1843 (at Jones 240); Moore (173-75); Moore to George W. Hill, July 21, 1843 (at Moore 179-80); Gray (11); Wells (161) (citing *U.S. Diplomatic Correspondence* 12:290); *Houston Morning Star*, July 15 and 18, 1843; New Hampshire *Patriot*, September 14, 1843 (SRM); Fuller (233); and Vázquez (340).

Mexico's peace offer, which Houston parlayed into a truce, was noted by *New Orleans Tropic*, June 10, 1843 (reprinted in Augusta *Chronicle and Sentinel*, June 17, 1843); Worley 24-26 (citing Elliott to Anson Jones, July 24, 1843); Haley 276 and Fehrenbach 262.

THIRTY-FIVE: THE WAR AT HOME

The squadron's arrival at Galveston was documented in Walke Journal, July 14, 1843; *Houston Morning Star*, July 18, 1843; Dienst document 274 (CAH) (copy of J. M. Allen to Edwin W. Moore, July 14, 1843); Moore to H. M. Smythe, July 14, 1843 (Moore, *Brief Synopsis* 21); Fuller (234); Moore to G. W. Hill, July 21, 1843 (Moore 180-81).

Secretary Hill's discharge of Moore, Lothrop, and Snow was reported in Hill to Sam Houston, November 30, 1843 (TSLA); William Bryan and William C. Brashear to Moore, July 25, 1843 (at Moore 181); Hill to Moore, July 9, 1843 (at Moore 182-83); Hill to J.T.K. Lothrop, July 19, 1843 (at Moore 183); Moore, *Brief Synopsis* (10-11); Bryan and Brashear to Lothrop, July 25, 1843 (at Moore 183); Wells (164, citing *Journals of Ninth Texas Congress*, Appendix 75-90); and Hill to Charles B. Snow, July 19, 1843 (at Moore 184). Background on Brashear comes from Houston to Brashear, January 7, 1843 (Houston 3:269, 270 n.2); and Handbook of Texas Online, "Brashear, William C." entry.

Moore's disputes with Samuel May Williams and James Love were recounted in Moore to Samuel May Williams, July 20, 21, and 24, 1843 (Rosenberg SMW); Williams to Moore, July 21, 1843 (Rosenberg SMW); Henson, SMW, pp. 121-22; and Wells p. 163 (citing James Love to Albert Sidney Johnston, August 18, 1843).

Moore's battle for popular support was documented in James Morgan, "To the Public," July 16, 1843 (*Telegraph*, July 25, 1843); Moore, "To the People of Texas," (*Telegraph*, July 25, 1843); and *Telegraph*, July 25, 1843 (editorial).

The departure of Moore and Lothrop and the resignation of the bulk of the officer corps was described in Walke Journal, July 26, 1843; Lothrop to Hill, July 28, 1843 (Rosenberg TNC); and Hill to Houston, November 30, 1843 (TSLA).

The efforts of Moore, Lothrop, and Snow to obtain a court-martial were documented in Moore to Bryan and Brashear, July 25, 1843 (at Moore 188); Lothrop to Hill, July 28, 1843 (at Moore 189); Moore to editor, *Houston Citizen*, August 12, 1843 (at Moore 185–86); Wells (164–65, citing Moore, "To the Honorable the Senate and House of Representatives of Texas," January 11, 1844); in Moore, *Reply* (28, quoting *House Journal, Ninth Texas Congress, Second Session* 86); Gammel 2:1030 (act approved February 5, 1844); *Civilian and Galveston Gazette*, September 23, 1843; *Senate Journal, Eighth Texas Congress* 108 (Dienst copy); Charles S. Mason, Account of J.T.K. Lothrop, May 31, 1844 (ROT Claims, J.T.K. Lothrop); Claim, Charles B. Snow, n.d. (ROT Claims, Charles B. Snow); Dienst 4:116–17 (quoting Naval Committee Report), 122; Senator Jones, August 2, 1854, speech to the U.S. Senate; and *Weekly Mirror*, October 19, 1844, (quoting *New Orleans Bulletin*) (Dienst copies). Lothrop's reinstatement was noted in Mason, account of J.T. K. Lothrop, May 31, 1844, approved by G.W. Hill May 31, 1844 (ROT Claims, J.T. K. Lothrop). Lothrop's death was referred to in James S. Holman, affidavit, April 2, 1852, and Moore to James B. Shear and J. M. Swisher, January 19, 1849 (ROT Claims, Edwin Moore, "Letters of Administration of E.W. Moore on the Estate of J.T. K. Lothrop, Dec'd.").

The courts-martial of Snow and Moore were documented in Moore to Snow, January 31, 1843 (Moore 188); Snow to Maj. Gen. Richard Bache, March 30, 1845 (Rosenberg JGT); on Wells p. 167 (citing Joint Resolution for the Relief of Charles B. Snow, passed January 25, 1845, and quoting *Houston Morning Star*, July 1, 1844), 168 (citing Houston to Senate, July 15 1854), 169 (citing *New Orleans Tropic*, June 18, 1844), 170 (citing William Kennedy to Lord Aberdeen, September 23, 1844, *New York Herald*, January 8 and 13, 1844, and *LaGrange Intelligencer*, October 8, 1845.); Dienst 4:117; M. C. Hamilton to Fleming T. Wells, March 15, 1844 (TSLA); Witness subpoeanae to Brashear, Snow, Bryan, Lloyd, H. Washington, Tennison, Lothrop, James Moore (Rosenberg TNC); *Weekly Mirror*, October 19, 1844 (quoting *New Orleans Commercial Bulletin*) (Dienst copy); Hill, pay approval dated July 18, 1844; Sidney Sherman, pay voucher, June 28, 1844 (ROT Claims, J.T. K. Lothrop); Thomas Johnson to Moore, December 7, 1844 (Dienst copy); *Journal of the Ninth Texas Congress*, 244; and Moore to Sen. James A. Pearce, March 28, 1853 (CAH). Snow's reinstatement is found in "Claim of C. B. Snow Against the Republic of Texas," (ROT Claims, Charles B. Snow).

Popular reaction to the court-martial verdict was documented by the *Telegraph*, January 15, 1845, quoted by Nance at 182. Houston's efforts to reverse the decision of the court-martial were documented at Moore, *Reply*, 28 (citing *House Journal, Ninth Texas Congress, Second Session* 86); Dienst document 392 (preamble to January 11, 1845 publication signed by members of the court); *Journal of the Ninth Texas Congress* 155, 224 (Dienst copy); Wells 173 (citing Morgan to Samuel Swartwout, August 16, 1845, and TSLA Executive Record Book 47, June 27, 1845 entry); Dienst 4:122 (citing *Senate Journal, Ninth Texas Congress, 2nd Session* 75); Veto of President Anson Jones, June 27, 1845 (Buchanan et al. 11 (NARA); and Moore, "Brief in Case of Captain E.W. Moore" (NARA).

The deaths of Commander Lothrop and Lieutenant Crisp were recounted in Wells p. 167 (citing William Kennedy to Lord Aberdeen, July 29, 1844 and *Telegraph*, June 12, 1844), and 168 (citing D. F. Duerr Diary); James S. Holman, affidavit, April 2, 1852 (ROT Claims, J.T. K. Lothrop); Moore to Shear and Swisher, January 19, 1849 (ROT Claims, J.T .K. Lothrop); "Letters of Administration to E.W. Moore on the Estate of J.T. K. Lothrop, Dec'd.," (ROT Claims, E.W. Moore); in Cartwright pp. 74–75; Handbook of

Texas Online, "Lothrop, John T.K." entry (citing *Telegraph*, April 3, May 15, June 12 and August 21, 1844); and Handbook of Texas Online, "Crisp, Downing H" entry.

THIRTY-SIX: A SLOW DEATH

The administration of the Navy in ordinary in preparation for sale was documented in William C. Brashear and William Bryan to Fleming T. Wells, July 31 and August 10, 1843 (TSLA); *Austin* log, July 27-October 10, October 15 and November 11-22, 1843 (NARA); Wells to Anson Jones, August 3, 1843 (Jones 239) and George W. Hill to Wells, August 27, 1843 (TSLA); Houston to Charles Elliott, October 5, 1843 (Houston 4:224); and Houston to Gail Borden, Jr., September 23, 1843 (Houston 2:167).

Houston's attempts to sell the Navy were documented in Hill to Houston, November 30, 1843 (TSLA); *Civilian and Galveston Gazette*, September 23 and October 7, 1843; *Houston Morning Star*, October 17, 1843; Wells (165-66, citing *Telegraph*, October 18, 1843 and James Love to Albert Sidney Johnston, November 6, 1843); Galveston *News*, October 20, 1901, and Houston, Speech to Presbyterian Church (Huntsville), November 8, 1843 (Houston 3:449, 451).

Appropriations for and administration of the Navy in ordinary after the vessels failed to sell were documented in Hill to Houston, November 30, 1843 (TSLA); *House Journal, Eighth Texas Congress*, 69 (Dienst copy); *Senate Journal, Eighth Texas Congress* 44, 221-23 (Dienst copy); Petition of Pursers F.T. Wells and J. F. Stephens, and Lieutenants Downing H. Crisp and Thurston M. Taylor, January 9, 1844 (TSLA); Wells (167-68, citing John C. Calhoun to Isaac Van Zandt and J. Pinckney Henderson, April 11, 1844 and Brower to Van Zandt, April 11, 1844); Charles S. Mason to Texas Senate, January 19, 1844 (TSLA); John Grant Tod to Gustavus A. Parker, December 11, 1844 (Rosenberg JGT); Gammel 2:976-77, 1011 and 1027, 1028 (Dienst copy); Dienst 4:119; Sullivan (31, citing Special Report of the Secretary of War and Marine, December 24, 1844); J. B. Gardiner to M.C. Hamilton, August 29, 1844 (Rosenberg TNC); Committee Report, Committee on Federal Relations, November 23, 1857 (Dienst copy); Hill to Houston, January 1, 1844 (TSLA); and Senate Documents, 29th Cong., 1st Sess., Report 443, 1, 6-9 (survey of Texas coastal defenses dated January 21, 1846).

The effect of annexation on protection of the Texas coast was documented in *Galveston News*, March 1, 1903 (Dienst collection CAH); Schroeder 154 (citing David M. Plecher, *The Diplomacy of Annexation: Texas, Oregon and the Mexican War* (Columbia, Missouri 1973), 132-33); Eisenhower, *So Far From God* (24-25, (re: Stockton orders); and Wells (166).

The decline of the ships while annexation talks were pending was chronicled in the *Austin* log, February 2-3, 1844; William A. Tennison to Hamilton, September 11, 1844 (Dienst collection); Hamilton to Tennison, September 23, 1844; Tennison, "Summary of the Property Belonging to the Navy of the late Republic of Texas transferred by Lieutenant Wm. A. Tennison to Hiram C. Runnels Esq., U.S. Commissioner on the 11th May 1846," (NARA) (hereafter, "Tennison Inventory"); Hill to Tennison, September 23, 1844 (Dienst collection); *Brashear v. Mason*, 47 U.S. 92, 99 (6 Howard 92) (1848); contract between Commander William C. Brashear and James Denny, November 26, 1844 (TSLA); Joint Resolution, May 1, 1845 (*Brashear*, 47 U.S. at 93); purser's log, January 2, 1846 (Rosenberg TNC); Brashear to Cooke, March 27, 1845 (TSLA); Adjutant General C. L. Mann to Moore, February 8, 1848 (at Moore, *Reply*); Secretary of War and Navy William G. Cooke to Brashear, January 26, 1846 (Moore, *Reply*, 33); and Houston to Brashear, September 24, 1844 (Houston 4:372).

The transfer of the Texas Navy's vessels to the United States Navy was documented in Wells on p. 174; Cooke to Tod, February 10, 1846 (NARA); Symonds on p. 14 (re: Randolph); USN Archives, Commander Victor M. Randolph (NHC); Thomas J. Rusk to Tod, April 25, 1846 (Rosenberg JGT); Hiram G. Runnels, Report and Inventory of Texas Navy, July 3, 1846 (NARA); Tod to Thomas F. McKinney, April 9, 1846 (Rosenberg JGT); J. Pinckney Henderson to Tennison, April 25, 1846 (Dienst collection, CAH); Tennison

Inventory; Tennison, "List of Officers in the Texas Navy," April 26, 1846 (Rosenberg TNC); *Houston Morning Star* (quoting *Telegraph*, May 20, 1846); Tennison document 394 (Dienst collection CAH); Moore to Sen. James A. Pearce, March 28, 1853 (CAH); Tod to Runnels, May 15, 1846 (Rosenberg JGT); George Bancroft to Victor M. Randolph, June 27, 1846 (USN Archives, NHC); Navy Secretary Josephus Daniels to Robert L. Rogers, June 17, 1915 (USN Archives, NHC).

The final disposition of the Texas Navy warships by the U.S. government is found in Randolph to Bancroft, July 31, 1846 (extracted in USN Archives, NHC); Charles Morris to Bancroft, August 15, 1846 (extracted in USN Archives, NHC); *Houston Morning Star* (quoting *Telegraph*, July 1, 1846); Bauere (23); Bancroft to James K. Polk, August 19, 1846 (extracted in USN Archives, NHC); Tennison document 294 (Dienst Collection CAH); John Y. Mason to Randolph, September 19 and October 12, 1846 (extracted in USN Archives, NHC); Capt. H. C. Cooke to Jim Dan Hill, May 8, 1931, 486 (USN Archives, NHC); Mason to Polk, October 8, 1846 (USN Archives, NHC); Polk to Mason, October 9, 1846 (extracted in USN Archives, NHC); Report of the Secretary of the Navy, November 7, 1846, 383, 462 (extracted in USN Archives, NHC); Randolph to Mason, November 9 and December 1, 1846 (extracted in USN Archives, NHC); William K. Latimer to Secretary of the Navy, May 13, 1848 (extracted in USN Archives, NHC).; and Secretary of the Navy, Report for the Year 1849, November 1, 1848 630 (extracted in USN Archives, NHC).

THIRTY-SEVEN: FLOTSAM AND JETSAM

Commodore Moore's financial audits for his years in command of the Texas Navy are documented in Senator Jones's August 2, 1854, speech, 8; State Comptroller James B. Shaw to Edwin W. Moore, May 11, 1846, (TSLA); Charles S. Mason to Shaw, April 25, 1844 (ROT Claims, E.W. Moore); William G. Cooke, List of Naval Officers, January 24, 1846 (NARA); Naval Committee Report, December 20, 1847 (Jones's August 2, 1854, speech); Gammel 2:1720 (Dienst copy); Gammel 3:251, 334-36, 357-58; Gammel 4:682; Wells (176, citing Public Debt Papers, February 4, 1856 (TSLA)); General Land Office Certificate 2453/2554, June 8, 1852 (duplicate of certificate dated May 10, 1844).

Texas officers' efforts to be inducted into the U.S. Navy are found in *Telegraph*, May 27, 1846; *Brashear v. Mason*, 47 U.S. 92, 100-101 (6 How. 92) (1848); Moore to James A. Pearce, March 28, 1853 (CAH); Handbook of Texas Online, "Brashear, William C." (citing *Texas State Gazette*, November 24, 1849); *New York Mirror*, March 7, 1844 (Dienst copy); Speech of Sen. Sam Houston to U.S. Senate, July 31, 1846 (CAH); H. R. 589, 29th Cong., 2nd Sess. (Rosenberg TNC); Brashear to John Grant Tod, September 23, 1848 (Rosenberg JGT); *Senate Journal, 30th Cong., 1st Sess.* (Rosenberg TNC); Moore, *Brief Synopsis*; Moore et al. *Memorial of the Officers of the Late Texas Navy* (USN Archives, NHC); H. R. Rep., 288, 31st Cong., 1st Sess., May 2, 1850 (Rosenberg TNC); *New York Daily Tribune*, March 17, 1846 (SRM); Will T. Hale, "Great Southerners: Franklin Buchanan," *Children's News*, n.d. (Dienst collection, CAH); Buchanan et al. *In Relation to Claims of the Officers of the Late Texas Navy* (CAH); Moore, *Reply to the Second Pamphlet* (CAH); Joint Resolution of the Texas Legislature, February 16, 1852 (Gammel 3:1005) (Dienst copy); Resolution of the Texas Legislature, August 20, 1856 (Rosenberg TNC); Dienst 4:124 (citing Tennison document 296, Gammel 4:1152, and *Congressional Globe*, 34th Cong., 3rd Sess. Appendix 427), 125; Houston to Tod, April 20, 1857 (Rosenberg JGT); Gammel 4:682, 705 (Dienst copy); Gammel 5:315 (Dienst copy); Tod to Anson Jones, April 28, 1857 (Jones 512); and Wells (178).

The war of words between Houston and Moore in the 1840s and 1850s, and the underlying factual disputes, were recounted in the *New York Mirror*, May 31, 1845; Moore to Houston, May 5, 1845 (reprinted in Moore to Pearce, March 28, 1854); Houston to Maggie Houston, August 3, 1843 (Houston, *Personal Correspondence*, 1:283-84); Moore to Pearce, March 28, 1854 (CAH); Speech of Sen. Sam Houston, July

15, 1854 (CAH); Houston to J. Pinckney Henderson, February 20, 1844 (Houston 4:269); Moore to Mason, February 7, 1848 (NARA); A. Taney, memorandum, January 27, 1858 (NARA) (re: Tod claims); Speech of Sen. James C. Jones, August 2, 1854 (CAH). Houston's accusations about Wells' estate evidently were based on the case *Richard Wells v. Moore et al.* (order enjoining payment of estate funds to Moore) and A. J. Hamilton, Memorandum, April 8, 1853 (ROT Claims, E.W. Moore).

The State of Texas also voted a small pension for surviving Revolutionary naval officers on August 13, 1870, but by then most of the naval officers were dead or lost for all time. Comptroller of Public Accounts, Certificate No. 871, November 13, 1870 (ROT Claims, James G. Hurd). The act was amended on April 21, 1874. Hurd affidavit, July 15, 1874 (ROT Claims, James G. Hurd).

The post-republic years of Texas Navy officers are documented at Fuller 226 (re: Fayssoux);Tod, "Memorandum of Service" (NARA); Charles B. Snow to Houston, April 2, 1858 (Houston 4:373 n.1); Henry I. Garlick to Callender I. Fayssoux, June 6, 1860 (Fayssoux Collection, UNC) (Lieutenant Garlick and Midshipmen Fayssoux, C. L. Betts and Robert H. Clements); memorandum of service, n.d. (Fayssoux Collection, UNC); James G. Hurd to A. Bledsoe, Comptroller, December 18, 1870 (ROT Claims, James G. Hurd); affidavit of Hurd, October 31, 1870 (ROT Claims, James G. Hurd); Handbook of Texas Online, "Lewis M. H. Washington," "Alfred Gilleat Gray," "Edward Johns," "John Grant Tod," "James Morgan," "Norman Hurd," "Lent M. Hitchcock," and "Albert Moses Levy"; Charles B. Snow to Tod, December 23, 1845 (Rosenberg JGT) (Lt. Snow); "James Morgan," n.d. (Rosenberg James Morgan Papers index); Sullivan n. 33 (Lt. Snow, Midshipman Kintzing); Houston to Margaret Houston, February 8, 1847, (*Personal Correspondence* 2:208) (Tennison); Brashear to Tod, September 23, 1848 (Rosenberg JGT) (Tennison); *Dallas News*, May 26, 1902 (Dienst collection, CAH) (Midshipman John E. Barrow); Gammel 3:364 (act for relief of O. P. Kelton's family approved March 1, 1848); and Dienst Collection (CAH) (correspondence of John Grant Tod, Jr.).

Edwin Moore's twilight years were recounted in *Telegraph*, September 13, 1849; in Wells pp. 177-80 (citing Federal District Court Record of Wills and *Clarksville Northern Standard*, December 22, 1849); and Houston to Tod, January 12, 1857 (CAH, Tod Letters; and *Augusta (Georgia) Daily Constitutionalist*, May 25, 1860); *New York Herald* obituary, n.d. (Fayssoux Papers, UNC).

THIRTY-EIGHT: GHOSTS AND GRAVES

Efforts of NUMA and others to locate the *Zavala, Invincible,* and *Brutus* are documented in Cussler, *The Sea Hunters*, (44-51); Oertling, 1992, (14-39); Oertling, 1997 (10-24); *Brutus* cannon file, Texas Seaport Museum; Wayne Gronquist, conversation with author, August 19, 2000; Clive Cussler, conversation with author, January 20, 2001; Thomas Oertling, July 3, 2001, conversation with the author; John Hooper, e-mail to author, June 14, 2001. The line from "If I Had a Boat" is (c)1987 Michael H. Goldsen, Inc./Lyle Lovett (ASCAP), all rights reserved. Used by permission.

EPILOGUE: THE VERDICT

Commentary on and tributes to the Texas Navy can be found in Semmes, *Service Afloat and Ashore* 49; Resolution, Ladies of Galveston, May 24, 1845 (Walke, reprinted in *Houston Chronicle*, June 13, 1937); William R. Crim, letter to author; Handbook of Texas Online, "Robert Potter," "Edwin W. Moore," and "S. Rhoads Fisher" entries; Brig. Gen. Theodore Roosevelt, Jr. (Hill foreword); Adm. Chester W. Nimitz, January 16, 1944 (Eller 39, quoting remarks to "The Texas Roundup," Moana Park, Honolulu); Wilson 18; James 334-35; and Haley 262.

BIBLIOGRAPHY

ARCHIVAL COLLECTIONS

Archivo General Nacional, Mexico City, Mexico
Brazoria County History Museum, Angleton, Texas
    Captain Jeremiah Brown Residence File
Daughters of the Republic of Texas Library, The Alamo, San Antonio, Texas
    J.G. Burrows File
    Robert M. Potter File
    Texas Navy File
    Yellow Stone File
Historic New Orleans Collection, New Orleans, Louisiana
National Archives and Records Administration, College Park, Maryland
    U.S. Naval Records
Naval Historical Center, Washington Navy Yard, D.C.
Newberry Library, Chicago, Illinois
    Edward E. Ayers Collection
Rosenberg Library, Galveston, Texas
    James Morgan Papers
    John Grant Tod Collection
    Map Collection
    S. Rhoads Fisher Collection
    Samuel May Williams Collection
    Texas Navy Collection
Sam Houston Library and Research Center, Liberty, Texas
    Nancy Burch Collection
Texas General Land Office, Austin, Texas
Texas Maritime Museum, Rockport, Texas
Texas Seaport Museum, Galveston, Texas
    Brutus Cannon File
Texas State Library and Archives, Austin, Texas
    Andrew Jackson Houston Collection
    Department of State Records
    Diplomatic Correspondence
    Domestic Correspondence
    Executive Records
    Navy Papers
    Republic of Texas Claims
Texas Tech University, Special Collections Library, Lubbock, Texas
    Elizabeth Howard West Papers
Tulane University, Howard-Tilton Memorial Library
    Albert Sidney Johnston Papers
    Joseph S. Copes Papers

University of North Carolina at Chapel Hill, Southern Historical Collection
    William McClennan Fayssoux Papers
University of Texas, Center for American History, Austin, Texas
    Alex Dienst Collection
    Bexar Archives
    Charles G. Bryant Papers
    Christian F. Duerr Papers
    Lewis Miles Hobbes Washington Papers
    Midshipman Edward Johns Collection
    Thomas F. McKinney Collection
University of Texas, Benson Latin American Library, Austin, Texas
University of Texas at Arlington
    R. A. Irion Family Papers Collection
    Texas Navy Collection
Yale University, Beinecke Rare Book and Manuscript Library, New Haven, Connecticut

OFFICIAL RECORDS

Almonte, Juan Nepomuente, *Memoria del Ministerio de Guerra y Marina*, etc., (Mexico: Imprenta del Aguila, 1841), Archivo General de la Nacion, Mexico City

An Accurate and Authentic Report of the Proceedings of the House of Representatives, from the 3d of October to the 23d of December. First Congress—First Session (Columbia, Texas: G. & T. H. Borden, Public Printers 1836)

Bulnes, Manuel de, *Escalafon de los Señores Gefes y Oficiales del Cuerdo de Guerra de la Armada Nacional cerrado hasta fin de Agosto de 1839* (Mexido: Imprenta del Aguila, 1840), Archivo General de la Nacion.

Brashear v. Mason, 47 U.S. 92 (6 Howard 92) (1848)

Correspondencia que ha Mediado entre La Legacion Extraordinaria de Mexico, etc., (Mexico: Reimpreso por Jose M. F. de Lara, 1837), Archivo General de la Nacion, Mexico City

Gammel, Hans Peter Nielsen, *The Laws of Texas*, 1822-1904 (13 vols., Austin: Gammel-Statesman Publishing, 1904)

Hererra, José J. de, *Memoria del Secretario de Estado y del Despacho de la Guerra*, etc. (Mexico: Imprenta del Aguila, 1834), Archivo General de la Nacion, Mexico City

House of Representatives Documents, 25th Cong. (United States), 2nd Sess.

Journals of the Consultation Held at San Felipe de Austin, October 16, 1835 (Houston: Telegraph Power Press, 1888)

Journal of the Proceedings of the General Council of the Republic of Texas, Held at San Felipe de Austin, November 14th 1835 (Houston: National Intelligencer Office 1839)

Journal of the First Congress, House of Representatives, First Session (Columbia: G. & T. H. Borden, 1836)

Journal of the House of Representatives of the Republic of Texas, at the Second Session of the First Congress, Held by adjournment at the City of Houston, Commencing May 1st 1837 (Houston: Telegraph Office, 1838)

Journal of the House of Representatives of the Republic of Texas: Second Congress, Adjourned Session (Houston: Telegraph Office, 1838)

Journal of the Second Congress, House of Representatives, First Session (Houston: Telegraph Office, 1838)

Journal of the House of Representatives, 2nd Congress, Called Session (Houston: National Banner Office—Niles & Co., Printers, 1838)

Journal of the House of Representatives of the Republic of Texas, Regular Session of Third Congress (Houston: Intelligencer Office, 1839)

Journals of the Senate of the Republic of Texas, First Session of the Third Congress (Houston: National Intelligencer Office, 1839)

Journals of the Fourth Congress of the Republic of Texas, 1839-1840: to which are added the relief laws (Harriet Smither, ed.) (3 vols. Austin: Von Boeckmann-Jones Co., 1931)

Journals of the House of Representatives of the Republic of Texas: Fifth Congress, First Session, 1840-1841 (Austin: Cruger & Wing, 1841)

Journals of the Sixth Congress of the Republic of Texas, 1841-1842, to which are added the special laws (Harriet Smither, ed.) (Austin: Von Boeckmann-Jones Co., 1940-1945)

Journals of the House of Representatives of the Eighth Congress of the Republic of Texas (Houston: Cruger & Moore, Public Printers, 1844)

Journals of the House of Representatives of the Ninth Congress of the Republic of Texas (Washington, Texas: Miller & Cushney, 1845)

Journals of the House of Representatives of the Extra Session, Ninth Congress, of the Republic of Texas (Washington, Texas: Miller & Cushney, 1845)

Report of the Chairman of the Committee on Naval Affairs, on the President's Message (Austin: Whiting's Press, *1840*)

Report of the Minority of the Select Naval Committee of the House of Representatives, November 22, 1841 (Austin: Texian Office, 1841)

Reprimand Delivered by the President of the Senate to Hon. Robert Wilson, by order of the Senate, January 13, 1839 (Houston: Telegraph Power Press, 1839)

Senate Documents, 24th Congress (United States), 2nd Sess.

Senate Documents, 30th Congress (United States), 1st Session (Misc. 27—Dawson Petition)

Senate Journal, 30th Congress (United States), 2nd Sess.

Senate Journal, 2nd Congress, Regular Session (Houston: National Banner Office—Niles & Co., Printers, 1838)

Tornel y Mendivil, José Maria, *Memoria del Secretario de Estado y del Despacho Guerra y Marina*, etc. (Mexico: Impreso por Ignacio Cumplido, 1835), Archivo General de la Nacion, Mexico City

Tornel, José Maria, *Memoria del Secretario de Estado y del Despacho de la Guerra y Marina*, etc. (Mexico: Impreso por Ignacio Cumplido, 1839), Archivo General de la Nacion, Mexico City

Winkler, Ernest W., ed., *Secret Journals of the Senate of the Republic of Texas, 1836-1846* (Austin: Austin Printing Co., 1911)

UNOFFICIAL ACCOUNTS, COMPILED CORRESPONDENCE, JOURNALS, PAMPHLETS, AND MANUSCRIPTS

Adams, Ephraim Douglas, ed., "Correspondence from the British Archives Concerning Texas, 1837-1846," in *Texas State Historical Association Quarterly* 15 (January and April, 1912)

Allen, W. Y., "Extracts from the Diary of W.Y. Allen, 1838-1839," William S. Red, ed., *Southwestern Historical Quarterly* 17 (January 1914).

Anonymous, *Texas in 1837*, Andrew Forest Muir, ed. (Austin: University of Texas Press, 1988)

Barker, Eugene C., ed., *The Austin Papers*, 3 vols.; (Austin: University of Texas Press, 1926)

Bass, Jr., Ferris A. and B. R. Brunson, eds., *Fragile Empires: The Texas Correspondence of Samuel Swartwout and James Morgan, 1836-1856* (Austin: Shoal Creek, 1978)

Binkley, William C., ed., *Official Correspondence of the Texan Revolution*, 2 vols; (New York: D. Appleton & Co., 1936)

Bryan, Moses Austin, "Personal Recollections of Stephen F. Austin," *The Texas Magazine*, 3 (September-November 1897)
Buchanan, Franklin, S. F. Dupont and George A. Magruder, *In Relation to the Claims of the Officers of the Late Texas Navy* (New York: Office of "Parker's Journal" 1850)
Buchanan, Franklin, S. F. Dupont and George A. Magruder, *Reply to the Report to the House of Representatives of the Congress of the United States*, n.d.
Castañeda, Carlos E., trans., *The Mexican Side of the Texas Revolution* (Dallas: P. L. Turner, 1928)
Clopper, A. M., "The Clopper Correspondence, 1834-1838," *Texas State Historical Association Quarterly* 13 (October 1909)
Cox, Cornelius C., "Reminiscences of C. C. Cox," *Texas State Historical Association Quarterly* 6 (October 1902 and January 1903)
Crisp, Downing H., *Statement*, Edward E. Ayers Collection, Newberry Library, Chicago, Illinois
Cushing, S. W., *Adventures in the Texas Navy and at the Battle of San Jacinto* (Austin: W. M. Morrison Books 1985)
De la Peña, José Enrique, *With Santa Anna in Texas*, trans. Carmen Perry (College Station: Texas A&M University Press, 1997)
Duerr, Christian Frederick, *Diary of Christian Frederick Duerr*, Center for American History, University of Texas
Duval, John C., *Early Times in Texas* (Lincoln: University of Nebraska Press, 1936)
Filisola, Vicente, *Evacuation of Texas: Translation of the Representation Addressed to the Supreme Government by Gen. Vicente Filisola in Defence of His Honor*, etc. (Waco: Texian Press, 1965)
Filisola, Vicente, *Memoirs for the History of the War in Texas*, trans. Wallace Woolsey (Austin: Eakin Press, 1985)
Fuller, George F., "Sketch of the Texas Navy," *Texas State Historical Association Quarterly* 7 (January 1904)
Gaillardet, Frédérick, *Sketches of Early Texas*, James L. Shepherd III, ed. (Austin: University of Texas Press, 1966)
Gardiner, John Burrows, *Abstract of Medical Journal of the Sloop of War* Austin, Daughters of the Republic of Texas Library, San Antonio, Texas
Garrison, George P., *Diplomatic Correspondence of the Republic of Texas*, 3 vols. (Washington: Government Printing Office, 1907-11)
Gaulick, Jr., Charles Adams, et al., eds., *The Papers of Mirabeau Buonaparte Lamar* 6 vols. (Austin: Von Boeckmann-Jones, 1921-1927)
Gray, Alfred Gilleat, "The Battle of Campeche Described," ms. ca. 1857, reprinted by the Texas Navy Association, 1980, DRT Library, San Antonio, Texas
Green, Thomas J., *Journal of the Texian Expedition Against Mier: Subsequent Imprisonment of the Author . . .* (New York: Harper & Bros., 1845)
Hall, Edward, et al., *A Vindication of the Conduct of the Agency of Texas, in New Orleans* (New Orleans: Louisiana Advertiser Office, 1836)
Harkort, Edward "The Journal of Col. Eduard Harkort, Captain of Engineers, Texas Army, February 8-July 17, 1836," Brister, Louis E., ed., *Southwestern Historical Quarterly* 102 (January 1999)
Haugh, George F., ed., "The Public Letters of Morgan and Moore in Regard to their Naval Actions," *Southwestern Historical Quarterly* 64 (July 1962)
Houston, Sam, *The Personal Correspondence of Sam Houston*, Madge Thornall Roberts, ed. 4 vols. (Denton, Texas: University of North Texas Press, 1996-2001)
Houston, Sam, *The Writings of Sam Houston* 1813-1863, Amelia W. Williams and Eugene C. Barker, eds. 8 vols. (Austin: University of Texas Press, 1938)

Houston, Sam, "Speech of Senator Sam Houston of Texas," July 15, 1854 (Washington: Congressional Globe Office, 1854)

Houstoun, Matilda Charlotte Fraser, *Texas and the Gulf of Mexico, or Yachting in the New World* (Austin: W. Thomas Taylor, 1991)

Jenkins, John H., ed., *Papers of the Texas Revolution*, 10 vols. (Austin: Presidial Press, 1973)

Jones, Anson, ed., *Memoranda and Official Correspondence Relating to the Republic of Texas, its History and Annexation* (New York: D. Appleton, 1856 reprint, Chicago: Rio Grande Press, 1966)

Jones, James C., "Speech of Senator James C. Jones of Tennessee," August 2, 1854 (Washington: Congressional Globe Office 1854)

Kokernot, D. L., "The Battle of Anahuac," *Galveston News*, May 12, 1878, reprinted in *Pioneer Magazine*, n.d., on file at DRT Library, San Antonio, Texas

Mabry, James, "Journal of Midshipman James Mabry," *Galveston News*, January 9 and 16 and February 13, 1893

Manning, W. R., ed., *Diplomatic Correspondence of the United States, Inter-American Affairs*, 12 vols. (Washington: Carnegie Endowment for International Peace 1932-1939)

McKinney, Thomas F., *To All Who May Have Seen and Read the Dying Groans of Wm. Bryan, E. Hall and Saml. Ellis, Ex-Agents of Texas, etc.* (Columbia: Office of the Telegraph 1836)

Mier y Terán, Manuel de, *Texas by Terán*, Jack Jackson, ed., trans. John Wheat (Austin: University of Texas Press, 2000)

Moore, Edwin Ward, *To the People of Texas: An Appeal in Vindication of the Conduct of the Texas Navy* (Galveston: November 1843)

Moore, Edwin Ward, *A Brief Synopsis of the Doings of the Texas Navy under the Command of Com. E. W. Moore: Together with his Controversy with Gen. Sam Houston, President of the Republic of Texas; In Which He Was Sustained by the Congress of that Country Three Different Sessions; By the Convention to form a State Constitution; and by the State Legislature, Unanimously* (Washington: T. Barnard, 1847)

Moore, Edwin W., Letter to Senator J. A. Pearce, March 28, 1853 (on file in Center for American History, University of Texas)

Moore, Edwin Ward et al., *Memorial of the Officers of the Late Texas Navy to the Congress of the United States* (Washington: T. Barnard, 1850)

Moore, Edwin Ward, *A Reply to the Pamphlet by Commanders Buchanan, Dupont & Magruder of the U.S. Navy, Addressed to the House of Representatives, in Relation to the Officers of the Late Texan Navy* (Washington, 1850), National Archives and Records Agency

Morgan, James, *To the Public* (Houston: Telegraph Office, 1843)

Ripley, Eliza Moore Chinn McHatton, *Social Life in Old New Orleans; Being Recollections of My Girlhood* (New York: D. Appleton & Co., 1912) (electronically reproduced by the University of North Carolina at http://docsouth.unc.edu/ripley)

Santa Anna, Antonio López de, *The Eagle: The Autobiography of Santa Anna*, Ann Crawford, ed. (Austin: State House Press, 1988)

Seguín, Juan N., *A Revolution Remembered*, Jesús F. de la Teja, ed. (Austin: State House Press, 1991)

Sheridan, Francis C., *Galveston Island, or a Few Months Off the Coast of Texas: The Journal of Francis C. Sheridan 1839-1840*, Willis W. Pratt, ed. (Austin: University of Texas Press, 1954)

Smith, Ashbel, "Reminiscences of the Texas Republic," December 15, 1875 (reprinted at Sons of DeWitt Colony website)

St. John, Percy B., "The Dismasted Brig; Or, Naval Life in Texas," *Colburn's United Service Magazine and Naval and Military Journal* (London: Henry Colburn, 1845)

Turner, Amasa, "Colonel Amasa Turner's Reminiscences of Galveston," Francis Harwood, ed., *The Quarterly of the Texas State Historical Association* 3 (July 1899)
Williams, Mrs. Floyd, ed., *Research Notes on the Ships of the Texas Navy*, Chambers County, Texas Historical Commission (on file in Sam Houston Regional Library and Research Center, Texas State Library and Archives, Liberty, Texas)
Winkler, E. W., ed., *Manuscript Letters and Documents of Early Texans, 1821-1845* (Austin: Steck 1937)
Winthrop, John, *Report of the Trial of Thomas M. Thompson, for a Piratical Attack Upon the American Schooner San Felipe, Before the United States Court for the Eastern District of Louisiana* (New Orleans: E. Johns & Co., 1836)

NEWSPAPER SOURCES
Augusta (Georgia) Daily Constitutionalist, 1843, 1860
Augusta (Georgia) Chronicle and Sentinel, 1840
Austin City Gazette, 1840
Boston Daily Times, 1843
Civilian and Galveston Gazette (Galveston, Texas), 1843
Daily National Intelligencer (Washington, D.C.), 1836
Dallas News, May 26, 1902
Diario del Gobierno (Mexico City), 1835-1843 (trans. Jamie Fernandez and Benjamin C. Mendoza III)
Houston Citizen, 1843
Houston Morning Star, 1843, 1846
Louisiana Advertiser, 1836
Mobile Commercial Register, 1836
New Hampshire Patriot, 1843
New Orleans Bee, 1836, 1842
New Orleans Bulletin, 1843
New Orleans Commercial Bulletin, 1836-37, 1842
New Orleans Courier, 1836-1843
New Orleans Daily Picayune, 1837, 1842
New Orleans Tropic, 1842, 1843, 1844
New York Daily Tribune, 1846
New York Herald, 1845
New York Journal of Commerce, 1839-1840
New York Mirror, 1845
New York Times, 1837, 1843
Niles' National Register, 1843
Semanario Politico del Gobierno de Nuevo Leon, 1843
Telegraph and Texas Register (San Felipe de Austin, Harrisburg, Columbia, and Houston, Texas), 1835-1846
True American (New Orleans), 1836
Texas Republican (Austin, Texas), 1835
Texas Sentinel (Austin, Texas), 1840, 1841

EARLY HISTORIES
Bancroft, Hubert Howe, *History of the North Mexican States and Texas*, 2 vols. (San Francisco: San Francisco History Co., 1889)
Bollaert, William, *William Bollaert's Texas* (Norman, OK: University of Oklahoma Press, 1956)
Bonnell, George W., *Topical Description of Texas, to which is Added, an Account of the Indian Tribes* (Austin: Clark, Wing and Brown, 1840; Waco: Texian Press, reprint, 1964)

Burnet, David G., *Compendium of the Early History of Texas* (1860; reprint, San Marcos: Southwest State Teachers College, 1935)
Jenkins, John S., *The Life and Public Services of General Andrew Jackson* (New York: Miller, Orton & Mulligan 1855)
Kennedy, William, *Texas: The Rise, Progress and Prospects of the Republic of Texas* (2 vols.; London: R. Hastings, 1841)
Newell, Chester, *A History of the Revolution in Texas, Particular of the War of 1835 & '36* (New York: Wiley & Putnam, 1838)
Richardson, W. & D., *Texas Almanac for 1860* (Galveston: Galveston News, 1860)
Semmes, Raphael, *Service Afloat and Ashore During the Mexican War* (Cincinnati: W.H. Moore & Co., 1851)
Semmes, Raphael, *Memoirs of Service Afloat During the War Between the States* (Baltimore: Kelley, Piet & Co., 1869; 1996, Louisiana State University Press)
Thrall, Homer S., *A Pictorial History of Texas, from the Earliest Visits of European Adventurers, to A.D. 1978* (St. Louis: N.D. Thompson & Co., 1879)
Yoakum, Henderson, *History of Texas, from its First Settlement in 1685 to its Annexation to the United States in 1846*, 2 vols. (New York: J. S. Redfield, 1855)

MODERN SOURCES
Journal Articles

Baldwin, Elizabeth R, "T. S. S. *Zavala*: The Texas Navy's Steamship-of-War," *The INA Quarterly* 22 (Fall 1995)
Barker, Eugene C., "The San Jacinto Campaign," *The Quarterly of the Texas State Historical Association* 4 (April 1901)
Barker, Eugene C., "Difficulties of a Mexican Revenue Officer in Texas," *Studies in Texas History, Chiefly of the Revolutionary Period*, 2 vols. (Austin: University of Texas Press, 1900–25).
Barker, Eugene C., "President Jackson and the Texas Revolution," *American Historical Review* 12 (July 1907), reprinted in *Studies in Texas History* 1 (Austin: University of Texas Press, 1900–25)
Brack, Gene, "Mexican Opinion and the Texas Revolution," *Southwestern Historical Quarterly* 72 (October 1968)
Bugbee, Lester G., "Slavery in Early Texas," *Political Science Quarterly* 3, (September–December 1898) (reprinted at Sons of DeWitt Colony Web site, www.tamu.edu/ccbn/dewitt/slaverybugbee.htm)
Carroll, H. Bailey, "Texas Collection," *Southwestern Historical Quarterly* 55 (July 1951)
Christian, A. K., "Mirabeau Buonaparte Lamar," *Southwestern Historical Quarterly* 23 (April 1920)
Crimmins, M. L., ed., "Notes and Documents: Texas Items in the *Army and Navy Chronicle*, 1836," *Southwestern Historical Quarterly* 49 (January 1946)
Denham, James M., "Charles E. Hawkins: Sailor of Three Republics," *Gulf Coast Historical Quarterly* 5 (Spring 1990)
Denham, James M., "New Orleans, Maritime Commerce, and the Texas War for Independence, 1836," *Southwestern Historical Quarterly* 97 (January 1994)
Dienst, Alex, "The Navy of the Republic of Texas, Part I," *The Quarterly of the Texas State Historical Association* 12 (January 1909)
Dienst, Alex, "The Navy of the Republic of Texas, Part II," *The Quarterly of the Texas State Historical Association* 12 (April 1909)
Dienst, Alex, "The Navy of the Republic of Texas, Part III," *The Quarterly of the Texas State Historical Association* 13 (July 1909)
Dienst, Alex, "The Navy of the Republic of Texas, Part IV" *The Quarterly of the Texas State Historical Association* 13 (October 1909)

Ellenberger, Matthew, "Illuminating the Lesser Lights: Notes on the Life of Albert Clinton Horton," *Southwestern Historical Quarterly* 88 (April 1985)
Ellis, L. Tuffly, "Southwestern Collection," *Southwestern Historical Quarterly* 81 (April 1978)
Franklin, Ethel Mary, "Memoirs of Mrs. Annie P. Harris," *Southwestern Historical Quarterly* 40 (January 1937)
Haugh, George F., "History of the Texas Navy," *Southwestern Historical Quarterly* 63 (April 1960)
Haugh, George F., "The Texas Navy in New York," *Southwestern Historical Quarterly* 64 (January 1961)
Hill, Jim Dan, "Hawkins of the Texas Navy," *Southwestern Review* (Autumn 1936)
Hutton, Margaret, "The Houston-Fisher Controversy," *Southwestern Historical Quarterly* 76 (July 1972)
Neu, C. T., "The Case of the Brig *Pocket*," *Southwestern Historical Quarterly* 12 (April 1909)
Nichols, Ruth G., "Samuel May Williams," *Southwestern Historical Quarterly* 56 (October 1952)
Pohl, James W. and Stephen L. Hardin, "The Military History of the Texas Revolution: An Overview," *Southwestern Historical Quarterly* 89 (January 1986)
Roach, M. Baptista, "The Last Crusade of Mirabeau B. Lamar," *Southwestern Historical Quarterly* 45 (October 1941)
Schroeder, John H., "Annexation or Independence: The Texas Issue in American Politics, 1836-1845," *Southwestern Historical Quarterly* 89 (October 1985)
Steen, Ralph W., "Analysis of the Work of the General Council of Texas, 1835-1836," *Southwestern Historical Quarterly* 42 (July 1938)
Stenberg, Richard R., "Jackson's Neches Claim, 1829-1836," *Southwestern Historical Quarterly* 39 (April 1936)
Vázquez, Josefina Zoraida, "The Texas Question in Mexican Politics, 1836-1845," *Southwestern Historical Quarterly* 89 (January 1986)
Wilson, James E., "Notes on Commercial Relations Between New Orleans and Texas Ports, 1838-1839," *Southwestern Historical Quarterly* 34 (October 1930)
Winfrey, Dorman H., "Mirabeau B. Lamar and Texas Nationalism," *Southwestern Historical Quarterly* 49 (October 1995)
Worley, J. L., "The Diplomatic Relations of England and the Republic of Texas," *The Quarterly of the Texas State Historical Association* 9 (July 1905)

Books

Bate, W. N., *General Sydney Sherman: Texas Soldier, Statesman and Builder* (Waco, Texas: Texian Press, 1974)
Bauere, K. Jack and Stephen S. Roberts, *Register of Ships of the U.S. Navy, 1775-1990: Major Combatants* (New York: Greenwood Press, 1991)
Blake, Nicholas and Richard Lawrence, *The Illustrated Companion to Nelson's Navy* (Mechanicsburg, PA: Stackpole Books 2000)
Bocanegra, José M., *Memorias para la Historia de Mexico Independiente, 1822-1846* (San Angel, Mexico: 1892)
Brands, H. W., *Lone Star Nation* (New York: Doubleday, 2004)
Cantrell, Greg, *Stephen F. Austin: Empresario of Texas* (New Haven: Yale University Press, 1999)
Cardenas de la Peña, Enrique, *Semblaza Maritima del Mexico Independiente y Revolutionario*, 2 vols. (Mexico City: Secretaria de Marina, 1970) (trans. Rose Buckley)
Cartwright, Gary, *Galveston: A History of the Island* (Fort Worth: TCU Press, 1991)
Chandler, David G., *The Campaigns of Napoleon* (New York: Macmillan Publishing Co., 1966)

Christensen, Carol and Thomas, *The U.S.-Mexican War* (San Francisco: Bay Books 1998)
Cohen, Eliot A., *Supreme Command: Soldiers, Statesmen, and Leadership in Wartime* (New York: Free Press, 2002)
Connor, Seymour V., et al., *Capitols of Texas* (Waco: Texian Press, 1970)
Curtis, James C., *Andrew Jackson and the Search for Vindication* (Boston: Little, Brown & Co., 1976)
Cussler, Clive, and Craig Dirgo, *The Sea Hunters: True Adventures With Famous Shipwrecks* (New York: Pocket Star Books, 1996)
Deveraux, Linda Ericson, *The Texas Navy* (Nacogdoches, Texas: Ericson Books 1983)
DeVoto, Bernard, *The Year of Decision: 1846* (New York: Truman Talley Books 1842, 2000 ed.)
Dimmick, Gregg J., *Sea of Mud: The Retreat of the Mexican Army After San Jacinto, An Archeological Investigation* (Austin: Texas State Historical Association, 2004)
Douglas, Claude L., *Thunder on the Gulf: The Story of the Texas Navy* (Dallas: Turner Company, 1936)
Eisenhower, John S. D., *Agent of Destiny: The Life and Times of General Winfield Scott* (New York: Free Press, 1997)
Eisenhower, John S. D., *So Far From God: The U.S. War with Mexico, 1846-1848* (Norman: University of Oklahoma Press, 2000 ed.)
Fehrenbach, T. R., *Lone Star: A History of Texas and the Texans* (second ed., Da Capo Press, 2000)
Fischer, Ernest G., *Robert Potter: Founder of the Texas Navy* (Gretna: Pelican Publishing, 1976)
Francaviglia, Richard V., *From Sail to Steam* (Austin: University of Texas Press, 1998)
Francaviglia, Richard V. and Douglas W. Richmond, eds., *Dueling Eagles: Reinterpreting the U.S.-Mexican War of 1846* (Fort Worth: TCU Press, 2000)
Gambrell, Herbert P., *Anson Jones: The Last President of Texas* (Garden City, NY: Doubleday, 1948)
Garrison, George P., *Westward Extension, 1841-1850* (New York: Greenwood Press, 1906)
Guthrie, Keith, *Forgotten Texas Ports,* Vol. II (Austin: Eakin Press, 1993)
Guthrie, Keith, *Forgotten Texas Ports,* Vol. III (Austin: Eakin Press, 1995)
Hafertepe, Kenneth, *A History of the French Legation in Texas* (Austin: Texas State Historical Association, 1989)
Haley, James L., *Passionate Nation* (New York: Free Press, 2006)
Haley, James L., *Sam Houston* (Norman, OK: University of Oklahoma Press, 2002)
Haley, James L., *Texas: From the Frontier to Spindletop* (New York: St. Martin's Press, 1985)
Hardin, Stephen L., *Texian Iliad: A Military History of the Texas Revolution* (Austin: University of Texas Press, 1994)
Henson, Margaret Swett, *Juan Davis Bradburn: A Reappraisal of the Mexican Commander at Anáhuac* (College Station: Texas A&M University Press, 1982)
Henson, Margaret Swett, *Samuel May Williams: Early Texas Entrepreneur* (College Station: Texas A&M University Press, 1976)
Hill, Jim Dan, *The Texas Navy: In Forgotten Battles and Shirtsleeve Diplomacy* (Chicago: University of Chicago Press, 1937)
Hogan, William Ransom, *The Texas Republic: A Social and Economic History* (Austin: University of Texas Press, 1986 ed.)
Holt, Michael F., *The Rise and Fall of the American Whig Party* (Oxford: Oxford University Press, 1999)
Jackson, Donald, *Voyages of the Steam Boat Yellow Stone* (New York: Tiknor and Fields, 1985)
James, Marquis, *The Raven* (New York: Paperback Library, 1929, 1967 ed.)
King, Dean, *A Sea of Words* (New York: Henry Holt & Co., 1997)

Koury, Michael, *Arms for Texas: The Weapons of the Republic of Texas* (Ft. Collins, Colorado: Old Army Press, 1973)
Lack, Paul D., *The Texas Revolutionary Experience* (College Station: A&M University Press, 1992)
Lambert, Andrew, ed., *Steam, Steel & Shellfire: The Steam Warship 1815-1905* (London: Conway Maritime Press, 1992, 2001 reprint by Chartwell Books)
Lamego, Gen. Miguel A. Sanchez, Mex. Army (ret.), *The Second Mexican-Texas War, 1841-1843* (Hill Junior College Monograph, 1972)
Leckie, Robert, *From Sea to Shining Sea* (New York: HarperCollins Publishing, 1993)
Marshall, Bruce, *Uniforms of the Republic of Texas* (Atglen, Pennsylvania: Schifler Military History, 1999)
Meed, Douglas V., *The Fighting Texas Navy* (Plano, Texas: Republic of Texas Press, 2001)
Miller, Edward L., *New Orleans and the Texas Revolution* (College Station: Texas A&M University Press, 2004)
Moore, Sir Alan, *Sailing Ships of War*, 1800-1860 (London: Halton & Truscott Smith, 1926)
Nance, Joseph Milton, *After San Jacinto: The Texas-Mexican Frontier, 1836-1841* (Austin: University of Texas Press, 1963)
Nofi, Albert A., *The Alamo and the Texas War for Independence* (Da Capo Press, 1992)
Powers, John, *The First Texas Navy* (Austin: Woodmont Books, 2006)
Ramsay, Jr., Jack C., *Thunder Beyond the Brazos* (Austin: Eakin Press, 1985)
Remini, Robert V., *Andrew Jackson and the Course of American Democracy, 1833-1845* (Baltimore: Johns Hopkins University Press, 1984)
Roberts, Randy and James S. Olson, *A Line in the Sand: The Alamo in Blood and Memory* (New York: Free Press, 2001)
Scheina, Robert L., *Latin America: A Naval History 1810-1987* (Annapolis: Naval Institute Press, 1987)
Schlesinger, Jr., Arthur, *The Age of Jackson* (Boston: Little, Brown & Co., 1946)
Shearer, Earnest C., *Robert Potter: Remarkable North Carolinian and Texan* (Houston: University of Houston Press, 1951)
Sibley, Joel H., *Storm Over Texas: the Annexation Controversy and the Road to the Civil War* (Oxford University Press, 2005).
Silverstone, Paul H., *The Sailing Navy 1775-1854* (Annapolis: Naval Institute Press, 2001)
Stephenson, Nathaniel W., *Texas and the Mexican War: A Chronicle of the Winning of the Southwest* (New Haven: Yale University Press, 1921)
Tijerina, Andrés, *Tejanos & Texas Under the Mexican Flag, 1821-1836* (College Station, Texas: Texas A&M University Press, 1994)
Weems, John Edward, *Dream of Empire: A History of the Republic of Texas 1836-1846* (New York: Simon & Schuster, 1971; reprint, Barnes & Noble, 1995)
Wells, Tom Henderson, *Commodore Moore and the Texas Navy* (Austin: University of Texas Press, 1960)
Wilson, R. L., *Colt: An American Legend* (New York: Abbeville Press, 1949, 1986 ed.)

Magazine Articles

Arnold, Linda, "Too Few Ships, Too Few Guns, and Not Enough Money: The Mexican Navy, 1846-1848," *The Northern Mariner* (April 1999)
Drake, Jerry C., "The Lone Star's Wooden Walls: The Texas Navy," *Heritage* (Fall 2004)
Goldthwaite, Carmen, "The Sidewheeler that Saved Texas," *Wild West* (June 2002)
Milton, Keith, "Battle of the Downs," *Military Heritage* (October 2002)
Moore, Marc A., "Marines of the Texas Republic," *Marine Corps Gazette*, (August 1978)
Symonds, Craig L., "Rank and Rancor in the Confederate Navy," *MHQ: The Quarterly Journal of Military History* (Winter 2002)
Sullivan, David M., "The Republic of Texas Marine Corps," *The Sheet Anchor* (Summer 1997)

Newspaper Sources

Allen, Winnie, "Texas Navy: Two Youths in that Service Have Left Us Thrilling Tale of Stirring Scenes at Sea," *Dallas Morning News*, March 13, 1927

Ashford, Gerald, "Texas Hero Tombs Face Destruction," *San Antonio Express News*, September 11, 1954

"Lost Texas Navy Vessel Surfaces," *Dallas Morning News*, November 17, 1986

Pruett, Jackie L., "Texas Sampler: *The Yellow Stone*," *Texan Express*, November 14, 1874

Roark, Garland, "Famous Ships of Texas," *Houston Chronicle*, October 1, 1961

"Sale of Texas Navy and Troubled Events of Republic Recounted," Houston *Chronicle*, June 13, 1937

"Texas Battle Ship Excavated," *Lubbock Evening Journal*, November 17, 1986

"Three Officers of Texas Navy Are Given Final Resting Place in State Cemetery," *Beaumont Sunday Enterprise*, January 16, 1955

Theses, Dissertations, and Other Papers

Adair, A. Garland, "The Navy of the Republic of Texas," Information Circular No. 32 (November 1943), Texas Memorial Museum, Austin, Texas

Arnold, J. Barto III, Clive Cussler, and Wayne Gronquist, "The Survey for the *Zavala*, a Steam Warship of the Republic of Texas," in *Underwater Proceedings of the Society for Historical Archeology Conference 1990*

Bidwell, Robert Leland, "The First Mexican Navy 1821–1830" (University of Virginia 1960) (unpublished Ph.D. dissertation)

Borgen, Amy Anne, "Analysis of the Pass Cavallo Shipwreck Assemblage, Matagorda Bay, Texas," (Texas A&M University, 2004) (unpublished M.A. thesis)

Crane, Robert E. L., "The History of the Revenue Service and the Commerce of the Republic of Texas" (University of Texas 1950) (unpublished Ph.D. dissertation)

Drake, Jerry C., "The Cruise of a Forgotten Flotilla: A Historiographical Survey of the Texas Navy" (copy on file with author)

Eller, E. M., ed., *The Texas Navy* (Washington: Naval History Division, Department of the Navy 1968)

Jenkins, John H., *The Texas Navy: Los Diablos Tejanos on the High Seas* (Palo Alto: American West Publishing 1968)

McKee, Gary E., *Saga of the Republic of Texas's Schooner of War Invincible* (Gary E. McKee, 1995)

Oertling, Thomas J., *Survey for the Texas Navy Warship, Invincible* (Galveston, Texas 1992)

———, *Archeological Testing and Survey for the Texas Navy Vessel, Invincible, Galveston County, Texas* (Austin: National Underwater and Marine Agency, 1997)

Robinson, Adm. Samuel Murray, *A Brief History of the Texas Navies* (presentation to the Sons of the Republic of Texas, Houston, 1961)

Robinson, Adm. Samuel Murray, *The Texas Navy, John G. Tod Letters, 1835–1839, and Short Sketches* (copy on file with NHC)

Stone, Howard L., "A History of the Texas Navy, 1835–1846," (unpublished M.A. thesis, Stephen F. Austin State College, 1951)

Online Sources

Handbook of Texas Online, www.tsha.utexas.edu/handbook/online

National Underwater & Maritime Agency, www.numa.net

Naval Historical Foundation, www.mil.org/navyhist

Sons of DeWitt Colony Texas, www.tamu.edu/ccbn/dewitt/main.htm

Texas Navy Association, www.texasnavy.com

Texas State Library and Archives, www.tsl.state.tsc.us/exhibits/navy

University of Michigan, www.clements.umich.edu/webguides/arlenes/np/porter.html

INDEX

Abispa, 96, 112
Adams, John Quincy, 314
Adkins, Thomas, 269
Adventure, 95, 96, 112
Aguila, 199, 205, 228
   Battle of Campeche and, 234, 253, 254, 255, 262, 264-267
Alamonte, Juan, 7-8
Alcedan, Pablo, 165, 167
Aldana, José de, 96, 98-99
Allen, Augustus, 26, 40-41
Allen, Isaac, 245, 251
Allen, John, 70, 271, 279
Allen, William, 203
Almonte, Juan, 67
Ampudia, Pedro de
   challenges Moore, 263-264
   siege of Campeche and, 232, 246-247, 258, 270, 277
Ana Maria, 171
Anáhuac, Mexico, 2-5, 9-11
Anaya, Juan Pablo
   Canale's letter to, 154, 156, 157
   Moore and, 157, 158, 171-174
   taken hostage, 197
Anderson, Dr. Thomas P., 175, 195
   Battle of Campeche and, 267-268, 269
   San Antonio mutineers and, 244, 252
Andrade, Juan, 310
Andrews, Edmund, 39
Arcas Islands, 156-157, 169
Archer. *See Branch T. Archer*
Archer (modern escort vessel), 309
Archer, Dr. Branch, 37, 38, 183, 189, 195, 215
Argyle, 159
Arista, Mariano, 116
Arnold, J. Barto, III, 305
Asia, 6

Asp, 130, 149
Austin, 153, 183, 190-191, 244
   Battle of Campeche and, 248, 252-257, 260-262, 264-270, 277
   condition of, 210, 214, 215, 216, 220, 221, 226, 230, 239-240, 292-293
   current location of, 306
   Houston offers to return to Dawson, 238
   illness on, 175
   Moore departs from, 282
   off Mexican coast, 154, 156-159, 161, 162, 165-167, 168, 172-176, 195, 197, 199, 200, 205-206
   San Jacinto and, 170-171
   Segunda Fama and, 165-167
   Texas renamed as, 149
   Thornton and mutiny plans, 174
   transferred to US Navy, 294-296
Austin (modern transport vessel), 309
Austin, Henry, 51
Austin, John, 3
Austin, Stephen F., 21, 76
   aboard *San Felipe*, 11-14
   appointed commissioner to US, 25
   first fleet purchases and, 37, 38
   on Mexican anarchy, 17-18
   warned of need for navy, 20

Bancroft, George, 292, 293
Barbachano, Miguel, 234, 253, 277-278
Barnett, Thomas, 268-269
Barragan, Matias de la Peña y, 246, 258, 270
Barrington, William, 202-203, 245, 250-251
Barton, George, 268
Baudin, Charles, 116-117
Beatts, William, 204
Beatty, George, 136
Bee, Barnard E., 153, 187, 211

Belgium, 153
Benjamin R. Milam, 72
Borden, Gail, Jr., 112, 194, 217, 238
 after annexation, 302
 Galveston and, 110
Boston, 71, 82, 126, 128, 295
Bounty, 33-34
Bowers, William, 131
Boxer, 226
Boylan, James D., 69, 90-100, 102
 Battle of Campeche and, 234, 254, 256-257
 commands *Brutus*, 80
 commands *Viper*, 72
 Sea Fencibles and, 212
Bradburn, John Davis, 2-4
Branch T. Archer, 99, 155, 191
 Brazos renamed, 149
 condition of, 210, 212, 217, 218, 220, 224, 226, 227-228, 230
 current location of, 306
 offered for sale, 288-290
 transferred to US Navy, 294-295, 296
Brannum, William T., 136, 137, 210
Brashear v. Mason, 298
Brashear, William
 Moore, Lothrop and, 280-281
 sale of Navy and, 287, 288, 290, 292
 US Navy and, 298
Bravo (also known as *General Bravo*), 6, 55, 72
 balance of power and, 58, 310-315
 Invincible attacks, 52-53
 Moctezuma renamed as, 21
 privateers and, 30
Brazoria, 4-5
Brazos, 134, 149
Brief Synopsis, A (Moore), 298-299
Brigham, Asa, 112
Brilliante, 284
Brown, Jeremiah, 57, 70
 balance of power and, 58, 310-315
 Hawkins, *Brutus* and, 66-67
 Invincible and, 47, 52-55, 71-72
 Pocket affair and, 65-66
 removed from command, 80
 Vencedor and, 69-70
Brown, William S., 33
 death of, 72
 Hawkins has arrested, 66
 Liberty and, 47, 64
 Pelicano's capture and, 49-52
Brutus, 56, 66-67, 69-70, 90-100
 acquired and outfitted, 40-41
 Boylan given command of, 80
 current location of, 305
 damaged in Racer's Storm, 100
 Hurd given command of, 47
 in New York for repair, 71-72, 77-79, 192
 Pocket's officers and, 54
Bryan, Moses Austin, 13, 130, 219
Bryan, William, 55, 274
 first fleet purchases and, 37, 41, 46
 on Hurd, 47
 Moore, Lothrop and, 280-281, 285
 on *Pelicano*'s capture, 51
 Pocket affair and, 65-66
 reports on Mexican naval buildup, 68
 sale of Navy and, 238-240, 242, 287, 290
Bryant, Andrew Jackson, 221, 234, 267, 269
Buchanan, Franklin, 299
Burnet, David G.
 in anti-Houston faction, 103, 104
 appoints Potter as Secretary of Navy, 45
 Battle of San Jacinto news and, 57
 calls for election in 1836, 74
 commissions Hawkins, 46
 designates Galveston naval depot, 56, 111
 disposition of vessels and, 54, 64, 67-73
 flag of Texas and, 48
 Houston defeats, 193
 privateers and, 32, 35
Burton, Isaac, 68-69
Bustamente, Anastasio, 80, 81, 116, 121, 186
Butler, Anthony, 313

Calder, Robert, 56-57
Campeche, battle of, 247-249, 252-271, 276-278
Campecheana, 7
Campecheano, 188
 Battle of Campeche and, 232, 234, 254, 255
Canale, Antonio, 153, 154
Carbajal, José, 30-31
Carleton, Henry, 16-17, 41
Carson, Samuel, 32
Cayuga, 33, 56, 72, 104
Celarayn, Juan, 200
Censor, El, 160
Chalco, 6
Champion, 76, 81, 86
Charleston
 acquired, 122-123
 renamed *Zavala*, 130
Charleswood, E.P., 229, 257
Charlotte, 269, 276
Christy, William, 239

City Gazette, 180
City of Dublin, 199
Clark, John, 287
Clark, John C., 180-181
Clark, Michael, 175
Clark, R.M., 175
Clay, Henry, 124
Cleaveland, Richard, 229, 257
Clements, Robert, 199
Climax, 81
Cluskey, C.B., 302
Coahuila y Tejas, 1-5
coastal survey project, 184-185, 198
Collingsworth, George, 21
Colonel Hanson, 212
Colorado, 134, 148
   in New York, 139-141
   renamed *Wharton*, 149
   Wheelwright given command of, 142-143
Colt pistols, 132, 182, 202, 203, 308
Colt, Samuel, 132, 308
Columbia, 134
Columbus, 34
Comanche, 69
Commercial Bulletin, 65, 78-79, 276
Comus, 182, 185
Conchita, 166
Conciliador, 160
Congress, 34, 65
Conner, David, 293
Constante, 6, 7
Constellation, 6
Cooke, Louis P., 150, 180
   Moore's communications with, 64, 159
   orders *Wharton* dismantled, 155
   as Secretary of Navy, 130, 133, 134, 135, 143
   Zavala refit and, 136-138
Cooke, William G., 293
Copano Bay, Texas, 68-69
Correo de Mexico Segundo, 52, 70, 97
Correo de Tabasco
   damaged in Racer's Storm, 100
   Fisher's offensive and, 96, 112
   Shepherd's plan for, 110
Correo Mejicano, 11-18
Cós, Martín Perfecto de, 10, 11, 17, 21
Courier, 17, 80, 164-165
Cox, Charles, 271
Cox, Cornelius C.
   on Galveston, 129
   on life at sea, 145, 146, 147
   on *San Jacinto*, 143
   on *Zavala* in storm, 164

Cox, Emma Matilda Stockton, 302, 303
Creole, 301
Crim, Billy Bob, 308
Crisp, Downing H.
   death of, 284
   given command of *Potomac*, 143
   sale of Navy and, 291
   in *San Bernard*, 183, 185, 189, 191, 221, 223-224, 227-228
   Segunda Fama and, 165
Culp, Fielding R., 224
Cummings, Cyrus, 197, 204, 206, 244
   US Navy and, 301
Cussler, Clive, 304-306

Dallas, A.J., 64, 65, 71
Damon, lieutenant on *Brutus*, 54
Daniel, Price, 309
Davis, Fernando R., 53, 83, 86
Davis, Mike, 305
Dawson, Frederick, 122, 148-149, 179, 211, 238
de la Peña, José Enrique, 310-311
de León, Fernando, 31
Dearborn, M.H., 202
Diario del Gobierno, 17, 86
Dienst, Alex, 301, 308
Dinsmore, Silas, 28
Doloritas, 205
Dolphin, 148, 149
Doric, 205
Dos Amigos, 205-206, 212
Doyle, Percy, 247
Duffus, James, 175
Dunlap, Richard, 139, 141
Dupont, Stephen, 299
Durango, 32, 33

Edgerton, Samuel, 128, 175
Edwin W. Moore, 309
Eliza Russell, 96, 104, 112
Elizabeth, 174
Elliot, Charles, 231-232, 273-274
Elliot, G.B., 247
Elys, Eugene, 173
England. *See* Great Britain
Escuadrilla del Mar del Norte, 83

Fairfield, 126
Falmouth, 293
Fannin, James, 20, 31
Fanny, 263-264
Fanny Butler, 69

Fayssoux, Calender I., 221, 295, 301
Félix, 6
Filisola, Vicente, 19, 21
  after Battle of San Jacinto, 56, 58, 310–313
Fisher, J.P., 131
Fisher, Samuel Rhoads
  appointed Secretary of Navy, 76
  death of, 105
  Navy Yard plans and, 111
  offensive of, 89–105, 159, 192
  privateers and, 30, 31, 33
  rebuilding of Navy and, 77
  response to blockade, 80–81, 82
  Senate hearing about, 104
  Texas county named for, 308
  Tod and, 124
flag, of Texas, 48
Flash, 31–32, 56, 81
Flora, 34
Forsyth, John, 18, 140–141
Fort Davis, 3
Fort Velasco, 2, 4–5
Fortune, 195
Fowler, Rev. Littleton, 104
France, 6, 115–117
  recognizes Republic of Texas, 153
Franklin, Benjamin, 56–57
Franklin, Benjamin C., 64–65, 289–290
Frederick Dawson & Sons, 122
Frier, George, 269
Fuller, Charles F., 171, 202–203
Fuller, George
  on Battle of Campeche, 267, 268
  on Campeche, 261
  on mutineers' punishment, 250–252
  on Navy, 144
  US Navy and, 301
Fuller, John, 132, 202

Gaines, Edmund, 313–314
Galveston, Texas, 32, 55–56
  described, 129
  Racer's Storm and, 100
  reaction to Battle of Campeche, 271, 279–280
  reaction to sale of Navy, 289–290
  Shepherd's plan for defense of, 110
  Texians' victory over, 4
  women's resolution of thanks in, 307–308
Gaona, Antonio, 310
Gardiner, Dr. John Burrows, 166, 174–175, 221
Garlick, H.L., 295

Garro, Máximo, 186
General Bravo. *See Bravo*
General Terán, 80, 81
General Urrea, 55, 72, 80, 81
Gibbons, James, 142, 146
Glide, 270
Godines, Blas, 83
Goldsborough, H.A., 182
Gray, Alfred
  after annexation, 301
  Austin and, 195–198, 282
  Battle of Campeche and, 246, 253, 254, 255, 257, 261, 265, 268, 269, 270, 277
  on life at sea, 145, 146–147
  San Antonio court-martials and, 243–244
  San Jacinto and, 169–170
  takes Mexican hostages, 197–198
  US Navy and, 301
Grayson, Peter, 17, 122, 125
Great Britain
  Eliza Russell incident and, 112
  mediates between Mexico and France, 117
  Mexico, Texas, US and, 6, 231–233, 247
  Republic of Texas and, 152–153, 158, 177–178, 179
  sell ships to Mexico, 229, 231–232
Green, Thomas Jefferson, 68, 257
Guadalupe, 228–229, 292
  Battle of Campeche and, 232, 234, 253–257, 259, 262, 264–267, 269
Guerrero, 6
Gutierrez, centralist commander, 172, 173

Hall, Edward, 27, 37, 40–41
Hall, John, 193
Hamilton, James, 122, 124, 135, 177–178, 179, 237, 250
Hamilton, Morgan C., 222–227, 229, 240, 286
Hanks, Wyatt, 28
Hannah Elizabeth, 30–31
Hardeman, Bailey, 68
Harriet Lane, 304
Harris, William, 39
Hawkins, Charles Edward, 55, 56, 57, 77
  background of, 45–47
  Browns and, 66–67
  death of, 79–80
  Nimitz on, 308
Hays, Jack, 292
Henderson, J. Pinckney, 294
Henrieta, 11
Hermon, 6
Hernandez, Antonio, 270

Herrera, José de, 7
Hidalgo, 80
Hill, George Washington
  charges against Moore and Lothrop, 262, 280-281, 284
  sale of Navy and, 238-239, 287-290, 292-293
  Tod and, 124-125, 136
Hill, Jim Dan, 308
Hinton, Addison C.
  on Wright, 139
  Zavala refit and, 130, 136-138, 192
Hitchcock, L.M., 110
Hockley, George W., 114, 222
  Colt pistol and, 132
  naval funding and, 209-222
  orders Moore home, 194, 205-207
  resigns, 222
Holland, 153
Horse Latitudes, 214
Houston, Maggie, 193, 214
Houston Morning Star, 226, 258, 269, 271, 275, 277, 279, 290
Houston, Sam
  appointed commander in chief, 25, 74-75
  background of, 74-75
  Battle of Campeche and, 248-249
  Battle of San Jacinto and, 56, 310-311
  calls for privateers, 111
  criticizes Lamar's policies, 134-135, 179
  death of, 303
  elected president of Republic of Texas, 74, 76, 190-191, 192, 193
  Fisher's offensive and, 90, 91, 92, 101-105
  Great Britain/US relations and, 372-374
  on Hawkins, 46
  Hockley and, 222
  Lamar contrasted to, 123-124
  Mexican occupation of San Antonio and, 211-212
  Moore and, 194, 212, 217-219, 223, 225, 237, 240, 248, 272-276, 286, 298-300, 302
  Naval Act of 1837 and, 121-122
  naval strategy of, 75-78, 80-81, 87, 114, 192-193, 208, 212-213
  Navy's funding and, 112-113, 209-210, 214-230, 236-245, 291
  opposes *Potomac*'s refit, 110
  policies regarding Mexico, Great Britain, and US, 231-233
  on Potter, 45
  proclamation regarding Moore and Navy, 274-276
  Santa Anna and, 67-68, 75
  Tod and, 125
  transported for medical care, 34, 63-64
  as US senator, 298, 300
  visits *Colorado* and *Texas*, 148
  warned of need for navy, 20
Howard, William, 131
Howes, Elijah, 53-54, 65
Hoyt, Charles, 175
Hoyt, Nathaniel, 78-79
Hudgins, James, 245, 251
Humphreys, Peter W., 102, 125
Hunt, Memucan, 124, 130, 132, 135-136
Hunter, Charles, 140
Hurd, James Gardner, 302
Hurd, Norman, 175, 195, 301-302
Hurd, William A., 12, 54, 67
  arrested and tried for piracy, 18
  in battle with *Correo Mejicano*, 13-16
  commands *William Robbins*, 30-31
  given command of *Brutus*, 47
  removed from command, 80
  takes *Brutus* to New York for repair, 71-72, 79
  at Thompson trial, 17
  treatment of crew by, 146

Iguala, 116, 159
Illness
  scurvy, 166
  tropical fevers, 175-176, 257, 259, 284
Iman, 228, 232, 234, 254, 255
In Relation to the Claims of Officers of the Late Texas Navy (Buchanan, Dupont, and Magruder), 299
Independence, 55, 56, 57, 66, 69-70, 80, 82
  acquired and outfitted, 40, 46
  captured by *Libertador*, 83-87
  current location of, 306
  Hawkins death and Wheelwright's command of, 79-80
Independencia, 72, 96, 254, 270
Ingham, 8, 40
Invincible
  acquired and outfitted, 38-40
  balance of power and, 58, 310-315
  Bravo and, 52-53
  current location of, 305-306
  fired upon by *Brutus*, 66-67
  in Fisher's offensive, 90-99

at Galveston with refugees, 56
J. Brown given command of, 47
in New York for repairs, 71-72, 77-79, 192
news of Battle of San Jacinto and, 56-57
Pocket and, 53-55, 64-66
Santa Anna held on board of, 67-68
Thompson abandons, 99-100, 102
Thompson given command of, 80
Venceder and, 69-70
Iturbide, 96, 98

Jackson, 203
Jackson, Andrew, 74, 152, 313-314
Jane, 100
Jefferson Davis, 301
John Adams, 293
John M. Bandel, 52
Johnson, Francis, 3, 66-67
Johnson, Thomas "Ramrod," 284, 285
Johnston, Albert Sidney, 132, 150, 194, 230, 233
Jones, Anson, 130, 193, 286, 293
　annexation and, 293-294
　Houston appoints as minister to US, 122
　on Lamar's naval appointments, 134-135
Jones, Ezekiel, 8
Jones, James, 300
Jones, Oliver, 134-135
Josepha, 11
Julius Caesar, 33, 81, 86
J.W. Zacharie & Company, 51

Keenan, Edward, 203, 245
Kennedy, William, 153
Kerr, Peter, 30
Kinsey, Dr. Peter, 31
Kintzing, Matthew, 301
Kokernot, David, 3

LaBranch, Alcée, 54
Lady Byron, 271
Lafitte, 212
Lamar, A.L., 302
Lamar, Mirabeau Buonaparte, 68, 76, 151-155
　in anti-Houston faction, 103, 104
　appoints Moore commander in chief, 125-128
　appoints naval officers, 131-132, 134-135, 161
　Hinton and *Zavala* refit and, 137
　justifies actions against Mexico to Congress, 178-180

Moore and, 302-303
political support for Navy and, 148
presidential policies of, 123-124, 135
renames ships, 149-150
sends diplomatic missions to Mexico, 153-154, 157-160, 182-183, 185-187
Yucatán and, 152, 157, 160-161, 188-190, 193-194
Landois, Antonio, 203, 245, 251
Lansing, J.P., 182, 204, 244
Latimer, William, 296
Laura, 12, 13, 14, 15-16, 18, 123
Lawrence, 293
Lemus, José, 197
Lemus, Pedro, 166, 171, 196-198, 200, 207, 246, 258
LeRoy, captain of *Sisaleno*, 267
Letters of Marque and Reprisal. *See* privateers
Leving, William, 53, 54
Levy, Dr. Albert Moses, 67, 85, 86
Lewis, Armstrong Irving, 159, 221, 270
　after annexation, 301
　Louisa and, 197
　San Bernard and, 182-183
Lewis, Ira, 28, 30
Lewis, W.T., 282
Libertad, 6, 80, 199
Libertador, 72, 96, 98, 262
　Independence's battle with, 83-87
Liberty, 64, 306
　acquired and outfitted, 38
　captures *Pelicano*, 49-52
　W. Brown given command of, 47
Liberty, Mexico, 3, 10
Lion, 244
Lipscomb, Abner, 153-154, 160
Little Penn, 96, 112
Lloyd, Daniel, 285
López, Francisco de Paula, 80, 96
　Battle of Campeche and, 252-253, 257, 259, 263
　Independence's battle with *Libertador* and *Vencedor* and, 83-87
Lothrop, John T.K., 132, 154, 158, 181, 217, 220
　Battle of Campeche and, 255, 256, 266
　death of, 284
　discharged and court-martialed, 280-284
　given command of *San Jacinto*, 130
　at Moore's court-martial, 285
　sale of Navy and, 241-242
　Zavala and, 142, 162-165, 172

Louis Philippe, King of France, 186
Louisa, 197-198
Louisiana, 81
Louisiana State Marine and Fire Insurance Company, 66
Louisville, 130, 306
Love, James, 179, 281
Lubbock, Thomas, 205
Luciana, 6

Mabry, James, 160, 172
Magruder, George, 299
Margarita, 232
Maria, 11
Marín, Tomás, 186, 232
　Battle of Campeche and, 259, 263-265, 270, 277
Marshal, Francis, 149
Marshal, Perry, 149
Marstella, captain of *Flash*, 32
Martha, 8
Mary Elizabeth, 212
Mary Jane, 33
Mason, Charles, 181, 297
Mason, John, 295-296, 298
Matagorda Committee of Safety, 28, 30
Mateo, lieutenant on *Bravo*, 30-31
Matilda, 70-71
Mayfield, James, 285
McGregor, John, 166, 171
McKinney & Williams, 12, 38
McKinney, Thomas F., 12-13, 149
　first fleet purchases and, 37, 39
　Invincible and, 39, 47
　Lamar and, 124
　privateers and, 26, 28, 29, 30
　sale of Navy and, 290
　wounded, 15
Mendez, Santiago, 157, 158, 235
　Battle of Campeche and, 246, 258, 260, 270, 276-277
Mentor, 78
Merchant, 214, 217, 223
Mexía, José Antonio, 46
Mexican War, 59, 314
Mexicano, 234, 254, 255, 262
Mexico, 6-8, 212-212, 247. *See also specific ships*; Yucatán
　attempts to control Coahuila y Tejas, 1-5
　blockades Texas ports, 80-83
　diverse cultures in, 151-152
　fleet rebuilding in, 63, 68, 72, 190, 198-199, 209, 228-229
　France and, 115-117
　land-based strategy of, 19-22
　political situation in, 10, 115, 152-155
　signs armistice with Republic of Texas, 277
　Texas, Great Britain and, 231-233
Middleton, Peyton, 221
Mississippi, 293
Moctezuma (schooner), 7-8
　renamed *Bravo*, 21
Moctezuma (steam frigate), 228-229, 292
　Battle of Campeche and, 234, 246-247, 253-257, 262, 264-267, 269
　Great Britain and, 232
　illness on, 257, 259
Moore, Alexander, 125, 128, 171, 183
Moore, Edwin Ward, 81-82, 151-155, 183
　after annexation, 302-303
　appointed commander in chief, 125-128, 132, 134
　background of, 125-126
　Battle of Campeche and, 253-257, 260-271, 276-278
　coastal survey project and, 184-185
　Crisp writes to of *San Bernard*'s condition, 224
　death of, 303
　discharged and court-martialed, 280-286
　Galveston welcomes, 279-280
　Gray's hostage-taking and, 197-198
　Houston and, 194, 212, 217-219, 223, 225, 237, 240, 248, 272-276, 286, 298-300, 302
　Houston's decision to sell Navy and, 238-245
　Huston fleet recall and, 190-191, 194
　Lamar and, 302-303
　letter to public, 282
　on Mendez, 157
　Mexican coast cruise in 1840, 157-171
　naval funding and, 212-230, 217, 234, 297
　naval officers and, 131-132, 142-143, 151
　political support for Navy and, 148
　recruits men in New York, 139-141
　San Antonio mutiny and, 204, 250-252, 280, 285
　Semmes on, 307
　State of Texas audit and reimbursement of, 297-298
　Texas county named for, 308
　Tod and, 135, 210
　treatment of crew by, 146
　treatment of Mexican civilians by, 159
　unrest in Navy and, 204-205

US Navy and, 125-128, 298-300
Williams and, 281
Yucatán and, 171-174, 189-200, 205-207, 232-235, 248-249
Zavala refit and, 136
Moore, Francis, 148
Moore, James W., 215-217, 277, 285
Morehouse, Edwin, 284
Morgan, James, 31-32, 56, 66, 274
   after annexation, 302
   Battle of Campeche and, 247-249, 253, 255, 256, 258, 260, 262, 264, 276
   death of, 302
   letter to public, 281-282
   on Moore, 286
   at Moore's court-martial, 285
   on mutineers' punishment, 251
   sale of Navy and, 238-244
Morris, Charles, 295
Murphy, William, 292

Nacogdoches, Mexico, 2, 5
Napian, Evan, 186
Natchez, 81
National Underwater & Marine Agency (NUMA), 304-306
Naval Act of 1837, 121-122
Nelson, Lord Horatio, on privateers, 34
Neptune, 191, 284
Neride, 116, 117
Nevill, Francis Scott, 47
New Castle, 52
New Orleans *Bee*, 34, 65, 79
New Orleans, Louisiana, 37-38, 51-52, 65
New Orleans *Tropic*, 228-229, 258, 260
New York *Albion*, 91-92
New York *Herald*, 303
New York *Mirror*, 298, 299
New York, NY, 71-72, 139-141
Nimitz, Chester W., 308
Norris, John, 267, 268
North Carolina, 140

Ocampo, Jiminex Carlos, 11, 14, 16, 17, 53, 54
Ocean, 68, 70
Odell, T.H., 203
Ohio, 10
Oliver, Robert, 224, 301
Ontario, 244, 295
Orizaba, 6
O'Shaunessy, James
   commands *San Jacinto*, 162, 167-171, 176
   deserts, 182

   given command of *San Antonio*, 142
Oswald, Seymour, 202-203, 243

Packenham, Richard, 155, 158, 169, 187
Palmerston, Lord, 177-178
Papaloapan, 6, 7
Parker, John, 139
Passaic, 72
Paterson revolver, 132
Patrick Henry, 214
Paulding, James, 128
Pearce, James, 295, 299
Pelicano, 50-52
Penguin, 159
Pennoyer, James, 123
Pennsylvania, 32, 34
Pensacola, Florida, 6
Peraza, Martín, 187, 188-190, 196, 234
Perdenal, 6
Perez, Lino, 15
Phoenix, 90-91, 110-111
Picalina, 157
Picayune, 276
Pocket
   Fisher accused of embezzling from, 104
   Invincible captures, 52-55, 64-66
Polk, James, 295-296
Pompilly, Benjamin, 203, 243
Porpoise, 293
Porter, David, 7, 45-46, 124
Postell, John, 204
Postell, William, 142, 157-158, 162, 301
Potomac (brig), 109-110, 114, 130, 143, 155
   current location of, 306
   sinks, 179
Potomac (US frigate), 293
Potter, Robert M., 44, 45, 56, 64, 66, 69, 181
   Texas county named for, 308
Press, 226
Princeton, 293
privateers, 25-35, 70-72, 78, 111
Progreso, 199, 213

Racer, 100, 167
Racer's Storm, 100
Rafaelita, 97
Ramírez y Sesma, Joaquín, 21, 58
Randolph, Victor, 294, 295, 296
Rawle, Edward, 65
Red River, 3-4
Regenerador, 199, 205, 228, 234, 260, 262
Reily, James, 284, 285
Rejón, Donanciano, 188

Rejón, Joaquin, 196, 197-198, 207, 234
Remini, Robert V., 313
Renshaw, James, 140
Republic, 276
Republic of Texas, 1-2, 9. *See also* Republic of Texas Navy
   1836 elections in, 74, 76
   annexed by US, 293
   early rebellion against Mexican control, 2-5
   flag of, 48
   forms provisional government, 25
   Lamar's policies and, 123-124
   Mexico signs armistice with, 277
   Naval Act of 1837, 121-122
   recognized but not accepted into US, 152
   recognized by European countries, 152-153
   Santa Anna recognizes independence of, 63
   US history and, 59
Republic of Texas Navy. *See also specific ships*
   after independence declared, 63-73
   balance of power and, 311-315
   discipline and training in, 142-150, 166-167, 221, 224
   early ranks in, 42-48
   early fleet purchases and, 36-41
   under Fisher, 89-105
   history's verdict on, 307-309
   Houston and funding for, 112-113, 209-210, 214-230, 236-245, 291
   Houston's strategy for, 75-78, 80-81, 87, 114, 192-193, 208, 212-213
   Navy Yard and, 111-112, 143, 210, 226, 292
   placed in ordinary, 178-183, 287-294
   privateers and, 25-35, 70-72, 78, 111
   sailors' lives in, 143-148
   under Shepherd, 109-114
   ships' conditions, 208-230
   ships, men, and materiel rebuilt after Naval Act of 1837, 121-141
   transferred to US Navy, 294-296
   unrest in, 201-205
   US history and, 59
   US Navy and officers of, 298-301
Republicano, 271
Retrieve, 212
Richardson, Dr. William, 195
Ridgley, Charles, 128
Rio Grande River, as southern boundary of Texas, 2

Rivas, Joachim, 167
Roberts, Samuel, 188-189
Robertson, Arthur, 47
Robinson, James, 25, 40, 47
Roo, Andréas Quintana, 196, 197, 232
Roosevelt, Theodore, Jr., 308
Rosario, 246-247
Ross, John E., 32
Rosseter, N.T., 131
Rowan, Henry, 175
Rowan, Thomas, 203-204, 280
Rowland, John G., 4
Royal Navy. *See* Great Britain
Royall, R.R., 29
Runaway Scrape, 32, 33
Runnels, Hiram G., 294
Rusk, Thomas J., 68, 103
Russell, William J., 4-5

Sabine, 47, 50, 185
Sam Houston, 98
San Antonio, 130, 133-134, 139, 181
   Ana Maria and, 171
   coastal survey project and, 184
   condition of, 210, 214, 215
   mutineers' court-martial and sentencing, 250-252, 280, 285
   mutiny on, 200-204, 220, 243, 244-245
   off Mexican coast, 154, 159, 161, 162, 169, 189-191, 195, 198, 200, 205-207
   O'Shaunessy given command of, 142
   Scorpion renamed as, 130, 149
   vanishes, 215, 221, 225-226, 230
San Antonio, Texas, Mexican occupation of, 211, 231-232, 233
San Bernard, 130
   Asp renamed as, 149
   condition of, 210, 214, 215, 221, 223-224, 226, 227-228, 230, 295
   current location of, 306
   illness on, 175-176
   mutiny plotted in, 202
   off Mexican coast, 154, 157-159, 161, 162, 167-168, 172, 173, 175-176, 182-183, 185, 189-191, 195, 198-199, 205-207
   offered for sale, 288
   San Jacinto's grounding and, 169-171
   transferred to US Navy, 294-295, 296
   Williamson given command of, 142
San Felipe
   Correo Mejicano and, 13-18
   McKinney & Williams and, 12, 18
   as privateer, 28-29, 30

San Jacinto, 34, 70-71, 130
   current location of, 306
   Gibbons given command of, 142
   off Mexican coast, 154-155, 157-159, 161, 162, 167-168
   O'Shaunessy given command of, 162
   O'Shaunessy runs aground, 169-171, 176
   Viper renamed as, 130, 149
San Jacinto, Battle of, 56-57, 310
San Jacinto (modern carrier), 309
San Juan de Ullúa, 116
Santa Anna, Antonio López de
   Austin on, 12
   centralists and, 10, 178
   Battle of San Jacinto and, 56, 66-67, 75
   French at San Juan de Ullúa and, 116
   land-based strategy of, 19-22
   Navy's capture of supplies for, 51, 52, 53-54, 55, 58
   recognizes Texas independence, 63
   regains power, 1841, 211
   Texian rebels claim to be supporting, 5
Santiago, 34
Sappho, 169
Saratoga, 293
Sayre, Charles, 79
Scorpion, 130, 149
Scott, William, 3
Scott, Winfield, 59, 314
Sea Fencibles, 212
Seegar, Augustus, 181
Seeger, William, 191, 196, 197
   San Antonio mutiny and, 201-203
   San Antonio's disappearance and, 215, 221, 225-226
Segunda Fama, 165-167, 198
Semmes, Raphael, 307
Sentinel, 179, 183
Seypert, Thomas, 284
Shepherd, Frederick, 203-204, 245, 250, 268
Shepherd, Joseph, 244
Shepherd, William M., 102-105, 109-115, 124
Sheridan, Francis C., 147, 209
Sherman, Sidney, 284, 286, 301
Simons, James, 94
Simpson, William, 203, 245, 251
Sisaleno, 228, 232, 254, 267
slaves/slavery, 11, 152-153, 178, 314
Smith, Ashbel, 199, 229, 232, 233
Smith, Benjamin, 28
Smith, Henry
   first fleet purchases and, 36-40, 48
   on Hawkins, 46
   Houston and, 74-75, 76
   privateers and, 26-28, 35
   as Texas's provisional governor, 25, 40
Smythe, H.M., 280
Snow, Charles B.
   accused and acquitted of desertion, 281, 284
   after annexation, 301
   at Moore's court-martial, 285
   relieves Crisp, 228
   US Navy and, 301
Somers, 293
Somervell, Alexander, 284
Soulé, Pierre, 16-17
Spain, 6
Spillman, James, 3
St. Mary's, 293
Stephen F. Austin, 3-4
Stephens, George, 269
Stephens, J.F.
   Moore and, 204
   sale of Navy and, 238, 241-242, 291
   US Navy and, 301
Stockton, Robert F., 293
Streachout, Dick, 268
Striped Pig, 306
Swartout, Samuel, 79
Sylph, 198, 201

Tampico, 6
Taylor, John W., 85-86, 114, 130, 291
Taylor, Thurston M.
   given command of Navy Yard, 143
   given command of *San Jacinto*, 170
   Segunda Fama refugees and, 166
   theft ring and, 182, 204
Telegrafo, 95, 96, 112
Telegraph and Texas Register, 33, 70, 79-80, 89-91, 104, 121, 173, 281, 294-295
Tennison, William A., 55, 164, 199, 281
   after annexation, 301
   at Moore's court-martial, 285
   places vessels in ordinary, 287-288, 290, 292-293, 294
   US Navy and, 301
Tenorio, Antonio, 9
Terán, Manuel de Mier y, 1, 7
Terrible, 70-71, 126
Texas
   Houston visits, 148
   as new flagship, 141
   Postell given command of, 142
   renamed *Austin*, 149

Texas Sentinel, 165
Texas, State of. *See also* Republic of Texas
   audit of Moore's finances, 297-298
   Houston as senator from, 298, 300
Texas Times, 248-249, 275
Texian and Brazos Farmer, 284
Thomas Toby, 72, 78-80, 90-91, 100
Thomas Toby & Brother, 64
Thompson, Alexander, 111
Thompson, Henry Livingston
   death of, 102-103
   in Fisher's offensive, 90-99, 101-102, 192
   given command of *Invincible*, 80
   recommendations for *Correo de Tabasco*, 110
   recommendations for *Phoenix*, 111
   treatment of crew by, 94
Thompson, Thomas "Mexico," 10-11, 53
   arrest and trial of, 16-18
   on *Correo Mejicano* in battle with *San Felipe*, 11-16
   death of, 114
   Navy Yard plans and, 111-112
   Wharton's release and, 86-87
Thornton, Edward, 174
Thruston, Algernon S., 80, 98-99
Timothy, Owen, 269
To the People of Texas (Moore), 283
Toby, Thomas, 65-66, 71, 77-78
Tod, John Grant, 111, 149, 180-181, 209-210, 286
   after annexation, 301
   audits Navy, 112, 114
   death of, 301
   dismissed from service, 181
   Hunt and, 135-136
   Love's warning to, 179
   on Moore, 126
   as naval agent to US, 122, 124-125, 129, 134, 148-149
   receives captain's commission, 293
   relieved of duties, 184
Tom Salmon, 215
Tornel y Mendivil, José María, 7, 17, 59, 68, 116
Travis, William Barret, 3, 8, 10, 11, 21-22
Treat, James
   death of, 171
   sent to negotiate with Mexico, 153-154, 157-160, 161, 169, 187
Tremont, 12, 12-13
Triplett, Robert, 64

True American, 81
Tyler, John, 292, 296

Ugartechea, Domingo de, 4-5, 9, 17
Union, 70, 94
United States. *See also* United States Navy
   annexes Republic of Texas, 293
   army size in 1846, 314
   Mexico and, 59, 231, 247
   Neutrality Act and Moore's recruitment of men, 139-141
   recognizes Republic of Texas, 152
   Republic of Texas Navy and, 198
United States Navy, 6, 81
   Moore and, 125-128
   patrols Mexican coast prior to annexation of Texas, 293
   Republic of Texas officers petition for place in, 298-301
United States v. Thompson, 16-17
Upshur, Abel, 292
Urchin, 80
Urrea, José de, 21, 58, 310

Van Buren, Martin, 122
Van Zandt, Isaac, 247, 292
Vásquez, Rafael, 206, 211
Vencedor del Alamo, 63, 69-70, 72, 80, 83-86
Veracruzana, 7, 17, 21
Victoria, 6
Vigilante, 81
Viper, 72, 110
   renamed *San Jacinto*, 130, 149

Waite, Alfred, 181, 202, 204
Walke, Alfred, 176, 252, 257, 276, 282-283
Warren, 64, 65, 184, 185, 205, 295
Washington, 200, 212
Washington, Lewis M.H., 45, 214
Watchman, 68-69
Water Witch, 3-4, 72
Webb, James, 183, 185-187
Webster, Daniel, 198
Wells, Fleming T.
   on Moore, 134
   at Moore's court-martial, 285
   reports misconduct, 221
   sale of Navy and, 287, 291
   on Taylor, 114
Wells, James, 55
Wells, Tom Henderson, 308
West, William, 268

Wharton, 149
  Battle of Campeche and, 248, 253–257, 260–262, 264–270, 277
  condition of, 210, 215, 216, 220, 221, 226, 228, 230, 239–240, 292–293
  current location of, 306
  Houston offers to return to Dawson, 238
  Lothrop departs from, 282
  midshipmen resign from, 234
  off Mexican coast, 154–155, 159, 161, 162, 191
  transferred to US Navy, 294–296
Wharton, John A., 33, 47, 87, 104
Wharton, William H., 37, 38, 86–87, 124
Wheeler, Asa, 269
Wheelwright, George Washington, 47, 80
  Correo de Tabasco and, 110
  dismissed by Houston, 113–114, 125, 192
  given command of *Colorado*, 142–143
  given command of *Independence*, 80
  given command of *Liberty*, 64
  Independence's battle with *Libertador* and *Vencedor* and, 83–87
  Navy Yard plans and, 111–112
  relieved of command, 162
  in *Wharton*, 154–155
White, George, 224
Wilbur, D.C., 244, 267, 269
William Robbins, 306
  acquired and renamed *Liberty*, 38
  as privateer, 28, 30–31
  San Felipe's guns and, 29, 30
Williams, Henry, 122, 149
Williams, John, 203, 245, 250–251
Williams, Samuel May
  first fleet purchases and, 12, 37, 39, 130
  Moore and, 281
  as naval agent to US, 122, 124
  privateers and, 28, 31
  sale of Navy and, 238
  Tod and, 136
Williamson, William S., 142, 167, 170
Woll, Adrian, 231–232, 233
Wright, Francis, 20, 110, 143
  Fisher's offensive and, 94, 96, 100
  Hinton on, 139
  Phoenix and, 111

Yellow Stone, 31, 32–33, 56
Yucatán
  Battle of Campeche and, 247–249, 252–271, 276–278
  federalism declared in, 152
  Mexico launches war to regain, 232–235
  moves closer to reconciliation with Mexico, 196–197
  Republic of Texas support of federalists in, 152, 157–161, 171–180, 188–200, 193–194, 205–207, 232–235, 248–249
Yucateco, 228, 234

Zavala
  condition of, 209, 210, 212, 214, 217, 218, 220, 221, 222, 226, 230, 288, 292
  current location of, 304–305
  in Gulf storm, 162–165
  Hinton and refit of, 130, 136–138
  Lothrop given command of, 142
  off Mexican coast, 154–155, 158–159, 162–165, 171–174, 176, 183, 190–191
Zavala, Lorenzo de, 68, 130
Zavala, Lorenzo de, Jr., 234

ABOUT THE AUTHOR

JONATHAN W. JORDAN has written about historical topics for such publications as *Military History Magazine* and *Military History Quarterly*. A graduate of Vanderbilt University Law School, he is a practicing attorney. He lives in the Atlanta area.

www.ingramcontent.com/pod-product-compliance
Lightning Source LLC
Chambersburg PA
CBHW031611160426
43196CB00006B/95